PARLIAMENT, POLICY AND POLITICS
IN THE REIGN OF WILLIAM III

HENRY HORWITZ

Parliament,
policy and politics
in the reign of
William III

NEWARK: UNIVERSITY OF DELAWARE PRESS

© MANCHESTER UNIVERSITY PRESS 1977

Library of Congress Catalog Card Number: 76–27126

Associated University Presses Inc
Cranbury, New Jersey 08512

ISBN 0–87413–124–3

Printed in Great Britain

CONTENTS

PREFACE

After a generation or more when historians of Stuart England have been pre-occupied with the coming and course of the 'Great Rebellion' of mid-century, there has been a resurgence of interest in the 'Glorious Revolution' of 1688–89 and its consequences. Works by John Carswell, James Jones, and John Western have shed new light upon James II's aims and measures and upon the process of his overthrow. Stephen Baxter has published a substantial biography of William III, Peter Dickson has produced an impressive analysis of the 'financial revolution' that began in the 1690s, and J. H. Plumb has provided a stimulating re-interpretation of 'the growth of political stability' in the post-Revolution decades. Then, too, Dennis Rubini has valiantly sought to impose order on the complex political developments of William III's reign by a topical treatment of the conflict between 'Court' and 'Country'. Nevertheless, students of the politics of the 1690s have continued to be greatly dependent upon the relevant chapters of Sir Keith Feiling's perceptive history of the 'first' Tory party, and, even more fundamentally, upon Lord Macaulay's *History of England*. Macaulay's narrative of William III's reign, though unfinished and often criticised for its 'Whig' bias, has stood without a successor for well over a century.

It would be rash to suggest that the present study, even though it offers a full scale narrative of the political history of William III's reign, can displace Macaulay. Much new evidence has become available since Macaulay wrote, but the principal reason for choosing to attempt a narrative was that more recent studies of William III's reign, in adopting topical approaches, have left us without a sense of how events transpired, how things happened. Without a sense of process derived from an account of how decisions were made or avoided, topical analysis is in danger of distortion by way of abstraction and of omission. Yet, as anyone who has tried his hand at narrative knows, the very process of arranging occurrences in sequences may convey a spurious sense of causation and an unwarranted impression of purposefulness.

These and other pitfalls are easier to identify than to avoid. All that can be said here is that in shaping my narrative, I have sought (at the risk of repetition) to tell the story in depth and to give that story form and meaning by concentrating on themes suggested both by the materials themselves and by the work of other students of early modern English history. The interaction between crown and parliament was the dominant motif of the traditional historiography of Stuart England, and for all its familiarity it should remain a fundamental one. Of late, perceptions of the relationships between King, Lords, and Commons have been enlarged by research upon the county communities of gentry that sent members of their leading families up to Westminster and upon the expanding electorate in the counties and the boroughs which participated in the choice of M.P.s when the local notables would not or could not settle the matter among themselves. Thus, while the focus of this study is on decision-making at the national level, I have tried to take into account local and 'popular' inputs in this process, as manifested, for instance, in the 'provincial' positions adopted by members at Westminster, in the views expressed on 'national' questions in the proliferating pamphlet literature of the day (whose authors both articulated and sought to mobilise opinion 'out of doors'), and in the interplay between local circumstances and national controversies as revealed in the conduct of the general elections of the reign.

Understanding of the relations between crown and parliament in early modern England has been advanced in recent years by research along other lines as well. One of the most fruitful, in my judgement, has been the new emphasis on parliament's legislative functions. Demands for statutes came not only from the King and his administration but also from other quarters: from the local communities of shire and town, from a growing and diverse assemblage of commercial and business entities, and from individual families (as exemplified in estate acts). These demands were translated into action, by way of the evolving procedures for lawmaking in the Lords and in the Commons, through the initiative and persistence of individual peers and Commoners who, for one reason or another, were willing to assume active roles in the legislative process. In turn, these working members—who have been isolated by dint of collation of the evidence embedded in the *Journals* of the Commons and in the diaries of M.P.s who recorded some of the debates—were able to call upon specialists in the service of the two Houses, as well as others in the central administration and among the capital's lawyers. Thanks to the work of the late O. C. Williams and the more recent studies of Sheila Lambert and Peter Thomas, we have learned a good deal about these officials and other legislative specialists, and also about parliamentary procedure and the physical setting in which the members operated. These works have left me free to concentrate on telling how the 'King's business' was transacted in parliament and on tracing the origins and fate of those bills whose authors aimed to reform the 'constitution', regulate the conduct of politics, and improve the workings of the royal administration. Limitations of space have precluded a full treatment of all parliament's activities; however, I have sought to suggest the range and extent of other types of legislation and to indicate some of the interest groups and individual M.P.s who were involved in those areas of lawmaking.

While I have sought to frame my account of the policy-making process during William's reign in the light of current scholarly work, my research in the 1690s has culminated in a conviction that King William's war was the single most important influence on the politics of the day. The conduct of the war against France and the raising of the money to pay for it were the principal concerns of king and parliament for much of the reign. Even in the interlude between the Peace of Ryswick and the new conflicts that followed Carlos II's death, war-related issues and problems tended to dominate the business of the now annual parliamentary sessions. Then, too, the growth of the army, the expansion of the executive, and the new ties between the government and London financiers both kept alive and modified traditional fears of arbitrary rule and Court 'corruption'.

Moreover, the complex and fluid parliamentary alignments of the reign can be seen in large measure as reactions to the problems and the possibilities posed by wartime administration and finance, and they also help to account for the frequent ministerial alterations that William felt it necessary to make during the 1690s. In these and in other ways as well, William's policies ended by making him a parliamentary king in a fashion unforeseen when the crown and the Declaration of Rights were tendered to him in February 1689.

As these perspectives and themes have shaped the narrative chapters, so they also figure in the topical chapters (IV, IX, and XIII). Each topical chapter is intended to provide a moving review of the political developments, constitutional changes, and administrative innovations that were taking shape gradually during the reign; each also includes extended discussions of points arising out of the narrative along with analyses of the available evidence about voting patterns, placemen, and elections that is tabulated in the appendices. Thus, it may be that some readers, and students certainly, will find it easier—having read the first chapter—to skim through these analytical chapters before essaying the narrative chapters.

In preparing this study, I have drawn upon the wealth of manuscript materials that has become accessible in recent decades. Most important have been the Harley and Bentinck papers of the Duke of Portland, the former on loan to the British Library and the latter deposited in the University of Nottingham Library. Other substantial collections include the Locke MSS. in the Bodleian Library, the Trumbull MSS. of the Marquess of Downshire on deposit in the Berkshire Record Office, and the Lowther MSS. of the Earl of Lonsdale on deposit in the Cumberland Record Office. Invaluable, too, are the Commons' diaries of Narcissus Luttrell (now in print) and of Sir Richard Cocks (Bodleian Library) and the 'Entring Book' of the ejected Nonconformist Rev. Roger Morrice (Dr Williams's Library). I have also drawn widely from other collections, while no little effort has been devoted to tracking down the dispersed papers of William Blathwayt in both the U.K. and the U.S., and I should like to thank the Duke of Buccleuch, the Duke of Devonshire, the late Duke of Marlborough, the Marquess of Bath, the Earl Spencer, and Colonel John Chandos-Pole for allowing me to examine and to cite materials in their possession.

Many archivists and librarians in England and elsewhere have expedited my researches, among them Mr M. F. Bond, Clerk of the House of Lords' records, Mr B. C. Jones, Archivist of Cumberland and Westmorland, Mr P. I. King, Chief Archivist of the Northamptonshire Record Office, Mr Stephen Parks, Curator of the Osborn Collection of Yale University Library, Miss J. C. Sinar, County Archivist of Derbyshire, Mr F. B. Stitt, County Archivist of Staffordshire and Librarian of the William Salt Library, Mr Peter Walne, County Archivist of Hertfordshire, and Mrs M. A. Welch, Keeper of Manuscripts in the University of Nottingham Library. And as always, the Bodleian Library and the Institute of Historical Research of London University have been open as well-stocked and quiet havens for the student.

Often, I have been led to specific collections and individual documents by the work of other researchers. Most of all, I am indebted to the labours of Edward L. Ellis and John P. Kenyon, and the latter helped by lending transcripts too. I have also been informed and enlightened by several as yet unpublished works by younger scholars: Colin Brooks on projectors and taxation; Lionel Glassey on the commissions of the peace; Robert Hopkinson on Cumberland and Westmorland elections; J. A. Johnston on parliament and the navy; D. W. Jones on the London mercantile community and government borrowing; and Louis Waddell on William's army in the Low Countries. Three older doctoral dissertations —those of E. L. Ellis on the Whig Junto, J. H. Plumb on elections during William III's reign, and Alan Simpson on the Convention Parliament—were also most instructive. I should like to thank all of them for making their dissertations accessible to readers; specific findings have been cited at various points in my notes.

Another kind of assistance was given me by Clayton Roberts, who criticised painstakingly an earlier draft of this book. I am not sure he will approve even of this version, but I know his comments weighed with me as I prepared it.

Similarly, my readings of Dutch materials owe much to Professor R. P. Meijer of Bedford College; he gave freely and extensively of his time to help me, particularly with some of the more cryptic passages in Huygens's *Journaal*.

Thanks are also due to Betty Kemp of St Hugh's College, Oxford, for allowing me to take a copy of her transcription of Sir Richard Cocks's diary, to Dr J. F. A. Mason of Christ Church College, Oxford, for providing transcripts from the Weston Park MSS., to Professor Henry Snyder of the University of Kansas for securing microfilm copies of the Bonnets's dispatches from the Merseburg archives and for sending me proof copies of some of the Marlborough–Godolphin letters, and to Dr P. D. G. Thomas of the University of Wales for supplying information about the Welsh constituencies.

During the years I have been studying William III's reign, I have incurred many other obligations. My own university twice awarded me research assignments, and I have also been greatly assisted by grants and fellowships from the National Endowment for the Humanities, the American Council of Learned Societies, and the Folger Shakespeare Library. The labour of gathering biographical data about the 1,354 M.P.s who sat in the Commons between 1689 and 1702 was expedited enormously by the very generous access to their files extended me by the 1660–1690 section of the History of Parliament Trust, and a great deal of further information about Commoners and peers was compiled by my research assistants in the History Department of the University of Iowa. I should also acknowledge the permission of the editors of the *Journal of British Studies* and of the *Bulletin of the Institute of Historical Research* to make use in this book of materials that first appeared in those publications.

Finally, I welcome this opportunity to record my deep gratitude to the Graduate College of the University of Iowa for a generous subvention which has made possible the publication of a manuscript whose length might otherwise have deterred even the most sympathetic of university presses.

Iowa City
March 1976

NOTES ON DATES AND STYLE

Throughout the text of this study, *old style* dates have been used, though with the year taken to begin on 1 January. However, in the footnotes contemporary letters dated *new style* in the original have been cited under both *old* and *new style* dates.

All transcriptions have been modernised. In the footnotes, the place of publication is London unless otherwise indicated. Contemporary pamphlets have been identified by the numbers assigned them by Donald Wing in the first edition of his *Short Title Catalogue*, except in cases where they were subsequently reprinted in one of the standard collections. Citations of pamphlets not listed by Wing and not reprinted include a library call number. Other printed works are cited by their full title, with date and place of publication, the first time they are referred to in each chapter, unless they are cited by one of the following abbreviations.

ABBREVIATIONS

ARA—Algemeen Rijksarchief (The Hague)

Archives—*Archives ou correspondance inédite de la maison d'Orange Nassau*, 3rd s., 1689–1702, ed. F. J. L. Krämer (Leyden, 1907–9)

BAGR—*Britain after the Glorious Revolution 1689–1714*, ed. Geoffrey Holmes (1969)

BIHR—*Bulletin of the Institute of Historical Research*

BL—British Library (formerly the British Museum), followed by the name of the manuscript collection or by the printed book number

Bodl.—Bodleian Library, followed by the name of the manuscript collection or by the printed book number

Baxter, *William III*—Stephen Baxter, *William III* (1966)

Boyer, *William the Third*—Abel Boyer, *The History of King William the Third* (1702–3)

Browning, *Danby*—Andrew Browning, *Thomas Osborne Earl of Danby and Duke of Leeds 1637–1712* (Glasgow, 1944–51)

Burnet, *History*—Gilbert Burnet, *Bishop Burnet's History of His Own Time* (Oxford, 1833)

Burnet, *Supplement*—*A Supplement to Burnet's History of My Own Time*, ed. H. C. Foxcroft (Oxford, 1902)

CJ—*Journals of the House of Commons*

CSPD—*Calendars of State Papers, Domestic series*

CTB—*Calendar of Treasury Books, 1660–1718*, ed. William Shaw

CUL—Cambridge University Library

Clar. Corr.—*Correspondence of Henry Hyde, Earl of Clarendon, and of his brother, Laurence Hyde, Earl of Rochester*, ed. S. W. Singer (1828)

Correspondentie—*Correspondentie van Willem III en van Hans Willem Bentinck, eersten graaf van Portland*, ed. N. Japikse (The Hague, 1927–37)

DWL—Dr Williams's Library

Dalrymple, Memoirs—*Memoirs of Great Britain and Ireland*, ed. Sir John Dalrymple (1771–3)

EHR—*English Historical Review*

FSL—Folger Shakespeare Library

Foxcroft, Halifax—H. C. Foxcroft, *The Life and Letters of George Savile, Bart., first Marquess of Halifax* (1898)

Grey, Debates—Anchitell Grey, *Debates of the House of Commons from the Year 1667 to the Year 1694* (1769)

Grimblot, Letters—*Letters of William III and Louis XIV*, ed. P. Grimblot (1848)

HJ—*Historical Journal*

HLM—*The Manuscripts of the House of Lords*, old and new series

HMC—Historical Manuscripts Commission, various reports

Hatton Corr.—*Correspondence of the family of Hatton*, ed. E. M. Thompson (Camden Society, 1878)

Horwitz, Revolution Politicks—Henry Horwitz, *Revolution Politicks. The Career of Daniel Finch second Earl of Nottingham, 1647–1730* (Cambridge, 1968)

Hunt.—Huntington Library, followed by the name of the manuscript collection or by the printed book number

Huygens, Journaal—*Journaal van Constantijn Huygens, den zoon, van 21 October 1688 tot 2 Sept. 1696* (Historisch Genootschaap, Utrecht, 1876–8)

KAO—Kent Archives Office

KU—University of Kansas Library, microfilm copy of the dispatches of the Bonnets to the Elector of Brandenburg, 1689–1702; originals in Deutsches Zentralarchiv, Merseburg, German Democratic Republic, as Acta Bonet, Repertorium xi, 73 England

JMH—*Journal of Modern History*

Klopp, Der Fall des Hauses Stuart—Onno Klopp, *Der Fall des Hauses Stuart und die Succession des Hauses Hannover* (Vienna, 1875–88)

LJ—*Journals of the House of Lords*

Lacey, Dissent—Douglas Lacey, *Dissent and Parliamentary Politics in England, 1661–1689* (New Brunswick, New Jersey, 1969)

Lamberty, Mémoires—[Guillaume de Lamberty], *Mémoires de la derniere Revolution d'Angleterre* (The Hague, 1702)

Luttrell, Brief Relation—Narcissus Luttrell, *A Brief Historical Relation of State Affairs from September 1678 to April 1714* (Oxford, 1857)

Luttrell, Parliamentary Diary—*The Parliamentary Diary of Narcissus Luttrell 1691–1693*, ed. Henry Horwitz (Oxford, 1972)

MSP—*Miscellaneous State Papers, from 1501–1726*, ed. Philip Yorke, Earl of Hardwicke (1778)

Macaulay, History—Thomas Macaulay, *History of England*, ed. C. H. Firth (1913–15)

Memoirs of Ailesbury—Memoirs of Thomas, Earl of Ailesbury, Written by Himself, ed. W. E. Buckley (1890)

NU—Nottingham University Library

PH—Cobbett's Parliamentary History of England (1806–20)

PRO—Public Record Office (where not otherwise specified, London)

RO—Record Office

Ralph, History—James Ralph, The History of England during the Reigns of K. William, Q. Anne, and K. George I (1744–6)

Ranke, History—Leopold von Ranke, A History of England Principally in the Seventeenth Century (Oxford, 1875)

SR—The Statutes of the Realm (1810–28)

ST—A Collection of State Tracts, Publish'd During the Reign of King William III (1705–7)

Shrewsbury Corr.—Private and Original Correspondence of Charles Talbot, Duke of Shrewsbury, with King William, Etc., ed. William Coxe (1821)

Somers' Tracts—A Collection of Scarce and Valuable Tracts, ed. Sir Walter Scott (1809–15)

Tindal, The Continuation—Nicholas Tindal, The Continuation of Mr. Rapin's History of England from the Revolution to the Present Times (1757–9)

Vernon Corr.—Letters Illustrative of the Reign of William III from 1696 to 1708 addressed to the Duke of Shrewsbury, by James Vernon, Esq., ed. G. P. R. James (1841)

I

THE STAGE IS SET

1688-1689

The joyous reception accorded Charles II at his landing at Dover on 29 May 1660 attests, above all, to that yearning for settlement shared by so many Englishmen after the traumatic experiences of the 1640s and 1650s. Restoration, for most, meant not merely the return of the monarchy in the Stuart line but also the reinstatement of civilian rule and parliamentary authority. Once again, men of standing and property would take up their traditional places in local affairs, while at the centre the 'ancient constitution', as redefined by the reform legislation of 1640–41, would hold sway.

Nevertheless, the experiences of nearly twenty years could not so easily be erased, and the Restoration 'settlement' as it took shape between 1660 and 1662 left open the possibility of disruption on several fronts. In the State, the arrangements of 1660–62, coupled with the repeal in 1664 of the triennial act of 1641, did not resolve the problem 'of achieving co-operation between a king shorn of some of his prerogatives, and increasingly financially dependent on the Commons, and a House of Commons which, though aggressive and privileged, yet depended for its existence upon the King'.[1] In the Church, the failure of the restored Anglican episcopate and the moderate Puritan clergy to reach a compromise led to the ejection of over 1,700 parish incumbents. The heirs of the 'old Puritans' were driven into the wilderness and left to consort there—if they so chose—with Baptist sectaries, Quaker enthusiasts, and even perhaps Catholic recusants.

Neither of these oft-remarked deficiencies of the Restoration arrangements might have seemed subsequently so momentous had it not been for the political inclinations and religious preferences of Charles II and of his brother James. Even after the débâcle of the second Anglo-Dutch war, the goodwill displayed by the 'Cavalier' parliament during the 1670–71 session suggests that a royal stance of 'Church and King', coupled with a Protestant foreign policy, 'could almost certainly have been successful' in promoting harmony between the King and the Commons. Had the amicable atmosphere of the 1670–71 meeting been 'maintained, perhaps for one more session', 'Charles might [have] secure[d] a permanent "ordinary" revenue sufficient to free him from ever having to meet parliament again'.[2]

Instead, the King and his brother, who took on the part of heir presumptive as it became increasingly apparent that Charles's marriage of 1661 would remain childless, sought to free the crown from parliamentary shackles by allying with France and by unilaterally proclaiming religious toleration for all, including

Catholics. And though Charles, under financial pressure from the Commons in 1673–74, reluctantly rescinded his declaration of indulgence and made peace with the Dutch, apprehensions of his leanings towards 'popery', France, and arbitrary rule mounted. Moreover, James's conversion to Catholicism, which was publicly signalled by his refusal to take the anti-Catholic 'test' imposed upon all office-holders by statute in 1673, accentuated these doubts and fears and so helped to undermine the Earl of Danby's attempts in succeeding years to patch up relations between king and parliament.

Between 1674 and 1678, Danby sought to reunite Charles and the Cavalier parliament by appealing once more to 'Church and King' sentiments and by deploying the growing patronage resources available to him as Lord Treasurer. But Danby's muster of a 'Court party' in the Commons was turned against him by his critics and rivals, chief among them the Earl of Shaftesbury, who inveighed against official 'corruption' and warned of the loss of parliament's pristine independence. Paradoxically, Danby could never quite command the necessary majorities in the Commons to secure the additional revenues he needed to keep his royal master to an anti-French line abroad, even though the Lord Treasurer did arrange the marriage in 1677 of the King's nephew William of Orange to James's elder daughter Mary. Consequently, Danby's 'neo-Cavalier' strategy and his tactics of parliamentary management only postponed temporarily the controversy over the royal succession that had been likely ever since James's conversion was disclosed.

The catalysts that brought on the Exclusion crisis of 1679–81 were the ex-Jesuit Titus Oates's alleged discoveries of a 'popish plot' in favour of James and the former ambassador Ralph Montagu's revelation of Charles's secret dealings with Louis XIV after 1674. In an attempt to forestall further disclosures of his relations with Louis, Charles dissolved the Cavalier parliament in January 1679 and then sought to dissipate his subjects' discontent by calling three new parliaments within two years. To each of them, the King offered to accept any expedient they could devise, short of excluding James from the succession, in order to avert the dangers posed by a Catholic coming to the throne. But expedients, whether 'limitations' on the power of a Catholic successor or a regency to govern in his stead, seemed impractical to the Commons' majorities in these parliaments, and throughout Shaftesbury and his compeers kept up a barrage of propaganda and petitions in favour of exclusion. Even so, by November 1680, Charles was ready to risk a division in the Lords on the second exclusion bill, and in the event Lord Halifax's appeal to moderate opinion among the peers helped the bill down to defeat by a vote of 63 to 30. Meanwhile, the royal Court and the Anglican bishops had begun to rally loyalist support out of doors by stressing the links between the Exclusionists and the Protestant Nonconformists and by invoking the spectre of 1642. By 1680, as one royal official later recalled:[3]

the nation was in a great ferment, most persons being distinguished by the opprobrious names of Whig [Exclusionist], and Tory [loyalist]: but there was a third sort of persons, who had the appellation of Trimmers, who . . . pretended great impartiality.

Once Charles perceived that the Whig tide had crested, he dissolved the third Exclusion parliament in March 1681 and indicated that he would not summon another for the time being. Deprived of their parliamentary forum, the Whigs during the next two years were subjected to mounting political and legal pressures which in effect confronted them with the choice either of conceding defeat or of resorting to force. Most chose the former, only to find themselves still at risk when a few, rasher men turned to conspiracy. In any case, by the time the Rye House plot was uncovered in mid-1683, many Whig notables who had not promptly made their peace at Court in 1681 had already been purged from the county commissions and replaced, for the most part, by long-standing local rivals whose influence had been temporarily eclipsed during the Exclusion crisis. So strong was this 'Tory reaction' that when Charles died unexpectedly in January 1685 James succeeded peacefully. Furthermore, when James called parliamentary elections that March, after publishing his pledge to preserve the established church, barely forty former Exclusionists secured seats in the new House of Commons.

If our brief sketch of English politics between 1670 and 1685 appears to exaggerate the rapidity and the extent of fluctuations in political sentiment, the sharpness of these swings is at least partially attributable to the politicians' intensifying exploitation of a variety of manipulative techniques. Danby concentrated on the management of the Cavalier parliament, though he did not neglect by-elections. Besides distributing the increasing patronage at his disposal, derived in part from the crown's resumption of direct collection of the customs and from the pensions funded from the new farm of the excise, the Lord Treasurer devoted considerable attention to the day-to-day direction of the Commons, even offering to make himself available to friendly M.P.s every evening during the spring session of 1675.[4] Nor were Danby's enemies able to displace him until they finally manoeuvred the King into dissolving this long-lived parliament. Thereafter, Shaftesbury and his associates, taking advantage of the lapse of the statutory censorship, bent their efforts to mobilising anti-Catholicism in order to gain the election of 'worthy' candidates who would support a change in the royal succession. And by concentrating so singlemindedly upon exclusion, the Whig leaders helped to polarise politics more severely than at any time since 1660.

While Danby systematised the dispensation of government patronage for purposes of parliamentary management and Shaftesbury elaborated the dissemination of propaganda for purposes of electioneering, perhaps the most far-reaching political innovation of the Restoration era was the 'remodelling' of parliamentary boroughs carried out by the government during Charles II's closing years. The imposition of new charters in nearly a hundred boroughs between late 1681 and the general election of 1685 was executed in conjunction with, and largely for the benefit of, local Tories. And one result was to swell the loyalist majority returned in 1685.[5]

Yet for all the apparent volatility and malleability of political opinion both in parliament and in the constituencies, a closer look suggests an underlying continuity from the Restoration onwards. A substantial majority of those men who, as electors (perhaps two hundred thousand *in toto* in the 269 English and Welsh constituencies), local notables, or members of parliament, were involved in the political process, appear to have favoured strongly the maintenance of the established order in church and state. Most were opposed both to arbitrary rule and to republican schemes, and they were almost as easily roused by charges of Nonconformist plots for 'the good old cause' as they were by tales of Catholic conspiracies. In this sense, there was a strong commitment to the *status quo* that persisted below the surface, and those politicians and propagandists who realised this were most likely to succeed.

However, James II was more impressed with the seeming efficacy of the political techniques that had been utilised by friend and foe during the second half of his brother's reign than he was cognisant of the conservative temper of the political nation. The new King—influenced perhaps by the Earl of Sunderland, the most dextrous political technician of the later seventeenth century—seems to have adhered consistently for most of his brief reign to the view that a show of determination on his part, coupled with the application of the appropriate methods of political manipulation, would suffice to achieve his objectives in church and state on behalf of his fellow Catholics. So, James forthrightly enjoined his parliament when it first met in May 1685 to 'use me well' when it came to the settlement of royal finances, and he did secure both a lifetime grant of the ordinary revenue (now worth perhaps as much as £1,600,000, thanks to the boom in foreign trade) and the vote of additional sums to pay off outstanding royal debts.[6] Encouraged by these parliamentary successes and emboldened by the ease with which his forces crushed the Duke of Monmouth's rising during the summer of 1685, James announced to the members when parliament reassembled that November that he intended to retain in service the Catholic military officers he had appointed during the recent emergency and that he wished a further supply to keep up his now-enlarged army. But at this, the loyalist-dominated parliament balked, and rather than risk a direct rebuff over the Catholic officers the King abruptly prorogued the two Houses.

Despite this initial setback, James still hoped to have his way with this parliament, and in succeeding months he sought to overcome resistance by 'closeting' (personally interviewing) leading members, particularly those holding posts in his disposal. 'Closeting' was a blatant attempt to pressure men by exploiting both the royal presence and the crown's patronage. But it failed, in part because at the same time James introduced more Catholics into his service by way of individual dispensations from the test act of 1673.

By the end of 1686, the King abandoned the attempt to revive his initial majorities in the parliament of 1685, and in the spring of 1687 he began to prepare the ground for the choice of a new House of Commons which would do his will. His declaration of indulgence of April 1687 freed all Protestant Nonconformists from the intense persecution they had endured during the Tory reaction, for James was now bent on wooing them and their Whig friends in order to forge a new electoral coalition. Those Tories and Trimmers such as Halifax who were unwilling to pledge support for the repeal of the Test acts and the penal laws were to be removed from their positions in county administration or municipal government as part of a new 'remodelling', which was in effect to reverse the results achieved between 1681 and 1685. And after James's queen, Mary of Modena, became pregnant in the autumn of 1687, the electoral 'regulators' directed by Sunderland redoubled their efforts, even though this entailed relying on many men who lacked any local standing.

However, the prospect that the Queen might bear a son, who would displace his Protestant half-sisters Mary and Anne in the line of succession, also galvanised those who feared that the balance in England was tilting decisively in the King's favour. After all, if control of the government and disposal of royal patronage were to remain in Catholic hands beyond James II's own lifetime, 'men of fortune' might, as Edward Russell gloomily anticipated, 'be governed by their present interest'.[7] It was, then, the birth of a male heir to the King in early June 1688 which sealed the understanding that had been lacking during the Exclusion crisis between James's more determined opponents in England and William Prince of Orange, the guiding spirit in a revitalised European coalition against Louis XIV. And once William secured promises of support directly and indirectly from many prominent Englishmen, he committed himself to intervene against James both to preserve his wife's and his own claims to the throne and to bring the island kingdoms into the alliance against France.

The Prince's landing in the West of England at the head of 15,000 professional troops on 5 November 1688 allowed all those who disliked their King's measures to come out into the open. By this time, the spectrum of opposition was very broad. James's Catholicising efforts, his attempts to 'pack' parliament, and his maintenance of an army more and more staffed by Catholics seemed almost as grievous as the rule of the 'godly' and the generals had been three decades earlier. So, among the leaders of the risings for a 'free' parliament in the North and the Midlands were to be found not only such former Exclusionists as the Earl of Devonshire and Lord Delamere but also the Earl of Danby. Again, prominent among those who joined the Prince of Orange during the first un-certain weeks after his landing were Sir Edward Seymour, the former Speaker of the Cavalier House of Commons during the 1670s and an outspoken foe of exclusion, and the Earl of Abingdon, Danby's brother-in-law. Furthermore, Princess Anne's husband, Prince George of Denmark, followed the lead of Lord Churchill and deserted the King's army to join William, while Anne and her favourite Sarah Churchill fled the Court and were escorted personally by Bishop Compton of London to Lord Devonshire's headquarters at Nottingham.

Even those loyalist peers and bishops who did not abandon James in November were active in pressing the King to repudiate his pro-Catholic measures and to summon parliament. At first, the lead in London was taken by James's brothers-in-law by his first marriage, the Earls of Rochester and Clarendon. But after the King returned from his demoralised army on 26 November, the Marquess of Halifax and his friend the Earl of Nottingham, both advocates of expedients in the Exclusion crisis and untainted (as Rochester was) by any involvement in James's administration, were foremost in urging him to seek an accommodation with William and to call a parliament to settle the kingdom's affairs. And since James seemed ready to yield to these importunities, Clarendon left London to pay his court to the Prince of Orange, while loyalists in the Midlands such as Lords Chesterfield and Ferrers made their way to Nottingham to offer their respects to Princess Anne.

Hitherto, James's major miscalculation had been his failure to take seriously until too late the possibility of William's direct intervention. Yet though the King by early December 1688 had lost all hope of securing religious and political equality for his co-religionists, the Prince was well aware that his own situation was still problematical. From the outset of his expedition to England, William had made the summoning of a 'free and lawful' parliament his central demand, even though he knew that to entrust his 'destiny' to a parliament was 'no small risk'.[8] Yet force alone could not achieve his objectives, and as one of the under-secretaries of state observed at this critical juncture:[9]

Almost all people in the nation of all ranks and condition are set upon a parliament as the only means that can restore and settle a lasting peace in the kingdom, and I cannot tell how to think that so many of the nobility and chief gentry as seem to be on the Prince's side could have taken those measures if they had not been induced to it by some reasons of that nature.

Hence, when James in early December sent Halifax, Nottingham, and William's old acquaintance Lord Godolphin to the West to negotiate and simultaneously ordered the dispatch of writs for an election, the Prince felt he must make every show of being reasonable. Although some of his Whig adherents such as Sir Henry Capel and William Harbord feared that immediate elections would hinder them from being chosen, William overruled their objections while remarking that 'we may drive away the King; but, perhaps, we may not know how easily to come by a parliament'.[10]

In fact, James's strategy at this juncture was to deny the Prince a legally-constituted parliament, and his offers of accommodation were only a ruse. Amidst his last hasty preparations for flight to France, the King—who had countermanded an earlier set of writs in September 1688 upon the first reports of William's expedition—destroyed on 11 December all the new writs that had not yet been dispatched by the Chancery. James's bonfire of these writs, coupled with his disposal of the Great Seal in the Thames, created (as he intended) formidable procedural obstacles in the way of convening a parliament in his absence.[11] Thus, though the King had failed either through patronage or by packing to gain a parliament which would do his will, he still hoped to frustrate the Prince's own designs. In this, he was sadly mistaken and his flight played into his enemies' hands. Nonetheless, only after the throne that James aban-doned was again filled did William find it possible to secure a parliament.

In the often tumultuous days following James's departure, a variety of ways to secure that 'tool called parliament' were canvassed.[12] One alternative, pursued resolutely by James's remaining supporters, was to contrive a summons, in one form or another, under the King's authority. Within hours after James left London on 11 December 1688, the peers in and about the capital were sum-moned to the Guildhall by letters under Archbishop William Sancroft's signa-ture. These missives had been prepared for just such a contingency by Bishop Francis Turner of Ely (James's most devoted servant among the episcopate) in consultation with the Earl of Rochester. But though the loyalists were a majority among the twenty-nine peers who responded, they were not able to dictate the terms of the declaration drawn up at this gathering late on the 11th. Lords Montagu (Danby's accuser in 1678) and Wharton (the leading Nonconformist peer), joined by Viscount Newport and Lord Culpepper, generated enough resistance to Turner's original draft to compel the omission of a key clause that explicitly affirmed James's right to the throne. So, the loyalists had to be satisfied with a statement avowing the peers' readiness to assist William in procuring a 'free parliament'.[13]

However, the loyalists' flagging spirits were momentarily revived by James's return to London on 16 December. Turner again took the lead in a renewed search for an acceptable compromise, and in an interview with the King on the morning of the 17th he emphasised the need for a parliament and for far-reaching concessions on James's part if he hoped to preserve his title. Later that day, Turner told his colleague William Lloyd of St Asaph 'that now he believed his Majesty was willing to do all that could be required of him, and even to be reduced to the state of a Duke of Venice'. 'This way', Turner ingenuously added, would be 'most agreeable to his Highness's declaration', though others were quick to observe that Turner and his associates were part of a 'powerful faction that labours to narrow and enervate the Prince's design'.[14]

Precisely how numerous the loyalist group was at this time is impossible to determine, for before that assembly of peers—summoned by the Prince on 20 December 'to advise the best manner how to pursue the ends of my declaration in calling a free parliament'—confronted the main question, the King (with William's connivance) had successfully escaped to France.[15] Certainly, the assembly of peers, which met for the first time on the 21st, did include a significant proportion of loyalists. After the peers gathered on the 21st, there were predictions that they would send to the King (then at Rochester) 'to desire his concurrence and for calling a new parliament', and the Nonconformist (but well-connected) diarist Roger Morrice noted that before the news of James's second flight reached London late on the 23rd there had been a meeting of the loyalists to confer on the limitations upon the King they should propose on the 24th.[16] Then, too, though the peers refused on the 24th to read James's parting letter from Rochester, the Earl of Nottingham was still prepared to argue that the kingdom 'cannot come to have a parliament but by the King'. In the same spirit, the Earl of Clarendon proposed that those members who had been or could be returned on the writs issued before the 11th (184 of a total of 513) should meet and then authorise the other constituencies to choose representatives.[17] So when the Earl of Rochester wrote to his absent friend Lord Dartmouth on the 25th that 'I am very confident if the King had not again withdrawn himself, the peers would have sent to him before they made any address to the Prince', he was not simply whistling in the dark.[18]

Diametrically opposed to the loyalists' efforts to safeguard James's title by invoking his authority to convene parliament were the notions of some of William's adherents. In the wake of the news of the King's first flight, they had begun to talk of a cession of the crown. The lawyer Henry Pollexfen, for instance, told a startled Clarendon on 15 December 'that the King, by withdrawing himself, had left the government; that he had made a cession and forfeited his right'.[19] Similarly, when the Prince consulted those peers in attendance upon him at Windsor on the 17th about the disposition of the King's person after James's return to London, several spoke of a 'desertion' or 'dissolution of the government' as a result of the King's first flight.[20] Again, Bishop Lloyd had the 'way of cession' in mind when he talked with Turner in London that same day.[21] Gilbert Burnet (who had returned from exile with William and was in close touch with Lloyd) knew, then, of what he spoke when he later related in his History that 'the lawyers' had advised the Prince 'to declare himself King', as Henry VII had done, and that afterwards 'he might call a parliament which would be a legal assembly, if summoned by the King in fact, though his title was not yet recognised'.[22]

But as James's second flight helped to frustrate the schemes of the loyalists, so William's reservations about so blatant a violation of his own declaration undermined the position of the advocates of a 'cession'. The Prince, after hesitating for two days upon his arrival in London, decided instead to seek guidance from

the peers and others on how to convene a parliament. The lords were the first
to be consulted, and in their deliberations on 24 December still one other way
to call a parliament was suggested by Lords Paget and North. They proposed to
treat the King's flight and his dispatch of the 'pretended Prince' to France as
evidence of a legal demise, to declare that the crown had devolved on the Princess
of Orange as his rightful heir, and then to have Mary issue the writs for a
parliament. This alternative was backed by Bishop Compton (Danby's long-time
associate), but it appealed neither to the loyalists nor to most of William's
adherents. On the one side, Nottingham and his learned friend the Earl of
Pembroke spoke against it; on the other, Delamere roundly asserted that 'nothing
can be done but by the body of the people in their representatives'.[23]

In this fashion, all conceivable means for securing a parliament were rejected,
and so at last the peers decided to recommend the summoning of a convention—
that is, a meeting of the two Houses without royal authorisation. Pembroke,
reportedly, first suggested this expedient, and the assembly finally adopted it
after sitting for nearly eight hours on the 24th. As the Brandenburg envoy in
London remarked, the English, who always sought historical precedent for their
acts, could cite the case of 1660 in this instance.[24] Further, as Burnet explained
to Admiral Arthur Herbert (the commander of the flotilla that had borne the
Prince to England), a convention 'will be the true representative of the kingdom and that, though they have no legal writs, yet they being returned
upon a free choice, this will be upon the matter a free parliament' which will
'judge both the King's falling from the crown and the birth of the pretended
Prince; and that then a parliament may be legally held after they have declared
in whom the right of the crown lies'.[25]

Pembroke's expedient of a convention was also recommended in an address of
27 December made by a second assembly, which consisted of those Commoners
then in London who had served in Charles II's parliaments and of the London
aldermen and fifty common councilmen of the City.[26] After this body's concurrence with the peers, the Prince announced his acceptance of the plan on the
28th. And on the 29th, William's temporary secretariat, headed by William
Jephson, began sealing and dispatching the letters of summons.

In the three and a half weeks between the decision to call a convention and
its assembly on 22 January 1689, the political temperature in the capital remained
feverish. Already, the main alternatives its members would consider in resolving
the issue of who had or should have title to the throne had been mooted: (1)
making the Prince a regent and effective ruler in James's name (as Nottingham
had advocated on 24 December); (2) declaring the Princess the successor on the
grounds of James's 'demise' (as Paget and North had proposed); and (3) proclaiming William king on the basis of James's 'cession' (as Pollexfen had suggested).
Now, the merits of each of these proposals, as well as of the recall of James or
of the establishment of a commonwealth, were debated in a flood of pamphlets
and broadsides. The capital was also the scene in early and mid-January of a
series of 'consults' among the bishops and their noble friends. And these gatherings at Ely House and at Lambeth Palace (where Archbishop Sancroft was still
refusing to take any action himself) attracted so much attention that one newsletter writer felt obliged to deny the report that a convocation of the Church
had been meeting.[27]

It is harder to gauge the political temperature in the provinces in January

1689. Morrice, a Londoner, noted that the elections to the Convention were 'contended fervently in very many places'; yet, only thirty-one results were controverted in petitions to the Commons, while evidence of polls survives for twenty-nine other constituencies.[28] This total of sixty contests is substantially larger than the figure for the 1685 elections. Even so, the dynastic question only surfaced occasionally in these contests, and there were also relatively few flare-ups of the political and religious animosities that had been aroused during the Exclusion crisis and the Tory reaction.[29] Then, too, the fears voiced by some Whigs with William in early December 1688 that they might find it difficult to secure seats were obviated by James's departure and by the subsequent delay in the elections. In fact, Harbord was returned for three widely-separated constituencies! Overall, the new Commons included among its 513 members 341 who had sat before; of this number, 238 had served in at least one of the Exclusion parliaments but only 193 had been elected in 1685.[30]

In turn, when the Commons assembled in St Stephen's Chapel of Westminster Palace on 22 January, a majority of those present signalled their sympathy with the Prince's cause by choosing Henry Powle (a Whig barrister and the speaker of the ad hoc assembly of Commoners the previous month) over Sir Edward Seymour as their Speaker. Seymour's hatred of Catholicism had prompted him to come in early to William in the West. But by the time the Convention met the haughty Sir Edward, known as 'his highness' even to his friends, was disturbed by the 'countenance' given to Whigs and Nonconformists and offended by the lack of attention paid him after the Prince's arrival in London, and it was expected he would oppose the offer of the crown to William.[31]

Sir Henry Capel then sought to follow up Powle's selection by proposing that the Commons should go into committee of the whole to consider 'the state of the nation' on the 23rd. Others, however, urged delay, and chief among them was Sir Thomas Clarges, a staunch Churchman and one of the thirty 'old parliament men' in this House whose service dated back at least to the 1650s. Sir Thomas, who was acting 'upon concert with Lord Nottingham and Mr [Heneage] Finch' (Nottingham's younger brother and formerly Solicitor-General), pointed out that many members were still on the roads to Westminster and so moved an adjournment until the 28th.[32]

The loyalists' aim was to allow the Lords the initiative in sorting out the constitutional conundrum James had left behind; their hope was that the peers would provide, as they had in December, a more conservative lead than could be anticipated from the Commons. But though the lower House did agree to Clarges's motion, William's supporters in the Lords quickly reacted. Prompted by Halifax, who had committed himself to the Prince after James's first flight and who was now chosen over Danby as Speaker pro tem. of the Lords, the peers on the 25th voted in favour of Devonshire's motion to adjourn until the 29th.[33]

All eyes now were on the Commons, and 417 members answered to the Clerk's call of the roll on Saturday, 26 January.[34] Then on the 28th, the lower House began by once more passing over Seymour. Amid shouts of 'No Seymour, No Seymour' from the backbenches, the Commons chose Richard Hampden (once a member of Oliver's 'other House' and the leading Nonconformist sympathiser in this House) to preside over the committee of the whole.[35] The committee then took only a few hours to come to a voice vote, with but three negatives, that James had broken 'the original contract', 'abdicated the government', and left the throne 'vacant'. The full House promptly approved this resolution and rose by 3 p.m.[36]

However, the apparent consensus of 28 January masked some important differences. Gilbert Dolben (the barrister son of the late Bishop of Rochester) had spoken not of James's 'abdication' but of his 'demise' in opening the debate in the committee, and his usage had been followed in a number of other speeches.[37] The weight men might give to these distinctions was to be clearly demonstrated eight days later when 151 members and two tellers (Francis Gwyn, the Earl of Rochester's long-time friend, and Sir Joseph Tredenham, Seymour's brother-in-law) left their seats to vote in favour of accepting the amendments that the Lords had subsequently made to the Commons' resolution of the 28th.[38]

The changes the peers made and communicated to the lower House on 2 February reflected the greater conservative strength and the deeper divisions among them. Three main groups may be distinguished. First, there was a numerous, though not altogether unanimous, band of loyalists. Some such as Bishop Turner and the Earls of Clarendon and Ailesbury remained loyal to James both out of personal devotion to him and from concern to maintain the Church's doctrine of non-resistance.[39] Others such as the Earls of Nottingham and Pembroke were more concerned to preserve James's title to the crown and feared that acceptance of the Commons' vote would open the door to an elective monarchy.[40] The former still hoped against hope that James might yet be recalled, and many of the bishops among them were to refuse the oaths to the new monarchs; the latter were quite prepared to serve William and Mary faithfully once their constitutionalist scruples were eased.[41] Both loyalist elements joined on 29 January in support of Rochester's amended motion for the creation of a regency in James's name during his lifetime, though Turner subsequently stated that he and his friends thought a regency *for life* 'as liable to as great objections as the deposing' and supported it only 'to amuse and gain time'.[42] In the event, the motion for a regency was rejected late that evening by a vote of 51 to 48.[43]

The second group in the Lords were adherents of the Prince, and they were almost as numerous as the loyalists. These men were ready to adopt the Commons' resolution of 28 January and to install either William alone (as Halifax seems to have favoured) or William and Mary jointly on the throne.

But the balance among the Lords, as the proceedings of 30 and 31 January revealed, was held by a third, much smaller group headed by the Earl of Danby, who had been absent in the North till early January. Danby's flying squadron, which included Bishop Compton and perhaps as many as six other peers, voted against a regency on the 29th. But during the next two days, they combined with the loyalists to amend the Commons' resolution by substituting 'deserted' for 'abdicated' and by deleting the clause of 'vacancy'. This coalition also turned back, by a vote of 52 to 47, a motion to proceed immediately to proclaim William and Mary, for Danby and his friends favoured the declaration or recognition of Mary as James's hereditary successor. In turn, this same combination of loyalists and 'Maryites' was in evidence on 4 February when the Lords reaffirmed their earlier amendments to the Commons' resolve by margins of 55 to 51 and 54 to 53.

These divisions in the Lords finally provoked a formal division in the Commons on 5 February, though the vote of 282 to 151 for maintaining the original terms of the resolution of 28 January only exposed the Tory minority to subsequent 'black-listing' by their Whig foes.[44] The deadlocked Houses then proceeded to a conference the next morning in which their 'managers' disputed precedents from English history and bandied definitions from continental legal texts. Yet, the confrontation between the spokesmen for the Lords and for the Commons was curiously inconclusive. Full agreement was impossible since the Commons' managers, prominent among them such rising Whig lawyers as Sir George Treby and John Somers, were unwilling to answer the question posed by Nottingham (and reiterated by Rochester and Clarendon) as to whether the 'vacancy' applied only to James or to his heirs as well. Similarly, the Lords' spokesmen were almost as reticent when the Commoners sought to find out who, in their view, did occupy the throne if it were not now vacant.[45]

This stalemate was to be resolved not by learned debate but by outside pressure, chiefly from the Prince. William had moved cautiously heretofore, if for no other reason than to avoid alienating potential supporters. Despite his need for speedy action lest the Dutch Republic 'be lost before England can be settled or ready to act' against France, he had decided against a unilateral assumption of the crown.[46] Moreover, though he had written Danby on 12 December 1688 that the best service the gentry who had risen with the northern peers could then do was to preserve 'their inclination for me' and 'stand to be chosen parliament men', the Prince had avoided direct involvement in the election campaign.[47] With James's 'regulating' attempts fresh in many men's minds, William even refused—despite repeated importunities—to commit any of the letters of summons to the Convention 'to any private gentleman's hands'.[48] Now, however, he confirmed earlier hints of Willem Bentinck and others of his intimates that he would settle for nothing less than the crown in his own right.[49] He made this statement at a private gathering probably held the evening of 3 February; among those present were Halifax, Danby, and the Whig peers Shrewsbury, Winchester, and Mordaunt. William also told this group he was prepared to have Mary be queen in name and to give preference in the succession to Anne and her offspring before any children of his own by a possible second marriage.[50]

William's private statement, Mary's refusal to countenance Danby's efforts in her behalf, and Anne's public declaration (in the form of a message to the peers on 6 February) that she would waive temporarily her claim to the throne should Mary predecease William all but settled the question.[51] After receiving Anne's message and hearing their managers' report of the abortive free conference of the 5th with the Commons, the peers voted on the 6th to swallow both 'abdication' and 'vacancy'. And after some further debate, they also approved the Marquess of Winchester's motion to make William and Mary king and queen.[52] This time, the ranks of William's adherents were swelled by new recruits absent from earlier votes, and the margin of victory was further enlarged by the abandonment of resistance on Danby's part and by those loyalists who either absented themselves on the 6th as Viscount Weymouth did or left the House before the decisive votes were taken as Godolphin did.[53]

Yet just as the Lords and the Commons seemed on the verge of an agreement to install William and Mary on the throne, another obstacle appeared in the shape of the proposed statement of subjects' rights and liberties. The desirability of drawing up a detailed condemnation of James's misdeeds had first been broached in the Commons on 29 January, and the long and wandering debate which followed had sidetracked a motion by Thomas Wharton (the rakehell heir of the Puritan peer) to supply the vacancy voted the previous day with both

Prince and Princess. In the debate of the 29th adherents of William such as William Garroway and Hugh Boscawen found themselves aligned with 'Mary-ites' such as Clarges and Sir Christopher Musgrave. Musgrave argued that the House 'can not answer it to the nation or Prince of Orange till we declare what are the rights invaded'; Garroway claimed that the Prince 'cannot take it ill if we make conditions to secure ourselves for the future' in order to 'do justice to those who sent us hither'. At the same time, other supporters of William such as Pollexfen joined with 'Maryites' such as Dolben in warning of the dangers of delay involved in any elaborate recasting of the constitution and in denouncing the distrust of the Prince that such a course might appear to suggest.[54] Finally, it was agreed that a committee would be appointed to draw up 'heads' in the form of a declaration which could, as Clarges suggested, 'be presented to our chief governor, when declared'. Treby reported back twenty-three articles from the committee on 2 February, and the Commons with a 'ready concurrence' (which surprised some observers) approved them and added a few more of their own devising.[55] But on the 4th, the lower House partially reversed itself and decided, as Seymour and others had suggested on the 29th, to instruct the committee to distinguish between 'such of the general heads, as are intro-ductory of new laws, from those that are declaratory of ancient rights'.[56]

Thus matters stood on the morning of 7 February when, with the news of the Lords' votes of the 6th common knowledge, Lord Wiltshire (the Marquess of Winchester's heir) rose in St Stephen's Chapel to propose that the Prince and Princess be named to fill the vacant throne. But the Commons put off his motion until they could consider the revised declaration of rights, which was reported and approved that afternoon. Then on the 8th, after instructing a committee to embody in a single text the declaration (now shorn completely of the heads 'introductory of new laws'), the resolution of 28 January, the Lords' vote in favour of William and Mary, and the Lords' proposals for a revised oath of allegiance, the Commons passed the entire document without a division and dispatched it to the Lords.[57]

However, the Lords' acquiescence in the declaration was by no means a foregone conclusion. Certainly, Sir Edward Harley (Hampden's kinsman and once a parliamentarian captain) did not think so, for when he heard of the Lords' acceptance of the main points of the declaration on 9 February, he wrote excitedly to his eldest son Robert in Herefordshire: 'This is a special instance of divine providence, for the contrary was extremely endeavoured and skilfully insinuated, though false, of the Prince's displeasure to have terms of mistrust put upon him'.[58]

The abortive manoeuvres which explain Harley's sigh of relief were recorded by his friend Morrice. Morrice's story is that on the evening of 8 February 'divers bishops and divers lords' went to William and 'told him those stipula-tions argued great disingenuity and distrust, that they were usurpations upon the crown' to which the Lords would never agree, and that a majority among the peers 'could carry all without any such stipulations.' With rumours spreading that William was opposed to at least some of the articles in the declaration —reports which gained credence because it was known that 'most of those about the Prince' were of this mind—Seymour offered in the Commons on the morning of the 9th to 'lay any wager there was no king or queen proclaimed till Tuesday fortnight or longer'. But at the same time, some of William's adherents sent to St James's to assure him that the 'articles contained nothing in them but the known laws' and to warn him of the political dangers in any opposition to the declaration. The Prince's response, Morrice was told, was that he had never 'expressed his sense one way nor another' and that 'his sense in this case was what the Lords and Commons thought fit'. When these sentiments of William were made known in Westminster Palace around midday on the 9th, those peers who that morning 'had exerted themselves to exalt the dispensing power, etc., and to make a fatal breach between the two Houses' over the terms of the declaration now 'saw that they were mistaken and that this was none of the sense of the Prince'. So, 'they and all their party veered about', 'laboured to bring themselves off with all the art they could, and lowered some passages in some articles they had already passed over'.[59]

Morrice's testimony is corroborated and amplified by a second report of this episode. Seymour, so Lord Yester wrote to his father in Scotland, declared in the Commons on the morning of the 9th that 'he had it from Monsieur Bentinck that the Prince was not satisfied with the restrictions and limitations they were putting upon the crown and that if it had been left to himself he would have done better and more for their security'. His tale 'almost fired' both Houses, especially the Lords 'where it was said by Nottingham that the Prince ought to consider that the crown of England with whatever limitations . . . was far more than anything the States of Holland were able to give him'. But all was 'calmed' after Colonel Henry Sidney (one of the seven signers of the 'invitation' to William and the Prince's chief English confidant) returned post-haste from an audience with William and assured members 'that any such thing was far from his thoughts'.[60]

William's disavowal of Bentinck was probably somewhat disingenuous; after all, William later in 1689 told Halifax he would not have 'all the articles' of the declaration confirmed by statute.[61] But in early February, his chief concern was to prevent any miscarriage or further delay in the impending offer of the crown. In the event, the two Houses were able to settle quickly their differences over the terms of the declaration, and the three alterations agreed upon on the 12th were all in the direction of qualifying the Commons' formulations.[62] The Commons' condemnation of the dispensing power was limited to its exercise 'of late' on the grounds that, however abused by James II, dispensation was a traditional royal prerogative. The Commons' assertion that all Protestants were entitled to bear arms was restricted to weapons 'suitable to their conditions, as allowed by law', probably because the peers felt it 'savour[ed] of the politics to arm the mob'.[63] And the Commons' pronouncement that parliaments 'ought to be held frequently, and suffered to sit' was narrowed by the omission of the last four words.

In final form, then, the thrust of the declaration was threefold. In the first place, the legislative supremacy of parliament was stressed. Parliaments were to be held often, and parliament's consent was needed to suspend statutes, to levy taxes, and to maintain an army in peacetime.[64] In the second place, a variety of 'illegal' acts of preceding reigns (especially James II's) were condemned: they included the flood of dispensations, the establishment of the commission for ecclesiastical causes, the prosecution of petitioners, the disarming of Protestants, and several abuses of the legal processes. In the third place, a deep concern was manifested for the 'freedom' of parliament, with respect both to the choice of members and to debates at Westminster. Yet severe as the framers of the declaration were in denouncing past royal measures, the text was also vague at critical points, particularly in failing to specify how often parliament was to meet and how free elections were to be secured.

Given the declaration's omission of the heads 'introductory of new laws' and the lack of precision in some of its critical articles, the 'constitution'—at least as members of parliament between 1660 and 1688 had understood it—was not fundamentally altered. The declaration certainly left intact the royal prerogatives to make war and to command the militia, to appoint to governmental posts, and to summon, prorogue, and dissolve parliaments. Nor did the declaration outlaw those devices by which Charles II and James II had sought to alter the composition of parliament and to influence its members. William and Mary would continue to have the right to select new bishops, to create new temporal peers, even to issue new borough charters; it also remained open to them to use grants, places, and pensions to sway individual peers and Commoners.

The declaration, then, did not really speak to the future conduct of relations between the crown and the two Houses, and much would depend—as at the Restoration—on the terms of the financial settlement, which was still to be worked out. Yet the tender of the crown, along with the declaration, to William and to Mary (newly arrived from Holland) on 13 February did, at last, allow William to secure a parliament. The way chosen, after consultation with the lawyers, was by a bill to 'declare' the Convention a parliament from 13 February 'in the first year of their Majesties' reign'.[65] A measure to this effect was introduced in the Lords on the 18th and with the often reiterated plea of 'necessity' it secured a quick, though not unopposed passage in five days. Thus, by 23 February 1689 William finally had both the crown and the parliament that James had sought to deny him. Now, the new monarch would have to discover how to translate the negative consensus against the old king into the parliamentary support he needed to sustain the new government against its enemies and to achieve the other goals of his expedition to England.

Notes to Chapter I

1 B. Kemp, *King and Commons 1660–1832* (1965), p. 3.

2 D. Witcombe, *Charles II and the Cavalier House of Commons 1663–1674* (1966), pp. 126, 125.

3 *Private Memoirs (Never Before Published) of John Potenger*, ed. C. Bingham (1841), p. 57. See also R. Willman, 'The Origins of "Whig" and "Tory" in English Political Language', *HJ* XVII (1974), 247–64.

4 *The Diaries and Papers of Sir Edward Dering, Second Baronet, 1643–1684*, ed. M. F. Bond (1976), p. 63.

5 J. R. Jones, *The Revolution of 1688 in England* (1972), pp. 46–7.

6 C. Chandaman, 'The Financial Settlement in the Parliament of 1685', in *British Government and Administration*, ed. H. Hearder (Cardiff, 1974), pp. 144–54.

7 Burnet, *History*, III, 240. And see Lacey, *Dissent*, p. 240.

8 *Correspondentie*, I, i, 49.

9 BL Add. MS. 45731, f. 71, R. Warre to E. Poley, 4 December.

10 *Clar. Corr.*, II, 222, and 219, 221.

11 F. Mazure, *Histoire de la Révolution de 1688 en Angleterre* (Paris, 1825), III, 264.

12 *HMC Buckingham etc.*, p. 452.

13 R. Beddard, 'The Guildhall Declaration of 11 December 1688 and the Counter-Revolution of the Loyalists', *HJ* XI (1968), 403–20, and ' "The Violent Party": the Guildhall

Revolutionaries and the Growth of Opposition to James II', *Guildhall Miscellany* III (1970), 120–36. And see *CSPD*, 1687–1689, pp. 379–80.

14 Dalrymple, *Memoirs*, II, app. i, 336 (and see *CSPD*, 1687–1689, p. 381); DWL Morrice MS. Q, 379–81.

15 *PH*, V, 21.

16 Bodl. Ballard MS. 45, f. 22 [R. Sare to Dr A. Charlett], 22 December; DWL Morrice MS. Q, 401.

17 Althorp Savile MSS., box 4, Halifax's notes of the debate of 24 December. See also *Clar. Corr.*, II, 234–5.

18 HMC *Dartmouth*, III, 141 (also Gwyn's letter of the same date).

19 *Clar. Corr.*, II, 225–6.

20 Althorp Savile MSS., box 4, Halifax's notes of 17 December.

21 *Clar. Corr.*, II, 228; Dalrymple, *Memoirs*, II, app. i, 337. And see DWL Morrice MS. Q, 378, 382; *Hatton Corr.*, II, 127.

22 Burnet, *History*, III, 361. And see his memorandum in *Diary of the times of Charles the Second by the hon. Henry Sidney*, ed. R. W. Blencoe (1843), II, 288–91.

23 Althorp Savile MSS., box 4, Halifax's notes; *Clar. Corr.*, II, 235. See also E. Thompson, 'Correspondence of Admiral Herbert during the Revolution', *EHR* I (1886), 535.

24 Althorp Savile MSS., box 4; KU, F. Bonnet, 25 December/4 January.

25 Thompson, 'Correspondence of Admiral Herbert', p. 535.

26 Morrice noted that at first some of this assembly spoke of urging William to assume the crown immediately; DWL Morrice MS. Q, 396–7.

27 BL Egerton MS. 3929, f. 130, 19 January. And see A. Simpson, 'The Convention Parliament 1688–1689' (unpublished D.Phil. thesis, University of Oxford, 1939), pp. 67–72 and Appendix E.

28 DWL Morrice MS. Q, 436. For the contested seats, see Appendix A.

29 For examples, see H. Horwitz, 'Parliament and the Glorious Revolution', *BIHR* XLVII (1974), pp. 41–2.

30 These totals have been calculated to include those men chosen in by-elections to replace members who, like Harbord, were elected in more than one constituency.

31 *Clar. Corr.*, II, 238; KU, F. Bonnet, 22 January/1 February and 25 January/4 February; Huygens, *Journaal*, I, 70, 72.

32 *Clar. Corr.*, II, 252–3. And see Grey, *Debates*, IX, 4–6; DWL Morrice MS. Q, 437.

33 *Clar. Corr.*, II, 253–4; A. Simpson, 'Notes of a Noble Lord, 22 January to 12 February 1688/9', *EHR* LII (1937), 92.

34 *The London Intelligence*, No. 5 (24–9 January), Bodl. Nichols Newspapers.

35 Huygens, *Journaal*, I, 72; BL Egerton MS. 3929, f. 133, newsletter, 2 February; DWL Morrice MS. Q, 444. And see Lacey, *Dissent*, p. 224.

36 Grey, *Debates*, IX, 7–25; MSP, II, 401–12; DWL Morrice MS. Q, 444; House of Lords RO, Hist. Collection 155, 'A Jornall of the Convention at Westminster begun the 22 of January 1688–9'.

37 BL Stowe MS. 840, ff. 1–9, 'Mr Dolbin's speech concerning the vacancy'. I owe this reference to Professor L. G. Schwoerer.

38 The 'blacklist' is given in Browning, *Danby*, III, 164–72.

39 R. Beddard, 'The Loyalist Opposition in the Interregnum', *BIHR* XL (1967), 101–9; Bodl. Clarendon MS. 90, ff. 11–19; *Memoirs of Ailesbury*, pp. 229–37.

40 Horwitz, *Revolution Politicks*, p. 72 and ff.; *Memoirs of Ailesbury*, pp. 232–3; Simpson, 'Notes of a Noble Lord', p. 97.

41 Burnet, *History*, III, 377–8.

42 Beddard, 'The Loyalist Opposition', p. 108. And see Danby's notes of the debate in Horwitz, 'Parliament and the Glorious Revolution', pp. 50–2.

43 The forty-eight 'regencyites' plus their teller Clarendon are listed in *Clar. Corr.*, II, 256 note. For the composition of the other two groups, see Horwitz, 'Parliament and the Glorious Revolution', pp. 43–5.

44 Bodl. Rawlinson MS. D1079 (diary of a London dissenter), f. 12, and compare DWL Morrice MS. Q, 459. See also Grey, *Debates*, IX, 90.

45 *PH*, V, 66–108.

46 Thompson, 'Correspondence of Admiral Herbert', p. 535.

47 This letter is printed in *Cambridge Historical Journal* V (1937), 107–8.

48 DWL Morrice MS. Q, 408.

49 Foxcroft, *Halifax*, II, 203; *Clar. Corr.*, II, 246–7; Dalrymple, *Memoirs*, II, app. i, 342.

50 Burnet, *History*, III, 395–6; Huygens, *Journaal*, I, 81; C. F. Sirtema van Crovestins, *Histoire des luttes et rivalites politiques entre les puissances maritimes et la France* (Paris. 1851–4), VI, 19–20.

51 FSL Newdigate newsletters 1971, 7 February; Bodl. Rawlinson MS. D1079, f. 13. And see Horwitz, 'Parliament and the Glorious Revolution', p. 46 n. 5.

52 DWL Morrice MS. Q, 459–61.

53 Horwitz, 'Parliament and the Glorious Revolution', p. 46.

54 Grey, *Debates*, IX, 29–37; MSP, II, 413–25; DWL Morrice MS., Q, 447. Cf. R. Frankle, 'The Formulation of the Declaration of Rights', HJ, XVII (1974), 265–79.

55 MSP, II, 420; DWL Morrice MS. Q, 453; CJ, X, 17; Grey, *Debates*, IX, 42–5.

56 CJ, X, 19; MSP, II, 415, 419.

57 Grey, *Debates*, IX, 70–1; CJ, X, 21–2, 23–4. For the Lords' revised oath, see Horwitz, *Revolution Politicks*, p. 82.

58 BL Add. MS. 40621, f. 20, 9 February (my italics).

59 DWL Morrice MS. Q, 463–5.

60 House of Lords RO, Willcocks MSS. (transcripts), VI, 21, to Lord Tweeddale, 11 February. See also Horwitz, 'Parliament and the Glorious Revolution', p. 49, n. 2.

61 Foxcroft, *Halifax*, II, 217, 223. And see *Correspondencia entre dos embajadores*, ed. G. Maura Gamzao (Madrid, 1951–2), I, 86.

62 LJ, XIV, 122–5; CJ, X, 25–8.

63 Luttrell, *Parliamentary Diary*, p. 444.

64 L. G. Schwoerer, 'No Standing Armies!' (Baltimore, 1974), pp. 150–4.

65 HLM, 1689–1690, p. 30. Cf. SR, VI, 23; Grey, *Debates*, IX, 84–106.

II

THE CONVENTION PARLIAMENT

1689-1690

In the three and a half months since William's expedition had set sail from Dutch shores, his skill and James's folly had produced a startling and dramatic revolution in England. But the 'great acclamations of joy' in London at the proclamation of the new King and Queen on 13 February 1689 were no guarantee of the success of their reign.[1] Indeed, their first year on the throne was to be troubled by a host of difficulties. Although there were good grounds to believe that Scotland would follow England's lead in accepting William and Mary, earlier hopes for the peaceful implementation of their authority in Ireland soon faded. Negotiations with the Earl of Tyrconnel failed to bring the old king's viceroy to terms, and on 15 February James left his new residence at St Germain for Ireland, intent on regaining his lost kingdoms with French backing and Irish Catholic assistance. Even in England, the new monarchs' situation was problematical. The physical security of the government continued in some doubt, partly because of the uncertain loyalty of those regiments of James's army still in being, partly because of the conspiracies being concerted by busy Jacobite plotters. Besides, there remained many controversial questions attendant upon the Revolution that had to be resolved by the King and the two Houses.

William's decision to transform the Convention into a parliament was prompted, then, by a desire to avoid both the delay and the possible disorders that a new general election would entail. But after the Convention was 'declared, enacted, and adjudged' a parliament by statute on 23 February, the King's relations with the assembly which had voted him the crown were beset by disagreements that stemmed in part from William's unfamiliarity with English affairs and his initial choice of measures and men, in part also from the medley of actors and motives which had made the Revolution itself.

William came to the throne with few fixed points of reference in domestic affairs beyond his desire to dampen down internal differences in order to pursue a vigorous foreign policy and his determination to defend the legitimate prerogatives of his predecessors. Yet the majority of those Englishmen with whom he had been in close contact before and immediately after his arrival were long-time opponents of the Stuart Court. The King began, then, with an exaggerated notion of the strength of the Whigs or, as he referred to them, the 'Commonwealth party', and the largest contingent of his initial appointees to high office was drawn from the ranks of former Exclusionists and their friends.[2] Perhaps the most influential of these men was to be the young and still untested Earl of Shrewsbury. Shrewsbury, appointed southern Secretary of State at the age of twenty-eight, had been one of the motley band of seven who signed the 'invitation' to the Prince in June 1688, and his charm won for him a special place in William's affections. Other Whig peers rewarded for their parts in the Revolution were Viscount Mordaunt and Baron Delamere, and they were joined on the Whig-dominated Treasury Commission by Richard Hampden and Sir Henry Capel, while William Jephson was named to the lucrative post of Secretary to the Treasury. The royal bedchamber and the household, too, were mainly Whig preserves, save for the King's Dutch servants. Four of the six English peers selected as Gentlemen of the Bedchamber were Whigs, including Lord Lumley, another signer of the invitation. The Earl of Devonshire (a third signer) was named Lord Steward, the Earl of Dorset was made Lord Chamberlain, and below them were several important Whig Commoners—particularly 'Honest Tom' Wharton as Comptroller and his friends, Charles Lord Wiltshire and 'Jack' Howe. Furthermore, the majority of the new judges and royal legal officers were Whigs such as Speaker Henry Powle (Master of the Rolls), Sir John Holt, Henry Pollexfen, Sir George Treby, and John Somers. And though the Admiralty Board was headed by the independent and irascible Admiral Herbert, most of his colleagues were Whigs, including such old House of Commons men as William Sacheverell and Sir Thomas Lee. Moreover, Edward Russell, a cousin of the Whig martyr Lord Russell and himself a fourth signer of the invitation, was chosen as Herbert's principal subordinate at sea and also as Treasurer of the Navy. Altogether, then, Whigs constituted the preponderant element among the thirty-two-man Privy Council, in which William at first thought 'the government was to reside'.[3] And in lesser posts were to be found many other Whigs and former Exclusionists, including John Wildman (once a Leveller) as Postmaster-General, and Robert Ferguson, the Dissenting minister who had accompanied the Duke of Monmouth in 1685.

From the outset, however, William had no intention of being a 'Doge of Venice', and in any case two former servants of Charles II, the Marquess of Halifax and the Earl of Danby, had strong claims on his favour. Danby (along with his old protégé, Bishop Compton) was another of the signers of the invitation; earlier, he had been the sponsor of William's marriage to Mary, and during the Convention he supported the Princess's enthronement until William spoke his mind. At the age of fifty-seven, the pasty-faced Danby was not in the best of health, but he was ready to serve once more as Lord Treasurer. In the event, he had to settle for the Lord Presidency and a step up in the peerage as Marquess of Carmarthen, while only some of his numerous tribe of kinsmen and dependants —principally Charles Bertie and Sir Henry Goodricke (both appointed to posts in the Ordnance under the Huguenot Duke of Schomberg)—were given places. To add to Carmarthen's disappointments was the appointment of his perennial Yorkshire rival and contemporary, the Marquess of Halifax, to the more lucrative post of Lord Privy Seal. The 'black marquess' (as the dark-complexioned Halifax was sometimes nicknamed to distinguish him from Carmarthen) was both by repute and by self-profession a 'trimmer' *par excellence*, yet he had committed himself wholeheartedly to securing the throne for William, even to the exclusion of Mary, after he had joined the Prince at Windsor in mid-December. Halifax also quickly struck up an intimacy with William that Danby never attained, and fortunately Halifax's jotted notes of some of their conversations between late December 1688 and May 1690 survive to illumine the King's thinking during these critical months. Yet despite their many differences, Carmarthen and Halifax did have at least two points in common in early 1689. Both disclosed some doubts about the permanence of the new government: Halifax tried to reinsure himself with James through Lady Oglethorpe, while Carmarthen's request to William for the governorship of Hull was interpreted by some as the provision of a retreat in case the old King returned.[4] Nor was either marquess much to the taste of most Whigs—Danby by reason of his long-standing commitment to 'Church and King' policies, Halifax because of his part in the defeat of exclusion and his reputed share in the direction of the 'Tory reaction'.

Whig influence in the new administration was further curtailed by two other appointments. One was William's choice of the assiduous though timorous Baron Godolphin, a loyal servant of Charles II and James II, to be the fifth (and the only experienced) member of the Treasury Commission. Second, and politically the more important, was William's selection of the Earl of Nottingham as northern Secretary, for it was anticipated when this earl's appointment was announced in early March that he, Shrewsbury, Carmarthen, and Halifax would be the leading English ministers.[5] Nottingham, at forty-one, was a great deal older than his fellow Secretary Shrewsbury, and he had a considerable reputation among the Tories and the clergy. The Earl had led the struggle in the Lords for a regency, but he was ready to support the new government and he refused to be party to a projected loyalist walk-out from the Lords. Thus, once the King failed to lure his old friend Sir William Temple out of retirement, he decided to name Nottingham rather than to rely on the more experienced Whig candidate, Ralph Lord Montagu, who was suspected of still harbouring Francophile sympathies.[6] Nottingham agreed to serve, but he also bluntly told William that 'he foresaw that there were many steps yet to be made in which he would oppose that which would be pretended to be his [the King's] service'.[7]

Initially, then, the new administration's make-up epitomised that essentially negative consensus against James whose limits had been underlined by the divisions within the Convention over the disposition of the crown. And to add to the discord that might be anticipated within a patchwork ministry, handicapped by partisan animosities and personal rivalries, was the administrative inexperience of many of the new officials. Not that a lack of previous service troubled all the King's new servants: while Nottingham solicited memoranda on the duties of his unfamiliar post from old hands such as his kinsman Sir Robert Southwell, the brasher Mordaunt—whose ability was only outdistanced by his conceit—was convinced 'at his first entrance into the Treasury that he would understand the business of it as well as Lord Godolphin in a fortnight'.[8]

If such a government was to be effective, William would have to give a strong lead and also rely heavily upon the trusted Dutch servants who had accompanied him. Yet some of them, notably Zuilestein and Ouwerkerk, were wary of involvement for fear of exposing themselves to parliamentary attack, especially as they quickly perceived that William's reliance upon Willem Bentinck stirred up English resentment.[9] To be sure, Dijkvelt, who formerly had served as William's envoy in England, did not engender the same ill will that Bentinck provoked, and it was reported early in 1689 that some English peers hoped he would stay and be naturalised.[10] But Dijkvelt did not get on with Bentinck, and the King showed where his favour lay between the two in his bestowal of coronation honours in

the spring of 1689. Bentinck was created Earl of Portland and at the same time
the leading English 'favourite' Henry Sidney (the seventh signer of the invitation) was ennobled as Viscount Sidney. They were joined by the new Marquess
of Carmarthen and by the Marquess of Winchester (made Duke of Bolton),
Viscount Fauconberg (raised to an earldom), Viscount Mordaunt (made Earl of
Monmouth), Lord Montagu (elevated to an earldom), Lord Churchill (made Earl
of Marlborough), Lord Lumley (promoted to a viscountcy), and the Irish peer
Cholmondeley (created an English baron). But Dijkvelt was omitted from this
honours list, and late in 1689 he returned to the Continent, along with his
servant Lamberty (who later compiled a very informative narrative of
William's first year on the throne), leaving Bentinck without a rival in the royal
entourage.

Englishmen's suspicion of Dutch favourites reflected the ambiguity of
William's position as 'dual monarch' of England and the United Provinces, and
it also points up the difference between the King's European perspective and the
more parochial outlook of most of his new subjects. William's prime objective in
intervening in the British Isles, beyond safeguarding his wife's and his own
claims to the succession, had been to further his lifelong struggle against Louis
XIV. And once on the throne, both his public declarations and his private statements attested to his overriding concern with France. Yet for most Englishmen
who had participated in James's overthrow, it had been the threat 'popery' posed
to the established order within the British Isles (and not least in Ireland) that had
impelled them to run the dangers, physical and moral, of helping to cast out an
anointed monarch. There still were, it is true, some Englishmen such as Justice
Rokeby who could mesh insular and continental affairs into an integrated
(though somewhat old-fashioned) vision of an all-encompassing struggle for 'the
cause of God and Christ against Satan and Anti-Christ'.[11] But there were many
more who, like Halifax, were startled by the priority their new king accorded to
the Continent, even after the news of James's landing in Ireland reached London
in mid-March.[12]

In the light of the differences over domestic affairs within parliament and the
ministry and of the divergence on external affairs between the King and his new
subjects, it is understandable that William's relations with the Convention
parliament were often troubled. Then, too, the questions before the members
were complex and sometimes novel. The securing and supporting of the new
government, the formulation of the terms of settlement in church and state, the
financing of foreign policy and the management of the war, stand out as the
three principal sets of issues with which parliament, and particularly the Commons, had to deal in 1689. And in some respects, the Commons were ill-equipped
to handle them in a constructive and expeditious fashion. In the first place, their
deliberations—recorded unofficially by the Nottinghamshire M.P. Anchitell
Grey, who had begun to keep a diary of debates in 1667—were bedevilled by the
clash of those groups whom contemporaries sometimes referred to as Whigs and
Tories, sometimes as the 'Commonwealth party' and the 'Church party'. In the
second place, the tradition that the Commons' primary role was to serve as the
'grand inquest' of the kingdom, exposing the 'Country's' ills and investigating
the misdeeds of the 'Court', was not easy to reconcile with the need to support
a new government. Similarly, the lingering tradition that supplies should be
proposed by backbenchers, rather than by the King's servants in the lower

House, did not facilitate effective justification or provision of the government's unprecedentedly large fiscal requests.[13]

But these are retrospective judgements; when William addressed the Convention on 18 February he did not anticipate a lengthy or difficult session. Rather, in indicating his wish to avoid new elections, the King stressed the need for 'speedy care' first 'of our allies abroad', particularly the Dutch, and second 'of affairs here', particularly the state of Ireland.[14] And once he formally approved the bill declaring the Convention a parliament, the two Houses did take up a series of bills covering a wide range of subjects—prominent among them measures to support and secure the new regime by providing the legal authority to sustain it against its enemies.

The Commons made quick work of two very useful bills. After Richard Hampden, speaking as a Privy Councillor, informed members on 1 March of the urgent need to provide for the continued detention of Jacobite suspects, the lower House responded by drafting and twice reading that same day a bill to suspend temporarily the habeas corpus act.[15] Similarly, a fortnight later when the news of a mutiny at Ipswich by one of James's former regiments reached the capital, the Commons swallowed their distaste for martial law and rapidly approved what would become the first mutiny act.[16] But the bills introduced in both Houses in early March to impose the oath of allegiance were not so quickly adopted, for the question of the enforcement of the oath became entangled with the ticklish problem of relations between Anglicans and Protestant Nonconformists, both in the state and in the church. So, from mid-March to mid-April much parliamentary time was devoted to a series of bills that bore upon those relationships.

The specific difficulty raised by the oath bills was whether any pledge of allegiance to the new sovereigns should be exacted from incumbent Anglican clergy, for it was widely anticipated that many would scruple even the appearance of violating their previous oath to James or of repudiating their fervid advocacy in the past of the doctrine of passive obedience to duly constituted authority. It was to mitigate such scruples that Nottingham had offered during the Convention's debates a revision of the existing oath. His version, incorporated in the Declaration of Rights and then imposed on all members of both Houses by the act declaring the Convention a parliament, differed from the Jacobean oath in two key respects. Instead of acknowledging William and Mary as 'lawful and rightful' king and queen and binding the oathtaker to 'bear faith and true allegiance' to them and to their 'heirs and successors', men were simply obliged to swear to be 'faithful and bear true allegiance' to the new rulers.[17] But while only a handful of lay peers (most prominently, Clarendon) and even fewer Commoners refused the new oath, the possibility that a significant proportion of the clergy would decline it was brought home in early March by the failure of at least eight bishops (including the Archbishop of Canterbury) to comply with the 1 March deadline for members of parliament to take it.[18]

As the Tories' fears of a division among the clergy over the question of allegiance mounted, many Protestant Nonconformists and their sympathisers in the two Houses seemed bent upon pressing for full political equality with members of the Church of England. Old Lord Wharton, in a memorandum drawn up in early March and headed 'to be discoursed with Mr [Richard] Hampden', gave first priority to this objective.[19] His aim was to end the formal exclusion of Nonconformists from positions in local and central government by abolishing the requirements laid down by the corporation act of 1661 and the test act of 1673 that office-holders must take communion under Anglican auspices at least once yearly. Already, too, the two issues of the imposition of the new oath upon the clergy and the easing of the sacramental test for the Nonconformists' benefit were being linked in parliament's deliberations. As soon as the Commons agreed on 25 February to bring in a bill to revise the Jacobean oath, Sacheverell and Capel proposed the abrogation of the corporation act and secured leave to introduce a bill of repeal, and both measures were read a first time on 7 March. In turn, the Lords upon reading their own oath bill a second time on 15 March entertained a motion to end the sacramental test and charged a select committee with the task of drafting a clause for this purpose.

To this point, the Churchmen in parliament had not directly challenged these and other moves on behalf of the Protestant Dissenters. But Tories had murmured since William's arrival in London at the 'countenance' he gave the Dissenters, and when the King interjected his own views on the test simmering resentment rose to a boil.[20] William's intervention, which was counselled only by Richard Hampden, came on 16 March when he took the occasion of passing a bill to deliver a speech to parliament in which he urged speedy passage of an oath bill and avowed it was his hope that 'all Protestants, that are willing and able to serve', might be made eligible for secular preferment.[21] In response, the Churchmen in the Commons openly organised in opposition. Meeting at the Devil Tavern in the City that evening, Sir Robert Sawyer, Heneage Finch, Sir Thomas Clarges, Sir Christopher Musgrave, Sir Joseph Tredenham, and more than 150 other like-minded M.P.s joined in denouncing the King's speech and in vowing to do all possible to blunt any challenge to the Anglican monopoly on office.[22]

The first real test of strength came at the third reading of the Commons' oath bill on 18 March when a Whig rider in favour of those Protestant Dissenters who had taken office under James without complying with the test was offered and rejected. As one Anglican clergyman jubilantly reported: 'we have been very apprehensive of the Dissenters and some unreasonable men in the House of Commons, but we find their party is not so formidable as was feared'.[23] And just as many of the majority in the lower House who had voted to make William king did not seem prepared to permit him to employ Dissenters, so in the Lords Nottingham and Danby were joined by such earlier opponents as the Earl of Devonshire in their successful defence of the sacramental test on the 19th and again on the 21st and 23rd.[24] Moreover, when the Commons turned the following week to discuss the wording of the new coronation oath to be taken by William and Mary at the formal ceremony scheduled for 11 April, a similar majority carried the day for the formula 'to preserve the Church' as it is 'now established by law'. Although proponents of accommodation with the Dissenters urged the insertion of the phrase 'or shall be' before 'established' so as to allow the new monarchs to implement the changes included in a comprehension bill then under consideration in the Lords, this amendment was defeated by 188 to 149 in committee of the whole on 25 March and a similar rider was rejected by the full House on the 28th.[25]

These were significant triumphs. Nevertheless, the oft-quoted effusions of Churchmen in late March 1689 that they were in 'a majority in both Houses' and that 'the Devil Tavern Club are much the strongest party' in the Commons do not tell the whole story.[26] For while some Whigs joined with the Tories to uphold the sacramental test, the 'Church party' was losing ground over the issue of the imposition of the new oath of allegiance upon incumbent clergy. The two Houses' deliberations on this sensitive question are difficult to untangle, in part because each drafted its own bill and in part because Burnet's account has left the erroneous impression that the Lords' measure was more lenient than the Commons'.[27]

The Commons' oath bill did not, in fact, require clerical incumbents to subscribe; only incumbent civil and military office-holders had to. Professor Isaac Newton (serving for Cambridge University) informed his Vice-Chancellor on 16 March, the day the bill was engrossed, that he had kept a careful watch upon it since its initial stages and could assure the University 'that these new oaths are not designed to be imposed on them all, as I am told they still believe though I wrote formerly to remove this their prejudice'.[28] However, the Lords' bill, after it was revised in committee of the whole on 20 March, did include clerical incumbents. The peers stipulated that failure to take the new oath of allegiance by 1 August would be punished by deprivation of benefices; a subsequent refusal to swear, if the oath was again tendered such an individual, would render him liable to imprisonment. Thus, as Newton reported after the Lords transmitted their bill to the Commons: 'the bill about the new oaths sent up from our House to the Lords was there laid aside and a new one more severe sent down from them to us'.[29] Moreover, though 'the Churchmen thought they could gain anything after' their triumph 'in the business of the coronation oath', when the Lords' oath bill was read a second time in the Commons on 28 March they 'could not prevail for as much as a proviso to be added'. Even so, there was still the chance of amendment in committee, and Newton thought that the bill would 'be mollified' there.[30]

In voicing this hope, Newton may well have had in mind the possibility of a compromise between the Whigs and the Tories in which the *quid pro quo* would have been the elimination of the sacramental test. Certainly, many, including Burnet, interpreted the King's speech of 16 March as an indirect offer of 'a bargain' for 'excusing the clergy from the oaths, provided the Dissenters might be excused from the sacrament'.[31] Nor did William's efforts to promote such an arrangement cease after both Houses rejected, during the week of 18 March, amendments to their oath bills for abrogating the test. Among the gestures the King made by way of appeal to the Churchmen in succeeding days was the message he sent to parliament on 25 March in which he recommended the swift passage of a general act of indemnity.[32]

Just what the chances for compromise were remained in doubt during the first days of April. When the Commons resumed their deliberations on 1 April after a brief Easter recess, they seemed to be moved by contradictory impulses as they considered in sequence two possibly related questions. First, they read a second time (after a three-week lapse) and committed Sacheverell's bill to repeal the corporation act. But then the Churchmen proposed that the committee be instructed to preserve the sacramental test for municipal offices. A long debate ensued, ending only when the Whigs finally carried by 116 to 114 a motion to postpone further consideration of the proposed instruction until 10 April. Yet hard upon the heels of this close division came the uncontested appointment of a committee to prepare a bill to comprehend at least moderate Nonconformists within the Church, and in turn this select committee chose John Hampden as its chairman.[33] Was this, perhaps, a signal that the Commons were thinking of resolving the question of Dissenters' political rights by trying to reintegrate at least some of them in a more comprehensive state church?

Certainly, comprehension was seen in this light by some Tories, and particularly by the Earl of Nottingham. Comprehension, he hoped, would reunite Anglicans and moderate Dissenters and so prevent any future attempts to divide the 'Protestant interest' in England as both Charles II and James II had sought to do. Nonconformists who returned to a broadened state church would thereby become eligible for municipal and crown posts; those who would not accept the terms of accommodation offered in the comprehension bill Nottingham brought into the Lords on 11 March were to be accorded a limited freedom of worship. The terms of this toleration were set out in a companion bill Nottingham introduced on 28 February, and for those who chose to remain outside the national church the sacramental test would remain.[34]

There were, however, some difficulties in the way of Nottingham's projected solution. Some of the Nonconformists and their political associates were opposed to any scheme that would so divide the 'Dissenting interest'.[35] In addition, even moderate Dissenters found Nottingham's comprehension bill unappealing, especially by comparison to the proposals the Earl had helped to draft in the Exclusion parliaments, and Morrice characterised the 1689 terms as 'very narrow and stingy'.[36] To make matters worse, when the Lords read Nottingham's comprehension bill a third time on 8 April, they attached a proviso which would have barred anyone from qualifying for office by 'occasional conformity': those who received the sacrament under Anglican auspices to qualify themselves would forfeit their positions should they revert to attendance at Nonconformist meetings for worship.[37]

As the terms of Nottingham's already 'stingy' bill of comprehension were being further restricted, the younger Hampden was drafting a much more generous measure that would have broken effectively 'the neck of the sacramental test'.[38] Indeed, the differences between the two bills were only exceeded by the contrasts between their two authors. The younger Hampden may not have shared the deep religious commitment that his grandfather of civil war fame and his own father Richard held, but he did inherit their political views. He had been party to the Rye House plot, he was a useful member of the conspiracy that had culminated in William's expedition to England, and yet all that the new King was prepared to offer him was an embassy to Madrid, while Nottingham was made a Secretary of State. Thus, religious upbringing, political conviction, and personal frustration seem to have combined in impelling Hampden to bring in a comprehension bill that had much more appeal to Nonconformists.[39]

Before the Commons took up either comprehension bill, they debated once more the question of exacting the new oath of allegiance from incumbent clergy. This debate in committee of the whole on 5 April consumed several hours, yet the fullest account of it is provided by Morrice in a few sentences. At issue was[40]

whether or no the bishops ... should not be excused from taking the oath of allegiance etc. to the King ... Nota this seemed very strange to many that there should be any debate upon such a point as this, and seemed to have a very favourable aspect upon another thing [? the abrogation of the test], but at last it was carried that they should go on with their bill [that is, the Lords'] which enjoined all to take it. For many of those that would not have had any to have taken the oath of allegiance thought it too bold and daring a question to put...yet they did carry it 1. that the bishops should take it before 1 August or should be suspended. 2. that they should take it within six months after that or be deprived. There was a division upon this question whether the bishops should be deprived, if they took not the oaths within six months. Noes 138, Yeas 193.

Thus, though the Commons did 'mollify' the Lords' bill by allowing the clergy a grace period of six months after 1 August in which to master their scruples, attempts to exclude them from the bill or to give the King power to 'dispense' any from having to take the oaths 'would not be heard' either on the 5th or when the question was revived on the 6th.[41]

Still troubled by the question of the oaths, the Churchmen were probably in no mood to consider any proposal for comprehension, no matter how limited. And when Hampden's measure was read a first time on Monday, 8 April, its generous terms provoked one scandalised Churchman to move that a second reading be put off until 'Doomsday'.[42] A heated debate followed, and eventually the Commons postponed action on the measure for ten days.

But if the uncertain balance of forces in the Commons, with 'sometimes one side' and 'sometimes the other' in a majority, appeared to foreshadow an impasse on all aspects of Anglican–Dissenting relations, new possibilities were un-expectedly opened up on 9 April.[43] That morning, the Commons took up the Lords' comprehension bill, only to be diverted by a speech from the Whig Privy Councillor William Harbord. Acknowledging 'that very many had jealousies' of the King's inclinations to the Dissenters, Harbord declared 'he could assure them his Majesty was altogether of the judgement of the Church of England'. He then suggested that the Commons draw up an address 'to give thanks to his Majesty for declaring he would preserve the Church of England as by law estab-lished' and that this address include both a request for the summoning of a convocation (to consider detailed plans for comprehension) and an assurance that the calling of a convocation would 'no ways hinder the intended ease [i.e. toleration] for Dissenting Protestant subjects'.[44] In response, the Commons chose a committee and instructed it to prepare an address along the lines proposed by Harbord.

This new royal initiative—for Harbord was undoubtedly acting upon instruc-tions—was more even-handed than that of 16 March. And this time, so rumour had it, the King was taking not the elder Hampden's but Nottingham's advice.[45] The suggested compromise recognised the complexity of the comprehension question and would concede to the clergy, as Deans John Tillotson and Edward Stillingfleet had advocated, participation in the formulation of schemes of re-union.[46] Yet it also took account of most Dissenters' preference for freedom of worship outside the establishment, and, hopefully, the new arrangement would speed the passage of toleration. Certainly, the projected address was more to the taste of the Churchmen who resolved at a gathering the evening of 9 April at the Devil Tavern to support it.[47] The Dissenters' friends probably had more reservations, but when the text of the address was reported to the Commons, it was approved without a dispute. The Lords concurred in the Commons' address a few days later, and the two Houses then jointly presented it to William on 19 April. The King, in his reply the following day, restated his support of the Church, promised to summon a convocation 'as soon as conveniently may be', and took notice of 'the ease you design to Dissenters'.[48]

Although the two Houses promised to proceed with toleration while relegating comprehension to a convocation (to its 'ruin', so both Burnet and Halifax predicted), the address of 19 April did not settle the related questions of the sacramental test and the imposition of the revised oath of allegiance.[49] Even so, by mid-April the Commons at least had made up their minds on these points, too. No further action was taken on the bill to repeal the corporation act, so leaving the test for municipal offices intact. And despite Harbord's declaration in the House on the 12th that it was 'his opinion that his Majesty did not desire the oaths should be pressed upon the clergy', the Commons completed the committee stage of the Lords' oath bill that day without making any further provision to relieve clerical scruples and then returned the measure to the Lords for approval of their earlier amendments.[50]

However, a majority of the peers, led by Bishop Compton and by Burnet (newly raised to the episcopate), were now ready to make a bid for greater leniency, and on 17 April the upper House added a proviso to the Commons' amendments which would have allowed the King to refrain from tendering the oath to clerical incumbents. Yet if, to judge from Harbord's statements in the Commons, William preferred to have the incumbent clergy altogether exempted from taking the revised oath of allegiance, he was not eager apparently to exercise the discretionary authority the peers now proposed to vest in him. Indeed, the King's private secretary Constantijn Huygens was told by another of the Dutch circle at Court that Compton and Burnet 'had acted in direct opposition to the King's sentiments' in sponsoring this proposal.[51] Whatever William's views, the Commons clearly disliked the idea. Three conferences between the two Houses followed in quick succession. And finally the Lords yielded on the 24th by a vote of 45 to 42, after the Commons consented to a provision permitting the King to pay to no more than a dozen of the clergy who might be deprived a portion of the revenues of their former benefices.[52]

By mid-April, then, the Commons for their part had disposed of all the measures that bore upon future relations between Anglicans and Dissenters, save for those dealing with toleration. Moreover, the Lords were on the verge of giving Nottingham's toleration bill its final reading, and the Commons' own bill on the subject (drafted by Clarges) was read a first time on the 15th. Hence, the lower House was free now to give more attention to other problems, especially finance and foreign affairs.

Finance involved both the peacetime and the wartime expenses of the crown —that is, both ordinary and extraordinary revenue—and the lower House had run into difficulties on the first very early in the session. Before he approved the bill to transform the Convention into a parliament, William had secured the private opinions of five leading lawyers that James's revenue had 'not ceased by the demise of the King'.[53] Holt, Pollexfen, and Treby restated their views in the Commons on 26 and 27 February, but their learned presentations did not prevail as most members agreed that it would be necessary to regrant the ordinary revenue. To some extent, action was slowed by a lack of detailed information about the state of the ordinary revenue before 1689, yet the debates of 26–27 February also indicated that many members were thinking of terms bound to disappoint the new Court. There was talk of granting a lesser sum than that accorded James II, and a number of M.P.s spoke of limiting whatever was given to a term of years so as to ensure frequent meetings of parliament.[54]

On 1 March, William himself moved to expedite proceedings on the ordinary revenue by letting it be known he would consent to the elimination of the widely-disliked hearth tax; 'abuses and oppressions' in its collection had been among the heads in the preliminary version of the Declaration of Rights. However, even this costly gesture from the throne did not yield the desired results. After ten more days of intermittent debate, the most that the Commons would do was to order the preparation of a bill to allow the collection of the existing ordinary revenue until 24 June 1689. By that date, it was presumed, the terms and the amount of a more permanent arrangement could be worked out.[55]

While the settlement of the ordinary revenue raised in this fashion fundamental questions about the future relationship between crown and parliament that caused delay, the Commons did make some headway with extraordinary supply between late February and mid-April. On 27 February, they unanimously resolved to 'stand by and assist the King with their lives and fortunes, in supporting his alliances abroad, in reducing of Ireland, and in defence of the Protestant religion, and laws of the kingdom', and on the 28th they initiated a bill to provide an extraordinary aid of £420,000 which was to be raised by a six months' assessment on land.[56] During the next six weeks, the Commons then reviewed and agreed upon most of the estimates for extraordinary expenses for 1689. These totalled over £2,500,000: £600,000 to be repaid the Dutch for the cost of William's expedition (approved on 16 March), £714,000 for the reduction of Ireland (22 March), and £1,199,000 for the fleet as well as for summer and winter guards (5 April).

The votes on the estimates preceded any formal deliberations by parliament upon a breach with Louis XIV. In the face of earlier reservations about 'running the nation into a war with France' voiced even by such Whigs as Sacheverell, William preferred to delay consideration of a declaration of war until he felt confident it would pass 'without contradiction'.[57] And it is a measure of the concern aroused over the Anglican–Nonconformist problem both in Whitehall and in St Stephen's Chapel that not until that impasse was broken did the Commons take up the question of war with France. In fact, outward unanimity did prevail when the issue was broached on 15 April; both John Hampden and Sir Thomas Clarges spoke for war, and on the 16th a motion to this effect was approved *nemine contradicente* in committee of the whole. Even so, the lower House refused to approve the first text (drafted by the younger Hampden) of an address to the King in favour of war with France, apparently because of its scathing references to Louis XIV's bribery of Court and parliament in the 1670s.[58] So, it was not until the 25th that the Commons were ready to present a revised address to William.

Rather more difficult than either scrutinising the estimates or drafting addresses was the task of funding the military effort at sea, in Ireland, and on the Continent. Up to 25 April, the Commons had provided only the £420,000 aid towards the charge of the extraordinary estimates. To this they added on 26 April a poll tax measure and also the long-delayed bill to authorise the collection of the ordinary revenue (with the expiry date now pushed forward from 24 June to 24 December 1689). £600,000 of the ordinary revenue, it was agreed on the 25th, would suffice for the civil charges of the government, and so the Commons followed up their passage of the bill for its collection with a resolution that the ordinary revenue should furnish £700,000 towards the war.[59]

Even so, these votes left the Commons with a considerable sum to find, and still to be reckoned was the charge of the 10,000 men who had been dispatched to the Low Countries under the command of the new Earl of Marlborough in fulfilment of the terms of the Anglo-Dutch treaty of 1678.

To raise the additional money, the Commons resolved in late April to proceed with four of the many levies canvassed in sessions of the committee of the whole on ways and means: (1) an additional poll bill; (2) a tax on new buildings in the London suburbs; (3) the collection of the £500 penalty from those who had taken office during James's reign without complying with the requirements of the test and corporation acts; and (4) new excises on beer and other drinks. However, in succeeding days all save the last of these levies (which, it was estimated, would yield £200,000 yearly at most) encountered serious difficulties. An additional poll bill was approved and transmitted to the Lords on 6 May, but the peers' claim to appoint commissioners to rate themselves seemed likely to be unacceptable to the Commons. At the same time, the proceeds of the tax on new buildings (a levy oft mooted during the Restoration period but never adopted) proved impossible to estimate with any plausibility, and the bill died in the Commons. And the collection of the £500 penalty, which would have affected not only Catholics but also some Dissenters, ran into resistance from the latter's friends in the House, who by this time must also have been growing uneasy over the lack of progress on toleration.[60] To be sure, the Lords had passed Nottingham's toleration bill on 18 April and the Commons read it once, but since then they had taken no further action either on the Lords' or on their own version.

With toleration bills languishing and prospects for supply clouding over in early May even as William formally declared war on France, the kingship question was suddenly revived on the 8th on the Commons' third reading of the bill to give statutory form to the Declaration of Rights. This measure had not hitherto been a subject of controversy. But now, the Churchmen provoked a clash by proposing a rider which, according to the young Robert Harley (who had just taken his seat in the Commons), 'hath been long in contriving and was designed to overthrow all former proceedings'.[61] Specifically, the clause moved by Charles Godolphin (a brother of the Treasury Commissioner) stated that 'nothing in this act is intended to be drawn into example, or consequence, hereafter, to prejudice the right of any Protestant prince or princess, in their hereditary succession to the imperial crown of these realms'.[62] In the face of Whig denunciations of the amendment either as 'a stratagem from France' in favour of the Prince of Wales or the contrivance 'of some foreign minister' on behalf of the Hanoverian branch of the royal family, Musgrave and Clarges defended it as a useful preservative against a commonwealth should Mary, Anne, and William all die childless.[63] But their arguments did not find favour with the Commons. After a move by the advocates of the rider to amend it in order to exclude specifically the Prince of Wales was defeated 179 to 125, the clause was dropped and the bill was sent up to the Lords as reported from committee.

This dispute, coupled with the difficulties over supply, seemed to augur a resumption of full-scale partisan hostilities. But during the next few days, there were major breakthroughs on both supply and toleration. On 10 May, with Musgrave taking the initiative, the Commons resolved to lay one shilling on land, and this levy was reckoned to be worth at least £500,000.[64] Then, after

reading the £500 forfeitures measure a first time on the 15th, the lower House
revived both its own and the Lords' toleration bills. Each was given a second
reading that day, and then it was agreed to proceed with Nottingham's measure
since, in Clarges's words, it 'seemed very grateful to those it concerned'.[65] To be
sure, when this bill was reported out from committee on the 17th, Clarges
offered a rider to limit the term of the intended toleration to seven years. Yet,
he did not press his motion to a division, and that day the Commons returned
it to the Lords with only minor amendments.[66] No further action was taken on
the bill to collect the £500 forfeitures; instead, the Commons gave an initial
reading to the new land tax bill on 23 May, and on the 24th William gave his
consent to the toleration bill.

The sudden revival of the toleration bill in mid-May is not easy to explain.
All that Morrice, our only witness, knew or surmised is that the 'Devil Tavern
Club did call for it and did promote the passing of it', and to this he added that
'it's as certain they do now heartily repent they have passed it'.[67] As for the
Dissenters, they, too, had some reservations. Matthew Henry, a Nonconformist
minister, put it this way to his son: 'when you write to any of our lawmakers,
acknowledge their kindness and pains in procuring it with all thankfulness, but
till the sacramental test be taken off, our business is not done'.[68] Admittedly,
the toleration act did not give the Dissenters equal access to public office, but any
chances of such a concession had in all probability been extinguished by the
earlier decision to exact the revised oath of allegiance from clerical incumbents.
What is significant is that it was the Churchmen who took the initiative during
the second week of May both in proposing a new levy on land and in reviving
toleration. And though contemporaries did not link these two developments,
there was talk that Musgrave had been encouraged to propose the land tax on
the 10th by assurances that the Whigs were willing to act upon the King's
earlier recommendation of a general indemnity.[69] Furthermore, these reports are
reinforced by a Commons' order of 11 May, adopted over six weeks after the
King had sent his message in favour of an indemnity, which called for a committee of the whole to take up that subject on the 14th.

The indemnity question was an extremely sensitive one. Proceedings to identify and to punish 'the authors and advisers' of the objectionable policies and
illegal practices both of James's reign and of the Tory reaction had been started
by the Whigs early in March 1689.[70] The Whigs' concerns were twofold. Many
genuinely believed that at least some notorious offenders in former reigns should
be severely punished as a deterrent to any future attempts on the liberties and
religion of the realm. Many also bitterly resented the presence in the King's
councils of Halifax, Carmarthen, Nottingham, Godolphin, and some of their
friends. In turn, William's message of 25 March had been an attempt to calm
'all controversies' over the 'disorders in the late times'. The King urged the
adoption of an indemnity with 'such exceptions' only as 'shall seem necessary
for the vindication of public justice, the safety of their Majesties, and the settlement and welfare of the nation for the future'.[71] But though the King's exhortations were applauded by Churchmen such as Musgrave and Tredenham during
a debate on the royal message on 25 March, the Whigs were not convinced.
Jack Howe ironically reflected on 'a King so gracious as to admit such persons
into his presence, that have been against him', and William Harbord warned
'if there be not some examples made of persons who have overturned your laws.

you will never want those to overturn your government'.[72] Hence, until their
order of 11 May, the Commons had done nothing but thank the King for his
message on indemnity.

When the Commons did take up the issue of indemnity on 14 May, the
intensity of sentiment was reflected in the 'hot' dispute that broke out over the
choice of a chairman for the committee of the whole which was to formulate
the heads of the projected bill.[73] And once the committee got down to the
business of the day, with the Whig Sir Thomas Littleton in the Chair, sharp
differences between the parties over the appropriate method to adopt were
evident. The Churchmen advocated proceeding by naming 'persons'—that is, by
designating a few grievous offenders and pardoning all others. The Whigs
favoured 'inquiring into things first'—that is, beginning by defining the offences
to be punished and then ascertaining who had been guilty of them. After four
hours, the committee finally decided to recommend the latter course, despite
warnings that this 'will leave such jealousies in people, as that they will not
think themselves safe'.[74] This decision was followed on 23 May by the full
House's acceptance of ten categories of offences (later expanded to twelve), but
the task of determining who among the living and the dead should be named
as offenders promised to be long and contentious.

The Commons' decisions on indemnity were only one element in extending
an already lengthy session. In mid-May, the Spanish ambassador—taking note
of the tentative agreement on the land tax and also the lower House's order
of 13 May barring the introduction of any new private bills for the remainder of the session—predicted a recess within a few weeks.[75] But he reckoned
neither with the difficulties over the indemnity nor with the outbreak in
late May of new disputes between the two Houses. One item of controversy
was the peers' claim to rate themselves for the additional poll, for this met with
determined opposition from the Commons, who were adamant in resisting any
suggestion that the Lords could amend a money bill. The upshot was the loss
of this measure. Then, there were the Lords' alterations to the bill of rights.
Their omission of the section of that bill outlawing royal dispensations
threatened to revive earlier differences between the two Houses over this question. And their addition of the Electress Sophia and her offspring to the line of
succession also seemed likely to cause trouble. This amendment was proposed
by Burnet; it was also favoured by the King, at least partly for immediate
diplomatic purposes.[76] Yet in the light of the Commons' rejection of Godolphin's
rider of 8 May, the fate of Burnet's alteration appeared problematical.

However, before the Commons took up these changes to the bill of rights,
they had been provoked by another decision of the Lords. This was the rejection
of Titus Oates's attempt to secure, by writ of error, a reversal of the judgements
for libel and perjury found against him during the Tory reaction. Most peers
agreed that these verdicts had been erroneous and the sentences cruel, but Oates
himself had few admirers and his efforts to pressure the Lords by petitioning the
Commons for redress boomeranged. Carmarthen, incensed by reflections upon
his conduct which Oates had gratuitously included in his petition to the
Commons, took the lead in condemning the Salamanca doctor, and Oates was
committed for breach of privilege by the upper House on 25 May. Moreover,
after the judges informed the Lords on the 31st that if they reversed the perjury
verdict against Oates he could again serve as a witness, Halifax and Nottingham

joined Carmarthen in helping to carry a vote to uphold that judgement by 35 to 23.[77]

The principal reason for the Lords' reluctance to overturn the perjury verdict against Oates seems to have been the possibility that he might once again be used as a tool by the more violent Whigs. Yet, Carmarthen, Halifax, and Nottingham were vulnerable to other types of attack. Already, Sir John Maynard, a veteran Whig lawyer and one of the Commissioners of the Great Seal, had called in the Commons on 28 May for an inquiry into the Irish situation, and the state of Ireland certainly gave ample material for recrimination.[78] James's arrival in Dublin in March had been followed by further setbacks for the English interest in Ireland during the next two months as the Jacobite forces advanced into Ulster. The outnumbered allied fleet under Herbert failed to prevent French reinforcements from being landed and then was bested in a brief engagement in Bantry Bay.[79] In turn, the army officers in command at Londonderry decided that city could not withstand a siege and left the citizens to fend for themselves.

Admittedly, the responsibility for these miscarriages was not altogether clear. Carmarthen's sins were chiefly those of omission, for the new marquess had been sulking at Wimbledon since the coronation over the King's failure to accede to all his many patronage requests. In the public view, Halifax figured as the chief culprit, and the Lord President seems to have helped to encourage this notion. But Nottingham, who had already begun to play an important role in naval affairs, also came in for a share of the public criticism for his supposed part in the deficiencies of the allied fleet.[80]

None the less, the more rabid Whigs did not find it necessary to make fine distinctions among the ministers when the Commons took up the misconduct of the war effort on 1 June, with the Lords' vote of 31 May against Oates fresh in many members' minds.[81] The attack on the ministers was launched by Howe, who had recently been disappointed of a sizeable grant from the King. Arguing that the behaviour of the army officers who had deserted Londonderry and also the faults of other subordinate officials must have 'had encouragement from greater persons than themselves', Howe declared that the House must 'come to the root'.[82] To do this, he proposed an address to William against those of his Privy Council who had served James II in the same capacity. Other Whigs, including the former Earl of Wiltshire (now styled Marquess of Winchester since his father's promotion to a dukedom), chimed in with similar suggestions. These culminated in a motion for an address asking the King to remove all those who had ever been impeached by the Commons (that is, Carmarthen and Halifax), regardless of whether those impeachments had been approved by the Lords. But Howe's targets were not without friends in St Stephen's Chapel, though none of the Privy Councillors present spoke in their behalf. Thus, after the Commons appointed a committee of investigation, they adjourned debate on the projected address until early the following week.[83]

The following days saw a flurry of activity out of doors and behind the scenes. On the night of 1 June, a petition was launched in the City by 'some fanatics', and by the 4th many hands had been secured to its call for an inquiry 'into several mismanagements, ancient and modern'.[84] In the meantime, the King himself sent Dijkvelt to Howe in hopes of quieting him. In the event, the City petition was not presented, Howe and his friends would not name names when challenged to do so on 4 June, and their motion was then laid aside.[85] So the only action the Commons took was to resolve (with reference to Carmarthen's plea of 1679) that a pardon was no bar to a parliamentary impeachment and that a report should be prepared of the Lords' handling of Oates's case.

Although the Commons were not yet prepared to countenance a frontal assault upon the ministers, speculation about a dissolution was now being heard. 'Things are here in so perplexed a condition', one Cheshire gentleman then in London lamented on the evening of 4 June, 'that I think the King must either give up the ministers or the parliament will be dissolved.'[86] Nor did developments during the next few weeks do much to improve this prognosis. The Commons' 'aking tooth' for the ministers continued to throb, flaring up in the abortive attack in late June upon the Earl of Nottingham for an alleged breach of privilege.[87] At the same time, the differences between the two Houses deepened, with the Commons resolving on 11 June to bring in a bill to reverse the judgement against Oates and then rejecting on the 19th and 20th the two principal amendments made by the Lords to the bill of rights. Then, too, by late June, the Commons had only managed to get to the individuals to be excepted under the third head of the indemnity bill, despite their prolonged deliberations on this measure. The eagerness of Howe, who set 'so many things . . . at once on foot', was partly to blame for the Commons' slow pace on indemnity.[88] But the delays may well have suited the Whigs who, so Burnet subsequently concluded, wanted 'to keep many under the lash'.[89]

Meanwhile, the funding of the war effort still remained unfinished in late June, and so did the settlement of the ordinary revenue. Indeed, it was not until 15 June that the Commons finally dispatched to the Lords the bill to levy one shilling on land. And then the peers came perilously close to adopting an amendment to name their own commissioners of assessment. Had this been approved, the result would probably have been that the land tax would have suffered the same fate as the abortive additional poll.[90]

These were the circumstances which prompted the King to come to Westminster on 28 June in a new effort to hasten his parliament's labours. Calling for 'union and vigour in your counsels', he urged members to expedite supply and the 'several acts yet to be passed for the safety and settlement of the nation'.[91] But while William was dismayed at the two Houses' delays, parliamentary and public distress at the government's seeming ineffectuality was also evident. During the Commons' debates of 18–19 June upon the conduct of the war, pointed (if not always well-informed) questions were raised as to where all the money already voted had gone and sharp complaints were voiced about 'the slowness' of the administration.[92] The King, it is true, could demonstrate that much less money was coming in, and that more slowly, than the Commons had expected. And he did announce in his speech of the 28th that detailed accounts would be laid before parliament.

Yet, it was not so easy for William or anyone else to justify the seemingly dilatory proceedings in Ireland and elsewhere. An investigation, instigated by the Duke of Bolton, into the management of the war was under way in the Lords, and on 18 June the peers had felt it necessary to vote an address advising William of the need to put the Channel Isles and other strategic places in a fit state of defence.[93] Criticism of the Dutch was also mounting, and anti-Dutch sentiments were openly voiced in the Commons by a few bold members, most notably Seymour. The King's confidence in Bentinck (who was now being accused in the coffee-houses of selling places) had been a sore point from the start, but to this was added now resentment both at the delayed arrival of those Dutch ships which should have been with Herbert at Bantry Bay and at continued Dutch trade with France.[94] Nor was William himself exempt. Even in March, the deteriorating situation in Ireland had provoked comment about his 'slothful, sickly temper' and 'dilatory' conduct; in mid-May, Dijkvelt was concerned over complaints of the King's 'lack of dispatch' and of his seeming preoccupation with the hunt; and by mid-June, the normally sympathetic Spanish ambassador observed that William 'displayed the same slowness' as many of his officials.[95]

Certainly, by late June the King was almost at a loss as to how to proceed on the home front. Earlier in the year, he had seemed 'to be complaisant to all parties', but by mid-year William was thoroughly disgusted.[96] He was annoyed by the attacks upon his ministers made by the 'angry party' among the Whigs, and he was even more displeased at the failure of his Whig Privy Councillors in the Commons to press for supply. Their reluctance to move the consideration of ways and means to provide the promised repayment to the United Provinces was particularly galling, and William excused the Dutch failure to provide their full naval contingent on the grounds that they had been anticipating prompt payment from England of the £600,000 that had been tentatively agreed upon in March. William also had harsh words for many individual Whigs: he distrusted the Earl of Monmouth as a convinced Commonwealthman, thought old Hugh Boscawen a 'blockhead', and was ready to consign John Hampden to Bedlam. At the same time, he found the conduct of Carmarthen's friends in the Commons 'insufferable' and objected to Nottingham for 'caballing' with the Lord President. And as the King vented his anger at both Whigs and Tories to Halifax, he also lamented the limitations upon his own freedom of action. In particular, he complained 'that a king of England who will govern by law as he must do, if he hath conscience, is the worst figure in Christendom—He hath power to destroy the nation and not to protect it'.[97]

In this perplexity, William at times during June talked of taking some dramatic step to remedy affairs. Again and again, he spoke of leaving England to take command of the allied forces in the Low Countries and of allowing Mary, who, he believed, 'would govern us better', to rule in his stead. But in the end he had to admit that his departure was impossible, at least for the moment. What he did finally resolve upon was to put an end to the session. Despite Halifax's arguments against such a move, by 10 July the King seemed to have made up his mind. Two days later, he sent a message to parliament to announce that all he desired before a recess was that the two Houses should complete their work on those money bills already begun and pass an indemnity bill.[98]

Forewarned, perhaps, of the King's intentions, the Commons on 8 July reviewed the bills pending before them and decided to concentrate upon thirteen. Three were bills of extraordinary supply, a fourth was for settling the revenue, and a fifth was for establishing a fund to repay the Dutch. Others were the bill of rights, the bill of indemnity, and a bill to restore corporate charters. In turn, there was a brief spurt of activity on supply. The Commons sent up an additional customs bill (begun in late June) to the Lords on 10 July and the additional excise bill on the 18th, and they also finally committed the bill for settling the revenue. Even so, only the excise measure was finished by the end of July. There had also been further progress on the ordinary revenue by the end of the month, but the Commons' resolution in committee of the whole on 30 July to give the excise for life but the customs only for three years was little to the King's liking.[99] Furthermore, the additional customs bill was foundering on the rock of the Lords' determination to make good their claim to amend supply measures.

Nor was it only the additional customs bill that provoked renewed clashes between the two Houses during the second half of July. The Lords also objected to the Commons' bill to settle the militia, at least in part because the measure sharply reduced the powers of the lords lieutenant.[100] Then, too, the treatment of Oates and the terms of the bill of rights continued in dispute. The Lords refused to accept the Commons' bill to reverse the judgement against Oates unless it included their clause disqualifying him as a witness, and after several conferences between the Houses the peers voted 48 to 30 on 30 July to adhere to their amendment. The Lords also declined to yield on their provision in favour of the Hanoverian line, though they did give up their efforts to maintain a dispensing power in the crown. Reinforced by William's declaration in council late in July that he, Mary, and Anne all favoured the Hanover clause, the Lords voted 38 to 29 on the 31st to adhere to this amendment despite the birth, a week earlier, of a son (christened William) to Princess Anne.[101]

While both bills of supply and of settlement continued to be impeded by disputes between the two Houses, attacks upon the ministers further diverted the attention of the dwindling number of Commoners still in attendance. A new outburst came on 13 July when the King, for a second time, let it be known that he would refuse the Commons' unprecedented requests in pursuit of their Irish inquiries for access to the minutes of the Privy Council and its Irish committee. The lower House responded by unanimously approving a resolution which branded the unnamed persons who had delayed the relief of Ireland and advised William to refuse access to the minutes as 'enemies to the King and kingdom'.[102] Then, for the first time in the long session, a motion for an address against particular ministers, Halifax and Carmarthen, was proposed. Among those who spoke for it were two senior Whig Privy Councillors, Sir Robert Howard and Sir Henry Capel, and Jack Howe and Lord Winchester chimed in as well. Finally, the combined forces of the two ministers' friends managed to get the debate adjourned *sine die*.[103] None the less, William heeded the warning, and the following week he agreed to permit an inspection of the Council's records.

Neither the Privy Council's nor the Irish committee's minutes furnished the evidence the Commons were seeking, yet the more violent Whigs did make one further attempt against Halifax early in August. This time, it was Sir John Guise (the Duke of Bolton's nephew and a colonel of one of the new regiments) who proposed an address against the Lord Privy Seal on 2 August. The debate on his motion was first postponed to the 3rd. When it was resumed that day, Halifax's supporters, led by his son Lord Eland, found they had the advantage, called the question, and carried it 90 to 76. Among the minority were several of Carmarthen's friends, a sign of the continuing ill will between the two ministers; among the majority were a number of moderate Whigs, who, it was reported, 'have no kindness' for Halifax 'but thought it better he should escape at present to be a balance to the rest of the same stamp' in the King's service.[104]

Amidst these disputes and delays, William seems to have decided to lower his sights even further. He was now prepared to forgo the indemnity bill, the grant of the additional customs, and even the settlement of the ordinary revenue. It is true that on 4 August he remarked to Halifax that 'the revenue once settled, he would take his measures'. But at the same time, he was unhappy with the Commons' vote of 30 July to give him the customs for only three years. As he angrily remarked to Halifax on 1 August, 'there was but one reason to make him accept the revenue upon the terms proposed, which was because the money given to the Dutch is comprehended in it'.[105] However, if William was prepared to acquiesce in the Commons' resolution of 30 July, he was not willing to accept the vote passed in committee of the whole on 5 August that Princess Anne's provision out of the revenue should be raised from £30,000 to £70,000 and that she should have this sum for life. That was to add insult to injury, and when the Princess's clause was reported on 9 August, it encountered substantial opposition that was probably inspired by the Court.[106] Eventually, the debate on that clause was adjourned. And instead of going ahead with the revenue bill, the lower House agreed to proceed with a separate measure which provided for paying the Dutch their £600,000 by charging the ordinary revenue with that sum. This bill was dispatched to the Lords on the 12th and they passed it three days later.

All that remained now was for parliament to complete action on the projected measure to halt English trade with France. And as soon as the Lords' amendments to that bill were approved by the Commons on 20 August, the King finally brought the session to an end. Even so, the closing days of the session were nearly disrupted by the demonstrations staged in the precincts of Westminster Palace by thousands of silkworkers from Spitalfields, who were protesting against a measure to encourage the wearing of woollens and to prohibit the import of silk.[107]

The protest of the silkworkers was a fitting coda to the dissonance of the lengthy session. During the six months since the Convention had been transmuted into a parliament, fifty-five more bills had been approved, but many major measures had either failed of passage or were left unfinished at the adjournment. And, not surprisingly, though William realised that the need for further supply would compel him to meet a parliament before year's end, he was reluctant to recall this one. Even before the adjournment, he was mulling over the possibility of dissolving the Convention parliament and summoning a new one. He told Halifax that he still hoped to 'go upon the bottom of the trimmers' or 'the middle party', but as the Lord Privy Seal observed, 'the practice is difficult'. 'To form a party between the two extremes' and to call a new parliament would, the King realised, entail a greater reliance upon the Churchmen, for the events of the session had only reinforced his fears that the Whigs had a 'design of a commonwealth'.[108] In particular, their efforts to delay the grant of the revenue or to limit it to a term of years, along with their attempt in the militia bill to restrict his prerogative, had angered William. He now also regarded Whig advice to give up the hearth tax in a similar light, and he appeared to be hearkening to Nottingham's reports of the schemes of the 'angry cabals' in parliament and in the City. As yet, however, the King was not certain 'whether he might rely upon the Church party'; Whig charges that they inclined 'to return to a regency' still troubled him.[109] Thus, he remained uncertain as to the course he should steer amidst the shoals of domestic politics.

Fortunately, the fate of the new regime was not solely dependent upon crown–parliamentary relations. By early autumn, the Jacobite forces in Scotland no longer constituted a serious military threat. Furthermore, in Ireland the unexpected relief of Londonderry in late July had been followed quickly by the landing in Ulster of a sizeable army under the Duke of Schomberg's command. Meanwhile, on the Continent a series of diplomatic successes late in the spring was succeeded by a summer campaign that went unexpectedly well for the allies.[110]

Perhaps it was these improvements in the external situation that led William to decide to meet the Convention parliament again in the autumn of 1689. But though he was not yet ready to make a sharp break with the Whigs, there were signs that he was increasingly relying upon Nottingham's advice, at least in ecclesiastical affairs. Persuaded that Archbishop Sancroft was 'an honest man' who might still 'come off from his present opinion', the King sent the northern Secretary to Lambeth Palace to assure the metropolitan he need not leave his official residence despite his suspension on 1 August for refusing the oaths. William also decided to pass over the Whigs' candidate for the bishopric of Worcester; Dean Stillingfleet was named instead, and most of the crop of ecclesiastical promotions made at the beginning of September also went to clerics drawn from the circle of Nottingham's friends and clients.[111] At the same time, William—without even troubling to consult his Whig Secretary—authorised his Tory Secretary to convene a clerical commission to draft detailed plans for comprehension and other reforms; these were then to be submitted to a meeting of the Convocation of Canterbury planned for November.[112]

These decisions can be read as signs of the King's and Nottingham's continuing hopes of averting a schism over the oaths and of achieving a union with the moderate Dissenters; they can also be seen as gestures to attract the support of the Churchmen in parliament. Certainly, William let it be known during the parliamentary recess, both directly and indirectly, that he would take care 'in preserving the Church of England'.[113] Again, in his opening speech on 19 October to the reassembled Convention parliament, the King (who drafted his own text in French) included a flattering reference to the Church as 'one of the greatest supports' of European Protestantism, though this did not satisfy Clarges who complained that William had not designated the Church 'as established by law'.[114]

The chief burden of the King's speech was the need for prompt provision of ample supplies. He apologised for recalling the members so soon, and his only other specific request was that they pass a bill of indemnity.[115] Initially, there seemed a good chance they would quickly comply. The Commons immediately voted their thanks and then agreed to a preconcerted motion offered by two Whigs, Sir John Thompson and Sir Thomas Lee, that they request a brief prorogation from the King.[116] William was only too happy to agree; a prorogation would erase all bills still pending before the recess in August and so allow a fresh start, especially on the measures that had been in dispute between the two Houses.

The brief prorogation from 19 to 23 October did serve some purpose. The Commons let their bill for reversing the judgement against Oates sleep. Similarly, when the lower House sent up a new bill of rights on 6 November, the peers forbore to raise the Hanoverian question. The Lords did express reservations about the bill's absolute prohibition of royal dispensations, and they were also interested in giving more precision to the section calling for 'frequent parliaments'. However, the peers decided to proceed on these points by separate bills, and neither was in the event adopted by the upper House.[117] The result was that only one controversial amendment to the bill of rights was proposed. This came at the third reading on 23 November when some of Carmarthen's enemies moved, in a half-empty chamber, to add a clause to void all pardons in cases of impeachment. But while Nottingham spun out the debate, the upper House filled, and then the motion was overwhelmingly rejected.[118] The bill was sent back to the Commons that same day, and they approved the Lords' minor amendments on 10 December.

The easing of tensions between the two Houses was accompanied by other favourable portents during the early days of the autumn session. On 24 October, the Commons voted unanimously to assist the King in the reduction of Ireland and in 'a vigorous prosecution' of the war against France.[119] And once the accounts of the charges of the war in 1689 and the estimates for 1690 had been laid before them, they resolved on 2 November upon £2,000,000 in extraordinary supply. Nevertheless, the hope voiced by Sir Joseph Tredenham on 24 October that 'there might be no divisions this session' was not to be fulfilled.[120] The brief prorogation could neither assuage partisan rivalries nor salve resentments against the ministers. Even during the first weeks of the autumn session, there were many signs that the divisions of the first session did not lie far below the surface calm.

In the first place, the question of relations between Anglicans and Dissenters was again up for consideration, this time not only in parliament but also in convocation. During October and early November, the clerical commission which William had convened was hard at work on proposals to be submitted to the forthcoming meeting of the convocation. Yet, walk-outs from the commission by some of its more rigid members boded ill for these plans, as did the choice of many like-minded clergy in the sometimes-contested elections for members of the lower house of convocation. Meanwhile, the Commons were also making a contribution to intensifying ill will on this front. After the lower House ordered on 30 October the preparation of a new bill to restore corporate charters and another to impose severer penalties for failure to take the new oaths, the members fell into a heated debate when the latter was read a first time the next day. The Churchmen, who were clearly on the defensive in this matter, could only argue that many Dissenters had also failed to take the oaths—an assertion that provoked Whig denials and jibes about the suspended bishops.[121]

In the second place, storm clouds were gathering again over the treatment to be meted out to offenders in the late reigns. The Commons did set on foot a new indemnity bill on 1 November, with the Churchmen 'extraordinarily fervent' for it, but they also agreed on 26 October to bring in a bill of pains and penalties.[122] Even more disturbing were the Lords' orders of 2 November. First, the peers revived their committee to investigate the Earl of Essex's mysterious death in the Tower during the Tory reaction. Then they appointed another which was charged with identifying those responsible for the prosecution of the Whig martyrs of the 1680s, for the campaign against the corporations and their subsequent 'regulation', and for the maintenance of the dispensing power. These inquiries were moved by some of the 'hotter' Whig lords, with the Duke of

Bolton once more in the van, and they were chiefly aimed at Halifax. But the Lord Privy Seal, who had been the target of similar inquiries in the Commons during the first session, was as capable of defending himself as was the Lord President. Despite the testimony of a host of witnesses, including John Hampden, by late November it was evident that there was no real case against Halifax.[123]

In the third place, the conduct of the war was under scrutiny in the Commons once more. Grave concern was expressed about the general lack of success in Ireland where Schomberg's army had been plagued by problems of supply and disease, and also at sea where there had been substantial losses of merchant shipping. And sharp criticism was heard of specific instances of maladministration in the Victualling Office, at the Admiralty Board, and in the provisioning of the Irish army. Thus, in early November, the Commons appointed two select committees, one to inspect the government's accounts which was chaired by Sir John Guise, the other to investigate miscarriages which was headed by Paul Foley.[124] The choice of two outspoken Whigs to chair these committees would seem to suggest that partisan enmities prompted their establishment. And many Whigs did continue to claim that the employment of men who had been the servants of former monarchs was the basic cause of the misconduct of the war. Yet from the outset of the autumn session, these inquiries were also strongly supported by some Churchmen, particularly the disgruntled Sir Edward Seymour and his brother-in-law Tredenham who were at odds with Carmarthen.[125] Then, too, given the mottled complexion of the administration, the issue was not intrinsically a partisan one. The old Victualling Commissioners, whom William dismissed late in October, were mostly Tories; the Admiralty Commissioners were mostly Whigs. Again, the two officials chiefly responsible for Schomberg's supply problems were the Whig Paymaster for Ireland William Harbord and Commissary John Shales, a former official of Charles II and James II.

As the Commons' investigation into miscarriages progressed, questions about the appropriate relationship between the executive and parliament were aired anew. In July, William had finally given in to the Commons' requests to examine the minutes of the Privy Council and its Irish committee, but their inspections did not reveal which (if any) of the King's servants had been at fault. Now, the Commons tried a different tack to ascertain ministerial responsibility; this was to address William to ask him who had recommended Shales for his post.[126] The two votes about the proposed address on 27 November divided members mainly along Court–Country lines. Most office-holders, anticipating the King's reluctance to answer such a question, opposed it, along with some Churchmen such as Seymour and Tredenham. But after the previous question was carried 188 to 142, the motion for an address was approved 195 to 146.[127]

William's reply on 2 December to this address was a flat refusal: 'It is impossible for me to give you an answer'. But his denial was preceded by another message on 30 November which raised a separate, though related issue for the Commons. Without referring to the inquiry about Shales's appointment, the King declared his resolution 'to prosecute the war in Ireland with the utmost vigour' and offered to allow the lower House to recommend commissioners in place of the ousted Shales.[128] The Commons' first reaction on 30 November was to vote their thanks for the message. But many members had second thoughts over the week-end, and their reservations came to the fore on Monday, 2 December, when the House deliberated on its response to the King's offer.

Speakers in the confused and sometimes wandering debate on 2 December addressed themselves to two questions: (1) should the Commons make any nominations? and (2) should they recommend any of their own number? All five speakers who were ready to have members recommended, or at least were against excluding them from consideration, were strong Whigs: two, Capel and Howe, had places; the other three, Guise (who had resigned his regiment in September), Sir William Williams (the Speaker of the second Exclusion parliament), and John Hawles (a barrister), did not. But a majority of the speakers that day were against making any recommendations, members or no. The argument chiefly invoked against the naming of M.P.s was that there were already too many placemen in the Commons. Moreover, those who opposed making any nominations, including Paul Foley, Clarges, and Musgrave, contended that acceptance of the King's offer would be to assume executive responsibilities outside the Commons' purview and that it would also tie their hands politically should there be further miscarriages in Ireland. Finally, the lower House voted 201 to 128 (with all four tellers being Whigs) against naming members and then resolved 'to leave it to his Majesty's great wisdom to nominate fit persons' for the task.[129] It was, then, only after these resolutions were adopted that the King's refusal to reply to the address about Shales was announced. By this time, members, apparently, had had their fill of the matter. And so William succeeded in denying the address without either raising a storm or having to pay the price of accepting the Commons' nomination of Shales's replacement.

Although the Commons drew back from direct involvement in executive appointments, their pursuit of miscarriages certainly slowed work on other fronts. No progress was made on indemnity during November and the lower House also lagged in devising ways and means to supply the £2,000,000 which it had authorised at the beginning of the month. Many fiscal proposals were canvassed in committee of the whole, but few were found acceptable. Some, such as the idea of a general excise on staple commodities, failed in committee. Others, including a levy on office-holders which was carried by a single vote in committee, were rejected upon report to the full House. Still others, such as the revived scheme for the collection of the £500 forfeitures and a new project to levy £100,000 on the Jewish residents of England, were accepted in principle by the full House only to be held up afterwards by strong opposition.[130] By the end of November, then, the only tax bill that had reached a second reading was the two-shilling levy on land. Even so, it was becoming apparent that in deciding to raise this by way of a pound rate (rather than by a monthly assessment), the bill would not come close to yielding the £1,400,000 originally estimated.[131]

From the King's point of view, the first weeks of December brought no real improvement. At Westminster Abbey, hopes of an ecclesiastical reconciliation were foundering on the rock of the lower house of convocation's barely-concealed hostility to anyone or anything that appeared to have royal backing. Not only was the Clerk of the Royal Closet, John Tillotson, rejected as Prolocutor, but also a majority of the lower house refused even to concur in the upper house's address of thanks for William's opening message. Thus, on the 14th convocation was adjourned amid predictions it would not sit again, while behind the scenes one last attempt at a compromise was made with Bishops Burnet and Lloyd acting as intermediaries between the Court and their suspended colleagues. However, Turner and the other endangered bishops were not willing either 'to barter and break' the Anglican political monopoly or to pledge support for a generous scheme of comprehension in order to save themselves and other non-jurors from the deprivation that was in store for them at the end of January 1690.[132]

Meanwhile, at Westminster Palace, there was only halting progress on supply. On 11 December, the Commons finally passed the land tax, yet how they would raise the other half of the £2,000,000 was still in doubt. As for the ordinary revenue, all the lower House seemed prepared to do was to pass another interim measure allowing the government to continue to collect it up to the end of 1690. Moreover, it took determined Court efforts to overcome a renewed bid by Princess Anne's friends (including many Churchmen) to attach to this measure an amendment raising her income to £70,000 yearly and settling that sum upon her for life. Instead, an address requesting the King to provide her with £50,000 for the coming year was adopted on 18 December. So the dispute between the two courts was compromised and Anne subsequently accepted William's offer in 1690 of an annual settlement of £50,000, but the affair set Queen Mary at odds with her sister and with her sister's confidante, Lady Marlborough.[133]

The Commons also showed they were not yet wearied of the problem of war miscarriages when they revived their consideration of the state of the nation on 14 December. This time, the debate was conducted amidst heated partisan recriminations. Alarmed, apparently, by rumours of an impending dissolution and of a change of ministers in the Churchmen's favour, the hotter Whigs again sought to fix the blame for miscarriages on the employment of those who had served in former reigns. And their chief fire was now concentrated upon the three peers—Halifax, Nottingham, and Godolphin—who had been sent by James II to William just a year earlier. In response, Churchmen such as Clarges warned 'that we have none to fear but sectaries and commonwealthmen'.[134] Some speakers on the 14th did deplore these partisan 'distinctions', and Sir Robert Howard cautioned that it would 'prove fatal' to the nation to stand upon 'Whig and Tory'. But despite some signs of a 'moderate healing' spirit, the Commons concluded by ordering the preparation of an address to recount 'the ill conduct and success of our affairs' and to urge that William employ 'persons unsuspected, and more to the safety of his Majesty, and satisfaction of his subjects'.[135] Furthermore, when John Hampden reported a text of the proposed address from committee on 21 December, Whigs such as Howe and Hawles found it not 'home enough', while Churchmen such as Serjeant Wogan denounced it as a 'libel' upon the ministers. Thus, objections from extremists of both sides led to its recommittal, this time to a group chaired by Foley.[136]

Yet if the Whigs had been aroused by reports such as the story Morrice noted in his entry for 13 December 'that the parliament would be adjourned that they might keep their Christmas, and then not be called to sit again, but dissolved, and that there would be a Lord Chancellor and Lord Treasurer and a Lord High Admiral or Vice-Admiral, to wit Nottingham, Danby [Carmarthen], and Herbert', these rumours were not altogether accurate.[137] Herbert, who had been raised to the peerage as Earl of Torrington the previous summer, was in fact on the verge of resigning his post as first Commissioner of the Admiralty since he felt the King no longer had confidence in him.[138] Yet it was true that Nottingham, at least, was 'very industrious' in encouraging the belief that William was now ready to 'entirely espouse' the 'interest' of the Church. The Tory Secretary also seems to have let it be known that the King would gratify the Churchmen in their desire for a long Christmas adjournment.[139] But with the political temperature climbing as the holiday season neared, even the length of the parliamentary recess became a matter of partisan dispute. Shrewsbury opposed a long adjournment and advised William on 22 December that 'your resolution in this must be suitable to what you determine, either to join or not join with the Church of England'.[140]

In the event, the King asked parliament on 23 December to take only a week's adjournment. But the exodus from the capital, especially of Churchmen, brought him no relief. Those who remained in town were convinced that the King was under 'a necessity of declaring' one way or the other, and so they redoubled their efforts to sway him. Thus, Shrewsbury, Tom Wharton, and several other Whig office-holders again warned William in a series of outspoken letters of the dangers of trusting the Churchmen. 'Even the very best of them', in Shrewsbury's view, had 'a regency still in their heads'. Once more, these Whigs made the argument so often heard in St Stephen's Chapel during 1689; it was the employment of former servants of Charles II and James II that had led to the military setbacks and lost the new government much of its initial support. Shrewsbury conceded that the Churchmen were 'the properest instruments to carry the prerogative high', yet he reminded William that 'they have so unreasonable a veneration for monarchy as not altogether to approve the foundation yours is built upon'.[141]

While Shrewsbury and his associates were importuning the King, Nottingham was also active. In the face of the threat against him in the Commons' projected address, Nottingham reiterated his earlier stand to William that 'he would not go' unless dismissed. Simultaneously, he bent his efforts 'to make it appear to the King the Church party was the strongest' as he tried to gain support for supply from Seymour, Clarges, and Musgrave by holding out the prospect of official appointments to them.[142] Then, too, the Earl was also trying to mobilise the Churchmen in parliament against a Whig attempt, anticipated after the recess, to amend the bill to restore corporate charters (committed by the Commons on 19 December) by leaving out the sacramental test for municipal officers.[143]

Confronted by these conflicting pressures, William still hoped to be able to keep on trimming. He dissuaded Halifax from resigning and chose to act on the advice of Sir John Trevor (the Tory Speaker of the 1685 Commons) to see 'whether this parliament would give more money before he took his resolution'.[144] William did, however, accept Torrington's resignation from the Admiralty Board, only to confront strong Whig objections to Sir Richard Haddock as his successor. Haddock was recommended by Nottingham, while Shrewsbury, Wharton, and Sir Robert Howard were all reported to have argued against him, ostensibly on the grounds that as a member of the recently dismissed Victualling Commission he still lay under a Commons' charge of malfeasance. The King was persuaded to omit Haddock from the new commission ordered on 6 January 1690; instead, he named the Tory Earl of Pembroke, who had recently returned from a spell at The Hague as ambassador to the States General. Moreover, when the new commission was issued a fortnight later, two of the hotter Whigs, Sir Michael Warton and William Sacheverell, who had signalled their disenchantment by failing to attend the Board at all for some months, were omitted along with Torrington.[145]

By the time the new Admiralty Commission was announced, the clash of the parties in parliament had, if anything, intensified. When the members reassembled on 30 December 1689, the Whigs had the advantage in the Commons since so many Churchmen were still out of town. Whig strategy in this situation was to try to appease William by moving ahead with supply and by abandoning direct attacks on the ministers; instead of fighting with the Churchmen in the Commons they would try to undo them in the constituencies by altering the terms of the corporation bill. So, the projected address on miscarriages was laid aside, on New Year's Day 1690 the Commons gave a first reading to an additional poll bill, and on 3 January a motion for an additional one-shilling tax on land was carried. None of these moves provoked a division, and on the 2nd the Whigs exploited their numerical superiority to carry a series of additions to the corporation bill that would have had the effect of proscribing a host of Tories for their involvement in the surrender of charters during the 1680s. And in anticipation that William would find these amendments objectionable, some Whigs were so bold as to let it be known that if the King 'interposed or meddled' against the disabling clauses (somewhat misleadingly attributed to William Sacheverell), they 'would not finish the money bills'.[146]

William's reaction to such threats was not long in doubt. Reports were soon circulating that he had declared 'he would not be dealt with as King Charles II. for he would neither have bills of another nature tacked to money bills nor money bills delayed till other bills were signed by him'.[147] Similarly, after the King dined at Shrewsbury's on Twelfth Night, it was rumoured that he had taken the occasion to say that 'though some wished to make him a Doge of Venice, he would, since he had been called to the throne by God, maintain the authority reposed in him'.[148] His stand, coupled with the return of many Tories, doomed the proscriptive amendments when the corporation bill came up for a third reading on 10 January.[149] Heartened by intimations of royal support, the Churchmen attended in force, remained through a sitting that lasted nearly twelve hours, rejected Whig motions either to moderate the 'Sacheverell clause' or to recommit the bill by margins of from five to twelve votes, and eventually had the objectionable sections completely removed from the bill.[150] Their bluff called, the Whigs made no attempt to delay the supply measures; on the 13th. the additional poll bill was read a second time and the additional land tax measure was dispatched to the Lords.

With the rest of the supply at last in train, William's thoughts turned more and more to his expedition to Ireland. According to the Imperial envoy, the King had tentatively decided to take personal command in Ireland as early as the beginning of December, when he had made his pledge to the Commons to take vigorous action there.[151] And in all likelihood, the famous but hitherto undated episode when William was only dissuaded by tearful ministerial entreaties from returning to the Continent and leaving the English government in Mary's hands also took place late in November or early in December, for Burnet's version of this incident concludes with the King deciding to go to Ireland instead.[152] What is certain is that by late 1689 William had had to abandon his earlier notions of reducing Ireland by attacking France. As he explained to Prince Waldeck (his general in the Low Countries) in early January 1690, he saw no alternative but to concentrate his own and the realm's efforts in Ireland for the coming campaign.[153]

As the news of William's decision to take personal command in Ireland began to spread in London early in January, opposition quickly developed. The most vociferous objections came from the Whigs; some even alleged that only traitors could have counselled exposing the King and the kingdom to such grave danger. Fear of possible parliamentary attempts to forestall him prompted the King to avoid any mention of his plan when he came to parliament on 16 January to accept the land tax bill, but 'weary of the parliament' as he was he did not yet end the session. The additional poll bill still needed the Lords' approval, and the King had some hope that the indemnity bill—at last given a second reading by the Commons that day—might yet be passed.[154]

However, the Whigs were in no mood to be generous to the offenders of previous reigns, especially after the failure of their amendments to the corporation bill. And the Tories still could not muster a majority on indemnity. This became clear on the 21st when a Tory motion to proceed with that bill by naming particular offenders to be excepted from it was defeated on a previous question 190 to 173. William's reaction to this vote was to anticipate an early end to the session. As he wrote that night to Portland, then in Amsterdam: 'There seems little chance that this business [the indemnity] will be finished. And so it is likely the session will be short, there being no more money to hope for. And the feelings of each side against the other become more and more embittered.'[155]

Yet even after the Lords passed the additional poll bill on 22 January, William held his hand a little longer. What finally determined him was a motion started in the Lords on the 25th to request him not to go to Ireland. With most of the Tory peers, save Rochester, and all the bishops present opposing the putting of that question, the debate was adjourned till the 27th.[156] And before the peers could resume that day, William made an early appearance in the Lords on the 27th to accept the poll bill and to announce a prorogation to 2 April 1690.

For all the earlier speculation, the actual prorogation came as a surprise; William himself told Portland that he had informed only one person beforehand. Still, as the King observed the unschooled reactions of the members to his announcement, it was evident to him that 'the Tories were quite satisfied with it, but not the Whigs'.[157] In fact, Nottingham and Carmarthen had been urging a new parliament for some time, and they had intensified their pressure in the wake of the controversy over the Sacheverell clause, contending that 'the breaking upon this point, as it would make the new elections sure to the Church party in many places, so it would oblige them to the King, since he preserved them from the fury of this bill'.[158] Then, two days after the prorogation was announced, some 150 Tory members, headed by Sir John Lowther of Lowther (the King's Vice-Chamberlain), gathered at the Devil Tavern and agreed to thank the King 'for his firm adhesion to the Church of England'.[159] Meanwhile, their chiefs at Court were assuring William that if he would call a new parliament it 'would immediately settle a revenue upon him'.[160]

Although the King had not determined upon a dissolution when he prorogued the Convention parliament, he soon found he had little room for manoeuvre. He told Halifax on 5 February that 'he wished he could trim a little longer, but things pressed so, he could not'. What William now realised was that he did not have sufficient ready funds to leave for Ireland without holding another session. And he was also aware that it would be futile to reconvene the existing parliament. Not only were its Whig members 'incensed' by the prorogation, but in any case he could not legally alter the term of the prorogation. Thus, on 6 February the King took what seemed the only way out of this dilemma by issuing a proclamation to dissolve the old parliament and to summon a new one to assemble at Westminster on 20 March.[161]

After twelve hectic months, then, the Convention parliament received its *quietus*. In retrospect, it would seem that the first parliament of the new reign had substantial accomplishments to its credit. After all, the declaration of war against France, the passage of the toleration act, and the enactment of the bill of rights now stand out as milestones in the course of English history.[162] But contemporaries had a different perspective; they were more conscious of the wide gulf between their initial expectations and the parliament's actual achievements.[163] From William's vantage point, the failure to settle the ordinary revenue, to approve an act of indemnity, and to agree upon comprehension were major disappointments. As for the Whigs and their Dissenting friends, their sense of frustration was even keener since they had begun the new reign with such high hopes. Only the Churchmen had any cause for satisfaction; even so, they had not been able to avert a schism among the clergy over the new oaths and most of their parliamentary successes had been defensive in nature.

Nevertheless, the fact that the new regime did survive its traumatic first year confounded Jacobite predictions and belied the gloomy prognoses of many of its adherents. And if the prospects for the coming year were uncertain, it was clear that the outcome of the general election and the temper of the new parliament would be critical. No one was more conscious of this than William; even after he issued the summons for a new parliament, second thoughts rose to perturb him. Above all, he still was fearful that a parliament dominated by the Churchmen might 'question the validity of all done' in the last, 'and consequently the kingship'. Hence, he spoke to Halifax on 8 February of putting off the new parliament if he could borrow sufficient funds for the Irish campaign, though he acknowledged that 'the Church party would take it ill, being now prepared to meet'. For the time being, then, William postponed a final decision. As he told Halifax, he would 'first see some of the elections returned' before committing himself either to meet the new parliament as scheduled or to proceed with the reconstruction of his administration.[164] Thus, for the moment, the focus of politics shifted from Westminster to the constituencies.

Notes to Chapter II

1 Luttrell, *Brief Relation*, I, 501.

2 Baxter, *William III*, p. 250; Foxcroft, *Halifax*, II, 203, 212. However, the list of appointments suggested in Burnet's memorandum of early 1689 included a good many Churchmen; BL Add. MS. 32681, ff. 317–18.

3 Foxcroft, *Halifax*, II, 204. At the outset, the council was meeting 'almost constantly, even in the King's absence'; House of Lords RO, Willcocks MSS., VI, 208, Lord Yester to Lord Tweeddale, 5 March 1689.

4 *Memoirs of Sir John Reresby*, ed. A. Browning (Glasgow, 1936), pp. 553, 557–8, 561, 563–5.

5 BL Add. MS. 25377, f. 381, Terriesi's report of 8/18 March. See also Morrice's strong and fearful reaction; Lacey, *Dissent*, p. 232.

6 Horwitz, *Revolution Politicks*, pp. 82–5; Lamberty, *Mémoires*, II, 136, 161: KU, F. Bonnet, 15/25 February.

7 Burnet, *Supplement*, p. 315.

8 Chatsworth MSS., Devonshire House notebook, *sub* 'Monmouth Lord'. And see BL Add. MS. 38863, ff. 45–9; Hunt. Blathwayt MS. 418, printed in M. G. Hall, *The Glorious Revolution in North America* (Chapel Hill, 1964), pp. 67–9.

9 Huygens, *Journaal*, I, 57, 70–1, 77; J. Scheltema, *Geschied en letterkundig Mengelwerk* (Utrecht, 1817–36), III, ii, 143–4.

10 Scheltema, *Geschied*, III, ii, 140, also 139. Lamberty credited Dijkvelt with helping to persuade Nottingham to accept the Secretaryship; Lamberty, *Mémoires*, II, 161.

11 A *Brief Memoir of Mr Justice Rokeby*, ed. W. Collins (Surtees Society, vol. 37, 1861), p. 35.

12 For Clarges's and Halifax's reactions to this 'inadvertancy', see Grey, *Debates*, IX, 108; Foxcroft, *Halifax*, II, 219, and *passim*.

13 For an example from mid-June 1689, see Lamberty, *Mémoires*, II, 463; KU, F. Bonnet, 21 June/1 July.

14 *CJ*, X, 30.

15 Grey, *Debates*, IX, 129–36. This temporary act was renewed twice, first in May and then in the autumn.

16 C. Ellestad, 'The Mutinies of 1689', *Journal of the Society for Army Historical Research* 53 (1975), 421. And see DWL, Morrice MS. Q, 503.

17 *SR*, V, 1074; *LJ*, XIV, 119–20. See also Horwitz, *Revolution Politicks*, p. 82.

18 Besides Clarendon, Lords Newcastle, Lichfield, Exeter, Yarmouth, and Griffin never took them. Lords Ailesbury, Strafford, and Stawell eventually did.

19 Bodl. Carte MS. 81, f. 752. See also Lacey, *Dissent*, pp. 232–3.

20 *Clar. Corr.*, II, 238; *Memoirs of Reresby*, pp. 541, 557.

21 *CJ*, X, 51. No one wished to take credit for advising this abortive initiative, but Hampden's role is noted in *Correspondencia entre dos embajadores*, ed. G. Maura Gamzao (Madrid, 1951–2), I, 160; Chatsworth MSS., Devonshire House notebook, *sub* 'Hambden senior'; Burnet, *History*, IV, 12–13.

22 DWL Morrice MS. Q, 505; KU, F. Bonnet, 26 March/5 April. See also Huygens, *Journaal*, I, 103.

23 CUL Buxton MS. 60, J. Herne to R. Herne, 19 March. See also DWL Morrice MS. Q, 507; Bodl. Ballard MS. 45, No. 57a, [R. Sare] to A. Charlett, n.d.

24 *HLM*, 1689–1690, pp. 53–4; DWL Morrice MS. Q, 507, 511; Bodl. Ballard MS. 45, f. 58, newsletter, [23 March]; *Memoirs of Reresby*, p. 567 (who says Halifax was one of the principal advocates of repeal).

25 Grey, *Debates*, IX, 190–8, 200–4.

26 BL Add. MS. 36707, f. 62, A. M. to [J. Harrington], 21 March; Bodl. Ballard MS. 22, f. 48, J. Newton to A. Charlett, 28 March. See also HMC *Portland*, III, 435, 436; Bodl. Ballard MS. 30, f. 26.

27 Burnet, *History*, IV, 12, 14–16.

28 *The Correspondence of Isaac Newton*, ed. H. W. Turnbull (Cambridge, 1959–   ), III, 18. See also *HLM*, 1689–1690, pp. 63–6.

29 *HLM*, 1689–1690, pp. 53–5; *SR*, VI, 57–60; *Correspondence of Newton*, III, 19.

30 BL Add. MS. 36707, f. 63, A. M. to [J. Harrington, 28 March]; *Correspondence of Newton*, III, 19.

31 Burnet, *History*, IV, 13, and *Supplement*, pp. 315–16.

32 Another was his intercession behind the scenes to inhibit any punitive action by the Lords against Archbishop Sancroft for his failure to respond to the upper House's summons.

33 BL Loan 29/140 (unfoliated), Sir E. to R. Harley, 2 April.

34 Horwitz, *Revolution Politicks*, pp. 87–9, 92; R. Thomas, 'Comprehension and Indulgence', in *From Uniformity to Unity 1662–1962*, ed. O. Chadwick (1962), pp. 247–50.

35 Burnet, *History*, IV, 20–1.

36 DWL Morrice MS. Q, 496. And see Bodl. Ballard MS. 39, f. 57, ? to G. Smallridge, 14 March.

37 Horwitz, *Revolution Politicks*, pp. 90–1.

38 The phrase is Matthew Henry's; *Diaries and Letters of Philip Henry*, ed. M. M. Lee (1882), p. 364. And see Lacey, *Dissent*, p. 235.

39 Foxcroft, *Halifax*, II, 229; Lamberty, *Mémoires*, II, 674–5; Lacey, *Dissent*, pp. 401–2.

40 DWL Morrice MS. Q, 525–6. See also HMC *Downshire*, I, 306.

41 Bodl. Ballard MS. 45, No. 34a, [R. Sare to A. Charlett], 6 April.

42 Bodl. Ballard MS. 45, f. 35, newsletter, 9 April. See also DWL Morrice MS. Q, 527–8; *Hatton Corr.*, II, 128; *Memoirs of Reresby*, p. 572.

43 *Memoirs of Reresby*, p. 570.

44 DWL Morrice MS. Q, 530–1.

45 Bodl. Ballard MS. 45, f. 35.

46 HMC *Finch*, II, 194; *The Works of Dr John Tillotson* (1820), I, cxviii–cxix.

47 Bodl. Ballard MS. 45, f. 35.

48 CJ, x, 97.

49 *Memoirs of Reresby*, p. 572.

50 Bodl. Ballard MS. 45, No. 52a, [R. Sare?] to A. Charlett, 13 April.

51 Huygens, *Journaal*, I, 117. See also Foxcroft, *Halifax*, II, 219. Cf. G. Every, *The High Church Party 1688–1715* (1956), p. 36.

52 Capel had earlier suggested this in the Commons; Chester RO, Earwacker letters, f. 66, [Sir W. Aston] to Sir J. Crewe, 16 April.

53 DWL Morrice MS. Q, 479; Grey, *Debates*, IX, 108–10, 113–23.

54 Note particularly the speeches of Birch, Clarges, and Sacheverell; Grey, *Debates*, IX, 119, 123, 149. Cf. R. Reitan, 'From Revenue to Civil List, 1689–1702', HJ XIII (1970), 576–7.

55 Grey, *Debates*, IX, 148–50, 153–8.

56 CJ, x, 36.

57 HMC *Portland*, V, 645; Foxcroft, *Halifax*, II, 210; KU, F. Bonnet, 16/26 April.

58 KU, F. Bonnet, 16/26 April; CJ, x, 94–5, 105, 111; Foxcroft, *Halifax*, II, 214; DWL Morrice MS. Q, 536, 546; HMC *Portland*, V, 645; Grey, *Debates*, IX, 230–3.

59 These sums reflect the fact that the government in 1689 was still collecting all the revenue (save the hearth money) that had been given to James, even though the Commons had tentatively resolved to settle only £1,200,000 upon William and Mary.

60 Lamberty, *Mémoires*, II, 311; KU, F. Bonnet, 30 April/10 May; DWL Morrice MS. Q, 548, 549.

61 BL Loan 29/164, bundle 2, to Elizabeth Harley, 11 May.

62 CJ, x, 126.

63 Grey, *Debates*, IX, 237–42; DWL Morrice MS. Q, 552.

64 Boyer, *William the Third*, II, 86.

65 DWL Morrice MS. Q, 557; Grey, *Debates*, IX, 253–4; Lamberty, *Mémoires*, II, 402.

66 Grey, *Debates*, IX, 258–62. A similar rider had failed in the Lords.

67 DWL Morrice MS. Q, 558. And see Lacey, *Dissent*, p. 237.

68 *Diaries and Letters of Philip Henry*, p. 362. There was a petition from the City for the abrogation of the sacramental test in June, but the Commons did not proceed upon it.

69 Lamberty, *Mémoires*, II, 382–3; KU, F. Bonnet, 14/24 May.

70 CJ, x, 41–2; Grey, *Debates*, IX, 137–41. And see *Letters of Richard Thompson to Henry Thompson*, ed. J. Cartwright (Camden Society, n.s., vol. 31, 1883), p. 7.

71 CJ, x, 64.

72 Grey, *Debates*, IX, 186–8.

73 Bodl. Ballard MS. 45, f. 54, [R. Sare] to A. Charlett, n.d.; DWL Morrice MS. Q, 556.

74 Grey, *Debates*, IX, 244–51.

75 *Correspondencia entre dos embajadores*, I, 207.

76 HLM, 1689–1690, pp. 345–7; Burnet, *History*, IV, 28; *Memoirs of Mary, Queen of England* (1689–1693), ed. R. Doebner (Leipzig, 1886), pp. 72–6.

77 Browning, *Danby*, I, 450–1; Boyer, *William the Third*, II, 94–6; HLM, 1689–1690, pp. 76–80; DWL Morrice MS. Q, 563–4.

78 KU, F. Bonnet, 28 May/7 June.

79 None the less, Herbert was soon raised to the peerage as Earl of Torrington.

80 Browning, *Danby*, I, 449–50; Foxcroft, *Halifax*, II, 76–81; Horwitz, *Revolution Politicks*, p. 96.

81 Grey, *Debates*, IX, 277; Lamberty, *Mémoires*, II, 445–6; Huygens, *Journaal*, I, 140.

82 DWL Morrice MS. Q, 564; Grey, *Debates*, IX, 280.

83 CJ, x, 162; DWL Morrice MS. Q, 564; Luttrell, *Brief Relation*, I, 541; KU, F. Bonnet, 4/14 June.

84 Luttrell, *Brief Relation*, I, 542; DWL Morrice MS. Q, 566–7. And see Chester RO, Earwacker letters, f. 72, [Sir W. Aston] to Sir J. Crewe, 4 June.

85 Boyer, *William the Third*, II, 119; Lamberty, *Mémoires*, II, 445–6; DWL Morrice MS. Q, 574; Grey, *Debates*, IX, 281–2.

86 Chester RO, Earwacker letters, f. 72.
87 Horwitz, *Revolution Politicks*, pp. 96–7.
88 Bodl. Carte MS. 239, ff. 334–5, W. Jephson to [T. Wharton], 13 June.
89 Burnet, *History*, IV, 26.
90 Chester RO, Earwacker letters, f. 74, [Sir W. Aston] to Sir J. Crewe, 20 June. In early June, an anonymous calculation arrived at the sum of £2,300,000 still to be raised; *CSPD*, 1689–1690, p. 139.
91 *CJ*, X, 200.
92 KU, F. Bonnet, 21 June/1 July; Grey, *Debates*, IX, 333–6, 347–51.
93 *HLM*, 1689–1690, p. 134 and ff.; Bodl. Carte MS. 79, ff. 28–9, R. Hampden to T. Wharton, 15 June.
94 Chester RO, Earwacker letters, f. 74; Scheltema, *Geschied*, III, ii, 151, 157; Huygens, *Journaal*, I, 134; Foxcroft, *Halifax*, II, 219, 223; Lamberty, *Mémoires*, II, 465–6; P. Scheltema, *Aemstel's Oudheid* (Amsterdam, 1855–85), V, 94. See also Wing W94.
95 *The Diary of John Evelyn*, ed. E. S. de Beer (Oxford, 1955), IV, 631–2; *Memoirs of Reresby*, p. 571; Huygens, *Journaal*, I, 132; *Correspondencia entre dos embajadores*, I, 222.
96 'Letters of Richard Thompson to Henry Thompson', pp. 5–6.
97 Foxcroft, *Halifax*, II, 219, 221, 222, 224. And see Scheltema, *Geschied*, III, ii, 156.
98 Foxcroft, *Halifax*, II, 220, 222, 224.
99 BL Loan 29/142 (unfoliated), Sir E. to R. Harley, 30 July: Foxcroft, *Halifax*, II, 227; Lamberty, *Mémoires*, II, 528–9, 532–3.
100 Burnet, *History*, IV, 25; *HLM*, 1689–1690, pp. 206–17.
101 *HLM*, 1689–1690, pp. 259–61, 347; Lamberty, *Mémoires*, II, 528; KU, F. Bonnet 23 July/ 2 August.
102 *CJ*, X, 201, 206, 217; Lamberty, *Mémoires*, II, 500. For an attempt to oust Halifax from the Chair in the Lords on 10 July, see Foxcroft, *Halifax*, II, 86.
103 DWL Morrice MS. Q, 590; Ralph, *History*, II, 133.
104 Chester RO, Earwacker letters, f. 84, [Sir W. Aston] to Sir J. Crewe, 7 August. And see *Clar. Corr.*, II, 122; KU, F. Bonnet, 6/16 August; Foxcroft, *Halifax*, II, 89.
105 Foxcroft, *Halifax*, II, 228, 227, and also 224, 215.
106 Lamberty, *Mémoires*, II, 548; [N. Hooke], *An Account of the Conduct of the Dowager Duchess of Marlborough* (1742), p. 30.
107 *Hatton Corr.*, II, 137–8; BL Loan 29/140 (unfoliated), Sir E. to R. Harley, 17 August; *HLM*, 1689–1690, pp. 261–4.
108 Foxcroft, *Halifax*, II, 230, 232, 226, 227.
109 Foxcroft, *Halifax*, II, 226, 225, and also 230, 229, 227; Burnet, *History*, IV, 25, 5. See also Scheltema, *Geschied*, III, ii, 159.
110 Baxter, *William III*, pp. 251–5.
111 Foxcroft, *Halifax*, II, 222, 223, 232, 233; Luttrell, *Brief Relation*, I, 567, 577–8; G. Bennett, 'William III and the Episcopate', in *Essays in Modern English Church History*, ed. G. V. Bennett (1966), p. 118.
112 Bodl. Carte MS. 228, f. 133, ? to [T. Wharton], 17 September; CUL Buxton MSS., box 34, J. Herne to his sister, 5 September. And see Horwitz, *Revolution Politicks*, p. 100.
113 E.g., his reply to an address from Cambridge University; *The London Gazette*, No. 2496, 10–14 October. See also DWL Morrice MS. Q, 615; *Clar. Corr.*, II, 291; Luttrell, *Brief Relation*, I, 606.
114 Lamberty, *Mémoires*, II, 615; DWL Morrice MS. Q, 616–17; KU, F. Bonnet, 22 October/ 1 November.
115 As late as mid-September, Carmarthen did not think any parliament would sit before late November; HMC *Finch*, II, 247.
116 DWL Morrice MS. Q, 617; KU, F. Bonnet, 22 October/1 November. Seymour and a few others did oppose the motion for a prorogation.
117 *HLM*, 1689–1690, pp. 348–9, 343–4, 364–7.
118 Huygens, *Journaal*, I, 210; *LJ*, XIV, 351.
119 *CJ*, X, 273. And see *Archives*, III, i, 40.
120 DWL Morrice MS. Q, 623–4.
121 DWL Morrice MS. Q, 637–8.
122 DWL Morrice MS. Q, 640.
123 Foxcroft, *Halifax*, II, 91–105. Bolton later told Halifax he 'was now satisfied of the

falseness of imputing Lord Russell's death to me'; Chatsworth MSS., Devonshire House notebook, *sub* 'Bolton Duke'.

124 DWL Morrice MS. Q, 638–9.

125 DWL Morrice MS. Q, 642.

126 In general, see C. Roberts, *The Growth of Responsible Government in Stuart England* (Cambridge, 1966). For a report that Shales had been recommended to Portland by Harbord and that a sizeable sum of money changed hands in the process; DWL Morrice MS. R, 16.

127 DWL Morrice MS. R, 13; Grey, *Debates*, IX, 454–8, 461–4.

128 CJ, X, 300, 299.

129 CJ, X, 300; Grey, *Debates*, IX, 466–73.

130 DWL Morrice MS. Q, 654, 656; Grey, *Debates*, IX, 400–2; CJ, X, 281, 282; KU, F. Bonnet, 8/18 and 12/22 November.

131 A motion to substitute a levy by monthly assessment was lost on a previous question 182 to 139 on 30 November, in part for procedural reasons. CJ, X, 283, 299; BL Add. MS. 29573, f. 350, C. to Viscount Hatton, 9 November; DWL Morrice MS. R, 18.

132 Bodl. Rawlinson Letters 98, ff. 93–4, [Bishop F. Turner to his brother Thomas, 20 December]. See also Horwitz, *Revolution Politicks*, p. 101; BL Egerton MS. 3337, f. 149, Bishop Frampton to Carmarthen, 24 December; Bodl. Ballard MS. 27, f. 88, [M. Theobald] to A. Charlett, 24 December; DWL Morrice MS. R, 87.

133 Grey, *Debates*, IX, 477–80, 490, 504. See also *Account of Duchess of Marlborough*, pp. 29–35; *Memoirs of Mary*, pp. 17–18, 26–7; KU, F. Bonnet, 20/30 December and 24 December/ 3 January.

134 For this and the following quotation, see Grey, *Debates*, IX, 480–90.

135 Bodl. Ballard MS. 33, f. 100, V. Bathurst to A. Charlett, 14 December; CJ, X, 308–9.

136 Grey, *Debates*, IX, 504–10. And see DWL Morrice MS. R, 56, 63.

137 DWL Morrice MS. R, 44. See also BL Add. MS. 17677 II, f. 255, van Citters, 16/26 December; BL Add. MS. 29573, f. 366, C. to Viscount Hatton, 14 December, and 29578, f. 230, Sir C. Lyttleton to same, 14 December; Luttrell, *Brief Relation*, I, 617.

138 For Torrington's fall from William's graces, see J. Ehrman, *The Navy in the War of William III 1689–1697* (Cambridge, 1953), pp. 316–21; E. B. Powley, *The Naval Side of King William's War* (1972), pp. 281–92, 322–4.

139 BL Add. MS. 33923, f. 465, Sir John Knatchbull's diary; *Clar. Corr.*, II, 296–7.

140 *Shrewsbury Corr.*, pp. 14–16.

141 *Shrewsbury Corr.*, pp. 14–16. And see Dalrymple, *Memoirs*, II, app. iii, 84–95; HMC *Seventh Report*, pp. 230–1.

142 Foxcroft, *Halifax*, II, 242, 243; BL Add. MS. 33923, f. 465; Chatsworth MSS., Devonshire House notebook, *sub* 'Nottingham Lord'; BL Add. MS. 29594, f. 185, Nottingham to Viscount Hatton, 24 December.

143 Lacey, *Dissent*, p. 241 and n. 116; BL Add. MS. 42592, ff. 49–54 (drafts of the bill).

144 Foxcroft, *Halifax*, II, 241, 242; Dalrymple, *Memoirs*, II, app. iii, 80–4.

145 DWL Morrice MS. R, 71, 75. Cf. Ehrman, *The Navy*, p. 322.

146 Lacey, *Dissent*, pp. 239–42; Foxcroft, *Halifax*, II, 243.

147 DWL Morrice MS. R, 82. See also *Correspondentie*, I, i, 64.

148 KU, F. Bonnet, 17/27 January. See also Bodl. Ballard MS. 38, f. 125, W. Helyar to A. Charlett, 11 January.

149 For speculation as to why the third reading had been delayed till the 10th, see DWL Morrice MS. R, 77; Ralph, *History*, II, 182–3.

150 Grey, *Debates*, IX, 511–18; *A Letter Concerning the Disabling Clauses* (1690, Wing L1351), p. 5; CJ, X, 329–30; DWL Morrice MS. R, 84. The bill died in the Lords with the adjournment.

151 Klopp, *Fall des Hauses Stuart*, V, 64–5, 339. See also Lamberty, *Mémoires*, II, 693.

152 Burnet, *Supplement*, pp. 338–9, and *History*, IV, 70–1. See also C. Firth, 'The Memoirs of the first Lord Lonsdale', EHR XXX (1915), 94; *The Conduct of the Earl of Nottingham*, ed. W. A. Aiken (New Haven, 1941), pp. 56–8 and n. 38.

153 *Wilhelm III von Oranien und Georg Friedrich von Waldeck*, ed. P. L. Müller (The Hague, 1880), II, 210.

154 Foxcroft, *Halifax*, II, 243; *Correspondentie*, I, i, 69–70, 74, 81.

155 *Correspondentie*, I, i, 85–6. And see Grey, *Debates*, IX, 523–47.

156 Horwitz, *Revolution Politicks*, p. 106; KU, F. Bonnet, 28 January/7 February.

157 *Correspondentie*, I, i, 95. See also KU, F. Bonnet, 28 January/7 February; DWL

Morrice MS. R, 103; *Diary of Evelyn*, V, 5. Both Evelyn and Morrice reported that Carmarthen knew beforehand of the prorogation.

158 Burnet, *Supplement*, p. 338.

159 *Diary of Evelyn*, V, 5. See also DWL Morrice MS. R, 106; Ralph, *History*, II, 186 and n. 2.

160 Foxcroft, *Halifax*, II, 247.

161 Foxcroft, *Halifax*, II, 247, 246. And see BL Add. MS. 25378, f. 317, Terriesi, 31 January/10 February; BL Add. MS. 29573, f. 392, C. to Viscount Hatton, 1 February.

162 In addition to the fifty-six acts passed in the first session, seventeen were passed in the second.

163 *Diary of Evelyn*, V, 4.

164 Foxcroft, *Halifax*, II, 246, 249.

III

THE ASCENDENCY OF THE CHURCHMEN

1690–1692

It would be difficult to stress too much the importance of William's decision to dissolve the Convention parliament. That he chose to keep the Scottish Convention on foot throughout his reign is some measure of the gamble he was now taking in England. What the King was proposing, as he put it to Halifax, was 'to declare for one party more than for another', while reserving the option 'if his kindness was not answered' of 'tak[ing] the others by the hand' in turn. Nor did he need Halifax to tell him that the 'experiment was doubtful and dangerous'.[1] Hence, after the issuance of the new Admiralty Commission on 20 January 1690, William held his hand on further ministerial changes until the election returns were in. He did reluctantly accept Halifax's firmly tendered resignation on 8 February, but in the Marquess's stead he named a commission consisting of three Commoners, with no marked partisan bias, to hold the Privy Seal for the time being. Furthermore, though Godolphin was anxious to resign from the Treasury and the government was pinched for ready money, especially since after the dissolution some City Whigs did not renew their short-term loans to the crown, the King put off reconstituting the Treasury Board.[2]

William also demonstrated a reluctance to put the crown's electoral influence at the disposal of party or even of particular individuals. He did indicate to those who came to take their leave of him before going into the provinces for the election campaign that he favoured the return of 'moderate men of the Church party', and his financial generosity towards the six deprived non-juring bishops seems to have helped to sweeten the tempers of the Churchmen.[3] Yet, he declared in the midst of the campaign, when informed that letters invoking his name had been written to the Cinque Ports, that he 'had nor would not recommend to any place, nor any way interpose'.[4] Similarly, though he agreed to Nottingham's and Carmarthen's importunities for an alteration in the Whig-controlled lieutenancy of London, he informed them that in that affair (as well as in any changes in the commissions of the peace) he would 'not agree to put out whom we propose, only he would add whom we please to the number'.[5] And in the face of Whig objections to the new list of deputy lieutenants submitted by Bishop Compton, the King postponed the issuance of the London commission until the election was over.

William's caution was, undoubtedly, irksome to the Tory ministers and their friends. Carmarthen grumbled in mid-February that the King 'makes such slow steps' in implementing 'his good intentions to the Church party' that it 'does us no good in this chief business of elections'. Similarly, Clarendon lamented: 'To have a Church of England House of Commons when those who by their employments most influence elections are . . . either professed enemies to our Church or, at best, unconcerned for any church, will I doubt be very difficult.'[6] But while the Churchmen received less direct assistance than they had hoped, and also had to put up with Postmaster Wildman's tampering with the mails on the Whigs' behalf, by mid-March they had little reason to regret the results of what developed as the most widely contested general election to this time in English history.[7]

At least 106 constituencies are known to have been polled by rival candidates in February and March 1690—nearly double the total of the 1689 campaign.[8] Moreover, the clergy were 'very busy in most places', usually in favour of those candidates esteemed Churchmen. Bishop Compton not only sent out circular letters to his clergy to remind them 'at this time how highly the Church of England is concerned to send good members to the next parliament'; he also appeared with his retinue at the Middlesex and Essex county polls. Similarly, Bishop Trelawney of Exeter wrote to his clergy in Cornwall to recommend the Tory incumbents for the shire as 'persons of sound principles to the Church and crown', men 'who in debating the form of the coronation oath were for the religion which is already established' and who had 'lately assisted in the throwing out of the act settling the corporations, the incapacitating clauses'.[9] Partisan controversies in the Convention parliament were also the focal points of two widely dispersed 'blacklists'. The first to be published was a Whig effort; it listed the names of 150 Commoners, who were stigmatised as 'Jacobites' for voting against 'abdication' and 'vacancy'. The second was a Tory counter-attack; it listed 146 M.P.s, who were labelled 'Commonwealthmen' for voting for the Sacheverell clause.

In this fashion, the partisan dissonance that had disrupted the deliberations of the Convention parliament was superimposed upon the perennial jostling of local interests which, in turn, was sharpened in some boroughs by charter disputes stemming from the corporate remodelling of the 1680s. Just what effect the clash of Whig and Tory had upon the frequency of contests or upon the outcome of the general election is impossible to calculate precisely. For all the clamour, blacklisted and non-blacklisted incumbents fared equally well, and of the 513 members of the new Commons 352 (69 per cent) had sat in the last.[10] None the less, it is striking how often the surviving sources refer to the divisive impact of the national issues and rivalries at the local level; Viscount Weymouth was not alone in observing how the 'interest of a party' had triumphed over 'affection to the persons standing'.

Overall, the results of the 1690 election appeared to favour the Tories, and known Whigs had a particularly difficult time. Of the 150 blacklisted 'Jacobites', 103 were returned again and only 9 of these men found it advisable or necessary to shift their constituencies; of the 47 who were not re-elected, only 10 are known to have been candidates again. Of the 146 'Commonwealthmen', 100 were returned, 14 in different constituencies; of the 46 not re-elected, at least 27 are known to have stood unsuccessfully, some for more than one seat, with perhaps the outstanding casualty being John Hampden whose quarrels with his father hindered his re-election at Wendover.[11]

The anti-Whig trend apparent in these computations can be amplified by a survey of the 110 members chosen to sit in the Commons for the first time. This group included a number of vocal Tory country gentlemen who henceforth would be returned time after time, among them Sir Jacob Astley, Sir John Bolles, William Bromley, Sir John Packington, and Peter Shakerly. By contrast, the new Whig crop, though it did not lack for numbers, was thin in quality. Whereas Jack Howe, Sir Thomas Littleton, Charles Montagu, and Edward Russell were returned for the first time in 1689 (not to mention Robert Harley, who was chosen at a by-election), perhaps the most noteworthy of the Whig recruits in 1690 was John Locke's and Sir John Somers's friend, Edward Clarke.

Contemporary verdicts on the 1690 election also indicate that the Tories had the better of it. As early as 28 February, with only very partial results in, there were reports that the Church party would have a two to one or even three to one advantage.[12] Subsequent accounts were more restrained, but there was general agreement that the Churchmen were 'much pleased' and that their rivals had 'sad apprehensions'.[13] Even Somers, the Whig Solicitor-General, was discouraged; on the eve of the new parliament he wrote to Locke that he would probably go on circuit since the list of returns printed in the official *Gazette* 'inclines me to believe' that 'there be no hopes' of a good session.[14]

Once most of the results were in, the King moved ahead with the alterations he had been holding in abeyance. The new commission for the London lieutenancy, which contained a majority of Churchmen, passed the seals in mid-March.[15] A few days later, changes at the Treasury were announced. Godolphin and three Whig members of the old commission, Lords Monmouth and Delamere and Sir Henry Capel, were omitted from the new one, which consisted of only four members; William's failure to appoint a fifth was a mark of his desire to leave a place for Godolphin should he change his mind. The only hold-over on the new commission was the elder Hampden, who was now appointed Chancellor of the Exchequer in Delamere's stead. Joining him were Sir Stephen Fox (an old courtier who had served on the Board before the Revolution), Sir John Lowther of Lowther (an associate of the Tory ministers), and Thomas Pelham (a Whig, recommended by Halifax, who had been serving on the Customs Commission). William had told Halifax before the Marquess resigned that 'he must employ such as would advance money', and personal wealth was the principal common attribute of the new Treasury lords.[16] And their willingness to lend sizeable sums seems to have spurred subscriptions to the large loan being floated in the City late in March.[17]

The composition of the new Treasury Commission indicates that though the Whigs' intransigence had antagonised the King and weakened them in the country, the governmental changes of early 1690 did not all go in the Tories' favour. In partisan terms, the revamped commissions of the Treasury, the Admiralty, and the London lieutenancy were no longer Whig-dominated, but each still contained a substantial Whig contingent. Then, too, the ousted Delamere was consoled with the earldom of Warrington and a generous pension, and Monmouth retained his Bedchamber place and his regiment. Equally significant are the appointments William did not make. Nottingham had been hoping to bring in three of the leading Tory Commoners—Seymour, Clarges, and Musgrave—but none was given office. Neither was the Secretary's brother Heneage Finch, despite the coffee-house pundits who had designated him Lord

Keeper.[18] At the same time, such prominent Whig Commoners as Attorney-General Treby, Solicitor-General Somers, and Comptroller Wharton retained their posts, and among the leading ministers Shrewsbury continued as southern Secretary. Finally, in assessing the political import of the ministerial changes, the enlargement of the courtier element is of some note. Granted, Fox merely replaced the more capable Godolphin at the Treasury. But there was also William's choice of Henry Guy (Jephson's predecessor as Secretary to the Treasury) to succeed Pelham on the Customs Board. Even more telling was the selection of Sir John Trevor as the Court's candidate for the Speaker's Chair in the new Commons, for in August 1689 William had characterised Sir John as 'such a knave, that it would be objected, if he was employed'.[19] In sum, as the new parliament assembled late in March 1690 with the total number of place-men up to 119 from 101 in the old parliament, the Tory and courtier elements in the King's service had been increased, chiefly at the Whigs' expense. Yet, William still hoped to retain the more manageable Whigs in place, and one member of the new Commons spoke now not only of Whigs and Tories, but also of 'Court Whigs' and 'Tory Whigs'.[20]

The fissure in Whig ranks was apparent when the Commons took up the choice of a Speaker on 20 March 1690. A total of 385 members were in atten-dance as Trevor's name was put forward by Sir John Lowther and Sir Henry Goodricke (just named a Privy Councillor), who were to serve as ministerial spokesmen during this and several subsequent sessions. An attempt to re-elect Henry Powle was made by a group of backbench Whigs, with Sir John Guise and Sir John Thompson in the lead, but Trevor was supported by the elder Hampden. And since the Whigs were, in Morrice's words, 'not united' and 'dispirited', the Court's candidate was seated without a division.[21]

During the next few weeks, the King's business also fared reasonably well. In his opening speech on 21 March, William stated his intention of going to Ireland and announced he would make an end of the indemnity issue by submit-ting to parliament an act of grace that would except 'some few persons only'. His principal requests were for supply to carry on the war and for the settlement of the ordinary revenue, and the King sought to advance both by adding that 'if no quicker or more convenient way' could be devised 'for the raising of ready money' he would 'be very well content, for the present' to have the ordinary revenue used as 'a fund of credit' to secure loans to supply the armed forces'.[22]

The King's suggestion was readily taken up by the Commons in their delibera-tions on supply in late March and early April. First, the terms of the grant of an ordinary revenue of £1,200,000 were thrashed out. In addition to the crown's hereditary revenues, the excises that had been settled upon Charles II and James II were voted for the lives of William and Mary. However, the customs (tunnage and poundage) granted in 1660 and 1685 for life were limited to four years—a marginal improvement over the three-year term tentatively voted in July 1689. Second, an extraordinary supply of £1,200,000, above and beyond the moneys voted in the second session of the Convention parliament, was agreed to be necessary for the support of the war during 1690. Furthermore, it was decided that £1,000,000 of this should be raised by loans upon the royal revenue, with the remaining £200,000 to be made up by the imposition of a new poll tax.

To judge by Lowther's initial requests on the King's behalf for all the ordinary revenue to be granted for life and for war supply of £1,400,000, the Commons' resolutions fell considerably short of royal desires, and William was said to be particularly disappointed at the Commons' determination to limit the grant of the customs to four years so as to assure frequent meetings of parliament.[23] It was also reported that the King had not expected to have any more than half the extraordinary supply charged upon the revenue, but this was not the impression conveyed by his financial spokesmen in the Commons, Lowther and Pelham. In fact, the only division on supply came on 1 April in committee over an attempt to reduce the amount for the war from the £1,200,000 figure, which the Court's managers had already accepted, to £1,000,000, and this motion was rejected 229 to 165.[24]

Although the Commons quickly reached agreement on supply and on the revenue, it was perhaps too much to expect that they would heed the King's exhortations in his opening speech against 'differences and disagreements'. From the outset, it was evident that the sores opened up during the last parliament and exacerbated in the recent elections still rankled with many. On 22 March, the Commons ordered an inquiry after the 'authors and dispersers' of the black-lists as violators of the House's privileges. That same day, a complaint was entered against Sir Thomas Mompesson for assaulting another member, William Okeden, in the Lobby; the 'bottom reason' for that attack was that Okeden had tried to prevent Mompesson's re-election for Salisbury by telling the electors Mompesson 'was for the corporation bill, and that he was a favourer of the Presbyterians, etc.'[25] This was the only physical confrontation of the session, but it was followed by several long and well-attended sittings on contested elections in the committee of privileges and elections, otherwise known as 'the committee of affections'.[26] On 11 April, that committee (in which all who came could vote) sat till 11.45 p.m. on the Hertford case, with 300 members lasting out the evening. As one disappointed Whig observed:[27]

It was very late for so ancient a man as Sir Thomas Clarges and Sir Robert Sawyer and many other old parliament men to stay; however, they commend their zeal for the Church by their diligence and constancy to effect what they desire, which they have done at all the committees that have sat to hear disputable returns.

For all the wrangling in the Commons, the sharpest clashes came in the Lords during the early weeks of the 1690 session. To start with, there were complaints from some of the more extreme Whig peers about the late dissolution, the King's intended Irish venture, and the proposed act of grace.[28] But it was the Duke of Bolton's bill 'for declaring' the acts of the Convention parliament 'to be of full force and effect by the laws of the realm' and 'for recognising' William and Mary as 'rightful and lawful' rulers that made tempers flare the highest, for this measure aroused all the Churchmen's scruples about the legality of the Revolution. Since William was anxious to avoid disputes on this sensitive point, Halifax, Devonshire, and Shrewsbury joined Nottingham and Carmarthen in criticising the Duke's bill when it was read a first time on 26 March. Yet there was general agreement that some form of affirmation of the Convention parliament's actions was desirable, and the bill was committed on the 28th on the understanding that it would be altered to make it more acceptable.[29]

The Lords' deliberations in committee of the whole were mainly taken up with the first section of the bill, which dealt with the statutes of the Convention parliament. Nottingham and his friends pressed to have those acts 'confirmed', rather than 'declared' legal, in accord with the Restoration precedent, but a majority could not be mustered for either wording. Clauses containing the opposing formulae were reported by the divided committee to the full House on 5 April, and both were rejected. Nevertheless, there was considerable sentiment that 'a matter of so great a consequence ought to receive some determination', especially as it was 'beginning now to be blown about that the Lords were against recognising the King and Queen, though that matter had never yet been under any debate'.[30] In this spirit, a compromise resolution put forward by the Lord President was carried late on 5 April; by this, the Lords stated it to be their 'opinion' that the acts of the Convention parliament 'were and are good laws, to all intents and purposes whatsoever'.[31] Then on Monday, the 7th, the peers took up the bill once more, and at last they managed to devise a text which could command a majority. The phrase 'rightful and lawful' was dropped from the clause recognising William and Mary, and it was 'enacted' that the acts of the previous parliament 'were and are' statutes. But not all the peers could be brought to accept this version. After the measure was passed on 8 April, Nottingham and sixteen other Tories entered a formal protest in which they denounced the 'were and are' formula as 'neither good English nor good sense'.[32] This was too much for the rest of the Lords, and a majority which included Carmarthen then voted to expunge the protest from the Journal.[33]

The Lords' prolonged debates on the recognition bill attracted considerable attention out of doors. Some found them ludicrous. Such 'politic distinctions', jibed the non-juror Charles Hatton (Nottingham's uncle by marriage), 'do far, as to niceness, exceed the philosophical distinctions of the schoolmen'.[34] Yet it was widely expected that the bill would also provoke an extended controversy in the Commons. So it came as a surprise that the lower House passed the measure in two days without even the usual formality of a committal.

Why the Commons acted with such dispatch on the bill of recognition is not easy to determine. In the first version of his *History*, Burnet attributed it to the Churchmen's desire 'to give the King this early assurance of their fidelity to him; and the leaders of the Tory party drew in their followers (before they were aware of it) to consent to it'. In his later version, however, Burnet stated that the Tories had intended to oppose the measure after it was committed, but that their design was prematurely revealed and so forestalled, thanks in part to a very able speech by Somers.[35] As best as can be ascertained, both his accounts contain a measure of fact. Some Churchmen, among them Clarges, Sawyer, and Musgrave, did voice objections similar to those of the Lords' minority and spoke for committal. But Lowther, presumably inspired by Carmarthen, joined the Whigs in urging immediate passage. Thus, in the Commons, as in the Lords, the Tories divided over the bill, and, as Rochester himself told Clarendon, he and Nottingham were by mid-April 'quite out' with the Lord President.[36]

Nor was this the only occasion during this session when the Churchmen fell out with one another. Seymour and Musgrave had earlier opposed Lowther and Goodricke in the debates over the settlement of the revenue and the grant of extraordinary supply. Moreover, there was no love lost between Lowther and Goodricke, and Musgrave: Sir John and Sir Christopher were rivals of long standing in Westmorland, and Sir Henry as Lieutenant-General of the Ordnance occupied the position that had been Musgrave's between 1681 and 1687. Even so, it was Seymour who most openly displayed his resentment at his continued exclusion from office. In a speech 'much taken notice of' during the debates on the revenue, Sir Edward had scathingly referred to the 'white horse' Halifax who had sought to manage the Convention parliament and to the 'black horse' Carmarthen who 'governs' its successor, and six weeks later he joined with other Churchmen at odds with Carmarthen in a direct attack on the Lord President.[37]

However, when the Churchmen did unite, they usually could muster a majority during the 1690 session, as in the proceedings upon the London charter and the City lieutenancy. On 8 April, the Tories succeeded in rejecting both the London common council's proposals and the Whigs' attempts to 'declare' void the 1683 judgement against the City's charter; instead, they carried it 194 to 139 that a bill should be brought in to 'reverse' the verdict and to restore the corporation to its *status quo ante*.[38] Then on the 24th, the Churchmen—aroused by reports that the King might be considering a reversal of the recent changes in the London lieutenancy—pushed through 185 to 136 a resolution to thank William 'for the great care he has expressed of the Church of England in the late alteration he has made in the lieutenancy'.[39]

Even so, the Whigs had more than one arrow in their quiver. As 'a Roland for the Oliver' the Tories 'had given in addressing' on 24 April, they sought to turn the flank that the Churchmen had exposed in the Lords' debates over the act of recognition.[40] Late on the 24th, Comptroller Wharton—in a surprise and preconcerted move—proposed a bill to oblige all office-holders to take an oath abjuring James II. His motion was carried without a division, he was made chairman of the committee which was named to bring in the measure, and on the 25th the Commons read it once and ordered a second reading for the following morning. That evening, so Morrice noted, the Churchmen gathered 'in many taverns' to mobilise against the abjuration.[41] Their objections to it, which they repeatedly voiced in the debate on the 26th, were that (1) the oath denominated William and Mary as 'rightful and lawful' sovereigns; (2) it was to be imposed upon clerics as well as lay officials; and (3) it could be tendered by any two justices of the peace, who were to be empowered to commit without bail any who refused it.[42] Even Goodricke and Lowther, who had spoken for abjuration on the 25th, now turned against Wharton's bill, and Lowther explained that 'his mind was changed upon very weighty reasons, which he received from a very great person'. Whether that 'great person' was the Lord President, as Grey assumed, or the King, as Morrice and others inferred, the united Churchmen first defeated a motion to commit the bill by 192 to 178 and then secured its rejection.[43]

However, the Commons' votes of 26 April did not end the disputes over abjuration, for when the Lords turned to consider the state of the nation on 1 May, the Whig peers sought to reverse the defeats their friends had suffered in the lower House. Their attempt that day to have a select committee appointed to investigate the new London lieutenancy was voted down 45 to 43, but the peers did agree to pursue the matter in committee of the whole and they also gave a first reading to a modified abjuration bill.[44] The following afternoon, with the King attending incognito, the peers deliberated for four hours upon the measure. Carmarthen, Nottingham, Pembroke, and Halifax spoke against both the terms of the oath and its imposition upon all subjects, and only two of the eleven bishops present (Burnet and Stratford of Chester) supported it. Nevertheless, the bill was committed by a vote of 51 to 40.[45]

Meanwhile, the controversies over recognition and abjuration helped to feed continuing speculation about new alterations at Whitehall. Reports of ministerial changes began to spread in mid-April, and some thought that Nottingham's bitter opposition to the bill of recognition presaged either his resignation or his dismissal. But the Tory Secretary was willing to swallow that act, though he declared in the Lords that he would resign if an abjuration were adopted, and William was not prepared to remove him, even if he was 'too violent for his party'.[46] Rather, it was the Whig Secretary who was ready to retire, as he had already spoken of doing the previous autumn. Shrewsbury was weary of the burdens of his office and resentful of the influence of his Tory colleagues, and it was apparently William's wavering over abjuration that finally determined him. Subsequently, he told Halifax that 'the King encouraged him about the bill of oaths but afterwards changed his mind', and on 28 April he returned the seals to William.[47]

Some observers were surprised at Shrewsbury's decision, and the Brandenburg resident remarked that 'up to now it had not been believed that his attachment to his party had been so great'. But Whig reactions were rather different. Colonel Thomas Tipping explained to an acquaintance that Shrewsbury was resigning because 'he sees the kingdom is ruined and so, etc.' And Mary Kemys (*née* Wharton) spelled out Whig views when she wrote, in response to her husband's report that the Earl and other Whigs were giving up their places: 'I wonder they did not do it sooner, for since it was not in their power to keep the ruin of the nation off, they are to be (I think) commended for letting the world see that they have no hand in the furthering of it.'[48] For the moment, William did manage to induce the southern Secretary to keep the seals. Nevertheless, Shrewsbury, pleading ill health, left town to go to the Newmarket races early in May in the company of Comptroller Wharton and Lord Steward Devonshire.[49]

The well-publicised departure of these Whig notables did not put an end to the partisan affrays in parliament, yet it seemed to take some of the sting out of their friends' attack. In the Lords, the Whigs' oath bill was so extensively amended that they lost interest in pursuing it, and their inquiry into the City lieutenancy bogged down in a swamp of depositions and counter-depositions at the Bar.[50] At the same time, the Churchmen's bill to reverse the judgement against the City was approved, though only by narrow margins: 179 to 171 by the Commons on 8 May, 47 to 44 by the Lords on the 13th. In addition, the Churchmen, perhaps as a goad to the King to bring forward the promised act of grace, revived the measure proposed twice in 1689 for the collection of the £500 forfeitures from those who had taken office under James II without complying with the test.[51]

Still one more sign of the Whigs' discouragement by mid-May 1690 was their failure to follow up the attacks against Carmarthen launched by his personal enemies. Guise and Thompson did join Seymour and John Granville (a younger son of Carmarthen's old antagonist, the Earl of Bath) in moving an address against the Lord President on the 14th, but Harbord spoke against it and Paul Foley vainly tried to avert the division that the movers then lost by at least sixty votes. Again, though some Whig peers seconded Halifax's bid of the 20th to exclude Carmarthen from the act of grace, that debate was eventually adjourned without a division.[52]

However, these clashes did slow progress on the King's business. Although most of the major money bills had been approved by the beginning of May, the measure to vest the hereditary revenues in William and Mary and to authorise loans upon them was not even reported from the Commons' committee until the 16th. The lower House was also troubled by the legal conundrums some discerned in the Lords' bill to make Mary regent during the King's absence in Ireland. For the most part, it was the Whig lawyers and their friends who found difficulties in the way of William's departure, and a few of them openly declared their dislike of the projected expedition.[53] Even so, by 13 May this measure was also ready for the royal assent. Four days later, the Commons read the hereditary revenues bill a third time, but they attached to it a rider to bar William and Mary from alienating any portion of them.

The amendment to the hereditary revenues bill was not to William's taste, and so little did he care for the bill with this restriction that his feelings on this score may have influenced the timing of the ensuing adjournment. On 19 May, the day the Lords read the hereditary revenues bill a first time, the King finally sent them the long-awaited act of grace. After this measure (which needed only a single reading in each House) had been approved, and just as the Lords were about to give a third reading to the revenues bill, William unexpectedly came to Westminster Palace on the 23rd. He accepted the last of the twenty-eight bills completed during the session and then announced he could 'no longer delay my going into Ireland, and therefore I think it necessary to have an adjournment'.[54]

What the King's objection was to the hereditary revenues bill, beyond the obnoxious rider, is not clear, but he may have felt that no parliamentary authorisation was necessary either to collect or to borrow upon them. All that is known is that after the adjournment, William told Halifax that the bill 'would bring him no credit', even though it contained a provision to allow loans of up to £250,000 on the hereditary revenues. In any case, the King lingered in London for almost another fortnight before setting out for Ireland, and after his departure the Treasury was able to raise substantial loans upon the security of the hereditary excises.[55]

The sudden adjournment not only forestalled the hereditary revenues bill; it also prevented the completion of several other measures. One prominent casualty was a bill to establish an enlarged East India Company on a statutory footing. This measure was drafted by counsel for the old Company and submitted to the Commons in an attempt to outflank the Company's interloping rivals and in response to criticism levelled against the corporation in the Convention parliament.[56] During the spring session of 1689, the Commons had condemned the old Company for issuing martial law commissions at St Helena in James II's reign. And in the autumn session, a Commons' committee had been on the verge of recommending the dissolution of the old royally-chartered Company and the creation of a new one to be endowed by statute with quasi-sovereign powers comparable to those exercised by the Dutch East India Company.[57] But instead of proceeding either with the Company's bill or along the lines of their earlier proposals, the Commons prepared another draft which would merely have confirmed the Company's charter until such time as parliament established a new one. This interim measure suited neither the Company nor the interlopers, and after it was committed on 8 May no further action was taken.

Another notable victim of the early adjournment was the Commons' bill to establish a commission to examine the crown's receipts and disbursements since

November 1688, and subsequently some were to attribute William's early close of the 1690 session to his dislike of this proposal. Roger Kenyon (member for Clitheroe) expressed this opinion in a speech of December 1690, and George Tollet (later Secretary to the Commission of Accounts) was also of this view.[58] But they were in error. Parliament was not adjourned, as Tollet asserted in January 1691, 'the very day in which the bill should have passed'; rather, the Commons were debating a rider offered at the measure's third reading and before it was sent up to the Lords when the King came on 23 May to end the session. Nor, for that matter, was William opposed to the bill. He had accepted the principle of providing accounts to parliament in his speech of 28 June 1689, and he had fulfilled this promise in the two subsequent sessions. It is true that the Commons had not been able to learn as much as they had hoped from the accounts laid before them, and the bill of May 1690 did represent a new attempt to get to grips with the problem of finding out where the taxpayers' money was going. Yet this approach (which was that of the Brooke House commission of 1667–68) also was acceptable to William. In the very conversation with Halifax in which the King expressed his dislike of the hereditary revenues bill, he also indicated his disappointment at the loss of the accounts measure. Moreover, before he left for Ireland, he ordered his ministers to try to implement the scheme by creating a royal commission consisting of the nine men the Commons had named in their abortive bill. This design did not succeed, but that was chiefly because the four Whig nominees were reluctant to serve on such a basis. As Sir John Trevor informed the King in June: 'pains have been taken to prevent them from acting, and to put all imaginable misconstruction on your good intentions of that commission'.[59]

The sabotage of the projected royal commission of accounts was not the only instance of Whig dissatisfaction at the close of the spring session of 1690. William had not intended to make any major alterations in the ministry before setting out for Ireland. To be sure, Trevor received the first reward for his services by being named to replace the aged and cantankerous Serjeant Maynard as chief commissioner of the Great Seal. Yet at the same time, three Whigs were added to the Admiralty Board: Sir Richard Onslow (head of a prominent Surrey family) and two experienced seamen, Admiral Edward Russell and his follower Captain Henry Priestman. Little partisan significance was attached to these changes, but William's choice of the council of nine to advise Mary in his absence does reflect his growing dependence upon the Tory ministers.

The King delayed naming the council until the eve of his departure in the hope that Shrewsbury could be induced to keep the seals, even if not to act for the time being. William went so far as to assure that Earl that 'if he would stay in, his party should be the major part', though he also warned that 'if he left him, he would force him to put himself into Lord Carmarthen's hands'.[60] But Shrewsbury sent up the seals to the King from the country on 3 June, and so William omitted him from the list of nine he had first drawn up in February. Those named to the council on the evening of the third included six from William's earlier list (Lords Carmarthen, Devonshire, Dorset, Nottingham, Pembroke and Sir John Lowther) and three more recent choices (Lords Monmouth and Marlborough and Admiral Russell). Dropped with Shrewsbury from the earlier list were Comptroller Wharton and Lord Chief Justice Holt.[61] Monmouth and Russell were, it is true, as staunch Whigs in their own ways as Shrewsbury

and Wharton, and when Shrewsbury and Devonshire departed to Newmarket
in early May they left their proxies as members of the House of Lords with
Monmouth.[62] But Monmouth and Russell had little regard for one another.
Moreover, with Shrewsbury's departure Carmarthen was especially recommended to Mary by William, Nottingham was left as sole Secretary, and
Nottingham's elderly kinsman Sir Robert Southwell was chosen to accompany
the King as Secretary for Ireland.

After William set out for Ireland on 4 June, Mary took up the exercise of the
royal authority under the terms of the regency statute adopted in May. Heretofore, the Queen had remained very much in the background, 'declin[ing]
always to declare herself till she ha[d] heard the King's opinion'; now, she
could hardly avoid decisions.[63] At the outset, she was prey to doubts about her
own abilities and fears of a Jacobite uprising in England should William's campaign falter. Nor did she at first repose much confidence in the councillors the
king had left her. Carmarthen, she wrote, was 'of a temper I can never like';
Devonshire, 'weak and obstinate'; Dorset, 'lazy'; Pembroke, 'not very steady';
Nottingham, 'suspected by most as not true to the government'; Monmouth,
'mad'; Lowther, 'weak'; Marlborough, 'can never deserve either trust or
esteem'; and even Russell 'had his faults'.[64]

In the event, it was not the Irish campaign but the defeat of the allied fleet at
Beachy Head on 30 June that most severely imperilled the regime. Torrington,
who was in command of the outnumbered allied fleet that day, sought to avoid
an engagement. But he was overruled by direct orders from Whitehall, which
Mary issued after she was assured by Russell and Nottingham that 'good
success from the ships now together' could be expected.[65] The fact that the
unfortunate Admiral left the Dutch contingent to bear the brunt of the engagement only intensified the ensuing outcry against him. As recriminations over the
defeat mounted, Mary and her council called upon William to return to England
and anxiously discussed whether parliament should be reconvened in order to
vote emergency funds.[66] Fortunately, neither expedient proved necessary, thanks
in part to William's victory at the Boyne early in July and in larger part to
French unpreparedness to make a landing in force in England.

Although the immediate threat of invasion from without or rebellion from
within receded quickly, divisions within the royal administration were a constant
concern to Mary. The problem was not between Carmarthen and Nottingham;
so far as the Queen could discern, their breach of the spring was now a thing of
the past, and as the summer went on Mary was more and more impressed by the
Secretary's 'hearty' and 'sincere' conduct.[67] It was, rather, the ever unpredictable Monmouth who was stirring up trouble. At first, he seemed bent on discrediting Nottingham, but Mary—alerted by Carmarthen, and also by Russell
and Marlborough—was not taken in by his attempts to cast suspicion on the
Secretary's faithfulness. Thus, in an interview with Monmouth early in July the
Queen sharply rebuked him for his meddling and she also vigorously asserted the
royal prerogative in the choice of ministers. As Mary subsequently related to
William, she told Monmouth that[68]

I found it very strange you were not thought fit to choose your own ministers; that they
had already removed Lord Halifax, the same endeavours were used for Lord Carmarthen,
and would they now begin to have a bout at Lord Nottingham too; it would show they
would pretend ever to control the King in his choice, which, if I were he, I would not suffer.

Unabashed, Monmouth continued to make trouble, with some help from his friend Bolton. The Earl tried to exploit the government's need for loans to tide it over the summer by obstructing the council's requests to the City after Beachy Head, while promising the Queen himself to secure £200,000 at low interest from his own friends in the City (among them, the goldsmith Charles Duncombe) provided a new parliament was called.[69] However, as Nottingham had anticipated, the necessary loans were raised without any such commitment, though this did not deter Monmouth and some other Whigs from continuing to press for a dissolution.

Monmouth also had a hand in the prolonged squabble over the choice of Torrington's replacement. He began by putting himself forward as a candidate, telling Mary he had 'reason to expect the command'. Then, after his own and also Shrewsbury's offers to go to sea were politely declined, Monmouth joined with some of the Whig Admiralty lords in opposition to the council of nine's nomination of Sir Richard Haddock to head a joint commission to command the fleet. Among the objections advanced against Haddock were the charges that had been levelled against him by the Commons in the autumn of 1689. And though the Admiralty Commissioners were not willing to take the responsibility for Torrington's trial because he was a peer, they claimed that the council should have solicited nominations for his successor from them. In Whig eyes, Haddock was also suspect as Nottingham's candidate, and Monmouth and Bolton busily denounced him as anti-Dutch and a Jacobite to any who would listen, including the Dutch ambassador. Not until 8 August, after two stormy interviews between the Queen and the Admiralty Board, was the commission for the three co-admirals finally signed by four of the seven Admiralty lords.[70]

In the face of such difficulties, Mary's relief at William's return to London on 10 September was understandable. As for the King, he could take some comfort in the results of the summer's campaign, despite both Beachy Head and the allied army's setback at Fleurus on 1 July. His belief that he could leave England to the Queen's administration had been vindicated and, as Mary subsequently noted, he now was prepared to talk 'more freely' to her of business.[71] Then, too, William's victory at the Boyne and his personal valour in that battle not only furthered the reconquest of Ireland but also restored his tarnished image in English eyes. Thus, reinforced by Carmarthen's arguments against a dissolution and knowing that 'the Treasury will be at a stand at the beginning of November', the King announced on 12 September that he would meet his second parliament again early the following month.[72]

While the Court made preparations for the assembly of parliament, Lord Sidney and Thomas Coningsby (M.P. for Leominster) wrote jointly from their new posts in Dublin as Irish Lords Justices to advise Portland on the management of the English House of Commons. Their letter of 27 September recommended reliance on the Speaker and the enlistment of members 'who have fair reputations in the House' to join with Trevor and other Court managers in nightly consults. They specifically instanced three members who, they asserted, 'have the greatest influence over the three parties in the House that are not for King James: [William] Sacheverell of the Whigs. [Sir William] Leveson-Gower of the middle party, and Sir Thomas Clarges of the high Church'.[73] Yet there is no reason to suppose that William and Portland were dependent on such belated suggestions from across the Irish Sea, especially with Trevor and Carmarthen in

London. The King also had other useful M.P.s in his service—among them William Jephson, Secretary to the Treasury. In his official capacity, Jephson dispensed the government's 'secret service' funds at the King's command. And though Godolphin would lament Jephson's premature death in mid-1691 as an 'irreparable' loss to the administration because of his adroitness in handling the King's financial business in the Commons, the critics of the government eagerly sought sight of his secret service accounts in the hope of confirming their allegations that he, like his predecessor Charles Bertie in the 1670s, was making payments under the table to susceptible Commoners.[74] No doubt, such suspicions were easily aroused since Carmarthen (Bertie's brother-in-law and patron) was at the helm once more, and the Lord President's papers indicate that he was hard at work in the weeks before the autumn session opened, consulting with the King, preparing organisational memoranda, and writing in William's name to 'friends in both Houses to be as early as they can' at Westminster.[75]

None the less, only about 150 Commoners were present to hear the King's opening speech on 2 October 1690. Among those missing was Sacheverell (who was absent most, if not all, of the session) and also his old friend Anchitell Grey, and Grey's failure to come up to town for this session leaves us without a detailed account of the debates.[76] However, the King's speech—as was the usual practice —was officially printed and widely distributed. William began by calling to mind the successes in Ireland, his own nearly fatal wound at the Boyne, and the mortgaging of the ordinary revenue, and he announced that the 'public accounts' would be laid before parliament to explain how the military departments had accumulated their large debts. He went on to urge the grant of extraordinary supplies at least as large as those voted for 1690 and also of funds for 'the clearing of my revenue'.[77] Specifics were then provided in the estimates for the fleet and the figures for the army presented to the Commons on 9 October by Sir Thomas Lee for the Admiralty Commission and Lord Ranelagh as Paymaster of the Army. These revealed that the King wanted £1,800,000 for the fleet and an army of 69,000 men.

The government's requests met with an unexpectedly favourable response. Just before the session opened, under-secretary Robert Yard had anticipated that the Commons would be 'a little out of humour at several things that have happened this summer', but his prediction was made before news reached London a few days later that Cork had surrendered to Marlborough's expeditionary force on 28 September.[78] In any event, when the lower House took up the naval estimates on 10 October, they were approved with little dispute. The troop requests did provoke some arguments as a few members, notably Seymour and Clarges, spoke for a sharp cutback in the army and the pursuit of a maritime strategy. However, optimism was now the order of the day, and Lord Manchester observed that 'most of the speeches tended as if they did expect 40,000 men to land in France' the coming year to bring the war to a speedy end. The result was that the full House approved the request for 69,000 men on the 13th *nemine contradicente* and then resolved on the 14th to raise £2,300,000 to pay for them.[79] That evening Bishop Burnet wrote jubilantly to his kinsman Johnston:[80]

I was never more surprised in my whole life than I am to see the House of Commons in such a temper. All that I know say plainly, they dare not go back into their country if they do not give money liberally.... In a word, the French fleet, by lying so long on our coast, . . . and the King's behaviour in Ireland, as well as King James's meanness, has made so wonderful a change in all men's minds with relation to them both, that we seem now not to be the same people, that we were a year ago, . . .

Even so, it did not prove easy to devise ways and means to raise the sums voted with such alacrity. By mid-November, William was beginning to complain to Pensionary Anthonie Heinsius at The Hague of the delays, and not until early in the new year was the King free to leave for the Continent to confer with the other leaders of the anti-French alliance.[81] By then, grants calculated to yield roughly £4,600,000 had been approved. Yet the Commons' readiness to vote supply was qualified in several respects. Despite William's renewed plea midway in the session for the clearing of the loans taken up on the ordinary revenue during 1690, the lower House eventually authorised only an extension of these borrowings. Then, too, a much larger proportion of the supply for 1691 than for either 1689 or 1690 was to be raised by loans on future revenues; only the land tax and the doubled excise on drink were voted for a single year. The new customs proposed by Clarges and the other increases in existing excises were to be imposed for terms of up to five years in the future, and the acts for their collection included clauses of credit for the raising of loans on the security of these taxes in order to pay for the coming year's outlays.[82]

The hypothecation of the additional customs and excises proved necessary because two other widely canvassed projects did not get through the Commons. One was a general excise which was favoured, among others, by the official author (probably Richard Hampden) of a presessional financial memorandum to the King.[83] Reports that such a levy, which had been denounced as a means to 'enslave our nation' when mooted by Sir Thomas Lee in the previous session, would be suggested by the Court circulated widely in November.[84] But no formal proposal for a general impost on domestic commodities was ever offered, perhaps because it was doubted that it could be carried, though the Commons did discuss schemes to excise barley and malt.

The second project that came to naught was to raise a large sum either by the sale or upon the security of the forfeited estates of the rebels in Ireland. On 17 October, the Commons did tentatively approve such a proposal and it was reckoned that it might yield as much as £1,000,000. But from the outset, there were doubts that anything like this sum could be realised from the Irish lands, at least in the near future.[85] For this reason, and possibly also because the King feared his prerogative of disposing of forfeitures was being challenged, 'the supporters of the Court' were quick to oppose an address proposed in late October to request from the government a list of the names and estates of the Irish rebels.[86] Yet the Commons two months later did pass a forfeiture bill which would have applied the estates of the rebels to the support of the war, though even the measure's advocates were ready to concede that for the time being those lands would not yield much.[87] In this form, the King had every reason to object to the bill, and when the Lords effectively blocked its passage by voting to hear counsel for the many petitioners against it, their action was quite plausibly attributed to Court influence.[88] In the event, the Commons had to rest content with William's assurance, offered in his speech at the close of the session on 5 January 1691, that he would not make any grants of the Irish forfeitures 'till there be another opportunity of settling that matter in parliament in such manner as shall be thought most expedient'.[89]

Although the Irish bill failed to reach the statute book, the King did give his consent to a measure to set up a commission of accounts. This, too, had nearly gone astray in the Lords after its passage, with the Court's acquiescence, by the Commons on 26 December 1690. The stumbling block was the Lords' vote of 29 December to add four peers to the nine Commoners who had been chosen by ballot in the lower House. The Commons responded by delaying the transmission of the additional excise bill, and the peers gave in to this pressure on the 31st. In this fashion, the failure of the previous session's measure was made good, and the first of a notable series of parliamentary commissions of accounts was born.[90]

Other potentially useful reform bills were not among the forty-one statutes enacted during the 1690–91 session. Among the casualties were the Commons' bills to prohibit the sale of offices, to reform the procedure in treason trials, and to facilitate the determination of controverted elections. The Commons' interest in the speedier resolution of election disputes may well have reflected the considerable amount of time taken up, both in committee and on the floor, by election petitions in this and in the previous session. Many controverted election cases had been held over from the spring, and as Philip Foley warned his kinsman Robert Harley (a petitioner) early in the 1690–91 session: 'when you come here you will find the same humour of Whig and Tory as formerly.'[91] Often, too, the votes in these cases were very close: the Whig Edward Brent of Sandwich carried the first petition to be reported by 175 to 174 on 30 October, with 'the two parties appear[ing] in their full strength in this cause'; a month later, the Tory candidates from Chester were seated by margins of a single vote in divisions first in committee and then on the floor.[92]

While both parties could claim some victories on election petitions, the Whigs gained the upper hand in the one other hotly disputed partisan affray of the 1690–91 session. At stake was control of the bench of aldermen (and hence the mayoralty) of the City. The Tories thought they had recaptured control in London when parliament passed in May 1690 the bill to reverse the 1683 judgement against the City. But that act contained some large loopholes which the City Whigs had promptly exploited so that once again the Churchmen looked to parliament to redress the balance in London.[93] A petition from 124 Tory common councilmen was presented to the Commons by Sir Samuel Dashwood on 2 December, immediately after the Churchmen had triumphed in the division over the Chester election. Their petition, setting out a series of alleged irregularities committed by the Whig Lord Mayor and his aldermanic colleagues, was received by a vote of 192 to 167, and the Tories savoured the taste of success. But when counsel for both sides were heard the following week, the petitioners failed to make out a strong case. In turn, on 11 December a Whig motion of adjournment was carried, 'beyond the expectation of all mankind', by 197 to 184, so leaving the 'high party' again 'much broken and discontented'.[94]

Whig and Tory were not the only poles of politics during the 1690–91 session. Although the *contretemps* over the Earl of Torrington's case did take on the appearance of a party quarrel—'the Whigs', it was observed, 'wish to oust him, this is enough to make the Tories work to bring him off'—the question of how to deal with the fallen Admiral also offered an opportunity for the 'outs' to harass the 'ins'.[95] Torrington's case, briefly referred to by William in his opening speech, raised several different legal problems. On 6 October, the Earl petitioned the Lords to be released from the Tower, where he had been committed by the

Privy Council after Beachy Head, on the grounds that his imprisonment was a breach of the peers' privileges. Despite Nottingham's spirited defence of the Council's order, the Lords upheld his claim 32 to 17 on 21 October. Uncharitable commentators remarked upon the prominent role taken by Halifax and Rochester on Torrington's behalf, for in this instance, at least, their zeal for the peers' privileges appeared to have been fortified by their enmity towards the Lord President of the Council.[96]

A similar political pattern was evident in the parliamentary debates that followed over a government bill, brought in upon Carmarthen's and Nottingham's advice, for the purpose of clarifying the powers of the reluctant Admiralty Commissioners to court-martial Torrington. Before the bill was adopted, its backers had to overcome a vocal opposition put up by the Lord President's personal enemies including Seymour and Granville in the Commons, Rochester and Bolton in the Lords.[97] Then, much to William's anger and dismay, Torrington's fellow officers who served upon the court-martial jury found him not guilty. So the King could do little to punish the Earl save to revoke his remaining commission as Vice-Admiral of England. Simultaneously, William turned out John Granville, Torrington's principal defender in the Commons and in the fleet, from all his military and naval appointments on the grounds that he had made derogatory remarks about one of the Dutch officers who was a witness at the court martial.[98]

Although Carmarthen's advice on the disposition of Torrington's case had not taken into account the sentiments of the English fleet officers, the Lord President showed all his old skills when his enemies threatened him on familiar parliamentary ground. One attack against the Marquess was mounted in the Lords early in the 1690–91 session, and on this occasion Shrewsbury and the Whigs were joined by Halifax, Rochester, and Godolphin.[99] This storm quickly blew itself out, but a second assault upon the Lord President, again principally inspired by Shrewsbury, was planned towards the end of the session in the Commons. As Morrice noted:[100]

A great number of the House of Commons from different principles and for different ends had agreed to make an address to his Majesty to remove the Marquess of Carmarthen from his council and presence. They had thought to have had moved it in the House upon Tuesday [30 December], and after that upon Thursday (so that the business took air and was noted at Court), but Friday the 2nd instant was the day they finally agreed on, and other business was put off. But when Friday came, and there had been a long expectation in the House, nobody spoke a word about it. And so those of the other side laughed at them, for some had been spoke to and some were false.

In outmanoeuvring his opponents at the turn of the year, Carmarthen was assisted by the discovery of a Jacobite conspiracy. The plot was unravelled by the Lord President's son Danby's capture on the night of 31 December of a vessel bound for France with Lord Preston, once Secretary of State to James II, on board. Among those who, according to Preston's papers and his subsequent confessions, knew of his voyage to France (if nothing more) were both acknowledged Jacobites such as Lords Clarendon and Dartmouth and professed Williamites including Seymour, Halifax, and even some Whigs. The credit that Carmarthen garnered by his management of this discovery, coupled with the discomfiture of some of his leading enemies, was more than enough to silence for the moment those who sought his ouster.[101]

Despite Carmarthen's success at the close of the 1690–91 session, there was some substance to the reports of ministerial changes that had circulated throughout the autumn. Those who had predicted Godolphin's return to business were vindicated in mid-November when he took up the vacant seat that had been left for him at the Treasury. But those who anticipated Rochester's 'coming into play' were disappointed, at least for the time being.[102] Furthermore, the King's eventual choice to take the seals returned by Shrewsbury came as a surprise to all. Those whose names had been bruited about for the vacant Secretaryship— Shrewsbury himself, Lowther, Sir William Trumbull (recently recalled from his embassy to the Turkish Porte), Monmouth, and Comptroller Wharton—were either unwilling to accept or were not judged worthy. Instead, William made it known in mid-December that he would recall his old friend Sidney from Ireland and make him Secretary.

The King's selection of Sidney had all the appearance of a choice *faute de mieux*. William himself was reported to have described the Viscount as merely a temporary stopgap; others were more scathing, among them Carmarthen, who characterised Sidney as a man 'who could not write'.[103] The Lord President's denigration of the new Secretary was not without justification, but Carmarthen's sharpness of tone is also suggestive. Although popularly believed to be 'the only man in credit', the Marquess had not been consulted over either of the two appointments of late 1690.[104] It is true that both Godolphin and Sidney were primarily courtiers and not party men, though the former's associations were mainly with the Tories as the latter's were with the Whigs. Nevertheless, both men were 'known to be his enemies', and Godolphin was also on good terms with other foes of Carmarthen, especially Shrewsbury and Marlborough. Nor was the Lord President a friend to Russell, the commander-designate of the fleet, and the Admiral was soon complaining to William of the difficulties he laboured under in having Carmarthen as 'my professed enemy'.[105]

The Lord President also had little, if any, part in the lesser official changes made after the King departed early in January 1691 for The Hague where he was to confer with his princely allies. Godolphin was chiefly responsible for the alterations to the Excise Commission which were made in the hope that new men would improve the efficiency of that service.[106] Nor did Carmarthen approve of the political logic behind the appointments made at the Admiralty and in the Post Office. In both cases, the new men were M.P.s, but they were not all of the same political persuasion. At the Admiralty, the resignation of Lord Carbery over the handling of Torrington's case and the removal of Russell to serve at sea led to the appearance of two new faces—the Whig Robert Austen (also one of the new Commissioners of Accounts) and the Churchman Lord Falkland (a former Treasurer of the Navy before the Revolution). Similarly, the removal of Major Wildman from the Postmastership—presumably for tampering with the mails once too often—was followed by the joint appointment of Sir Robert Cotton (of Cambridgeshire) and Thomas Frankland (who had served for a time in 1689 as a Commissioner of the Excise). Carmarthen could hardly have been sorry to see the last of Wildman, though John Hampden was furious at this new instance of the King's ingratitude to the Whigs. Yet the Lord President could not refrain from openly questioning the selection of the Major's successors: 'one is a Whig [Frankland] and the other a Tory, which', so Sidney reported Carmarthen to say, 'is the most destructive method your Majesty can take'.[107]

Perhaps it was these signs of Carmarthen's limited credit with the King that encouraged talk of further high-level changes after the King returned to London in early April 1691. Certainly, William's reception of the Earl of Sunderland at Court and the King's dinner at the Earl of Rochester's house in Surrey added fuel to the flames. The penitent Sunderland, after fleeing to Amsterdam during the Revolution, had returned to England in mid-1690 with William's permission, secured by the pleas of his Countess and the good offices of their old friend Sidney. Yet the Earl had been one of those excepted from the act of grace of May 1690, and his political infamy as James II's chief adviser, coupled with his own trepidation at exposing himself to parliamentary attack, made him an unlikely candidate for office. Even so, Shrewsbury bitterly remarked to Halifax in April 1691 that it seemed that 'the King had as much mind to have my Lord Sunderland in again, as anybody'.[108] Whether or not Shrewsbury's suspicions were justified, William did not accept the advice that the grateful Sunderland later claimed he had offered at this juncture. Sunderland's counsel was that the King should revert to relying upon Shrewsbury and that Earl's Whig friends.[109] But in the spring of 1691, William seems to have been rather more inclined to try to bring Rochester back into business. To be sure, the King began his reign believing that Rochester was a 'knave' who should be 'pinched' even more severely than the Earl of Mulgrave for having served on James II's ecclesiastical commission. But already by mid-1689, Burnet was urging Rochester's employment upon the Queen, by the autumn of 1690 the Earl's appointment to one major office or another was anticipated by many, and in early 1691 Rochester himself told Halifax 'that he could have a place at Court if he would'. But for the time being, all that he accepted from the King was the resumption of payments on the pension he had been granted by Charles II.[110]

Thus, the council the King named to assist the Queen during the summer of 1691 included seven of the nine who had served the previous year. Monmouth was replaced by Godolphin and Marlborough, who was going to accompany William back to the Low Countries, was to be succeeded by Prince George. From the outset of the reign, the King had found his stolid Danish brother-in-law an 'encumbrance', and he was not prepared to be troubled with George on this campaign as he had been in Ireland in 1690. William may have thought that a seat on the council for George was a gracious gesture in Anne's direction. But after William's return to the Continent, Mary undid whatever good might have been accomplished by forbidding the Prince to go to sea with the fleet as a volunteer.[111]

For all the speculation, then, the major changes in personnel that William did make in April 1691 were not in the state but in the church. For over a year, he had allowed the deprived bishops to remain in their episcopal residences and to draw the revenues of their sees. But the discovery among Preston's papers of a letter from Bishop Turner to James II in which that prelate conveyed the good wishes of his brethren to their former master brought renewed pressure to fill the vacant bishoprics. As Sir John Trevor warned Turner's colleague, Lloyd of Norwich, in an interview of late January 1691:[112]

the whole Court . . . were very angry with us upon the accompt of the late discovery. And that London [Bishop Compton], St Asaph [Bishop Lloyd], and Carmarthen and Nottingham vehemently pressed the filling up the vacant bishoprics . . . even before the King went to Holland but . . . he said he would consider of that matter after his return.

The refusal of the non-juring prelates to purge themselves of the sentiments with which Turner had credited them sealed their fate. John Tillotson reluctantly accepted the Archbishopric of Canterbury (much to Compton's chagrin), and most of the other vacancies on the episcopal bench were supplied by men drawn from the circle of Tillotson's and Nottingham's friends—among them, John Sharp as Archbishop of York, Simon Patrick, John Moore, Richard Kidder, and Edward Fowler.[113]

Reaction to the new appointments in the church was mixed. Burnet, in the first draft of his *History*, lauded William's and Mary's care in seeking out the 'worthiest and learnedest men' who 'could be found'.[114] But some Whigs denounced the new prelates as 'the most rigid' of churchmen, while they were objectionable to many Anglican clerics who disapproved of the support they had given in 1689 and still gave to projects of internal reform and of reconciliation with the moderate Dissenters. The Queen, indeed, was fearful that the 'high churchmen' within the establishment would join with the non-jurors outside it to 'form a party' against Tillotson and his colleagues which might be led by the disappointed Bishop Compton.[115] But for the time being at least, the non-jurors and their sympathisers among the clerical incumbents mainly vented their spleen against Tillotson personally. Even before his appointment had been announced, he was reported to be odious to many clergy; afterwards, so Robert Harley noted in June 1691, 'the rage is as high and gall overflowing' as 'if Mr Baxter [the great Nonconformist] had been made' archbishop, and among the calumnies put about was that he had never been baptised and that he was a Socinian.[116]

William, however, did not linger in England to witness the storm over the new prelates, for the campaigning season was already well under way by the time he returned to the Continent in mid-May 1691. The initial developments were not auspicious; in early April the French took Mons, and a month later they managed to get a supply convoy through to Ireland before the allied fleet put out to sea. When the Anglo-Dutch fleet did get out, French evasive tactics forestalled any chance of revenging the disgrace at Beachy Head. To make matters worse, early autumn storms destroyed several English men-of-war kept at sea in the forlorn hope of meeting the enemy. The campaign in Flanders was equally unproductive, though the fact that William's army did contain the French after Mons fell might be said to constitute a success of sorts. But the public grumbling over heavy taxes with which the year opened was hardly likely to be assuaged by accomplishments of that order, and Carmarthen, for one, had been nervously warning William for months that 'without such a success as will be valued here . . . our condition will be very deplorable'.[117]

Fortunately for William's regime, the army under Ginckel's command in Ireland had more positive achievements to its credit. News of the capture of Athlone and of the victory of Aughrim (12 July) even led the ministers to hope that a small-scale descent upon France might be possible before the summer was over. This would be 'a little thing', yet one which Nottingham, Godolphin, and Carmarthen agreed would 'please better than a very great one done in Flanders'.[118] But there were no troops as yet available for such a project, and the reconquest of Ireland was not completed until early October when generous terms were conceded the besieged Jacobite forces at Limerick.

By the time the tidings from Limerick reached London, the start of the 1691–1692 parliamentary session was only a few days away. Rumours of Carmarthen's resignation (for reasons of physical and political health) and of a dissolution had circulated throughout the summer, but success in Ireland relieved the King of any immediate need to change hands. Even so, the ministry was no more united in the autumn than it had been the previous spring. The relative position of its discordant elements—Tories, courtiers, and Whigs—was aptly illustrated in the manoeuvring during June 1691 over the choice of a new Secretary to the Treasury after William Jephson died unexpectedly. Those Whigs still in office were anxious to secure the lucrative place for the young Charles Montagu, but they realised that without Godolphin's backing as first lord of the Treasury Montagu's chances were slim. At the same time, Carmarthen and Nottingham were reported to be pushing a candidate of their own. However, it was Trevor's former associate Henry Guy who was named to the post which he had held until 1689, while Godolphin was gratified by the appointment of his brother Charles (despite his opposition to government measures in the Commons during previous sessions) to replace Guy at the Customs Board.[119]

As the King's servants jockeyed for places at Whitehall, trouble for the administration was brewing in nearby York Buildings where the new Commissioners of Accounts had recently taken up rented quarters. The nine commissioners selected by their fellow Commoners in December 1690 were mostly Whigs, by contrast to the more evenly balanced group named to the stillborn commission of May 1690. Six of the men voted onto the new body had supported the Sacheverell clause in January 1690, and one of their number, Sir Robert Rich, had headed the ballot. The most experienced and knowledgeable commissioner was that zealous Churchman, Sir Thomas Clarges, and his views might have been expected to set him at odds with colleagues like Rich, Sir Samuel Barnardiston, Paul Foley, and Foley's nephew by marriage Robert Harley, for they all came from families distinguished by their Nonconformist sympathies.[120] Besides the popular Rich and the veteran Clarges, a third formidable member of the Commission was Paul Foley, and not merely by reason of his well-connected family in Herefordshire, Worcestershire, and Staffordshire. Known as 'Heavy Paul' for his grave manner and sober disposition, Foley combined a training in the law with financial connections inherited from his father, the greatest ironmaster of his day. Together, Foley and Clarges were to make a most effective duo once the commissioners agreed to lay aside their previous differences in order to concentrate on exerting 'to the utmost' the 'very large powers' vested in them by parliament.[121]

In turn, the Commission of Accounts' busy inquiries into official irregularities and their eager pursuit of Jephson's 'secret service' accounts help to explain the reports made to William by Carmarthen in May and by Sir Robert Howard in July of 'schemes to put all things in disorder when a parliament shall meet' and 'of a design' that 'the war both by sea and land, should be managed by a committee of parliament'.[122] Admittedly, both the King's correspondents had their own reasons for uttering such dire warnings, but to judge by subsequent developments the Commissioners of Accounts were eager to make the most of their mandate.[123] And as a result, much of the interest of the 1691–92 parliamentary session derives from their campaign to remedy the deficiencies and abuses they claimed to have detected in the management of the war effort.

William's own response to the uncertain prospects abroad and at home was to be unusually forthright in his requests when he came to Westminster to open

the session on 22 October 1691. He began by alluding to the 'good success' in
Ireland and he asked for funds to pay the arrears of the army there, while
promising 'to keep that kingdom, as far as it is possible, from being burdensome
to England for the future'. He went on to call for the setting out of a fleet for
1692 as strong as that of 1691 and to state that at least 65,000 men would be
needed 'not only to defend ourselves from any insult, but also to annoy the
common enemy, where it may be most sensible to them'.[124]

The Commons' initial response to William's requests was favourable. Robert
Harley noted that 'the gentlemen generally come up with no other apprehension
but to give all that is asked', and on 27 October a motion offered by Sir Richard
Temple (one of the Customs Commissioners) to assist the King 'to the utmost'
in the war against France was approved *nemine contradicente*. But the House
was still 'very thin', and Harley anticipated that a better gauge of sentiment
would come on the 30th.[125] This was the day appointed to take the King's
speech under consideration and a moment for which Harley and his fellow
Commissioners of Accounts had long been preparing. Thus, though some 'expected that money should be immediately moved for' by the ministerial spokesmen on the 30th, Paul Foley took the lead and opened to his audience 'the state
of the nation, especially in reference to the navy and army'. False musters in the
forces and incompetent officers in the fleet headed Foley's and his colleagues' list
of grievances, and Harley thought their speeches 'a little opened the eyes of
some gentlemen that come out of the country'.[126] The upshot was that the
Commons decided to put off supply until 6 November and to go first upon the
state of the nation on the 3rd.

However, it was not only Foley and 'honest gentlemen' who favoured the
discussion of grievances before supply. There were also those whom Harley
referred to as the 'men of intrigue'—Whig partisans bent on discrediting the
Tory ministers by whatever means that came to hand.[127] This difference in aim
among the critics of the administration resulted in disappointments for Foley
and his friends on 3 November. Safeguards against false musters were agreed on,
and they were to be incorporated in this session's mutiny bill. But when Foley,
seconded by Clarges and Musgrave, went on to offer a measure for 'informing
his Majesty in sea officers', he was charged with seeking to encroach upon the
King's prerogative. No text of the scheme he offered survives; apparently, it
involved the creation of a system for examining and certifying naval officers.[128]
However, it was attacked, notably by Sir John Guise, as being but one step away
from dictation to the King on executive appointments, and in the end the plan
proved too novel for the Commons. Guise, who had supported the nomination
by the lower House of commissioners to direct the Irish provisioning when he
had temporarily been out of place in December 1689, was not only concerned
with the maintenance of the royal prerogative; he and his Whig friends in office
also sought to exploit the dissatisfaction over the fleet's inactivity that had been
voiced by Clarges and others by pinning the blame for all disappointments upon
Carmarthen and Nottingham.[129] Thus, after Lord Brandon and Jack Howe loudly
denounced the 'cabinet council' of the past summer, Comptroller Wharton
moved at the end of the long sitting that the Commons should resume their
consideration of the state of the nation on the 7th to inquire into 'who have been
the occasion' of the 'miscarriages'.[130] As Harley gloomily observed to his father
that evening, 'the men of intrigue imposed upon others and at present laid that

[the plan for certifying naval officers] aside to hunt as they preferred nobler game'.[131]

Little came of the projected Whig attack upon the Tory ministers, for William, fearful of disruption of the session, stepped in to patch up a truce between those the Brandenburg resident labelled 'les Carmarthens et les Russels'.[132] It was his intervention that accounted for the unaccustomed silence in committee of the whole on 7 November when the subject of Russell's conduct of the fleet was to be taken up. After the members 'had sat still for half-an-hour and nothing said', as Narcissus Luttrell (a newly elected member for Saltash) noted in the diary of debates he assiduously kept during this and the following session. Charles Montagu proposed that the Speaker resume the Chair.[133] However, no sooner had his motion been approved 147 to 115 (with Guise telling for the majority) than Clarges arrived in St Stephen's Chapel, having been warned belatedly of what was afoot. Sir Thomas's lateness did not prevent him from airing anew his criticisms of Russell's conduct, and in support he now adduced fresh evidence derived from a log-book given him by Admiral Henry Killigrew. Yet for all intents and purposes, the inquiry into naval miscarriages had been effectively stifled.[134]

Nevertheless, the case of nerves that had been plaguing the Lord President for months persisted after the truce with Russell and his friends. Fearful of attack from other quarters, Carmarthen resorted to his usual tactic of trying to keep his enemies off balance. One of the devices he employed during succeeding weeks was to encourage the Commons to follow up Preston's confessions implicating Halifax and Seymour and to inquire into William Fuller's promised disclosures. Fuller, once a page of Mary of Modena at St Germain, seemed prepared to implicate many prominent Englishmen in Jacobite intrigues, among them Godolphin.[135] Another of Carmarthen's evasive moves was to try to dissociate himself from the generous, and hence unpopular terms of the Articles conceded to the Irish rebels at Limerick, and this he did in a speech to the Lords in which he also claimed 'ignorance of what is done at the cabinet council'.[136] The Lord President may even have connived at 'a foolish plot set up by the Duke of Bolton's contrivance' whose aim was to 'blacken Lord Nottingham'.[137] Certainly, Carmarthen's son Danby had a hand in this affair, and the Lord President's involvement was suspected since even before the session there had been talk of 'dissension' between the two ministers. Moreover, after the session got under way Carmarthen was reported to be unhappy at Nottingham's renewed efforts to win round those Churchmen who were in opposition to the ministry, while the Secretary was said to be displeased with the Lord President's dealings with Russell and the Whigs.[138] But whatever the differences between the two, the danger of an attack upon either one receded after the Commons allowed their inquiry into naval miscarriages to lapse. In retrospect, Robert Harley's younger brother Edward accurately told the pulse of the lower House when he informed his father on 10 November that 'there seems no disposition' now 'to meddle with the ministers of state' as 'Whigs and Tories unite against the Court in endeavouring to be frugal by good management'.[139]

A concern with 'good management' was very evident in the Commons' proceedings on supply during November 1691. Clarges and Foley took the lead, usually followed closely by Musgrave and Harley, in subjecting the administration's requests to intensive scrutiny. Despite Court objections to this novel procedure, the naval estimates were entrusted on the 9th to a select committee. On the 14th, Harley reported the committee's recommendations which called for £279,000 to be cut from the original request for £1,855,000. And his report was then adopted virtually *in toto*, with the only division going against the Court by 174 to 147.[140]

Forewarned by the setback over the fleet, the Court rallied its forces in support of the army estimates which in past years had encountered more opposition than those for the navy. The first major confrontation came in committee of the whole on 19 November after Paymaster Ranelagh submitted a detailed list of the intended disposition of the 65,000 men which William had requested: 13,000 were to remain in England and Scotland, another 13,000 in Ireland, and almost all the rest were to serve overseas. Foley, Clarges, Musgrave, and Harley, with support from other backbenchers, questioned the need for so many men and urged the Commons to proceed upon the list 'head by head'. But Lowther, Hampden, Guise, and Temple, with support from other placemen, opposed any attempt either to reduce the total or to bind the King by vote to the precise disposition of men which Ranelagh had announced. Finally, the list was approved in general without a division after Seymour unexpectedly weighed in upon the Court's side and some of Sir Edward's West Country friends repeatedly interrupted opposition speeches with noisy calls for the question.[141]

However, the next sitting in committee of the whole on supply on 25 November did not go so well for the Court once it emerged that officers had not been included among the 65,000 total approved on the 19th. In reaction to this unwelcome disclosure from Ranelagh, the committee approved an opposition resolution that the 13,000 men intended for Ireland should be taken to include officers.[142] Three days later, the Commons resumed this debate. But now the placemen had an answer. Goodricke declared:[143]

that the King himself has taken notice of your *Votes*. He pulled them out of his pocket in Council. And he has empowered us to say that he was resolved to make a descent in France, and withal that if you did strike off the number as proposed (and is done in Ireland by including the officers) you would spoil all.

Although Clarges and others protested that 'it is not usual to hear the King's name used herein so as to influence our debates', this new instance of royal outspokenness, however unparliamentary, worked. Seymour again came to the Court's aid, and at last the opposition was overborne 176 to 151.

The overall result of the prolonged review of the estimates was that of the £2,256,000 originally requested for the army, the Commons eventually authorised £2,101,000 (with £165,000 of this to be borne upon the Irish revenue). For all their pains, then, Foley and his fellow commissioners had less success in paring the army askings than in cutting the naval ones. Still, a reduction in the combined estimates of the order of 10 per cent was a significant saving, and the Court had had a difficult time to limit the cuts to £434,000.[144]

The Commissioners of Accounts had also prepared a detailed report of the results of their months of investigation into finances and administrative practice. This report, along with thirty-one critical 'observations' (signed by all nine commissioners), was laid before the Commons on 1 December and debated at length on the 3rd and the 12th.[145] The Commission's work did not pass unchallenged. The report indicated government receipts (excluding loans) of £10,132,881 between November 1688 and Michaelmas 1691. This total was already markedly below the figure of £12,000,000 that Foley and others had bandied about in the earlier debates upon supply. Even so, as Lowther observed with some warmth, the Commission's accounts contained other 'mistakes' and still exaggerated net government income by some £1,439,550.[146]

Lowther's critique of the Commissioners of Accounts' figures was followed by the rebuttal of some of their observations, especially the ninth in which it had been suggested that substantial secret service payments might have been made to many M.P.s by the late William Jephson. Much of the sting was taken out of this question when Comptroller Wharton and Sir Robert Rich (recently made an Admiralty lord in succession to the late Sir Thomas Lee) affirmed that their friend Jephson had told them before his death that 'there were not above four persons in this house [who] had received those moneys for secret service and that what they had was . . . to dispose of to some persons employed to make discoveries for their Majesties' service'.[147] In the end, the Commons did not even trouble to discuss all the observations so that, as one placeman cynically observed, 'like a hot eager lover after a long struggling, they lay panting out of breath and did little or nothing'.[148]

Although the Commons did not give much heed to the 'observations' of the Commissioners of Accounts, the Court did not oppose, at least openly, the continuation of the Commission for another year. Moreover, when that body's principal supporters moved a clause on 9 January 1692 to reappoint seven of the incumbents and to omit the two placemen, Rich and Austen, the amendment was approved 'without one advocate' for the two.[149] It was the Lords, again intent upon adding commissioners of their own to act with those named by the Commons, who threatened the renewal measure. The Lords' amendment, Harley believed, was 'covertly designed to spoil the bill'; in his view, many in office were eager 'to get a bridle out of their mouths'.[150] And this year, the peers, led in this instance by Rochester, were ready to insist on their addition. The Commons were equally adamant in defence of their fiscal prerogatives; after all, it was they, not the Lords, who granted the supplies. This stalemate meant that the Commission's only chance for survival was by way of a 'tack' of a renewal clause by the Commons to one of their supply measures yet to be sent up to the Lords.[151]

By mid-February 1692, two major tax bills had already reached the King—a continuation of the double excise on beer and spirits calculated to yield £400,000 net and a land tax by assessment reckoned to be worth £1,570,000. In addition, the Commons had settled on a compromise figure of £200,000 as the portion of the ordinary revenue for the coming year to be applied to the war.[152] So there was still about £1,350,000 to be found, and this proved no easy task especially because the Treasury Board was not prepared to give a clear lead. During January, a variety of proposals were canvassed, among them two different projects for creating a long-term funded debt. One, espoused by Foley and backed by Treasury Commissioner Hampden, looked back to the kind of perpetual interest arrangements established *ad hoc* after the Stop of the Exchequer of 1672; the other, sponsored by Sir Walter Yonge (another of Somers's and Locke's coterie), backed by Treasury Commissioner Lowther, and apparently devised by the Scots projector William Paterson, looked forward to the type of national bank that would be adopted two years later. In the end, however, the lower House settled upon a much more traditional device—a poll tax which was proposed by Seymour on 18 January.[153] It was to the poll bill, then, that the backers of the Commission of Accounts sought to 'tack' a renewal clause.

The chances of success for the amendment in the Commons were uncertain. Clarges, kept away by illness, assured Harley that the addition of such a clause to the poll bill could be justified by the precedents and by William Hakewill's treatise on legislative procedure. But perhaps just as persuasive as these authorities was a widespread resentment among members at the rough treatment the Lords had already meted out during the 1691–92 session to other Commons' bills.[154] One clash had come over the Irish oath bill.[155] Another was in the making over the mutiny bill, which incorporated the new safeguards against false musters.[156] But the most prolonged disagreement had been provoked by the Lords' amendments to the bill to reform the procedure in treason trials. This bill, like its predecessor in the 1690–91 session, was aimed at correcting those abuses in treason trials that had been denounced in the preliminary version of the Declaration of Rights. In the Commons, its supporters, headed by the barrister Sir William Whitlock, had had to overcome opposition from royal servants such as Lowther and Treby, who argued that the adoption of such reforms while the realm was still at war would imperil national security.[157] But it was not the reforms themselves that occasioned the quarrel with the Lords; it was the peers' desire to secure the elimination of the crown's discretionary power in the selection of the jury in the Lord Steward's court, the tribunal in which peers were tried when parliament was not in session. The Lords' own trials bill of 1689 had run up against Commons' objections to this innovation, and most members of the lower House regarded it as too great a concession to be allowed the peers. As Charles Montagu put it in the critical debate of 31 December 1691; the Lords 'have power over your estates by their pretended judicial power, over your tongues by their *Scandalum Magnatum*, and now' this change will 'instead of a monarchy set up an aristocracy'.[158] It is true that some Commoners, among them the bill's heartiest proponents, were willing to accept the peers' addition, but they were outvoted 186 to 120, and the result was that the measure died in a stalemate between the two Houses.

These differences with the Lords must have been prominent in men's minds when John Granville moved on 15 February 1692 to tack the clause renewing the Commission of Accounts to the poll bill. First to speak against the amendment was Seymour, and his condemnation of the tack as unparliamentary and undesirable was seconded by a dozen placemen, among them Hampden and Somers. But upon the question, 'the Whig and Tory country party joined together' and triumphed 145 to 104.[159] Buoyed by this victory, some of the majority were ready to use the amended poll bill as a lever to exert even more pressure upon the peers and, behind them, upon the Court. After the bill was given a third reading on the 18th, a motion was offered to let it 'lie on the Table' until the 22nd; in the meantime, the Commons should send 'to the Lords to put them in mind' of the House's measure to dispose of the Irish forfeitures, which was still awaiting action by the peers. Clarges and several others spoke in support of the motion but they were not prepared to divide the Commons on this point, at least partly because it was felt that Court hostility had already left 'no prospect' of the Irish bill's 'passing this sessions'.[160]

'Many good bills were left unfinished', then, when William came to Westminster on 24 February 1692 to end the session.[161] The tack of the accounts bill did succeed, since the Court did not wish to lose the poll bill. Caught in the middle, the Lords swallowed the tack and salved their injured dignity by entering a protestation in their Journal 'that they will not hereafter admit, upon any occasion whatsoever, of a proceeding so contrary to the rules and methods of parliament'.[162] But though the poll bill reached the statute book, along with fifty-six other measures, there were numerous entries on the other side of the ledger. Besides the treason trials bill, the Commons' mutiny bill was also lost in a disagreement over the Lords' amendments, and its loss did pose some problems in the maintenance of military discipline during 1692.[163] Then, too, the Lords' failure to take action on the Commons' forfeitures bill left William free, so he thought, to dispose of the Irish estates as he saw fit.

Besides these casualties, another dozen bills which had passed one but not the other House failed of enactment, despite a series of formal reminders which passed between the Lords and the Commons during the final days of the session. Of these, perhaps the most controversial were the Commons' measures to reduce the maximum rate of interest in private transactions from 6 to 5 per cent and to reorganise the lucrative trade to the East Indies.[164] Debates on the East India bill suggest that on economic and commercial questions the lines of division in the lower House tended to cut across not only Whig–Tory groupings but also Court–Country ones. Among the supporters of the old Company were Sir Richard Temple, Sir Thomas Clarges, Sir Thomas Littleton, and John Howe; among the advocates of a new company were Sir Edward Seymour, Sir Christopher Musgrave, Sir Robert Howard, and Richard Hampden.[165] Opposition to the old Company, stimulated by the lobbying activities of a new syndicate of interlopers, was mounting, and on 22 January the Commons voted 171 to 116 to give a second reading to a bill to establish 'an' East India Company.[166] Against this, the old Company's friends in the lower House, including the corporation's Governor, Sir Joseph Herne, fought a successful delaying action. On 6 February, the Commons, who had yet to read their own bill a third time, decided not to proceed further with it since it was evident it would face further and probably decisive delays in the Lords. Instead, they agreed to address the King to dissolve the old Company and to establish a new one 'in such manner as his Majesty, in his Royal Wisdom, shall think fit'.[167] This news produced a rise in the 'actions' of the old Company on the stock exchange, since it was assumed that the corporation 'would find better quarter at Whitehall than Westminster'.[168] William did promise 'a positive answer' to the Commons' address and the Company's affairs were reviewed by the King and his advisers at this time, but for the moment no answer was returned to the Commons—an omission remarked upon by some M.P.s.[169]

Another surprise to many members of the Commons, so the Brandenburg resident noted, was the King's veto on 24 February of the bill 'for ascertaining the commissions and salaries of the judges'.[170] William used the first veto of the reign against an attempt to mandate his voluntary practice of appointing judges during 'good behaviour', instead of 'at pleasure' as had been their tenure for most of the seventeenth century. Judicial security of tenure had been called for in the preliminary version of the Declaration of Rights. Yet Burnet's later statement that the judges themselves advised the King to use his veto is confirmed by the Brandenburg resident's contemporary report, though just why that advice was tendered was a point which the former could no longer recall when he prepared the final version of his *History* and which the latter did not trouble to explain.[171] It is possible that the chief reason for the veto was that the bill 'would render judges independent upon the crown' and that William, though willing for the moment to issue judicial patents during good behaviour, did not want to bind himself or his successors in this matter.[172] But it is more likely the immediate objection to this measure was that the judges' salaries would thereby become a fixed charge upon the hereditary excise and that its sponsor, Sir Walter Yonge, had neglected to secure prior royal leave for the inclusion of this pro-vision.[173] Certainly William had displayed two years before an acute sensitivity to parliamentary legislation affecting the hereditary revenues. But whatever the reason, when Bishop Burnet reported upon the results of his summer visitation of the diocese of Salisbury to Nottingham in September 1692, he warned that there was 'a general resentment of the denial of the judges' bill'.[174]

All in all, there can be little doubt that the 1691–92 session had been more difficult for the Court than that of 1690–91. And not surprisingly, reports of extensive ministerial changes, with Rochester and the suddenly good-natured Seymour figuring as the leading candidates for high office, had already begun to spread by the beginning of 1692.[175] Then, Marlborough's dismissal from all his posts on 21 January 1692 opened up the prospect of even more far-reaching alterations. The cause of Marlborough's sudden fall was the subject of wide-spread comment at the time, and Burnet's original account probably comes as close to the truth as is now possible. Noting the Earl's discontent at his failure to be given the 'great rewards' he expected for his services, especially the capture of Cork and Kinsale in the autumn of 1690, Burnet went on to relate:[176]

The King said to myself upon it that he had very good reason to believe that he had made his peace with King James and was engaged in a correspondence with France; it is certain he was doing all he could to set on a faction in the army and nation against the Dutch and to lessen the King; [and that he] as well as his wife, who was so absolute a favourite with the Princess that she seemed to be the mistress of her whole heart and thoughts, were alienating her both from the King and Queen.

The fall-out from Marlborough's ouster was certainly substantial. The Princess stood by the Churchills and refused to drop Lady Marlborough from the Cockpit entourage despite pressure from the Queen. Thus, the breach between the royal sisters—first publicised in the disputes over Anne's financial settlement in 1689 and then aggravated by the Queen's veto in 1691 of Prince George's plans to go to sea—widened. And despite attempts to mediate by Tillotson, Compton, and the Earl of Rochester, Anne left the Cockpit in February and took up residence out of court at Syon House, with Lady Marlborough still in attendance.[177]

It was under this cloud that the ministerial reshuffle finally took place. The quarrel between Mary and Anne may have made William all the more eager to conciliate the leading Tories in opposition, since they would be the Princess's most likely advocates should the quarrel be taken up in parliament, but the King's inclination in the direction of 'the interest of the Church of England' had been anticipated before Marlborough's ouster.[178] The chief plums went to the friends of Secretary Nottingham, whose wife was also now high in the Queen's favour. With Pelham and Lowther both quitting the Treasury for personal reasons, first Musgrave and then Seymour were offered seats on that Board. While Musgrave might have been tempted by such an offer in 1689 or early 1690, he now refused, though his son did accept the deputy-governorship of Carlisle Castle a few months later. But Seymour, who had hung back from Clarges's and Musgrave's new alignment with Foley and Harley, was only too eager. Besides a seat on the Treasury Commission, Sir Edward was named to the cabinet council and favourably recommended to Mary by William.[179] The other new member of the cabinet council was Rochester.[180] In addition, Pembroke—who offended nobody and was at least minimally competent—was advanced from being first lord of the Admiralty to the Privy Seal, an office which had been in commission since Halifax's resignation. Moreover, Carmarthen was gratified by two instances of the King's favour. Royal patience with Jack Howe had finally run out and he was replaced as the Queen's Vice-Chamberlain by the Lord President's nephew, Peregrine Bertie junior.[181] At the same time, Carmarthen's newest son-in-law was raised to the peerage as Baron Leominster.

Although William declined to accept Sunderland's renewed counsel in early 1692 to rely mainly upon the Whigs, the King did not feel he could dispense with their services altogether.[182] At the beginning of the 1691–92 session, he had named Sir Robert Rich to the Admiralty in succession to his fellow Whig Lee. Then, in early 1692, the King intervened in Admiral Russell's feud with his Tory colleague Killigrew in order to retain Russell's services at sea, and Killigrew was induced to give up his commission in return for a pension.[183] Furthermore, the second vacancy at the Treasury Board was filled by Charles Montagu, Pembroke was succeeded at the Admiralty by Lord Cornwallis (Monmouth's brother-in-law and a fervent Whig), and the Whigs also retained their grip upon royal legal posts in the promotions that followed chief justice Pollexfen's demise. Treby succeeded Pollexfen, Somers replaced Treby as Attorney-General, and Thomas Trevor was named Solicitor-General. Then, too, the second Secretaryship—which was now vacated by Sidney's appointment as Lord Lieutenant of Ireland—did not go to Sir William Trumbull, though he had been touted widely for it. Instead, William deliberately left the post vacant after he persuaded Secretary-at-War William Blathwayt to serve informally in the capacity of a Secretary of State in Flanders.[184]

Behind William's decision to do without a second Secretary of State, at least for the time being, lay some careful political calculations which can be reconstructed from the entries in Trumbull's diary.[185] The first relevant entry, dated 26 February 1692, is the record of an interview Sir William had that day with the Earl of Portland. Portland explained he had sent for Trumbull because

> upon the King's going away, there would be many changes of officers . . . [and he] would be glad to know my inclinations; and (among other things) to know of what party I was . . . Whig or Tory, as commonly called. For my affection to [the] government he knew that well. But as to the other, would desire me to inform him, the Whigs being many in number, rather more than the others, and would expect (upon a removal) to have one they could confide in, and would take it ill if had not such a one, etc.

Trumbull, after disclaimers as to his personal merits, replied that 'as to any party, I had never been of any, that I was of the Church of England . . . and wished well to the government and the Protestant Religion and to all that were wellwishers to it'. However, when Portland repeatedly pressed to know whether 'the Whigs would trust' him and were his 'friends', Trumbull answered: 'I believed not, and thought they had no reason. But my religion was that of the two Archbishops and the Bishop of Worcester who knew me well and, if his Lordship pleased, he might inform himself from them, etc.'

On this note, Trumbull's interview with Portland came to an end. A week later, Trumbull had a frank conversation with Nottingham, and he also entered this in his diary. He had gone to call upon the Secretary at his office in Whitehall, and after he put in a word for one of his protégés in the diplomatic service, Nottingham said

that he hoped I should be a [? part] to do it myself ere long, and was sorry not done before. But that he was to ask my pardon, for he kept me out, being (as was said) so great a Tory, that I (who was reputed of the same [stamp]), was not to come in with him.
I replied it was very true, for I had put an end to my own employment by a confession of my faith my Lord Portland desired me to make to him.

After Trumbull related his interview with Portland, Nottingham informed Sir William that

he had spoken with the King and Lord Portland also about me. That he told the King he judged it fit for him to appoint another Secretary before he went: (1) that the world might not say he was a covetous man to engross all the business; (2) that if he fell sick, nobody to assist him or go on with the thread; (3) to exclude all suspicion of Lord Sunderland, who [was] false to kings, and man, and G[od]. The King said to this that he might be satisfied Lord Sunderland was not thought on, but he would not name anybody yet.

Moreover, when Nottingham raised the question of Trumbull's appointment to Portland, the Secretary was told that 'the Whigs must not be made desperate' lest they 'resort to etc.'—presumably, St Germain.

Despite Nottingham's failure to secure Trumbull's appointment before William's departure for Flanders in March 1692, there can be no doubt that the 1691–92 political season closed with the Churchmen in greater favour and strength at Court than ever before in the reign. Furthermore, Nottingham, at least, was confident that the King's leanings towards the Churchmen 'as the only sure support of the monarchy' (a claim the Secretary made to Portland) would carry him still further down the road he had taken in dissolving the Convention parliament. As Nottingham put it to Trumbull in ending their conversation of 5 March: 'If the King had success this summer and returned without needing the Whigs or thinking he did so, he believed I would be the man.'

However, Nottingham was to prove no prophet in this respect. The King's return in the autumn of 1692 found him in great need of the Whigs, and when Trumbull finally took office in 1694 it was under Sunderland's auspices, not Nottingham's. And as the spring of 1692 marks both the high point of the Churchmen's influence in the King's councils for the rest of the war and a shift in focus of England's war effort from Ireland to the Continent, it may be useful to take stock of the governmental arrangements and political alignments that had taken shape in the course of the three years since the Revolution.

Notes to Chapter III

1 Foxcroft, *Halifax*, II, 244.
2 Foxcroft, *Halifax*, II, 246; *Correspondentie*, I, i, 140; *CTB*, IX, 364; Burnet, *Supplement*, pp. 339, 341.
3 Ralph, *History*, II, 1000. And see BL Lansdowne MS. 1013, f. 17, W. Kennet to Rev. Blackwell, 8 February; E. Cardwell, *Documentary Annals of the Reformed Church of England* (Oxford, 1844), II, 376.
4 DWL Morrice MS. R, 119. And see *CSPD*, 1689–1690, pp. 467, 484; BL Add. MS. 42586, ff. 77–85; Ralph, *History*, II, 1000.

5 Shropshire RO, Attingham MS. 112/3, Carmarthen to [Earl of Abingdon], 15 February. See also Foxcroft, *Halifax*, II, 247; Burnet, *History*, IV, 72.

6 Shropshire RO, Attingham MS. 112/3; Newberry Lib., Case MS. E5, c5434, f. 27, to Abingdon, 16 February.

7 In general, see H. Horwitz, 'The General Election of 1690', *Journal of British Studies* XI (November 1971), 77–91. Only materials not used in that essay are cited in the succeeding four paragraphs.

8 See Appendix A, and compare D. Hirst, *The Representative of the People?* (Cambridge, 1975), app. iv.

9 'Collectanea Trelawniana', p. 268 (I am indebted to Dr G. V. Bennett for this reference). See also A. T. Hart, *William Lloyd 1627–1717* (1952), p. 270.

10 Of the 161 new members, fifty-one had previous parliamentary experience.

11 William Salt Lib., Plas Newyd MSS., box xvib, D. to Lord Paget, 14 March; Verney MSS., reel 44, J. to Sir R. Verney, 26 February.

12 KU, F. Bonnet, 25 February/7 March and 28 February/10 March; Berkshire RO, Trumbull Add. MS. 102, newsletter, 28 February.

13 BL Stowe MS. 746, f. 125, ? to T. Hulton, 6 March. And see Burnet, *History*, IV, 72.

14 Peter Lord King, *The Life and Letters of John Locke* (1884), p. 234.

15 *A List of the Commissioners of the Lieutenancy of the City of London, as constituted in the Year 1690* [?1692, Wing L2416a]. The 1689 commission, erroneously listed as 1690, is in CSPD, 1689–1690, pp. 501–2.

16 Foxcroft, *Halifax*, II, 247, and 249. Lowther kept his place as Vice-Chamberlain.

17 DWL Morrice MS. R, 124, 125, 127; Luttrell, *Brief Relation*, II, 25.

18 Foxcroft, *Halifax*, II, 242, 243, 249; Chatsworth MSS., Devonshire House notebook, sub 'Nottingham Lord'; BL Add. MS. 29573, f. 407, C. to Viscount Hatton, 18. February.

19 Foxcroft, *Halifax*, II, 228.

20 HMC Portland, III, 446. See also *Correspondencia entre dos embajadores*, ed. G. Maura Gamzao (Madrid, 1951–2), II, 132. And see Appendix D.

21 DWL Morrice MS. R, 125. And see CJ, X, 347; KU, F. Bonnet, 21/31 March.

22 CJ, X, 349.

23 Grey, *Debates*, X, 9, 31–4; Burnet, *History*, IV, 77. I am indebted to Professor C. Roberts for allowing me to read his unpublished essay on the financial settlement of 1690.

24 HMC Portland, III, 446; DWL Morrice MS. R, 130; KU, F. Bonnet, 4/14 April; *Correspondencia entre dos embajadores*, II, 167.

25 DWL Morrice MS. R, 125, 127; CJ, X, 349–50, 355. See also *An Answer to a Letter sent to the Mayor of Salisbury* (1690, Guildhall Lib. 111). On 2 May, the Whig 'blacklist' was formally censured.

26 Churchill College, Erle MSS. 2/24, H. Flory to T. Erle, 21 December 1688.

27 BL Loan 29/184, f. 321, Philip Foley to R. Harley, 15 April. See also Exeter City Lib., Pine Coffin letterbook 'A', R. Lapthorne to R. Coffin, 12 April.

28 LJ, XIV, 438–9; DWL Morrice MS. R, 128; Verney MSS., reel 44, A. Nicholas to Sir J. Verney, 25 March.

29 Bodl. Ballard MS. 48, f. 78. See also *An Impartial Inquiry into the Causes of the present Fears and Dangers* (1692), reprinted in ST, II, 228.

30 Bodl. Ballard MS. 48, f. 78. And see HLM, 1690–1691, pp. 2–3.

31 LJ, XIV, 451. And see Hatton Corr., II, 146–7.

32 HLM, 1690–1691, pp. 3–7; PH, V, 577.

33 Horwitz, *Revolution Politicks*, p. 114.

34 Hatton Corr., II, 147.

35 Burnet, *Supplement*, p. 340, and *History*, IV, 75.

36 Browning, *Danby*, I, 481 n. 2. And see Grey, *Debates*, X, 45–52.

37 Exeter City RO, Pine Coffin letterbook 'A', R. Lapthorne to R. Coffin, 29 March; Grey, *Debates*, X, 13–15. See also BL Loan 29/189, f. 83, [E. to Sir E. Harley], 1 April [1690].

38 DWL Morrice MS. R, 132; Grey, *Debates*, X, 41–5.

39 CJ, X, 388, 381. And see BL Add. MS. 17677KK, f. 91, van Citters, 22 April/2 May; KU, F. Bonnet, 22 April/2 May.

40 Bodl. Ballard MS. 22, f. 51, J. N[ewton] to A. Charlett, 26 April.

41 DWL Morrice MS. R, 138. And see Grey, *Debates*, X, 86, 73–5.

42 Grey, *Debates*, X, 75–87; Bodl. Rawlinson MS. A79, ff. 70–9; BL Add. MS. 29594, f. 205,

Nottingham to Viscount Hatton, 26 April; All Souls College MS. 153, vol. I (unfoliated), text of bill.

43 DWL Morrice MS. R, 138; HMC *Portland*, III, 447; KU, F. Bonnet, 29 April/9 May; Grey, *Debates*, X, 84.

44 HLM, 1690–1691, pp. 47–8; DWL Morrice MS. R, 139–40.

45 BL Egerton MS. 3345, bundle 3, Carmarthen's notes of the debate; DWL Morrice MS. R, 140; KU, F. Bonnet, 2/12 May.

46 *Memoirs of Mary, Queen of England (1689–1693)*, ed. R. Doebner (Leipzig, 1886), p. 30; Horwitz, *Revolution Politicks*, pp. 115–16; KU, F. Bonnet, 9/19 May.

47 Chatsworth MSS., Devonshire House notebook, *sub* 'Shrewsbury Lord'. And see *Memoirs of Mary*, pp. 28–9; DWL Morrice MS. R, 139; D. H. Somerville, *The King of Hearts* (1962), pp. 66–7; Burnet, *History*, IV, 80–1; Foxcroft, *Halifax*, II, 250; KAO, Chevening MS. 78, J. Vernon to A. Stanhope, 29 April.

48 KU, F. Bonnet, 29 April/9 May; Huygens, *Journaal*, I, 268; NLW, Kemys Tynte correspondence (unsorted), to Sir C. Kemys, 2 May.

49 DWL Morrice MS. R, 141.

50 HLM, 1689–1690, pp. 38–44, 45–69. William was again present for lengthy debates over the oath on 8 and 12 May.

51 Ralph, *History*, II, 200; HLM, 1690–1691, pp. 76–81. Pamphlets relating to this controversial bill include Wing C1756, D1686, L1632, S3529a.

52 Grey, *Debates*, X, 136–45; *Hatton Corr.*, II, 149; DWL Morrice MS. R, 146; KU, F. Bonnet, 16/26 and 20/30 May; KAO, Chevening MS. 78, J. Vernon to A. Stanhope, 27 May.

53 Grey, *Debates*, X, 98–108, 114–33; BL Add. MS. 42592, f. 117, W. Brockman's notes; HLM, 1690–91, pp. 38–40.

54 LJ, XIV, 506–7. Morrice believed the adjournment was decided upon only the night before; DWL Morrice MS. R, 150.

55 Foxcroft, *Halifax*, II, 252; HLM, 1690–1691, pp. 81–7; CTB, IX, 737; Bodl. MS. Eng. hist. b23, W. Lowndes's copy of Treasury accounts, 1690–91.

56 East India Office Lib., old Co. Court Book B/39, ff. 263, 295, 301–2; CJ, X. 363. In general, see D. W. Jones, 'London Overseas-Merchant Groups at the end of the Seventeenth Century and the Moves against the East India Company' (unpublished D.Phil. thesis, University of Oxford, 1970), chapter 7.

57 East India Office Lib., old Co. Dispatch Book E/3/92, p. 78, to Bombay, 31 January 1689[–90]; Luttrell, *Brief Relation*, II, 7–8. And see Huygens, *Journaal*, I, 265.

58 Lancashire RO, Kenyon MS. DDKE 6/38; Trinity College MSS., King correspondence, No. 110, G. Tollett to W. King, 24 January 1691.

59 CSPD, 1690–1691, p. 29. And see Foxcroft, *Halifax*, II, 251; CTB, IX, 396; HMC *Finch*, II, 439, and III, 379, 380; CJ, X, 422. Cf. J. A. Downie, 'The Commission of Public Accounts and the Formation of the Country Party', EHR LXXXXI (1976), esp. 36.

60 Chatsworth MSS., Devonshire House notebook, *sub* 'Shrewsbury Lord'. See also *Memoirs of Mary*, p. 28.

61 For William's initial list, see *Memoirs of Mary*, pp. 24, 28; Shropshire RO, Attingham MS. 112/3.

62 KU, F. Bonnet, 6/16 May.

63 Bodl. Ballard MS. 45, No. 31a, [R. Sare] to A. Charlett, 17 March 1689. For William's initial reservations about allowing the Queen any real power, see Foxcroft, *Halifax*, II, 246, 247, 248; *Memoirs of Mary*, pp. 21, 22.

64 *Memoirs of Mary*, pp. 29–31.

65 HMC *Finch*, II, 312. And see J. Ehrman, *The Navy in the War of William III 1689–1697* (Cambridge, 1953), pp. 344–50.

66 Browning, *Danby*, II, 172, 175–6; Horwitz, *Revolution Politicks*, p. 119. Parliament had only been adjourned, not prorogued, on 23 May.

67 Dalrymple, *Memoirs*, II, app. iii, 133, 134.

68 Dalrymple, *Memoirs*, II, app. iii, 134. And see Horwitz, *Revolution Politicks*, pp. 120–1. For William's doubts whether Monmouth would be more troublesome in Ireland or in London, see Foxcroft, *Halifax*, II, 215, 245.

69 For Monmouth's City connections, see DWL Morrice MS. R, 58.

70 Horwitz, *Revolution Politicks*, pp. 121–2.

71 *Memoirs of Mary*, p. 34.

72 HMC *Finch*, II, 447. And see Chester RO, Earwacker letters, f. 106, [Sir W. Aston]

to Sir J. Crewe, 4 September; Dalrymple, *Memoirs*, II, app. iii, 157, 159; DWL Morrice MS. R, 200–1.

73 NU, Portland MS. PwA 299.

74 *CSPD*, 1691–1692, p. 353 (misdated 1692).

75 Huygens, *Journaal*, I, 335–6, 343; Browning, *Danby*, III, 176–9; BL Add. MSS. 46554–9 (unsorted), to Lord Lexington, 20 September.

76 PRO (Belfast), DOD 638/6/7, Lord Ranelagh to T. Coningsby, 4 October; HMC *Portland*, III, 453.

77 CJ, x, 425. For some pre-sessional calculations on supply, see PRO, SP 8/7, No. 185, a memorandum (probably in R. Hampden's hand) summarised in *CSPD*, 1690–1691, p. 132.

78 KAO, Chevening MS. 78, R. Yard to A. Stanhope, 30 September.

79 PRO (Belfast), DOD 638/5A/31, to T. Coningsby, 14 October. And see KU, F. Bonnet, 10/20 and 13/23 October; Huygens, *Journaal*, I, 349; Trinity College MSS., Clarke correspondence, II, 228, 238.

80 Quoted in Tindal, *Continuation*, XIII, 420–1. See also *Archives*, III, i, 102.

81 *Archives*, III, i, 126. And see Ranke, *History*, VI, 153.

82 HMC *Portland*, III, 453; SR, VI, 243; Dorset RO, D60/F56, Sir J. to H. Trenchard, 21 October; Luttrell, *Parliamentary Diary*, p. 403.

83 PRO, SP 8/7, No. 185. See also a tract roughly of this date; Wing S4633.

84 Grey, *Debates*, X, 35–8. And see BL Loan 29/184, f. 359, [R. Harley] to his father, 13 November; HMC *Portland*, III, 452.

85 DWL Morrice MS. R, 212; Ranke, *History*, VI, 150; National Lib. of Ireland MS. 2055 (unfoliated), Sir R. Southwell to W. King, 22 November.

86 Ranke, *History*, VI, 151.

87 Burnet, *History*, IV, 118–19; HMC *Portland*, III, 454; HLM, 1690–1691, pp. 228–30.

88 Boyer, *William the Third*, II, 240–1. Cf. Ralph, *History*, II, 248.

89 LJ, XIV, 618. And see Burnet, *History*, IV, 119.

90 Burnet, *History*, IV, 116, 117, and *Supplement*, p. 351; PRO (Belfast), DOD 638/13/14, J. Pulteney to T. Coningsby, 1 January 1691. For the Commons' inquiry into accounts during the 1690–91 session, see CJ, x, 495–9, 515–19.

91 BL Loan 29/135 (unfoliated), 16 October. However, Harley's own rival was another Whig, Sir Rowland Gwynne, Treasurer of the Chamber.

92 DWL Morrice MS. R, 281 (who notes the defection of Seymour and Falkland on the Sandwich and on several other petitions); Verney MSS., reel 44, J. to Sir R. Verney, 3 December.

93 BL Add. MS. 29573, ff. 448, 451, C. to Viscount Hatton, 22 and 29 May; KU, F. Bonnet, 30 May/9 June; DWL Morrice MS. R, 151; Verney MSS., reel 44, A. Nicholas to Sir R. Verney, 3 June; Luttrell, *Brief Relation*, II, 46–7, 49.

94 Bodl. Ballard MS. 22, f. 10, J. Harrington to A. Charlett, 11 December; HMC *Portland*, III, 455, 454. See also BL Loan 29/184, f. 371; Verney MSS., reel 44, J. to Sir R. Verney, 3 December; Luttrell, *Brief Relation*, II, 141; BL Add. MS. 42592, ff. 107–13.

95 Ranke, *History*, VI, 148.

96 HLM, 1690–1691, pp. 93–6; Ranke, *History*, VI, 152; Trinity College MSS., Clarke correspondence, III, 271, J. E[disbury] to G. Clarke, n.d. See also Ehrman, *The Navy*, pp. 359–66.

97 LJ, XIV, 535; Ranke, *History*, VI, 154–5.

98 BL Loan 29/184, f. 381, [R. Harley] to his father, 13 December; Luttrell, *Brief Relation*, II, 141, 145; Huygens, *Journaal*, I, 379; CSPD, 1690–1691, p. 95; PRO (Belfast), DOD 636/13/1, J. Pulteney to T. Coningsby, 23 December.

99 Browning, *Danby*, I, 482–3, and III, 179–81.

100 DWL Morrice MS. R, 226. And see Burnet, *History*, IV, 121–2; HMC *Portland*, III, 456.

101 Browning, *Danby*, I, 484–5. Preston's confessions are printed in HMC *Finch*, III, 308–20.

102 Chatworth MSS., Devonshire House notebook, *sub* 'Shrewsbury Lord'; William Salt Lib., Plas Newyd MSS., box xvib, H. Ashurst to Lord Paget, 28 October; DWL Morrice MS. R, 219.

103 Dartmouth's note in Burnet, *History*, IV, 8; Chatsworth MSS., Devonshire House notebook, *sub* 'Carmarthen Lord'. And see BL Add. MS. 36662, f. 231.

104 Burnet, *Supplement*, p. 353; Chatsworth MSS., Devonshire House notebook, *sub* 'Carmarthen Lord'.

105 Burnet, *Supplement*, p. 353; CSPD, 1690–1691, pp. 440, 262. See also HMC *Seventh Report*, p. 208; NU, Portland MS. PwA 1347.

106 CSPD, 1690–1691, p. 290; CTB, XVII, 507, 508; NU, Portland MS. PwA 1328, [Sunderland to Portland], 13 July 1694.

107 Dalrymple, *Memoirs*, II, app. iii, 181 (cf. HMC *Finch*, III, 30). And see HMC *Portland*, III, 461; BL Loan 29/185, f. 19; Bodl. Locke MS. C15, f. 9.

108 Chatsworth MSS., Devonshire House notebook, *sub* 'Shrewsbury Lord'.

109 Kenyon, *Sunderland*, p. 249.

110 Foxcroft, *Halifax*, II, 202, 219, 232; Chatsworth MSS., Devonshire House notebook, *sub* 'Rochester Lord'; CTB, XVII, 510.

111 Chatsworth MSS., Devonshire House notebook, *sub* 'Hanover Prince'; *Memoirs of Mary*, p. 38; [N. Hooke], *An Account of the Conduct of the Dowager Duchess of Marlborough* (1742), pp. 39–40.

112 Bodl. Tanner MS. 27, f. 237, [Lloyd to Sancroft], 24 January. See also Burnet, *History*, IV, 128–9; *The Letters of Rachel Lady Russell*, ed. Lord John Russell (1852), pp. 53–4; Berkshire RO, Downshire MSS., D/ED/c32.

113 Horwitz, *Revolution Politicks*, p. 125; E. Carpenter, *The Protestant Bishop* (1956), pp. 171–5.

114 Burnet, *Supplement*, pp. 359–60. And see G. Bennett, 'Conflict in the Church', BAGR, esp. p. 161.

115 HMC *Seventh Report*, p. 198; *Memoirs of Mary*, p. 39. And see H. Horwitz, 'Comprehension in the later Seventeenth Century: A Postscript', *Church History* XXXIV (1965), 342.

116 BL Loan 29/185, f. 96, to Sir E. Harley, 6 June. And see HMC *Seventh Report*, p. 198; Berkshire RO, Downshire MSS., D/ED/c32. Tracts in defence of the new bishops include Wing V534 and S5679.

117 Browning, *Danby*, II, 221. See also *Correspondencia entre dos embajadores*, II, 400.

118 Browning, *Danby*, II, 203; Godolphin's letter of 13 July 1691 in CSPD, 1691–1692, p. 366 (misdated); HMC *Finch*, III, 98–9, 141, 188, 202.

119 Bodl. Carte MS. 79, f. 369, J. Vernon to T. Wharton, 11 June; HMC *Seventh Report*, pp. 199, 200.

120 Thus, Morrice noted that Clarges and Sir Benjamin Newland were 'of a sense different from all the rest'; DWL Morrice MS. R, 224. The three other commissioners were Sir Matthew Andrews, Robert Austen, and Sir Peter Colleton—all also Whigs. Andrews, Colleton, Foley, and Harley had not been chosen in May 1690; the other five had been.

121 CSPD, 1695 and Addenda, p. 168. Their activities can be followed in their formal minute book at BL Harleian MS. 1489 and in Colleton's rough notes in BL Harleian MS. 6837, ff. 135–206. I am grateful to Mr J. A. Downie for allowing me to read in draft 'The Commission of Public Accounts', in which he identifies Colleton's hand.

122 Browning, *Danby*, II, 203; CSPD, 1690–1691, p. 465. Jephson's secret service accounts are printed in CTB, XVII, 515–626.

123 HMC *Portland*, III, 467; BL Loan 29/185, f. 98, C. Musgrave to R. Harley, 8 June; CSPD, 1690–1691, p. 465.

124 CJ, X, 538. Godolphin's draft of this speech is in PRO, SP 8/8, No. 1 (misdated in CSPD, 1690–1691, p. 134, and see also p. 512).

125 HMC *Portland*, III, 479, also 482; PRO (Belfast), DOD 638/13/58, J. Pulteney to T. Coningsby, 27 October. And see Foxcroft, *Halifax*, II, 137–9; BL Loan 29/185, f. 228.

126 BL Loan 29/185, f. 230, [R. Harley] to his father, 31 October. And see PRO (Belfast), DOD 638/13/60.

127 BL Loan 29/185, f. 232, [R. Harley] to his father, 3 November.

128 *Het Archief van den Raadpensionaris Antonie Heinsius*, ed. H. J. van der Heim (The Hague, 1867–80), I, 34.

129 HMC *Seventh Report*, p. 205; BL Add. MS. 42592, f. 175; HMC *Portland*, III, 481.

130 CJ, X, 545; Ranke, *History*, VI, 162–3; HMC *Seventh Report*, p. 205; PRO (Belfast), DOD 638/13/58.

131 BL Loan 29/185, f. 232.

132 Ranke, *History*, VI, 165; *Het Archief van Heinsius*, I, 36 (should be dated 10/20 November).

133 Luttrell, *Parliamentary Diary*, pp. 5–6.

134 Luttrell, *Parliamentary Diary*, pp. 6–7; Ranke, *History*, VI, 164.

135 Browning, *Danby*, I, 490–1, and II, 192. For the proceedings on Fuller, see HMC *Portland*, III, 485; Luttrell, *Parliamentary Diary*, pp. 57, 67, and *passim*.

136 HMC *Downshire*, I, 390; PRO (Belfast), DOD 638/13/78, J. Pulteney to T. Coningsby, 5 December.

137 HMC *Downshire*, I, 390. And see Browning, *Danby*, I, 493–5; KU, F. Bonnet, 20/30 November and 24 November/4 December.

138 Huygens, *Journaal*, I, 510; HMC *Seventh Report*, p. 208.

139 HMC *Portland*, III, 481.

140 Luttrell, *Parliamentary Diary*, pp. 8, 9–11, 17–20; HMC *Portland*, III, 481, 482. The decision that the 'ordinary' of the Navy should be shifted to the ordinary revenue accounted for £92,000 of the reduction.

141 Luttrell, *Parliamentary Diary*, pp. 28–33; Grey, *Debates*, X, 175–80; PRO (Belfast), 638/13/69, J. Pulteney to T. Coningsby, 19 November; HMC *Seventh Report*, pp. 207, 208; Ranke, *History*, VI, 169.

142 Luttrell, *Parliamentary Diary*, pp. 39–42; Grey, *Debates*, X, 184–6.

143 Luttrell, *Parliamentary Diary*, pp. 47, and 48–9.

144 Of the £434,000, £185,000 had simply been shifted on to the ordinary revenue.

145 Text in HLM, 1690–1691, pp. 356–99, 404–8.

146 Luttrell, *Parliamentary Diary*, pp. 58–60, and also 4, 9, 11–12; Grey, *Debates*, X, 188–93. The figures used in this passage are derived from Shaw's in CTB, IX, esp. clxiv.

147 Luttrell, *Parliamentary Diary*, p. 61; Grey, *Debates*, X, 199–200.

148 PRO (Belfast), DOD 638/13/77, J. Pulteney to T. Coningsby, 3 December.

149 BL Loan 29/79, bundle 2, [R. Harley] to his father, 9 January.

150 BL Loan 29/186, f. 19, and 29/79, bundle 2, [R. Harley] to his father, 28 January and 2 February.

151 HLM, 1692–1693, pp. 50–1.

152 Luttrell, *Parliamentary Diary*, pp. 112–14, 120–3; PRO (Belfast), DOD 638/13/94, J. Pulteney to T. Coningsby, 12 January.

153 Luttrell, *Parliamentary Diary*, pp. 123–5, 136, 137, 138, 140; CJ, X, 631–2.

154 HMC *Portland*, III, 479; BL Loan 29/79, bundle 2, [R. Harley] to his father, 2 and 9 February.

155 BL Add. MS. 36662, f. 213, J. Pulteney to Sir W. Colt, 17 November; HLM, 1690–1691, pp. 315–19; Luttrell, *Parliamentary Diary*, pp. 49–50, 62–3.

156 HLM, 1692–1693, pp. 62–3.

157 Grey, *Debates*, X, 171–5; Luttrell, *Parliamentary Diary*, pp. 24–5; HLM, 1690–1691, pp. 319–27.

158 Luttrell, *Parliamentary Diary*, pp. 99–100. Compare BL Loan 29/141 (unfoliated), Sir E. to R. Harley, 9 January 1691[–2].

159 Chester RO, Earwacker letters, f. 127, [Sir W. Aston] to Sir J. Crewe, 16 April. And see Luttrell, *Parliamentary Diary*, pp. 186–9; BL Loan 29/187, f. 30.

160 Luttrell, *Parliamentary Diary*, pp. 193–4, and also pp. 177–8, 182.

161 Bodl. Rawlinson MS. D1362, f. 181 recto (anonymous diary for part of 1692–93 session). And see Ranke, *History*, VI, 180.

162 LJ, XV, 90.

163 L. M. Waddell, 'The Administration of the English Army in Flanders and Brabant from 1689 to 1697' (unpublished Ph.D. thesis, University of North Carolina, 1971), pp. 222 ff.

164 Sir Edward Hussey was the sponsor of the interest bill, which had been defeated in the 1690–91 session 158 to 155. For its opponents' use of Locke's arguments, see *The Correspondence of John Locke and Edward Clarke*, ed. B. Rand (1927), pp. 330–1; Luttrell, *Parliamentary Diary*, pp. 116–17, 150–1.

165 HMC *Seventh Report*, p. 205; Luttrell, *Parliamentary Diary*, pp. 16–17, 43–6.

166 Bodl. Rawlinson MS. C449, ff. 18–33 (minutes of the syndicate).

167 CJ, X, 655; Luttrell, *Parliamentary Diary*, pp. 173–6.

168 KAO, Chevening MS. 78, R. Yard to A. Stanhope, [February 1692]. Soon, rumours of bribery began to spread, with Portland being said to have taken £50,000 from the old Company; HMC *Finch*, IV, 442.

169 CJ, X, 661; Ranke, *History*, VI, 181; East India Office Lib., old Co. Court Book B/40, f. 104; Bodl. Rawl. MS. C449, f. 18.

170 Ranke, *History*, VI, 181.

171 Burnet, *History*, IV, 154; KU, F. Bonnet, 1/11 March.

172 See D. Rubini, *Court and Country 1688–1702* (1967), p. 120. For the quotation, see Luttrell, *Parliamentary Diary*, p. 325.

173 Macaulay, *History*, V, 2139; HLM, 1692–1693, pp. 76–9.

174 HMC *Finch*, IV, 442.

175 HMC *Downshire*, I, 390; Luttrell, *Brief Relation*, II, 326.

176 Burnet, *Supplement*, pp. 368, 373. See also Churchill, *Marlborough*, I, 392; Ranke, *History*, VI, 177–8; HMC *Seventh Report*, p. 220.

177 Churchill, *Marlborough*, I, 394–6; Luttrell, *Brief Relation*, II, 343; KU, F. Bonnet, 1/11 March; KAO, Chevening MS. 78, R. Yard to A. Stanhope, 15 March.

178 HMC *Downshire*, I, 389, 390.

179 *Memoirs of Mary*, pp. 42–3; KU, F. Bonnet, 1/11 March; C. Firth, 'The Memoirs of the First Lord Lonsdale', EHR XXX (1915), 96; BL Loan 29/79, bundle 2, [R. Harley] to his father, 2 February; BL Add. MS. 17677MM, f. 139, Baden, 8/18 March; KAO, Chevening MS. 78, R. Yard to A. Stanhope, 28 March. And see BL Add. MS. 56242, f. 21; CSPD, 1691–1692, pp. 352–3.

180 Mary was pleased at Rochester's appointment, but not Seymour's; *Memoirs of Mary*, p. 46.

181 Bertie was also Tom Wharton's nephew, but he voted as a Tory.

182 Kenyon, *Sunderland*, pp. 250–2. There had been reports that Nottingham would be made Lord Chancellor in order to make way for Sunderland at the seals; e.g., BL Add. MS. 17677MM, f. 89, Baden, 2/12 February.

183 KAO Chevening MS. 78, R. Yard to A. Stanhope, 19 January. And see Horwitz, *Revolution Politicks*, p. 132.

184 HMC *Finch*, IV, 20. See G. A. Jacobsen, *William Blathwayt: A Late Seventeenth Century Administrator* (New Haven, 1932); R. Preston, 'William Blathwayt and the Evolution of a Royal Personal Secretariat', *History*, n.s. XXXIV (1949), 28–43.

185 BL Add. MS. 52279 (unfoliated), 26 February and 5 March.

IV

THE REVOLUTION UNSETTLEMENT

1689-1692

The constitution

'The key question about 1689', as one scholar recently observed, 'is whether it established a new king on the throne, or a new type of monarchy?'[1] That this question can still be posed so long after the event may be symptomatic of the vagaries of historical interpretation, yet it also attests to the ambiguity of the 'Revolution' and to the varying perceptions of it by contemporaries. The yoking of the offer of the crown to the Declaration of Rights gave and still gives the appearance of at least an implied contract between the new sovereigns and their subjects—a contract which ushered in a new type of monarchy even if it was still clothed in the garb of the 'ancient constitution'. The hallmark of this new 'frame of government' was the subordination of the monarch to the law as made in parliament. James II had sought in a host of ways to 'subvert and extirpate the Protestant religion, and the laws and liberties of this kingdom'; his successors were to be bound to maintain the 'undoubted rights and liberties' of the realm which the Declaration arrayed under thirteen heads.[2] Furthermore, in the words of the revised coronation oath William and Mary swore to rule 'according to the statutes in parliament agreed on and the laws and customs' of the kingdom.[3] And among the statutes of 1689 was one incorporating the Declaration itself, along with a further provision restricting the throne to Protestants.

However, other features of the work of the Convention parliament lend support to the view—enunciated, though for different reasons, by both Jacobites and Williamite Tories—that the principal change in 1689 was one of 'persons', not of 'things'.[4] There was no systematic redefinition of the constitution before the tender of the crown; instead, many of the twenty-eight heads of the first version of the Declaration of Rights were excised from the final text because they were 'introductory of new laws', and even some that remained were worded more as general exhortations than as specific limitations upon the King's discretion.[5] Furthermore, by the time the Convention parliament was dissolved, only the revised coronation oath (head fifteen of the initial draft of the Declaration), the grant of toleration to Protestant Dissenters (sixteen), and the abolition of the hearth tax (twenty-seven) had reached the statute book.

The reasons for the failure to legislate on others of the twenty-eight heads during the first parliament of the reign were quite diverse. Some failed from apparent lack of interest: heads eighteen (judges' tenure), twenty-two, twenty-three and twenty-five (abuses in the legal system), and twenty-eight (abuses in the excise) seem to have been ignored; proposals on heads twenty (shrieval administration) and twenty-four (sale of offices) did not proceed beyond Commons' orders for the preparation of bills on those topics. But some of the heads were the subject of heated debate in one or both sessions, particularly the comprehension bills of the first session (sixteen), the attempts in both Houses to bar royal pardons to impeachments (twelve), the corporation bills (three) considered by the Commons in the spring and by both Houses in the autumn, the militia bills (five) discussed by both Houses in the spring and by the Commons in the autumn, and the Lords' proposals for the trial of peers (seventeen) and for triennial parliaments (nine, ten and eleven).[6]

The record of William's second parliament during its first three sessions was even less impressive. Granted, between March 1690 and February 1692 parliament did consider more than a score of bills that touched upon one or another of the twenty-eight heads. The Commons were seemingly the more energetic, and the great majority of these measures originated with them. During these years, the lower House displayed particular interest in bills relating to heads five (the militia), eight (regulation of elections), thirteen (corporation charters), seventeen (trials for treason), and twenty-four (sale of offices); the upper House, with the judges as their assistants, concentrated upon the remedy of abuses in the legal system.[7] Yet of these bills, only six were approved even by one House, and three of these failed of adoption in the other.[8] In addition, the Commons' treason trials measure of 1691–92 was lost in a quarrel with the Lords, and William vetoed their bill to secure the tenure of the judges. So only the bill to abrogate the Lord Warden's claim to nominate to parliamentary seats in the Cinque Ports actually reached the statute book in May 1690, after a similar bill had been lost by the dissolution of the Convention parliament.[9]

By the spring of 1692, it would seem, then, that little had altered in the constitution since a Jacobite pamphleteer (writing in the guise of a disillusioned Whig) had denounced the Convention parliament just after its demise for making William king without making it 'impossible for that king to be like the kings that went before him'.[10] As the anonymous author of that tract went on to point out:

He has the same power over parliaments that his predecessors had, . . . Their elements are as insecure as ever. Their meetings as uncertain, . . . Neither are they masters of their own sessions, to adjourn and prorogue as they please. And if they have prepared the most useful or necessary law in the world, . . . he may refuse to pass it, . . . Much less does the parliament nominate his council, or is he obliged to act in the intervals of parliament by the advice and approbation of a council. . . . He picks and chooses his council: he names all the great officers of the state, navy, army and church . . . and he absolutely commands the militia.

However, there are two features of the monarch's situation in the early 1690s which do not figure in this assessment, and both omissions are significant. One is the terms of the settlement of the ordinary revenue. Harbord, in an oft-quoted speech delivered on 29 January 1689 in which he was arguing against the delays that would occur if the Commons sought to formulate a new 'Magna Charta' before settling the crown, had reminded his colleagues: 'You have an infallible security for the administration of the government; all the revenue is in your own hands, which fell with the last king, and you may keep that back.'[11] This is exactly what the Commons did a month later, and their debates of 25–27 February 1689 demonstrate that many M.P.s were intent upon rectifying the errors they believed had been made in the revenue settlements of 1660 and 1685. The relatively low figure of £1,200,000 was tentatively fixed upon without much dispute in March 1689, and when the requisite legislation was finally passed a year later it was decided to give tunnage and poundage for a fixed term of years. It is true that one of the reasons that was offered for this decision during the critical debates of 27–28 March 1690 was that a grant for a definite period of time would make the revenue more attractive to lenders as a 'fund of credit' for the war. Yet, as William Ettrick pointed out on the Court's behalf, and as the act granting the excise for lives illustrates, it was perfectly possible to provide a clause for the protection of lenders 'in case the King and Queen die before the debt is paid'. Thus, there can be no doubt that the Commons' principal concern in agreeing to limit the grant of tunnage and poundage to four years was, as both Sir William Williams (once a rabid Exclusionist) and Sir Joseph Williamson (formerly Secretary of State to Charles II) urged, to ensure 'that parliaments may be frequent' as the Declaration of Rights had enjoined.[12]

The second omission in the Jacobite pamphleteer's assessment of the constitution relates to the effects of the war against France. It is true that the Declaration of Rights had not restricted the monarch's power to declare war and to make peace, though Halifax subsequently observed that 'some thought' this question 'would' or should 'have been more thoroughly considered' in 1689.[13] Rather, the Declaration and the bill of rights simply prohibited the maintenance of a standing army within the realm in time of peace without parliamentary consent. This was a novel restriction upon the crown nor was it realised in 1689 how prolonged the war with France would be. Moreover, even if the Commons were not, in Sir William Williams's words, to 'meddle' with 'war and peace', it was clear from the outset that they were 'to supply' most of the cost of the fighting.[14] Hence, William delayed a formal breach with France until he had secured parliamentary backing for the war in late April 1689.

In turn, the King's efforts to secure the necessary financial support to continue the war had already by early 1692 set in motion important changes in the relations between the crown and the Commons. And despite Halifax's fears that parliament might become little more than a fund-raising mechanism (a 'Parlement of Paris' was the analogy often invoked) out of 'the necessity of self-preservation' once the war was under way, the alterations tended more in the direction of making the monarch a 'Doge of Venice'.[15] Most important, William was compelled to acquiesce in the burdening of his ordinary revenue, once granted, with loans to help finance the military effort, and these debts were not subsequently provided for by parliament. At the same time, the unprecedentedly large requests for extraordinary grants prompted the Commons to elaborate their supply procedures. The King's servants were asked to provide increasingly detailed estimates of the ways in which the money was to be spent, and during the 1691–92 session the lower House carefully scrutinised and significantly reduced the figures for the 1692 campaign. Furthermore, the inclusion in supply measures of clauses appropriating the moneys granted to specified uses was becoming common practice. During the 1690–91 and 1691–92 sessions, all the money voted was appropriated either for specific services or for the conduct of the war in general. And from the outset of the reign, the Commons displayed a keen interest in securing full accounts of the sums actually raised and the uses to which they had been put. The act of June 1689 to

grant the one shilling aid enjoined 'that an account shall be given' to the
Commons of 'every sum' collected 'by virtue of this' or 'of any other act' passed
'during the present sessions', and this included the ordinary revenue.[16] Subsequently, dissatisfaction with the quality of official accounts presented to them
led the Commons to press for and to secure the establishment of a Commission
of Accounts staffed by their own members and responsible to parliament.

The creation of the Commission of Accounts early in 1691 may also be seen
as a sign of a new readiness on the Commons' part to interfere with, perhaps
even to usurp, the conduct of administrative tasks. There was, already, after all,
the precedent in August 1689 of the establishment of the Commissioners for Wool
whose charge was to prevent the smuggling of that precious material out of the
realm, though against that somewhat mysterious instance of a penchant for
parliamentary administration must be set the lower House's wary refusal a few
months later of the opportunity to make recommendations of Shales's successors.[17] In any case, some of the critics of the Commission of Accounts thought
that its activities, as well as Foley's scheme for examining and certifying naval
officers, betokened a design against royal control of the executive, though it
remained to be seen whether such suspicions were really justified.[18]

However, there can be little doubt that the grant of a portion of the ordinary
revenue for a term of years, coupled with the King's dependence upon the
Commons for extraordinary supply so long as the war lasted, was capable of
producing a profound shift in the relations between crown and parliament, and
especially the lower House. Even so, it would be misleading to read into the
developments of the first three years of the reign a clearly conceived or fully
conscious constitutional design. Although the men of 1689 wanted frequent
parliaments, they did not demand annual sessions. And while they supported a
breach with France once James was given aid by Louis XIV, most would have
recoiled with shock could they have foreseen the length and the expense of the
war. In 1690 and in 1691, many M.P.s seem to have hoped that an amphibious
'descent' in force upon France would bring Louis very quickly to his knees, and
some of the ministers—particularly Nottingham—were also of this opinion.
Hence, the Commons' willingness to vote large supplies in 1691–92 despite the
lack of success in the previous campaign; hence, too, the shocked dismay of John
Evelyn when he heard from Lord Dover, who had just returned from France in
late 1691, of 'the strength of the Fr[ench] King, and the difficulty of our forcing
him to fight'.[19]

Then, too, it was difficult for many, even as late as 1692, to anticipate the
transformation of the current practice of annual parliamentary sessions into a
constitutional convention. Rather, there were some influential members such as
Sir Christopher Musgrave who looked forward to the time when there 'will not
be such needs of an annual sessions'.[20] But if the future was difficult to predict,
what was evident for the present was that the bulk of the King's business in the
yearly sessions was the provision of supply for the war and that the main task
of the royal administration was the organisation of the war effort.

The King's administration

The most notable feature of the operation of the royal administration during the
early years of William's and Mary's reign was the leading role personally played

by the King. Granted, William held the crown jointly with Mary, and her claim by dynastic right was far stronger (at least in English eyes) than his own. Yet if it was relevant to ask at the beginning of the reign which of the royal couple would 'touch for the [King's] evil', there was no doubt who would have the direction of affairs.[21] It was not simply that William had stated he would be neither regent nor king consort and so had received 'the sole and full exercise of the regal power'.[22] Rather, William's demands upon the Convention reflected his knowledge of Mary's readiness to accept the subordinate place of a wife, just as Mary's own statements to Danby and Burnet's dissemination of her views facilitated the disposition of the 'regal power'.

Nevertheless, the Queen soon showed that she was not a cipher. Sometimes, as in her deepening estrangement from her sister Anne, Mary's involvement complicated affairs, but usually the results were positive. Her devotion to the Church not only personally fortified her against the anguish of opposing a father in support of a husband; it also smoothed the way for Nottingham and Tillotson to emerge as the King's leading advisers in matters ecclesiastical. Still more evident was the courage and judgement the Queen demonstrated in her role as regent during the summer of 1690. In sum, Mary lacked neither commitment nor ability, and she put her resources at William's service, so enhancing his position. That the King still occasionally saw his one-time mistress Lady Betty Villiers may have grieved the Queen, but that relationship posed no real threat to Mary as wife or queen.[23]

Backed up by Mary, William was the working head of an administration that he operated, so it is generally said, on a 'departmental system'.[24] Certainly, he was his own first minister—a position to which his chief confidant Portland never aspired. Rather, Portland's principal role as Groom of the Stole and first Gentleman of the Bedchamber was to act as an intermediary between William and those who did not normally have direct access to him.[25] William's chief officials in Scotland and also in Ireland after the reconquest communicated with him via Portland on all important matters, and in English affairs the Earl's intervention was chiefly sought by all those outside the narrow circle of leading ministers and personal attendants (especially the other Gentlemen of the Bedchamber) who saw the King regularly in the course of their duties.[26] Portland, in other words, was a trusted and beloved confidential man of affairs, secretary, even nurse, who screened his master from suppliants and others whom William had neither the time nor the inclination to see. It was because Portland was the principal channel of approach to the King that even the Earl's doorkeeper was exceedingly well tipped and that he himself was sought out by so many leading Englishmen, whatever their personal feelings for the Dutchman. Thus, even when Portland returned alone to England in May 1692 to assist the Queen and the ministers in the face of a possible French invasion, no fewer than thirty-two peers, not to mention others of lesser rank, were counted in attendance upon him one morning at his apartments in Kensington.[27]

While Portland never sought to be the King's first minister for English affairs, William deliberately denied that role to Carmarthen, not least by keeping him out of the Treasury. The King told Halifax in 1689 that 'there were two places which should ever be in commission, viz. admiralty and treasury', and though he changed his mind on other points of administrative practice he never appointed a Lord Treasurer.[28] Yet to speak of a 'departmental system' in operation during the early years of the reign may be misleading, especially if this phrase conveys the impression of a tightly-knit and well-oiled administrative apparatus at work. William, after all, was a 'stranger' to the practice of English government, prey to errors such as supposing that the Privy Council could or should function as the effective centre of the executive.[29]

A further problem was that many of William's initial appointees to key posts were lacking in any administrative experience. The first Secretary of State, Shrewsbury, had never before held office, and the principal prior service of his colleague Nottingham had been at the Admiralty. Admittedly, their lack of diplomatic training was not a matter of grave concern to the King since he intended to keep the main threads of foreign affairs in his own hands.[30] Nottingham might busy himself with the details of the Anglo-Dutch treaty in 1689, but though he was taken along to The Hague conference of allied princes in early 1691 he was not admitted to the working sessions.[31]

Similarly, it might be supposed that the King's financial and military expertise would ease problems met on those fronts. Even so, William was glad to avail himself of Godolphin's service at the Treasury in 1689, and he was eager to persuade him to return after his resignation in March 1690. Furthermore, after Godolphin rejoined the Board as first Commissioner in late 1690, William cajoled him into remaining despite Godolphin's talk in early 1691 of remarrying and resigning and despite his continued intimacy with Marlborough after that Earl's fall from favour in early 1692.[32]

However, it was in naval affairs that William was most dependent on others' experience and assistance.[33] And apart from the initial setbacks in Ireland, the most obvious failures of 1689 and 1690 came at sea, where the unfortunate Arthur Herbert, Earl of Torrington, was serving as both the head of a weak Admiralty Board and the commander of the Anglo-Dutch fleet. In the spring of 1689, there were costly delays in setting out the English contingent as well as the late arrival of most of the Dutch ships. In the autumn, there was a furore over provisioning; this finally led to the dismissal of the old Victualling Commissioners who had been continued from James II's reign and the selection of their successors by ballot at an extraordinary joint sitting of the Treasury and Admiralty Boards (reinforced by the leading ministers).[34] In turn, a new low point was reached the following summer with the disgrace of Beachy Head, though naval historians have since vindicated Torrington's strategy and joined him in criticising Nottingham and the rest of the Queen's council for a failure in the evaluation of the available intelligence about French strength—a failure which led the council to insist that the Admiral give battle despite a serious disadvantage in numbers.[35]

Yet the administrative problems the English government encountered during the early campaigns of the war cannot be ascribed solely to the inexperience of many of those in office. On the one hand, some of the most serious problems arose in the work of those who, like the Commissioners for Victualling or the infamous Shales, were old hands. And on the other hand, in making his initial selections for major posts William had in many cases been more concerned with the men's political standing than with their expertise. Nor was it only at the top levels that political considerations intruded. Thus, the removal of Lord Dartmouth and Samuel Pepys from their positions of trust in the navy was followed by a massive reshuffle among those holding command posts at sea. Nearly two-thirds of the sixty captains in Dartmouth's fleet in 1688 did not serve at sea at any time between 1689 and 1697; again, of those commanding ships at the war's end, over half received their commissions during the first four years of the reign.[36] Not surprisingly, this rapid turnover of old hands, prompted chiefly by fears as to the loyalty of many of the pre-Revolution captains, took its toll in terms of the general level of competence in the fleet.

Similar difficulties plagued the army. Both resentment and disloyalty were apparent among some of James II's regiments, and roughly one-quarter of the higher officers and one-fifth of the junior officers left the service with the change of regime in 1689.[37] Then, too, the units raised by William's adherents during and immediately after the Revolution were lacking in training and often deficient in equipment, too. The reports of the special commissioners to inspect the army whom William dispatched to the provinces in May 1689 must have made depressing reading for the King; for instance, the Earl of Monmouth, in a private letter, castigated one of the new units in saying that 'it wanted nothing to be a complete regiment but clothes, boots, arms, horses, men, and officers'.[38] Monmouth may not have been an unprejudiced witness since the regiment in question was organised by his despised colleague at the Treasury, Lord Delamere, but overall there can be no doubt that the task of making the English army a disciplined and effective force was not a matter of months but of years.[39]

To the difficulties of specific departments and of the fighting forces must be added a noticeable lack of co-ordination within the executive. A 'departmental system' presupposes central supervision and direction, but though William was said 'to labour unceasingly, working and writing day and night', he found it difficult to keep pace with the multiplicity of demands upon him.[40] The weight of the burdens he bore must be taken into account in evaluating the persistent complaints made during these years by his English ministers—Carmarthen, Shrewsbury, Nottingham, even Sidney—that they could not get prompt decisions from him on the most pressing affairs. Sidney, reputed lazy and incompetent himself, went so far as to say that he had been 'deceived' in William, 'that he thought him more a man of business than he found him'; similarly, Shrewsbury, who found the routine of Whitehall tedious and prejudicial to his health, confided to Halifax (after both had resigned) that the King's 'often refusing to hear him . . . to business he had appointed, turned his stomach'.[41] But though William was both by temperament and by experience averse to making snap decisions, royal dilatoriness was not the real difficulty, while the King's penchant for the hunt becomes more explicable when one realises that it was his only escape from business. Rather, the main problem was that if the King did not personally provide direction, no one else could or would. There were frequent meetings in 1689 of the committee for Irish affairs (a subcommittee of the Privy Council established in February 1689), but it was only after William concentrated his attention on the reconquest that matters began to take a turn for the better. And even as he was leading his troops to victory in Ireland during the summer of 1690, Secretary-at-War William Blathwayt was complaining in London that 'nobody has a particular charge of general matters so as to watch and pursue the dispatch of them in the several places'.[42]

Oversight of this sort might have been provided by some kind of co-ordinating body within the executive, and there was some pre-Revolution precedent for the use of what contemporaries usually referred to as a 'cabinet council'—that is, a select group of key ministers and advisers meeting frequently, yet distinct from the Privy Council. The Irish committee was too large and disparate a body to serve this function, and at the close of the first session of the Convention parliament there were reports that 'his Majesty is ordering a cabinet council to consist of Halifax, Carmarthen, Portland, and the two Secretaries of State'.[43] During 1689, William did on occasion confer with select groups of councillors, chiefly the five mentioned in these reports, about key decisions, especially naval measures.[44] But such gatherings were convened on an *ad hoc* basis. And despite recurrent conversations with Halifax in which the King acknowledged the necessity of a 'cabinet council', nothing more was done for the time being so that, as Sir John Lowther later recalled, 'there was no council but only for form'.[45]

Two obstacles inhibited action. One was the discord among the leading ministers in 1689; as William lamented to Halifax early in 1690, 'he did not know of [? four] men, who would speak freely before one another'.[46] A second was the prospect of competition among the King's servants for inclusion in such an inner council; if all those with either personal or *ex officio* claims were to be summoned, little would be accomplished. Both these problems did handicap even the advisory council of nine which the King set up for the summer of 1690. Subsequently, William revived this body in the early months of 1691 during his stay at The Hague and he reconstituted it when he went back to the Low Countries for the 1691 campaign. Yet it was not until the winter of 1691–92 that he began to hold at least occasional meetings of a 'cabinet council' while he was in England. Curiously, this innovation did not attract much contemporary notice, and since only one minute of such a gathering has survived from these months later students of the development of the cabinet have passed these meetings by as well. Even so, sufficient evidence is extant to remove all uncertainty. On 30 November 1691, Secretary Sidney informed a subordinate in matter-of-fact tones that 'the cabinet council meets this evening about 6 o'clock at Kensington'; on 18 December, the King's Dutch secretary Huygens noted in passing that he was unable to speak to his master until 9 p.m. that evening when William 'came out of a cabinet council'; on 9 and 23 January 1692, Nottingham communicated decisions to the Treasury Board that 'the King has resolved this day at the cabinet council'; and in March, the records of both the old East India Company and the interloping syndicate note summons to them from 'the Lords of his Majesty's Cabinet Council' while under-secretary Yard referred to several cabinet councils held at this time in which the settlement of the East India trade was one item of business.[47]

Just why William finally resorted to holding cabinet councils in his presence during the winter of 1691–92 is impossible to determine. Yet the increasing ascendency of the Churchmen in his administration at this time is suggestive. Moreover, the coincidence in time between the demise of the Irish committee with the completion of the reconquest in the autumn of 1691 and the first passing allusions to meetings of the cabinet council reinforce the hypothesis that the former body had 'acted as a quasi-cabinet' hitherto.[48] None the less, the immediate precursors of the cabinet councils held at Kensington in the King's presence during the winter of 1691–92 were the advisory councils which William had named to assist the Queen the two previous summers. Thus, those recorded as present on 21 October 1691 in the only extant minute of a cabinet council in these months were eight of the nine councillors who had been designated in May 1691, plus William himself along with Marlborough and Sidney who had been with the King on the Continent during the past summer.[49] In turn, during the next six months the membership of the cabinet council must have been affected by the quarrel between the two royal courts which undoubtedly put an end first to Marlborough's attendance and then to Prince George's. But their removal did not bring any reduction in the cabinet's size, for Rochester and Seymour were made members in March 1692, just before the King's departure for the Low Countries.

Although William only decided to meet with a cabinet council in 1691–92, he had from the outset of the reign often attended the Treasury Board while he was in England. Yet not even his presence could halt the government's slide into debt. Already by the autumn of 1690, Richard Hampden calculated the debt of the various military agencies as £3,000,000, and in addition there was another £1,000,000 anticipated on the ordinary and hereditary revenues. Moreover, though the supplies voted in the 1690–91 session did just cover the military estimates for 1691, nearly half the money was to be raised by anticipating tax returns as far ahead as 1695. The result was that Godolphin had considerable difficulty in getting the necessary loans and unfunded departmental debts continued to mount. And meanwhile, Londoners and others with ready cash were speculating in Exchequer tallies and official salaries were heavily in arrears.[50]

Given these financial problems, there was considerable sentiment at the Treasury in favour of recourse to other expedients to raise supply. Both Hampden and Lowther voiced support in the Commons during the 1691–92 session for schemes to create a funded long-term debt, but the two were not of one mind as to which of the various plans under discussion should be adopted. Another project, mooted as early as the autumn of 1689 and repeatedly alluded to thereafter, was the imposition of a general excise on domestic commodities. Such a levy was advocated by the elder Hampden in his memorandum to William in the autumn of 1690, and Godolphin, too, was leaning in this direction. Thus, in the summer of 1691, the first lord of the Treasury reported to William that he was encouraging Dr Charles Davenant to polish his already 'very good scheme' for a general excise.[51]

But while those in charge of the King's finances tended to see a general excise almost as a panacea for their problems, parliamentary reaction was in a different key. When Sir Thomas Lee broached the advantages of a 'home excise' in the Commons on 2 April 1690, he found few to support him even though he held out the prospect that its adoption would obviate the need of regular land taxes. John Swynfen's reply, in effect, was the majority opinion: 'I am not', so the Staffordshire veteran of the Long Parliament declared, 'for saving our lands to enslave our persons by excise.' Similarly, when there was talk of a general excise during the autumn of 1690, Robert Harley wrote home to his father of it in fearful tones, while noting that Sir Christopher Musgrave 'was positive against it'.[52] The dangers that members perceived in excises were more fully spelled out in a number of pamphlets of the 1690s, among them a diatribe from the pen of the younger Hampden. Excises, it was said, were hardly ever terminated once granted precisely because they were less burdensome personally to M.P.s than was the land tax; they necessitated the employment of large numbers of salaried officials, by contrast to the unpaid commissioners who assessed the land tax and also the polls; and the excisemen would invade the houses of the subject in pursuance of their duties and also interfere in parliamentary elections, while their employment would add to the patronage resources at the disposal of the crown and its ministers. This by no means exhausts the list of objections; it was also alleged that excises burdened the poor and that the end result of a general excise would be to lower gentlemen's rentals.[53]

In the face of such vehement and deep-seated objections to anything that savoured of a general excise, it is not surprising that the government, even with Dr Davenant's scheme in hand, again drew back from actually proposing this levy in the 1691–92 session. Not since the days of the Protectorate had the country been committed to so ambitious a foreign policy with its unprecedented requirements in manpower, *matériel*, and money. But while Oliver and the generals could dispense with parliamentary authorisation of excises and even with parliaments themselves, William had little alternative but to work through and with the Commons and the Lords.

Patterns of politics

'Whilst there was war', William acknowledged to Halifax in July 1689, 'he should want a parliament'. However, the task of parliamentary management was a demanding one for which the King was not well suited. Ideally, it called for close personal contact with leading members of both Houses, for careful attention to the distribution of patronage, and for the skilful presentation of coherent justifications of government measures both in parliament and out of doors. William's own inclination to 'do what was right and [? leave] it there' was not, as Halifax observed, 'enough for a king, and especially here'; rather, 'the world is like a beast that must be cozened before it be tamed'.[54] Then, too, William's 'cold and reserved' ways (at least with those whom he did not particularly like or trust), the prominent place of Dutchmen in his entourage, and his preference for residences (Hampton Court and Kensington) away from the injurious smoke of London's hearths all worked to isolate him from easy contact with members of parliament. Indeed, early in the reign, Sir Rowland Gwynne, Treasurer of the Chamber and Whig M.P. for Radnorshire, noted with dismay that there were not even enough tables at Court at mealtimes to 'treat' the members who attended.[55]

It is true that William had not expected to bear the burdens of parliamentary management when he came to the throne. This was to be the work of those politicians he appointed, and apparently the King had hoped that by including men representing a wide spectrum of opinion it would be possible to sustain broad-based support for his measures, and especially the war. But this calculation soon proved erroneous, partly because of the reawakening of party antagonisms and partly because of the military setbacks incurred in 1689. In fact, the disputes in the Convention over the settlement of the crown did not subside, and already in mid-February 1689 there was talk 'as if the members of both Houses who have been in the affirmative and negative for and against abdication' were 'to be exposed in print'.[56] Thus, as Sir John Lowther later recalled, 'the buried names of Whig and Tory' were 'revived' in the first parliament of the reign, 'dispersed through the nation' in the general election of 1690, and then kept up in renewed confrontations during the first three sessions of the second parliament.[57]

At first glance, the recrudescence of the party divisions of Shaftesbury's day may appear somewhat surprising. To be sure, there was considerable continuity of personnel both at the top and among the generality of members of parliament. Of the 116 peers who attended the Lords during the debates over the bestowal of the crown, eighty-one had sat in one or more of the Exclusion parliaments, including eighteen who had then been members of the Commons. Similarly, 238 of those elected to the Commons in January 1689 had served between 1679 and 1681. Nevertheless, many who had earlier opposed exclusion were not in 1689 prepared to allow James to retain even his title to the throne: the margin of victory in the Lords on 29 January 1689 was provided by a dozen peers who had voted against the second exclusion bill in November 1680 and who now divided against the motion for a regency in James's name.[58] Similarly, men of divergent political backgrounds joined together in the Commons to forward the Declaration of Rights and to deny William title to those revenues that had been voted to James for life. But though James's behaviour on the throne, followed by his flight to France, settled his personal fate, his ouster did not resolve all the outstanding issues of the Exclusion crisis nor did it settle the many scores left from the days of the Tory reaction.

From the outset, the Whigs were disgruntled by their failure to monopolise William's favour and outraged by the prominence within the new government of Carmarthen, Halifax, and Nottingham. The young Edward Harley observed in early March 1689 that 'the preferment of some men to places of trust that were the promoters of tyranny and the disregard of those that always opposed it occasions some discontents', and simultaneously some of his father's friends in the Commons were setting on foot inquiries into the attack on London's charter and exclaiming against 'the old instruments' of arbitrary government.[59] Nor did their fury abate in succeeding months as first they sought to turn the King's proposals for indemnity into a bill of pains and penalties, then they attempted to secure addresses against the ministers, and later they tried to add their proscriptive amendments to the corporation bill.

The Tories, too, contributed their share to partisan animosities by their campaign in defence of the sacramental test for office. They also signalled their continuing differences of principle with the Whigs by their ingenuity in devising justifications for their adherence to William and Mary that eschewed arguments based upon the 'original contract' or the subject's right of resistance. Nottingham and his friends among the clergy were especially prominent in their exposition of the notions that the Revolution was an act of divine providence and that the new sovereigns were to be obeyed only as *de facto* rulers.[60] And while the Tories were reluctant to recognise William and Mary as 'rightful and lawful', much less to abjure James, they sought to add to the bill of rights an explicit affirmation of the principle of hereditary royal succession.

However, the ferocity of the partisan conflict in the Convention parliament should not obscure the looseness of party ties. Not all members were partisans—witness Sidney's and Coningsby's reference in 1690 to a 'middle party'. Nor did all partisans always vote consistently; as Morrice observed gloomily in April 1689, 'the House of Commons was stronger by 80 to 100 voices to reform things in the state than in the church'.[61] Thus, the Whigs were unable to secure a repeal of the sacramental test just as the Tories were unable to carry an indemnity bill. It is also significant that both abrogation of the test and passage of a general indemnity had been specifically recommended to parliament from the throne. William's measures to promote domestic reconciliation and unity were not only the chief victims of the party clash; they also brought to the fore questions of principle which both intensified and served to dignify the competition for power between Whigs and Tories in parliament and within his mixed and divided ministry.

Already by the summer of 1689, it was painfully apparent to the King that his initial political moves both on men and on measures left much to be desired. In the months that followed, he hesitantly and gradually adopted a number of expedients that he had not originally contemplated. After he resigned himself to the fact that he could not just go off and leave Mary to deal with parliament, he consciously tried to improve his personal relations with key members of the two Houses, particularly the Lords. In October 1689, the King journeyed to Newmarket for the races; after his return, he and Mary dined for 'the first time publicly at Whitehall ... as their predecessors did'; in January 1690, he partook of a 'debauch' at Shrewsbury's town house in the company of Marlborough, Godolphin, Sidney, Mulgrave, Dorset, and Tom Wharton; and in May 1690, he finally took the trouble, as Halifax had earlier pressed him to do, to attend informally or incognito several lengthy debates in the Lords, as Charles II had done in his time.[62]

In the meantime, William had embarked on a new experiment in ministry-making by deliberately favouring the Tories over the Whigs. After signalling his opposition to the Whigs' amendments to the corporation bill and then dissolving the Convention parliament, he publicly recommended the choice of moderate Churchmen in the general election and removed some of the more violent and less able Whigs from office. Then, in the new parliament, the King took the sting out of the indemnity question by bringing in an act of grace, and as he accepted Carmarthen's compromise over 'recognition' so he also came out against the Whigs' scheme for an abjuration oath.

During these months, the King also acted to mobilise more effectively the Court's potential influence in parliament. In considering the composition of the revamped Treasury Board in early 1690, he showed a new consciousness of the importance of selecting able House of Commons men and he rejected Baptist May on the grounds that 'he was no speaker'.[63] Even more striking was his designation of Trevor for the Speakership of the new Commons and the re-emergence of Carmarthen in his old role of parliamentary manager.

To judge by the course of the first and even more the second session of 1690, the King's expedients were reasonably effective. Partisan tensions, which had been so high in the Convention parliament and which carried over into the first meeting of the new parliament, diminished after William made it known in September that he would not give in to Whig importunities for a new dissolution. Although Whigs continued to pit themselves against Tories during the 1690–91 session, especially in the continuing struggle for ascendency in the City and in a series of controverted elections, a reaction against the 'high flyers of both' parties was observed. Whereas the spring session of 1690 was marked by twenty-four divisions in the full House in which more than half the total membership voted (with nine of these being occasioned by contested elections), during the fall session there were only fifteen large divisions (nine of them on election petitions) even though it lasted a month longer. It was also remarked that during the autumn session the parties seemed 'to vie with one another who shall give most', and the ready grant of £4,600,000 was facilitated—if the evidence of a memorandum drafted by Carmarthen before the session is to be accepted at face value— by the activities of a set of 'managers of the King's directions', who were assisted by a number of Privy Councillors.[64] The managers designated by Carmarthen were chiefly Tories, with the list headed by Lowther, Goodricke, and Clarges, though in fact Sir Thomas opposed the maintenance of a large land army during this session; the latter were Whigs such as Wharton, Richard Hampden, and the Marquess of Winchester. Furthermore, Carmarthen wanted the Commissioners of the Treasury to mobilise all members with 'employment [or] advantage under the crown' to 'forward' supply, while army officers in the Commons (said by one Jacobite pamphleteer to number four score) were 'to be spoken to by the King'.[65]

Just how far the Commons' 'universal concurrence' during the 1690–91 session is to be attributed to Court management is somewhat uncertain. We do not know how far Carmarthen's plans were actually followed. And even if they were implemented, there were substantially fewer placemen in the Commons in 1690 than enemies of the government alleged. Upon examination, the 'four score' military men dwindle to at most twenty-five (some also holding garrison commands), and the total number of officers and officials in late 1690 was about 120.[66] At the same time, it is necessary also to take into account, though we cannot reckon the effects in numerical terms, the favourable reaction to Beachy Head and the Boyne and also the optimism about the future course of the war that was observed among backbenchers by Burnet and Lord Manchester.

Then, too, renewed backbench support for the government and for the war during the 1690–91 session was not without qualifications. The government's requests for extraordinary supply were answered, but a general excise was still anathema and a substantial proportion of the levies that were voted consequently entailed anticipation of future revenues. Furthermore, despite William's renewed plea in November 1690 for supply to pay off the loans on the ordinary revenue, his suit was in effect denied, to the accompaniment of a widely-publicised speech from Sir Charles Sedley (a prominent Court wit in his younger days) bewailing 'the want and misery' of a heavily-taxed country and denouncing the 'crafty old courtiers' who were deluding 'a brave and generous prince' while they 'wallow in wealth and places'. Subsequently, Sir Charles put his speech in print and as far away as Worcester it drew 'abundance of company to the coffee house'.[67]

As Sedley's speech suggests, any respite in party hostilities that had been induced by the 'Carmarthen art' might go hand in hand with the revival of that 'distinction of Court and Country party' that had prevailed 'in that long parliament of Charles the Second' when the Lord President had last held high office.[68] Already in the autumn of 1689 there had been complaints in the Commons that there were too many placemen in the House; moreover, the motion to address William to find out who had recommended Shales divided members along Court–Country lines. In turn, Foley's proposal of May 1690 that ministers sign their advices was another backbench attempt to resolve the knotty question of how to assign responsibility for maladministration without falling into partisan recriminations.[69]

Admittedly, Country slogans might serve merely as rhetorical ammunition to cover the assaults made by ambitious politicians out of office on their entrenched rivals—as, for instance, in the addresses projected against Carmarthen in the

Commons in May 1690 and January 1691. But suspicion of the Court was also manifested in other ways during the 1690-91 session. Fears of arbitrary power lay behind the opposition stirred up in the Commons to the sweeping terms of a Lords' bill to indemnify Privy Councillors and other royal servants for any illegal actions, such as the committal of suspected Jacobites, they might have taken in the wake of Beachy Head.[70] Similarly, fears of corruption lay behind the amendment, moved by Sedley, to the bill establishing the Commission of Accounts; his successful rider sought to give the Commissioners the power to inquire into government payments from any source (including secret service funds) to members of either House.[71]

Even more ominous, at least from the Court's point of view, was the conduct of the Commissioners of Accounts. Although Richard Hill could tell Trumbull in early 1691 that 'all ... the nation ... is Whigs and Tory' and others could assess the disposition of the individual Commissioners in like terms, the 'hot words' that passed among the nine at their first meeting were quickly smoothed over.[72] They were soon hard at work, and they exhibited a keen interest in probing rumours that the 'buying off men' was being practised by way of Jephson's disbursements of secret service moneys.[73] Furthermore, it was members of the Commission and their 'grumbletonian' friends, as one Whig courtier called them, who took the lead during the 1691-92 session in challenging the administration.[74] Whigs such as Foley and Harley, supporters of the Sacheverell clause in January 1690, joined with Churchmen such as Clarges and Musgrave, opponents of 'abdication' and 'vacancy', to try to shape the diffuse and often negative Country outbursts of previous sessions into an effective campaign on behalf of 'good management', with the result that Sir Thomas and Sir Christopher had already gained by late 1691 'the character of Commonwealth men'.[75] Moreover, when 'the Court party' (including the newest convert, Seymour) opposed the tack of the bill of accounts to the poll bill in February 1692, it was carried by the juncture of 'the Whig and Tory country party'.[76]

However, the new backbench alignment did not sweep all before it during the 1691-92 session, for there were many obstacles to overcome. Two of the Commissioners of Accounts themelves accepted places after being elected to serve on that body, and altogether the number of placemen (civil and military) in the Commons had risen to 130 by the beginning of the 1692-93 session.[77] Then, too, Whig-Tory animosities remained, and the Whig 'men of intrigue' still in office continued to exert an influence over many of their old friends in the Commons. Although Harley found 'the parties ... very much intermixed and jumbled together' in the early days of the 1691-92 session, Hill observed a month later that 'so soon as the mouse appeared the lady turned cat again, I mean the parties flew out for their interests and hopes of prey'.[78] In addition, the King succeeded in securing most of his troop requests by holding out the prospect of a descent upon France, and the Court frustrated at least some distasteful measures, especially the bill to reform treason proceedings, by exploiting the conflicting pretensions of the two Houses.

Nevertheless, William was compelled to admit the need for some ministerial changes by the end of the third session of his second parliament, and so the practice that Burnet characterised later as the 'taking off parliament men, who complained of grievances' was carried further by bringing Seymour into the cabinet and the Treasury. The news of Sir Edward's appointment came as no surprise after his sudden shift of position in the Commons during the previous months, but it did provoke Sir Robert Holmes (Governor of the Isle of Wight and M.P. for one of the island's boroughs) to complain resentfully to Nottingham that while 'many employments', 'pensions', and 'sums of money' were 'given daily' to those who 'talk and mutiny in the House of Commons' his own loyal and valuable services were being overlooked.[79] But it is also of significance that it was Churchmen whom the King chose to try to detach from the opposition in parliament. Seymour's appointment, Rochester's entry into the cabinet as a minister without portfolio, and the offer of a place to Musgrave were undertaken on Nottingham's advice. And William's acceptance of his Secretary's urgings was both a mark of his and the Queen's esteem for Nottingham, who was also making himself useful as a kind of minister for naval affairs, and a clear indication of their acceptance of his claim that the Tories would loyally defend the royal prerogative.[80]

Yet in early 1692 William still sought to retain a Whig presence in his government, and so he declined—at least for the present—to accept Nottingham's recommendation of Sir William Trumbull for the second Secretaryship. In part, the King's decision not to give Sir William the seals, along with his successful efforts to keep Russell in his service and the choice of the young Charles Montagu to fill the other vacancy at the Treasury, reflects his hesitancy to commit himself unreservedly to either party lest he become subject to it. William, after all, was a 'trimmer' by preference. In part, too, the King was anxious not to exclude the Whigs from all hope of his favour lest their alienation lead them into desperate measures. Certainly, there had been fears in Court circles as early as the winter of 1689–90 that some of the more extreme Whigs 'were beginning to treat with King James'; in the summer of 1690, William and Carmarthen had been alert to the risk of a Jacobite rising in the City of London which might possibly be linked to the conspiracies in Scotland by way of Ferguson, Wildman, and Monmouth; and in the winter of 1690–91, these apprehensions had been reawakened by Lord Preston's confession that several leading Whig peers (Monmouth, Shrewsbury, and Dorset, among others) had participated in conferences with William Penn about the possibility of James II's restoration.[81]

The danger of an accommodation between disappointed Whigs and at least some of the Jacobites is, indeed, a good measure of the instability and uncertainty just below the surface of English politics during the early 1690s, just as the fact of such an alliance in Scotland at this time attests to the far greater disarray prevailing in that kingdom. Evelyn characterised the English government in mid-1691 as 'very lose and as it were on floats, the sum of all seeming to depend on the issues of this summer'.[82] There was considerable Jacobite activity in both London and the provinces, and the lenience many in office displayed towards known Jacobites was interpreted by critics of the Tory ministers, if not as outright sympathy, at least as if they and their subordinates 'feared that [the Jacobites] would one day be uppermost' again.[83]

It is true that the Jacobites themselves were increasingly divided between the largely Protestant 'Compounders' and the primarily Catholic 'non-Compounders' over the terms on which James could or should be restored, but both wings could join in denouncing the government.[84] Numerous Jacobite broadsides and tracts survive from the early 1690s, and the topics that their authors, often writing in the guise of disgruntled Williamites, chose can serve as a useful guide to what

were perceived to be the most vulnerable characteristics of the new government:
the alleged failure to fulfil the promises of William's declarations in favour of
the kingdom's liberties and subjects' rights, the mismanagement of the war and
the heavy taxes, the influence of Dutch 'favourites' and the damage to English
commercial interests as a result of the alliance with the States General.[85] At least
ten such Jacobite pamphlets survive from 1690 alone, and their effectiveness was
enhanced by their appeal to Country sentiments. Nevertheless, Jacobite plans
for a counter-revolution were based neither on propaganda nor on unaided
domestic conspiracy. Rather, 'all their hopes', so William Carstares was informed
early in 1692, 'depend on a foreign force'.[86] Thus, just as the conduct of the war
was making for far-ranging changes in the constitution and in the King's
administration, so for Williamites and Jacobites alike the unpredictable course
of that struggle was more and more coming to shape their outlook and to dictate
their political course.

Notes to Chapter IV

1 J. Carter, 'The Revolution and the Constitution', *BAGR*, p. 40.
2 *CJ*, x, 28–9. For the text of the thirteen heads and the twenty-eight preliminary ones,
see App E.
3 *SR*, vi, 56.
4 See below, pp. 86, 95, 100.
5 Note also the much more sweeping proposals in the papers of two members of the
Convention, Thomas Erle and Tom Wharton: Churchill College (Cambridge), Erle MS. 4/4;
Bodl. Carte MS. 81, f. 766.
6 Drafts of militia bills considered in the Commons in the spring and autumn of 1689,
which are considerably more sweeping than the bill the Lords rejected in July 1689, are in
BL Loan 29/278 (unfoliated) and BL Harleian MS. 1250, ff. 219–319.
7 See BL Add. MS. 42592, ff. 61–85, 167–9, drafts of and notes on the abortive corporation
bill of 1691–2; BL Harleian MS., ff. 320–51, a draft of the militia bill of November 1690.
8 For the three bills which passed one House, see *HLM* 1690–1691, pp. 251–2, 308–13;
HLM, 1692–1693, pp. 48–9.
9 The electioneering of Colonel John Beaumont (Governor of Dover) in early 1690 kept
this question alive; Dover City MS. 199x, J. Mascall to T. Bedingfield, 12 February 1690.
10 *The English Man's Complaint* ([1690], Bodl. Pamphlet 206 No. 3), p. 1.
11 Grey, *Debates*, ix, 36; *MSP*, ii, 415.
12 Grey, *Debates*, x, 8–22. And see *SR*, vi, 164. I am indebted to Professor Clayton
Roberts for this point.
13 Foxcroft, *Halifax*, ii, 138.
14 Grey, *Debates*, ix, 110.
15 Foxcroft, *Halifax*, ii, 138.
16 *SR*, vi, 85.
17 R. Lees, 'The Constitutional Significance of the Commissioners for Wool of 1689',
Economica xiii (1933), 147 ff. and 264 ff.
18 Note Bonnet's assumption that Foley and his friends wished to set up a commission
to review army musters; Ranke, *History*, vi, 142. And see the heads for such a measure in
Harley's hand in BL Harleian MS. 7018, f. 103.
19 *The Diary of John Evelyn*, ed. E. S. de Beer (Oxford, 1955), iv, 72.
20 Luttrell, *Parliamentary Diary*, p. 406.
21 Verney MSS., reel 43, C. Gardiner to Sir R. Verney, 17 February 1688[–9]. In fact,
neither did so as both found some of the traditional ceremonies 'superstitious'.
22 *CJ*, x, 29.
23 For contemporary reference to Lady Betty's role as a political contact during the
early 1690s, see HMC *Portland*, iii, 452; Chatworth MSS., Devonshire House notebook, *sub*
'Falkland Lord'. See also H. and B. Van der Zee, *William and Mary* (New York, 1973),
pp. 288, 358.

24 Baxter, *William III*, pp. 272–3. See also S. Baxter, 'The Age of Personal Monarchy in England', *Eighteenth Century Studies Presented to Arthur M. Wilson*, ed. P. Gay (Hanover, New Hampshire, 1972), esp. p. 8.

25 For the layout at Hampton Court, see H. Baillie, 'Etiquette and the Planning of the State Apartments in Baroque Palaces', *Archaeologia* CI (1967), 169–99.

26 For William's reduction of the number of household offices, see J. Beattie, *The English Court in the Reign of George I* (Cambridge, 1967), p. 17.

27 NU, Portland MS. PwA 163, [Blancard to Portland], 30 July/9 August 1697.

28 Foxcroft, *Halifax*, II, 221. That William spoke of a Lord Admiral in the same breath as a Lord Treasurer is another mark of his unfamiliarity with English government.

29 Foxcroft, *Halifax*, II, 204.

30 G. Gibbs, 'The Revolution in Foreign Policy', *BAGR*, p. 67.

31 Horwitz, *Revolution Politicks*, p. 109; Burnet, *History*, IV, 129.

32 Dalrymple, *Memoirs*, II, app. iii, 224, and also 227.

33 J. Ehrman, *The Navy in the War of William III 1689–1697* (Cambridge, 1953), p. 259.

34 *CTB*, IX, 65.

35 For Torrington's rebuttal of the charges against him, see Bodl. Rawlinson MS. A87, esp. pp. 4–5.

36 These figures are derived from J. A. Johnston, 'Parliament and the Navy 1688–1714' (unpublished Ph.D. thesis, Sheffield University, 1968), pp. 416–17.

37 J. Western, *Monarchy and Revolution* (1972), p. 142.

38 Bodl. Locke MS. C16, f. 105, to J. Locke, [9 June 1689].

39 See L. M. Waddell, 'The Administration of the English Army in Flanders and Brabant from 1689 to 1697' (unpublished Ph.D. thesis, University of North Carolina, 1971).

40 De la Tour's 1692 character of William; *Archives*, III, i, xxix.

41 Chatsworth MSS., Devonshire House notebook, *sub* Carmarthen, Shrewsbury, and Sidney; Huygens, *Journaal*, I, 362, 429; *Archives*, III, i, xxix.

42 To Sir R. Southwell, 27 July, quoted in Ehrman, *The Navy*, pp. 368–9. See also Dalrymple, *Memoirs*, II, app. iii, 221.

43 Verney MSS., reel 43, J. to E. Verney, 14 August 1689. And see HMC *Roxburghe*, etc., p. 118; Luttrell, *Brief Relation*, I, 568.

44 HMC *Finch*, III, 424, 428–9; *CSPD*, 1689–1690, p. 322.

45 Foxcroft, *Halifax*, II, 236, 244; C. Firth, 'The Memoirs of the first Lord Lonsdale', *EHR* XXX (1915), 94.

46 Foxcroft, *Halifax*, II, 244. And see Firth, 'Memoirs of Lonsdale', p. 94.

47 *CSPD*, 1691–1692, pp. 21, 90, 107, and also 430; Huygens, *Journaal*, I, 531; KAO, Chevening MS. 78, R. Yard to A. Stanhope, 16 February and 1 March [1692]; East India Office Lib., old East India Co. Court Book B40, f. 104; Bodl. Rawlinson MS. C449, f. 18. And see HMC *Fitzherbert*, p. 31; *CSPD*, 1690–1691, p. 553.

48 J. Carter, 'Cabinet Records for the Reign of William III', *EHR* LXXVIII (1963), 97 n. 3. And see PRO, PC 6/2, Irish committee minutes.

49 HMC *Finch*, III, 412.

50 *CSPD*, 1690–1691, pp. 241–2; *CSPD* 1691–1692, p. 353 (misdated 1692); *CTB*, IX, 1368; BL Add. MS. 24905, ff. 5–6, William to Godolphin, 7/17 February 1691; Luttrell, *Parliamentary Diary*, p. 137.

51 *CSPD*, 1691–1692, p. 353; PRO, SP 8/7, 185.

52 Grey, *Debates*, X, 35–8; BL Loan 29/184, f. 359, 13 November 1690. And see Luttrell, *Parliamentary Diary*, p. 34.

53 For pamphlets pro and con, see *PH*, V, app. vi, esp. lvi–lxiii; Wing G498, P3891, S4633, T258; *ST*, II, 308–9. Note also the clause attached to the 1691–92 act for renewing the double excise which barred excisemen from meddling in parliamentary elections; *SR*, VI, 253 (later re-enacted).

54 Foxcroft, *Halifax*, II, 223, 210 (my interpolation), 211.

55 Burnet, *History*, III, 131; Chatsworth MSS., Devonshire House notebook, *sub* 'Dutch ambassador'; Huygens, *Journaal*, I, 93; Baxter, *William III*, p. 248.

56 NLW, unsorted Kemys correspondence, ? to Sir C. Kemys, 17 February [1689].

57 Firth, 'Memoirs of Lonsdale', pp. 93–4.

58 For lists of the voters on the second exclusion bill, see Bodl. Carte MS. 81, f. 654; BL Add. MS. 36988, f. 159; Northants RO, Finch–Hatton MSS. 2893 A and D. For lists of the voters on regency, see Appendix B.

59 BL Loan 29/184, f. 169, to R. Harley, 5 March 1689; *Letters of Richard Thompson to Henry Thompson*, ed. J. Cartwright (Camden Society, n.s. vol. 31, 1883), p. 7. See also *Memoirs of Sir John Reresby*, ed. A. Browning (1936), p. 564.

60 G. Straka, *Anglican Reaction to the Revolution of 1688* (Madison, 1962), chapters 4–6; Horwitz, *Revolution Politicks*, pp. 82–5; R. Beddard, 'Observations of a London Clergyman on the Revolution of 1688–9', *Guildhall Miscellany* II (1967), 416; 'London in 1689–90 by the Rev. R. Kirk', ed. N. Brett-James, *Transactions of the London and Middlesex Archaeological Society*, n.s. VII (1937), 305–6, 307. Cf. J. Kenyon, 'The Revolution of 1688: Resistance and Contract', *Historical Perspectives: Studies in English Thought and Society in honour of J. H. Plumb*, ed. N. McKendrick (1974), pp. 47–54.

61 NU, Portland MS. PwA 299, 27 September 1690; DWL Morrice MS. Q, 534. And see Kirk's equation of 'the moderate church party' with the 'trimmers', in 'London in 1689–90', p. 306.

62 Luttrell, *Brief Relation*, I, 595; Huygens, *Journaal*, I, 225; KU, F. Bonnet, 2/12, 9/19, 12/22 May 1690; Foxcroft, *Halifax*, II, 218, 244. And see Lamberty, *Mémoires*, II, 481.

63 Chatsworth MSS., Devonshire House notebook, *sub* 'May Bab'.

64 Chester RO, Earwacker letters, f. 106, [Sir W. Aston] to Sir J. Crewe, 4 September 1690; DWL Morrice MS. R, 202; Browning, *Danby*, III, 178–9.

65 Browning, *Danby*, III, 178–9; *The Dear Bargain* [1690], reprinted in *Somers' Tracts*, X, 355.

66 For the placemen in the Commons, see Appendix D. The proportion of peers with Court connections was considerably higher; thirty or so of the seventy-five peers who attended at least half the Lords' sittings during the Convention parliament held offices of profit under the crown.

67 *Somers' Tracts*, X, 331; Bodl. Ballard MS. 35, f. 58, R. Taylor to A. Charlett, 5 January 1690[-1]. For a reply, see Wing R940.

68 See the Jacobite *A Letter from an English Merchant* ([1690], Wing L1446).

69 Grey, *Debates*, X, 142; BL Harleian MS. 1243, f. 197.

70 HMC *Portland*, III, 454; Lancashire RO, Kenyon MS. DDKE 6/38 (R. Kenyon's speech against the bill); HLM, 1690–1691, pp. 187–8; SR, VI, 246.

71 PRO (Belfast), DOD 636/13/1, J. Pulteney to T. Coningsby, 13 December 1690; CJ, X, 528.

72 Berkshire RO, Downshire MS. D/ED/c32; DWL Morrice MS. R, 224; HMC *Portland*, III, 459.

73 Burnet, *History*, IV, 76. See also S. Baxter, *The Development of the Treasury 1660–1702* (1957), pp. 235–6.

74 NLW MS. 5303E, ff. 60–1, notes for a speech [by Henry Herbert, late 1690]. Herbert suggested that the 'grumbletonians' consisted of some who were active in the Revolution and others who were not; the latter, he alleged, were more violent in their attacks upon the administration.

75 HMC *Portland*, III, 485.

76 Chester RO, Earwacker letters, f. 127, [Sir W. Aston] to Sir J. Crewe, 16 April 1692.

77 See Appendix D.

78 BL Loan 29/185, f. 240, to his father, 7 November; HMC *Downshire*, I, 390.

79 Burnet, *History*, IV, 153; HMC *Finch*, IV, 18.

80 HMC *Downshire*, I, 389. For Nottingham's naval role, see Horwitz, *Revolution Politicks*, pp. 109, 124–5.

81 Burnet, *Supplement*, p. 339; *Memoirs of Mary, queen of England* (1689–1693), ed. R. Doebner (Leipzig, 1886), p. 31; Burnet, *History*, IV, 111–13; Chatsworth MSS., Devonshire House notebook, *sub* 'Shrewsbury Lord'; BL Lansdowne MS. 885, f. 12; HMC *Finch*, III, 309.

82 *Diary of Evelyn*, V, 60.

83 HMC *Seventh Report*, p. 197. See also HMC *Portland*, III, 481.

84 *Memoirs of Ailesbury*, p. 273. And in general, see G. H. Jones, *The Main Stream of Jacobitism* (Cambridge, Mass., 1954).

85 *Somers' Tracts*, X, 314, 349, 559; Wing E2935, F1119, H309, L1383, L1446, O200, T895.

86 Quoted in Jones, *Main Stream of Jacobitism*, p. 23.

V

THE CASUALTIES OF WAR

1692–1693

As the 1692 campaign got under way, it seemed that the war might be about to take a decisive turn. Preparations were in train in both England and France for seaborne descents, one upon the other. The French mobilisation outstripped the English, yet it was only in late April that the cabinet council in London realised that the enemy was aiming not at the Channel Isles but at the mainland.[1] The ministers, reinforced by Portland's return from the Low Countries, took hasty counter-measures, including the arrest of known and suspected Jacobites—among them, Marlborough. At the same time, Sunderland expatiated to Portland on the unfortunate impression that William's failure to leave sufficient troops in England had created, and James's adherents in the provinces were reported to be refusing to pay their taxes in anticipation of the exiled king's imminent return.[2] But Jacobite prospects, buoyed by their hope that some English captains would join the French, were confounded when the opposing fleets met off Barfleur on 19 May. Favourable winds had enabled the English and Dutch contingents to join, so putting Admiral Tourville at a severe numerical disadvantage. Still, the French commander, like Torrington two years before, had positive orders to fight, the English commanders proved to be loyal, and Admiral Russell was victorious.

The defeat of the French fleet appeared to open the door to a successful English descent—a venture which, in Nottingham's opinion, would assure 'the establishment of their Majesties' throne, the perpetual security of this island, and the peace of Europe'.[3] However, not all were as sanguine as the Secretary. Earlier, some of his ministerial colleagues, particularly Godolphin and Rochester, had balked at the projected cost of a descent.[4] Now, as Russell came to Portsmouth to confer on its execution with Portland, Sidney, and Rochester, 'Shrewsbury and his gang told everybody that Mr Russell had gained a great victory and that there was three lords gone to spoil it'.[5] In late May, the Admiral still shared the Secretary's enthusiasm for a descent. But when the transport vessels for the troops were delayed until late July, he declined to proceed with any of the various schemes that had been mooted. So the French vessels that had taken refuge at St Malo eventually managed to rejoin the main enemy fleet at Brest. And while regiments which William badly needed in Flanders were kept in England for the abortive descent, the French captured the great fortress of Namur late in June and then inflicted heavy casualties upon the English forces at Steenkirk early in August.

The setbacks in the Low Countries, the descent that never was, and the recriminations that broke out late in the summer of 1692 between Russell and the cabinet council did not augur well for the coming session. The King did let his ministers know he was resolved 'to support the committee' against the Admiral, yet he found their projections of the parliamentary prospects very disturbing.[6] Most pessimistic were the newest cabinet councillors. Rochester advised William in mid-August that he might have to accept a drastic cutback in the English contingent in Flanders, and his view was reiterated, with some qualifications, by the entire cabinet council a few days later. However, Carmarthen, Nottingham, and Pembroke did hold out some hope.[7] They agreed that Rochester's proposal to reduce the army and to enlarge the fleet was impracticable and undesirable, and Nottingham went so far as to say that it was a 'pernicious' and 'fatal' scheme. Instead, the three suggested that the Commons could be induced to give as much for 1693 as they had for 1692, provided M.P.s were assured that most of the troops authorised would be utilised for a descent. Carmarthen underlined the importance he attached to this change in military strategy by warning that many country gentlemen now believed that the 'sending an army into Flanders is not the way to put an end to the war' and 'that the war there exhausts the species of the money out of the kingdom, which they account worse than payment of the tax'. Nottingham, for his part, was of the same mind, but he argued the case in positive terms: 'to invade France next year with a powerful army' would, he thought, minimise the loss of specie, and a 'considerable success' there could 'cause a revolution' against Louis XIV and so 'put an end to the war'.[8]

Although William was dismayed by the cabinet council's gloomy forecasts since they 'differ so much from what the state of Europe certainly requires', he did heed some of the counsel offered by Carmarthen and Nottingham.[9] In his opening speech to parliament on 4 November 1692, the King requested not only 'assistance' but also 'advice' in the continuing struggle against 'the excessive power of France'. And while he asked for forces at sea and on land as large as those of the past summer, he promised to hearken to any scheme parliament could offer to lessen 'the inconvenience of sending out of the kingdom great sums of money'. In addition, William announced that despite the 'disappointment' of this year's projected descent, he was planning an attempt in 1693 'with a much more considerable force'. Finally, he pledged his utmost efforts on behalf of the common interest and assured his listeners that as 'we have the same religion to defend', so 'you cannot be more concerned for the preservation of your liberties and properties than I am that you should always remain in the full possession of them'.[10]

The King's speech (translated from his French text by Nottingham) was, in Robert Harley's judgement, 'quite other than his former ones', and it was much applauded. It was also remarked that William's manner upon his return from the Continent in late October was 'much more open than his usual', and he was at special pains to make much of Russell and the Admiral's friends.[11] Archbishop Tillotson was 'the first man the King took into his closet after his arrival', and on 27 October William and Mary attended a service in which the Archbishop eulogised the Admiral and glorified his victory.[12] Moreover, Russell was offered a peerage, though he declined, pleading that his income was not sufficient to maintain that honour.[13]

For all this, the omens for the fourth session of William's second parliament were generally unfavourable. To be sure, the Brandenburg resident was confident on the eve of parliament's assembly that eventually supplies would be voted, but he and other reporters also indicated that discontent was rife.[14] In the City, petitions were being circulated, one against the Admiralty to protest the heavy losses of merchant shipping, another against Nottingham condemning his interference in the recent mayoral election (won by the Whigs). Meanwhile, the Commissioners of Accounts had been busy, and plans were afoot to broaden the scope of parliamentary inquiries to cover the King's alliances and his subsidies to foreign princes. And when Harley heard the King's speech on 4 November, his conclusion was that the royal request for advice offered 'a very good handle . . . to lay hold upon . . . for the good of the public'.[15]

Since the Commons adjourned from 4 to 10 November to await the arrival of some of the many absentees, the Lords became the forum for the first confrontation of the 1692–93 session between the ministers and their critics. The specific question the peers addressed themselves to upon the 7th was the legality of the Privy Council's committal the previous spring of Lords Marlborough, Huntingdon, and Scarsdale on suspicion of Jacobite activities.[16] Marlborough had many advocates: among the Privy Councillors, Lords Devonshire, Newport, Montagu, and Ranelagh had avoided signing the warrant for his arrest, and then Lords Halifax, Shrewsbury, and Carbery had stood bail for him in mid-June after Robert Young's forged evidence against him had been discredited.[17] But with the ministers staunchly defending the initial arrests in the light of the threatened French landing, the malcontents in the Lords more and more concentrated their fire during succeeding days upon the questionable legality of the continued imprisonment of Huntingdon upon the evidence of a single witness.[18] On the 14th, the peers resolved that there should be two witnesses against any and every treason suspect who was remanded, but no further proceedings were taken after the government arranged on 18 November for the discharge from bail of the three peers. Even so, this compromise did not alter the prevailing mood in the Lords, and the 1692–93 session was to be characterised by unusually cordial relations between the 'Cockpit interest' which Marlborough managed and the discontented Whigs headed by Shrewsbury.[19]

However, in mid-November it was still uncertain what tack the Commons would take. Thus, as soon as Clarges seemed to suggest on 11 November that Russell might not be wholly blameless in the failure to follow up the initial victory off Barfleur, the Admiral's friends sprang to his defence. In order 'to prevent all reflections' upon Russell, Charles Montagu moved, Goodwin Wharton (the Comptroller's younger brother) seconded, and a thin House agreed, without dividing, to a resolution commending 'his great courage and conduct in the victory obtained at sea last summer'.[20] Yet on the 15th, the lower House also agreed, this time at the urging of 'the country party' to put consideration of the accounts, alliances, and advice before supply, despite pleas from Sir Stephen Fox and other officials that 'the Exchequer was never barer than now'.[21]

This resolution gave Harley 'hopes (which before were low) that God hath mercy for us', and he was further cheered by the outcome of the first sitting on advice in committee of the whole on 21 November.[22] With the Commons 'very full about 400', the members took up the report of a select committee, chaired by John Granville, on the losses of merchant shipping. This report by and large accepted the exaggerated figures contained in the London petition and laid the chief blame upon the Whig-dominated Admiralty Commission, 'as if they had been very careless in the appointing cruisers'. 'After some warm and digested speeches touching the general state of the nation', notably from Clarges, Thomas Sackville (a kinsman of the Earl of Dorset), Harry Mordaunt (Lord Monmouth's brother), and Goodwin Wharton, 'a question was formed' by Harley and his friends and 'calmly debated for five hours' that the Admiralty be entrusted to 'such persons as have known experience in maritime affairs and that all orders to the fleet may pass through the said Commissioners' (rather than by way of the Secretary's office).[23] Admittedly, the House was not unanimous. Seymour and Lowther justified Secretary Nottingham's dispatch of orders to the fleet as long-standing practice; Russell, Somers, and other ministerial Whigs defended their colleagues' conduct at the Admiralty. None the less, those who spoke against the motion did not choose to divide against it.

The next day, the Commons turned to supply, and it became apparent that many M.P.s were ready to be generous with assistance as well as with advice. Despite objections from Musgrave, a general resolution of supply for carrying on a 'vigorous' war against France was voted on 22 November. And after the official estimates were reviewed in succeeding days, a total of 54,000 men was approved on 3 December.[24] This was 11,000 fewer than the 1692 figure, but the bulk of the reduction resulted from the placement upon the Irish revenue of the units to be stationed there. Furthermore, when the review of all the military estimates was completed on 10 December, the total expenditure authorised was £4,017,000—only £188,000 less than had been requested. Thus, despite the disappointments of the 1692 campaign, the Commons cut less than 5 per cent from the administration's estimates (as compared to roughly 10 per cent in 1691–92), and Harley was left to console himself with the thought that he and his friends 'have done the part of honest men and lovers of our countries . . . against all the placemen'.[25]

By this time, Harley had other reasons to lament the course of the 1692–93 session. One was the fate of Whitlock's bill for the reform of treason trials which had passed both Houses, though in differing terms, the previous winter. This year, the Court's 'piebald voters', as Harley stigmatised them, carried an amendment in committee of the whole on 28 November by 175 to 140 that would have delayed the implementation of the projected reforms until the end of the war. This amendment was then accepted by the full House on 1 December by only a slightly narrower margin, and so the bill's sponsors did not protest when the amended measure was left to lie on the table. Instead, Attorney-General Somers and Solicitor-General Trevor were instructed to bring in a bill for 'the better preservation of their Majesties' persons and government'.[26]

An even greater disappointment to Foley, Harley, and their friends was the Commons' proceedings on advice after the resolution that had been adopted on 21 November. Granted, the second sitting on advice, held on the 23rd, did end with some hope of relief in the galling situation of foreign general officers commanding in the royal armies. The greatest resentment was reserved for Count Solms's supposed misconduct at Steenkirk which, it was alleged, had resulted in the heavy English casualties of that engagement, and some members were eager to press Thomas Tollemache's claims as a fit replacement for Solms. Most agreed, however, with Musgrave that it would not be 'decent in the House to name one to his Majesty', and so Harley's motion 'that the English foot might be commanded by a native of their Majesties' dominions' was approved without any designation of who should succeed Solms. Yet it was also pointed out by several of the serving officers present in the Commons that there were few Englishmen besides Tollemache who had sufficient experience to be given general posts, and it was also observed that many of the present generals had accompanied William on his expedition to England in 1688. In the end, then, it was agreed over Foley's and Musgrave's opposition simply to request that 'for the future, as often as vacancies shall happen' natives should be appointed to other posts of command in the army.[27]

When the deliberations on advice were resumed on 26 November, the conduct of the ministers was the principal topic. Foley offered a wide-ranging review of the mismanagement of the war, and his motion that William be advised to employ 'men of known ability and integrity' was carried *nemine contradicente*. Next, Sir William Strickland and a few others denounced the cabinet council as a 'dangerous and destructive' novelty, but Temple and Lowther countered with the claim that 'there is no government but has a secret council for some matters'. Foley and the Lincolnshire backbencher Sir Edward Hussey responded to this argument for secrecy with a motion that 'all who give any advice' ought 'to set their hands to it by way of assent to or dissent from it' so that parliament could ascertain who was responsible for decisions, but this proposal 'fell' without a division, as it had the last time that Foley had offered it.[28]

The Commons took up the topic of advice for a fourth time on 30 November, and that day discussion centred on the long-awaited select committee report on the descent. The committee's findings, which were presented by the influential Yorkshire Whig William Palmes, seemed in Speaker Trevor's judgement to be directly 'levelled' against Nottingham. Yet the ministerial Whigs, who 'managed the debate' on the 30th, deliberately refrained, as Comptroller Wharton put it, 'from coming to particulars'.[29] They sought, instead, to take advantage of the Secretary's and other Churchmen's *de facto* views, and the Comptroller offered a resolution to advise William to employ only those who 'will come up both to the principles and his Majesty's right to this government'. In support, his brother Goodwin instanced an anti-Jacobite tract by Bishop Lloyd which had been licensed by the Secretary's office even though it seemed to transform the King from a 'deliverer' into a 'conqueror'. But the Tories did not rise to this bait, and Wharton's motion, like Foley's motion of the 26th, was carried *nemine contradicente*. None the less, Palmes's report on the descent did not pass unchallenged. Seymour attacked it as both incomplete and partial, charging that not all the relevant documents had even been considered and that this additional material would demonstrate that Russell and the generals had actually been consulted well in advance about the plans for the descent. Sir Edward's remarks brought angry retorts from both Palmes and Russell, and when 'the friends to the Lord Nottingham' moved later on the 30th that 'all the papers relating to the descent might be laid' before the Commons, 'it was opposed by his enemies, the Whigs; so carried in the negative'.[30]

In this way, then, the ministerial Whigs took the lead in the proceedings on advice, and the stage was set for the confrontation of 5 December. Since Wharton, Russell, Somers and their associates had failed to provoke the Tories by their motion of 30 November, they now sought to press home the findings of Palmes's committee. Somers's friends Yonge and Clarke offered a motion 'expressly levelled' at the Secretary, while Foley vainly tried to amend it to make it less pointed. The partisan character of the motion was further underlined when Musgrave joined Seymour and Lowther in speaking against it, as based 'upon a report *ex parte*'.[31] Finally, the committee of the whole divided on the main question, and the Whigs carried it 156 to 155.

This condemnation of Nottingham left Harley in a glum mood. As he lamented to his father, 'the disparity is so small, and the selfishness of those that attack him so much, and for other ends than public good, it seems to me this matter in this way will not be carried much further'.[32] Certainly, the proceedings on advice were not, even though Temple and other members were eager to offer expedients to lessen the export of coin. In fact, so far as the Whig ministerialists were concerned, the committee on advice had served its purpose. As Harley bitterly remarked, 'those who had made great noise before now let every thing fall, and left their friends as they have formerly done on like occasions'.[33] A few desultory sittings of the committee were held after 5 December, but nothing of moment was done, and early in the new year, the Whig and Tory placemen joined to put an end to its work by a vote of 135 to 112.[34]

As the Commons' deliberations on advice flagged, so the Lords' proceedings in that vein began to attract attention. The peers had begun on 28 November by passing a resolution against foreign general officers, and in succeeding sittings they had moved on to the naval miscarriages. It was to their inquiries on the descent that Seymour was alluding on 5 December when he warned the Commons that 'if you will go on to judge persons without hearing' them, 'assure yourself they will be heard in another place'.[35] Now, Nottingham, aroused by his condemnation below, sought to redress the balance above. On 6 December, he brought in the official papers the Lords had earlier requested from him. On the 7th, he joined with the other cabinet councillors present (save Devonshire) and all the bishops in attendance (save Watson of St David's) to defeat by 48 to 36 a motion, backed by Shrewsbury, Monmouth, and Mulgrave, for proceeding by way of a joint committee of the two Houses. Two days later, the Secretary took the floor in the upper House to justify himself, and in his lengthy speech he added further details 'which more nearly touched Mr Russell, as if he had been wanting in several things that were incumbent upon him'.[36] The Secretary's 'circumstantial' presentation was favourably received in the Lords, and at Court the Queen justified him publicly. Thus, Nottingham triumphantly informed his father-in-law a few days later: 'I was sure that nothing could be laid to my charge', and Admiral Russell now 'has reason to repent of his bringing upon the stage the last season's transactions'.[37]

Nevertheless, the ministerial Whigs' campaign against their Tory colleagues was not yet over. The day after the Secretary launched his counter-attack in the Lords, Somers submitted to the Commons the draft bill 'for the preservation of their Majesties' persons and government' that he had been asked on 1 December to prepare. The measure had two main provisions: (1) severe penalties were to be imposed on any who in speech or in print asserted or implied that William and Mary were only rulers 'in fact', and not 'of right'; and (2) a new oath was to be exacted from all holding offices of profit under the crown who were to swear to defend the government against James II and his adherents. When the bill came up for committal on 14 December, it drew heavy fire, chiefly from the Churchmen. They contended that making words treason 'will in effect make all gentlemen slaves to their servants' and they denounced the oath as 'a snare' that would only 'catch good, conscientious men and will not hold the bad'. Lowther and Lord Falkland, perhaps under Carmarthen's influence, did speak for committal, but most other Churchmen, including Seymour, Sir Stephen Fox, and Rochester's son Lord Hyde, seem to have voted against it.[38] But it was the avowed opposition of Foley and Harley, who disdained the measure 'as brought in to serve a turn', that explains the town's talk that 'the Jacobites and Commonwealthmen joined together' to defeat it 200 to 175.[39]

This new check left the ministerial Whigs in an ugly mood, and there were recriminations against Foley and Harley for 'too great a familiarity' with Clarges and Musgrave.[40] Moreover, when the Commons on 20 December took up the papers relating to the descent (prepared by Nottingham) that the Lords had just transmitted to them, there were renewed attacks on the Secretary.[41] After Russell denounced the materials as intended 'to cast a reflection' upon him, Tom Wharton declared:[42]

I think it not fit for the safety of this government that all things should depend on one man who is not of an opinion for the title of this King and Queen. . . . For my part I cannot act, nor I think any honest man, as long as he is at the helm, and therefore I move you for an address to his Majesty to remove this lord from his presence and councils.

However, the Commons were not prepared to go all the way with the Comptroller. After a heated debate, thanks were again voted to Russell, this time worded so as to cover the whole of his transactions the past summer, but Wharton's motion for an address was not followed up.

Even so, the Commons' vote of 20 December was enough to set the two Houses off upon a procedural quarrel which threatened to disrupt the session. What the outcome would have been had not William himself intervened early in January 1693 to ask Nottingham to halt his struggle for vindication is not clear. But in any event, the King's move came too late to dissuade Russell from making good his earlier threat to resign if he would have to receive his orders for the next campaign via Nottingham, and simultaneously the Comptroller left town and did not return for months.[43] Hence, in selecting Admirals Delaval, Killigrew, and Shovell to serve in commission to command the fleet, William was only pouring salt into Whig wounds. The announcement of these appointments on 22 January was received, so Pepys noted, 'to the declared satisfaction of the Lord Nottingham and his friends', while the Whigs denounced the first two as Jacobites and Lord Cornwallis resigned from the Admiralty Board in protest.[44]

Most Whig placemen were not prepared to follow Wharton's or Cornwallis's examples, though Sir Richard Onslow also resigned from the Admiralty Board in February 1693 and Wharton's friend Charles Godfrey resigned his regiment.[45] But the Whigs who remained in place and their friends in the Commons were unquestionably aggrieved, and their ill-humour helps to account for the parliamentary progress of several Country reform proposals from late December onwards. One was Sir Edward Hussey's place bill, which sailed through the Commons on 22 December. Admittedly, this measure to bar office-holders from sitting in the lower House was only to apply to members elected after February 1693, either to this or to future parliaments. Still, it would have sharply restricted royal influence in years to come, and yet what opposition there was was confined almost entirely to the Tory placemen.[46] Even more ominous was the support that the bill attracted in the Lords. The peers committed it on 31 December by a vote of 48 to 33, spurred by a powerful speech from the Earl of Mulgrave, who, having failed to ingratiate himself at Court and envious of Rochester's new-found favour there, was now bent on making himself indispensable in parliament. Three days later, after intensive Court canvassing against it, Hussey's bill came up for a third reading. The outcome was its rejection by 47 to 45; some peers who had previously spoken for the bill, among them Burnet, stayed away, and proxies provided the margin of victory for the Court. Ranged in support of the bill were frustrated Whigs such as Monmouth, Stamford, Warrington, and Wharton; known or suspected Jacobites, particularly Ailesbury, Scarsdale, and Bishop Watson; the 'Cockpit interest', consisting chiefly of Prince George and Marlborough; and two other prominent malcontents, Halifax and Mul-grave.[47] Opposed to the bill were Portland and Sunderland, all the members of the cabinet council then present, and no fewer than seventeen bishops.[48]

Despite the loss of the place bill, the Lords continued in their unaccustomed, unruly ways. On 10 January 1693, the peers revived their proceedings on advice; on the 12th, Shrewsbury laid before them a bill to require annual parlia-ments; and on the 16th, with Mulgrave in the van, they attached an amendment to the Commons' land tax bill to allow them to appoint their own commis-sioners of assessment.[49] Not all these challenges were pursued, but the upper House did go ahead with the proposals to secure more frequent parliaments that were offered in lieu of the lost place bill. Shrewsbury's measure, which also included enforcement provisions analogous to those of the triennial act of 1641, was laid aside, and a new draft was brought in which stipulated annual sessions, new elections at least every third year, and dissolution of the present parliament no later than 1 January 1694. This substitute the Court did not choose to oppose, and it was sent down to the lower House on 21 January.[50]

When the Commons gave the Lords' triennial bill a first reading on 28 January, the chief opposition came from Seymour and Tredenham, Lowther and Temple, and Heneage Finch, while the absent Wharton was informed that 'your friends were most of them (officers and all) for the bill'.[51] The support the Whig careerists gave the measure, despite 'great solicitations' by the Court against it in St Stephen's Chapel, was somewhat of a surprise, and Harley remarked that he could 'name near seventy that voted for the bill [who] before had declared against it'.[52] To be sure, some of the Whig placemen did support the ameliorative amendments Lowther offered after the bill was committed. The first, which would have eliminated the requirement of annual sessions, was backed by Somers, Montagu, and Guise, and it failed by only 179 to 168. The second, which affirmed the King's right to dissolve a parliament before three years were up, was also narrowly rejected. Even so, thirty-four Whig placemen were reported among the majority of 200 to 161 when the unamended bill was passed on 9 February.[53]

As soon as the Commons finished the Lords' triennal bill, speculation began whether William would consent to it when it was presented to him. But after the bill's passage, the King did not choose to come to parliament until the very end of the 1692–93 session.[54] In turn, William's delaying tactics may have con-tributed to new anti-Court moves in both Houses. On 16 February, the Lords revived once more their proceedings on advice in order to pass new heads against the employment of foreigners and other grievances. Then on the 17th, just when it appeared the peers 'were at an end' of their recommendations, old Lord

Wharton moved to include a head to condemn the Tory-dominated London lieutenancy. Only the ill-timed presentation on the 20th of a scurrilous anti-Tory tract against the lieutenancy prevented further ventilation of this topic.[55]

Although his father's manoeuvre went awry in the Lords, Goodwin Wharton was more successful in the Commons. Taking the occasion of a debate on 14 February on the bill to renew the Commission of Accounts once more, he raised the subject of the Irish army's accounts—a question that Foley and the other Commissioners were only too ready to discuss. On the 22nd, there ensued a long debate on the general state of Ireland; this was managed by the younger Wharton and enlivened by the testimony of witnesses he and his friends had taken care to have waiting in the lobby. The brunt of the attack was directed against Lord Sidney and his protégé, Thomas Coningsby, who had recently been created an Irish viscount and named to succeed the late William Harbord as Vice-Treasurer of that kingdom.[56] When this debate was resumed on the 24th, Coningsby did successfully vindicate himself, but the Commons also voted to prepare an address summing up the miscarriages in Irish administration that had been reported to them and asking for their redress.[57] The Lords, too, readied an address on this subject. Still, the Commons' text, drafted by a committee chaired by Goodwin Wharton, was noticeably more pointed than the Lords' and it included an ominous request that no grants of the forfeited estates be made 'till there be an opportunity for settling that matter in parliament'.[58] So as the session drew to a close, William was presented not only with the Lords' articles of advice on 23 February, but also with addresses from both Houses on Ireland on 9 March.

If the King was distracted by the turmoil in parliament, especially the 'insolent' conduct of many of his Whig servants, at least he could console himself that the ways and means to finance the war for another year had been found.[59] The lead in formulating proposals to raise the £4,700,000 needed (the sum of the estimates plus the £700,000 deficiency left as a result of the partial failure of the 1692 poll tax) was taken not by the Commissioners of the Treasury but by the Commissioners of Accounts. Fearful, apparently, that a general excise might be pressed by the ministry, they took the initiative in offering alternatives.[60] The sources for the bulk of the £4,700,000 were agreed upon by the Commons, at least in principle, in mid-December, when the House began work on a land tax, additional customs duties proposed by Clarges, and a £1,000,000 loan scheme suggested by Foley. Foley's plan, advanced as a counter to one offered by Thomas Neale (the Groom Porter and a well-known 'projector') for a 'perpetual fund', called for the sale of annuities with a tontine or survivorship provision; payment was to be secured by the grant of additional excises upon beer to be given for a ninety-nine-year term.[61]

Despite the novelty of Foley's proposal, it encountered little opposition, but there was some controversy over the land tax. At the outset, the Commons divided 226 to 148, largely along regional lines, in favour of a four shilling in the pound levy, in place of the monthly assessment employed during 1691 and 1692. Then, as the bill made its way through the final stages in the lower House in early January 1693, unsuccessful attempts were made to attach to it clauses to renew the Commission of Accounts (rejected as 'more proper' for a separate bill) and to bar the payment of any pensions by the Crown for the duration of the war.[62] Finally, the bill, which it was reckoned should yield £2,000,000, was dispatched to the Lords on 12 January. Eight days later, it became the first aid of the session to be tendered to the King, and it was followed on the 26th by the bill embodying Foley's 'million project'. Progress on the additional customs duties was slower, chiefly because the rates on a host of individual items had to be reviewed. But by early February, the Commons had completed this job, and by this time they had also resolved that the ordinary revenue (still burdened by debt) should furnish £400,000 towards the costs of the war in 1693.[63]

This left the Commons with £1,300,000 to find, and the House again followed Clarges's and Foley's lead in (1) agreeing on 6 February upon a tax on joint stock holdings, coupled with a continuation of existing duties upon wine, vinegar, and tobacco, and (2) voting on the 8th the new customs duties for a four-year term. The former, it was calculated, should be worth £500,000 over their full term, the latter £510,000.[64] Admittedly, the Treasury Commissioners were not enthusiastic about these resolutions, partly because they were 'so much upon credit' and partly because they thought the estimated yields were set too high. But as Musgrave retorted to such complaints on the 6th; 'we must do as men in debt do and be contented to pay interest for what we raise since we can't raise it without', unless the Court would consent to the floating of a large loan upon the security of the forfeited Irish estates 'which we were once promised should be applied towards carrying on the war'.[65] The Treasury Commissioners were in no position to respond to this sally, since the King had begun granting out the Irish estates after the end of the 1691–92 session, so the Commons went on with the customs proposals.

However, the Commissioners of Account were miffed by the Court's lack of appreciation for their work on ways and means and so left it to the Treasury lords to offer a way to raise the £300,000 still outstanding. As Harley remarked to his father on 9 February, 'we will leave them for one day to show their skills to whose posts it more properly doth belong'.[66] So, it was Seymour who suggested on the 10th that a review of the last year's poll be employed, and his proposal was readily accepted. In this fashion, then, the total of £4,700,000 was finally agreed upon, though the bills imposing these levies still remained to be processed.[67]

Supply bills were not the only measures pending during February 1693. Among other unfinished business were several controversial economic bills, particularly a new bill to regulate the East India trade which had taken up many hours in the Commons since that issue had been thrown back in their laps by a royal message on 14 November 1692. The gist of the King's message was that efforts to implement the Commons' address of 6 February 1692 had been stymied by the fact that the present Company was entitled by its charter to three years' notice before its monopoly could be revoked. William had been warned by several of his ministers that if he did issue this notice, the Company was likely to allow the trade to decay during this interim period; at the same time, the Company's directors, confident of their position, refused to accept a new royal charter if it included regulations formulated in the spirit of the Commons' abortive bill of 1691–92. In response to this stalemate at Whitehall, the Commons decided to proceed with a bill to establish a new joint stock company to conduct the valuable trade. Heads for such a bill were agreed on in early December 1692, but the Company's obstructive tactics held up this year's bill, too. Once more, then, the Commons fell back upon an appeal for royal action.

On 25 February 1693, the lower House passed an address over the objections of the Company's adherents which requested William to dissolve the Company upon the three years' notice guaranteed them by their present charter.[68]

During the closing weeks of the 1692–93 session, parliament did take action on a number of other bills of interest to the government. One was the royal mines bill, brought in by the friends of Sir Carbery Price; its purpose was to protect him from any further suits brought by private persons seeking to block his exploitation of the rich lead mine discovered on his estate on the grounds that he was illegally mining a mineral that belonged to the crown. A similar measure had failed the previous winter in the Commons, but this year his bill was approved, despite objections from the King's Counsel, by the lower House on 27 January and by the upper House on 16 February.[69]

A second was the bill for the renewal of the Commission of Accounts for a third year. This had been brought in by John Granville on 13 January after 'the courtiers and some angry men' had defeated an earlier attempt to attach a renewal clause to the land tax bill.[70] Despite Seymour's and Sir Robert Howard's doubts about the Commission's usefulness, the bill was committed on 14 February. When it was reported out on the 17th, Somers and Montagu joined Seymour in support of an amendment to empower the Commissioners to review the bankers' debt created by Charles II's Stop of the Exchequer. But this clause was opposed by Clarges and others who were 'jealous that the design' was 'either to throw the said debt upon the parliament or else to obstruct the bill'.[71] The placemen did not press the point to a division, the clause was dropped, and the bill was approved by both Houses without further difficulty.

A third measure of interest to the government was the Lords' bill to indemnify Privy Councillors for the arrests and other extraordinary measures ordered in the spring of 1692 when a French invasion had been feared. In its original form, this bill differed little from the indemnity act passed two years earlier, but before sending it down to the Commons in January 1693 the peers made a series of significant amendments. These amendments, which provoked 'high debates' in the Lords, aimed at specifying, and thereby restricting, the conditions under which the Privy Council might arrest suspects. But the peers' proposals found few supporters among the Commons. Most, like Musgrave, suspected the additions as an attempt to undo the habeas corpus act. The bill did survive a first reading on 27 February by 124 to 76; subsequently, all but the indemnity section was dropped, and in this reduced form it eventually became law.[72]

A fourth measure of concern to the crown was the omnibus bill for the continuance of expiring acts, for among the statutes due to be extended once more was the licensing act of 1662. In late December 1692, the Commons voted that it should be renewed and left it to the group to whom it was committed to fix a term. On 20 February, the committee reported the bill, indicating that the licensing act was to be continued for 'one year' from 13 February 1693 'and from thence to the end of the next session of parliament'. Yet even this limited extension seems to have been too long for some members, though the committee's recommendation was upheld by a vote of 99 to 80.[73] Growing opposition to the operation of the censorship was also apparent in the Lords when they took up the measure a fortnight later. Mulgrave, Halifax, and Shrewsbury backed an amendment that would have allowed unlicensed printing, provided the author's or the printer's name was given, and this clause was only rejected by a margin of 26 to 18.[74] To what extent the parliamentary opposition derived from the complaints loudly voiced earlier in the session that the official Licenser, a subordinate of Nottingham's, authorised Tory tracts while denying the *imprimatur* to Whig ones and to what extent it arose from the printers' and booksellers' petitions to both Houses against the Stationers' monopoly is not clear.[75] But it was evident that the future of the censorship was increasingly in doubt, and especially, as one Tory M.P. noted the following session, 'because one side of our House is against any restraint of the press'.[76]

When William came to the Lords on 14 March 1693 to close the session, the last of the fifty-nine bills passed by both Houses were ready for his approval. But two of them were not to reach the statute book, at least this year, because the King saw them as unwelcome restrictions on his prerogative. The veto of the royal mines bill provoked little comment, but his refusal of the triennial bill— though presaged by his delay in acting upon it—aroused an outcry. As Archbishop Tillotson sadly observed, this veto is a 'great matter of joy to his greatest enemies and much resented by many of his true friends'.[77]

Nevertheless, William was not wholly unmindful of Whig feelings and he was preparing a salve for this new wound. The first application of this royal preparation was his offer, shortly after the end of the session, of the Lord Keeper's place to Somers and of the second Secretaryship to Sir John Trenchard (chief justice of Chester since 1680). Somers's elevation to the Lord Keepership, after Nottingham refused the opportunity to make a 'seasonable retreat' from the Secretary's office by taking the Great Seal, was not unexpected, for Sir John was recognised as one of the ablest lawyers of his day and suitors in Chancery 'were now grown weary of the Great Seal's being in commission'.[78] But the choice of Trenchard was a surprise. As late as 14 March, under-secretary Yard could 'not meet with anybody that can do so much as to make a tolerable guess who is to be the new Secretary'.[79] And Nottingham, though he had again urged William to appoint a second Secretary, surely had not expected a former adherent of the Duke of Monmouth to be chosen and charged with the task of corresponding with the fleet.

William accompanied these offers to Somers and Trenchard with some very obvious gestures in Russell's direction. Among the lesser Whigs who were rewarded at the end of the session, the Admiral's cousin Lord Edward Russell was named Treasurer of the Chamber (to fill a vacancy left by Sir Rowland Gwynne's ouster a year earlier) and the Admiral's brother Francis was appointed Governor of Barbados. Russell himself retained the Treasurership of the Navy, he continued to come to Court, and he was even consulted on naval affairs.[80]

In seeking to appease the ministerial Whigs and their friends as a means of bolstering the government's sagging position in parliament, William was at least partly acting on Sunderland's advice. That Earl, who had taken his seat in the Lords in November 1692 for the first time in the reign, had been preaching to the King and to Portland for the past two years the need to invigorate the royal administration and to assure the 'generality of mankind' that sufficient care to secure the kingdom was being taken.[81] Moreover, it was Sunderland's opinion that the King's business had been grossly mismanaged during the 1692–93 session and that William's earlier turn to the Churchmen had been a grave error.[82] Probably he was not eager for office for himself. Although there were recurrent rumours as the session drew to an end that he would be appointed to a ministerial position, Sunderland's strong instincts of self-preservation still militated against such exposure. Godolphin's comment at this juncture was that it would be 'as easy to have the general excise as to bring Lord Sunderland into business', and the Earl may have shared Henry Guy's view that his appointment 'would hurt the King'.[83] What would help William, he firmly believed, was to extend royal confidence to the Whigs at the expense of the Tories since, as he later put it, 'the whole of [the former] may be made for [the government], and not a quarter of the other ever can'.[84]

However, the King was still reluctant to accept Sunderland's thesis in full. Although the setbacks of the 1692 military campaign and the turmoil of the 1692–93 parliamentary session led him to choose Trenchard rather than Trumbull for the second Secretaryship, he was only restoring the partisan balance within the ministry that had tipped well over to the Tory side since 1690—'a sort of trimming betwixt the parties', as one contemporary put it.[85] Thus, none of the leading Tory councillors was displaced; the Whig appointees were named to offices already vacant and the cabinet council was simply expanded to include Somers and Trenchard.[86] Even so, there were many at Court who had little liking for these changes. The Queen felt her husband was being forced to 'court those who use him ill and will never be satisfied', and she vehemently disapproved of Sunderland.[87] Indeed, she took this moment to dismiss her Treasurer Lord Bellomont (a protégé of Shrewsbury) for his 'impertinent conduct' in and outside St Stephen's Chapel, particularly for his share in stirring up the agitation about maladministration in Ireland and also his 'talking too freely' against the veto of the triennial bill.[88] Nor did the Tory ministers trouble to conceal their anger and dismay. Somers and Trenchard were accused of being 'disaffected to the Church' despite being vouched for by Archbishop Tillotson, the King was charged with 'breach of his word' in choosing them, and Nottingham proceeded to block Somers's recommendation of Sir Thomas Trevor as Sir John's successor as Attorney-General.[89]

While the Tory ministers grumbled, some of the malcontent Whigs were little mollified. Among them was Monmouth, who confided to Locke: 'I rather wish we had our Whiggish laws.'[90] Another who felt very strongly about the veto of the triennial bill was Shrewsbury. And unbeknownst to one another, both these Earls seem to have made at least a tentative commitment to a new scheme to 'compound' with the exiled James II.[91] The key figure in this project was the Earl of Middleton, Secretary of State in James's reign and a kinsman of Shrewsbury. Middleton's return to James's service, as the representative of the 'compounders', had been under negotiation since the French defeat at Barfleur, and late in March 1693 he left England for France. In turn, among the promises that James made in his conciliatory declaration of April 1693 was that after his restoration he would assent to a triennial bill, should one be passed in parliament.[92]

Meanwhile, the 'clutter' in London over the new Whig appointments persisted even after William's departure for the Continent in early April, and the Tory ministers showed themselves ready to obstruct any further changes. In May, Rochester discouraged Trumbull from taking up an offer, pressed by Sunderland, to serve with Lord Capel (the former Sir Henry) as one of the Lords Justices who were to succeed Sidney in Dublin, as Sidney was to be made Master of the Ordnance in hopes that his transfer would calm the clamour over Irish maladministration. Again, later in the summer, Nottingham was able to pressure Somers into issuing the Earl of Bath's long-delayed lieutenancy commissions for Cornwall and Devon, thereby undermining Sunderland's attempt to bring that peer and his two sons (Lord Lansdowne and John Granville) to heel.[93] Even worse, the enlarged cabinet council was now 'more than ever divided' so that, as Carmarthen observed, the Queen's advisers were on 'such reserves to one another that we do not speak out enough to be understood amongst ourselves'.[94]

The tension within the cabinet council may have contributed to the major setback of the 1693 campaign. This year, preparations for a descent had been renewed, despite a shortage of funds and over Godolphin's earnest protests.[95] But when news came in May that the enemy's Atlantic and Mediterranean squadrons had joined at Brest, the main allied fleet was diverted to escort the often-delayed merchantmen bound for the eastern Mediterranean out of danger. Even so, the joint admirals left the 400 richly laden English and Dutch vessels exposed to attack by deciding not to convoy them further than fifty leagues south-west of Ushant—a choice that was the product both of their own failure to gather intelligence of French dispositions and of a misunderstanding in the cabinet between the two Secretaries over who was to dispatch fresh and alarming reports of the enemy's movements to the fleet.[96] In this way, scarce cash was diverted to another descent that never materialised; the Turkey merchantmen suffered heavy losses by capture and scuttling, though the majority escaped; and, to cap these reverses, the main fleet was then forced back into Torbay to revictual in early July, so forfeiting any chance for it to seek out and engage the French. Meanwhile, the news—at first exaggerated—of the damage to the Turkey ships nearly destroyed the government's credit in the City at a time when the allied army in Flanders was under heavy pressure. As Godolphin warned William on 14 July, 'the consternation [is] so great in the City at present that it is impossible to hope for any money from thence'.[97]

Despite the disaster at sea and the enforced retreat of the outnumbered allied army after a bloody encounter with the French at Landen on 19 July, there was some improvement during the next few weeks. Granted, there was a great outcry against the old ministers, especially Nottingham, and against the three admirals. At a meeting of the London common council on 20 July, a petition (already signed by over fifteen hundred) was presented by the merchant Peter Houblon; this called in strident tones for an inquiry into the recent débâcle and also into past miscarriages. But Sir John Fleet (the moderate Whig mayor) abruptly adjourned the meeting, and when the petition was offered to the Queen a week later, care had been taken to couch it 'in modest words'.[98] The government, meanwhile, delayed putting its request to the City for a loan on the deficient supplies of the 1692–93 session until mid-August. Then, the Whig-dominated common council, in response to an eloquent plea from Somers, subscribed 'a great sum themselves' and voted 'to congratulate his Majesty's deliverance' after he had exposed himself so valiantly in the engagement at Landen.[99] As James Johnston observed, 'the Whig party in the City, by lending and addressing so seasonably, have restored matters here'.[100]

The London Whigs' conduct reflected the growing *rapprochement* between their chiefs and the Court that had begun with the appointment of Somers and Trenchard. Since then, Sunderland had worked closely with the new ministers, while employing his old associates of pre-Revolution days, Speaker Trevor and

Treasury Secretary Guy, to sweeten other malcontents' tempers for the next session. At first, Sunderland was quite optimistic, provided William would hearken to his advice and ignore the complaints of the Tory ministers. Early in May 1693, he informed Portland:[101]

I have been several times with my Lord Keeper and Mr Secretary. We have looked over and considered the list of p[arliament] men and agreed upon the best means of persuading them to be reasonable. But as I have writ to the King, the strongest arguments are such as they must not use. I and my other two friends hope to let you know pretty exactly what is to be done in relation to both Houses and I believe the King will not dislike the account he shall have of that matter. Sir R. Howard will prepare things for excises. Secretary Trenchard will employ some able men to the same purpose, and so will Mr Guy.

However, even at this juncture there were some who were wary of involvement with Sunderland and his schemes. Particularly notable was Robert Harley's reaction to the approaches Sunderland was making to Paul Foley. As Harley informed his father in mid-June:[102]

Earl Sunderland is ... setting up to be premier ... [and] in order to it driving barters with several. Our friend is again solicited to meet him. I wish he get clear; it is hard to sit amongst tobacco takers and not carry away the smell, though one partakes not. However, care will be taken not to involve us in that inconvenience as last year.

The 'inconvenience' to which Harley referred was, probably, the Commissioners of Accounts' role in the work of ways and means during the 1692–93 session. Now, feeling that their initiatives had not been appreciated and unwilling to act with Sunderland, Harley, at least, was more attracted by the advances being made by Sunderland's 'brother[-in-law]' Halifax, who 'offers to join upon a square foundation if anything forms' in the coming session.[103]

But while Foley and Harley seem to have stood out, Sunderland was reporting to Portland that 'Speaker, Mr Guy, and myself have done a great deal in order to persuade men to serve the King, and I think with good success'. Some, especially a few indigent peers, were to have money. Others demanded special acts of favour for which Sunderland would need the King's consent. Mulgrave sought a marquessate and indicated that his pride would not allow him to accept one amongst a general promotion of others, Bath's wayward sons were to be appeased by a restoration to their former posts, and Lord Brandon (the Earl of Macclesfield's heir) wanted a regiment and a major-general's posting. All these William eventually agreed to, spurred on by the fate of the Turkey merchantmen and by Sunderland's new outbursts against the ministers. In the event, the Granvilles were not willing to play, but Sunderland continued to tell Portland that the King 'may be greater than ever' if he 'govern[s] with as much vigour as he fights'.[104] He put it this way in a letter of 14 August:[105]

The misfortunes of this year have not taken away our courage here ... and I believe men will be ready to give as much as ever if they can have a prospect of good management ... I am persuaded the King may yet cure all, if he pleases. But it must not be done by patching but by a thorough good administration, and employing men firm to this government and thought to be so.

In other words, it would not be sufficient in the wake of the loss of the Turkey ships to buy support in parliament with cash, places, and honours. It would also be necessary to make more ministerial changes. And in the light of his patronage of the joint admirals, Nottingham was the most obvious sacrificial victim, particularly if his departure would bring Shrewsbury and Russell back to their former posts. Sunderland did not spell this out, but Nottingham's name was certainly the most frequently mentioned in the rumours of official alterations that began circulating in London in the late summer.[106]

Reports of ministerial changes were given an added fillip by the widely-publicised gathering over which Sunderland presided at his country house in Northamptonshire late in August. This conference was convened just after Sidney left London for the Continent, presumably having been 'sent for to give the King an account of the present dispositions here in order to his Majesty's forming his resolutions against the approaching parliament'.[107] Those present at Althorp included Russell, Tom Wharton, and Lords Montagu, Shrewsbury, Devonshire, Marlborough, and Godolphin.[108] But despite the gossip that had Sunderland ready to take up Nottingham's post, the King had not yet agreed to remove one 'who had served him longest and most faithfully'.[109]

When William finally returned to London late in October 1693, he found himself at the centre of a political maelstrom. Earlier in the month, the Privy Council had begun a formal inquiry into the loss of the Turkey ships, with Nottingham assisting the admirals in framing their defence and with the Admiralty Commissioners (especially Lord Falkland) in the van of the attack.[110] But this investigation was not sufficient to allay the 'general discontent' that the King and others observed in the weeks before the 1693–94 session. There were predictions that 'some high propositions' would be advanced when the members assembled on 7 November including, perhaps, a bid for parliamentary control of the fleet, and there was talk that some would claim (in a fashion reminiscent of 1677) that the present parliament was dissolved under the terms of the medieval statutes stipulating annual parliaments.[111] Moreover, when Sir Robert Atkins (chief Baron of the Court of the Exchequer) came to the City on 30 October to preside at the installation of the new Lord Mayor, Sir William Ashurst, he took the occasion to deliver a 'republicarian sermon' that 'reflect[ed] much upon the Lord Nottingham and the Church'.[112]

Worst of all, from the King's vantage point, was the despair of the Tory ministers at the prospects for supply in the coming session. Their pessimism, coupled with the Whigs' and Sunderland's assurances, finally convinced the King that 'his case [was] so bad' that at least Nottingham would have to go immediately. As he told Heinsius on 3 November, 'I see well I shall have to do things I do not care for.'[113] So when the Tory Secretary jibbed at resigning, lest he appear to be admitting culpability, William sent Trenchard for the seals on the morning of 6 November, and later that day he reappointed Russell as commander of the fleet.[114]

However, Nottingham's ouster was not enough to induce Shrewsbury to return as Secretary. As Yard informed Stanhope on 7 November:[115]

It seems the thing had been advanced so far by my Lord Sunderland and others that his Majesty had taken the resolution to confer that place upon him. But my Lord Shrewsbury coming on Saturday last [4 November] to the King...it's said he told his Majesty he could not resolve to take upon that office unless his Majesty would promise to pass the triennial bill in case it was presented to him by the parliament, to which his Majesty in some anger answered that he would never pass it, upon which they parted with some coldness. All my Lord Shrewsbury's friends blame him for so indecent a proceeding.

Among the critics was Lord Capel, who wrote from Dublin to Russell:[116]

My Lord Shrewsbury...has often been blamed, by men of prudence, as a person quite unintelligible; and unless he has had the concurrence of Lord Canterbury [Tillotson] and Lord Keeper, I doubt the world will have reason to think so. We have often been blamed as men contented with nothing; and if the church, the law, the fleet, the army (in regard to Tollemache's great station), and the offering of both seals to be in the hands of our friends ... will not give content, what must?

As Capel's remarks suggest, William had done much during the past nine months 'to please a party' which Mary, at least, feared 'he cannot trust'.[117] Yet while some Whigs could be attracted to the Court by places, there were others who would demand 'Whiggish laws' as well. Shrewsbury was the most recent and prominent instance, but Foley's and Harley's coldness towards Sunderland's approaches is also suggestive. Thus, the parliamentary session of 1693–94 began under very uncertain auspices. Sunderland's planned reconstruction of the ministry was still incomplete and William did not know whether the alterations he had made in the face of military and political reverses would 'be successful or not'.[118]

Notes to Chapter V

1 J. Ehrman, *The Navy in the War of William III 1689–1697* (Cambridge, 1953), pp. 381 ff.

2 NU, Portland MSS. PwA 1209–10, 5 and 16 May; *Letters of Humphrey Prideaux ... to John Ellis*, ed. E. Thompson (Camden Society, 2nd s., 15, 1875), p. 151.

3 HMC *Finch*, IV, 232.

4 BL Add. MS. 37991, ff. 5–6, Nottingham to the King, 11 March. And see CSPD, 1691–1692, pp. 198–9; Dalrymple, *Memoirs*, II, app. iii, 242.

5 NU, Portland MS. PwA 1348, Sidney to [Portland], 31 July.

6 Horwitz, *Revolution Politicks*, pp. 131–4, quoting HMC *Finch*, IV, 374.

7 Dalrymple, *Memoirs*, II, app. iii, 240–3; HMC *Finch*, IV, 418, 425–8; Browning, *Danby*, II, 212–13.

8 Browning, *Danby*, II, 213; HMC *Finch*, IV, 427, 428.

9 HMC *Finch*, IV, 440.

10 CJ, X, 696.

11 BL Loan 29/186, f. 196, to his father, 5 November; ARA Heinsius MS. 247, L'Hermitage, 1/11 and 8/18 November. See also Peter Lord King, *The Life and Letters of John Locke* (1884), pp. 238–9.

12 *The Correspondence of John Locke and Edward Clarke*, ed. B. Rand (1927), p. 355. See also Ranke, *History*, VI, 182.

13 *Hatton Corr.*, II, 185; Chatsworth MSS., correspondence, 1st s. 43–4, Queen to Lady Russell, 8 October; BL Add. MS. 51511 (Halifax's 'Holland House notebook'), f. 69.

14 Ranke, *History*, VI, 182. And see HMC *Finch*, IV, 442.

15 BL Loan 29/186, f. 124, Sir T. Clarges to R. Harley, 20 September, and f. 139, P. Foley to same, 1 October, and f. 196, [R. Harley] to his father, 5 November; BL Loan 29/135 (unfoliated), [P. Foley] to R. Harley, 17 September; KAO, Chevening MS. 78, R. Yard to A. Stanhope, 11 October; Luttrell, *Brief Relation*, II, 580, 587, 616, 631; King, *Locke*, p. 239.

16 HLM, 1692–1693, pp. 86–91; T. Sharp, *The Life of John Sharp*, ed. T. Newcome (1825), I, 293–4; Foxcroft, *Halifax*, II, 158–9, 255–6.

17 HLM, 1692–1693, p. 91; *Hatton Corr.*, II, 180. Halifax and Shrewsbury were subsequently struck off the list of Privy Councillors, ostensibly for non-attendance; HMC *Finch* IV, 260.

18 BL Add. MS. 7080, f. 10, 'Timon' to R. Newport, 12 November; ARA Heinsius MS. 247, L'Hermitage, 15/25 November; KAO, Chevening MS. 78, R. Yard to A. Stanhope, 8 November.

19 HMC *Finch*, IV, 438, 478; *Memoirs of Ailesbury*, p. 308; Burnet, *History*, IV, 187–8.

20 Luttrell, *Parliamentary Diary*, pp. 218–19.

21 Bodl. Carte MS. 310, f. 341, R. Price to [Duke of Beaufort], 17 November; Luttrell, *Parliamentary Diary*, pp. 227–31. See also *Archives*, III, i, 298–300.

22 BL Loan 29/186, f. 207, to his father, 17 November.

23 BL Loan 29/186, f. 213, [R. Harley] to his father, 22 November; Luttrell, *Parliamentary Diary*, pp. 239, 241–8.

24 Luttrell, *Parliamentary Diary*, pp. 249, 287–92; Bodl. Carte MS. 130, f. 339, R. Price to [Duke of Beaufort], 24 November; BL Add. MS. 34096, ff. 230–1, R. Yard to Sir W. Colt, 6 December; BL Loan 29/186, f. 223, [R. Harley] to his father, 3 December.

25 BL Loan 29/186, f. 223.

26 Luttrell, *Parliamentary Diary*, pp. 264–5, 280–2.

27 Luttrell, *Parliamentary Diary*, pp. 251–7; Ranke, *History*, VI, 186.

28 Luttrell, *Parliamentary Diary*, pp. 262–3.

29 HMC *Finch*, IV, 512; HMC *Portland*, III, 508; Luttrell, *Parliamentary Diary*, pp. 263, 275.

30 Luttrell, *Parliamentary Diary*, pp. 271–7.

31 BL Loan 29/186, f. 224, [R. Harley] to his father, 6 December; Luttrell, *Parliamentary Diary*, pp. 294–5.

32 BL Loan 29/186, f. 224.

33 BL Loan 29/186, f. 226, to his father, 8 December. And see Luttrell, *Parliamentary Diary*, pp. 301–3, 310–11, 324–5.

34 Luttrell, *Parliamentary Diary*, p. 364.

35 Luttrell, *Parliamentary Diary*, p. 295.

36 BL Add. MS. 34096, f. 232, R. Yard to Sir W. Colt, 9/19 December. Notes for this speech are in Leicestershire RO, Finch MSS., Naval & Military Papers 29; Hunt. Ellesmere MS. 9161.

37 ARA Heinsius MS. 247, L'Hermitage, 9/19 December; BL Add. MS. 29594, f. 265, 13 December. And see KU, F. Bonnet, 13/23 December.

38 Luttrell, *Parliamentary Diary*, pp. 314–20; All Souls College MS. 152, v. 1 (unfoliated), text of bill. And see ARA Heinsius MS. 247, L'Hermitage, 16/26 December; BL Add. MS. 34096, f. 239; Ranke, *History*, VI, 197–8; Bodl. Carte MS. 130, f. 343.

39 BL Loan 29/186, f. 227, [R. Harley] to his father, 10 December; Bodl. Carte MS. 130, f. 343.

40 BL Loan 29/79 (unfoliated), E. to Sir E. Harley, 10 January. And see HMC *Portland*, III, 510.

41 BL Add. MS. 34096, ff. 232, 236–7, 239, 242; ARA Heinsius MS. 247, L'Hermitage, 13/23 December.

42 Luttrell, *Parliamentary Diary*, pp. 330–2. See also BL Harleian MS. 6867, ff. 23–6, endorsed by R. Harley, 'Admiral Russell's answer to Lord Nottingham's paper . . . received from the Admiral's own hand'.

43 Horwitz, *Revolution Politicks*, p. 139; Bodl. Carte MS. 79 (Wharton correspondence), f. 473 and ff.; Grey, *Debates*, X, 293.

44 Horwitz, *Revolution Politicks*, p. 139, quoting *Samuel Pepys's Naval Minutes*, ed. J. Tanner (Navy Record Society, 1926), p. 290.

45 Luttrell, *Brief Relation*, III, 19, 36; ARA Heinsius MS. 297, L'Hermitage, 14/24 February. Killigrew and Delaval were subsequently named to fill the vacancies at the Admiralty Board.

46 HLM, 1692–1693, pp. 279–80; Luttrell, *Parliamentary Diary*, pp. 335–6; BL Loan 29/186, f. 234, [R. Harley] to his father, 24 December.

47 HMC *Seventh Report*, p. 212; PH, V, 748–51. For Halifax's move into opposition and his many Jacobite associations, see Foxcroft, *Halifax*, II, 140–5; KAO, Chevening MS. 78, R. Yard to A. Stanhope, 31 January.

48 HLM, 1692–1693, pp. 280–1; Ranke, *History*, VI, 198–200; BL Loan 29/187, f. 1, [R. Harley] to his father, [4] January. Neither Carmarthen nor Shrewsbury is recorded as attending on the 3rd, though the former had opposed committal.

49 HLM, 1692–1693, pp. 186, 305–6; Burnet, *Supplement*, p. 381.

50 HLM, 1692–1693, pp. 299–302; Foxcroft, *Halifax*, II, 162–4.

51 Bodl. Carte MS. 79, f. 475, [C. Godfrey], 28 January. And see Luttrell, *Parliamentary Diary*, pp. 390–4.

52 BL Loan 29/187, ff. 17–18, [R. Harley] to his father, 28 and 31 January.

53 Luttrell, *Parliamentary Diary*, pp. 405–8, 412–16; ARA Heinsius MS. 297, L'Hermitage, 14/24 February; Ranke, *History*, VI, 212.

54 For Mulgrave's bid on 7 March to get William to commit himself on the triennial bill before the end of the session, see CSPD, 1693, p. 61; LJ, XV, 278; KU, F. Bonnet, 10/20 March.

55 DWL MS. 201:38, p. 38, [Bishop J. Moore] to Bishop E. Stillingfleet, 21 February; HLM, 1692–1693, p. 187.

56 Luttrell, *Parliamentary Diary*, pp. 421–2, 438–43.

57 Luttrell, *Parliamentary Diary*, pp. 446–8; Ranke, *History*, VI, 213–14; Bodl. Carte MS. 130, f. 345, R. Price to [Duke of Beaufort], 25 February.

58 CJ, X, 842–3; LJ, XV, 274–5. See also BL Add. MS. 34096, ff. 294, 298. The principal official victim of the Irish inquiry was William Culliford, an M.P., who lost his post as an Irish Revenue Commissioner.

59 *Memoirs of Mary, Queen of England* (1689–1693), ed. R. Doebner (Leipzig, 1886), pp. 58–60.

60 BL Loan 29/135 (unfoliated), [P. Foley] to R. Harley, 17 September 1692.

61 Luttrell, *Parliamentary Diary*, pp. 311–13, 321–3, 326–7. Cf. P. G. Dickson, *The Financial Revolution in England* (1967), p. 52.

62 Luttrell, *Parliamentary Diary*, pp. 312–13, 355–6, 358–60.

63 Luttrell, *Parliamentary Diary*, pp. 389, 403–4. And see BL Add. MS. 9735, Godolphin to W. Blathwayt, 5 July 1692.

64 Luttrell, *Parliamentary Diary*, pp. 400–1, 403–5.

65 Luttrell, *Parliamentary Diary*, p. 404. See also *Archives*, III, i, 313–14.

66 BL Loan 29/187, f. 22.

67 Luttrell, *Parliamentary Diary*, pp. 417–18, 419.

68 Luttrell, *Parliamentary Diary*, pp. 336–7, 351–2, 372–3, 436, 449.

69 Luttrell, *Parliamentary Diary*, pp. 313, 367–8, 376, 389; HLM, 1692–1693, p. 337; W. R. Scott, *The Constitution and Finance of English, Scottish and Irish Joint Stock Companies to 1720* (Cambridge, 1910–12), II, 443–4; *Seventeenth Century Economic Documents*, ed. J. Thirsk (Oxford, 1972), p. 319, extracting a tract of Sir W. Waller who suggests that Capel, with 'a promise of the grant' of Price's mine, was behind the law suits.

70 BL Loan 29/79 (unfoliated), E. to Sir E. Harley, 10 January.

71 BL Add. MS. 34096, f. 284, R. Yard to Sir W. Colt, 17 February. See also Luttrell, *Parliamentary Diary*, pp. 420–1, 430–1; BL Loan 29/187, f. 21.

72 Luttrell, *Brief Relation*, II, 630, and *Parliamentary Diary*, pp. 455–6, 473; HLM, 1692–1693, pp. 175–7.

73 Admitedly, this is a speculative reading of Luttrell, *Parliamentary Diary*, pp. 433–4. Compare Macaulay, *History*, V, 2308.

74 HLM, 1692–1693, pp. 379–80.

75 For the *contretemps* in January over *de facto* tracts, see Macaulay, *History*, V, 2279–2307. For Locke's views at this stage, see *Locke–Clarke Correspondence*, pp. 366–7. See also *Supplement to the Paper called, Reasons humbly offered to be considered before the Act for printing be Continued, etc.* ([1693], Guildhall 2068).

76 CUL, Sel. 3.238 No. 416, W. Cooke to [E. Bohun], 18 January 1693[–4].

77 DWL MS. 201:39, p. 29, to E. Stillingfleet, 16 March. And see Macaulay, *History*, V, 2316–20.

78 Burnet, *History*, IV, 193. And see Horwitz, *Revolution Politicks*, p. 141.

79 BL Add. MS. 34096, f. 310, to Sir W. Colt, 14 March.

80 ARA Heinsius MS. 297, L'Hermitage, 14/24 February; KU, F. Bonnet, 17/27 March; NU, Portland MS. PwA 1092, Russell to [Portland], 8 May.

81 Burnet, *History*, IV, 194. Note that the letter in Guy's hand (*Correspondentie*, I, ii, 245) was probably a copy of one from Sunderland to William; cf. Kenyon, *Sunderland*, p. 245.

82 NU, Portland MS. PwA 1219, memorandum [June] 1693.

83 BL Add. MS. 51511, ff. 73, 58, and also f. 74.

84 NU, Portland MS. PwA 1240, to [Portland], 5 August 1694.

85 BL Add. MS. 33573, f. 171, W. Norris to R. Cecil, 25 March.

86 Sunderland, indeed, at first asserted he did not want to 'interfere between Whig and Tory'; NU, Portland MS. PwA 1222, to [Portland], 10 July.

87 *Memoirs of Mary*, pp. 58–9. And see Kenyon, *Sunderland*, p. 256.

88 Bellomont refused the pension offered him at the time of his dismissal and worked to revive the Irish inquiries during the 1693–94 session: *Memoirs of Mary*, p. 59; BL Loan 29/187, ff. 1, 92; Bodl. Rawlinson Letters 98, f. 206; ARA Heinsius MS. 297, L'Hermitage, 31 March/10 April.

89 BL Add. MS. 33573, f. 171; NU, Portland MS. PwA 1219. And see Burnet, *History*, IV,

194; Horwitz, *Revolution Politicks*, pp. 141–2; Grey, *Debates*, x, 313; KAO, Chevening MS. 78, R. Yard to A. Stanhope, 28 March.

90 King, *Locke*, p. 239.

91 D. H. Somerville, *The King of Hearts* (1962), pp. 77–9. See also Bodl. Locke MS. C24, ff. 200–2; BL Add. MS. 51511, ff. 71–2; CSPD, 1694–1695, p. 228; *Memoirs of Ailesbury*, pp. 371, 391–2.

92 G. H. Jones, *Charles Middleton: The Life and Times of a Restoration Politician* (Chicago, 1967), pp. 248–54. See also NU, Portland MS. PwA 419, Trenchard to [Portland], 29 August 1693.

93 J. Kenyon, 'Lord Sunderland and the King's Administration, 1693–5', *EHR* LXXI (1956), 585.

94 *Memoirs of Mary*, p. 59; Browning, *Danby*, II, 215. And see NU, Portland MS. PwA 1218, [Sunderland to Portland], 27 June.

95 CSPD, 1693, pp. 102–3, 140; Yale Univ. Lib., Osborn Collection, Phillipps MS. 10074, pp. 17–20, Godolphin to W. Blathwayt, 5 May. For the campaign at sea, see Ehrman, *The Navy*, pp. 491–3, 500–3; A. Ryan, 'William III and the Brest Fleet in the Nine Years War', *William III and Louis XIV*, ed. R. Hatton (Liverpool, 1968), pp. 59–62.

96 Horwitz, *Revolution Politicks*, pp. 143–4.

97 Koninklijk Huisarchief (The Hague), A16–XI G 171.

98 *Correspondentie*, I, ii, 40; Luttrell, *Brief Relation*, III, 141, 142; Bodl. Carte MS. 233, f. 214, J. Vernon to T. Wharton, 26 July, and ff. 221–3, Sir R. Howard to same, 27 July.

99 Bodl. Carte MS. 233, f. 223; KAO Chevening MS. 78, R. Yard to A. Stanhope, 15 August; Luttrell, *Brief Relation*, III, 163; CSPD, 1693, pp. 274–5.

100 HMC *Johnstone etc.*, p. 611. See also NU, Portland MS. PwA 1174, Somers to [Portland], 18 August.

101 NU, Portland MS. PwA 1212, 3 May.

102 BL Loan 29/187, f. 95, 17 June.

103 BL Loan 29/187, f. 95. See also Foxcroft, *Halifax*, II, 170–1; HMC *Portland*, III, 542.

104 *Correspondentie*, I, ii, 38–41; NU, Portland MS. PwA 1225, 28 July.

105 NU, Portland MS. PwA 1228.

106 Horwitz, *Revolution Politicks*, p. 144.

107 KAO, Chevening MS. 78, R. Yard to A. Stanhope, 15 August.

108 Kenyon, *Sunderland*, p. 261 (who mistakes Charles Montagu for the Earl of Montagu). See also Leicestershire RO, Finch MSS., Secretarial Papers for 1693, G. Dolben to Nottingham, 3 September.

109 *Memoirs of Mary*, pp. 58–9. And see Baxter, *William III*, p. 437 and n. 25.

110 BL Add. MS. 17677NN, ff. 288–9 and ff., L'Hermitage's October dispatches; BI Add. MS. 9764, ff. 78–80, 'State of the Case concerning the differences between the Admirals and Lord Falkland', 19 October.

111 *Archives*, III, i, 332; Ranke, *History*, VI, 216; Bodl. Ballard MS. 35, f. 68, [R. Taylor] to A. Charlett, 2 November.

112 Bodl. Ballard MS. 35, f. 68; Luttrell, *Brief Relation*, III, 217; ST, II, 361. See also HMC *Finch*, III, 138.

113 *Memoirs of Mary*, p. 61; Burnet, *History*, IV, 222; *Archives*, III, i, 332.

114 Horwitz, *Revolution Politicks*, pp. 145–6; HMC *Seventh Report*, p. 213.

115 KAO, Chevening MS. 78. And see BL Add. MS. 51511, f. 70.

116 Sir J. Dalrymple, *Memoirs of Great Britain and Ireland* (1790), iii, 57.

117 *Memoirs of Mary*, p. 61.

118 *Archives*, III, i, 332.

VI

A TURN TOWARDS THE WHIGS

1693-1694

Although William and Mary had been beset by dark forebodings at the outset of the 1693–94 parliamentary session, by the time that the Christmas recess arrived, even the Queen was ready to acknowledge that the King's business had gone 'pretty well, far beyond what could be hoped'.[1] Most reassuring was the Commons' positive response to William's call, in his opening speech of 7 November, for a renewed effort against the enemy that entailed *increases* in both the navy and the army. Admittedly, the lower House began on the 13th by ordering an inquiry into the miscarriages at sea of the past summer. But while Clarges advocated 'the ancient way of parliament' that 'grievances may be redressed before we give aid', the Commons also agreed that day at Russell's urging to move ahead simultaneously with supply. Then on the 19th the Admiral's motion for an immediate vote of credit for £400,000 was approved, though an entry was made in the Journal that this 'manner of proceeding shall not be drawn into precedent hereafter'.[2]

The Commons also took other unprecedented steps in dealing with supply. In late November, they accepted most of the naval estimates; in addition, they decided to provide a special supplement of £500,000 to reduce the existing arrears in seamen's wages. This step was intended to lessen the need to keep virtually all seamen in the King's service on ship the year round; this had been the prevailing practice because the Navy Office lacked the funds to pay any of them off.[3]

After these initial successes for the Court, the Commons turned in early December to the army estimates. The government was seeking an additional 30,000 men and Ranelagh submitted an estimate that totalled £2,881,000—almost £800,000 more than had been voted for the army in 1693. When these figures were first discussed on 5 December, Clarges, Musgrave, and Sir John Thompson denounced the projected increases as new instances of 'Dutch counsels', and Harley warned that so large an army would probably bring down a general excise upon the realm.[4] Yet there were many who seemed disposed to approve a sizeable addition to the English forces, especially as the Court could show that the allies were also going to augment their troops by 30,000. In fact, when the figures for the army were reviewed in committee of the whole on 12 December, the Commissioners of Accounts were on the defensive, and a general motion for enlarging the army was carried 248 to 78 that day. On the 14th, the number of additional men was debated. Comptroller Wharton and other ministerial spokesmen had apparently been authorised by William to accept any reasonable total offered from the floor, and in this manner an increase of 20,000 troops was carried without a division.[5] So when the Commons adjourned for a brief Christmas holiday on 23 December, they had approved a total of £5,031,000 for the navy and the army—a figure only £196,000 less than that requested and a startling £1,014,000 higher than the previous year's.

Nor was supply the only cause for the Court's improved spirits. Another tonic was the fate of the triennial legislation brought before parliament during the autumn of 1693. On 14 November, the three major reform measures of the 1692-93 session were revived in the Commons: the bill for free and impartial proceedings (exclusion of placemen) which was brought in again by Sir Edward Hussey; the bill for regulating trials of treason introduced for a fourth time by Sir William Whitlock; and the bill for more frequent parliaments presented by William Brockman, a Kentish squire characterised by one of his detractors as 'of the [16]48 size and cut'.[6] The place bill, couched in terms virtually identical to the last year's unsuccessful measure, sailed through the Commons and was sent up to the Lords on 4 December. This session, the Lords accepted it, though only after amending it. The principal change was to allow the re-election of members who accepted offices of profit under the crown after their initial election, and this alteration was accepted by the Commons on 21 December. But the lower House bridled at the peers' omission of a clause to exempt the Commons' Speaker from the terms of the projected act. At the Christmas recess, then, it was not yet clear whether the two Houses could agree on a place bill whose terms, by comparison to its predecessor's, had already been relaxed considerably.[7]

Meanwhile, the treason trials bill appeared to be bogged down in the Commons; by late December, it had got no further than a second reading. And by this time the fate of the bill for more frequent parliaments had already been settled. Brockman's measure ran into difficulties from the moment he introduced it. The draft he brought in on 14 November stipulated biennial elections. But since the bill was 'presented without blanks' (that is, with the date of the dissolution of the present parliament already specified), Brockman was obliged on procedural grounds to withdraw it.[8] When reintroduced, it was couched as a triennial bill, and on 18 November the Commons committed it in this form. The committee of the whole then voted on the 24th that the present parliament would have to be dissolved no later than September 1694 and it added two other clauses: the King should not have to convene annual sessions and he should be free to dissolve subsequent parliaments before their three years expired. The inclusion of these two amendments, which the placemen had failed to carry in February 1693, was in effect sustained on the 28th in the full House by a vote of 129 to 80. The result was to cool the ardour of some, like Granville, who had been most fervent in advocating triennial legislation. And when the Commons divided on the question of passing the bill on the 28th, the amended measure was unexpectedly rejected 146 to 136.[9]

The loss of the Commons' bill did not quite end the controversy over triennial legislation, for on 30 November Monmouth introduced in the Lords a measure identical to the one vetoed by William in March 1693. The peers passed the Earl's bill on 8 December, but only after they voted 59 to 41 in favour of a rider offered by Devonshire which explained that a session might be said to be 'holden' even if 'no act or judgement shall pass within the time of their assembly'. Obviously, some peers had also undergone a change of heart. Shrewsbury, who had left town to escape renewed importunities to take up the seals, was absent, and other former adherents including Mulgrave, Marlborough, Abingdon, and Bishop Sprat of Rochester now backed Devonshire's amendment.[10]

The issue of annual sessions was again the most controversial in the Commons' deliberations on Monmouth's bill. And once Devonshire's addition was upheld in committee on 18 December and on the floor four days later by 209 to 139 and 222 to 131, the fate of the measure was predictable. Some ministerial Whigs, among them Secretary Trenchard, did vote for passage, but Tory placemen such as Lowther who had opposed triennial bills all along joined with sticklers for the last year's bill such as Thompson, and Monmouth's amended measure was rejected 197 to 127.[11]

Nevertheless, the Court did not have it quite all its way during November and December 1693, and the most noticeable setbacks came in the course of the inquiry into the misconduct at sea. From the outset, the ministerial Whigs and their friends were bent upon laying the blame upon Nottingham and the admirals, and in this they had the vociferous support of the other Admiralty Commissioners, especially Falkland. The other Tory placemen, however, were joined by their fellow Churchmen on the backbenches, including Clarges, Musgrave, and Granville, in opposing their partisan rivals' handling of the investigation. Still, the admirals' critics had the upper hand initially. On 17 November, the Commons voted 140 to 103 'that there hath been a notorious and treacherous mismanagement of the fleet this year', and ten days later the House resolved 188 to 152 that the ships under the admirals' command had on board sufficient provisions for them to have escorted the merchantmen out of danger from the Brest fleet.[12] However, when the Whigs sought to press home their attack during the next fortnight, they suddenly found themselves in a minority. On 29 November, a motion that the admirals had left the merchantmen exposed, though they knew the Brest fleet was out, was rejected 170 to 161, and on 6 December a resolution condemning them for 'a high breach of trust' was defeated in a relatively full House, 185 to 175. The blatantly partisan nature and harsh terms of these two motions, coupled with the attendance of some usually distinguished by their absence, helps to explain their rejection. It was also reported that the Tories had been joined by 'some Whigs', and one of the tellers for the majority on 6 December was Harley's friend, Henry Boyle. Once again, it would seem, some country Whigs had been put off by the tactics of the 'men of intrigue'. And it may well have been their votes that allowed the admirals, as Blathwayt commented, to be 'cut down after hanging'.[13]

While the admirals escaped the severer censures moved against them in the Commons, William made his own position very clear on 10 December by removing Killigrew and Delaval from both their seats at the Admiralty Board and their other employments. But if the Commons were content to let the matter rest there, the Lords were not. On the 11th, the peers agreed, at the instance of the Whig Earl of Oxford, to begin their own inquiry. And in this case at least, the Lords' investigation turned out to be rather more revealing than the Commons'. The upper House found the testimony of one of the principal witnesses against the admirals, John Rutter, who claimed he had brought word to them of the enemy's movements, so suspect that they voted to exonerate Killigrew and Delaval on 10 January 1694.[14] Furthermore, Nottingham's statement that he had received and brought to the cabinet council advice that the Brest fleet was out, but that the admirals never were sent this intelligence by Trenchard, led the Lords to vote an address the next day in which they asked that the members of the cabinet be given permission by William to explain their proceedings. The King's reply that he would 'consider of it, and give you an answer' was little to the taste of many peers, who construed it as a refusal, and Marlborough even suggested on the 12th that the Lords adjourn until they were given a more definite reply. But Carmarthen hastily smoothed over the matter by assuring his fellows that they would be given 'a more satisfactory answer'. [15]

William did comply with the Lords' request, so allowing Nottingham to submit documentary support of his earlier claim. Next, Godolphin and other cabinet councillors explained that they had assumed that this intelligence had been sent on to the admirals by Secretary Trenchard, whose brief included correspondence with the fleet. The upshot was that on 15 January the Lords decided to communicate their findings to the Commons and to ask them to inqure of those of their own number who were cabinet councillors why the news had not reached the fleet. As in the last session, however, the lower House was not about to have its proceedings directed from above, and unsympathetic Churchmen alleged that the Whigs now showed themselves 'as backward' when 'it is too manifest it will stick upon a brother, I mean Secretary Tr[enchar]d' as they were 'too precipitate in their first vote' because 'they thought of striking only at the admirals'.[16]

The new turn the Lords had given the debate over the loss of the Turkey convoy was not the only problem for the ministerial Whigs and also for the Court after the Christmas recess. Another loomed up on 5 January 1694 when the peers voted 36 to 25 to yield on their second amendment to the Commons' place bill, for William was now left 'unscreened' to face the unwelcome choice of either accepting this distasteful new reform or creating an uproar by another veto. Nor could he postpone a decision on this bill until the end of the session, save at the cost of an inordinate delay in enacting the two supply bills the Commons had initiated in December—one to make good the deficiency of £118,000 on the last year's 'million project' by recasting the terms of the unsold annuities, the other a land tax designed to raise £2,000,000.

While William pondered the place bill, the Commons struggled to adjust the terms of the land tax so as to prevent a recurrence of the nearly £200,000 deficiency incurred on the four-shilling levy of 1693. Soon, however, the ministerialists found a more pressing reason for concern over the substance of the land tax bill, for on 17 January an amendment was offered which would have had the effect of obliging the Admiralty to appoint forty-three cruisers specifically for the protection of trade. Harley had suggested such a provision six weeks earlier in the wake of reports that the King intended to appoint 'a select committee of the Council and to join with them several eminent merchants to take care of their trade and of appointing sufficient convoys for the protection of it'.[17] But William had done nothing further, and the ministerialists were caught by surprise when Harley revived his plan and the House approved it 125 to 81. Nor were the placemen successful in overturning this decision when the bill came up for the third reading on the 22nd. Despite warnings that the amendment constituted a tack that might provoke the Lords to obstruct the bill, Harley and his friends stood fast claiming that theirs was a cheaper and more effective remedy against French privateers than anything the Admiralty had hitherto done. When the question was finally put, the amendment was upheld 187 to 123. Thus, the

Admiralty's freedom of action was curtailed, but at least the Lords did not choose to regard this addition as a tack so that by 25 January they had read the land tax bill three times and it was ready for the King's approval.[18]

When Speaker Trevor returned from the Lords late on 25 January 1694 to announce that William had accepted the land tax but refused the place bill, a hubbub such as few could remember arose. So agitated were the members that nothing more could be done that afternoon save to approve unanimously a resolution to go into committee of the whole the next morning to consider the state of the nation. After the doors of St Stephen's Chapel were locked on the 26th, Clarges opened the debate by condemning those who had advised the veto, hinting particularly at Portland, and he was supported by Harley and Thompson, among others. Then, the committee resolved, with only two or three 'noes', that whoever had counselled the veto of a measure which was 'to redress a grievance and take off a scandal upon the proceedings of the Commons' is 'an enemy to their Majesties and the kingdom'.[19] Next, it was proposed that the King be addressed to 'discover' who had advised his refusal, but this suggestion was greeted with a loud chorus of 'noes'. Instead, it was agreed—with only Goodricke, Montagu, and Sedley objecting—to accept Harley's motion that a 'representation' be drawn up to inform William 'how few the instances have been, in former reigns, of denying the royal assent to bills for redress of grievances, and the great grief of the Commons for his not having given the royal assent to several public bills, and particularly' to the place bill, especially 'after their having so freely voted to supply the public occasions'.[20]

By the time Granville reported the draft representation on 27 January, tempers had begun to cool, and Montagu and Temple succeeded in securing the omission of a section asking that the King 'direct some expedient' whereby the nation 'might reap the fruit' of the place bill. They reminded their colleagues that to adopt this veiled call for a prorogation, which would permit Hussey's measure to be reintroduced, would also necessitate beginning from scratch with the many other pending bills and would thus badly slow preparations for the next summer's campaign.[21] Even so, some members were anxious to carry the matter further after William's response to the amended representatation was received on the 31st. Foley and the Warwickshire Churchman Lord Digby, Thompson and Granville, Harley and Musgrave all argued that the King's assurance that he would 'ever have a great regard to the advice of parliaments' was 'no answer at all', and they urged an address for a 'farther answer'. But most Whigs and also the Tory placemen were unsympathetic, and the question for a second address was defeated overwhelmingly 229 to 88.[22]

Still, there was further fall-out from the veto of the place bill. On 3 February, the Commons suddenly revived Whitlock's bill for the reform of treason trials, and on the 9th they ordered it to be engrossed. That same day, the Commissioners of Accounts brought in a second list, to supplement a briefer one presented on 11 December, of members who had received payments (apart from official salaries) from the crown. Among those named was Admiral Russell, who had been granted the proceeds of timber sales from the Forest of Dean (expected to be worth over £10,000) since his restoration to command of the fleet.[23]

Meanwhile at Whitehall, some mid-sessional official alterations were in train. Monmouth, who was apparently unable to restrain himself after the latest use of the veto against a 'Whiggish' bill, was removed from his colonelcy and his place as a Gentleman of the Bedchamber on 4 February. But at the same time, other less demanding or intemperate Whigs were being favoured. Lord Brandon, who had just succeeded his father as Earl of Macclesfield, was given the regiment he sought. And on the 6th, a major purge of the London lieutenancy was announced: forty incumbents, mainly Tories, were ejected, and in their places came thirty-four new men, virtually all Whigs. Then on the 8th, William had a long private interview with Shrewsbury, so reviving Whig hopes that the Earl would soon take up the seals again.[24] Just what would be the outcome of this conference was, for the moment at least, unclear, but Sir John Lowther took the occasion of the reshuffle at Whitehall and in the City to resign his last official post, the Vice-Chamberlainship. Despite the gossip which had named him a candidate for the seals in November 1693, Lowther had long been anxious to retire for reasons of health. Yet his departure at this juncture was taken by some observers as a gesture of his dissatisfaction at William's turn back to the Whigs. At the outset of the 1693–94 session, Sir John had spoken of his readiness to join his friend Nottingham in retirement, and the Brandenburg resident believed that the changes in the London lieutenancy were the last straw for him.[25]

These new indications of William's readiness to favour those Whigs who would support official measures may account for the fact that neither the Commons' inquiry into crown payments to members nor the proceedings on the treason trials bill ever came to very much. The former claimed but one victim— Lord Falkland. He had already had a narrow escape on 7 December when his maladroit attempts to suppress proof of his receipt of a £2,000 grant had aroused the lower House. Now, he was condemned by a vote of 143 to 126 on 16 February for 'begging and receiving' that money 'contrary to the ordinary method of issuing and bestowing the King's money'.[26] Yet Falkland's was a special case; his 'partial and furious animosity' against the admirals and 'his sudden turning' to the Whigs had done him no service with either the Tories or the Whigs. The remaining twenty-three members listed in the Commission of Accounts' report were all able to produce some justification or another for the moneys they had received, and on the 17th a desultory debate on the subject was adjourned by a vote of 98 to 78 and never resumed.[27]

By this time, the Commons had dispatched the bill for treason trials to the Lords, and on 22 February all the peers in and about the capital were summoned to attend an adjourned debate on the first reading. Eighty appeared on the 26th, and William was also present incognito. But in all likelihood, it was the absence in the bill of any provision to reform the Lord Steward's court that determined the outcome of that day's debate. Despite the advocacy of Monmouth and Marlborough, as well as Nottingham and Rochester, the bill was thrown out without a division.[28] A few days later, the Lords also put paid to their investigation of naval miscarriages. To be sure, when the Commons finally got round to communicating Trenchard's answers to the upper House on 12 February, the cause of the intelligence failure still was unclear. But Sir John had said enough to indicate that it would be very difficult to resolve the question of responsibility. And the upshot was that the Lords repeatedly adjourned further discussion of the matter until at last, after all in town had been summoned, the sixty-seven peers present on 3 March decided in effect to abandon the inquiry.[29]

Unfortunately, ways and means could not be disposed of so easily. By early February 1694, only the two supply measures William had accepted on 25

January had been completed, and two more bills were under consideration. One was the fruit of ministerial plans for a series of new excises whose proceeds were to be put up as security for the raising of substantial new loans. The first of the new excises, a levy on domestic and imported salt, was approved in committee of the whole on 14 December 1693 even though two prominent placemen, Seymour and Temple, joined backbenchers in declaiming against the dangers of a general excise on staples. These resolutions were ratified by the full House on 21 December, but in the weeks following the committee of the whole found it difficult to choose among the various loan schemes that were proposed.[30]

In the meantime, the Commons took up that favourite Country scheme of raising money from the Irish forfeitures. On 1 January 1694, a select committee was charged with the task of examining various proposals that had been offered for this purpose, and on the 12th Sir Rowland Gwynne reported that it appeared to be possible to secure up to £1,000,000 on those lands. A bill for this purpose was ordered that day; it was brought in by Boyle on the 24th; and despite Court distaste for the measure, it was committed without a division on 3 February.[31]

There was disagreement in the Commons, however, when the loan scheme to be linked to the salt excise was finally reported on 1 February. Among the various plans the committee of the whole on ways and means had discussed was a twenty-year loan bearing 15 per cent interest, a lottery suggested by Neale, and a revised version of William Paterson's 1692 bank project. The proposal recommended was for a £1,000,000 loan at 8 per cent, with the capital to be borrowed for an indefinite term but redeemable, after an initial period, at the crown's discretion. But the full House seemed to prefer Neale's lottery plan, and so the matter was recommitted to implement the majority's wishes.[32]

While the committee of the whole proceeded with the salt excise and Neale's lottery, the Court pushed the adoption of more new excises. Imposts on leather and on soap were carried in committee the next fortnight, but opposition to such levies was mounting. On 23 February, the report of the leather resolutions set off a lengthy debate, though the only division was carried in their favour by 149 to 118. Again on the 28th, the excise on soap was approved, but only after a substitute motion for anticipating the next year's land tax (that for 1695) was voted down 130 to 113. Even so, the foes of the new excises were not about to yield, and later on the 28th they moved for a call of the Commons in the hope that the return of the many absentees would, on balance, strengthen them.[33]

When the appointed day arrived on 14 March, 421 members answered to the Clerk's call of the roll.[34] However, among those absent was Anchitell Grey so that we lack any account of the debates during the weeks when the Commons discussed a variety of novel money-raising schemes, some of lasting significance. Even so, the division totals recorded in the *Journal* strongly suggest that while many M.P.s who came on the 14th did not attend regularly thereafter, enough did so to alter the House's position on excises. To be sure, the replenished Commons did reject a motion on 16 March to delay the passage of the lottery bill by a vote of 132 to 109, but the opponents of excises were able to secure committee approval for a new impost on wine (to be collected by the retailer) which they hoped to substitute for the soap and leather excises. And on 22 March, they succeeded in the full House in making this change by a vote of 168 to 145, despite the ministerialists' claim that the wine levy would not yield enough to fund the £1,500,000 more the Commons were talking of borrowing.[35]

Another potential fund-raising project also took on new life after the call of
the House in mid-March 1694, and on 23 March the Commons resolved to try to
secure a loan of £600,000 interest-free from the old East India Company for
which the Company would be given a twenty-year confirmation of its new royal
charter.[36] This charter, granted by William on the eve of the session, had not
satisfied those in the Commons who had been urging since 1689 the formation
of a new company. But the King, confronted with the obligation to give the
Company three years' notice if he wanted to divest it of its monopoly, chose
rather to impose upon the corporation most of the regulations that the Commons
had included in their abortive bills of 1691–92 and 1692–93.[37] Once it had
received this new charter, the Company opened its books to new subscribers in
an effort both to enlarge its working capital and to bring in at least some of its
interloping competitors. Yet many of the interlopers resisted the bargain offers
of stock privately made to them and had recourse, once more, to parliament.[38]

The East India Company's new royal charter was taken under consideration
by the Commons in January 1694, with the interlopers' attack being led by
Gilbert Heathcoate, whose ship (the *Redbridge*) had been prevented from sailing
by the corporation's representations to the Privy Council. The outcome was a
resolution, carried 91 to 90 in committee of the whole on 15 January and
approved without a division by the House on the 19th, that all Englishmen 'have
equal right to trade to the East Indies, unless prohibited by act of parliament'.[39]
Hence, in taking up again in late March the notion, first mooted in January, of
a loan from the Company, the committee of the whole seems to have been acting
upon the premise that the corporation would be willing to pay for a parliamentary act to remove the doubts earlier cast on the validity of its new royal charter
by the House's resolution of 19 January. At best, however, the Company
appeared only lukewarm, and after a motion to delay consideration of the scheme
failed 136 to 80 on 26 March, the full House immediately decided not to proceed
any further with it.[40]

Although the plan to borrow a sizeable sum interest-free from the East India
Company came to naught and the Irish forfeitures bill continued to languish in
committee, on 26 March the Commons made an important step towards cutting
through the knotty problem of ways and means by approving a committee
resolution of 24 March for a tax on shipping. A similar levy had been offered a
year earlier by Paul Foley; it is not clear if he was responsible for its revival, but
he and other opponents of the leather and soap excises now displayed a willingness to concede the validity of earlier reservations about the additional wine
duties.[41] On 30 March, separate bills for levying the wine and the tonnage duties
were committed together on the understanding that they would be amalgamated
and that the wine duties would be dropped. In this tortuous way, the levy on
ships' tonnages came to stand as security for the projected loan of £1,500,000
that the ministerialists had originally intended to base on the receipts from the
abortive leather and soap excises.

The terms of the second major loan scheme of the 1693–94 session had been
tentatively agreed upon on 5 March: £300,000 of the new fund was to be raised
by the sale of the annuities, the remaining sum by a perpetual loan at 8 per cent.
But these aspects of the bill were also to be revised in the light of new proposals.[42]
Since early February, when the Commons had yoked Neale's lottery plan to the
salt excises, Paterson had been busy reworking the terms of his bank proposal

and he had also acquired influential new backers. His financial supporters were now headed by Michael Godfrey, a Whig citizen 'well known' at Whitehall and at Westminster, and the group included 'some of the late solicitors against the East India Company' (among them Heathcote), who were looking for new investment opportunities.[43] Just when the ministers committed themselves to Paterson's new plan cannot be determined, but there was little apparent disagreement in early April when the tonnage bill was amended in committee of the whole. The section providing for a perpetual loan of £1,200,000 at 8 per cent was altered to permit the subscribers of that sum to form a corporation to operate a bank, which was to be dissoluble at one year's notice after 1705.[44] Nor were there any divisions on the tonnage bill when it was reported to the full House on 12 April, though numerous amendments were offered then and on succeeding days, and among those passed were several to delimit more precisely the powers of the new corporation.

By the time the amended tonnage bill was transmitted to the Lords on 18 April, plans were also well advanced in the Commons to raise the last £1,000,000 needed to supply the £5,000,000 that had been approved for the navy and the army. None of the levies involved—a quarterly poll, a licensing scheme for hackney coaches, and a duty on paper and parchment—prompted any great disagreement in the lower House. But there was still one more battle over supply to be waged—the struggle in the Lords over the tonnage bill. On 23 April, the foes of the projected Bank of England aired their many objections in a debate which lasted from 9 a.m. to 6 p.m. Halifax, Monmouth, Nottingham, and Rochester were among the most vocal; among their arguments in opposition to the new corporation was that it would undermine royal authority for banks were only fit for republics, and they also warned that it would engross capital with the result that rents would be lowered and trade injured. In the end, what won the day for the bank scheme was not its own merits but the warnings of Carmarthen, Mulgrave, and Berkeley that to remove this project from the tonnage bill would be to begin a dispute with the Commons over the Lords' right to amend supply measures and that such a controversy would greatly delay the King's departure for Flanders and the sailing of the fleet. Even then, all thirteen bishops present, save Tillotson, divided with the opponents of the bank, but the bill was approved intact 43 to 31.[45]

After the Lords passed the remaining money bills in quick succession, William was at last able to bring the 1693–94 session to an end on 25 April. Although parliament had sat for nearly five and a half months, the legislative harvest on matters other than supply was not very distinguished. Only forty other bills reached the statute book, among them several that had failed in former sessions, including a measure for the relief of the City orphans and another for preventing disputes over royal mines.[46] But no one can question the significance of the session's supply acts, for both the amount they were intended to raise and the means that were devised to do it. From the King's point of view, what was perhaps most gratifying was that the Commons had voted unprecedentedly large sums despite the setbacks of the previous campaign and that in raising them the lower House had avoided imposing any new burden on the heavily-indebted ordinary revenue. And while the ministerial Whigs did suffer some reverses during the lengthy session, especially over the inquiry into naval miscarriages, their excise proposals, and their abortive bill for general naturalisation (christened by its enemies the 'bill to import beggars'), on the whole their record was quite impressive.[47] Moreover, they even managed to make a breach in that Country stronghold—the Commission of Accounts. Foley, Harley, and Clarges retained their seats on the Commission in the ballot of 11 April 1694 (the first since December 1690) to choose the seven members for the coming year. But in place of their four old colleagues (one recently deceased), the Commons chose three M.P.s with records as Court supporters and the Whig citizen Sir James Houblon.[48]

It was hardly surprising, then, that the end of the 1693–94 session brought substantial rewards for the Whigs and also for some of Sunderland's converts. Already, Shrewsbury had finally accepted the seals (after earlier declining the Lord Treasurer's staff), though precisely why the Earl gave in early in March to the King's importunities and to his friends' entreaties is still a mystery. Some thought he had finally secured a promise from William on the triennial question (and this is the most likely explanation); others speculated that either the prospect of official profits or the threat of prosecution for his dealings with the Jacobites inspired his return to business.[49] In any case, when Capel heard the news, he jubilantly declared that 'if we lose the King a second time, I think I may say our friends are bunglers in politics as well as in Court behaviour'.[50]

Before the King finally set sail for the Continent on 6 May, a host of new appointments and honours were announced. Seymour (prominent in his opposition to excises during the session) and Hampden (recently felled by a stroke) were replaced at the Treasury by Sunderland's nominee Trumbull and by Wharton's friend John Smith, and Montagu succeeded as Chancellor of the Exchequer. The Admiralty Board was also revamped; Admirals Russell and Rooke took Killigrew's and Delaval's places, and the prominent City Whig Sir John Houblon (brother of Sir James, and soon to be elected first Governor of the Bank of England) replaced the discredited Falkland in a bid to conciliate merchant opinion.[51] Rewards were also to be found for other Whigs in a purge of the revenue commissions to which William now consented, partly on administrative grounds and partly in response to Whig charges that the revenue services were 'filled generally with the most declared Jacobites of the country'.[52] In the meantime, the needy Henry Herbert was raised to the peerage, Harry Mordaunt was given the regiment that had been taken from his elder brother Monmouth, and Montagu's cousin Lord Irwin was made Governor of Scarborough. Nor were the government's chief supporters in the Lords overlooked. The new Earl of Macclesfield received his major-general's posting, Mulgrave was created Marquess of Normanby, Sidney was made Earl of Romney and Newport Earl of Bradford, and Shrewsbury, Carmarthen (as Leeds), Devonshire, Bedford, and the importunate Clare (as Newcastle) were all raised to dukedoms.[53]

Hardly had William landed in Holland, however, before difficulties arose in London over the conduct of affairs in his absence. One nagging issue for much of the summer of 1694 was the composition and character of the group named to advise Mary this year. Sunderland had long been harping on the defects of the existing cabinet council, claiming that body had 'neither secrecy, dispatch, or credit', and the King had finally resolved upon 'breaking' it, a decision which also offered a tactful way to ease Rochester out of the role he had assumed in 1692.[54] In place of the cabinet council, which had swollen since 1691 to a dozen (without including the King and Portland), only the 'great officers of the

crown'—that is, Lord Keeper Somers, Lord President Leeds, Lord Privy Seal
Pembroke, and Secretaries Trenchard and Shrewsbury—were to be regularly
consulted on 'secret and important' affairs. Others were to be summoned to such
conclaves, 'sometimes one, and sometimes another, as they should be judged most
proper for the business they were to advise about'.[55]

However, when the first meeting of the new 'committee' was held in Trenchard's office on 9 May 1694, Normanby—who had the impression he was to
take Rochester's place as a minister without portfolio—quickly learned of it
and indignantly protested that the King had promised he would 'be called to all
councils'.[56] The new Marquess refused to be placated by Sunderland, and he
sought unsuccessfully to enlist Devonshire and other former cabinet councillors
in his cause. At the same time, his first irate screeds to the King led William to
declare that 'if he forces us to have a regular cabinet council, merely that he
may attend, and when we do not deem it advantageous for the welfare of our
service, it is assuming too much'.[57] Yet Normanby had never been faulted for
lack of presumption. And after he managed by a 'stratagem' to be summoned
to a gathering at Trenchard's office on 21 June, it was decided that cabinet councils, as well as meetings of the more select 'committee', would be held. This was
an awkward arrangement which did not really satisfy Normanby. Its only merits
were that he continued to be excluded from meetings of the five and that when
the cabinet council did meet it could formally summon before it departmental
heads and other subordinate officers as needed.[58]

Another leading figure excluded from the 'committee' was first lord of the
Treasury Godolphin. Even though Sunderland had originally conceived of him
as a member of the inner council, he was not summoned to any of these meetings until late in the summer.[59] But it was the proposed purges of the Customs
and Excise Commissions that chiefly perturbed Godolphin during these months.
Rumours of the alterations planned began to circulate as soon as the 1693–94
session ended, but it was mid-June before Shrewsbury, Trenchard, Somers, and
Godolphin actually met in pursuance to royal command to review the two
commissions. The crux of Godolphin's objections to the changes proposed by his
three Whig colleagues was that they were intended 'to gratify party' without
reference to ability and experience. As he complained to William:[60]

I have long thought it necessary for the revenue of the Customs that there should be a
change made in that commission, but I never found that argument strong enough to
prevail for the doing of it. But now for the sake of removing some men that are of one
party and gratifying some that are of another in the Commission of Excise, your Majesty
is inclined to make a change in both.

The specific changes in the Customs Board recommended by the Whig minis-
ters were the removal of Godolphin's friend Sir John Werden and the ouster of
Sir Richard Temple and George Booth (a Whig M.P.): the charge against the
first two was that they had countenanced the continued employment of crypto-
Jacobites in that service and the complaint made against Booth was corruption.
In their stead, Somers and his colleagues proposed two Whig M.P.s, Sir Walter
Yonge and James Chadwick (Tillotson's son-in-law), and Samuel Clarke—a Tory,
but an experienced Customs officer. They also suggested that three Excise Com-
missioners, all men appointed in 1691 when Godolphin had presided over the last
revamping of that Board, be displaced. Two of these men were alleged to be
Jacobites; a third was said to have an interest in the brewing trade. In addition,

the Lord Keeper and the two Secretaries called into question, for poor attendance and lack of diligence, the continuation of the four City financiers on the two commissions: Sir Samuel Dashwood, Sir Stephen Evance, and Sir John Foche at the Excise; Sir Robert Clayton at the Customs. However, Shrewsbury, in transmitting these recommendations, added that 'it remains a question how far your Majesty in prudence will consider them as eminent citizens, and persons who all do or should promote loans, and other services you may expect from the City'.[61] To fill the six possible vacancies on the Excise Board, they nominated two Whig M.P.s, Edward Clarke and Foot Onslow (a younger brother of Sir Richard who was a not very successful Levant merchant), and four other Whigs including Robert Molesworth (the prickly author of the recently published *Account of Denmark*) and Thomas Tipping (a former M.P. who had been a supporter of the Sacheverell clause).

Faced with this disagreement between Godolphin and the three Whig ministers, William was inclined to temporise by accepting Godolphin's suggestion that the proposed alterations be submitted to the Treasury Board. But Shrewsbury and Sunderland vigorously protested. This, they told the King, would mean doing nothing, since the Whig Treasury lords Montagu and Smith 'will not say at the Treasury Board such a one is a Jacobite, such another takes bribes, and so forth'. Sunderland added ominously that 'if those commissions are not changed', then 'it was to no purpose to do anything else'.[62] At the same time, he suggested that the King need not be inhibited by any distaste he might have about those, particularly Molesworth and Tipping, whom the Whigs had nominated to fill the vacancies anticipated at the Excise; he might name others or simply keep in some of the City financiers.

In the end, William was won round. All the City men were retained on the new commissions issued early in August 1694, and the incumbents to whom the Whigs had most objected were displaced. The six vacancies were supplied by Samuel Clarke, John Danvers, and by the four Whig M.P.s, who would now be able to speak for the revenue services in the Commons.[63] And to add to Godolphin's 'mortification' at these changes, September brought a new encroachment upon Treasury patronage at the first lord's personal expense.[64] This time the M.P. to be rewarded was Guy's Yorkshire colleague, William Palmes, in the shape of his son's appointment to a newly-vacant Tellership of the Exchequer. The nomination of Guy Palmes was warmly endorsed by Sunderland, Speaker Trevor (who asserted that 'so much does he depend upon' the elder Palmes's 'assistance in the House of Commons that he hopes no importunity will prevail' against his son), and the Whigs. With this backing, William did not hesitate, and Godolphin had to be satisfied with a promise that the next Tellership to fall would go to his son.[65]

While the new ministers and their allies were consolidating their hold on office and provoking polemical complaints of the intrusion of 'the fanatical and Whiggish tribe' from outraged Churchmen, the 1694 campaign brought a distinct improvement in allied fortunes.[66] Thanks to the legislation of the previous session, English government finances were in better shape than they had been since the beginning of the war. The subscription to the lottery was nearly filled by the end of May, and the £1,200,000 for the Bank of England was rapidly pledged in June once the ground rules for setting up that corporation had been ironed out in the Privy Council.[67] The success of these projects led to a sharp decline in the discount rate on the sizeable amount of Exchequer tallies in circulation, and simultaneously the troop augmentation voted the previous winter had a visible effect in the Low Countries.

The new military balance in the Low Countries was signalled by the recapture of Huy in late September 1694; in effect, this meant that the allied forces had recovered much of the ground lost during the two previous years.[68] Moreover, the naval war was taking on a new face. The year 1694 saw the last of the many projects for a descent; after delays had given the French ample time to strengthen their defences at Brest, an amphibious assault failed miserably in early June. But against the death of the adventuresome Tollemache before Brest and the heavy toll of merchant shipping taken again this summer by the Dunkirk privateers must be set William's success in finally getting the allied fleet to the Mediterranean and then in keeping it there through the following year despite the hesitations of some of the ministers and despite Russell's own reservations. This was an important strategic departure, and its significance is suggested by the French withdrawal from Catalonia after the allied fleet made its appearance before Barcelona.[69]

Buoyed by the allies' seizure of the initiative in the war and by their own success in finding places for key parliament men, Sunderland and the Whig ministers were quite optimistic about the coming session of parliament. When Sunderland came up to town in September 1694, he did observe that 'all the art possible is used by some people to engage others in their ill humour', with 'the bank, the alliances, Dutch counsels, and the money which goes abroad' their chief topics. Some of these questions were also listed as items to exploit in one of the few surviving sets of instructions sent during the reign from St Germain to the small band of crypto-Jacobites who sat in parliament. The author of this memorandum also urged opposition to excises and to the dispatch of the fleet to the Mediterranean, and he suggested in addition 'that such popular bills be pressed as is supposed the P[rince] of O[range] will not pass'.[70] Still, measures were in hand to isolate the Jacobites and the irredeemable malcontents, and in late August Shrewsbury and Godolphin had opened conversations with Foley and Harley in the hope of 'prevent[ing] miscarriages in parliament, especially relating to excises'.[71] Overall, Sunderland was confident that 'it will be much easier this year than it was the last', and his prediction of mid-September was echoed by Trenchard two months later on the eve of the session.[72]

The only cloud on the horizon when the 1694–95 session opened on 13 November, at least in the view of James Vernon (once the Duke of Monmouth's secretary and now Shrewsbury's principal assistant), was the 'grumbletonians'' denunciations of the administration's handling of the Lancashire 'plot'. Indeed, the Commons' first sitting was largely taken up by this topic. Howe, Seymour, Musgrave, and Thompson sharply criticised the activities of Treasury Solicitor Aaron Smith 'and his myrmidons', and Foley and Harley were also upset over the 'scandalously vile' management of an affair which some suspected had been concocted either to strengthen the Whigs' electoral position in Lancashire or else to benefit the holders (among them Guise) of a royal patent for the discovery of concealed lands.[73] The arrests of a number of Lancashire and Cheshire gentry, most of them Catholics, had been authorised in July 1694 by the two Secretaries of State and the Lord Keeper, sitting jointly as the 'committee', on the strength of informations of a Jacobite conspiracy provided by three witnesses.[74] The principal witness was John Taafe, a former Catholic priest, who aspired to emulate Oates. But after Taafe failed to receive the sizeable reward he had expected, he secretly came to terms with the accused and then wrecked the prosecution's case at the trials at Manchester in October by swearing that he and the other witnesses had invented the original informations.

Nevertheless, the ministers were ready to defend their own proceedings in the Lancashire affair, especially because they were confident that Taafe had been suborned. So it was decided to take up the gauntlet flung down on the 13th in order to demonstrate, as Vernon put it, 'that those to whom the informations were brought have done but their duty'.[75] On the 22nd, the 'courtiers' carried by 117 to 102 a motion to summon both the defendants and Aaron Smith with his witnesses to the Bar for questioning. This show of determination appeared to quieten those who had hoped to exploit the handling of the plot, and when the Commons adjourned for Christmas exactly a month later the inquiry did not seem likely to be pressed to a conclusion unless the ministerialists chose to do so.[76]

In other respects, too, the course of the 1694–95 session up to the Christmas recess appeared to justify the optimistic forecasts of the King's advisers. Even though the Commons did not actually get down to work until 19 November, by 4 December the estimates for 1695 had been examined and approved. The relative rapidity of these proceedings owed much to that 'better posture' of military and naval affairs to which William alluded in his opening speech; it also reflected the renewed confidence of many members that a secure and advantageous peace —rather than the stiff conditions Louis had hitherto offered—could be gained by the vigorous pursuit of the war for another campaign or two.[77] There was, in fact, only one division over supply. That division, which, according to Harley, 'the Court forced upon us', came on 23 November, and the ministerialists carried it 157 to 98.[78] After this show of strength, the King's spokesmen did not strenuously resist some paring of the naval estimates, and on the 30th the Commons approved a total of £2,383,000 of the £2,603,000 originally requested. Similarly, when Foley—much to Clarges's disgust—proposed a lump sum of £2,500,000 for the army on 1 December, in lieu of a detailed review of the £2,705,000 estimate, Wharton immediately closed with this offer. Thus, Clarges could do little but murmur about 'corruption' when the full House, with only a few 'noes', confirmed this arrangement on the 4th.[79]

The Commons were also able to make considerable headway in the always difficult search for ways and means. In July 1694, Sunderland had reminded William that it is 'fit that next sessions all proposals of money' should 'come from the Court and not from country gentlemen', and later in the summer Godolphin seems to have been busy reviewing various possible projects.[80] Apparently, it was intended to raise the bulk of the supplies by another land tax and by anticipating a portion of the ordinary revenue, with the rest to be made up by new excises (possibly linked to another large loan).[81] But 'notions' such as these did not evoke much enthusiasm from Foley and Harley, and to avoid 'exorbitant excises and funds which will quickly destroy all the landed men of England' they formulated an alternative scheme. This was to finance the whole of the estimates by voting a one-shilling tax on land for a ten-year term, raising a loan on this security, and using the proceeds of that loan to mint special silver tallies in large denominations which would circulate with government backing and so help to relieve the shortage of specie.[82]

The outlines of Foley's and Harley's project were already being publicly discussed when the 1694-95 session began, and late in November Harley was writing to absent colleagues urging them to come up and support it. Hence, when Foley broached this scheme on 7 December in the first sitting of the committee of the whole on ways and means, the ministers had already had notice of it and had decided to oppose it, probably because they did not want to mortgage so far in advance the only reasonably effective direct tax in the government's repertory.[83] None the less, the ministerial leaders in the Commons 'thought fit to let it fall rather as if it had dropped than that it was thrown aside', on the view that their own suggestions would fare better 'if they took those along with them who were desirous to pause a little upon it [Foley's plan] without any ill meaning'.[84]

To allow time for the Commons to ponder Foley's scheme to hypothecate a portion of the land tax, the ministerialists urged the Commons to deal first with the King's request for the renewal of the duties of tunnage and poundage. These customs had been granted for four years in early 1690 as part of the settlement of the ordinary revenue, and that grant was due to expire on 24 December 1694. After the House agreed without dispute on 11 December upon a renewal, the length of the new grant and the question of whether there should be 'a little space to intervene between their expiring and being renewed, for asserting the people's right to grant them', were discussed.[85] On the 14th, it was decided—despite Seymour's arguments for a three-month interval—that tunnage and poundage should be renewed after only a single day's lapse, and it was also agreed that they should be given for five more years. The resolutions of this day did not indicate how these revenues were to be spent, but it was generally understood that some portion of them would be committed to paying off a loan to help finance the next campaign. William may still have preferred a grant of all the revenue for life, but, so Vernon reported, 'his Majesty has been told that the customs being thus given for a term certain makes it a better fund for loans than if it were for his life'.[86]

By this time, too, the Commons had agreed without dividing on 12 December not to proceed with Foley's proposal but instead to pass a conventional four-shilling levy on land for a one-year term. This, it was hoped, could be made to yield a full £2,000,000, despite the deficiencies of the past two years, provided more effective procedures were devised to assess 'personal estates'. Besides the land tax, the Commons discussed three other projects in committee during succeeding days, though without coming to any firm decision. One was Neale's suggestion of another lottery to be secured upon levies on soap and tobacco; the other two both involved the creation of 'something like a new bank'—one (put forward by Dr Nicholas Barbon) to be secured upon a revised hearth tax, the other to be funded by a duty on coal. Thus, after the presentation of the land tax bill to the Commons on 20 December and the dispatch of the tunnage and poundage bill to the Lords on the 21st, it appeared that the lower House had only to fix the sum to be borrowed on the customs and to select one or a combination of the schemes already under consideration in order to complete the year's deliberations on ways and means.[87]

By the Christmas recess, the Commons had also disposed, for the most part, of the three reform measures that now seemed hardy perennials—the place, treason trials, and triennial bills. The first was committed on 28 November by a vote of 138 to 116, with Foley telling for the majority. By mid-December it was ready to be reported, though, as Vernon remarked, the bill was drafted 'so carelessly as if people were unconcerned how it was drawn, not thinking it would be passed at last'.[88] The second was further advanced. After the committee of the whole voted 141 to 124 on 8 December to reject a clause to postpone until the war's end the implementation of the reforms in treason cases, the bill was sent up to the Lords on the 19th without further division.[89]

Of the three reform bills, the Commons devoted most attention to the triennial measure brought in by Harley on 21 November, a day after he had a long conference with Shrewsbury.[90] Harley's draft neither required annual sessions nor precluded early dissolutions, and the only point that divided the Commons was the date by which the present parliament must be dissolved. On 3 December, the committee of the whole decided upon 1 November 1695. But before the bill was reported on the 10th, an amendment was offered in committee to set back the terminal date to November 1696, and in a division marked by 'a great mixture of parties' this alteration was rejected 159 to 156.[91] Most ministerialists seem to have supported the later date, but Comptroller Wharton and some of his intimates (particularly Lord Winchester and Harry Mordaunt) voted for 1695 on the grounds that the Whigs were likely to gain by holding a new general election as soon as possible. In turn, the committee's vote of the 10th was reversed by the full House when the bill was read a third time. Because 'the House was not so full' and because 'those who stickled' earlier 'were grown passive now and took no pains to make converts', the Commons voted 155 to 147 that the present parliament could not sit beyond November 1696, so leaving it in 'the King's power to add a year to them or not'.[92]

The Commons' unwonted progress on supply and ways and means, coupled with the reports that William was likely to pass the triennial bill should the Lords approve it, lends colour to Burnet's view that a tacit bargain had been struck, perhaps as early as Shrewsbury's return to business in March 1694. This impression is reinforced by contemporary comment; as Blathwayt remarked to deputy Army Paymaster Richard Hill on 17 December 1694, 'our affairs go on merrily with relation to the land forces, for which the gentlemen will have the triennial bill'.[93] It is true that not all the government's critics had been silenced nor had Foley and Harley been 'corrupted'. Actually, Harley came away from the interview to which Shrewsbury had summoned him on 20 November with the sense that the ministerial Whigs were not so much interested in 'amendment' as 'to get men in, as they call it'.[94] Then, too, Foley and Harley had pressed hard for their own land tax scheme. And along with many other M.P.s, they still harboured a deep 'jealousy' of excises which, so Vernon predicted in mid-December, the Commons 'are not like to be brought to, but upon the failure of all other means'.[95]

Although the various Whig elements in the lower House remained at odds on some questions, there had been a noticeable easing of tensions between the ministerial group and the Foley–Harley squadron during the first phase of the 1694–95 session. In turn, the prospects of a further *rapprochement* were only enhanced by the Lords' proceedings on Harley's triennial bill. Despite some efforts, backed by both Devonshire and the Jacobite Ailesbury, to restore the 1695 terminal date, the measure was carried without any changes or any divisions by 19 December. Thus, when the King came to the Lords on the 22nd to accept the tunnage and poundage bill, the triennial bill was also submitted to him, and 'a great hum' of approval from the many Commons' members in attendance greeted William's assent to both.[96]

By late 1694, then, it seemed that the King, with Sunderland's assistance, had successfully carried off that 'dangerous experiment' against which Halifax had warned him in January 1690.[97] Having found the Tory ministers wanting in their capacity to assure parliamentary supply after the setbacks of the 1692 and 1693 campaigns. William had reluctantly and hesitantly turned back to the Whigs. And though there had been difficulties at first, not least with Shrewsbury, the outcome of the 1693–94 session was much better than the King had anticipated, and the financial measures approved by parliament had in turn contributed to the changed face of the war wrought by the 1694 campaign. At the same time, the choice of new ministers had been accompanied by the adoption of innovations in government funding (particularly the Bank of England), in naval strategy, and, now, in crown–parliamentary relations with the passage of the triennial bill. Whether these new departures in men and measures would suffice to bring victory against France in the continuing war remained to be determined. But for the moment, the King's and his subjects' attention was distracted by an unexpected calamity.

Notes to Chapter VI

1 *Memoirs of Mary, Queen of England* (1689–1693), ed. R. Doebner (Leipzig, 1886), p. 61.
2 *CJ*, XI, 7. And see Grey, *Debates*, X, 311–17; HMC *Seventh Report*, pp. 214, 215; *CTB*, X, 394–5.
3 HLM, 1693–1695, pp. 12–29; All Souls College MS. 152, vol. 1 (unfoliated), notes on naval supply, November 1693. See also J. Ehrman, *The Navy in the War of William III 1689–1697* (Cambridge, 1953), pp. 470–2.
4 Grey, *Debates*, X, 339–44; HMC *Seventh Report*, p. 217; HMC *Portland*, III, 548.
5 Grey, *Debates*, X, 358–64 (misdated 11 December); HMC *Seventh Report*, pp. 219–20; Ranke, *History*, VI, 224–5, 227.
6 HMC *Downshire*, I, 505.
7 HLM, 1693–1695, pp. 330–1.
8 *CJ*, XI, 3. And see Ranke, *History*, VI, 219–20; BL Add. MS. 42593, f. 9, text.
9 Grey, *Debates*, X, 329–31; HMC *Seventh Report*, p. 216; Ranke, *History*, VI, 223, 224; KAO, Chevening MS. 78, J. Vernon to A. Stanhope, 5 December.
10 HLM, 1693–1695, pp. 51–2; HMC *Hastings*, II, 232, 233, 234: ARA Heinsius MS. 297, L'Hermitage, 5/15 December; HMC *Seventh Report*, pp. 216, 218, 219.
11 Grey, *Debates*, X, 368–73; ARA Heinsius MS. 297, L'Hermitage, 19/29 December; KU, F. Bonnet, 22 December/1 January; BL Loan 29/187, f. 212, [Sir E. to A. Harley], 19 December.
12 *CJ*, XI, 5; Grey, *Debates*, X, 319–29; HMC *Seventh Report*, pp. 215, 216; Ranke, *History*, VI, 221–2; ARA Heinsius MS. 297, L'Hermitage, 21 November/1 December; Burnet, *History*, IV, 225.
13 BL Add. MS. 56241 (unfoliated), R. Hill, 8 December. And see Grey, *Debates*, X, 333–7, 344–8; HMC *Seventh Report*, pp. 216, 217–18; BL Add. MS. 17677 NN, ff. 364–5, 368, L'Hermitage, 1/11 and 8/18 December; BL Loan 29/27, bundle 1, Harley's draft speech of 22 November.
14 HMC *Hastings*, II, 234; HLM, 1693–1695, p. 101; BL Add. MS. 17677 OO, f. 155, L'Hermitage, 16/26 January.
15 *LJ*, XV, 341; BL Add. MS. 29574, f. 264, C. to Viscount Hatton, 18 January.
16 CUL Selden 3.238 No. 416, W. Cooke to [E. Bohun], 18 January. And see Horwitz, *Revolution Politicks*, p. 148; BL Add. MS. 29574, f. 265, C. to Viscount Hatton, 23 January.
17 KAO, Chevening MS. 78, J. Vernon to A. Stanhope, 21 November and 5 December 1693. See also *CSPD*, 1693, p. 408; J. Johnston, 'Parliament and the Protection of Trade 1689–1694', *Mariners' Mirror* LVII (1971), 399–413.

18 Ranke, *History*, VI, 234–5; BL Add. MS. 17677 OO, f. 161, L'Hermitage, 23 January/2 February. For merchant complaints later in the session, see CJ, XI, 154 ff.

19 CJ, XI, 70; Grey, *Debates*, X, 375–7; Ranke, *History*, VI, 236, 237; ARA Heinsius MS. 348, L'Hermitage, 26 January/5 February (noting a citation in the debate of Molesworth's *Account*); KAO, Chevening MS. 78, R. Yard to A. Stanhope, 30 January.

20 CJ, XI, 71; Grey, *Debates*, X, 377–9.

21 CJ, XI, 71–2; Ranke, *History*, VI, 236–7.

22 CJ, X, 75; Grey, *Debates*, X, 382–6; KU, F. Bonnet, 2/12 February.

23 For Russell's grant, see CTB, X, 412.

24 CSPD, 1694–1695, p. 21; Luttrell, *Brief Relation*, III, 265, 266, 267, 269; FSL Newdigate newsletters 2287, 13 February; Ranke, *History*, VI, 240.

25 HMC *Seventh Report*, p. 213; KU, F. Bonnet, 16/26 February. Lowther did, however, continue to support supply measures in the Commons.

26 CJ, XI, 98; Grey, *Debates*, X, 348–57.

27 BL Add. MS. 56241 (unfoliated). W. Blathwayt to R. Hill, 16 February; KU, F. Bonnet, 20 February/2 March.

28 BL Add. MS. 17677 OO, f. 192, L'Hermitage, 27 February/9 March; Bodl. Carte MS. 130, f. 347, R. Price to [Duke of Beaufort], 1 March.

29 Trenchard had given his answer orally on 23 January. BL Add. MS. 17677 OO, f. 162, L'Hermitage, 23 January/2 February; HLM, 1693–1695, pp. 102–3.

30 Ranke, *History* VI, 227–8; HMC *Seventh Report*, p. 219. See also CSPD, 1693, p. 423.

31 See also *Proposals for Raising a Million of Money out of the Forfeited Estates in Ireland: Together, with the Answer of the Irish to the same, And a Reply thereto* (1694, BL E1973 No. 5).

32 Ranke, *History*, VI, 231, 238; PRO, SP 32/5 No. 46 (Paterson's proposal summed up in Neale's paper). For Hugh Chamberlen's land back project, see CJ, XI, 22, 80.

33 BL Add. MS. 17677 OO, f. 194, L'Hermitage, 2/12 March; Bodl. Carte MS. 130, f. 348, f. 347, R. Price to [Duke of Beaufort], 1 March.

34 KU, F. Bonnet, 14/24 March.

35 Ranke, *History*, VI, 244–5; BL Add. MS. 17677 OO, f. 210, L'Hermitage, 20/30 March; Huygens, *Journaal*, II, 330–1.

36 BL Add. MS. 17677 OO, f. 63, van Citters, 23 March/2 April.

37 CSPD, 1693, pp. 108, 323–4, 389; CSPD, 1694–1695, p. 317: *Somers' Tracts*, X, 629–33.

38 D. W. Jones, 'London Overseas-Merchant Groups at the End of the Seventeenth Century and the Moves against the East India Company' (unpublished D.Phil. thesis, University of Oxford, 1970), pp. 346–55.

39 CJ, XI, 65; BL Add. MS. 17677 OO, f. 153, L'Hermitage, 16/26 January; Ranke, *History*, VI, 230–1, 233.

40 KAO, Chevening MS. 78, R. Yard to A. Stanhope, 26 March; BL Add. MS. 17677 OO, ff. 64, 216, van Citters and L'Hermitage, 27 March/6 April. See also CSPD, 1694–1695, pp. 364–5; KAO, Papillon MSS. U1015, O 16/9.

41 Luttrell, *Parliamentary Diary*, p. 417; BL Add. MS. 17677 OO, f. 64.

42 BL Add. MS. 17677 OO, f. 53, Baden, 2/12 March, who does refer to the possibility of a bank scheme being adopted.

43 J[erry] S[quirt], *Some Account of the Transactions of Mr. William Paterson* (1695, Wing S89), p. 4. See also Jones, 'London Overseas-Merchant Groups', app. cl; J. Horsefield, *British Monetary Experiments 1650–1710* (1960), p. 127.

44 BL Add. MS. 17677 OO, f. 73, van Citters, 10/20 April. Chamberlen retrospectively charged that Charles Montagu was 'pre-engaged' to the Bank; BL Loan 29/129 (unfoliated), to [R. Harley], 10 June 1701.

45 BL Add. MS. 17677 OO, ff. 243–4, L'Hermitage, 24 April/4 May; Ranke, *History*, VI, 247–8; Luttrell, *Brief Relation*, III, 298–9.

46 J. Kellett, 'The Financial Crisis of the Corporation of London and the Orphans' Act, 1694', *Guildhall Miscellany* II (1964), 220–7; BL Add. MS. 17677 OO, f. 177, L'Hermitage, 9/19 February; HLM, 1692–1693, p. 337.

47 BL Add. MS. 29574, f. 284, C. to Viscount Hatton, 17 March. And see *Somers' Tracts*, X, 591; Wing A3436.

48 The three omitted were Sir Matthew Andrews, Sir Samuel Barnardiston, and Sir Benjamin Newland; they were replaced by Sir Edward Abney, Sir Thomas Pope Blount, and Charles Hutchinson. A merchant Commissioner had previously been elected in May 1690.

49 BL Add. MS. 51511, ff. 54, 64, 70, 71; HMC *Buccleuch*, II, 762.

50 *CSPD*, 1694–1695, p. 60.

51 Falkland (who died suddenly in May) was slated to be sent as envoy to The Hague.

52 *CSPD*, 1694–1695, p. 219. The need for a purge of the staffs of the revenue services had long been argued by the Whigs; NU, Portland MS. PwA 2774. And see E. Hughes, *Studies in Administration and Finance 1558–1825* (Manchester, 1934), p. 188.

53 Sunderland claimed credit for the inclusion of Shrewsbury and Bedford in the honours list; BL Add. MS. 51511 f. 72.

54 NU, Portland MS. PwA 1238, [Sunderland to Portland], 13 July 1694, and see also PwA 1218, 27 June 1693.

55 *Shrewsbury Corr.*, pp. 38–9, 34.

56 *Shrewsbury Corr.*, pp. 35–6; NU, Portland MS. PwA 1232, [Sunderland to Portland, 12 May]; HMC *Buccleuch*, II, 61. To make matters worse, Romney was summoned both to this meeting and to one on the 14th.

57 *Shrewsbury Corr.*, p. 39. See also NU, Portland MSS. PwA 1235–6, [Sunderland to Portland], 4 and 18 June. Meanwhile, Leeds absented himself from London for over two months; Browning, *Danby*, I, 511–12.

58 NU, Portland MS. PwA 1237, [Sunderland to Portland], 6 July; *Shrewsbury Corr.*, p. 36. See also NU, Portland MSS., PwA 1157–8, [Normanby to Portland], 27 July and 7 August.

59 KAO, Chevening MS. 78, R. Yard to A. Stanhope, 10 April; NU, Portland MS. PwA, 1238, and PwA 472, Godolphin to [Portland], 3 August

60 PRO, SP, 8/15 No. 31, printed in *CSPD*, 1694–1695, pp. 184–5. And see Luttrell, *Brief Relation*, III, 300; KAO, Chevening MS. 78, R. Yard to A. Stanhope, 22 May.

61 *CSPD*, 1694–1695, pp. 179–82, 185–6.

62 NU, Portland MS. PwA 1238; *CSPD*, 1694–1695, p. 219.

63 *Shrewsbury Corr.*, pp. 62–3. And see *CSPD*, 1694–1695, p. 180.

64 NU, Portland MS. PwA 472. See also BL Loan 29/187, f. 267, [R. to Sir E. Harley], 7 August.

65 NU, Portland MS. PwA 1176, Somers to [Portland], 14 September, and also PwA 1243, [Sunderland to Portland], 13 September. See also *CSPD*, 1694–1695, pp. 297, 301–2.

66 [C. Leslie], *Querela Temporum* (1695, but written in 1694), reprinted in *Somers' Tracts*, IX, 517 note. And see *CSPD*, 1694–1695, p. 287.

67 For the Privy Council's sometimes contentious proceedings, see *CSPD*, 1694–1695, pp. 144–5, 168, 197; NU, Portland MS. PwA 1233, [Sunderland to Portland], 18 May; S. Bannister, *The Life and Writings of William Paterson* (Manchester, 1855), II, 67. See also BL Add. MS. 17677 OO, ff. 265, 314, L'Hermitage, 29 May/8 June and 3/13 August.

68 Baxter, *William III*, p. 318.

69 Ehrman, *The Navy*, pp. 490–505, 511–26; A. Ryan, 'William III and the Brest Fleet in the Nine Years War', *William III and Louis XIV*, ed. R. Hatton (Liverpool, 1968), pp. 63–5. And see NU, Portland MS. PwA 469, Macclesfield to [Portland], 16 July.

70 NU, Portland MS. PwA 1243; *The Herbert Correspondence*, ed. W. J. Smith (Board of Celtic Studies, Law Series XXI, 1965), p. 43.

71 BL Loan 29/187, f. 284, [R. to Sir E. Harley], 28 August. For references to subsequent meetings, see HMC *Bath*, I, 50–1; BL Loan 29/135, [P. Foley] to R. Harley, 23 October. Harley and Halifax were also in close touch; Foxcroft, *Halifax*, II, 182–3.

72 NU, Portland MS. PwA 1243; *CSPD*, 1694–1695, p. 338.

73 BL Add. MS. 46527, f. 22, J. Vernon to Lord Lexington, 13 November. *The Lexington Papers*, ed. H. Manners Sutton (1851), p. 16; HMC *Portland*, III, 559. For a recent review of the evidence, see also E. Lonsdale, 'John Lunt and the Lancashire Plot', *Transactions of the Historic Society of Lancashire and Cheshire* CXV (1964), 91–106.

74 *Shrewsbury Corr.*, pp. 50–1; HMC *Kenyon*, pp. 292–304.

75 *CSPD*, 1694–1695, p. 255; BL Add. MS. 46527, f. 23. And see BL Egerton MS. 920, ff. 69, 67, J. Vernon to W. Blathwayt, 26 and 30 October.

76 Bodl. Carte MS. 130, f. 353, R. Price to [Duke of Beaufort], 22 November; BL Add. MS. 17677 OO, ff. 395–7, L'Hermitage, 23 November/3 December; *Lexington Papers*, p. 37.

77 CJ, XI, 271; *Archives*, III, i, 366; HMC *Ancaster*, p. 436.

78 BL Loan 29/187, f. 345, to his father, 24 November. And see KU, F. Bonnet, 4/14 December.

79 All Souls College MS. 152, vol. 5 (unfoliated), proceedings in committee of the whole;

BL Add. MS. 17677 OO, f. 406, L'Hermitage, 4/14 December; KU, F. Bonnet, 4/14 December; BL Add. MS. 56241 (unfoliated), W. Blathwayt to R. Hill, 18 December.

80 NU, Portland MS. PwA 1238. And see CSPD, 1694–1695, pp. 217, 310.

81 In December 1694, Davenant finally published *An Essay upon Ways and Means of Supplying the War*. And see Ralph, *History*, II, 785 note c.

82 BL Loan 29/187, f. 344, draft to Sir H. Croft, 20 November. And see CSPD, 1695 and Addenda, p. 292; Bodl. Locke MS. C8, f. 178, J. Freke to Locke, 29 November.

83 HMC *Ancaster*, p. 436; BL Loan 29/187, f. 344; KU, F. Bonnet, 7/17 and 11/21 December.

84 BL Add. MS. 46527, f. 29, J. Vernon to Lexington, 11 December.

85 BL Add. MS. 46527, f. 29.

86 BL Add. MS. 46527, f. 32, J. Vernon to Lexington, 18 December. And see Ranke, *History*, VI, 258; BL Add. MS. 17677PP, f. 102, L'Hermitage, 21/31 December.

87 Ranke, *History*, VI, 257, 259; BL Add. MS. 46527, ff. 33–4, J. Vernon to Lexington, 18 and 21 December. And see CSPD, 1695 and Addenda, p. 292.

88 *Lexington Papers*, pp. 22–3.

89 BL Add. MS. 17677 OO, f. 414, L'Hermitage, 11/21 December.

90 HMC *Portland*, III, 560.

91 BL Add. MS. 46527, f. 29, and 17677 OO, ff. 407, 414, L'Hermitage, 4/14 and 11/21 December.

92 BL Add. MS. 46527, f. 31, J. Vernon to Lexington, 14 December. And see Huygens, *Journaal*, II, 437; KU, F. Bonnet, 11/21 and 14/24 December.

93 Burnet, *History*, IV, 238; BL Add. MS. 56241 (unfoliated), 17 December. And see Ranke, *History*, VI, 260–1; Luttrell, *Brief Relation*, III, 416.

94 HMC *Portland*, III, 560. And see HMC *Bath*, I, 52.

95 BL Add. MS. 46527, f. 31.

96 Luttrell, *Brief Relation*, III, 416. And see Ranke, *History*, VI, 260, 262; LJ, XV, 447.

97 Foxcroft, *Halifax*, II, 244.

VII

THE FORTUNES OF ROYALTY

1694-1696

The calm that had settled over the English political scene by late 1694 was first shattered by the sudden death of Mary, only a few days after William had assented to the triennial bill. On 21 December, Vernon reported that the Queen 'had been out of order this day or two', but her indisposition did not at first arouse serious concern.[1] On the 22nd, in fact, the King had lingered at Westminster, after passing the bills, for another two hours to hear the peers debate the current version of the bill to reform treason trials. Only when he reached Kensington that evening did he realise the gravity of Mary's illness which, amid conflicting diagnoses, was eventually confirmed to be smallpox.[2]

The court had been no stranger to sickness during the latter months of 1694. Since September, Secretary Trenchard had been able to attend only spasmodically to his duties because of respiratory problems, and in mid-November and again in December Shrewsbury had been laid up as well. Moreover, on 18 November Archbishop Tillotson had been felled by a stroke that carried him off five days later, to the great grief of both William and Mary. And now it was Thomas Tenison, another stalwart of the London clergy and Sunderland's and the Whigs' nominee for the primacy, who had the task of breaking the news to Mary that her condition was desperate.[3] Early in the morning of 28 December the Queen breathed her last, leaving the King in so distraught a condition that there were fears for his life as well. But though William could not bring himself to speak of affairs in the initial throes of his sorrow, the implications of Mary's death were not far from others' thoughts, with Burnet, for one, convinced that 'all is lost'.[4]

The principal legal question raised by the Queen's demise was whether the parliament, which had been convened by writs of summons bearing both William's and Mary's names, was dissolved. The contention that the parliament would be *ipso facto* dissolved had been advanced by the Jacobites as soon as the seriousness of the Queen's illness became apparent, and on 27 December a Privy Council was held to consider the issue. However, all those who attended—including some of the judges as well as the chief legal officers of the crown—were agreed that Mary's death would not necessitate new elections. And when the Lords and the Commons assembled to receive notification of the Queen's passing, 'none appeared to own' the Jacobite claim. 'If they had', so Vernon observed, 'they would have found themselves but coarsely treated', for Mary was widely mourned, save by a few indiscreet Jacobites, and her demise produced an upsurge of support for the regime.[5]

The Queen's death also became the occasion for an accommodation between the two royal courts. Anne had shown a deep concern for her sister's health during Mary's last days, and while the King grieved at Kensington in solitude, Sunderland and Tenison worked to consolidate the tentative reconciliation. Despite reports that these negotiations proceeded 'with so many precautions and so slowly' that it seemed 'as if it was a general peace' under consideration, the outcome, at least outwardly, was the restoration of cordial relations between the King and the Princess.[6] Once Anne recovered sufficiently from an indisposition of her own to go to Kensington on 13 January, William received her with 'extraordinary civility'; subsequently, it was 'expected and desired by both courts' that 'all the nobility and officers of state and all in office' should wait upon the Princess in turn.[7] Even more to the point, Anne now discouraged her non-juring uncle Clarendon from appearing at her court, and Marlborough suddenly shifted his anti-ministerial stance in the Lords. It was, then, the upsurge of support for the government and the reunion of the two courts that probably prompted Portland to predict on 15 January that 'there will be much less to apprehend at home than heretofore'.[8]

Yet as William began to pick up the threads of business again, some elements in parliament appeared eager to confound Portland's forecast. The first indication of political unrest growing out of Mary's death came on 15 January when the Commons went upon the report of the place bill. This measure stipulated that no member after election to the Commons should accept an office from 'his Majesty, his heirs and successors', and now the suggestion was made that this conventional formula ought to be altered lest at some future date it be interpreted to Anne's prejudice. Granted, she was designated by the bill of rights as the next 'successor' to the throne should she survive both Mary and William, but some members pointed out that the King would also have 'heirs', whether children by a subsequent marriage or simply relations such as the Elector of Brandenburg. In response, the Commons adjourned the debate on the place bill, first to 19 January and then to the 26th, and in the interim there were consultations between the two courts as well as talk by some of the Churchmen that perhaps Mary's death did necessitate a dissolution.[9] When the debate was resumed on 26 January, Comptroller Wharton was able to inform the lower House that William was willing to have 'heirs' omitted from the place bill (as it had been from the revised oath of allegiance in 1689) but that Anne thought this unnecessary. However, Wharton's message did not allay the agitation. Instead, a motion to omit 'heirs' was put to the question and carried 144 to 139, with Granville and Boyle telling for the majority against Wharton and Montagu for the minority.[10]

The union of backbench Whigs like Boyle with opposition Tories like Granville identifies the troublemakers, and it was also observed that Paul Foley had helped to round up signatures to the long-anticipated petition against the Bank of England that was submitted to the Commons on 19 January.[11] Nor was the 'notable clashing' confined to the Commons, for Mary's death severed the strongest of the remaining links to the Court of peers such as Nottingham, who now concluded that 'some things are more expedient to be done than have been formerly thought fit or necessary'.[12] So, the former Secretary not only spoke out in favour of the Commons' bill to reform treason trials (as he had the previous year), but also he and the Earl of Abingdon moved the Lords on 21 January for a day to consider the state of the nation.

When the Lords went into committee of the whole on 25 January to deliberate on the state of the nation, Nottingham led off with a long harangue which, though 'very respectful to the King', constituted a sweeping indictment of official policy since his ouster in late 1693. His main targets were the trials of the accused plotters in Lancashire, the ill state of the coinage and the deleterious effects of the Bank, the Brest fiasco, and the diversion of the fleet from its prime task of guarding against invasion. The late Secretary of State also reflected on Sunderland's influence at Court in his call for an address to request William, should he have to go to Flanders for the 1695 campaign, to entrust the management of affairs to 'persons of good sense, who were not odious to the nation'.[13]

Nottingham's bitter critique was seconded by Rochester, Halifax, and Torrington, yet neither these ex-ministers nor the new ministers' critics in the Commons were able to force any major reversal in official measures. Both Houses voted against undertaking a review of the complaints against the Bank—the Commons by 164 to 107 on 22 January, the Lords by 33 to 23 on the 25th.[14] And while the peers did agree to review the state of the fleet and to look into the Lancashire affair, the lower House—perhaps spurred on by the Lords' move—brought its own long-drawn-out investigation of the plot to a close on 6 February by sustaining the ministers' proceedings 136 to 109 and 133 to 97. Furthermore, the attempt in the Commons to revive the differences between the two courts was rebuffed by Anne and abandoned after a motion to amend the formula of 'heirs and successors' in the land tax bill was defeated 169 to 148 on 2 February.[15]

Although the Court succeeded in blunting the thrusts of the ministers' critics, the problem of ways and means was not so easily disposed of. The chief sticking point was the question of excises which, though 'hard digestion' to many M.P.s, were now being pressed by the ministerialists. This appears to represent a shift in Court strategy, for before the Christmas recess under-secretary Vernon had anticipated that the levies proposed on hearths and coals 'may be both made use of since neither of them singly is thought sufficient'. But on 4 January, Vernon gave notice to one of his official correspondents on the Continent that a proposal for a leather excise had been offered by the ministerialists that day in committee of the whole; this, he explained, was proposed 'that we may not delude ourselves in what remains of the supply'.[16] A general resolution in favour of an excise on leather and hides was carried in committee four days later by a vote of 126 to 121, yet the margin of victory was small and those who had strenuously resisted such levies during the 1693–94 session were no less determined now. As Harley informed his father on the 9th, they hoped their initial setback could 'be retrieved upon the report, wherefore it will be endeavoured on Saturday [the 12th] to oblige them to report before they go on further' in the committee on ways and means.[17] However, the ministerialists apparently were forewarned, the motion for an immediate report from chairman Sir Thomas Littleton was defeated on the 12th by 178 to 138, and the committee instead resolved to go on to examine the state of the ordinary revenue to determine to what extent it could bear new borrowings.

Nevertheless, the ministerialists' tactical success did not have quite the results they had wished. On 18 January, their proposal that £200,000 per annum from the grant of tunnage and poundage should be anticipated in order to help finance the 1695 campaign was laid aside; instead, it was carried by seventeen votes to take £300,000 yearly which, it was reckoned, would be sufficient to raise a loan

of £1,250,000. In succeeding days, the committee of the whole revived consideration of the hearth tax and also adopted a levy on births, marriages, and burials
(the rate to vary by the persons' status) in the hope that excises might be avoided.
And when the first of a series of resolutions to fix the rates for the leather excise
was put to the question in committee on 11 February, it was voted down 147
to 117, with Boyle telling for the majority and Wharton for the minority.[18]

In turn, both sides to the fight over excises mustered all the sympathisers they
could find in town for the sitting of 13 February when the full House was
scheduled to take up the committee's general resolution of 8 January in favour of
the excise on leather. But though the anti-excise forces even arranged to post one
of their number at the door of St Stephen's Chapel after the debate began so as
to discourage untimely departures by friends eager to fill their stomachs or to
empty their bladders, the resolution was confirmed 155 to 150. Still, the task of
finding the more than £1,800,000 needed over and above the sums expected from
the land tax and the anticipation of the customs was far from complete. The rates
on leather and hides remained to be fixed. And since the committee's other
recommendation for a new hearth tax was rejected without a division by the
Commons late on the 13th, it was also necessary to devise some substitute for it.[19]

For the moment, however, the Commons were diverted by unexpected developments in the inquiry that had begun a month before into the abuses committed
by regimental agents. Since their establishment, the Commissioners of Accounts
had encountered obstacles in getting some of the army agents to submit their
records, but the new probe was specifically sparked by a petition to the lower
House submitted on 12 January 1695 by the inhabitants of Royston (Herts.).
Their complaint was that soldiers who had been quartered amongst them had
also begun to demand that they furnish subsistence money. The Commons'
interrogation of the agent concerned, Tracy Pauncefort, revealed that he had
received the regiment's subsistence money from the Treasury and had failed to
make it over to the troops. Accordingly, he was committed to the custody of the
House's Serjeant at Arms on 28 January, and the further investigation of the
affair was entrusted to the Commission of Accounts. The Commissioners, in
turn, heard further complaints against Pauncefort from former officers of the
regiment who charged that the agent had collected a bribe fund of 500 guineas
from them and their colleagues to expend in securing the payment of the unit's
arrears. This Pauncefort did not deny, but he told the Commissioners on 7 February that 'he dare not' name the recipients of the money. Again on the 9th
and on the 12th, he refused, 'saying if death stood on one hand [of him] he
would not discover it'. And even after the Commission communicated his
refusals to the Commons later on the 12th, he kept silent, and so an irate House
committed him to the Tower.[20]

Three days later, Pauncefort informed the Commons he was now 'ready to
declare' what 'they shall think fit to require of him'.[21] Yet, when he was brought
to the Bar later that day, he seems to have said only that the transaction had
been handled by his brother Edward, another regimental agent who had an
interest in the clothing of the army and acted as deputy to Paymaster Ranelagh.[22]
The second Pauncefort, once catapulted into the limelight, put up much less resistance. When questioned on 16 February, first by the Commissioners (who could
administer an oath) and then by the Commons (who could not), he revealed that
200 of the 500 guineas had been paid to Treasury Secretary Guy, and he added

that 'since the bringing of this matter into the Commons' Guy had sent the money back.[23]

Edward Pauncefort's charges against Guy on 16 February did not come as a complete surprise. Vernon knew enough the day before to anticipate that were the Secretary to the Treasury to be named by Pauncefort, his friends in the Commons would try to have him sent to the Tower as a means of forestalling any more drastic steps, such as a vote of expulsion or an address for his removal from the Treasury. This was the course the Commons followed. First, Guy was heard in his own defence on the 16th, though his claim that he had taken the 200 guineas only after the back pay had been issued was denied by Pauncefort when he was called back in again and put to the question. Then, Guy was ordered into custody, and the Commons chose a committee to draw up a 'representation' to the King of the ill practices of the Paunceforts and other army agents.[24]

With Guy seemingly content to remain in the Tower until the storm against him subsided, the Commons turned back to the many other items of business before them.[25] For the moment at least, it did not appear that the new scandal was going to injure the Court. Only four days after Guy was committed, the two reform measures still pending were disposed of nearly simultaneously: on 20 February, the Lords voted 40 to 33 to adhere to their controversial amendments to the treason trials bill, so virtually ensuring its loss, and the Commons rejected the place bill 175 to 142. The peers then went on to conclude their examinations of the Lancashire plot and of naval affairs, with Nottingham and other critics in full retreat. Meanwhile, the Commons at last approved a series of resolutions in committee to fix the rates for proposed leather excise, after the first was carried by a vote of 130 to 128 on 22 February. And six days later, the anti-excise forces were again defeated 144 to 130 in an attempt to have the leather rates reported immediately to the full House.[26]

Even the two setbacks the Court did appear to suffer in the Commons during late February 1695 were not quite what they seemed. One was the adoption of a series of resolutions to regulate the civil list whose effect, had they been implemented, would have been to lessen the charge of the civil list by approximately 20 per cent, chiefly by compelling the suspension of most existing pensions and by forbidding new ones to be granted while the war lasted. Two years earlier, when backbenchers had sought to add similar restrictions upon the King to the land tax bill, they had been vigorously and successfully contested by the placemen. But this year no resistance was offered, perhaps because it was felt that resolutions had no legal force or perhaps because the Court was willing to concede them as a gesture of economy so as to expedite the proceedings on ways and means.[27]

The second of the seeming rebuffs to the Court in late February can also bear another interpretation. On the 26th, two ministerial Whigs, Papillon of the Victualling Commission and Clarke of the Excise Board, served as tellers for a motion to recommit the draft representation on army abuses. This motion was rejected 168 to 83. Yet its backers' objective was not to soften but rather to strengthen the document, particularly by adding an explicit reference to Guy's misconduct. As Vernon reported, 'those who were for recommitting the representation pretend it would have been a service to him [Guy] by referring him to the King'. But this is just what Guy's defenders had sought to avoid ten days earlier, and Vernon went on to observe that 'I don't find he [Guy] understands it [the motion] so or his friends for him'.[28]

Papillon's and Clarke's conduct on 26 February is consonant with Guy's later denunciation of Charles Montagu as his chief persecutor. At the time that the alterations in the revenue commissions were made the previous summer, Montagu had tried to tempt Guy to relinquish his lucrative post by promising to secure a peerage for him, and now the Chancellor of the Exchequer would appear to have been seeking to exploit his colleague's plight in an effort to make room for Sir Thomas Littleton.[29] In this and subsequent intrigues, Montagu was apparently working with Tom Wharton. These two leaders of the ministerial Whigs in the Commons made an odd but effective pair. Wharton's bluntness and *bonhomie* were complemented by Montagu's sarcasm and ingenuity, and both felt they had not yet been sufficiently rewarded for their services. There was some substance to Wharton's dissatisfaction; after all, in 1695 he was still only Comptroller of the Household and his aspirations for high preferment in Ireland (where his second wife had sizeable estates) remained unfulfilled.[30] Montagu, at first appearance, had less cause for complaint. He had entered the royal service as a Clerk of the Privy Council in 1689 under Halifax's patronage.[31] Yet by mid-1691, his tactical skills in the Commons led the Whigs to suggest him as Jephson's successor as Secretary to the Treasury; this suit was unsuccessful, but the following spring he had been appointed a Commissioner of the Treasury. Once in high office, Montagu quickly demonstrated that Jephson's loss was not, as Godolphin had feared, 'irreparable'. The 'little man's' flair for picking out feasible financial projects and his rising stature in St Stephen's Chapel had earned him the Chancellorship of the Exchequer when Hampden retired.[32] Yet despite or perhaps because of his rapid ascent from genteel obscurity to political prominence, thanks in part also to his marriage to the dowager countess of Manchester in 1688, Montagu's thirst for power and prestige was not yet quenched.

Despite his formidable enemies, it seemed at the end of February 1695 that Guy would weather the storm roused against him, and Vernon was not sure what those who had pressed for recommitting the representation on the 26th might now 'think of doing'. In fact, Guy, after waiting out the presentation of the representation to the King on 4 March, apparently judged that the time was ripe to seek his release from the Tower, and his friends had a petition ready to offer to the Commons on 7 March. But as Vernon reported on the 8th, a 'flame breaking out' on the 7th, 'it was not presented'.[33]

This 'flame' was a new and far more extensive series of accusations of corruption against members—accusations which took air in a seemingly accidental fashion. Early on 7 March, a private bill was being read. Members, who had just received their mail, were paying scant attention, 'everybody talking to his neighbour so that none could hear what was doing'. This 'great disorder' brought Seymour to his feet, and 'in a smart and weighty speech' Sir Edward admonished his colleagues and 'casually expressed himself that they appeared more like an assembly of trade or merchants than of legislators'. This censure spurred others to warn that without doors it 'was said both public and private business came to market there and neither could be done unless paid for'.[34] When specific instances of misconduct were called for, Sir Orlando Gee obliged by alleging that John Brewer had accepted thirty guineas for promoting a private bill. Gee's motive in falling upon Brewer was that the latter was chairman of a select committee which was on the verge of presenting a report in condemnation of the Commissioners for Hackney Coaches, among them Gee's younger brother Richard, for taking bribes in the allocation of new licences.[35] But whatever his animus, Sir Orlando's accusation set off a host of others and much was made of the large sums reputed to have been paid M.P.s by the East India Company and by the City of London in those corporations' pursuit of favourable legislation. So, not only did the Commons resolve to investigate Gee's charge, but they also named a committee of nine (chaired by Foley) to inspect the City's and the East India Company's accounts.[36]

When the Commons took up Brewer's case the morning of 8 March, he was able to vindicate himself, and Gee's allegations were dismissed as 'false, scandalous, and groundless'.[37] By now, however, some members were hunting much bigger game. As Vernon remarked that day, 'there is something working in the House of Commons that don't yet appear, not but it is sufficiently talked of without doors, particularly against the Speaker for having taken money to promote private bills'.[38] Despite his danger, Trevor was outwardly confident. In conversation, he did not deny accepting a gratuity of 1,000 guineas from the City after the passage of the London orphans' relief measure in 1694, yet he claimed that it was only just recompense for his pains and nothing improper was involved. He also declared that if anybody were daring enough to challenge him on this score, he could retaliate by disclosing 'things of greater import'.[39]

Friends did advise Sir John to stay away from Westminster on 12 March when Foley's committee was to report, but he chose to brazen it out. However, when the Commons debated the committee's findings, which included the City's payment to him and also the East India Company's expenditure of nearly £200,000 since 1689 for unspecified 'special service', Trevor found himself under unexpectedly heavy fire. Four hours of discussion concluded with the Speaker being compelled to state the question on a motion condemning him for 'a high crime and misdemeanour', and his friends chose to forbear a division in the face of an overwhelming voice vote against him. Trevor absented himself on the 13th and on the 14th upon a plea of illness, but he was too late in withdrawing. After his second letter of excuse was read on the 14th, Wharton rose to announce that the King was ready to 'give leave' for the election of a new Speaker so 'that there may be no delay in the public proceedings'.[40]

The suddenness of Trevor's fall, coupled with his own misjudgement of the strength of the forces aligned against him, lends credence to Guy's later account that the Speaker had been double-crossed by the Whig ministerialists. Guy's tale (unhappily lacking in dates) was that Trevor had first come to an understanding with Montagu at Guy's own expense. At a supper meeting, suggested by Montagu and arranged by Palmes, Trevor 'gave ... up' the Treasury Secretary and Montagu in return pledged 'a perfect friendship' to Sir John. Yet, 'in a week after' this understanding was concluded, Montagu turned 'violently' upon Sir John.[41] Admittedly, the ministerial Whigs alone could not have toppled Trevor, but Montagu and his friends seem to have learned a lesson from their unsuccessful attempt to recommit the army representation, and they were joined in the hue and cry against the Speaker by Foley and the country Whigs.

The zeal which Foley and his friends displayed in Trevor's downfall may have been encouraged by the Court's decision to abandon its two-month campaign for the leather excise—a decision that had been ratified by the Commons on 12

March, only moments before the report against Trevor was presented by Foley. In lieu of the leather excise and the hearth tax, the full House agreed that day to a levy on coal and glasswares which had been adopted in committee two weeks before. This new levy, coupled with the imposition of the tax on births, marriages, and burials for a five-year term, would suffice to raise the rest of the supply for the coming year. And so the Commons agreed on 12 March to put off the report of the resolutions fixing the rates on leather and hides till 10 May —a date well after the anticipated end of the 1694–95 session.[42]

If the abandonment of the leather excise was the result of a compromise, the arrangement did not include any firm agreement between Montagu and Foley over the choice of Trevor's successor. Possibly, some commitments had been made, for after the session was over Foley complained that Montagu had 'downright played him a trick or two, after a serious debate and a solemn promise passed between them'.[43] In any event, after Wharton delivered the King's message on 14 March to allow the Commons to choose a new Speaker, the Comptroller immediately went on to nominate Sir Thomas Littleton for the Chair. Sir Henry Goodricke seconded Wharton, thereby underlining that Sir Thomas was being offered as the Court's candidate. In response, Foley's name was put forward by two Churchmen, Musgrave and Lord Digby. The question for Littleton was put first and rejected 179 to 146, and then Foley was elected *nemine contradicente* and ceremonially escorted to the Chair by Boyle and Granville.[44]

Littleton's defeat was variously explained in the days following. Some thought that it was due to the irregularity of his nomination, and the *Journal* records that Wharton's speech was interrupted by shouts 'that it was contrary to the undoubted right' of the Commons 'to have any person, who brought a message from the King, to nominate one to them'.[45] Yet, since the minutes of the Commons' proceedings on the 14th were edited by a committee especially appointed for that purpose, too much weight cannot be placed on the *Journal*'s testimony. In addition, Vernon commented that he did not believe Wharton's indiscreet conduct 'influenced so many as Sir Thomas lost it by'. The under-secretary went on to observe that 'the Herefordshire and Worcestershire men' joined in support of their countryman 'with a party [the Churchmen] they seldom otherwise voted with' and that some other Whig backbenchers 'preferred Mr Foley purely upon opinion that he had the longer experience of the two'.[46]

Whatever the reasons for his success, once Foley was seated in the Chair he went out of his way to emphasise his independence. He concluded his acceptance speech to the Commons on 15 March with a pledge that 'whatever his failings might be, he would still preserve clean hands'.[47] Later, after a private interview of an hour with William (the two had never before met), Foley let it be known that he had declined a seat on the Privy Council as a gesture of the Chair's new dissociation from the Court.[48] Thus, though Trevor was expelled from the Commons on the 16th, it appeared that the Whig ministerialists had again failed in their attempts to supplant their Tory colleagues with men of their own choosing. Further disappointments were in store for them in the coming days. When the Commons balloted on 20 March for the next year's Commissioners of Accounts, Harley, Clarges, and Henry Boyle headed the poll, Foley was re-elected despite his new post, and Sir James Houblon was dropped. Furthermore, when Guy finally resigned his post early in April, William allowed him to name his former assistant William Lowndes as his successor under an arrangement whereby Guy retained a share in the profits of his former post. Finally, to add insult to injury a move to expel Guy from the Commons on 17 April failed on the previous question 103 to 66.[49]

Meanwhile, the 1694–95 session dragged on, despite William's eagerness to open the campaign in the Low Countries, and before it was over one of the King's former confidants, the Marquess of Halifax, breathed his last. Since his resignation in early 1690, the Marquess had gradually drifted into first limited and then virtually total opposition, and the record of his conversations that survives from these years attests to his commerce with a variety of Jacobite intriguers.[50] Yet he also continued to pay his respects to William each time the King departed for or returned from the Continent, and in early 1695 one well-informed placeman reported that Halifax had 'of a sudden run into the King's interest in parliament' and speculated that his aim was to prepare the ground 'to offer his service to settle Ireland as Lord Lieutenant thereof'.[51] But death unexpectedly intervened on 5 April just after his son Lord Eland was married to the eldest daughter of the Marquess's long-time friend, Nottingham.

While Halifax's body was being interred, the bribery inquiries in parliament continued to hold up the adjournment, and among the suspects were a number of the Marquess's former colleagues in office, including the Earl of Portland. Although Portland disdainfully shrugged off stories that he had accepted a substantial *douceur* from the East India Company, both the Commons and the Lords were eagerly pursuing all the leads they could turn up.[52] However, it was difficult to secure the necessary proof. Seymour's beneficial saltpetre contract with the East India Company turned out to be very skilfully drawn. Similarly, despite Monmouth's efforts, Normanby escaped formal censure for his activities in the City's behalf when the Lords rejected the motion against him by four votes.[53]

Nevertheless, it was widely believed that could Sir Thomas Cook, a former Governor of the East India Company and a present member of the Commons, be brought to tell what he knew, the bribery inquiries would yield noteworthy results. Cook was first interrogated by the Commons on 26 March, and his refusal to testify resulted in the introduction of a bill, over Seymour's objections, to compel Sir Thomas to account for the moneys spent for 'special service' during his term as Governor. The bill was sent up to the Lords on 6 April, and there Leeds—ingenuously protesting his own innocence—vehemently denounced it while Cook's counsel contended that their client was being forced to incriminate himself. The lawyers' arguments, when coupled with Sir Thomas's offer to testify if indemnified, persuaded the peers to proceed upon a bill of their own. This substitute offered the safeguards Cook sought on condition he explained his accounts by 23 April. And it was under the terms of this act, passed by the Commons on 19 April and approved by the King on the 22nd, that Cook at last appeared before a joint committee of both Houses on the 23rd.[54]

Despite the offer of an indemnity, neither Cook's papers nor his answers contained the revelations that had been anticipated, and he was returned to the Tower to languish there for over a year. But Sir Basil Firebrace—a former interloper, a friend of Seymour, and a key figure in the stock deals made by the Company with some of the interlopers in late 1693—was more forthcoming. At his first appearance before the joint committee on 24 April, Firebrace did little more than restate Cook's testimony. Yet after he was recalled at his own instance on the 25th, he proceeded to name names. Portland, he declared, had refused an offer of £50,000; Nottingham and Seymour had declined smaller sums; but Trevor and Guy had each accepted £5,000. In addition, he stated that 5,000 guineas had been made over to the Duke of Leeds's friend Charles Bates, and this money—he presumed—had found its way to Leeds. To this, Bates added on the 26th that he had indeed offered the guineas to the Lord President, that Leeds had refused them for himself, but that the Duke had allowed them to be placed in the hands of one of his own servants, the Swiss Robart, supposedly for purposes of 'telling' the coin which Bates intended to keep for himself. The money, Bates added, had been sent back to him in 'the past month' by Robart, and he in turn had given it back to Firebrace a few days before his own appearance as a witness.[55]

After the Commons heard the report of these depositions on 27 April, they did not hesitate to initiate an impeachment against Leeds, despite the sudden appearance the Duke made before them. Leeds's defence to the Commons was that he had never taken any of the money himself and that he could prove that the whole affair was 'a design laid against me long before the naming' of the joint committee and 'that Firebrace had been told he should be excused if he would charge' him.[56] Just who Leeds had in mind as his persecutors was made abundantly clear by Seymour a few weeks later in a private letter to the Duke: 'what you hinted at in the House of Commons...I shall be able to furnish materials to make out; namely, that it was a formed design begun and carried on by Mr Montagu and Mr Wharton'.[57]

When the Lord President's denial to the Commons did not avail, he and his supporters sought to hold up the lower House's passage of the last supply bill, arguing that, as this measure to tax coal and glassware had already been delayed while the measure against Cook was pending, so time should also be allowed for the Lords to try the charges that had been made against him.[58] Yet, the King—in giving his consent to the bill to indemnify Cook—had warned that he 'must put an end to the session in a few days'.[59] Then, too, Robart's disappearance after the Commons drew up articles against Leeds, though it reinforced the appearance of the Duke's guilt, made an immediate trial almost impossible. So once the coal and glass bill was approved by the Commons on 1 May and by the Lords on the 3rd, William promptly accepted the last of the fifty bills submitted to him during the long session and parliament was adjourned.

The twenty public acts of the 1694–95 session were only a minority of the many measures given serious consideration by at least one of the two Houses. Among the unsuccessful, in addition to the place and trial for treason bills, were a Commons' measure for the increase of seamen (a concern recommended from the throne at the beginning of the session), Edward Clarke's plan for the establishment of a land registry, and Lord Normanby's proposal to raise the penalties for perjury. But perhaps most noteworthy were the two bills in which John Locke and his 'college' (consisting of Edward Clarke, Sir John Somers, and the lawyer John Freke, with Sir Walter Yonge appearing as a close associate) were greatly interested. One was an attempt to extend the licensing act of 1685, which was due to expire at the end of the session. Locke and his friends, along with some other Whigs, were increasingly hostile to any prior restraint of the press, while many printers, publishers, and authors had a material interest in undoing the Stationers' monopoly. Yet, despite the Commons' vote on 11 February 1695 against a new extension of the act, only a minority cheerfully contemplated a complete end to the regulation of publishing. So, with encouragement from Somers, Clarke proposed a new printing bill in the wake of the Commons' vote of 11 February; this included provisions for the registration of all presses, the licensing of all new books, and the naming of the printer and publisher on the title pages of all publications. However, as Clarke and his friends anticipated, the college's bill did not go far enough to satisfy the Court, the bishops, or the Stationers Company, and it never emerged from committee. And so after the Commons rejected on 12 April an attempt by the Lords to include the old licensing act in the bill to renew expiring statutes, the censorship provisions simply lapsed.[60]

The second question in which the college took an active interest was the deteriorating state of the silver coinage—a problem that provoked extended discussions in both Houses during the 1694-95 session. The Lords were urged by Nottingham in his speech of 25 January to deal with the state of the coin, and they did subsequently pass a bill against counterfeiting and clipping which received William's assent on 3 May.[61] Meanwhile, a Commons' select committee, set up upon Harley's motion of 8 January, reviewed various proposals for a recoinage. This committee reported its recommendations to the lower House on 12 March, but the ministers showed no interest in taking up these proposals. As the college informed Locke, the Treasury still clung to the hope that the situation was manageable, and apparently they were also reluctant to impose any very severe limitation on the export of silver. Indeed, Montagu, when pressed on the need for some action on the coinage by Clarke, responded 'that when he thought of this matter he was like a monkey thrown into the water which always claps his paws or hands to his eyes and sinks to the bottom'.[62]

The effects of the lapse of the licensing act and of the failure to take effective measures to remedy the deterioration of the coinage would soon attract considerable notice. But as the long session drew to a close, more attention was focused on the potential impact of two new statutes—the triennial act of December 1694 and the general pardon of May 1695. The pardon, which excluded any involved in the bribery scandals, had encountered only token opposition even though it was generally interpreted to be chiefly for the benefit of 'the late excepted Ecclesiastical Commissioners' of James II's reign, and especially Sunderland.[63] Even so, that Earl was not one of the commission of seven Lords Justices which William established to administer the realm in his absence. The 'kinglings', as they were promptly christened in reference to the viceregal authority vested in them, were Archbishop Tenison, Lord Chamberlain Dorset, Lord Steward Devonshire, Lord Privy Seal Pembroke, Lord Keeper Somers, Secretary for the south Shrewsbury, and Godolphin as first lord of the Treasury. 'The town', it was remarked, 'are put to great straits here to make seven one, as much as the Deists have to make three one.' Yet, it was expected that the real burden would fall upon the last four members, as the first three were dismissed, perhaps a little too cavalierly, as 'ciphers'.[64]

The commission of Lords Justices was necessitated by Mary's death and by William's unwillingness to entrust any real power to Princess Anne.[65] Noticeable, too, was the omission of Prince George. Although this was rationalised by Vernon on the grounds that the Prince was 'certainly too great' to be 'one of seven', George had served on the advisory council to assist Mary in 1691.[66] In fact, the reconciliation between the two courts was still at a very tentative stage. Thus, Marlborough, who had helped to persuade Shrewsbury to take up the seals again in March 1694 and had hoped Shrewsbury's return would facilitate his own restoration to favour, found that all the King was prepared to do—despite the Duke's intercession for him and the subsequent accommodation between William and Anne—was to allow him to come to Court again. The penitent Marlborough was admitted to kiss William's hand in March 1695, but he remained on probation.[67]

However, Sunderland's omission from the commission of Lords Justices was principally a mark of his own reluctance to emerge from 'behind the curtain'. Certainly, he had a full measure of the royal confidence, and his success in recommending men to William in the spring of 1695 can be contrasted to the reception the King gave to the suggestions of Shrewsbury and to the pretensions of other Whigs. Shrewsbury seems to have backed Comptroller Wharton to be Lord Deputy in Ireland, but Sunderland—in conjunction with Portland—arranged instead that Lord Capel should be named to that post as part of the preparations for the calling of a new parliament in that kingdom.[68] Again, though Shrewsbury was reported to favour the choice of Lord Grey of Warke (who had gained 'great reputation' by his speeches in the Lords in support of the ministry during the past session) as Trenchard's successor after Sir John finally expired on 28 April, Sunderland secured the seals for Sir William Trumbull after 'a great deal of pains'.[69] Furthermore, Shrewsbury was unsuccessful in gaining Trumbull's seat at the Treasury Board for Sir Thomas Littleton. As Edward Clarke gloomily observed in mid-May, 'I doubt another gentleman, of a very different character' will 'have the place, that being still the prevailing interest and I fear will continue'.[70] Although William did not, as Clarke feared, appoint William Duncombe (one of the superseded Irish Lords Justices) to succeed Trumbull, he put off making any decision by allowing the new Secretary to keep his former place as well, even though Trumbull found it difficult to attend the Board regularly.

William, to be sure, was not opposed to gratifying those Whigs who had served loyally. Lord Grey was raised in the peerage as Earl of Tankerville, Somers was offered a peerage which he declined on the grounds he did not have an estate sufficient to support it, and Capel himself was a Whig of long standing. Moreover, after Sir Robert Atkins finally resigned from the Exchequer bench in October 1694, Whig lawyers were named to fill the ensuing vacancies, with Sir Thomas Trevor being made Attorney-General in May 1695. Even the egregious Monmouth was now reinstated in his Bedchamber post, having 'by his behaviour this sessions restored himself' to the King's good graces.[71] William, however, was determined that Montagu, Wharton, and such close associates of theirs as Littleton and Winchester should not profit from their attacks upon Guy, Trevor, and Leeds. So not only was Guy allowed to resign his post on quite favourable terms, but also Trevor retained his place as Master of the Rolls (which he held on 'good behaviour'), and Leeds stayed on as Lord President. Admittedly, the King did not feel it politic to name the Duke a Lord Justice or to allow him to attend the Privy Council in his own absence, but Leeds did not otherwise suffer despite the bribery charges brought against him by the Commons.

While Montagu complained that William had 'broken his promise to him in somewhat' and busied himself in devising new designs to harass his enemies in the Treasury (such as Auditor Done) and his foes in the Commons (such as Seymour), speculation mounted over the future of the present parliament now

that the triennial act was on the statute book.[72] The new legislation did not
require a dissolution for another year and a half, but already in early April 1695
Shrewsbury wrote to Russell (still in the Mediterranean) that the bribery
inquiries 'have thrown so much dirt that I conclude this same parliament can
never sit again'.[73] The King himself contributed to this speculation by confiding
his intention to dissolve to Sunderland, Shrewsbury, and Somers before he left
for the Continent. Although there was no public announcement of his intentions, Monmouth's indiscretion in 'positively affirm[ing]' that the King had
'declared the night before he went hence' in favour of a dissolution and stories
that Wharton had undertaken either to bring in eighty new members or to keep
out eighty old ones did circulate widely.[74]

The report that William had approved Wharton's election list and had specifically declared his displeasure with Harley led the latter to seek reassurance
from Henry Guy in mid-June 1695. Guy was ready to listen, not only because
he had promptly resumed his politicking once he was released from the Tower
but also because he was grateful to Harley for helping to forestall the attempt to
expel him from the Commons in mid-April 1695. Their meetings during the
summer of 1695 mark the beginning of an increasingly close relationship between this ill-assorted pair, and thereafter Harley would have in Guy a direct
contact with Portland and with William himself.[75]

For now, so Guy reported to Portland, Harley declared how 'much troubled'
he was by the story of Wharton's list and that he 'ever was and ever would be
as faithful to the government as any man living, and would as much assist to
support it, though he might sometimes differ in the method'. Nor were these
mere professions, for Speaker Foley at his own request had been meeting regularly with Guy since the adjournment in order to implement his 'resolution of
promoting every thing for the public'.[76] Foley's and Harley's willingness to
concert measures for the 1695–96 session with Sunderland and Guy sharply
contrasts with their reluctance to engage in such dealings two years earlier. But
though the Speaker and his kinsman were now profuse in their assurances of zeal
for the King's service, Guy warned Portland that it would be difficult to get Foley
to work with Montagu in the wake of the events of the past session. The Speaker,
he reported, showed 'a wonderful aversion' for the Chancellor of the Exchequer,
declared that Montagu's 'insolence' in the Commons would 'never be forgotten',
expressed concern at Somers's 'friendship to' Montagu, and even affirmed that
'by a little pains the Whig party will totally leave Mr Wharton and Mr Montagu'. At the same time, Palmes was advising Somers, 'who seemed much to
despond because the Whigs were divided', that Montagu would have to be
curbed. But this the Lord Keeper was either unwilling or unable to do, and it was
only when Sunderland returned to London in midsummer that some semblance
of order was restored.[77]

Sunderland's and Guy's reports of the discussions the Earl held with Shrewsbury and Somers in late July 1695 suggest that at least one reason for Wharton's
and Montagu's troublemaking since the King's departure was that neither the
Comptroller nor the Chancellor now favoured an early general election. To be
sure, Wharton had favoured a 1695 terminal date for the present parliament in
the debates over the triennial act, yet Sunderland and Guy believed that he and
Montagu feared that 'they shall have less power in a new' parliament. As later
events were to demonstrate, their anticipation of difficulties was not unfounded,

and even at the time Guy observed that 'it is the opinion of most men' that Foley would be re-elected Speaker in any new parliament.[78] None the less, Sunderland, Shrewsbury, and Somers agreed it would be 'impracticable' to continue the old parliament lest the bribery inquiries and Leeds's impeachment be revived to the detriment of supply. The three were also confident that 'the country will generally elect persons well-affected to the government'. William, they decided, should be informed that they saw no reason to alter their earlier recommendations for a dissolution, that they hoped he remained of 'the same mind', and that steps must be taken to chastise Montagu and Wharton since it appeared neither 'will be governed by friends or reason'.[79]

However, it did not prove necessary to 'force' Montagu and Wharton. Before Sunderland returned to Althorp in early August, he spoke 'very plain' to the Chancellor of the Exchequer, and his admonitions seem to have been seconded by Shrewsbury and Somers. Montagu's response was all that could have been wished; he denied that he was opposed to a dissolution and avowed that the Whigs 'should be undone without' Sunderland. Similar professions soon followed from the absent Wharton (despite complaints from Capel that the Comptroller 'endeavoured to do him all the hurt he could' during his stay in Ireland), and Guy was able to report some progress in his own conversations with Harley and Foley.[80] Harley, calmed by reassurances that William harboured no ill will towards him, intimated he would do what he could to dissipate resistance in the Welsh Marches to the large land grant the King intended there for Portland. Moreover, 'after much argument' Guy finally brought Foley to declare that 'he would ever live civilly with Montagu'; even so, the Speaker continued to believe that neither Montagu's 'understanding nor his principles are good', and he expressed the hope 'there would be others' among the King's servants 'with whom he might communicate' about the management of the Commons.[81]

It may, then, have been a mark of their good intentions that Harley and Foley opposed an attempt to revive the East India affair in late August by the Commission of Accounts. Their votes helped to make a majority of one on the Commission against accepting an offer from Sir Thomas Cook (still in the Tower) to testify, though the ostensible grounds for this refusal was that parliament had reserved the affair to itself.[82] In any event, by mid-August Sunderland was confident that 'if the King pleases all will do well', and on the 27th William responded by declaring that he had 'never entertained any other thought than to call a new parliament upon my return'.[83]

Even before the King's resolve was publicly known in London early in September, electoral preparations had begun in some constituencies. Somers, for instance, let his friends in Worcestershire know as early as the beginning of August that a new parliament was probable.[84] Later in August, Musgrave reported to Harley from the North that 'money' was already being disbursed from the 'overgrown purses' of some 'great men', especially his old rival, Sir John Lowther of Lowther.[85] Hence, by the time the dissolution was formally proclaimed by William upon his return to England on 12 October, the campaign was nearly in full swing. The ministerial Whigs and their friends had an advantage in terms of preparation, thanks to both earlier information about William's intentions and also the changes in local administration that had been effected during the past two years. Since early 1694, the London lieutenancy had been reconstituted in their favour; there had been efforts to purge the commissions of the peace and the revenue services of all who declined to take the oaths; and disputes over the charters of Plympton, Colchester, Dunwich, and Liverpool had been resolved to the advantage of local Whigs.[86]

The long run-up to the 1695 election distinguished it from that of 1690. Another contrast was that the many contenders for seats in 1695 are known to have carried their competition to the point of a poll in only seventy-nine constituencies—a sharp drop from the total of 106 recorded contests five years before.[87] Rising costs may explain some candidates' reluctance to fight to the finish against determined opponents, yet it would also seem that the old partisan animosities did not figure so prominently even in the contests that did occur.[88] Then, too, though the censorship had lapsed, the 1695 general election was surprisingly devoid of the controversial pamphleteering that had marked the 1690 campaign. It is true that in late August the Duke of Newcastle had anticipated 'great stickling between high and low church', and a few weeks later the Duke of Leeds sought to rouse his friends by invoking the safety of the Church and by warning of the 'schemes' being hatched by 'some of our grandees'.[89] Leeds did not specify what these dire designs might be, but others alleged that the 'juncto of three or four persons' which has 'for some considerable time . . . managed an interest with a powerful party' intended a new abjuration oath, a general excise, a confiscation of cathedral lands, and a new bride for William.[90]

Despite such ominous reports, most election contests appear to have been dominated by local rivalries and concerns, and the only 'national question' given much attention was continued support for the war. William's recapture of Namur in August 1695 had heightened expectations of a favourable peace in the near future, and the King's well-publicised tour of the Midlands during the election campaign served as useful reinforcement.[91] Admittedly, William was still not eager to make specific recommendations of candidates even in private, but the popular acclaim which greeted him on his progress may well have been a boon for those candidates willing to pledge full backing for the war.[92] Musgrave, after refusing Lowther's demand that he publicly promise full support to Court requests for supply, found it advisable to stand down in Westmorland; the returning naval hero Russell stood and was elected in three constituencies (two of them counties), as his friends sought to capitalise on his popularity; and several constituencies in the North and in the West sent up their members with addresses in favour of supply.[93]

These addresses were reported in the several bi-weekly London newspapers that had appeared after the licensing act had expired, and they also printed the returns as they came in. In private correspondence, the observation most often offered about the results was the high proportion of new members chosen—one in three, it was generally computed. More precisely, 174 men were returned who had not sat in the last parliament, and for all but thirty of them this would be their first term in the lower House. Yet, not one among the members, new or old, seems to have been prepared to fill the gap left by the departure of the two incumbent diarists of William's second parliament, Grey and Luttrell, so that all too often it is impossible for us to know in any detail who said what during the more important sittings of the new Commons.

The problem that contemporaries faced was how to assess the temper of an assembly which had so many untried members. And because they confined themselves for the most part to generalities, it is Burnet's retrospective characterisation of the election results that has most often been cited: 'the Jacobites', he wrote, 'were so descried, that few of them were elected; but many of the sourer sort of Whigs, who were much alienated from the King, were chosen'.[94] If we read 'Tories' for Burnet's 'Jacobites', the first part of the Bishop's description does seem to hold up. Clarges's death in early October 1695 was not the only loss the Tories suffered, and Musgrave's difficulties in Westmorland had a parallel in Seymour's problems at Exeter. Moreover, before Seymour's fate was known, Viscount Weymouth was bemoaning the poor showing the Tories had made in the West, while one of under-secretary Ellis's correspondents declared on 5 November that the returns 'already in print' made it apparent that 'God help the wicked'.[95] In Musgrave's and Seymour's cases, it was more a matter of divine help for those who helped themselves. Both found refuge in small boroughs— Musgrave at Appleby (after abortive canvasses in Westmorland and at Oxford University), Seymour at Totnes after he was outvoted (if not outspent) in Exeter.[96]

In other respects, however, Burnet's assessment of the 1695 returns diverged from the preponderance of evaluations offered at that time. George Tollett (secretary to the Commission of Accounts) reported in mid-November that 'the Court' believed 'the elections have succeeded as they would have them', though he added that 'we reckon all the new members are in the Court interest, only most of those in whose places these come were so, too'. Simultaneously, William Blathwayt observed to another royal servant that 'the choice of parliament promises very well but some of our friends are left out as well as others'. And a similar report 'that the majority' were 'truly disposed to support his Majesty and his interest' prompted Capel in Dublin to assume that 'things were never more promising in order to set the King upon a right bottom since his being upon the throne as now'.[97]

A closer look at the fate of the incumbent M.P.s and at the connections of the new men may help to flesh out the impressions offered by contemporaries. On the one hand, the success rate for the 120 incumbent placemen was about three in four, while the rate for the over 200 incumbents indicated as backbench opponents of ministerial measures on the Grascome list of 1693 was only one in two.[98] On the other hand, it would appear from the course of the ensuing session that when Tollett, Blathwayt, Ellis, and others spoke of the election of men 'known to be for the interest of his Majesty and the support of his government', they included many who were not likely to follow dutifully the emerging Whig Junto in their continuing bid for predominance in the Commons and at Court.[99] Thus, while there were seven Montagus (five of them new members) and four Russells in the new House, there were also five Foleys and three Harleys. Furthermore, new Whig members such as Anthony Ashley Cooper (styled Lord Ashley and the grandson of the first Earl of Shaftesbury), William Cavendish (styled Marquess of Hartington and the heir to the Duke of Devonshire), and Charles Lord Spencer (heir to the Earl of Sunderland) were soon to show that their Whiggery could carry them into opposition on some Court–Country questions.

Even before it became apparent that the Whig triumph in the 1695 general election would not necessarily redound to the Junto's or to the Court's benefit, the King had begun to exert himself to try to ensure a harmonious session. William 'in a manner commanded' Trevor not to seek re-election 'on purpose to prevent ... the reviving' of the bribery investigations.[100] Guy also did not stand,

and he used his interest at Hedon to have Trumbull returned along with Lord Spencer. In the meantime, the King assigned to Trumbull the unwelcome duty of telling Leeds not to attend the Privy Council, while Shrewsbury was deputed to urge Somers to see to it that the impeachment against the Lord President slept.[101]

The King was even more cautious once the returns were in. When Littleton's friends began 'soliciting' on his behalf for the Speakership, William ordered Sir Thomas to stay away from the Commons at their first meeting on 22 November so as to avoid a division. 'The Court', so the college disgruntledly informed Locke, 'was so wise as to join with their enemies and force their friends to comply with them by making Sir Thomas Littleton be absent at the choice.'[102] So Foley was returned to the Chair without contest as Trumbull moved and Paymaster Ranelagh seconded his nomination. In turn, Foley's friends apparently agreed that the new Solicitor-General Sir John Hawles should be chairman of the Committee of Elections and Privileges. Henry Boyle, earlier named as a possible candidate for that position, stayed away from the committee's first meeting. And when the Lincolnshire Tory Sir John Bolles nominated Harley, he left the chamber to avoid a contest with Hawles.[103]

The King's care to assure a peaceful start to the 1695–96 session reflected the government's pressing financial needs. As William indicated in his opening speech on 23 November, there were not only the supplies for 1696 to be considered but also the deficiencies of the levies voted in 1695 and the continuing debt on the ordinary revenue. Since lenders had been unwilling to make the desired advances upon the coal and glassware levy, among others, the supplies voted the previous session would fall short by nearly £1,000,000. In addition, by Michaelmas 1695 there was over £5,000,000 outstanding in temporary loans (mainly in the form of tallies), and some £3,000,000 of this total represented unfunded debts. Among these debts were arrears in civil list payments of nearly £450,000, at a time when the King's revenue was roughly £800,000 in debt. Furthermore, the repayment of the various unfunded temporary loans was hindered by the difficulties the government faced in making the scheduled payments on the funded debt (created by the tontine, lottery, bank, and annuity schemes of the past three sessions) because of the shortfall in the anticipated yield of such levies as the 1694 duty upon ships' tonnages.[104]

The government's financial problems were considerably complicated by the acceleration in the deterioration of the silver coin. The Lords' act against clipping and counterfeiting of the 1694–95 session had not really come to grips with the problem, and the abortive Commons' resolutions of April 1695 in favour of a recoinage and a devaluation only emphasised the existing divergence in gold–silver ratios between England and the Continent. In fact, it was during the first six months of 1695 that the gold guinea (worth 21s 6d in silver in 1690) soared in value to nearly thirty shillings, while the number of guineas coined in 1695 by the Mint but chiefly for private persons rose to more than twelve times the 1694 total.[105] The deterioration of the English silver coinage also was reflected on the international exchanges. Rapid exchange shifts may have stimulated English textile exports (especially undyed cloth), but they also aggravated the already difficult task of paying the army in the Low Countries. Godolphin had to inform William in early August 1695, while the siege of Namur was in progress, that 'the exchange is now fallen so very low' against sterling that 'the returns are become wholly impossible to be had'.[106] And even before this crisis point had been reached, Guy was assuming that a recoinage—at a cost of £1,500,000 'at the least'—would be necessary, and it was reckoned that with this charge and the supply deficiencies from previous years the 1695–96 session of parliament would have to raise over £7,000,000.[107]

Already in July 1695, Foley had 'drawn a scheme' to raise £7,000,000 or more, and both Guy and Godolphin thought it 'not an ill one'.[108] Yet the decision on recommending a recoinage to parliament was not taken until a fortnight before the members assembled. For one thing, the experts consulted by the government were by no means unanimous. A few, particularly Charles Davenant, still thought it possible to postpone a recoinage, at least until the war was over; among the rest, there was disagreement whether a recoinage should be accompanied by a devaluation. Chief among the adherents of the existing silver standard was Locke; his views were solicited by Secretary Trumbull in mid-July 1695 in the wake of a report from the Treasury Board to the Lords Justices. The Treasury, at least at this juncture, leaned towards a devaluation so as to bring the gold–silver ratio in England into closer conformity with that prevailing abroad. Although Godolphin did not sign this report, the recommendation for a devluation seems to have reflected both his own views and those of William Lowndes, and the new Secretary to the Treasury's advocacy of this course was made explicit in late September in the recoinage proposals he submitted.[109]

But it was not Lowndes's views but Locke's that William preferred, as the King made very clear at a cabinet meeting on 16 October.[110] Before he left for his tour of the provinces a few days later, William gave instructions that detailed proposals for implementing a recoinage at the old standard be drawn up, and Lowndes was charged with their preparation. At this stage, the King intended to act by way of proclamation, and on 4 November the 'expedients' Lowndes had drafted in conformity to his instructions were favourably reviewed by those ministers who remained in London. There were some reservations expressed at this meeting, however, about Locke's earlier suggestion (incorporated by Lowndes) that the badly-clipped coin should pass by weight; apparently, the ministers' fear was that this would produce an immediate fall in the price of guineas and might lead to a general stoppage of trade.[111]

Nevertheless, the principal division among the ministers and among the Commissioners of the Treasury, as Godolphin summed up their views to William on 10 November, was over the wisdom of taking any action before parliament considered the matter. Somers and Trumbull (Locke's principal friends in the administration) seem to have been the chief supporters of William's preference for executive action: they warned of the delays that parliamentary debates would bring and the resultant danger of a continued deterioration in the coinage. Shrewsbury and Devonshire were the most vocal in urging that the matter be put before the new parliament: they feared that the Commons would take it 'ill' if they were asked to finance a recoinage they had not first approved. In the face of this disagreement, even Somers had second thoughts. He brought to the cabinet on 13 November a draft of a proclamation embodying the Locke–Lowndes 'expedients', but at the same time he told William it would be better now to consult parliament.[112] So the proclamation was laid aside, and the King's speech of 23 November simply 'took notice' of the 'ill state of the coin', observed that a remedy 'may perhaps prove a further charge to the nation', and left the question 'entirely to the consideration of my parliament', without endorsing any specific measures.[113]

Besides supply and the coin, the King's speech directed parliament's attention to three other problems. Since the last parliament had not agreed upon means to increase the number of seamen available for the fleet, William again called for some 'good bill' for this purpose. He also suggested it would be desirable to provide a way to raise recruits to serve overseas in the army that would eliminate abuses in present practices and mute the perennial complaints and occasional riots against illegal impressment. In addition, William recommended the consideration of 'such laws as may be proper for the advancement of trade', especially 'that of the East Indies, lest it should be lost to the nation'.[114]

The King's mention of the East India trade was in direct response to a petition submitted to him by the Company. That corporation's stock had fallen in value by more than 40 per cent since midsummer in reaction to the Scottish parliament's establishment of an East India Company in that kingdom and to its own loss of five ships bearing cargoes valued at nearly £1,000,000 in recent months.[115] Whether it was the Admiralty which was at fault in the enemy's capture of the East India vessels (and also some of the Barbados fleet) remained to be investigated, but it did seem that neither the Commons' imposition upon the Admiralty in 1694 of the obligation to set out forty-three cruisers for the protection of trade nor the reconstitution of that Board by the King the following spring had brought relief from the French privateers. Anger at recent shipping losses was reported to have cost Sir John Houblon (Admiralty Commissioner and Lord Mayor elect) his chance to be chosen an M.P. by the City, and even Blathwayt had to admit that it was 'a great scandal that while we are so much superior at sea we should not in the first place and above all things take [care] to protect our trade'.[116] And just as the fear of drastic parliamentary action after the loss of the Turkey convoy had sparked ministerial interest in late 1693 in the establishment of a royal council of trade, so there was again talk in the cabinet council in the weeks before the new parliament met about the creation of such a body.[117]

Once the members assembled in late November 1695, the parallel with the events of two years earlier was carried further. As on the former occasion, ministerial preparations were held up by the King's hesitation; in turn, William's failure to take pre-emptive action again brought unwelcome parliamentary proposals on to the stage. Certainly, the state of trade was high on the list of members' priorities for consideration in both Houses. In the Commons on 25 November, as Robert Harley subsequently related:[118]

when the necessary forms were dispatching, the last whereof is the appointing the four grand committees, whereof one is for trade, a gentleman [presumably Harley himself] took the opportunity and made the first speech was uttered. By the sequel, it seemed to be designed, for he chalked out the lines of the whole proceedings until the plot's discovery interrupted the scheme. Amongst other things a council of trade was mentioned as absolutely necessary....

When the Lords first sat to do business on 2 December, it was Rochester who took the lead. Brushing aside suggestions for an address of thanks for the King's speech, he urged immediate consideration of the state of the coin and of trade, and he was seconded by Normanby and the Churchman Ferrers. During succeeding days, the Lords took up the danger posed by the new Scots company, the need for a recoinage, and the losses inflicted by French privateers. Similarly, the Commons resolved on 2 December to consider the two questions of the coin and of trade in alternate sittings in committee of the whole.[119]

But this evidence of parliamentary concern failed to persuade William to lay aside his reservations about a royal council of trade. A patent for a 'commission for trade and plantations' was ready for his signature by 9 December, but still he put off a decision 'from day to day'.[120] Hence, when the question of parliament's establishment of such a body was raised in the Commons' committee of the whole on 12 December, the placemen found themselves in a very awkward situation. As Monmouth informed Locke (who had already received intimations that he would be named to the projected royal commission):[121]

Our great managers, surprised, were forced to run up to some in our House [the Lords], others to go to Kensington, so that at last the Secretary [Trumbull] informs the House [of Commons] at the latter end of the debate (and much consultation), that the King had just formed such a commission, with all that could be said to prevent their further proceedings; ...

However, Trumbull's announcement was perceived by many M.P.s as a 'trick', and it was moved that the Commons should proceed with a bill of their own and that the members of such a commission should be named in the bill. The ministerialists complained that 'this was to clip the King's wings' and to alter the nature of the government. In reply, Howe proclaimed 'that we might be without a king but not without a trade'. He then went on to assert that 'he knew no other [government] than the King, Lords, and Commons, and though the executive part was in the King, yet they were to see what was fit to be done if he failed'.[122] For the moment, all that was done was to resolve to proceed with a bill, and then the question for adjourning the committee was moved and carried by the ministerialists 124 to 109, with Howe the minority's teller and Sir Walter Yonge the majority's. A few days later, the King did at last sign the warrant for the royal commission, but it remained to be seen whether this would suffice to appease the clamour.[123]

By contrast to the storm brewing over the council of trade, the estimates for the 1696 campaign were given a prompt and favourable hearing in the Commons. At each stage there was some opposition, especially on 13 December when Howe, Seymour, Musgrave, and Finch led an effort to reduce the number of troops from 87,000 to 62,000. But they could only find 135 members to support them against the 243 who divided for the larger figure, and it was observed that among the majority were such one-time Whig foes of large armies as Sir John Thompson.[124] By mid-December, estimates totalling £5,025,000 (£448,000, or 8 per cent, below the initial requests) had been approved. Moreover, by the end of December, the Commons—conscientiously taking only two days off for Christmas—had agreed on the ways and means to raise a substantial portion of the estimates and the past deficiencies. The means tentatively decided upon were another four-shilling tax on land, a new annuities offer, and the extension of existing customs on vinegar and wines, sugar and tobacco, and East Indian imports. Altogether, it was reckoned that these expedients should bring in nearly £3,700,000.[125]

During December, the Commons also made considerable progress on the coinage. To be sure, the first debate on this subject on 29 November aroused the fears of Locke's friends; Clarke felt he 'was deserted' by his official colleagues when he unsuccessfully proposed 'an address to make clipped money go by weight', especially since 'the night before the King had commanded the courtiers to press that matter'.[126] Then, too, Lowndes (newly elected for Seaford) took the opportunity of the next debate on the coin on 2 December to voice his own arguments in favour of a devaluation, and so the 'raw' country gentlemen became auditors to a restatement of the experts' earlier debates.[127] Yet with some prompting from the Lords who communicated their opinions on the coin to the Commons on the 5th, the lower House proceeded to formulate in committee eleven resolutions, and these were reported on 10 December by Granville as chairman.[128]

The resolutions of 10 December, in calling for a recoinage on the old standard with the cost to be borne by the taxpayer, followed Locke's thinking. But in choosing the means to implement the recoinage, the resolutions conformed to earlier suggestions offered by Isaac Newton (Montagu's Cambridge tutor and Locke's rival for the Mastership of the Mint). Like Shrewsbury, Montagu reckoned it would be 'impracticable' to have the clipped coin pass by weight, and he undoubtedly had a hand both in the ministerialists' failure to back Clarke's motion on 29 November and in the committee's decision to have the clipped coin recalled in stages, with special provision for its receipt in tax payments.[129]

When the committee's resolutions were reported to the full House, there was only one direct challenge made to them, and this motion in favour of a devaluation was decisively defeated on 10 December by 225 to 114. Next, the Commons addressed the King to issue a proclamation fixing deadlines for the use of the various denominations of the old coin and they also approved a resolution in committee to provide £1,200,000 to finance the recoinage. Then, Montagu's bill for 'regulating the coinage', which embodied the eleven resolutions of 10 December, was dispatched to the Lords, and on 31 December the Commons voted a window tax to pay for the charges of the recoinage.[130]

However, it soon became apparent that the Commons' proposals on the coin were defective in several respects. No provision had been made for counterfeit coin, with the result that holders of silver pieces of lower than sterling standard rapidly found it difficult to get them accepted, even in tax payments. They therefore petitioned the Commons for redress. Furthermore, the King's proclamation of 19 December, in which he declared that clipped half-crowns and crowns would cease to be legal tender after 1 January 1696 (save for tax payments), immediately discouraged the circulation of these coins and stimulated 'cunning fellows' to buy them up at low prices for use in tax transactions.[131] These difficulties prompted second thoughts among some members of the lower House. On 1 January 1696, Sir John Lowther, 'contrary to his former opinion', spoke out for having the clipped coin pass by weight and proposed a plan for 'registering the whole sum of clipped money all at once throughout all England in order to the stating and settling of every man's recompense'.[132] But after a prolonged debate, the Commons decided to postpone action in order to await the Lords' deliberations on Montagu's coinage bill.

As anticipated, the peers made extensive amendments to Montagu's measure on 2 January, so as virtually to make it 'a new bill', with Rochester, Leeds, and Godolphin himself taking the lead.[133] Their amendments were not without merit, but the Commons gave them short shrift on the grounds that the peers were tampering with money matters. Nevertheless, the Commons also decided to abandon Montagu's bill and to proceed with two new ones. These were to embody both the original eleven resolutions and six supplementary resolutions that were carried without a division on 9 January.[134]

The first of the new coinage bills was presented to the Commons on 13 January 1696. This measure 'to remedy the ill state of the coin' differed from Montagu's in extending the deadlines for the circulation of the clipped coins (the smallest denominations were to be legal tender until 4 May and to be received in tax payments until 24 June) and in treating all but completely counterfeit silver pieces as equivalent to clipped coin for purposes of recompense. The latter change greatly enlarged the government's financial liability, but no additional supply for the recoinage was voted. Despite ministerialist complaints on that score, the bill had a speedy and virtually unopposed passage; it was approved by the Commons on 17 January and by the Lords on the 21st.[135] Meanwhile, the second measure, which was intended to encourage holders of good silver coin and of plate to bring in what they had to be recoined, was committed by the Commons on the 21st, after the ministerialists voted down 110 to 87 a proposed instruction to the committee to 'consider of the price of guineas'.[136]

When William arrived in the Lords late on 21 January 1696 to give his assent to the bill 'to remedy the ill state of the coin', three other public measures were presented to him: the annuities bill, a bill to outlaw 'treating' after the *teste* of the writs of summons in parliamentary elections, and a bill to reform the procedure in treason cases. The last was a measure William knew well, for he had attended a number of the Lords' debates on previous versions. What was surprising was that this session the Commons had finally accepted the peers' insistence that the Lord Steward's court be revised as part of the general reform.[137] There was opposition to the Lords' amendment in the Commons on 17 January, but the lower House finally accepted it 192 to 150, with Boyle and Granville telling for the majority. Nor was the King disposed to risk a veto at this stage in the session, and so the reform measure most persistently pressed since the Revolution at last reached the statute book.[138]

At the same time, the King was having to swallow another bitter dose; this came in the form of a Commons' address on 17 January requesting that he halt the grant he had intended to make to Portland of a group of royal estates in Wales. From the outset, this grant had been controversial, and when it was first considered at the Treasury Board in May 1695 a number of Welsh M.P.s had attended to signal their opposition. Even so, Sunderland had advised William in August not to yield to the 'great noise' made about it, and in this he may have been encouraged by Harley's promise of assistance in the affair to Guy.[139] But in the event, the more pessimistic Godolphin proved a better prophet. When a petition against the grant was brought into the Commons in January 1696 by William Bromley of Warwickshire, the ministerialists sat silent since they realised it was 'to no purpose' to try to resist it. So William had no recourse but to give in, yet in replying on 22 January to the Commons' address he declared that as he would not have given Portland the Welsh manors 'if I had imagined the House of Commons could have been concerned', so I will 'find some other way of showing my favour to him'.[140]

Meanwhile, the contest over the projected parliamentary council of trade was coming to a head. After repeated postponements, the debate of 12 December 1695 was resumed in the Commons' committee of the whole on 2 January 1696. This lengthy sitting ended 'without resolving anything about the power this intended committee should have but agreeing that the nature of it should be perfectly different from that intended by the King'—his 'being only for speculations, as they said, about the improvement of trade in time of peace' and theirs being 'for the effectual security of it in war'.[141] However, it was resolved by a vote of 175 to 174, with Speaker Foley voting with the majority, that the members of the proposed council should be named by parliament.[142] The margin of victory was slim, yet the Court's defeat was disturbing, especially because Foley was joined not only by backbench Churchmen but also by such new Whig members as Devonshire's two sons, Lords Hartington and Cavendish, and Lord Spencer.[143]

Even so, the Whig ministerialists reckoned to recapture their wayward friends by a well-worn stratagem. When the council of trade project was next discussed in committee on 20 January, Comptroller Wharton (in his last notable contribution in the Commons before succeeding to his father's barony in early February) was ready with two supplementary resolutions. The first was to bar M.P.s from being named to serve upon the council and the second was to impose an abjuration oath upon those who were chosen.[144] Wharton's were wrecking amendments, yet the two resolutions passed without much dispute in committee. However, Foley then sought out Secretary Trumbull to ask if it was William's 'mind to break' the parliamentary council of trade and to warn the Secretary that to persist with the abjuration would 'destroy' the King's chances of gaining the civil list supply he had requested in his opening speech.[145] Trumbull did not record his reply to the Speaker, but he undoubtedly communicated Foley's remarks to Sunderland, and in turn the Earl must have renewed his earlier instances on the subject to William. As Burnet later related, although the King 'ordered his ministers to oppose it as much as possibly they could, the Earl of Sunderland, to the wonder of many, declared for' the parliamentary council of trade. Hence, the 'ministers' were 'much offended' at Sunderland's behaviour, and 'the King himself took it ill, and he told me, if he went on, driving it as he did, that he must break with him'.[146]

In this tense situation, Trumbull himself found reason to be out of town on Friday, 31 January, when the resolutions on the council of trade were reported from committee. Others, however, were early and assiduous in attendance; that day, 'the Court members attended at 8 in the morning [and] the House was full by 9'.[147] Two divisions were eventually called, and the project's supporters carried both. The resolution barring M.P.s from sitting on the council was overturned 209 to 188, though the 'Court party' was 'unanimous' for it. Then, the resolution for an abjuration oath was rejected 195 to 188, even though it was supported by 'divers that were against them [the Court party] in the first question', including Lord Spencer, Lord Ashley, and Robert Molesworth. The union of such new Whig members with their fellow Whigs in office did not suffice for two reasons. Both Harley brothers spoke against the abjuration and 'all the Foleys' voted against it in conjunction with the backbench Tories, and on this question they were joined by a number of Tory placemen—among them, Sir Stephen Fox and his son Charles, Lord Ranelagh, and Sir Robert Cotton (of Cambridgeshire). In addition, several more Tory placemen left the chamber to avoid either disobeying the King or betraying their principles.[148]

The strength of the opposition to the Court was then confirmed on 1 February in the ballot for the coming year's Commissioners of Accounts. Two lists were circulated, one by the 'Country Party, as it is called', the other by the minister-ialists. The highest number of votes for any of the latter list went to the incum-bent Sir Thomas Pope Blount (178), but his total fell far short of Harley's (243). Moreover, Harley was joined by six men of the same 'complexion': Foley (238), Boyle (228), Granville (227), Bromley of Warwickshire (200), Sir Thomas Dyke (185), and Francis Gwyn (180).[149]

The ballot of 1 February also attests to the new prominence in St Stephen's Chapel of Robert Harley. Foley's elevation to the Chair in March 1695 and Clarges's death the following October made the industrious Harley almost in-dispensable at the Commission of Accounts and in the Commons. 'All things stand still till he comes', wrote Foley to Sir Edward Harley in urging Robert's return to town in early November 1695, and when the new parliament opened a few weeks later it was Harley who made 'the first speech was uttered' and 'chalked out the lines of the whole proceedings' during the first half of the session.[150] But diligence, though a considerable asset, was only one of Harley's virtues. Later in life he was to be christened 'Robin the trickster', but at this stage in his career he radiated an aura of sincere 'patriotism', of empathetic understanding of backbench feelings and prejudices, that his more cosmopolitan rival Montagu never possessed. And while Montagu eagerly pursued place and profit, Harley—if we can rely upon his later memoirs—had already declined at least one tempting offer of office from William himself.[151]

Although both Harley and Foley appeared to be more than content with the leading posts they had been voted by their fellow Commoners, the divisions of 31 January and 1 February 1696 prompted a good deal of talk about ministerial alterations. Even before these setbacks to the Whig Junto, there had been rumours of Torrington's return to the Admiralty and of Delaval's reinstatement at sea, no doubt as a means of diverting the agitation for a parliamentary council of trade.[152] After the votes on the council of trade and the Commission of Accounts, one opposition sympathiser jubilantly, though perhaps exaggeratedly, observed: 'Sir Thomas Littleton and Mr Montagu, the Court managers, are become very contemptible, at Kensington neglected, despised in the House.'[153] Leeds, it was said, would again be summoned to council, while Nottingham's appearance at Kensington, ostensibly to present his son-in-law Halifax to the King, set off reports that the former Secretary would be made Lord Chancellor.[154] Meanwhile, Somers—the present holder of the Great Seal—was confined to his house with 'a colic and rheumatism', and his condition was subsequently diag-nosed by some of his acquaintance as 'of the nature of some great men's gout'.[155] Admittedly, there was a substantial element of wishful thinking in much of the talk, and the Churchman Robert Price, for one, was sceptical: 'there are mighty disorders at Court, the ministry are uneasy, a change is talked of but will not be hazarded'.[156]

Price, indeed, was writing in the wake of still one more ministerialist setback. This was the Commons' adoption of a land bank scheme that was 'chiefly managed by Foley, Harley, and the Tories', and 'much laboured' for by Sunder-land, who persuaded William to 'desire' it on the view that 'it would engage the Tories in interest to support the government'.[157] The project was first broached on 3 February in a committee of the whole on ways and means, and that day it was resolved that the remainder of the estimates should be met out of a fund to be raised upon the security of the salt tax at 7 per cent interest. The passage of this resolution was hailed by Harley as 'a good day's work', and he predicted to Sunderland that soon the Commons would be ready to act on the King's request for the civil list.[158] Others took a different view. The Whig ministerialists displayed 'great concern', and the Governor of the Bank of England appeared on 5 February before the Treasury Board (with the King in attendance) to 'represent the prejudice to his Majesty's service and to [the Bank] by setting up another bank'.[159]

When the Commons' committee again took up the matter on 10 February, they had not one but three fund proposals to consider. First in the field was the scheme sponsored by two of the three private land banks that had been launched in 1695: one was founded by John Briscoe and included Paul Foley among its many trustees, the other was established by Dr Barbon and numbered Robert Harley's younger brother Edward among its trustees. These two banks offered jointly to provide £2,000,000; in return, they asked to be incorporated as the 'land bank united'.[160] Second was the project the Whig ministerialists were supporting; this was to have the Exchequer issue interest-bearing bills for the sum needed and was the brainchild of Mordecai Abbot (Cashier of the Customs).[161] Third was the Bank of England's proposal to lend the necessary amount at 5 per cent.

The Bank's offer was quickly scouted on the 10th, 'they being instruments in the debasing and exporting our money, raising our guineas and also all commodities, breaking their faith with the parliament by trading and giving at credit bills beyond their capital sum'.[162] The Junto's plan was given a hearing, only to be rejected 196 to 112 with Yonge telling for the minority. Then without further division, a national land bank was approved, and to avoid 'all parties and interest' among the existing banks it was decided to have a new subscription and to exclude all those 'concerned' in the Bank of England from participation in the new corporation.[163] Ten days later on 20 February, the committee of the whole completed its work on the project with a resolution that the fund to be raised should total £2,564,000: £1,724,000 for the remainder of the estimates for 1696 and the other £840,000 in lieu of the deficient duties on coal and glassware and on ships' tonnages which were now to be abolished.[164]

Agreement on the means to raise the remainder of the supplies for 1696 appeared to herald an early adjournment, and speculation now began about the King's choice of Lords Justices to serve during the coming campaign, with the Dutch resident noting talk of a breach between Shrewsbury and Sunderland.[165] In the meantime, the ministerialists had suffered yet another setback, in this case over the vexed question of the price of guineas. Hitherto, the recoinage had not provoked sharp divisions within the Commons, especially because Foley and Harley showed no sympathy for a devaluation.[166] There had been an attempt on 21 January to take up the question of fixing a price for the guinea in conjunction with the second of the Commons' recoinage bills, but it had failed in the face of ministerialist opposition. Subsequently, representations from the Bank and from traders seem to have prompted a change of mind at Whitehall; by mid-February, the ministerialists were definitely of the opinion that to facilitate remittances to pay the army in the Low Countries during the coming campaign it would be necessary to lower the guinea's price substantially.[167] It was, then, on their initiative that this subject was taken up in committee of the whole on 13 February, with Palmes in the chair.

The debate of 13 February lasted from noon until 10 that evening, with 'all the halls, Painted Chamber, Speaker's [Chamber], and the lobby, and coffee-houses, full of people' awaiting the outcome.[168] The length of the discussion was a symptom of the diversity of opinion. Some members—notably Lowther, Howe, and Seymour—opposed any action on the grounds that it was the availability of good silver coin that would determine effectually the guinea's price. Others, such as Clarke, were for reducing it without delay to twenty-one shillings. But since most of the speakers favoured some degree of reduction, the principal clash came over the specific maximum to be set. Foley apparently advocated twenty-eight shillings, Montagu twenty-four. The only division came late in the day upon a motion for Palmes to leave the chair; after the ministerialists lost this vote 152 to 131, the question for twenty-eight shillings was put and passed. This resolution was affirmed by the full House on 15 February by a margin of thirty-five votes, and an amendment to this effect was ordered to be brought in to be added to the bill for renewing the customs on vinegar, wines, and other imports.[169]

Nevertheless, the Whig ministerialists and their friends were not ready to concede defeat on this critical point. At a meeting of their 'club' after the House rose on 15 February, there was talk of amending the amendment on the guinea's price, and a debate in committee on the 17th revealed that several backbenchers, particularly Sir Godfrey Copley (one of a handful of members of the Royal Society in the Commons), were now ready to alter their earlier votes for a twenty-eight-shilling ceiling.[170] But though the Junto and their friends still hoped it might be possible 'to recover our ground', the Commons' approval on the 21st of Sir William Williams's parliamentary qualifications bill did not indicate any revival of strength.[171] Williams's measure was potentially the most far-reaching of the various electoral reform bills taken up during the 1695–96 session in the wake of the heavy spending that had marked the previous campaign and of a seeming influx of 'officers, younger brothers [i.e. peers' younger sons], pettifoggers, blue-aprons [tradesmen] and such like' into the lower House.[172] By imposing a £500 per annum real estate qualification upon knights of the shire and one of £200 upon borough members, its backers aimed to preserve the landed gentry's predominance in St Stephen's Chapel. And despite the objections of the placemen and some M.P.s from the boroughs, the bill was adopted 173 to 150.

In late February 1696, another opposition project also appeared close to final approval by the Commons. Granville's bill to implement the resolutions of 31 January for a council of trade was committed without opposition on 18 February, and the lower House agreed to proceed upon it on the 24th. But that day, the Commons never got to Granville's measure. Instead, they were summoned to the Lords early on the afternoon of the 24th to hear William announce the discovery of a Jacobite conspiracy upon his life, chiefly organised by the non-Compounders, that was to have been coupled with a French invasion to reinstate James II. Reports of plotting and of French naval preparations had been coming into Kensington since early February, and on the 20th the Commons had been moved to address the King to 'hasten out' the fleet. That day, the motion was 'put off to another time', but after a fourth informer to the assassination conspiracy reached Portland on the 21st and provided new details, William finally took the threat seriously.[173] Additional troops were ordered over from the Low Countries on the 22nd, and that night and the following day a series of arrests was ordered.

Had the plot succeeded, England would have lost both a queen and a king within little more than a year. Yet in the event, William's escape worked to the government's advantage. In the midst of a mounting crisis over the coin, support for the regime was solidified. As one of Locke's correspondents remarked a fortnight later: 'I believe of all the sham plots you ever heard of or read of, none was so serviceable to the persons that forged and laid them as this real one, so miraculously discovered, will prove to the government.'[174] And there were to be other beneficiaries as well, chief among them the Whig Junto. How they succeeded in exploiting this unexpected opportunity to revive their faltering position in the Commons and at Court and then managed to provide for the maintenance of the war effort, despite the financial woes that followed the currency crisis, stand out as the most interesting developments of the months that followed.

Notes to Chapter VII

1 *The Lexington Papers*, ed. H. Manners Sutton (1851), p. 27.

2 Ranke, *History*, VI, 262.

3 Apparently, the Queen would have preferred Stillingfleet to Tenison: Burnet, *History*, IV, 244, and *Supplement*, p. 404; Bodl. Ballard MS. 34, f. 186, P. Stubs to A. Charlett, 8 December; Ranke, *History*, VI, 254–5, 257; Ralph, *History*, II, 538–9.

4 ARA Heinsius MS. 402, L'Hermitage, 4/14 January. And compare Ralph, *History*, II, 539; Baxter, *William III*, p. 320 and n. 5.

5 *Lexington Papers*, p. 35. And see Ranke, *History*, VI, 263. For Jacobite views, see Ferguson's tract extracted in Ralph, *History*, II, 542–4; Bodl. Carte MS. 256, f. 85, [Earl of Middleton] to Mr Sison, 3/13 January.

6 J. M. Kemble, *State Papers and Correspondence . . . from the Revolution to the Accession of the House of Hanover* (1857), p. 164. And see [N. Hooke], *An Account of the Conduct of the Dowager Duchess of Marlborough* (1742), pp. 105–11.

7 *The conduct of the Duchess of Marlborough*, p. 110; Bodl. Locke MS. C8, f. 180, J. Freke to Locke, 17 January.

8 *Lexington Papers*, pp. 49, 44 And see BL Add. MS. 29574. f. 369, C. Viscount Hatton, 10 January; *Shrewsbury Corr.*, p. 220.

9 BL Add. MS. 17677PP, f. 124, L'Hermitage, 15/25 January; BL Add. MS. 46527, f. 48, J. Vernon to Lexington, 25 January. See also BL Add. MS. 29574, f. 379, C. to Viscount Hatton, 12 February.

10 BL Add. MS. 17677PP, f. 139, L'Hermitage, 29 January/8 February; CJ, XI, 216 (which erroneously gives '44' as the noes' total and reverses the two sets of tellers); KU, F. Bonnet, 25 January/4 February.

11 ARA Heinsius MS. 402, L'Hermitage, undated slip [15/25 March]; BL Add. MS. 42593, ff. 36–7, text of petition.

12 BL Add. MS. 29595, f. 74, to Viscount Hatton, 3 January. See also BL Add. MS. 46527, f. 47, J. Vernon to Lexington, 22 January.

13 Horwitz, *Revolution Politicks*, pp. 151–2, citing L'Hermitage. See also Browning, *Danby*, I, 515–17.

14 HLM, 1693–1695, p. 459; Bodl. Locke MS. C8, f. 181, J. Freke to Locke, 4 February. In April, however, the Bank's attempt to gain permission to issue bank bills was rejected by the Commons: CTB, X, 1366; Bodl. Locke MS. C8, f. 194, J. Freke to Locke, 9 April.

15 The motion to amend was defeated despite Speaker Trevor's obstruction of Wharton's attempt to deliver another message from the Princess; BL Add. MS. 17677PP, f. 145, L'Hermitage, 5/15 February. See also Luttrell, *Brief Relation*, III, 436.

16 BL Add. MS. 46527, ff. 34, 41, to Lexington, 21 December, 4 January.

17 BL Loan 29/188, f. 1, [R. Harley] to his father, 9 January. And see Ranke, *History*, VI, 265; BL Add. MS. 17677PP, f. 123, L'Hermitage, 15/25 January.

18 Ranke, *History*, VI, 265, 266; BL Add. MS. 17677PP, f. 143, L'Hermitage, 1/11 February; All Souls College MS. 152, vol. 5 (unfoliated), note of abortive supply resolutions in committee.

19 KU, F. Bonnet 15/25 February; BL Add. MS. 17677PP, f. 156, L'Hermitage, 15/25 February.

20 BL Harleian MS. 1492, f. 51 and ff., Commission's minutes. See also BL Harleian MS. 7018, f. 107.

21 CJ, XI, 234.

22 BL Add. MS. 17677PP, f. 159, L'Hermitage, 15/25 February.

23 BL Harleian MS. 1492, ff. 62–3; ARA Heinsus MS. 402, L'Hermitage, 16/26 February.

24 BL Add. MS. 46527, f. 57, to Lexington, 15 February; BL Add. MS. 17677PP, ff. 160–161, L'Hermitage, 19 February/1 March; ARA Heinsius MS. 402, L'Hermitage, 16/26 February.

25 BL Add. MS. 46527, f. 62, J. Vernon to Lexington, 22 February.

26 HLM, 1693–1695, pp. 416–19; Horwitz, Revolution Politicks, p. 153; All Souls College MS. 152, vol. 5 (unfoliated), notes on supply.

27 BL Add. MS. 17677PP, ff. 165, 167, L'Hermitage, 22 February/4 March; BL Add. MS. 46527, f. 62.

28 BL Add. MS. 46527, f. 66, to Lexington, 1 March. And see BL Add. MS. 17677PP, ff. 170–1, L'Hermitage, 26 February/8 March.

29 NU, Portland MS. PwA 503, [H. Guy to Portland], 14 June 1694; HMC Portland, III, 455; Luttrell, Brief Relation, III, 443.

30 For Wharton's Irish aspirations prior to this time, see NU, Portland MS. PwA 2522, ? to the King, 29 May 1696; HMC Buccleuch, II, 145–6; D. H. Somerville, The King of Hearts (1962), pp. 185–6.

31 Dartmouth's note in Burnet, History, IV, 194; DWL Morrice MS. Q, 469.

32 Locke and his coterie regularly referred to Montagu as 'the little man' and also as 'the monkey'; e.g. Bodl. Locke MS. C8, f. 192; The Correspondence of John Locke and Edward Clarke, ed. B. Rand (1927), pp. 439, 440, 441.

33 Lexington Papers, p. 67.

34 Somerset RO, Sanford MSS., bundle 2980, E. Clarke to Lord Capel (draft), 23 March. See also CJ, XI, 258; BL Add. MS. 17677PP, ff. 182–3, L'Hermitage, 8/18 March; KU, F. Bonnet, 8/18 March.

35 CJ, XI, 258, 259–63.

36 The Privy Council's examination of the Company's accounts in the autumn of 1694 had brought to light its large expenditure on 'special service'; BL Add. MS. 9764, ff. 95–7, account of proceedings, 27 September 1694; BL Add. MS. 29588, ff. 3–6, E. Southwell to Nottingham, 27 September 1694.

37 CJ, XI, 263. Gee's brother eventually lost his place.

38 Lexington Papers, p. 67.

39 BL Add. MS. 17677PP, f. 193, L'Hermitage, 15/25 March.

40 CJ, XI, 267–71, 272; BL Add. MS. 17677PP, ff. 192–4; HMC Fitzherbert etc., pp. 36–7.

41 NU, Portland MS. PwA 503, [H. Guy to Portland], 14 June 1694.

42 BL Add. MS. 17677PP, f. 169, L'Hermitage, 26 February/8 March (who interprets the change as an attempt by the Court to avoid further delays); All Souls College MS. 152, vol. 5 (unfoliated), notes on supply.

43 NU, Portland MS. PwA 503.

44 CJ, XI, 272; HMC Johnstone, pp. 74–5.

45 CJ, XI, 272.

46 Lexington Papers, p. 69.

47 HMC Frankland–Russell–Astley, p. 82.

48 ARA Heinsius MS. 402, L'Hermitage, [?17/27 March]; BL Add. MS. 17677PP, f. 204, L'Hermitage, 22 March/1 April.

49 Kenyon, Sunderland, pp. 272, 273.

50 This is the 'Holland House notebook' in BL Add. MS. 51511. See also Foxcroft, Halifax, II, 142 and ff.

51 NU, Portland MS. PwA 2706, ? to Earl of Athlone, 'Victualling Office', 1 February 1695. See also ARA Heinsius MS. 348, L'Hermitage, 16/26 November 1694.

52 NU, Portland MS. PwA 2708, ? to Earl of Athlone, 22 March; Lexington Papers, pp. 72, 81. See also HMC Finch, IV, 442; BL Add. MS. 51511, f. 63.

53 BL Add. MS. 17677PP, ff. 209, 236, L'Hermitage, 29 March/8 April, 19/29 April; BL Add. MS. 46527, f. 77, J. Vernon to Lexington, 5 April; HMC Hastings, II, 247; LJ, XV, 546–58. Both Shrewsbury and Leeds voted to exonerate Normanby.

54 *Lexington Papers*, pp. 69–70; BL Add. MS. 17677PP, f. 224, L'Hermitage, 10/20 April; PH, V, 911; HLM, 1693–1695, pp. 549–51.

55 HLM, 1693–1695, pp. 552–61; CJ, XI, 316–18, 320–6; Browning, *Danby*, I, 518–19.

56 PH, V, 934–6; HLM, 1693–1695, p. 561.

57 BL Add. MS. 28051, f. 341, 12 May. See also Ranke, *History*, V, 91 n. 1; *An Answer to the Preceding Letter from a Friend in London* (1695, BL 100 i 70).

58 BL Add. MS. 17677PP, f. 253, L'Hermitage, 30 April/10 May; *The Norris Papers*, ed. T. Heywood (Chetham Society, vol. IX, 1846), p. 27.

59 CJ, XI, 314. For reports that the King did not want the bribery inquiries pursued, see *Lexington Papers*, pp. 72, 81; Ralph, *History*, II, 550; and cf. BL Add. MS. 46527, f. 82, J. Vernon to Lexington, 19 April.

60 Bodl. Locke MS. C8, ff. 185, 189, 192, J. Freke to Locke, 28 February, 8 and 14 March; CJ, XI, 301, 305–6; HLM, 1693–1695, p. 540. For the bill, see Bodl. Locke MS. B4, f. 77; BL Add. MS. 42593, f. 203; BL Harleian MS. 6847, ff. 99–104. For the college, see P. Laslett, 'John Locke, the great recoinage, and the origins of the Board of Trade: 1695–1698', in *John Locke: Problems and Perspectives*, ed. John Yolton (Cambridge, 1969), pp. 146–7.

61 HMC *Hastings*, IV, 310–12; BL Add. MS. 17677PP, f. 148, L'Hermitage, 8/18 February; HLM, 1693–1695, pp. 510–11, 516–19.

62 Bodl. Locke MS. C8, f. 192, also ff. 185, 188, 189. And see BL Loan 29/188, f. 1, [R. Harley] to his father, 9 January; All Souls College MS. 152, vol. 5 (unfoliated), notes of a debate on the coin; BL Add. MS. 17677PP, f. 246, L'Hermitage, 26 April/6 May.

63 BL Add. MS. 46527, f. 85, J. Vernon to Lexington, 30 April. And see Kenyon, *Sunderland*, p. 272 and note.

64 Bodl. Carte MS. 130, f. 355, R. Price to [Duke of Beaufort], 18 May.

65 Normanby had offered such a plan in the wake of Mary's death; PRO, SP 8/13 No. 7 (misdated in CSPD, 1691–1692, pp. 543–4). For his claim he had turned down an offer to be a Lord Justice, see NU, Portland MS. PwA 838, Lord Scarborough to [Portland], 20 July 1695.

66 BL Add. MS. 46527, f. 89, J. Vernon to Lexington, 18 June. See also BL Add. MS. 17677PP, f. 259, L'Hermitage, 7/17 May.

67 BL Add. MS. 51511, f. 54; NU, Portland MS. PwA 1239, [Sunderland to Portland], 20 July 1694; *Shrewsbury Corr.*, p. 47.

68 Somerville, *King of Hearts*, pp. 185–6, 188, 190; *Correspondentie*, I, ii, 46; NU, Portland MS. PwA 2708, ? to Earl of Athlone, 22 March 1695.

69 BL Add. MS. 46527, f. 66, J. Vernon to Lexington, 1 March; Lord Cutts to J. Dudley, 31 May, printed in *Massachusetts Historical Society Proceedings*, 2nd s. II (1885–6), 181. See also KU, F. Bonnet, 30 April/10 May.

70 Somerset RO, Sanford MSS., bundle 284, to his wife, 18 May. And see *Shrewsbury Corr.*, p. 90.

71 BL Add. MS. 46527, f. 74, J. Vernon to Lexington, 26 March.

72 NU, Portland MSS. PwA 501, [H. Guy to Portland], 31 May, and also PwA 935, C. Montagu to same, 11 June.

73 *Shrewsbury Corr.*, p. 226.

74 Bodl. Carte MS. 130, f. 355, R. Price to [Duke of Beaufort], 18 May. And see NU, Portland MS. PwA 1245, [Sunderland to Portland], 29 May; *Shrewsbury Corr.*, pp. 96, 104.

75 BL Loan 29/237 (unfoliated), C. Hutchinson to R. Harley, 1 October 1695.

76 NU, Portland MSS. PwA 504, 502, [H. Guy to Portland], 18 June, 31 May.

77 NU, Portland MSS. PwA 502, 503, [H. Guy to Portland], 31 May, 14 June.

78 NU, Portland MSS. PwA 1248, [Sunderland to Portland], 29 July, and PwA 510–11, [H. Guy to Portland], 30 July, 6 August.

79 *Shrewsbury Corr.*, p. 96; NU, Portland MSS. PwA 510 and 1248.

80 NU, Portland MSS. PwA 1248–9, [Sunderland to Portland], 29 July, 18 August, and PwA 511, [H. Guy to Portland], 6 August.

81 NU, Portland MS. PwA 511. And see *Correspondentie*, I, ii, 60–2; BL Loan 29/146 (unfoliated), R. Henley to R. Harley, 20 July.

82 BL Harleian MS. 1494, f. 78; HMC *Portland*, III, 466. See also BL Loan 29/188, f. 31, Sir J. Trevor to R. Harley, 27 August.

83 NU, Portland MS. PwA 1249; *Shrewsbury Corr.*, p. 104. The capture of Namur only reinforced Sunderland's confidence; NU, Portland MS. PwA 1363, Romney to [Portland], 17 September.

84 Surrey RO, Somers MS. J4, Sir J. Rushout to Somers, 3 August. Marlborough was also

aware at an early date of the impending dissolution, but Harley was not made party to the fact: BL Loan 57/1 No. 9, Marlborough to Sir B. Bathurst, [7 August]; BL Loan 29/188, ff. 30, 33, [R. Harley] to his father, 24 and 29 August.

85 BL Loan 29/312 (unfoliated), 21 August.

86 For an analysis of the changes in the commissions of the peace since Somers was made Lord Keeper, see L. Glassey, 'The Commission of the Peace, 1675–1720' (unpublished D.Phil. thesis, University of Oxford, 1972), pp. 164–71. For the other changes, see Luttrell, *Brief Relation*, III, 424, 435; HMC *Downshire*, I, 505, 510, 512; CSPD, 1693, p. 5, and 1694–1695, pp. 91–2; BL Add. MS. 34350, f. 8; Bodl. Carte MS. 239, f. 5.

87 See Appendix A.

88 Burnet, *Supplement*, p. 412. It is unlikely that many candidates spent as much as the £1,132 the Lowthers and Howards did jointly at Carlisle; Cumberland RO, Lonsdale MSS., section V.

89 KAO, Chevening MS. 32, Newcastle to A. Stanhope, 31 August; BL Add. MSS. 46554–9 (unarranged), Leeds to Lexington, 21 September; Gloucestershire RO, Lloyd–Baker MSS., box 4, K27, Leeds to Archbishop Sharp, 10 September.

90 Bodl. Rawlinson Letters 104, f. 104, ? to T. Hoskins, 4 May. And see Bodl. Ballard MS. 34, f. 142, A. Upton to A. Charlett, 11 October; *The Herbert Correspondence*, ed. W. J. Smith (Board of Celtic Studies, Law Series XXI, 1965), pp. 43–4; Wing W210.

91 HMC *Le Fleming*, pp. 337–8; *Archives*, III, i, 410.

92 The King made only one recommendation to the Earl of Bath for the Cornish constituencies, and that was a contingent one; BL Add. MS. 40771, f. 83, Shrewsbury to Ranelagh, 27 October.

93 For Westmorland, see HMC *Le Fleming*, pp. 337–8; HMC *Westmorland etc.*, p. 331. For the addresses, *Post Man*, No. 76 (Cumberland); *Post Boy*, No. 80 (Plymouth); *Flying Post*, No. 80 (Westmorland and Carlisle) and No. 88 (Exeter).

94 Burnet, *History*, IV, 288, and *Supplement*, p. 413.

95 Althorp Savile MSS., box 10, to Marquess of Halifax, 2 November (much gloomier than his of 21 October); BL Add. MS. 28879, ? to J. Ellis, 5 November.

96 Shrewsbury lent his aid to Seymour's opponent Tiley; BL Sloan MS. 2717, f. 47.

97 Trinity College MSS., King correspondence No. 477, 16 November; BL Add. MS. 56241 (unfoliated), to R. Hill, 15 November; HMC *Buccleuch*, II, 276. And see NU, Portland MS. PwA 659 [Portland] to R. Hill (draft), 22 November.

98 For the Grascome list, see Appendix C.

99 CSPD, 1695 and addenda, p. 345. The foreign envoys' reports echo these sentiments.

100 *Shrewsbury Corr.*, pp. 399–400.

101 Berkshire RO, Trumbull Add. MS. 116, cabinet notes of 16 and 24 October.

102 BL Loan 29/188, f. 107, [R. Harley] to his father, 16 November; Bodl. Locke MS. C8, f. 201, 30 November. See also *Lexington Papers*, p. 148.

103 Burnet, *History*, IV, 263–4; CJ, XI, 334; KAO, Chevening MS. 78, newsletter, 3 December. Littleton's candidacy for the chair of the committee of the whole on supply was also challenged, but there was no division.

104 Shaw's computations in his introduction to CTB, IX, have been amended here in the light of, but with some variations from, D. Waddell, 'The Career and Writings of Charles Davenant, 1656–1714' (unpublished D.Phil. thesis, University of Oxford, 1954), app. A.

105 J. Horsefield, *British Monetary Experiments 1650–1710* (1960), pp. 72–6.

106 Koninklijk Huisarchief (The Hague), Willem III, XI G, No. 176, 6 August. And see HMC *Portland*, III, 574; BL Add. MS. 17677QQ, f. 225, L'Hermitage, 17/27 January 1696.

107 NU, Portland MS. PwA 502, [H. Guy to Portland], 31 May. See also *Shrewsbury Corr.*, p. 231.

108 NU, Portland MS. PwA 506, [H. Guy to Portland], 5 July.

109 CTB, X, 1144–7 (the copy sent to Locke was signed by Montagu, Smith, and Fox); CSPD, 1695 and addenda, p. 71; Bodl. Locke MS. C22, f. 19, Sir W. Trumbull to Locke, 19 July, and C18, f. 158, Sir J. Somers to Locke, 21 September.

110 Berkshire RO, Trumbull Add. MS. 116, cabinet minute, 16 October. In general, these minutes confirm and amplify Burnet, *History*, IV, 264–5.

111 HMC *Buccleuch*, II, 242; Berkshire RO, Trumbull Add. MS. 116, minute, 4 November.

112 Berkshire RO, Trumbull Add MS. 116, minutes, 10, 12, 13 November.

113 CJ, XI, 339.

114 CJ, XI, 339.

115 Ming-Hsun Li, *The Great Recoinage of 1696 to 1699* (1963), p. 24; Luttrell, *Brief Relation*, III, 519, 539, 544, 550; Burnet, *History*, IV, 278; HMC *Buccleuch*, II, 256.

116 Koninklijk Huisarchief, Willem III, XI G, No. 178, to Godolphin (draft), 16/26 September; also Yale Univ. Lib., Osborn Collection, Phillipps MS. 10074, pp. 23, 29, Godolphin to W. Blathwayt, 10 and 24 September. And see BL Add. MS. 17677PP, f. 405, L'Hermitage, 22 October/1 November; KAO, Chevening MS. 78, R. Yard to A. Stanhope, 22 October.

117 See I. K. Steele, *The Politics of Colonial Policy: The Board of Trade in Colonial Administration 1696–1720* (Oxford, 1968), p. 11 and app. B.

118 HMC *Portland*, III, 577.

119 BL Add. MS. 17677PP, ff. 448–9, L'Hermitage, 3/13 December; HLM, 1695–1697, items 955, 959, 978; HMC *Hastings*, IV, 312–14; BL Harleian MS. 1274 (minute book of committee of the whole), f. 2, 2 December.

120 HMC *Buccleuch*, II, 275; Peter Lord King, *The Life and Letters of John Locke* (1884), p. 240.

121 King, *Locke*, p. 240. See also Bodl. Locke MS. C8, f. 206, J. Freke to Locke, 10 December.

122 HMC *Downshire*, I, 597–8.

123 BL Harleian MS. 1274, f. 7; CSPD, 1695 and addenda, p. 124.

124 KU, F. Bonnet, 13/23 December; BL Add. MS. 46525, f. 62, J. Ellis to Lexington, 13 December; BL Harleian MS. 1274, f. 8.

125 Luttrell, *Brief Relation*, III, 563, 567.

126 Bodl. Locke MS. C8, f. 201, J. Freke to Locke, 30 November.

127 KU, F. Bonnet, 3/13 December; Bodl. Locke MS. C8, f. 204, J. Freke to Locke, 5 December.

128 HLM, 1695–1697, p. 128 note; CJ, XI, 354, 358; BL Harleian MS. 1274, ff. 3, 4–6.

129 Newton was a devaluationist: Li, *The Great Recoinage*, pp. 68, 71–2, and app. A; *Shrewsbury Corr.*, p. 400; King, *Locke*, p. 221. For Montagu, see Bodl. Locke MS. C17, f. 27, R. Pawling to Locke, 7 January 1696.

130 BL Harleian MS. 1274, f. 9; Bodl. Locke MS. C8, f. 210, J. Freke to Locke, 17 December. Bonnet noted that one of the Treasury Lords voted with the minority on 10 December and that John Smith and Edward Clarke opposed the final stages of the coinage bill; KU, 10/20 December and 27 December/6 January. See also Boyer, *William the Third*, III, 119–20.

131 Bodl. Locke MS. C17, f. 27.

132 Bodl. Locke MS. C17, f. 219, W. Popple to Locke, 2 January. And see Luttrell, *Brief Relation*, III, 568.

133 Luttrell, *Brief Relation*, III, 566, 568; HLM, 1695–1697, pp. 128–31; BL Add. MS. 17677QQ, ff. 199, 204, L'Hermitage, 31 December/10 January and 3/13 January.

134 The goldsmiths vigorously lobbied for the supplementary resolutions; BL Add. MS. 17677QQ, ff. 214–15, L'Hermitage, 10/20 January.

135 The Commons' division of 16 January was an attempt to forestall further delay on the treason trials measure. See also BL Add. MS. 30000A, f. 7, F. Bonnet, 21/31 January.

136 CJ, XI, 400.

137 HMC *Hastings*, IV, 318–19; *Memoirs of Ailesbury*, p. 371; BL Add. MS. 17677QQ, f. 232, L'Hermitage, 21/31 January.

138 S. Rezneck, 'The Statute of 1696: A Pioneer Measure in the Reform of Judicial Procedure in England', JMH II (1930), 5–27.

139 *Calendar of Treasury Papers 1556/7–1696*, p. 437; NU, Portland MS. PwA 1249, [Sunderland to Portland], 18 August 1695.

140 CJ, XI, 409. And see *Correspondentie*, I, ii, 66; BL Add. MS. 46527, f. 104, J. Vernon to Lexington, 17 January; HMC *Kenyon*, pp. 396, 399.

141 Bodl. Locke MS. C17, f. 219. W. Popple to Locke, 2 January.

142 Luttrell, *Brief Relation*, III, 568; BL Add. MS. 5540, f. 92; BL Add. MS. 17677QQ, f. 205; BL Add. MS. 30000A, f. 3. All these are printed or cited in R. Lees, 'Parliament and the Proposal for a Council of Trade 1695–6', EHR LIV (1939), 49 ff. See also KAO, Chevening MS. 78, R. Yard to A. Stanhope, 6 January.

143 ARA Heinsius MS. 465, L'Hermitage, [3/13 January]. Cf. I. Burton *et al.*, *Political Parties in the Reigns of William III and Anne: The Evidence of Division Lists* (BIHR, special supplement 7, 1968), pp. 6–13 and app. A.

144 BL Add. MS. 17677QQ, f. 230, L'Hermitage, 21/31 January; BL Harleian MS. 1274, ff. 34–5, 37. See also HMC *Portland*, X, 29.

145 Berkshire RO, Trumbull Add. MS. 116, memo, 23 January. See also BL Add. MS. 17677QQ, f. 260, L'Hermitage, 4/14 February.

146 Burnet, *History*, IV, 295.

147 Hunt. Hastings MS. 954, D. Bret to Earl of Huntingdon, 3 February.

148 KAO, Chevening MS. 78, R. Yard to A. Stanhope, 11 February. Cf. Berkshire RO, Trumbull MS. 'Ellis' bound vol., J. Ellis to Sir W. Trumbull, 1 February. For the debates, see HMC *Kenyon*, pp. 398–9; HMC *Hastings*, II, 253–4.

149 CJ, XI, 429; HMC *Kenyon*, p. 399; Berkshire RO, Trumbull MS. 'Ellis' bound vol., J. Ellis to Sir W. Trumbull, 4 February.

150 HMC *Portland*, III, 573, 577.

151 BL Loan 29/165, misc. 97, pp. 2–3; HMC *Portland*, IV, 451.

152 FSL Newdigate newsletters 2577, 28 January. Delaval, despite the impression some had, thought it 'much better' for William to 'break this Admiralty' than 'to give way' to the demand for a parliamentary council of trade: HMC *Downshire*, I, 609; cf. Burton, *Political Parties*, app. A, for Delaval.

153 Hunt. Hastings MS. 954.

154 Berkshire RO, Trumbull MS. 'Ellis' bound vol., J. Ellis to Sir W. Trumbull, 3 February; BL Ad. MS. 29578, f. 543, Sir C. Lyttleton to Viscount Hatton, 12 February; BL Add. MS. 17677QQ, ff. 285–6, L'Hermitage, 21 February/2 March.

155 BL Add. MS. 46527, f. 110, J. Vernon to Lexington, 4 February; Bodl. Locke MS. C8, f. 213, J. Freke to Locke, 27 February.

156 Bodl. Carte MS. 130, f. 359, R. Price to [Duke of Beaufort], 11 February. See also KAO, Chevening MS. 78, R. Yard to A. Stanhope, 11 February.

157 Burnet, *History*, IV, 308. See Hammond's doggerel on this occasion in Bodl. Rawlinson MS. D174, f. 103, quoted in K. Feiling, *A History of the Tory Party 1640–1714* (Oxford, 1924), p. 327.

158 HMC *Downshire*, I, 618. And see BL Harleian MS. 1274, f. 39.

159 Berkshire RO, Trumbull MS. 'Ellis' bound vol., J. Ellis to Sir W. Trumbull, 4 February; CTB, X, 1430. See also Bank of England MSS., Court of Directors' Minute Book B, pp. 102–4.

160 Horsefield, *British Monetary Experiments*, pp. 201–6. During the 1694–95 session, Harley was apparently supporting Briscoe's proposal to incorporate his land bank by statute: BL Harleian MS. 1250, ff. 109–14; BL Loan 29/129, bundle 12, H. Chamberlen to R. Harley, 21 January [1695]; Wing B4757; London Univ., Goldsmiths' MS. 61, 'an account of the original and progress of the national land bank', f. 2.

161 The final version of this scheme (put out after those cited by Horsefield) can be seen in Berkshire RO, Trumbull Add. MS. 121.

162 Bodl. Carte MS. 130, f. 359. The last objection refers to the Bank's practice of issuing cashier's notes despite the Commons' refusal in the spring of 1695 to authorise the corporation to issue bank notes.

163 Bodl. Carte MS. 130, f. 359. And see BL Harleian MS. 1274, f. 42; Luttrell, *Brief Relation*, IV, 16.

164 BL Harleian MS. 1274, f. 47.

165 ARA Heinsius MS. 465, L'Hermitage, [18/28 February].

166 Northants RO, Buccleuch MSS., Vernon letters, I, No. 7, 12 October 1696.

167 Horsefield, *British Monetary Experiments*, p. 81.

168 HMC *Kenyon*, p. 403; *Locke–Clarke Correspondence*, p. 440.

169 House of Commons Lib. MS. 12 (fragmentary accounts of debates), f. 155. See also HMC *Hastings*, II, 256; [S. Grascome], *An account of the Proceedings in the House of Commons in relation to the Recoining the Clipp'd Money and Falling the Price of Guineas* ([1696], Wing W201), p. 8; BL Harleian MS. 1274, f. 43.

170 For Copley, see BL Stowe MS. 747, f. 62, G. C[opley] to T. Kirk, 15 February; *England's Enemies Exposed, And Its True Friends and Patriots Vindicated* (1701, BL T1688 No. 10), pp. 14–15.

171 Bodl. Carte MS. 103, f. 256, Sir R. Atkins to T. Wharton, 18 February.

172 Bodl. Ballard MS. 32, f. 188, [W. Moore] to A. Charlett, 10 March. See also BL Add. MS. 17677QQ, f. 286, L'Hermitage, 21 February/2 March.

173 Luttrell, *Brief Relation*, IV, 20; and, in general, see Baxter, *William III*, pp. 336–7 (though he confuses the days of the week). Note also Harley's curious account of this incident; BL Loan 29/165, misc. 97, pp. 4–6.

174 Bodl. Locke MS. C17, f. 37, R. Pawling, 14 March.

VIII

FINANCE AND POLITICS

1696-1697

Between Queen Mary's death in late December 1694 and the discovery of the assassination plot in late February 1696, a sharp struggle had broken out for mastery in the House of Commons. In early 1695, the Whig ministerialists succeeded in discrediting Guy, Trevor, and Leeds. But these triumphs had not yielded their expected rewards, for Montagu's arrogance and deceit undid their plans. Instead, Foley gained the Speaker's Chair, Trumbull succeeded Trenchard as Secretary, new elections were held in the autumn of 1695, and by early 1696 Sunderland thought it wise to speak up at Court in support of the parliamentary council of trade and the national land bank for which Foley and Harley appeared to command a majority in the new House of Commons.

However, the reaction to the Jacobite conspiracy led to a dramatic reversal of the tide that had been running against the leaders of the Whig ministerialists (the 'juncto' or junto). Apparently, Sunderland anticipated this possibility from the moment that the plot was uncovered, for after the first wave of arrests he went personally on the 23rd 'to the Speaker to acquaint him with all', while that evening Guy penned a note to Harley in which he conveyed the King's hope that, despite a recent bout of sickness, he would be able to attend the Commons the next day.[1] But if Harley did get to St Stephen's Chapel on the 24th, neither he nor Foley could forestall their rivals' exploitation of the discovery.

After the King on 24 February formally announced to parliament the news of the intended assassination and French invasion, the Commons promptly adopted Sir Rowland Gwynne's motion for an association which designated William 'as rightful and lawful king' and threatened 'revenge' upon all his 'enemies' should he die by violence.[2] This association, modelled on that of Queen Elizabeth's day, was to be 'voluntary', but on 25 February the Commons were called over to see who would and who would not take it. Of the 453 members present, 89—virtually all staunch Churchmen—refused.[3] That day, a similar subscription was set on foot in the Lords. Leeds did manage to have it worded that William 'hath right by law' to the crown, a somewhat less offensive formula to Tories, but the peers' association included a more explicit renunciation of James II and the 'pretended' Prince of Wales than the Commons'. And despite Leeds's efforts, no fewer than nineteen peers, headed by Nottingham, refused this voluntary association, though Lord Feversham (one of the sworn witnesses to the birth of the Prince of Wales in 1688) did subscribe after he was assured that the term 'pretended' referred only to parliament's abrogation of the child's claim to the throne and not to the facts of his birth.[4]

These associations, as Sir Christopher Musgrave observed during the lower House's debate, were simply abjuration in a somewhat different guise. Moreover, like earlier abjuration proposals such as those of 1690 and 1692, William had mixed feelings about the wisdom of such oaths. As he confided to the Earl of Chesterfield a few weeks later, when that peer explained to him in his closet why he had declined to subscribe, 'this was not a thing of his contriving, but that his cabinet council had advised him to it'.[5] Then, too, it is a measure of the rallying of sentiment to the throne that these subscriptions were carried so decisively in both Houses less than a month after the Commons had voted down the oath for members of the projected council of trade.

Mass signings of the associations were soon set on foot out of doors as well, and the widespread pro-Williamite reaction occasioned predictions that 'non-jurors and Jacks in most counties will be in danger, either as to their estates or persons'.[6] To be sure, Sir John Thompson's proposal on 27 February that all non-associators should be expelled from the Commons was not taken up, but the King clearly signalled his *official* position on 12 March at a meeting of the Privy Council. There, he 'declared he though it fit for his service that all who were in employment under him should sign the association, since it was begun in parliament and had gone so far in several parts of the kingdom', and he then 'called for the council book and struck out with his own hand' the names of three non-associating councillors—Nottingham, Normanby, and Seymour.[7]

A few weeks later, Sir John Thompson returned to the fray. In early April, he suggested that the Commons appoint a committee to examine some of the captured plotters; in turn, the committee's report prompted the lower House to order a bill for the 'better security of his Majesty's person and government'.[8] The progress of 'our glorious bill', as one Yorkshire Whig referred to it, was then speeded by the furore over the absolution administered to several of the conspirators at their execution on 3 April by three non-juring clerics. The bill imposed the association upon all office-holders (including members of the Commission of Accounts), extended the recusancy penalties to Protestant non-jurors, laid down penalties for those who 'by writing or otherwise' impugned William's title as 'rightful and lawful', and made returning from France without royal licence as serious an offence as going there without permission. In the heated debate over the bill, Seymour was nearly sent to the Tower for denouncing the measure as 'illegal'. Yet, stubborn opposition to the bill by the Tories only encouraged the attachment to it of a clause, approved by 139 to 103, that all members of subsequent parliaments must take the association. Again in the Lords, Nottingham and Rochester led a vocal opposition, but the measure was approved with only minor alterations in a long sitting on 13 April.[9]

By mid-April, the end of the first session of William's third parliament was approaching, with results very different from those that could have been predicted before the disclosure of the assassination conspiracy. No more had been heard of the parliamentary council of trade—'one of the benefits the plot has produced', so the Dutch resident observed.[10] Moreover, William did secure some supply for the civil list. When this topic was debated by the Commons on 16 March, the ministerialists at first spoke of £600,000, but they were apparently content to settle for £500,000 and an additional £15,000 for the relief of the Huguenot refugees.[11]

By the beginning of April, the long campaign to lower the guinea's price had also been concluded successfully. After fixing a maximum of twenty-eight shillings on 13 February, the Commons voted on the 28th to lower the ceiling to twenty-six shillings. But a further reduction to twenty-two shillings was narrowly rejected on 20 March by 167 to 163, and this setback was in no small part due to the feelings of a number of placemen (including Lowndes and Blathwayt) that 'the interest of the Bank' in the lower rate was not that 'of the King and old England'.[12] However, William promptly made it known to his servants that he favoured the twenty-two-shilling limit, and on 26 March the Commons adopted it by a vote of 166 to 146 and attached it to the bill to encourage holders of silver plate and good coin to bring them into the Mint to be recoined. Four days later, the Lords followed suit, 53 to 33.[13]

Yet, even as the college was reporting to Locke that we have 'got into a fair way of determining the mystery of this iniquity', the guineas clause remained to plague the King on another score—the parliamentary qualifications bill.[14] Sir William Williams's measure had been approved by the Lords on 9 March, with only limited Court opposition, so that all that it lacked was the King's assent. William's intention was to delay until the end of the session and then to veto it. However, the clause for guineas at twenty-two shillings in the coinage bill was to come in force on 10 April, so the King—after a reminder from both Houses—could not avoid deciding upon Williams's bill on the 10th when he came to Westminster to accept the coinage measure. His veto of the qualifications bill that day provoked demands in the Commons for an address against those who had advised it, and Sunderland's name was bandied about. Even so, when a motion for an address was proposed by the opposition Tories on 14 April, it was overwhelmingly defeated 219 to 70.[15]

All that remained of the Commons' agenda by mid-April 1696, then, were the final financial measures of the session, especially the long-delayed land bank bill. The King, despite the strong distaste for the project expressed by Montagu and his Treasury colleague John Smith, was willing to attempt it.[16] But before the bill was sent up to the Lords, the Commons made some important alterations in it. On 18 March, the lower House agreed to insert two additional sections at the instance of 'the friends' of the Bank of England, who were said to be trying 'to clog' the bill 'all they can'.[17] These additions—one to restrict the new bank to lending upon the security of land and to the crown, the second to enable the government to borrow the £2,564,000 by other means should the subscription for the new bank not be completed by some fixed date—were said, along with the lowering of the guinea's price, to be discouraging the original backers of the scheme. Soon there was talk that the land bank would, indeed, be 'turned into an Exchequer bank'.[18] But what the Commons actually did on 20 April was to approve an amendment to allow the Exchequer to issue interest-bearing bills up to a total of £1,500,000 before 1 August 1696 (the deadline for a 50 per cent subscription to the land bank). A further provision that the Exchequer could issue bills for the remainder of the £2,564,000, should the land bank fail to meet the deadline of 1 August, was also inserted, despite claims from the bank's supporters in the Commons that the scheme's financial backers already had 'amongst themselves a subscription of near £400,000' and were ready 'immediately' to open their books for a public subscription.[19] Whatever the validity of these claims, when William came to Westminster to close the session on 27 April, it must have seemed to him that one way or another the cash for the army would be forthcoming, despite his current difficulties in scraping up bullion to carry with him to the Continent.

In addition to the land bank bill, eighty others reached the statute book during the 1695–96 session. Among them was an act for affirmations for which the Quakers had long lobbied, an act for the encouragement of seamen (as William had requested from the throne), and an act allowing a parliament in being at the death of a sovereign to be continued for up to six months in the new reign. The last, brought in in the wake of the assassination plot, was seen as a signifi-cant innovation by the Brandenburg resident who thought it made parliament 'prior to the King', but this aspect did not trouble any considerable number in either House.[20] However, the Commons were not inclined to revive the censor-ship, despite a recommendation to this effect from their select committee on expiring laws, nor did they proceed with the college's printing bill after commit-ting it in March.[21]

Both Houses also devoted considerable time during the 1695–96 session to the East India Company's request for a parliamentary establishment, and each approved resolutions to regulate the trade by statute in order to 'obviate the inconveniences that may otherwise arise by the Scotch act' establishing a com-pany in that kingdom.[22] None the less, parliament adjourned without passing any legislation, in no small part because of the continuing disagreement between the Company and the interlopers. The eventual stalemate may also have owed some-thing to the shift in sentiment that was in evidence on other issues after 24 Feb-ruary. Up to that point, the Commons seemed to be leaning towards the old Company, and its request for a joint stock was approved 181 to 156 on 11 February over interloping suggestions for a regulated company. However, when the Company's accounts were examined in March, there was a noticeable drop in support for its proposals, and in the end it was reported that both sides were content to see the revised bill of establishment abandoned.[23]

Just as the discovery of the plot affected the fate of a variety of parliamentary measures, so it was expected that it would have considerable weight in the King's choice of his servants. After 24 February there was no more talk of a change of hands in the Tories' favour; rather, the rumours circulating in April 1696 of 'a great alteration' in 'divers places of trust' referred to alterations anticipated to the Whigs' advantage. No doubt Capel was not alone among the ministerial Whigs in using the plot as an argument to William for the ouster of those 'in great employments and trusts' who 'are esteemed dubious to your interest'. Among those considered most likely to be removed were Leeds and Godolphin, and prominent among those touted for office were the Whig peers Stamford, Monmouth, and Tankerville.[24]

Yet, though Harley believed that there had been 'a design' that was 'carried on to the last moment of the sessions' to secure 'an address against some great men', it never surfaced.[25] And contrary to many expectations, William left behind exactly the same set of Lords Justices who had served the previous summer. Places were offered to Stamford and Monmouth, but they were not grand enough to suit. Stamford declined a seat on the new Board of Trade; Mon-mouth, who had expected to succeed Russell as head of the Admiralty Commis-sion, declined to serve on that board after Russell was persuaded to remain. Hence, the only change among the upper echelon of royal officials was Littleton's long-delayed promotion from the Ordnance Office to Trumbull's seat at the

Treasury Board, thus giving the Whigs a majority on that commission for the first time since 1690.[26]

At the same time, the establishment of the royal Board of Trade created eight new paid positions at £1,000 a year, and among those gratified were Tankerville and John Locke. William also created two new peers. Sir John Thompson, a long-time 'grumbletonian' who had for years aspired to a peerage and had distinguished himself during the 1695–96 session in support of supply and of the association, was ennobled as Baron Haversham. Sir John Lowther of Lowther had much more considerable claims upon the King's favour for his loyal service in office between 1689 and 1694 and for his vigorous support of war measures thereafter, both in parliament and in the 1695 elections. In October 1695, Lowther—professing the fear that he would be 'condemned as long as I live to serve' in the Commons by his countrymen—had sought a peerage from William, and now he was created Viscount Lonsdale.[27]

Although the Junto Whigs still fell short in the spring of 1696 of that monopoly of royal favour to which they aspired, the position of those whom they regarded as their enemies or rivals was much weakened in the aftermath of the assassination plot. At Court, Sunderland was feeling the weight of their hostility for his sponsorship of Foley's and Harley's projects, his protégé Trumbull was being edged out of the continuing examination of the Jacobite network behind the attempt against William's life, and the Earl himself seems to have deliberately kept out of all but Irish affairs (complicated by Capel's death late in May) during the first part of the summer.[28] At Westminster, the Commission of Accounts was in danger of paralysis because of the requirement that its members take the association. Of the group chosen on 1 February, four—Granville, Bromley, Dyke, and Gwyn—were staunch Churchmen. And despite all Harley's persuasive talents, it was not till mid-June that one of them, Gwyn, finally qualified himself by taking the association and so established a quorum for business with Harley, Foley, and Boyle.[29] Meanwhile, in the provinces, a full-scale review of the lists of deputy lieutenants and justices of the peace was under way. The review was begun by the Privy Council in April with the aim of removing all whose support for the regime seemed less than wholehearted. Even the taking of the association was not sufficient; it was deemed necessary to have subscribed before the association had been made compulsory upon those holding the King's commission. Before William's departure, the Earl of Bath was ousted from his lieutenancies in Cornwall and Devon, and by late July 1696 it was reported that 86 justices and 104 deputy-lieutenants had been turned out with the review still far from complete.[30]

The recriminations that so extensive a purge of the county commissions might normally have provoked were muted by the general preoccupation with the liquidity crisis that gripped the realm during the King's absence. The root of the problem was the inadequacy of the measures adopted to implement the recoinage, once it had been decided in late 1695 that the matter was too urgent to postpone and that it was desirable to retain the old standard. On the one hand, Locke's recommendation that the clipped coin should go by weight had been overridden, and his subsequent criticism of the fixing of the guinea's price had gone almost unheard even by his college.[31] And on the other hand, the administrative preparations at the Mint were grossly inadequate, at least until Newton was named Master in April 1696. By mid-1696, the country mints were just beginning to function and the mills at the Tower had produced only £700,000 in new milled coin, even though clipped coin to the nominal value of £4,700,000 had been brought by that time into the Exchequer.[32]

In these circumstances, the virtual disappearance of coin of any sort after the May 4 deadline for the withdrawal of clipped silver money was almost predictable. As one of the Duke of Beaufort's correspondents wrote to him from London on 5 May:[33]

at this time all money is refused unless it be new money or very broad, of which there is but little stirring. I was forced to enter my name in a book to pay for my dinner, for they choose rather to trust than take even passable sixpences. The Exchequer has a double guard these two days, and the common people begin to grow a little mutinous.

The 'common people' were particularly disadvantaged, since they were unable to take advantage of the provision allowing the use of clipped coin for tax payments up to 24 June. Their superiors and the government itself were also in difficulties, since the liquidity famine rapidly spread to instruments of credit, particularly the Bank of England's cashier's notes. On 6 May, a run on the Bank started; this was 'probably set on by the goldsmiths' in the City, who had refused bank notes earlier in the year in pursuit of their rivalry with the Bank.[34] Now, instead of refusing bank notes, they sought to cash those they held. This left the Bank to face an unprecedented demand for coin which it could not even begin to satisfy because of the Mint's slowness.[35] The consequent discounting of bank notes was followed by similar difficulties for goldsmiths' notes; as a result, so Montagu informed Blathwayt, 'whereas formerly the paper money in London was more than all the cash of England, at present no bill or note will pass in payment'.[36]

These were the conditions prevailing when the newly organised commissioners to receive subscriptions to the national land bank asked the Treasury Board in late May for special allowances to facilitate the floating of the new project. Chief among their initial requests was for permission to accept up to a quarter of the total £2,564,000 in clipped money, and they also wanted to offer a premium of 10 per cent for payment in gold or in new coin.[37] Their insistence on these requests, and especially the former, brought a breakdown in negotiations between the backers of the land bank and the government, and this stalemate guaranteed the complete failure of the subscription when the commissioners opened the books on 4 June. As one of Blathwayt's correspondents observed: 'As to the new bank, though there at first appeared the most considerable merchants and the Jews and East India Company and all the lesser banks, yet since they find their demands not complied with by the Lord Justices, they all decline it.'[38]

In refusing to allow the land bank commissioners to receive clipped money, the Treasury, and the Lords Justices who finally determined the point, claimed to be following legal advice and were unanimous. However, the Lords Justices were also influenced by the fear that if some clipped money were at first allowed, 'the whole' subscription might be made in bad coin 'by which the King would lose one half and the money would be useless till it could be recoined, which it cannot be in a long time'.[39] Nevertheless, there were differences of opinion at the Treasury as to whether enough had been done to encourage the land bank, particularly after its backers abandoned their clipped money request. While Montagu informed his friend Blathwayt on 5 June that 'everything has been done to encourage them that could be reasonably expected', from the outset

Godolphin had warned Portland that 'other people' were not 'as uneasy as I am' over the prospects of the subscription's failure, and that some had been 'full of objections and difficulties'.[40]

The problem, as Godolphin perceived it, was that Montagu and his two Whig colleagues Smith and Littleton were not really worried about the land bank failing. They thought they could fall back upon their own scheme for Exchequer bills and believed they could secure the Bank of England's help in circulating them. Godolphin's own view was that it was preferable to allow 'almost any conditions to the land bank rather than venture' the risk of a collapse in supply to the army.[41] Hence, when the land bank commissioners renewed their approaches to the government late in June, just as the Treasury was about to launch the Exchequer bills, Godolphin urged acceptance of their offer even though it meant conceding a £300,000 premium. Yet, only Shrewsbury showed any signs of supporting Godolphin when the Treasury Board (with Fox absent) met the Duke and the Lord Keeper to review the new proposals, so they too were rejected.[42]

By this time, the government's financial situation was close to desperate. The Bank of England did remit £100,000 to the army overseas shortly after the King's departure from London, and in early June the directors agreed to send over another £100,000. But the second remittance was made upon a promise of prompt repayment which the Treasury was in no position to satisfy. As Godolphin warned William, in sending him the news of the second remittance on 17 June: 'I am confident it is the last we are to expect from them' nor would they 'have given it when they did, but to furnish an argument for not concluding with the other.'[43] In any case, when Blathwayt dispatched an express to Godolphin on 9 July to inform him that without prompt additional remittances the King would have to disband the army, Shrewsbury was forced to reply on behalf of the Lords Justices that there seemed no prospect of 'any speedy or considerable supply' from England.[44] As Godolphin explained the situation to Blathwayt a few days later:[45]

We are in no expectation of relieving . . . the wants of the army . . . since the disappointment of the land bank but from the credit of our Exchequer bills and that we can not propose to establish any farther at present than as we have money to support it, and the premium of tallies is now so great here that money is not to be borrowed at any rate for they give now 30 per cent to discount tallies at a year's distance. . . .

Starved of funds from London and unable to raise new loans on the Continent, William now decided to send Portland back to England, and the Earl was authorised even to assemble parliament if necessary. Portland arrived in London on 26 July and, after summoning Sunderland up to town by an express, plunged into a round of consultations.[46] A consensus against reconvening parliament quickly formed. As Shrewsbury informed William on the 28th: 'It was universally the opinion of all here that a session in your absence and in the divisions the nation labours under now would produce nothing but heat among themselves and petitions from all the counties about the state of the money.'[47]

Instead, talks with the backers of the land bank were resumed upon 'good encouragement from Mr Foley and Mr Harley that money will be got' from them.[48] These negotiations were conducted by Portland, Shrewsbury, and Godolphin, since the land bank men complained of past 'ill usage' from the Treasury Board. In addition, Sunderland employed Guy and the goldsmith

Charles Duncombe (Cashier of the Excise) to supplement the efforts of the government's negotiators. Hopes were high as the land bank men initially spoke of offering at least £200,000, and Gwyn reported that Foley 'thought he should get the better of his enemy Charles [Montagu] and the Bank of England'.[49] But on 4 August, the land bank men told Portland they could only advance £40,000, and that upon onerous terms—a result that left Foley and Harley 'in despair'.[50]

The King's servants now considered and discarded a variety of other expedients: the launching of a voluntary subscription to be begun among the officers of the crown, the request of a loan from the City, even the diversion of cash currently in the Exchequer though that money was appropriated by statute to other uses.[51] But each of these was, at best, very risky. Finally, the directors of the Bank of England were brought on 14 August to agree to furnish another £200,000; in return, they were promised full recompense for the remittance losses they had already incurred in the government's service. Portland celebrated the news of this relief by partaking of a drunken 'debauch' at Sir James Houblon's official residence in the City in the company of Shrewsbury, Montagu, and Smith. And the good news prompted the King to order Blathwayt 'to acknowledge the great service' done by the Bank which at least would suffice to 'bring us indeed into winter quarters'.[52]

Like it or not, then, William found himself more indebted to the Junto and to the Bank at the end of the disappointing 1696 campaign than he had been at the outset. The King had arrived in the Low Countries in May with high hopes of peace and with plans for forceful action in the field to stimulate movement in Louis XIV's negotiating position. But without funds, he had accomplished nothing. Moreover, while the Lords Justices failed to find suitable employ for the 'great useless' allied fleet after Rooke brought the Mediterranean squadron back home in the spring of 1696, the French were able to detach the Duke of Savoy from the alliance and to arrange a neutrality in Italy.[53] At home, the administration had been fortunate to weather the summer without serious disturbances. Had it not been for the rallying to the throne after the assassination plot, it is possible that the scattered riots and local tumults provoked by the recoinage would have escalated under Jacobite leadership at a time when the army in England lacked money to pay for either its quarters or its subsistence.[54]

The Whigs' reaction to the liquidity crisis was to draw in their horns. Although Sunderland had suggested to Portland in May 1696 that the Whigs were 'frighted' at the talk of a peace, 'thinking the King will get from them' once the war was over, by late July Shrewsbury, at least, was much more alarmed at the dismal prospects if the war were not soon ended.[55] Not only did the Duke express his fears to William (who promptly passed on the letter to Pensionary Heinsius for his perusal), but he also welcomed Sunderland warmly when the Earl came up to London after Portland's arrival.[56] Sunderland subsequently remarked that he had received from Shrewsbury 'more assurances of friendship than I thought him capable of' and that he had found the Junto 'tractable' and 'extremely desirous' to have 'things go well' in the next session of parliament.[57]

But while Sunderland, Shrewsbury, and Somers concerted matters in August 'as much as possible' for the 1696–97 session, they could not anticipate the unsettling effects of Sir John Fenwick's accusations.[58] Fenwick, once one of James II's generals and connected by marriage to the influential Howard clan headed by the young Earl of Carlisle, had been arrrested in June for his part in the assassination plot. Sir John, 'generally reputed a fearful man', did all he could after his arrest to avoid standing trial and he promised to make great revelations of Jacobite activities. The Lords Justices were willing to hear what he had to say, and Shrewsbury observed to William in late July that 'if he were well managed he might lay open a scene that would facilitate the business the next session'.[59] Little, then, did the Duke imagine he would be one of the accused in the 'confession' Fenwick made to Devonshire early in August—a confession that the Lord Steward dispatched to William without showing to any of his colleagues. Devonshire did so not only because he had promised secrecy to Sir John before he made his statement but also because he was himself shaken by the charges Fenwick levelled against Shrewsbury, Russell, and Godolphin, as well as Marlborough and a number of lesser men.[60] Sir John, in effect, had chosen to try to extricate himself by accusing those who had been involved, to one degree or another, in Middleton's 'compounding' schemes rather than by disclosing information about his own associates.

Whatever the half-truths embedded in Fenwick's allegations, the King wanted no part of his delaying tactics and divisive insinuations. In any case, as William frequently remarked, all Fenwick's accusations related to the years before the general pardon of 1695. Although the King did not inform the others Sir John denounced, he did dispatch the text of the 'confession' to Shrewsbury late in August accompanied by a letter in which he professed his 'astonishment' at its 'effrontery' and his 'entire confidence' in the Duke.[61]

Unfortunately for all concerned, it was not possible to allow Fenwick's case to rest there. When Sir John was again threatened with an immediate trial, he made a further confession on 23 September to Shrewsbury's under-secretary, James Vernon. This provided just enough additional information against known but unconvicted Jacobites such as the Earl of Ailesbury to induce the Lords Justices to put off his case once more. In the meantime, though the contents of Fenwick's papers were kept secret, speculation over their substance was rife. 'Everyone', Vernon told the vacationing Shrewsbury on 24 September, is 'tak[ing] a liberty at guessing who are accused'.[62] Among those whose names were frequently mentioned were Marlborough, Godolphin, and Rochester, but it was the story that Monmouth had been named that caused the most trouble. That unpredictable peer reported the gossip with concern over dinner with his friend Secretary Trumbull on 26 September, and Vernon was informed that the Earl was soon busy spreading accusations against Godolphin. Monmouth also told Vernon to his face that it was wrong for the Lords Justices to commit the second examination of Fenwick to a mere under-secretary. And it is possible, in the light of Monmouth's connections in the City, that he had a hand in the presentation on 28 September at a common hall (called to elect a new mayor) of a paper demanding a full parliamentary investigation of the assassination plot.[63]

For all the stir Fenwick's case was making, the King's principal concern on his return to London on 7 October 1696 was to see that measures were in hand to overcome the lingering liquidity crisis in order that Louis be convinced that England could finance at least one more campaign. So Sunderland renewed his 'courtship' of Foley and Harley, despite some ministerial Whigs' 'uneasiness', and on the 13th the King summoned the two to a two-and-a-half-hour conference.[64] The Junto also made their preparations; they and their friends were well aware they must 'stand' to their previous measures 'like men of mettle', and special care was taken to revive the meetings of the Whig 'club' of the 1695–96 session.[65]

Despite the continuing rivalry for ascendancy in the Commons between the Junto on one hand and Foley and Harley on the other, when parliament assembled on 20 October, prompt and nearly unanimous action was the order of the day. After the King warned members that 'the only way of treating with France is with our swords in our hands', the Commons resolved *nemine contradicente* to 'effectually assist him' in the war and to 'make good' the mounting total of deficient grants from former sessions.[66] That day, the Commons also specifically reaffirmed the last year's resolutions for a recoinage at the old standard so as to dispel continuing speculation about a devaluation. Altogether, these votes, as William happily informed Heinsius, were more than could have been expected in a single day's work, and the King was further reassured to find that all 'reasonable men' concurred in his negotiating posture.[67]

During the next fortnight, all attempts by a small group of Commoners led by Seymour, Musgrave, and Howe to delay or to obstruct supply were rejected by large majorities. On 26 October, a motion to adjourn for eight days until more members arrived was beaten 126 to 45; on 3 November, a move to take up consideration of past deficiencies before examination of the estimates for 1697 was overwhelmed 271 to 54; and on the 4th, the maintenance of an army of 87,000 men was approved 223 to 67. These successes Vernon attributed to the nearnightly meetings of the Whig 'club' at the Rose Tavern. As he remarked, 'whatever is pre-resolved is sure to be carried'. But the size of the majorities also attests to the backing for the estimates given, as in the two previous sessions, by Foley and Harley. And this point was implicitly conceded by Vernon himself when he commented that on ways and means the 'opposers will unite their strength and appear formidable'.[68]

Before reaching that hurdle, the Commons were asked to consider Fenwick's accusations. The decision to submit Sir John's case to parliament emerged from a month's agitated discussion and preparatory manoeuvres, set in motion by the news that reached William on 8 October of Shrewsbury's collapse at Eyford, the Duke's country retreat in Gloucestershire.[69] Shrewsbury's ailment, brought on by a hunting accident he suffered over a month after being informed of Fenwick's charges against him and a fortnight after leaving the capital for a brief vacation before the King's return, seems to have been the first attack of a type of tuberculosis.[70] But whatever caused Shrewsbury to spit blood profusely and repeatedly, he found himself in no condition to travel at a time when his presence in London was vital. Aware that his absence could be misconstrued, the Duke tried on 17 October to make the journey in a horse litter sent down to him at Portland's and Sunderland's instance, only to suffer a further attack. And this relapse prompted his first attempt to resign. However, his talk of giving up the seals was met by new representations from the King, Sunderland, and the Duke's Whig friends; they warned that for him to resign at this juncture would only compound the political damage his absence threatened. In response, the Duke promised to come up to London as soon as he could, and in the meantime he sent up a list of suggestions for dealing with Fenwick.

Shrewsbury's ideas concurred with Russell's and Somers's opinions that Sir John's allegations must be publicly refuted. The problem, as the Lord Keeper perceived it, was 'the time and the manner' of bringing the affair into parliament.[71] Above all, it was desirable to introduce the case at a moment of the ministers' own choosing and in a fashion that would indicate the King's disbelief in Sir John's charges while still treating them as of sufficient moment to justify the Commons' attention. To arrange all this was not easy. William's reluctance to have Fenwick brought before him for examination was overcome with Sunderland's aid. And Sunderland was also instrumental in devising a solution to another difficulty; this was the danger that some Whigs, urged on by Monmouth, might try to use Fenwick's revelations against Godolphin and thereby would hinder the vindication of Shrewsbury and Russell. So adroitly did Sunderland deal with Godolphin that even Somers and Wharton were left uneasy. What Sunderland did was to persuade Godolphin to offer his resignation to the King as a formal gesture on 30 October. William, who apparently felt that the events of the past summer indicated he could make do at the Treasury without Godolphin's assistance, then accepted the first lord's resignation, much to his chagrin. Thus, in Somers's judgement, Godolphin was 'directly tricked' into quitting.[72]

Just as Godolphin was leaving the stage, another removal considerably complicated the Fenwick affair. This was the flight of the actor Goodman to France, which was arranged and financed by Sir John's friends. Their aim was to block a trial, for the one witness remaining against Fenwick would not, under the terms of the 1696 statute regulating treason cases, suffice to secure a conviction. With Goodman out of the way, Fenwick felt safe in refusing either to substantiate or to disavow his confessions when he was brought before the King the evening of 2 November.[73] Even so, the Junto thought they had a counter for this in a parliamentary bill of attainder.

The recourse to attainder came on 6 November in the face of warnings from Sunderland that it would delay the King's business and create divisions in parliament.[74] As planned, the Commons' proceedings were initiated early that day by Russell. And Godolphin's resignation, the King's declared opinion of the falsity of Sir John's allegations, and Fenwick's own demeanour when he was interrogated at the Bar, ensured that when the question was put to condemn his papers in toto as 'false and scandalous', there were only 'one or two members who cried no'.[75] However, the subsequent motion to proceed with a bill of attainder was opposed both by some of the leading non-associators and by Harley, who had only been informed by Vernon that morning of this part of the Junto's plan. Despite warnings of the dangers to subjects' liberties in so extraordinary a proceeding, a large majority of 179 to 61 was mustered for the motion to bring in a bill to attaint Sir John. Hence, Vernon assured the absent Shrewsbury that he was 'confident', in spite of Sunderland's reservations, that 'the King's business will fare the better' for dealing with Sir John in this summary manner.[76]

However, it soon became apparent that the bill of attainder would consume more time and provoke more opposition, even in the Commons, than Vernon or the Junto had anticipated. Not only did the lower House grant Fenwick's request for counsel, but also a growing number of M.P.s began to question the wisdom of condemning to death even so obviously guilty a man on the testimony of only one witness. Thus, after the bill was committed on 17 November by a vote of 182 to 128, the sponsors gave some consideration to abandoning it. None the less, it was decided to proceed on the grounds that 'the matter having gone on so far, they must not flag in it' lest they 'give strength to the false accusations'.[77] The bill, then, was read a third time on 25 November, though now it was carried by only 33, 189 to 156. Among the minority were several prominent Whigs such as former Treasury Commissioner Thomas Pelham and former Admiralty Commissioner Sir Richard Onslow, while nearly a dozen crown servants stayed away, including Secretary Trumbull and Attorney-General Trevor.[78]

The mounting resistance that the bill of attainder had encountered in the Commons did not augur well for it in the Lords. From the outset, the bill's sponsors had expected greater opposition among the peers, not least because the Whig ministerialists were short of able speakers in the Lords if they could not count upon Monmouth.[79] So there were renewed importunities from the Junto and the King for Shrewsbury to come up to town, but another relapse hindered him from joining the 119 peers who answered the Lords' summons to be present at the first reading of the bill on 1 December. Yet, Shrewsbury's absence was more than counterbalanced by the zeal the King showed to get the bill passed. Portland did not 'stick to speak to anyone my Lord Keeper desire[d]', and William personally spoke to some of the bishops 'with a great deal of earnestness', though not always with success.[80]

However, no one could bridle Monmouth. Not content with his part in securing Godolphin's resignation, that Earl resisted all Somers's and Sunderland's efforts to quiet him. For some months, he had been patronising an informer, one Matthew Smith. And Smith, in hopes of a larger reward for his earlier disclosures about the Lancashire and the assassination plots, was prepared to charge Shrewsbury with stifling his reports. Moreover, while such former witnesses as Fuller and Young were once more offering their tainted services to the government in the autumn of 1696, Monmouth, who was apparently convinced Fenwick knew much more than he had said, was busily inciting Sir John to substantiate his earlier charges.[81] Monmouth had a hand in conveying papers of instruction to Fenwick when the bill of attainder was before the Commons, and some of Monmouth's friends in the lower House expressed, in Vernon's view, 'unintelligible notions of advantages to be made by Sir John's confession'. Similarly, when Fenwick appeared before the Lords on 1 December, Monmouth gave him 'all encouragement to have made out the accusations in his paper'.[82] But despite assurances both from the Lords and from the King that nothing he now revealed would be used against him, Fenwick was neither willing to disclose what he did know of his own associates' activities nor able to back up the major charges in his first paper.

Monmouth, then, was prominent among the majority in the Lords when the bill of attainder was passed on 23 December. Yet, the measure aroused such distaste it was approved by only 68 to 61 votes, although the Court canvassed for it strenuously and Marlborough succeeded in getting Prince George to vote with the majority on the final division. Among the minority were at least eight bishops and no fewer than four of the seven Lords Justices of 1696—Godolphin, Devonshire, Dorset, and Pembroke.[83] Much greater unanimity prevailed after the Christmas recess when Monmouth's troublemaking came under scrutiny. Enraged by Monmouth's outspoken backing of the attainder, Fenwick's Howard kinsmen retaliated, and the Earl was defended by only a few old associates such as Bolton and Stamford. On 15 January, Monmouth was found guilty of attempting to tamper with Fenwick, sent to the Tower, and stripped once more of his places at Court.[84] So he was near at hand when Sir John—all delaying tactics having failed—was beheaded on Tower Hill on 28 January 1697.

For all the furore generated by Fenwick's case, the opposition in the Commons was able to make little headway on other questions in the closing weeks of 1696. Critics of the ministers had a number of grievances they were eager to ventilate, chiefly the fleet's failure to prevent the junction of the Toulon and Brest squadrons and also the unpaid quartering of the army in England, but they could make little of them. Even the parliamentary qualifications bill encountered more resistance this year than the last, thanks in part to a petitioning campaign against it mounted by the boroughs. The bill was approved on 17 December by a margin of 200 to 160, but as a concession to the boroughs they were now to be permitted to return their own townsmen provided they had £5,000 or more in personal estates.[85]

In the meantime, the 'Lords of the Articles' (as Boyle sarcastically dubbed Montagu and Littleton), in frequent consult with the Rose Club, were moving ahead with plans to restore paper credit and to finance the 1697 estimates.[86] Despite Speaker Foley's emphatic defence of the land bank project, the Commons voted 200 to 124 on 11 November to accord the Bank of England its request for monopoly privileges during the term of its charter (to 1705); despite the fear that a general excise was lurking in the wings, they voted 202 to 105 on 19 November to raise all the supplies for 1697 out of current taxation; and despite the reservations of some Whigs such as Pelham and Onslow, they voted 211 to 134 on 2 December to extend a number of existing imposts, among them tunnage and poundage, to August 1706, to help to make good the deficiencies of past years' grants.[87]

The principal issue in the division of 2 December was not the extension of the various levies; it was Montagu's scheme to 'graft' the nearly £10,000,000 outstanding in tallies on to the Bank of England's stock. In return, the Bank would be paid the interest on the tallies it accepted as part of a new subscription of stock.[88] As yet, the terms of this scheme had still to be settled with the Bank, and so the Commons turned next to the ways and means to raise the supplies for the coming year. Members showed little enthusiasm for a ministerial proposal offered on 10 December for a 10 per cent levy on the sale of live cattle; instead, the lower House took up on the 11th a proposal for a 'capitation'. This project had been devised by Sir John Foche, and it was brought to the Commons' attention by Sir John Parsons, once Foche's colleague at the Excise Office.[89] Initially, Foche's combination of a poll, income tax, and land levy attracted wide support. The opponents of new excises were ready to embrace almost any alternative, and Seymour and Musgrave were prepared even to concede to the crown the power to nominate the commissioners to assess the proposed capitation. As for the ministerialists, they too were enamoured at first of a plan that could bring in £5,000,000 or even more, and so they laid aside their own projects for excises on live cattle and on malt.[90]

Despite these advances in the Commons' work on supply, the Treasury found itself strapped for cash in November and December 1696, just when William was receiving conflicting reports of French intentions. Although the French now indicated they were ready to make concessions in the preliminary peace negotiations on the critical question of the formal recognition of William's government, the enemy's simultaneous mobilisation of men and ships at Brest sparked fear a descent on some part of the British Isles was being readied. The Commons had not intended to leave the King short of ready money; on 9 November, harking back to the expedient adopted three years before, they authorised the government to borrow up to £600,000 on the strength of the taxes to be granted during the current session. The problem was finding lenders. So little had come in on the loan by late November that the government reverted to the practice of the early years of the reign and dispatched a delegation of Privy Councillors to the common council of London on the 27th. Even so, Vernon despairingly noted a month later that 'the public services [are] near at a stand for want of ready money and the loan goes on but slowly'.[91]

One impediment to the loan was the continuing hoarding of good coin, despite Newton's success in revitalising the Mint during the past six months and also the Commons' reaffirmation of the old standard on 20 October. To some extent, the good effects of the Commons' resolve had been undone by the disputes in the lower House during November over the terms of a new bill for 'further remedying the ill state of the coin'. Once more, Montagu seems to have dragged his feet over having the remaining 'hammered' coin (the remnant that was not badly clipped) pass by weight, and in the end this Lockean expedient was only carried 155 to 152 on the bill's final reading on 24 November.[92] No wonder, then, that Locke's friends put the blame for the problems in raising the loan upon the Chancellor of the Exchequer, and they were also highly critical of his suggestion in early December that a premium of 10 per cent be offered for any sums advanced by lenders in milled coin or in guineas.[93]

Locke's college also thought Montagu was at fault over another obstruction to the loan—the disagreement between the Treasury and the Bank of England over the 'engrafting' scheme. Indeed, they told Locke that the Chancellor of the Exchequer had not even consulted the Bank's directors before he offered this proposal in the Commons on 26 November. This was not altogether fair to Montagu, yet it was true that many of the directors, led by the Houblon clan, were fearful that engrafting would overburden the corporation and water down their personal equity in it.[94] The Houblons' view prevailed at a meeting of Bank stockholders on 7 December, and the general court concluded with a diplomatic but definite rejection of Montagu's first propositions.[95] All in all, then, the government was fortunate that by the turn of the year fears of a French descent had so far diminished that William felt free to announce his choice of the English plenipotentiaries—the Earl of Pembroke, Lord Villiers (Lady Betty's brother), and Sir Joseph Williamson—for the peace conference which was expected to begin in a few months.

As it was, the Commons took until mid-April 1697 to finish the financial tasks they had set themselves. The first of the money bills, the capitation, was sent up to the Lords on 26 January. By then it bore only a limited resemblance to Foche's original project, with its thirty-two categories of taxpayers and its estimated yield of £9,000,000. What remained was a three-shilling levy on land (with the crown to name the commissioners of assessment) coupled with various provisions designed to tax personal income as far down the socio-economic scale as servants' wages; all told, it was calculated that the revised capitation should bring in a total of £3,000,000. In addition, the capitation bill included authorisation for the Treasury to circulate £1,500,000 of the new Exchequer bills.

Before the capitation bill was transmitted to the Lords, the Commons were moved to tack Sir William Williams's parliamentary qualifications bill to it. After the original qualifications bill was rejected 62 to 37 by the Lords on 23 January, its backers in the Commons 'mustered all their strength' on the 26th to try to add it to the capitation bill as a rider. At first, so Vernon reported, it seemed that the tack would be approved, but then Speaker Foley, 'under pretence of speaking to order', refuted all the precedents its supporters had alleged and 'declared the like never was in parliament'. With this assistance from the Chair, the tack was rejected 163 to 135, though the two Cavendishes, Lord Ashley, and Molesworth voted with the minority.[96]

The next of the money bills incorporated Montagu's 'engrafting' project in a revised version which had been thrashed out in strenuous negotiations with the Bank.[97] The bill, as reported from committee of the whole on 3 February, provided that the Bank would take new subscriptions up to a maximum of £5,000,000; 80 per cent of the new subscriptions were to be in tallies, the rest in the Bank's own notes, and both were to be accepted at their full face value. This, it was hoped, would reduce the substantial discounts currently prevailing on them. In return, the Commons conceded, by a vote of 176 to 70, that the Bank's charter should be extended until 1710, that the Bank should be accorded exclusive privileges during that time, and that the Bank should receive 8 per cent interest on the tallies it took in. And all this was to be paid for out of the proceeds of those imposts which the Commons had previously voted to extend until 1706.

Once the terms of the engraftment had been worked out, the Commons turned to deal with the £840,000 deficiency on the discontinued levies upon ships' tonnages and upon coal and glassware. These levies had been adopted in 1694 and 1695 respectively in lieu of ministerial proposals for an excise on leather. So it was a particular pleasure for Montagu and his colleagues at the Treasury to secure the Commons' approval 159 to 132 on 17 February of a resolution for a 15 per cent tax on leather goods to replace those deficient imposts.

While the excise on leather provoked a relatively close vote in the Commons, the King's request for assistance in meeting payments on the civil list was somewhat less controversial. There were sharp words about royal grants to Dutch courtiers in the wake of William's recent gifts to the new Earl of Albemarle, but the Commons by a vote of 111 to 61 on 24 February again authorised £515,000 for the civil list and for the relief of the Huguenot refugees.[98] This left the lower House with just about £2,400,000 more to find to pay for the military and civil expenses of the coming year. Most of this was intended to come from a levy upon malt; the rest to be raised by new duties on wine and on textiles.

Approval of the malt levy on 12 February and of the wine and textile duties on 3 March should have concluded the Commons' deliberations on ways and means, but the lower House's initial resolutions had later to be revised. The chief problem was that resistance to the duties on wine and textiles grew, rather than diminished. The opponents included many West Country members who were concerned that these levies would damage the booming Anglo-Portuguese trade. Among them were such ministerial stalwarts as Edward Clarke and Sir Walter Yonge, and both of Locke's friends were prominent in the unexpected defeat of the wine duties bill on 3 April by 105 to 103.[99]

The rejection of the wine duties 'put our Ministry into great disorder and made them rage terribly' against the defectors.[100] Even so, the loss was quickly repaired. In lieu of the imposts on wine and textiles, a bill for doubling the duties of tunnage and poundage for the next two and three-quarter years and for levying a fourth shilling on land during 1697 was introduced on 7 April. Subsequently, this measure was amended to make provision for the circulation of £1,200,000 more in Exchequer bills. On the 7th, the Commons also agreed to add Thomas Neale's newest lottery project to the malt bill. And finally on the 14th, they dispatched to the Lords the last of the many financial measures of the session.

Supply bills loomed large among the sixty-five measures enacted during the 1696–97 session. Among the other new statutes was one to revise the defective 1695–96 act to encourage seamen and another to regulate the number and the activities of the new breed of 'brokers and stockjobbers' who had multiplied since 1689.[101] Among the casualties of the session were such not-so-hardy perennials as the Commons' bills to prohibit the sale of offices and to ease the financial responsibilities of sheriffs. The first was amended by the Lords in a fashion unacceptable to the Commons; the second, a project of Robert Harley's since his own term as sheriff in 1689, simply died in the upper House, despite two reminders from the Commons.[102] Harley also had a hand in another unsuccessful bill to regulate printing and publishing; this, like its predecessors of the last two years, never emerged from committee.

However, none of these measures attracted the attention given two others, both jointly sponsored by two staunch Whigs—Goodwin Wharton and Sir Henry Hobart. Hobart was a fiery-tempered country gentleman, a friend of Russell's, and chairman of the Whig assembly at the Rose Tavern; he served as knight of the shire for Norfolk and he was apparently acting to protect the interests of the East Anglian textile industry in promoting this year, as the last, a bill to ban the import for home consumption of East Indian textiles. This measure also had the enthusiastic backing of the London weavers who demonstrated in its favour outside Westminster Palace in late January 1697.[103]

After the Commons passed the bill against East Indian textiles by 140 to 139 on 6 February, Hobart and Wharton secured the House's leave by a vote of 134 to 106 to bring in a bill of general naturalisation. A similar measure had been pressed unsuccessfully by Palmes and other Whigs in 1693–94, and this year's bill was meted out the same fate. The opponents of general naturalisation contended that it would lead to a flood of impoverished immigrants and so undo the supposed benefits of the projected ban on the import of East Indian textiles, for the latter had been advocated as a means of protecting the numerous 'poor' employed in the domestic textile trades.[104] Thus, on 2 March, the Commons rejected 168 to 127 a motion to commit the naturalisation bill.

In the meantime, the Lords had approved the bill barring the import of East Indian textiles, but the friends of the East India Company also managed to secure the inclusion of several wrecking amendments. In particular, the peers' provision to impose a penalty of £50 for the wearing of the prohibited goods predictably set on the Commons to defend their fiscal prerogatives. After a series of conferences between the two Houses, the Lords 'adhered' to their amendments on 19 March by a margin of 42 to 40, and so the bill was lost.[105] That evening, the weavers reacted by putting to the torch the East End residence of the Governor of the East India Company. In response, the Company announced it was willing both to halt imports of Bengal silks and calicoes and to advance £400,000 in loans to the government, provided parliament would confirm its charter of 1693. This proposal had some official encouragement, for Governor Bohun reported to his fellow directors that it had been initiated from Whitehall. Nevertheless, the session ended without parliamentary consideration of the question.[106]

While the East India Company continued to function without parliamentary sanction, the 1696–97 session saw the demise of a parliamentary creation—the Commission of Accounts. The work of the 1696 commission had been hindered by the imposition of the association upon its members. Gwyn had finally taken the association in June 1696, thereby establishing a quorum of four, but even as he did so he had professed himself weary of the commission. Harley and Foley may not have shared their colleague's disillusionment with the work of the commission, but it is noteworthy that Lord Spencer (who had distinguished himself for his Whig views since entering the Commons in 1695) was the sponsor of the bill to renew the commission in the 1696–97 session. The ministerial Whigs, it would seem, were content to keep the commission in being and were intent (as in 1694) upon exploiting their ascendency in the Commons to pack it with their own nominees.[107] When the Rose Club's slate was put forward in early February 1697, it encountered only token opposition. Knowing that they 'could not bear up', most of their opponents voted with their feet, though a few stayed behind to 'put in some bantering names to ridicule the thing'.[108] But after the ministerialists' attention shifted to other topics, a motion to engross the bill was unexpectedly offered on 15 February and promptly voted down in a preconcerted move by 148 to 115. In this way, the Commission of Accounts passed, at least temporarily, from the Westminster scene, condemned by those who had once been its most enthusiastic proponents in order to prevent it from becoming a Court outpost.

The contrast between the Commons' massive financial commitments during the 1696–97 session and the demise of the Commission of Accounts did nothing to diminish William's pleasure at the results of the parliamentary campaign. When he came to the Lords on 16 April to close the session, the thanks he offered for its supplies were effusive and sincere. The Commons, he wrote Heinsius, 'had done more than I could have expected'.[109] What remained now was to make sure that parliament's provisions to restore credit were effectively implemented. Of these, none was thought more critical than the successful launching of the first issue of the £2,700,000 in Exchequer bills. Wharton was sent off into the City by Somers 'to dispose people's minds right', and William— sitting at the Treasury Board—personally recommended participation to the Governor and the directors of the Bank of England.[110] Furthermore, when the Whig financier Sir Robert Clayton compounded his earlier laxity in the King's service by 'discouraging' the subscriptions to the £400,000 fund being raised to circulate the bills, he was promptly ousted from the Customs Commission. With this kind of backing, the £400,000 was pledged by the time the King set sail for Holland late in April.[111]

Before departing, William presided over the annual round of official alterations and personal honours, and the Junto's efforts on the financial front during the 1696–97 session were duly rewarded. Two of their four leaders, Somers and Russell, now accepted peerages (as Baron Somers and Earl of Orford), and Somers was also named Lord Chancellor; the third, Montagu, was made first lord of the

Treasury and given an Irish grant; and the fourth, Wharton, was made Chief Justice in Eyre south of Trent and Lord Lieutenant of Oxfordshire, both positions formerly held by his local rival, James Bertie Earl of Abingdon. The Junto's friends and associates also did well. The Earl of Stamford was appointed Chancellor of the Duchy of Lancaster in place of Robert Bertie Lord Willoughby; the Marquess of Winchester was named to the new commission of Lords Justices of Ireland, along with two courtiers, Lords Galway and Villiers; and Thomas Pelham, Goodwin Wharton, and Sir John Austen were chosen to fill vacancies at the Treasury, the Admiralty, and the Customs respectively.

Naturally, not everyone was or could be satisfied. Russell grumbled that he would have preferred the Garter given to Portland, and Somers soon became embroiled with Portland over the fee farm grant William made to help the Lord Chancellor sustain his new peerage.[112] Wharton, too, believed he had grounds for complaint in the King's continued resistance to his Irish pretensions, which had been reawakened by Capel's death in May 1696. Upon the news of Capel's fatal illness, there had been much talk 'of Lord Wharton's succeeding singly' in Dublin.[113] Nor was this only gossip, for Shrewsbury put the Comptroller's name forward to William at that time 'with an assurance it is what he would cheerfully undertake'.[114] Simultaneously, the King was informed by another correspondent that Wharton himself 'owns that he declined being one of the Lord Justices when the last [Capel] went and that your Majesty promised he should be the next chief governor, upon which he depends, but will not press it'. Whatever William had promised in 1693, he was not prepared to send Wharton as Lord Deputy, perhaps because he feared that the Comptroller was too 'strongly wedded to a party' and that 'his heat and forwardness' would be disruptive in Dublin.[115] Instead, the decision on Capel's successor was put off, first until the King's return to England in the autumn of 1696 and then until the end of the parliamentary session. When Shrewsbury again proposed Wharton in April 1697, William professed his willingness to send him as one of a commission, but at the same time the King avowed that he thought Wharton would not be content for long to serve as one of three. In the event, the Comptroller did not, apparently, 'press' his candidacy, either in 1696 or 1697. Yet rightly or wrongly, he subsequently blamed Sunderland for his 'disappointment'.[116]

For the time being, it was Secretary Trumbull who was most vocal in his dissatisfaction. Already in October 1696, Sir William had sought leave from the King to resign, alleging his exclusion during the summer of 1696 from the continuing examination of the assassination conspiracy, the monopolisation of profitable official business by the Duke of Shrewsbury and Vernon at the other Secretary's office, and his own advancing age and lack of facility at 'treat[ing] parliament men, which [was] yet a necessary part of the business' of his office.[117] The events of the 1696–97 session had not changed Trumbull's inclination nor was his disposition any the whit improved by the fate of his recommendations on appointments. In early April 1697, Trumbull pressed Sunderland to see to the reward of three M.P.s whom he felt had done good service in the Commons: Sir Henry Hobart, John Arnold, and Arnold's kinsman John Dutton Colt. Hobart had strong support from the Rose Club's members, and his initial disappointment at failing to secure a place at the Customs in April was assuaged by the offer in June of a newly vacant seat on that commission.[118] But Arnold and Colt were *persona non grata* to Shrewsbury because of their association with Monmouth, and Sunderland was not prepared to exert himself in their behalf lest the Duke take it amiss.[119]

Sunderland's concern to maintain good relations with Shrewsbury, even if it meant disappointing Trumbull, is a mark of the Duke's pivotal position in the ministry. The King, the Junto, and Sunderland were all anxious to keep Shrewsbury in place in the face of his talk of resigning. Moreover, Sunderland, knowing the Duke's distaste for the burdensome routine of the Secretaryship, had begun promoting late in 1696 the idea of removing Leeds and of elevating Shrewsbury to the more honorific position of Lord President. But Sunderland's manoeuvring on this and other fronts alarmed the Junto; despite the restoration of outwardly amicable relations with him during the liquidity crisis, their suspicions of the Earl remained. Thus, Sunderland's seemingly devious conduct during and after the Fenwick affair, particularly his management of Godolphin's resignation in October 1696 and his part in securing Monmouth's release from the Tower in April 1697, was a recurrent source of uneasiness. The Junto also observed with dismay that Sunderland, in broaching the project of making Shrewsbury Lord President, said not a word to them about who would succeed the Duke as Secretary.[120] But while Wharton, Russell, and Somers each expressed his concern on these and other scores to the absent Shrewsbury in late 1696 and early 1697, the Duke seemed ready to fall in with Sunderland's plans. The two concurred, despite Somers's reservations, in procuring the newly-vacant Irish Lord Chancellorship for John Methuen.[121] And Shrewsbury, grateful for Sunderland's part in securing his vindication from Fenwick's charges and eager to be relieved of the seals, assured the Earl in mid-February 1697 that he was willing to deal with the King and 'with everybody, in such a manner as should be most to your own satisfaction'.[122]

However, after Shrewsbury finally returned to London in March 1697, the project of putting him in Leeds's place was not implemented. The King, to be sure, appeared ready to dismiss Leeds and complained that 'the whole family of Berties' had been in opposition during the session. What may have prevented Leeds's ouster was William's unwillingness to limit removals to wayward Tories. Although he complained to Shrewsbury and Sunderland at a conference with them in mid-April of the Berties' open insubordination, he also stated that 'punishment' should 'not be extended partially to one kind of men, but some should be displaced of different denominations'. Shrewsbury, taking alarm for Sir Walter Yonge and Edward Clarke, responded by trying to draw a distinction between 'those who had done wrong only once through ignorance' (that is, over the wine duties) and 'those who in the whole course of business had consistently opposed'. But this, the Duke reported to Somers (whose illness had prevented his attendance upon the King), met with a very 'cold' reception.[123] So, while Abingdon and Willoughby were put out, Leeds and several other of his kin were spared, as were Yonge and Clarke. And instead of Shrewsbury being named Lord President, it was Sunderland who accepted a change of position by emerging from 'behind the curtain' to succeed Dorset as Lord Chamberlain.

The initiative in this unexpected appointment, announced on 19 April 1697 after years of speculation about the Earl's return to office, was William's. He bought the Lord Chamberlainship for £10,000 from Dorset, who had been talking of retiring for some time, and he then persuaded Sunderland to accept it. Sunderland promptly used his own change of character as a means to induce Trumbull to soldier on in the second Secretaryship; now, he told Sir William, he need no longer feel 'alone' in 'the ministry'.[124] In turn, while Shrewsbury, beset by a new bout of haemorrhaging, returned to the country in late April to convalesce, Sunderland remained in London to serve as one of the nine Lords Justices the King named to administer the realm during the summer of 1697.[125]

William, too, was troubled by illness in April and again in May, and the 1697 military campaign opened on a sour note with the enemy taking Ath. Soon, however, a stalemate developed in the field. A similar deadlock prevailed at the conference table at Ryswick, but it was broken by the private negotiations begun in late June between Portland and Marshal Boufflers of France. The principal issue, so far as England was concerned, was France's recognition of the Revolution settlement of the throne upon William and his successors, as specified in the bill of rights. Shrewsbury was convinced that without satisfaction on this point it would be better to 'prepare to carry on the war', especially since England was 'now in a better condition to do [so] than we were the last year'.[126] In fact, Shrewsbury (who returned to London, seemingly much improved in health, in early July), Somers, and Sunderland were kept informed on the wording of the key articles being discussed by Portland and Boufflers.[127] By early August, formulae satisfactory to William had been worked out. None the less, there were renewed fears in late August and early September of a breakdown in the peace negotiations, particularly as Imperialist opposition to the projected settlement gave the French justification for seeking tougher terms on continental questions. Thus, the report of the final signing of the treaty on 10 September was greeted in England with both joy and relief. The news, so Sunderland exclaimed ecstatically to Portland, has 'made this a new world and has so mended it you will scarce know it'. Now, all that remained was for the King to 'come over quickly to settle it so that no accident shall be able to spoil it or alter it'.[128]

Notes to Chapter VIII

1 BL Loan 29/137 (unfoliated), H. Guy to R. Harley, 'Sunday evening'.

2 *England's Enemies Exposed, and Its True Friends and Patriots Vindicated* (1701, BL T1688 No. 10), p. 12.

3 HMC *Hastings*, II, 259. Subsequently, fourteen more declined as well. See Appendix C.

4 Horwitz, *Revolution Politicks*, p. 156; BL Add. MS. 17677QQ, ff. 298–9, L'Hermitage, 28 February/9 March.

5 BL Add. MS. 19253, f. 189, Chesterfield's memoirs.

6 *Calendar of Correspondence and Documents relating to the Family of Oliver Le Neve*, ed. F. Rye (Norwich, 1895), p. 38.

7 BL Add. MS. 35107, f. 35 (Privy Council memoranda); Bodl. Carte MS. 130, f. 361, R. Price to [Duke of Beaufort], 27 February. See also BL Add. MS. 35107, f. 20.

8 CJ, XI, 253. And see Bodl. Carte MS. 239, f. 77, J. Vernon to Lord Wharton, 2 April.

9 HMC *Various Collections*, VIII, 81–2; Luttrell, *Brief Relation*, IV, 38–40; CJ, XI, 545, 551–552.

10 BL Add. MS. 17677QQ, f. 320, 10/20 March.

11 BL Add. MS. 30000A, f. 66, F. Bonnet, 17/27 March; BL Harleian MS. 1274, f. 56.

12 BL Add. MS. 56241 (unfoliated), W. Blathwayt to R. Hill, 10 April. Meanwhile, the college was once again voicing suspicions of Montagu amid signs of renewed agitation for devaluation: Bodl. Locke MS. C8, f. 214, J. Freke to Locke, 10 March; BL Harleian MS. 1274, f. 54; BL Add. MS. 17677QQ, f. 355, L'Hermitage, 20/30 March.

13 BL Add. MS. 30000A, ff. 78, 81–2, F. Bonnet, 27 March/6 April, 31 March/10 April; *Shrewsbury Corr.*, p. 118; HLM, 1695–1697, pp. 234–5.

14 Bodl. Locke MS. C8, f. 217, 2 April.

15 BL Add. MS. 30000A, ff. 104, 112, F. Bonnet, 10/20 and 14/24 April; Luttrell, *Brief Relation*, IV, 42–3.

16 Montagu–Blathwayt correspondence, partly printed in Shaw's introductory volume to *CTB*, vols. XI–XVII, p. lx. Cf. D. Rubini, 'Politics and the Battle for the Banks 1688–1697', *EHR* LXXXV (1970), 693–714.

17 *CJ*, XI, 522; KAO, Chevening MS. 78, R. Yard to A. Stanhope, 24 March. See also Bank of England MSS., Court of Directors' Minute Book B, pp. 112–14, 123, 124, and General Court Book, I, 60, 61, 70.

18 Luttrell, *Brief Relation*, IV, 45. See also BL Add. MS. 17677QQ, ff. 379, 397, L'Hermitage, 10/20 and 20/30 April; BL Harleian MS. 1250, ff. 196–7.

19 *The Substance of the Clause Offered to the Land-Bank-Bill: with Remarks upon it* ([1696], Wing S6109A).

20 BL Add. MS. 30000A, f. 106, F. Bonnet, 10/20 April.

21 BL Add. MS. 30000A, f. 47, F. Bonnet, 20/30 March; Bodl. Locke MS. C8, ff. 203, 207, 210.

22 *LJ*, XV, 618. And see BL Harleian MS. 1274, f. 9.

23 HLM, 1695–1697, p. 3 and ff.; BL Add. MS. 17677QQ, f. 360, L'Hermitage, 3/13 April; KAO, Chevening MS. 78, R. Yard to A. Stanhope, 7 April. Cf. East India Office Lib., old Co. Dispatch Book E/3/92, p. 476, to Bombay, 4 May 1696.

24 FSL Newdigate newsletters 2605, 2614, 2617, 4 and 25 April, 2 May; HMC *Buccleuch*, II, 312.

25 HMC *Portland*, III, 575. This may be the 'old business' of removing Godolphin that Somers referred to in the fall of 1696; *Shrewsbury Corr.*, p. 415.

26 BL Loan 29/188, f. 128, R. Harley to J. Methuen (copy), 30 June; BL Add. MS. 30000A, ff. 122, 123, 126–7, F. Bonnet, 1/11 and 5/15 May; KAO, Chevening MS. 78, R. Yard to A. Stanhope, 7 May. In his self-defence in the Lords in January 1697, Monmouth alluded to his disappointments: BL Add. MS. 17677RR, f. 177, L'Hermitage, 12/22 January 1697; *Vernon Corr.* I, 150, 165.

27 Cumberland RO, Lonsdale correspondence, Sir J. Lowther of Lowther to Sir J. Lowther of Whitehaven, 13 October 1695.

28 Kenyon, *Sunderland*, pp. 278–9; Berkshire RO, Trumbull Add. MS. 125, Sir William's diary, undated entry for summer 1696.

29 BL Harleian MS. 1495, f. 1; Luttrell, *Brief Relation*, IV, 74; HMC *Portland*, III, 574–6.

30 Luttrell, *Brief Relation*, IV, 91.

31 *The Correspondence of John Locke and Edward Clarke*, ed. B. Rand (1927), p. 441. For William's later recognition that he had erred in pressing for the reduction of the guinea to twenty-two shillings, see *Shrewsbury Corr.*, p. 118.

32 Luttrell, *Brief Relation*, IV, 86; J. Horsefield, *British Monetary Experiments 1650–1710* (1960), p. 14. See also J. Craig, *Newton at the Mint* (Cambridge, 1946).

33 Bodl. Carte MS. 130, f. 363, H. Morgan.

34 KAO, Chevening MS. 78, R. Yard to A. Stanhope, 7 May.

35 BL Add. MS. 17677QQ, ff. 333–4, 420, L'Hermitage, 20/30 March, 8/18 May; CSPD, 1696, p. 178. And, in general, see Macaulay, *History*, VI, 2625–8.

36 *CTB*, Introduction to vols. XI–XVII, p. lxi. See also *CTB*, XI, 10; *Shrewsbury Corr.*, pp. 116, 119; Koninklijk Huisarchief (The Hague), Willem III, XI G No. 179, Godolphin to Blathwayt, 12 May.

37 *CTB*, XI, 16 and ff.

38 BL Add. MS. 9729, f. 142, R. Henley, 9 June. And see Baker Library (Harvard University), Ranelagh–Blathwayt letters, No. 3, 9 June 1696.

39 KAO, Chevening MS. 78, R. Yard to A. Stanhope, 2 June. And see *Shrewsbury Corr.*, p. 120.

40 *CTB*, Introduction to vols. XI–XVII, p. lxiii; NU, Portland MS. PwA 476, Godolphin to [Portland], 22 May. Blathwayt's letters to Montagu suggest that William at first was inclined to accept Montagu's arguments, but that by early July he was having second thoughts: BL Add. MS. 34355, ff. 5, 9. See also NLW, Penrice & Margam MS. L310, F. Gwyn to T. Mansell, 14 July.

41 CSPD, 1696, pp. 214, 239.

42 CSPD, 1696, p. 250; HMC *Buccleuch*, II, 365; *Calendar of Treasury Papers 1556/7–1696*, pp. 524–6.

43 CSPD, 1694–1695, p. 189 (misdated).

44 HMC *Buccleuch*, II, 367.
45 Koninklijk Huisarchief, Willem III, XI G No. 190, 20 July.
46 *Correspondentie*, I, i, 180.
47 *Shrewsbury Corr.*, p. 131, also p. 118.
48 *Shrewsbury Corr.*, p. 131.
49 Althorp Savile MSS., box 4, F. Gwyn to Marquess of Halifax, 3 August. See also CSPD, 1694–1695, pp. 242–3 (misdated); *Correspondentie*, I, i, 183; HMC *Buccleuch*, II, 386–7; Wing A3930, T2155.
50 *Correspondentie*, I, i, 187. The land bank men blamed Montagu and his friends for their difficulties in raising the money: compare Gwyn's letter (note 49); Montagu's in CTB, Introduction to vols. XI–XVII, pp. lxxi–ii; and Stockdale's in HMC *Various Collections*, VIII, 82.
51 *Correspondentie*, I, i, 187–96. *Shrewsbury Corr.*, pp. 134–5.
52 CTB, Introduction to vols. XI–XVII, p. lxxiii. And see HMC *Various Collections*, VIII, 82; BL Loan 29/188, f. 138, [R. Harley] to his father, 3 September; Baker Library (Harvard University), Ranelagh–Blathwayt letters, No. 8, 8 September.
53 The phrase is Godolphin's; CSPD, 1696, p. 223. And see J. Ehrman, *The Navy in the War of William III 1689–1697* (Cambridge, 1953), pp. 602–3.
54 CSPD, 1696, pp. 193, 221, 222, 227; Ehrman, *The Navy*, pp. 584–5; M. Beloff, *Public Order and Popular Disturbances 1660–1714* (Oxford, 1938), pp. 102–5.
55 NU, Portland MS. PwA 1251, 23 May.
56 *Shrewsbury Corr.*, pp. 128–9; *Archives*, III, i, 471–2; *Het Archief van den Raadpensionaris Antonie Heisius*, ed. H. J. van der Heim (The Hague, 1867–80), I, 226–7.
57 NU, Portland MS. PwA 1255, to [Portland], 6 September. See also *Correspondentie*, I, i, 188.
58 *Correspondentie*, I, i, 188, also 194.
59 *Shrewsbury Corr.*, pp. 131–2.
60 CSPD, 1696, pp. 337, 344; HMC *Buccleuch*, II, 393–6.
61 *Shrewsbury Corr.*, pp. 145–8.
62 *Vernon Corr.*, I, 6, 1–2. And see CSPD, 1696, p. 398.
63 *Vernon Corr.*, I, 7, 12–13; Berkshire RO, Trumbull Add. MS. 125; *Shrewsbury Corr.*, p. 408; HMC *Downshire*, II, 548; Ralph, *History*, II, 678 (cf. BL 816 m9 No. 55).
64 Northants RO, Buccleuch MSS., Vernon letters, I, 7, 12 October; HMC *Portland*, III, 580.
65 HMC *Various Collections*, VIII, 83.
66 CJ, XI, 566, 567.
67 *Archives*, III, i, 483, 485.
68 *Vernon Corr.*, I, 34, 28.
69 For these discussions, see *Shrewsbury Corr.*, pp. 154–61, 408–20; HMC *Buccleuch*, II, 414–21; Bodl. Carte MS. 233, f. 27a and ff. See also Kenyon, *Sunderland*, pp. 283–5.
70 For Shrewsbury's departure, see NU, Portland MS. PwA 1462, J. Vernon to [Portland], 22 September.
71 *Shrewsbury Corr.*, p. 414.
72 *Shrewsbury Corr.*, p. 420. And see KAO, Chevening MS. 78, R. Yard to A. Stanhope, 3 November; CSPD, 1694–1695, pp. 242–3 (misdated); *Correspondentie*, I, i, 193.
73 Berkshire RO, Trumbull Add. MS. 116, cabinet minute, 2 November.
74 *Shrewsbury Corr.*, pp. 427, 428; Bodl. Carte MS. 233, ff. 39–40, Shrewsbury to [Wharton], 14 November. Cf. Kenyon, *Sunderland*, p. 286.
75 CJ, XI, 579; *Shrewsbury Corr.*, pp. 424–7. The notes on the debates in BL Harleian MS. 7171 are slightly fuller than PH. V, 998–1149. And see also Wing P3545.
76 *Vernon Corr.*, I, 50, and 42, 45, 46–51, 52–3; HMC *Buccleuch*, II, 421–2.
77 *Vernon Corr.*, I, 59.
78 I. Burton et al., *Political Parties in the Reigns of William III and Anne: The Evidence of Division Lists* (BIHR, special supplement 7, 1968), pp. 21–6 and app. A. And see Burnet, *History*, IV, 329 note, 342 note.
79 *Shrewsbury Corr.*, p. 429; *Vernon Corr.*, I, 89, 94; Bodl. Carte MS. 233, f. 41, Shrewsbury to [Wharton], 15 November. Tankerville was made the bill's 'manager' in the Lords.
80 *Vernon Corr.*, I. 89; T. Sharp, *The Life of John Sharp*, ed. T. Newcome (1825), I, 295; Burnet, *History*, IV, 403–4 note.

81 Berkshire RO, Trumbull Add. MS. 125, entry for 13 May 1696; HMC *Downshire*, I, 694–5; CJ, XI, 584; Luttrell, *Brief Relation*, IV, 131.

82 *Vernon Corr.*, I, 85; *Shrewsbury Corr.*, p. 439. And see LJ, XVI, 50–3.

83 *Vernon Corr.*, I, 140. And see Appendix B.

84 *Shrewsbury Corr.*, pp. 444–5, 457; *Vernon Corr.*, I, 172–4. Subsequently, the Lords examined Smith's allegations against Shrewsbury and dismissed them as groundless.

85 *Vernon Corr.*, I, 56, 69, 70, 74–5, 86–7, 111; BL Add. MS. 17677RR, f. 149, L'Hermitage, 22 December/1 January. For the petitions, see CJ, XI, 590 and ff.

86 Northants RO, Buccleuch MSS., Vernon letters, I, 24, 19 November.

87 Luttrell, *Brief Relation*, IV, 139, 142, 147, 148; *Vernon Corr.*, I, 55–6, 83, 91, 94.

88 CSPD, 1696, pp. 482–3; CTB, XI, 65.

89 BL Add. MS. 17677QQ, f. 637, L'Hermitage, 11/21 December, Luttrell, *Brief Relation*, IV, 153; HMC *Le Fleming*, p. 345; *Vernon Corr.*, I, 121–2; All Souls College MS. 158, vol. 6 (unfoliated), text of Foche's proposal. See also Bodl. Carte 130, f. 357.

90 BL Add. MS. 17677QQ, f. 640, and 17677RR, ff. 143–4, L'Hermitage, 15/25 and 18/28 December; Klopp, *Der Fall des Hauses Stuart*, VII, 510–11; Luttrell, *Brief Relation*, IV, 155–6.

91 *Vernon Corr.*, I, 136, and 87–8. See also CTB, XI, 69.

92 Luttrell, *Brief Relation*, IV, 131, 140, 141–2, 143, 144; HMC *Le Fleming*, p. 344; KAO, Chevening MS. 78, newsletters, 13, 15, and 24 November.

93 Bodl. Locke MS. C8, f. 221, J. Freke to Locke, 5 December; *Vernon Corr.*, I, 111, 135; Bodl. Carte MS. 130, f. 367, R. Price to [Duke of Beaufort], 10 December.

94 Bodl. Locke MS. C8, f. 221. At the least, Montagu had sounded out some Bank directors; S. Bannister, *The Life and Writings of Sir William Paterson* (Manchester, 1855), II, xxxv–xxxviii; KAO, Papillon MSS. U1015, O 36/6 and O 36/8 (pp. 15–16).

95 BL Add. MS. 17677QQ, ff. 629–30, L'Hermitage, 8/18 December; Bodl. Carte MS. 130, f. 367; *Vernon Corr.*, I, 176–7. And see Bank of England MSS., Court of Directors' Minute Book B, p. 187.

96 Northants RO, Buccleuch MSS., Vernon letters, I, 59 26 January (cf. *Vernon Corr.*, I, 189). And see DWL MS. 201:38, p. 41, Bishop J. Williams to Stillingfleet, 23 January.

97 For pamphlet accounts of some of the arguments within the Bank, see Wing A3639 and L1640. The Bank's submission was facilitated by the King's decision late in January 1697 to pay it £75,000 to cover remittance losses incurred in 1695–96.

98 *Vernon Corr.*, I, 215–16; BL Add. MS. 30000A, f. 273, L. F. Bonnet, 26 February/8 March.

99 BL Add. MS. 30000A, ff. 290–1. L. F. Bonnet, 6/16 April; *Shrewsbury Corr.*, p. 479.

100 Bodl. Locke MS. C8, f. 227, J. Freke to Locke, 6 April.

101 For the latter, see P. G. Dickson, *The Financial Revolution in England* (1967), pp. 355–6, 516.

102 HLM, 1695–1697, pp. 511–13, 521–7; HMC *Fitzherbert*, p. 45. For Harley's involvement with the latter, and its precursors of 1689, 1690, 1693–94, and 1695–96, see BL Loan 29/278 (unfoliated), drafts of bills, and 29/136 (unfoliated), T. Foley to R. Harley, 16 October 1690.

103 HMC *Le Fleming*, p. 346; BL Add. MS. 17677RR, ff. 192–3, L'Hermitage, 22 January/1 February; Bodl. Carte MS. 130, f. 381, R. Price to [Duke of Beaufort], 11 February. See also H. Kearney, 'The Political Background to English Mercantilism, 1695–1700', *Economic History Review*, 2nd s. XI (1957), 481–96.

104 Bodl. Carte MS. 130, f. 381; BL Add. MS. 17677RR, f. 246, L'Hermitage, 2/12 March. See also C. Robbins, 'A Note on General Naturalization under the later Stuarts', JMH XXXIV (1962), 168–77.

105 DWL MS. 201:38, pp. 41–2, Bishop J. [Williams] to Stillingfleet, 20 March. See also HMC *Kenyon*, p. 415.

106 HMC *Bath*, III, 105; BL Add. MS. 17677RR, ff. 269, 281, L'Hermitage, 23 March/2 April, 30 March/9 April; East India Office Lib., old Co. Court Book B41, f. 156.

107 HMC *Portland*, III, 575–6; CJ, XI, 587; *Vernon Corr.*, I, 112.

108 Bodl. Carte MS. 130, ff. 381, 375, R. Price to [Duke of Beaufort], 11 and 18 February. See also *Some Remarks on the Bill for Taking the Public Accounts* (1701), quoted in CTB, Introduction to vols. XI–XVIII, p. clxx; CJ, XI, 703–5; Northants RO, Buccleuch MSS., Vernon letters, I, 67, 11 February.

109 Archives, III, i, 538.

110 Bodl. Carte MS. 228, ff. 126–7, Somers to [Wharton], 21 April. And see CTB, XII, 5; CSPD, 1697, p. 114.

111 *Shrewsbury Corr.*, p. 478; HMC *Bath*, III, 112; London Univ., Goldsmiths' MS. 65 No. 3 (list of subscribers).

112. BL Add. MS. 17677RR, f. 304, L'Hermitage, 23 April/3 May; Kenyon, *Sunderland*, p. 291.

113 NU, Portland MS. PwA 2522, ? to the King, 29 May 1696. See also *The Norris Papers*, ed. T. Heywood (Chetham Society, vol. IX, 1846), p. 32.

114 *Shrewsbury Corr.*, p. 113.

115 NU, Portland MS. PwA 2522.

116 MSP, II, 430; Northants RO, Buccleuch MSS., Vernon letters, II, 31, 3 April 1698. Vernon also observed that William defended Sunderland on this score, saying 'nobody was so earnest as he for his [Wharton's] being gratified in that particular'. Cf. Kenyon, *Sunderland*, pp. 289–90.

117 Berkshire RO, Trumbull Add. MS. 125, 18 October 1696.

118 HMC *Downshire*, I, 740, 772; NU, Portland MS. PwA 1256, [Sunderland to Portland], 30 April.

119 Berkshire RO, Trumbull Add. MS. 125, 8 and 11 April. And see Northants RO, Buccleuch MSS., Vernon letters, I, 78–9, 11 and 14 March 1697; HMC *Bath*, III, 108–9; HMC *Downshire*, I, 743.

120 *Shrewsbury Corr.*, pp. 415, 420, 429, 434, 454, 466–7, 472, 474; HMC *Buccleuch*, II, 446; *Vernon Corr.*, I, 187–8, 205; Bodl. Locke MS. C8, f. 227, J. Freke to Locke, 6 April.

121 *Vernon Corr.*, I, 146–7; *Shrewsbury Corr.*, p. 456. Cf. Kenyon, *Sunderland*, p. 287.

122 CSPD, 1697, p. 36. See also *Shrewsbury Corr.*, p. 474.

123 MSP, II, 431. And see Luttrell, *Brief Relation*, IV, 212–13; BL Add. MS. 30000A, ff. 300–1, L. F. Bonnet, 20/30 April.

124 Berkshire RO, Trumbull Add. MS. 125, 1–11 April. And see Kenyon, *Sunderland*, p. 289.

125 Lords Romney and Orford were also added to the previous year's seven Lords Justices, and Godolphin was left out. For speculation that Montagu would be made a Scots peer and a Lord Justice, see Bodl. Carte MS. 228, f. 126, Somers to [Wharton], 21 April; BL Add. MS. 30000A, f. 297, L. F. Bonnet 16/26 April. Cf. Kenyon, *Sunderland*, p. 290.

126 *Shrewsbury Corr.*, pp. 351, 171. And see BL Add. MS. 34355, ff. 27–59.

127 *Shrewsbury Corr.*, pp. 353–4, 358–9, 363; *Correspondentie*, I, ii, 75–6; NU, Portland MSS. PwA 1265, 1267, [Sunderland to Portland], 27 July, 10 August.

128 NU, Portland MS. PwA 1272, 17 September.

IX

THE EXPEDIENTS OF RULE

1692–1697

When William brought Rochester and Seymour into the cabinet council in March 1692, the war was entering a new phase. The reconquest of Ireland was completed, and the King was redeploying the realm's resources towards the continental conflict. And while William still hesitated to break entirely with the Whigs, the prospect of a successful descent on France buoyed Nottingham's spirits. In the event, the miscarriages of the 1692 campaign, and especially the failure to implement the descent, set the stage for a parliamentary session considerably more difficult than that of 1691–92—so difficult that the King was left little alternative save to begin to reverse his political course at home by promoting Somers and Trenchard.

Whether a change of men would suffice was uncertain. After all, the experiences of the 1691–92 and 1692–93 sessions seemed to indicate that continuance of the war and its heavy taxes would accentuate differences between 'Court' and 'Country', so that 'the names of Whig and Tory will at last', in Richard Hill's prediction of late 1691, 'change into English and Dutch'.[1] Certainly, William Brockman was not alone among the Whigs in asking in the early 1690s 'if the Prince of Orange be lost in the King?', and among the discontented who on one occasion distributed marked copies of William's declaration in the lobby of St Stephen's Chapel, in order to 'insinuate' that his earlier pledges had not been observed, was John Paschal (later to be named a Commissioner for Prizes in 1694 at Shrewsbury's instance over Godolphin's objections).[2] Then, too, the conduct of other Whigs, most notoriously Robert Ferguson, lent substance to Tory allegations that 'abundance of those that seemed fierce republicarians are in reality fierce Jacobites'.[3] Granted, charges of disloyalty against men of Foley's and Harley's views seem groundless, but when the Earl of Middleton crossed the Channel to St Germain in early 1693, he did bear tentative offers from such leading Revolution activists as the Earls of Monmouth and Shrewsbury, and these offers prompted James II to issue his conciliatory declaration of April 1693.[4]

The spring of 1693, then, saw new departures in both Williamite and Jacobite camps that were to culminate four years later at Ryswick. And en route, the constitutional position of the crown, the organisation of the royal administration, and the patterns of domestic politics had been transformed.

The constitution

The most obvious alteration in the English constitution between 1692 and 1697 was the new relationship between the monarch and the Commons laid down by the triennial act of December 1694. In final form, the bill for frequent parliaments did not enjoin annual sessions; its main provision was to limit a parliament to a maximum life of three years, thereby restricting the crown's power to keep on foot a compliant Commons. In fact, the agitation for triennial legislation was linked to the question of the placemen in the Commons from the outset. The first of the four bills for frequent parliaments considered between early 1693 and late 1694 was brought forward by Shrewsbury in the wake of the Lords' rejection of Sir Edward Hussey's measure in January 1693 to exclude in future all placemen from the Commons: his logic seems to have been that if the King's servants were not to be barred from sitting in the lower House their constituents should be given frequent opportunities to discard them. Yet, since the compromise triennial act of 1694 left the King free to dissolve a parliament before it reached its legal term, it became even more vital for monarch and ministers to weigh carefully the timing of elections within the new limits.

Significant though the triennial act was, the King's position vis-à-vis the Commons was weakened even more by his increasing financial dependence upon parliamentary grants, not only for war supply but also for payment of the civil expenditures of the crown—the 'civil list' as contemporaries called these charges. In this regard, it is suggestive that the triennial act of 1694 (unlike Shrewsbury's bill of January 1693) did not reimpose the self-enforcement provisions of its precursor of 1641, and one reason for the omission may have been that the grant of tunnage and poundage in 1690 for a limited term seemed a sufficient safeguard for the observance of the new statute. In addition to that new departure in the settlement of the ordinary revenue, continued by the grant anew of tunnage and poundage for a five-year term in December 1694, 1690 also saw the first of a series of loans for war supply raised on the security of the King's revenue. The loans taken out in 1690 were not paid off by parliament; instead, during the 1693–94 session there was talk of further loans to be secured upon the ordinary revenue. The approval of the long-term levies on salt and ships' tonnages obviated that necessity for the time being, but when the 1693–94 session was over William was warned by Coningsby that if peace did not come soon 'the next year's expenses will so anticipate those branches of the revenue that ever have been kept hitherto for the ordinary support of the government that [it] will be scarce possible that your Majesty should ever see an easy day'.[5]

However, at the end of the 1694 campaign, Louis was still not prepared to recognise the Revolution settlement of the throne (the minimum English condition for a peace), and so it was found necessary during the next session to hypothecate £300,000 annually from the new grant of tunnage and poundage in order to help finance the 1695 campaign. In addition, by the beginning of the 1695–96 session, the ordinary revenue was charged with nearly £800,000 in short-term loans and payments on the civil list were about £450,000 in arrears. That session, the Commons did vote a supply for the civil list, but the relief they provided was only temporary, and William was again compelled to come cap in hand to parliament in October 1696. Moreover, though the Commons did approve the King's request and this time provided £515,000 in new revenue, they also decided to extend the previous grant of tunnage and poundage from 1699 to 1706 and to use these customs duties, originally part of the ordinary revenue, to help pay the interest charges on borrowings upon parliamentary levies that had proved deficient.

While financing the war all but extinguished the distinction between ordinary and extraordinary revenues and left William heavily in debt by 1697, at least the King did manage to retain formal authority over the executive. This was no mean achievement in the face of persistent parliamentary pressure, especially for more effective protection of commerce. Heavy losses of English merchant shipping not only provoked repeated attacks on those entrusted with the management of sea affairs; they also prompted the formulation of alternate means to safeguard trade. As early as August 1692, Sir Edward Harley was convinced that 'securing the sea' would necessitate the establishment of 'a committee of trade, empowered for all the naval concerns relating thereto', and amid the outcry after the attack on the Turkey convoy a year later there were discussions within the ministry of the advisability of immediate establishment of such a body by the crown.[6] In late November, Secretary Trenchard instructed the Attorney-General to draft a commission for the projected committee of trade, and at the same time Sir William Ashurst (then Lord Mayor of London) was authorised to inform the City's common council that the King had decided to create such a body for the specific purpose of protecting trade and organising convoys for it.[7] But when no more was heard of the projected body, the Commons, over the objections of Trenchard and Russell, tacked a requirement to the land tax bill in January 1694 ordering the Admiralty to set out no fewer than forty-three cruisers to safeguard shipping.

Similar hesitation in the face of pressure for remedial measures almost cost William more dearly two years later. Only the discovery of the assassination conspiracy diverted the Commons from going ahead with their bill for a parliamentary council of trade during the 1695–96 session. The following autumn, there was again sharp criticism voiced in the Commons of the ineffective protection of shipping. Moreover, early in 1697, the Lords were moved by Godolphin and Rochester to take up the question, and Vernon believed that they intended 'some thing . . . like to what the House of Commons were framing last year'.[8]

Although the Lords' inquiry into naval affairs in 1697 raised new fears in the minds of the King's servants, the 1696–97 session did bring relief from the activities of the Commission of Accounts. Even at its most influential, the commission never posed the same threat to royal control of the executive that the proposed council of trade appeared to be in both William's and Somers's view.[9] The direction by such a body of perhaps as many as eighty of the King's ships would certainly have been more damaging to royal authority than were the Commissioners' precepts ordering officials to bring in their accounts.[10] Still, the usefulness of the commission to the advocates of 'good management' should not be underrated.[11] Although the Commissioners had only limited patronage at their disposal, the authority they had to administer an oath was a helpful complement to the Commons' own array of weapons, as the inquiry of early 1695 into the practices of the army agents demonstrated. In addition, the Commissioners were endowed with full power to search out and examine any payments (other than salaries) made by the crown to members of parliament. Admittedly, most of the instances of such disbursements they did turn up had perfectly plausible explanations, though this was not true in Falkland's case in 1693–94. Yet, to judge from the demeanour of members summoned before the commission to explain the payments they had received, it is likely that the very existence of the board restrained the temptation to offer or to accept under-the-table handouts.[12] But probably the commission's most important effect was the familiarity its more active members acquired with the workings of royal administration, so enabling them to function as more effective critics in the Commons. Thus, Harley, for one, developed a confidential relationship with Edmund Dummer (Surveyor of the Navy from 1692), and Dummer furnished him with useful ammunition even after the Commission of Accounts passed from the scene.[13] Even so, it does seem that the Commons' vote in February 1697 to throw out the bill to renew the commission for the coming year was more than a product of partisan manoeuvring; a certain measure of disillusionment with the board's efficacy had set in among some such as Gwyn, once one of its foremost proponents.

Coincidentally, the Commission of Accounts was laid to sleep at a moment when diplomatic interchanges had aroused new hopes of an end to the war. When a peace had been mooted in 1693–94, William was advised by Coningsby 'how much it will contribute to your future happiness that it should, if possible, be perfected before the meeting of . . . parliament'.[14] And it is likely that Lord Villiers was expressing his royal master's view when he observed on the eve of the 1696–97 session that 'a congress of peace will not be very consistent with a parliament sitting'.[15] In the event, the negotiations of Ryswick did not get under way until the following spring and the treaty was concluded during the summer recess. Nor was the treaty submitted to parliament after it was signed.

Nevertheless, the Commons' role in foreign affairs was not wholly passive. In the autumn of 1692, the lower House requested the presentation of the treaties of alliance, and the King delivered them, including the 'grand alliance'.[16] Thereafter, the Commons were kept informed of the terms of most of the additional subsidy agreements for the hiring of foreign troops. In turn, it was information from this source that Musgrave cited in April 1695 when he succeeded in securing approval in a thin House for an address to request William that in future England's share of such subsidies should be no larger than those of her principal allies.[17] Again, during the early weeks of the 1696–97 session, William was fearful that French obstinacy on the recognition issue might provoke a parliamentary address against further negotiations unless and until Louis gave in on that point, but the threat of interference passed when news of French concessions reached London. This information became public knowledge by way of a letter received by under-secretary Vernon while he was in attendance in St Stephen's Chapel on 7 December. He happened to mention the news to his 'next neighbour', and the tidings 'ran round the House like fire in a stubble'.[18] Yet, even after parliament recessed, William took care during the summer of 1697 to have Portland explain and justify the terms worked out on the question of recognition to Sunderland, Shrewsbury, and Somers.

While the Treaty of Ryswick seemed to set the seal of foreign acknowledgement upon Englishmen's successful defence of their 'liberties' in 1688–89, the years of war also brought at least a limited enlargement of those rights. Particularly important were the lapse of the licensing arrangements in May 1695 and the passage in January 1696 of the bill to reform procedures in trials for treason (so implementing, after many false starts, head seventeen of the preliminary version of the Declaration of Rights). Admittedly, the 1696–97 session saw both these advances in some danger. The new treason statute did not save Fenwick despite Goodman's flight, and another act of the session continued the imprisonment without trial of six other conspirators against whom there was only one witness.[19] Furthermore, the indiscretions of John Salisbury, the publisher of the *Flying Post*, raised a storm that momentarily threatened to engulf both his own and other newspapers founded since the end of the censorship. However, the furore over the notice in the *Flying Post*, which appeared to be an attempt to undermine confidence in the new Exchequer bills, abated quickly, and the bill ordered on 1 April 1697 to prevent the publication of unlicensed newspapers was rejected a few days later 200 to 16 by the Commons.[20] So members and the public were left free 'to divert [themselves] with some other newspapers besides the *Gazette*'.[21] And though these infant publications shied away from controversial domestic subjects and concentrated on foreign news, their continued appearance was one more step away from the days when English monarchs had been able to govern without visible consideration and frequent consultation of the interests and opinions of their subjects.[22]

The King's administration

The long years of war brought no diminution in William's directing role in the governance of the realm. On the contrary. Despite the physical toll his work load took, it was Mary who unexpectedly succumbed to disease. Her passing set in motion several other alterations in the royal entourage. The most immediate change was the King's new coldness towards his former mistress, Lady Betty Villiers. Nor was his conduct, as some reports had it, because he had in view 'a younger and fairer successor'.[23] Rather, William was overwhelmed with remorse after Mary's death, and he now arranged to marry Lady Betty off to a Scots nobleman. Before Mary's death, the new Lady Orkney may have had a part in Sunderland's return to Court and she is known to have served as an intermediary between William and Shrewsbury in the winter of 1693–94.[24] Yet she had never been cast to be another Duchess of Portsmouth. So it is surprising to discover Sunderland telling Portland in mid-1695 that Montagu and Wharton, amongst their other conceits, had 'swallowed' the notion of 'governing' the King 'by a lady'.[25] Sunderland professed to find the idea ridiculous, but even after her marriage Lady Orkney did continue to come to Court, and in the postwar years Wharton, at least on one occasion, did revert to his earlier scheme.[26]

Another prominent Court figure who underwent a change in status shortly after Mary's death was William's one-time page, Joost Keppel, who was named Master of the Robes in May 1695 in succession to Zuilestein, now made Earl of Rochford. An even more significant, though less public, sign of Keppel's high favour came the following autumn when the King had connecting doors installed between his own apartments and Keppel's quarters in a reorganisation of the layout of Kensington Palace, which left Portland's rooms without direct access to William's.[27] Thus, the rivalry between Portland and Keppel, which was already apparent to insiders at Court before Mary's death, increasingly became the subject of public comment, and in the summer of 1696 the older man's jealousy nearly brought on a duel between the two. Moreover, once Keppel was raised to the peerage as Earl of Albemarle in February 1697, not even the simultaneous bestowal of a Garter upon Portland could keep him at Court.[28]

There were malicious gossips in England who likened the young and attractive Keppel to James I's Villiers, but the new Earl—as Portland earlier—was not so much a favourite as a trusted and lavishly rewarded personal assistant upon whom William sought to devolve a portion of his administrative load, especially Scottish, Irish, and Dutch concerns. William's 'system' may itself be criticised; it is notable, as a measure of the King's lack of control over Scottish affairs, that he confessed to his cabinet on 10 November 1695 that he had never before heard of the Edinburgh parliament's incorporation of an East India Company.[29] But at least it can be said that the late nights William often kept alone with Albemarle were devoted not to sexual dalliance but to tedious deskwork, and the rivalry between Portland and Albemarle was a distraction and a disappointment to their master.[30] Even so, Albemarle was not simply a younger version of Portland; he was both more affable and less grasping, and consequently he did not arouse quite the same resentment among the English nobility. Albemarle was also not as diligent as Portland, though even before 1695 many lesser burdens had been shifted on to the shoulders of Blathwayt. From 1692 onwards, the industrious Secretary-at-War accompanied William on his campaigns and functioned as a Secretary of State in all but name and perquisites, and even during the winters in London he took on tasks that ranged far beyond his nominal responsibilities.

If Albemarle became Portland's successor, Mary had none. There was talk during the summer of 1696 of a bride for the King in the person of the young Electoral Princess of Brandenburg, so much so that Secretary Trumbull wrote over to secure 'an exact character' of the lady on the premise that there might be 'something in all this noise'.[31] However, nothing came of William's visit to Cleves in September 1696. Moreover, though the King's relations with Anne were formally correct, up to 1697, at least, he never seems to have seriously considered bestowing any official role upon her, even during his summer absences on the Continent. Instead, William appointed, as Normanby had suggested soon after Mary's death, a commission of Lords Justices with viceregal powers to govern the realm while he was abroad campaigning in 1695 and in succeeding summers.[32]

Although the new commission of Lords Justices was endowed with extensive powers, they have been characterised as 'the members of the cabinet meeting in a more formal guise'.[33] Certainly, the 'kinglings' functioned in practice much as had the advisory councils named in earlier years to assist Mary. They eschewed most of the ceremonial appropriate to their official dignity and they also tended to refer major and even minor decisions to the King, unless the pressure of time precluded delay. In some other respects, too, William's use of the cabinet before Mary's death foreshadowed the patterns of the later years of the reign. At least occasional meetings of the cabinet council in William's presence were held as early as the winter of 1691–92, and there are extant Secretary Trenchard's minutes of eighteen such meetings between mid-January and late April 1694. Furthermore, conclaves of a select inner group of ministers without the presence of either sovereign had been initiated by William in the summer of 1694, though that attempt to 'break' the existing cabinet council was hindered by Normanby's remonstrances.

None the less, it does seem that William's appointment of Lords Justices in 1695 and in the following summers was accompanied by a new regularity in cabinet meetings during the winters with the King in attendance.[34] The practice was to hold weekly meetings on Sunday at Kensington, and cabinet minutes survive for every Sunday but five that William was in London during the winters of 1695–96 and 1696–97. Occasionally, the King also held cabinet councils at Kensington on weekdays during these years; these meetings tended to cluster around the beginning and the end of the parliamentary sessions, when the pressure of business was greatest. There were also sometimes weekday meetings which William did not attend; usually, these were held at one of the Secretary of State's offices in Whitehall.

Gatherings of the cabinet councillors without the King appear to have been ordered by William on an *ad hoc* basis in order to prepare matters to be submitted for final action at subsequent cabinet councils at Kensington. These meetings at Whitehall do not seem to have been distinguished in any formal way from those at Kensington at which the King was present, but they did have a somewhat different character and their frequency was dictated by circumstance.[35] Minutes survive for only three such gatherings during the winter of 1696–97; by contrast, there are notes for over fifty during the winter of 1695–96. The great majority were held in March and April 1696; their business was the examination of the assassination conspirators, and so Lord Chief Justice Holt, Attorney-General Trevor and Solicitor-General Hawles were often present to assist.[36] Similarly, other officials or even entire Boards might be summoned as needed; the junior Treasury lords, for example, sat in on several Whitehall meetings about the recoinage during October and November 1695. But though such 'outsiders' might take part in sessions which the King did not attend, only 'regular' members of the cabinet council participated in those meetings at which William presided. And in 1695–96 and again in 1696–97, the 'regulars' consisted of the Lords Justices of the previous summer if they were still in office, afforced by Secretary Trumbull, Admiral Russell, Lord Portland, and Prince George.[37]

Apart from the special case of Treasury business—for William continued during these years to attend that Board frequently—virtually any type of administrative concern might be dealt with in cabinet council. The cabinet minutes kept by the four Secretaries of State in office between 1692 and 1697 give the impression that the single most frequent topic was sea affairs. To some extent this simply reflects the preoccupations of the minute-takers, though it is also a measure of the obvious need to provide the direction that the Admiralty Commission, however much its composition changed, seemed unable to furnish. Still, the 'institutionalisation' of the cabinet was no guarantee of more effective management of sea affairs, and in the wake of the sinking of the parliamentary council of trade it was thought vital to launch the royal alternative that had been under consideration in late 1695. Hence, in May 1696 the moribund Privy Council committee on trade and plantations was formally superseded by the new Board of Trade, and Locke was urgently summoned to town by Secretary Trumbull and told that this body 'must go on with effect, or the greatest inconveniences and mischief will follow'.[38]

Although the new members of the Board of Trade energetically got down to work in the summer of 1696, that body's future was still uncertain. The Board's relations to other agencies of the executive, particularly the Admiralty, lacked definition, and its reception by parliament was problematical.[39] Concern on the latter score prompted one of the new commissioners, John Methuen (member for Devizes and in 1696 serving as ambassador in Lisbon), to solicit the advice of Robert Harley. Harley's reply was reassuring, at least in a limited way: the need to resolve the liquidity crisis, he told Methuen, would preclude any concerted effort during the coming session to revive the bill for a parliamentary council of trade.[40] Yet as soon as parliament reassembled in the autumn of 1696, the Commons did request a report from the Board on 'the state of trade'. Moreover, the Board's report, submitted in late November, met with a cool reception; Seymour, in particular, urged that the new commission 'should meddle less with inland and more with the foreign trade'.[41] But for the moment, the proponents of a parliamentary council of trade lacked the votes to challenge the King's creation directly, while the ending of the war the following summer promised to take the sting out of the issue of the protection of merchant shipping.[42]

The approach of peace also eased the later stages of the recoinage and helped to overcome the credit crisis. By mid-July 1697, Shrewsbury was able to report that 'money [was] growing much more plentiful in the country and credit in town [was] beginning now to recover'; a month later, as anticipations of the coming of peace heightened, Montagu jubilantly proclaimed to Portland that 'after ages will not believe how great an alteration has been made in one year ... whether it be war or peace we will not be under such difficulties as we have gone through any more'; and in late September, the conclusion of the negotiations brought Bank bills back to par and Bank stock nearly so.[43] To record this happy ending to the liquidity crisis is not to suggest that the government's handling of the coinage and credit problems was beyond reproach or that Montagu deserves the accolades that have been showered upon him. Yet rather than weighing (once more) the merits of the steps taken to deal with these problems, it may be informative to examine the processes by which those measures were formulated, particularly the recoinage.

The first point of note is that when the soaring price of guineas and the 'turning' of the foreign exchanges against London during the summer of 1695 compelled the King's servants to confront the question of a recoinage, they were able to draw upon a large body of expert opinion. The difficulty was not any lack of considered advice but the experts' conflicting recommendations, and the clash of opinion stemmed in part from a paucity of reliable information on such critical points as the amount of silver coin actually held by the public. Some estimates of the amount were rather closer to the mark than others, but that became apparent only in retrospect.[44] A second noteworthy feature of the policy-making process is the parts played respectively by the King, the ministers, and the Commons. Trumbull's cabinet minutes demonstrate that it was William's opposition to a devaluation that was the determinative factor in resolving the debate within the royal administration over the standard. It is also evident that lack of unity within the cabinet council as to whether the Commons would fund a recoinage if they were not consulted beforehand eventually led William to refrain from proceeding, as he first intended, by way of proclamation. And third, it is of some interest to observe that though there were extensive deliberations on the recoinage in the cabinet (including meetings while the King was making his progress through the provinces) before it was decided to submit the matter to parliament, thereafter the cabinet does not seem to have concerned itself with the matter to any great extent.

The absence of involvement by the cabinet in the preparation of the recoinage bills does not mean that such questions were not discussed in other semi-official gatherings. After all, in 1695–96 the cabinet included only two members of the

House of Commons, Secretary Trumbull and Admiral Russell. Nor did it mean that parliamentary business was never discussed in cabinet council. During that winter, a draft bill to encourage seamen was a topic on several occasions, and the Commons' proceedings on this measure were discussed during the meeting of 9 February 1696.[45]

Similarly, the almost total silence of the extant Treasury minutes of the 1690s on the subject of ways and means to raise the supplies does not mean that it was simply left to the Commons to pick and choose among the schemes—often summarised and circulated in printed broadsides—that were devised by the fast-growing tribe of 'projectors'.[46] Admittedly, some of the most striking departures of the 'financial revolution', including the creation of the Bank of England, seem to have originated in projectors' proposals. Sometimes, individual projectors were summoned before the Commons to explain their schemes, as, for instance, Edmund Hemming was called before a committee of the whole on 18 December 1695 to speak to his plan for raising £8,000,000 by laying a tax on feather-beds![47] Then, too, there were other, more eminent practitioners of the trade, particularly Thomas Neale and Dr Barbon, who were able to exploit their membership in the Commons to press their projects, and in late 1695 the Bristol M.P.s reported to their brethren back home that they had been given copies of one of Neale's schemes by the author in St Stephen's Chapel.[48]

Nevertheless, even during the early years of the war, the ministers sought to provide M.P.s with some guidance, and Montagu eventually won for himself the sobriquet of 'projector general'.[49] Nor should Sunderland's contribution be obscured; the Earl took the view that 'all proposals of money should at least be intended to come from the Court' and he helped to see that such preparations were set on foot in the summer of 1693 and in succeeding years.[50] In May 1693, Sunderland informed Portland that Treasury Secretary Guy, Exchequer Auditor Sir Robert Howard, and Secretary Trenchard were having excise schemes readied, and in following summers we hear of repeated consultations between Godolphin, Guy and Foley.[51] Subsequently, the liquidity crisis, coupled with Montagu's triumph over Foley (and Godolphin) in the summer of 1696, was followed by the adoption of more formal procedures to prepare for the coming session. In September 1696, the Lords Justices discussed with the Treasury Board 'what proposals should be laid before parliament for next year's funds', and the Treasury lords then instructed the subordinate revenue boards 'to consider of funds to raise money for the ensuing year'.[52] Later, at a meeting of the Treasury Commission attended by the King on 21 October, a preliminary version of the engrafting scheme was 'debated' and ordered 'to be made as perfect as may be'.[53]

However, not even the most detailed preliminary planning could of itself assure the Commons' adoption of official proposals. Moreover, as Shrewsbury remarked to William in a letter the Duke wrote from Eyford in mid-October 1696, although 'your Majesty has often resolved to settle before the beginning of the parliament what should be the funds which your servants should endeavour to get the money raised upon for the ensuing year ... hitherto this could never be so agreed as to be well pursued'.[54] But what Shrewsbury did not realise was that even as he wrote the ministerialists in the Commons were on the verge of greater successes than ever before.

Patterns of politics

If politics is the art of the possible, then the state of the art would appear to have undergone a transformation between the beginning of the 1692–93 and the end of the 1696–97 sessions. 'Nobody', so Sir John Lowther despairingly exclaimed in August 1692, 'can know one day what a House of Commons would do the next', while Carmarthen glossed this comment by explaining to William that 'there [is] now no such thing as any particular interest that is considerable enough to do good' in parliament.[55] Yet, in the autumn of 1696, Montagu and Littleton met with their principal supporters to the number of fifty or so 'every night' at the Rose Tavern in order to 'settle what they will propose and how to manage it', so provoking vain opposition complaints of 'questions that were brought ready prepared' to the House.[56] Again, in 1692–93 the divided Treasury lords seem deliberately to have left the task of formulating ways and means to others, and Harley could justly claim towards the end of that session that it was the Commissioners of Accounts who 'have found out all the money hitherto'. By the autumn of 1696, however, only four of the seven Commissioners of Accounts elected for that year were acting, since three had declined to take the association, and Lowther's Whig successors at the Treasury had a 'scheme' which they opened 'by degrees at the [Rose] Club, as it is necessary to bring it on to a conclusion'.[57]

Besides the frequent assemblies at the Rose Tavern during the 1696–97 session, there would also appear to have been other gatherings of a more intimate sort attended by the principal royal advisers and the chief government 'managers' in the Commons. Unfortunately, the evidence of such conclaves is much sparser than the notices of meetings at the Rose. There are frequent references to ministerialist consultations just before and during the early weeks of the 1696–97 session, but these gatherings were convened specially to hammer out tactics for dealing with Fenwick's case.[58] For the more routine managerial meetings that presumably were held, perhaps the best evidence is an entry in Sir William Trumbull's diary for 28 November 1697; this records such a conclave that evening in the 'King's closet' at Kensington, probably just after the cabinet council had met. In attendance were four peers, Sunderland, Shrewsbury, Somers, and Orford, and eight House of Commons men—Secretary Trumbull, Treasury Commissioners Montagu, Smith, Littleton, and Pelham, Paymasters Ranelagh and Coningsby, and Admiralty Commissioner Rich. Their business, as Sir William briefly noted, was 'about the forces, navy, civil list, etc.'—that is, the estimates and other requests to be made of the House of Commons in the session which was scheduled to begin a few days later.[59] Although we cannot be sure, it is likely that the Commoners who met the King's principal ministers that evening were much the same group as 'those gentlemen of the House of Commons' whom Sunderland on another occasion requested Secretary Trumbull to summon of a Sunday to Kensington at 6 p.m.[60] They were the government's 'managers' both in the general sense that they were the leading spokesmen in St Stephen's Chapel for the administration and in the more specific sense that their executive responsibilities enabled them to speak in detail to questions bearing upon the main agencies of the executive—the secretariat, the financial boards, the army and navy. In the latter respect, at least, they differed from those 'managers of the King's directions' listed in Carmarthen's memorandum of the autumn of 1690; of the seven M.P.s he so designated, only Lowther, Goodricke, and Ranelagh then held responsible posts in the royal administration.[61]

Just how frequent 'managerial' conclaves were or when the practice of holding them began is obscure. Coningsby, in his memorandum to the King in 1694, alluded to being 'called' to a number of 'meetings' during the 1693–94 session 'to consider how to carry on your affairs', and it is likely that these gatherings were similar in character to the one recorded by Trumbull in late 1697.[62] This is only a hypothesis. Yet, since Sunderland's undated note to Secretary Trumbull (whose tenure in that post ran from May 1695 to December 1697) did not name names but simply instructed him to summon those Commoners 'who use to attend him [the King]', it would appear that whenever such meetings were initiated, by the war's end they had become common practice.

These 'strategy sessions' linked the King and his cabinet council to the supporters of the King's business in the Commons. And while neither the royal ministers, nor the group of Commoners summoned to the meeting Trumbull recorded, nor those who loyally voted for the administration's proposals in the Commons during the middle 1690s were exclusively Whigs (certainly, Ranelagh and Trumbull were not), the Whig 'Junto's' central role is undeniable. When an anonymous correspondent of an Oxford don first made use of the term 'juncto' in the spring of 1695 to denominate the 'three or four persons for some considerable time that have managed an interest with a powerful party', it was to these new Whig leaders that he referred.[63] Again, Montagu and Littleton were the 'lords of the Articles' who 'opened' the 'scheme' of the King's business step by step to those who met at the Rose, and the Rose Club itself was a Whig assembly.

Since the beginning of the reign (and even before), the Rose and Crown Tavern near Covent Garden had been known as a Whig rendezvous, though during the Convention parliament it was outshone by the Churchmen's assemblies at the Devil Tavern.[64] Again, when an anonymous satirist limned 'the clubmen of the House of Commons' in 1694, it was the Rose Club to which he referred. He observed that Thomas Wharton had the guise of 'the drawer at the Rose', and then listed as members twenty-nine other M.P.s, all but three of them Whigs.[65] And while Secretary Trenchard was not included among these 'clubmen', he was stigmatised at much the same time by a hostile pamphleteer (probably Robert Ferguson) as 'a Green Ribbon Secretary' who was 'perfected in the politics by the degrees he took at the Rose Club'.[66] Similarly, it was probably to gatherings at the Rose that Sir Richard Atkins referred when he kept the absent Wharton abreast of the views of 'our club' in February 1696.[67]

Although neither the managerial meetings at Kensington nor the Rose Club's assemblies were novelties in 1696–97, that session is distinguished by the high degree of unity that prevailed in Whig ranks. As Vernon remarked early in the autumn, 'while this union last[s], whatever is pre-resolved is sure to be carried'.[68] The Whigs' relative unanimity at this juncture appears to have developed out of the reaction to the assassination plot and it also reflected their determination to overcome the effects of the liquidity crisis and to bring the war to a successful conclusion. Even so, the ministerialists did not have it quite all their own way in the Commons during the 1696–97 session. The first levy they proposed, the excise on cattle, was discarded by the lower House and the capitation was adopted instead. It is true that on this occasion some cynics suggested that it was 'a piece of management to begin with an excise upon live cattle' in order to have a capitation 'better go down', but that was—so Vernon judged— to make 'accidents' pass as 'refined policies'.[69] Then, too, later in the session divisions among the ministerialists themselves led to the loss of the wine duties. Yet whatever qualifications may be adduced, the contrast between the parliamentary situations of 1692–93 and 1696–97 remains impressive. Morever, though the Whigs had not quite achieved a monopoly of place and favour by the spring of 1697, they had capitalised their parliamentary successes to claim a lion's share. The Junto of Somers, Orford, Wharton, and Montagu, along with their friend and patron Shrewsbury, held many of the principal posts in the King's service; a sizeable contingent of their friends in the lower House had been given places, so that at the war's end seventy-five or so Whig Commoners held civil or military commissions; and in a number of localities their kinsmen and supporters had been greatly strengthened at the expense of their Tory rivals.

However, there remain several puzzling features about the Junto's rise to power. Perhaps the most perplexing is the question of how they and their close associates were able in 1693–94 and 1694–95 to manage a House of Commons whose turbulence and unreliability had quite disheartened their Tory predecessors, despite the Churchmen's gains in the general election of 1690. It is true that Wharton and his friends had contributed to the difficulties of their predecessors, especially during the 1692–93 session. Still, it is noteworthy that a House of Commons which went out of its way in April 1690 to approve the alterations recently made in the Tories' favour in the London lieutenancy did not utter a murmur in February 1694 when that commission was reconstituted to the Whigs' advantage. The disillusioned John Hampden implied in the autumn of 1690 that this Commons had a higher than usual proportion of members who 'have no other rule than to be for those who spoke to them last', but his comment can hardly explain the differences in the way the King's business fared between the middle two and the last two sessions of the 1690–95 parliament.[70] Is this change in temper, then, to be accounted for in terms of the replacement of old members by men of differing views returned in by-elections? Or is it that the outlook of both old and new M.P.s was altered by the insidious effects of Court 'influence' in an assembly which came to be denigrated as the 'Officers' parliament'? Or is there some other explanation?

The composition of the Commons was in flux during the five-and-a-half-year life of William's second parliament. Altogether, ninety-one of the original 513 members had been removed from the lower House by May 1695—one by expulsion (Trevor), twelve by summons to the Lords, the rest by death.[71] Seventy of those men also had sat in the Convention parliament; of that number, fourteen had been blacklisted as 'Jacobites' and twenty as 'Commonwealthmen'. The Whigs were particularly hard hit by deaths during the early 1690s; they lost such stalwarts as Serjeant Maynard and Colonel Birch, Sir Thomas Lee and William Sacheverell, William Harbord and William Jephson. These losses may have facilitated the emergence of younger Whig leaders; none the less, the ninety-one new members returned in the ensuing by-elections were divided between Whigs and Tories in roughly the same proportion as their predecessors.[72] But the new members can be distinguished from their predecessors in another way. Taking as a gauge the list of ministerial supporters drawn up by the critical but well-informed non-juror Samuel Grascome early in 1693, the ratio of government supporters to opponents among the *new* members elected by that time was five to four, as compared to a four to five ratio prevailing among *all* the members sitting when the list was compiled.[73]

These very tentative computations reinforce other indications that though Whig numbers were not rising over the life of the 1690–95 parliament, the number of firm supporters of the King's measures was on the rise. For instance, while Comptroller Wharton pressed for an early general election when the Commons in December 1694 debated the timing of the implementation of the triennial bill and avowed that he did so because he thought the Whigs would gain in any new election (a view which Lords Monmouth and Devonshire had earlier acted on in urging a dissolution upon the Queen in mid-1690), the Court in 1694 appeared anxious to prolong the life of the 1690–95 parliament as long as it decently could. Moreover, the phenomenon of Court gains and stable Whig numbers can be linked to, and would seem to justify, contemporary allegations of, the 'corruption' of this House of Commons through the King's excessive bestowal of places, pensions, and other forms of favour upon its members. Perhaps the most sensational example of these accusations was levelled by the Jacobite author of the so-called 'hush-money paper' which appeared in the autumn of 1693; he claimed that Treasury Secretary Guy had handed out 'no less than £16,000 in three days' time for secret service' when 'the House was a little out of humour' during the 1692–93 session.[74]

Outright bribery of this sort certainly fell within the purview of the Commissioners of Accounts. Yet, save for the case they made out against Falkland in 1694, the Commissioners were not successful in uncovering much skulduggery among M.P.s, and even Falkland's misdeed was not so much the acceptance of a bribe as it was the diversion of public moneys to his own use. There may have been occasional cash payments from the Privy Purse to needy parliamentarians, but most of these seem to have gone to indigent peers over whom the Commission of Accounts exercised no real scrutiny.[75]

While the Jacobites had an undoubted interest in exaggerating the extent of corruption, what of the exertion of Court influence though the disposition of places? After all, Coningsby, in urging William to retain his second parliament until the end of the war, reminded his master in the spring of 1694: 'You have for the last four years past been giving all employments to members of the House, which, though it has not signified much in any party business, yet in that grand affair of carrying on the war, they have been of mighty service.'[76] Coningsby's statement may convey the impression that a dramatic increase in the number of placemen had occurred, but it is true that the number of civil office-holders and military men serving in the Commons did rise from roughly 120 in the spring of 1690 to 130 by the 1692–93 session.[77]

To counter this trend, parliament considered a variety of expedients. In 1692– numbers can be linked to, and would seem to justify, contemporary allegations exclude in future all placemen from the lower House; again, in January 1694 William had to resort to a veto to prevent the enactment of a less stringent bill which would have permitted the re-election of placemen. This was the closest a general measure against office-holding members came to the statute book during these years, but several more restricted place clauses were mooted and one was actually adopted as part of the lottery act of 1694. This provided that all those 'concerned directly or indirectly' in 'the farming, collecting, or managing any sums of money, duties, or other aid granted' by that act 'or that shall hereafter be granted by any other act of parliament', with the exception of Neale himself and of the Commissioners of the Treasury, Customs, and Excise '*not exceeding the present number in each office*', were to be barred from sitting in the Commons.[78] The problem posed by this provision in the lottery act was in interpreting how it should be applied. Did it mean, as some backbenchers alleged early in the following session, that the recent increase from one to three in the number of M.P.s serving as Excise Commissioners was illegal? Or did it mean, as the ministerialists urged, that the size of that Board could not be enlarged from its present total of nine in order to make additional places for M.P.s? In November 1694, the Commons accepted the ministerialists' reading; even so, the passage of this exclusionary clause limited substantially the possibility of instituting new places in future for members of the Commons either by the creation of new revenue boards or by the enlargement of existing commissions.[79]

Despite the loss of Hussey's general place bills and the limited applicability of the place clause in the lottery act, after 1693 the growth in the number of placemen in the Commons was halted and even reversed. Thanks to deaths and other removals, by the time William's second parliament was dissolved the total of placemen had dropped back to 120, though this figure does not include either members such as Palmes whose close relatives acquired places or others who voted with the Court in hopes of securing reward.[80] A striking case in point of a member openly seeking to trade his vote in the Commons for a place is provided by the merchant member for Grimsby in the 1695–98 parliament, Arthur Moore. In mid-1696, Moore was soliciting Secretary Trumbull for the fulfilment of a tentative commitment that had been made to his brother of a post in the military administration. Trumbull reported to Blathwayt that Moore had been told that his own conduct in the Commons during the 1695–96 session was the cause of the obstruction and that Moore had responded to this by avowing that he was now ready 'to serve the King in future' and that he would 'enter into measures with me the next winter for that purpose'.[81]

However, there were always more suitors than places, and in any event the relationship between a man's possession of office and his conduct in parliament was not necessarily that of *quid pro quo*. Admittedly, the bestowal of a position upon an M.P. by the King was usually a reward for services already performed and carried with it the expectation of loyalty in the future, too. Thus, Gwyn spoke of Clarke, Yonge, and the other M.P.s named to the revenue boards in 1694 as men who 'have at last had their bargain made good to them', and Musgrave observed in the same vein that 'it hath been evident very long that those gentlemen resolved to bring a duck in their mouths'.[82] Yet the possession of a place was hardly a cast-iron guarantee of obedience. Some offices were held for life or good behaviour (particularly the subordinate places in the Exchequer and in the legal system) by men who had secured these posts before the Revolution or purchased them since from the previous incumbents; such office-holders owed nothing to William and were difficult to discipline. For instance, the only way Montagu could think of dealing with Exchequer Auditor Thomas Done (the Tory M.P. for Newton, Hampshire) in 1695 was to seek a 'retrenchment' in the fees conventionally paid him.[83] Done and the like were exceptional cases, yet there are plenty of instances of placemen with tenure during pleasure opposing their nominal superiors over partisan questions. And occasionally one can find men holding quite responsible positions opposing ministerial proposals over ways and means, as Seymour and Temple opposed excises in 1693–94 and as Yonge and Clarke opposed the wine duties in April 1697.

Overall, then, the sharp fluctuations in the Commons' support for royal policy and in the enthusiasm members displayed for reform measures from the middle to the later sessions of the 1690–95 parliament cannot be explained as the result of any great increase either in corruption or influence. But the relative success of the King's business can be correlated to some extent with how well or poorly the previous summer's campaign had gone and also with M.P.s' sense of the prospects for the summer to come. The effects of the events of the preceding summer on the next parliamentary session have been traced in our narrative; it is harder to gauge the influence that the King's ministers and 'managers' themselves could exert over the lower House in shaping members' perceptions of the future course of the war. What is apparent is that even at their most numerous, a united band of King's servants in the Commons still needed substantial backbench support to carry any controversial question. Hence, it is necessary also to try to assess the quality of ministerial leadership as it affected both placemen and country gentlemen.

Here, the emerging Whig Junto had a considerable advantage over the Tory ministers and their spokesmen in the Commons during the early 1690s. Wharton and Trenchard along with Montagu and Littleton were more than a match in all respects for Lowther and Goodricke, while as soon as Seymour took office in 1692 he forfeited much of his influence over the Churchmen on the backbenches. But the difference was more than a matter of personality and ability, for as Sunderland observed: Whigs and Tories were not 'equal in relation to the government' since 'the whole of the one [party] may be made for it and not a quarter of the other'.[84] Sunderland exaggerated somewhat, but Whig support for the war, even if it had to be waged on a continental strategy, can be seen in the fact that in 1693–94 (and thereafter), by contrast to the 1691–92 and 1692–93 sessions, the principal divisions on supply came over ways and means, and not over the estimates. As Trenchard wrote joyfully to Capel a month after Nottingham's dismissal; 'I assure you the country gentlemen of the Whig party have adhered to the King's interest beyond what could be imagined.'[85] In turn, the commitment of the Whigs in office and on the backbenches to the continuation of the war—indeed, their readiness to vote an enlargement of the land army in late 1693 and then to maintain 87,000 men for the rest of the war—was reinforced both by the bestowal of places for the ambitious and by concessions on reform questions for the principled.

The change of hands in the ministry and in the Commons also had a healing effect on the breach in Whig ranks which had opened up during the 1691–92 and 1692–93 sessions. The coming together in those years of a band of self-styled 'patriots', which included men who had voted on different sides over 'abdication' and the 'Sacheverell clause', was in no small part a reaction to the Tory ministers' seeming inability to organise the costly war effort effectively. In Foley's and Clarges's eyes, this failure, coupled with their own desire for further safeguards for the 'laws and liberties' of the realm, sufficed to overcome previous differences over the legitimacy of the Revolution and over matters ecclesiastical. Thus, the 1692–93 session in particular was marked by a deepening division among the leading Whigs, with those in place at Whitehall and those sitting on the Commission of Accounts more and more at odds. In December 1692, Foley and Harley were 'aspersed' by their own kinsmen for their share in the defeat of the abjuration bill, and afterwards their 'desertion' was lamented by a pamphleteer in a frequently quoted passage:[86]

P. Fo[le]y turns cadet and carries arms under the general of the West-Saxons [Seymour]; the two Har[le]ys, father and son, are engineers under the late Lieutenant of the Ordnance [Musgrave], and bomb any bill which he hath once resolved to reduce to ashes, though it were for recognition, or anything else that is most necessary to our security.

Somewhat less familiar, yet equally trenchant, is the justification another pamphleteer advanced for the new Country alignment. Observing the continuing division of 'Williamites' into 'two sides' which are 'commonly distinguished by the names of Whig and Tory', he asserted that the two parties' chief 'labour is the gaining of the King and the getting those of their fraternity (whatever otherwise they be) into the government'. Then, too, 'the Court-followers' dominate the Commons and[87]

whoever calls this Court in question, whoever doubts its good intention to English men, to English liberties and government, whoever quotes past declarations, or instances a present grievance, nay, or that in discourse is but lukewarm towards the state, a way is found (and it seldom fails) to make that man ill thought of by the herd, suspected by the vulgar of his party, and shunned as a deserter: for with one party he is insured a Commonwealth's man, and with the other, a plain Jacobite.

What the sharpness of the exchanges between the Foleys themselves in the Commons or these pamphleteers out of doors obscures is that after the King began to turn back to the Whigs in 1693, his Whig servants, particularly Somers and later Shrewsbury, sought to reclaim their old friends. The Lord Keeper took pains to renew former ties so that, for instance, in January 1694 the pious Sir Edward Harley could happily report to Robert (then in Herefordshire) that he had been invited to 'a great feast' at Somers's where there had been 'no health drunk, no profane word uttered, thanks given before the meat'.[88] Furthermore, Shrewsbury—who complained in November 1693 that 'there is not such a thing left in being as a party of my mind' and who declined to take office unless the King made concessions for the 'good of England'—summoned Foley and Harley to him in August 1694 and began by declaring 'he was the same man as when we met' before his return to the Secretaryship.[89] It is true that the series of conferences that ensued did not produce agreement over Foley's scheme to hypothecate the land tax, but it was Harley who brought in the compromise version of the triennial legislation that the King approved in December 1694, and overall there was a noticeable easing of tensions between the Whig ministerialists and Foley and Harley in the opening weeks of the 1694–95 session.

If the key to the Whig ministerialists' successes in the latter stages of William's second parliament, at least up to Mary's death, lay in their party's commitment to continuing a war whose prospects began to improve during the 1694 campaign, along with their own adroitness both in 'getting men in' and in gaining the King's consent to a modified triennial bill, what, then, is the explanation of the mounting difficulties that the Junto encountered in the Commons between early January 1695 and late February 1696? Clearly, it was not any accession to Tory strength that frustrated Littleton's bid for the Chair in March 1695 or that prevented the imposition of an abjuration upon the members of the projected council of trade in February 1696. After Mary's death snapped that link to the Stuart past, Sunderland took care to consolidate the tentative *rapprochement* between the two royal courts, thereby preventing Rochester and Nottingham from exploiting Anne's potential role as the head of a 'reversionary interest'. Furthermore, contemporary and retrospective verdicts on the outcome of the ensuing general election do at least agree that the Tories, despite some efforts to revive 'the Church in danger' theme, fared poorly at the polls. Thus, a disproportionately large number of the M.P.s (almost all of them Churchmen) who refused to take the association in March 1696 were hold-overs: of the 103 non-associators, only 29 (28 per cent) had not served in William's second parliament; of the 410 members who signed, 145 (35 per cent) were newly elected.[90]

Rather, what seems to have precipitated the Whig ministerialists' difficulties in the early months of 1695 was Montagu's and Wharton's display of arrogant aggressiveness once Shrewsbury's and Trenchard's illnesses, Russell's absence, and Somers's usual passivity left the Comptroller and the Chancellor of the Exchequer temporarily unrestrained by cooler heads.[91] Francis Gwyn had remarked to Harley in September 1694 that 'our Rosicrucians are as restless as St Dunstan's clock and will let nobody rest that are near them', and certainly Montagu and Wharton gave no peace to their Tory colleagues after Mary's death.[92] Striking when the bribery inquiries offered the opportunity, they sought to exploit the country gentlemen's zeal against corruption and the Commission of Accounts' investigatory powers to rid themselves of their unwelcome associates in office. Yet in taking these measures, they failed to pay sufficient heed to the sensibilities and interests of Foley and Harley. It was unwise to seek to resurrect the leather excise (which would have burdened particularly the graziers and leatherworkers of the Welsh Marches) after the fierce resistance put up against it during the 1693–94 session, and it was foolhardy for Montagu to renege on understandings he had arrived at with Foley.

The costs of their imprudence were not long in catching up with Montagu and Wharton. It was galling enough that the King refused to let them profit from the wounds they had inflicted on their Tory colleagues and that they had to accept a dissolution about which they now had second thoughts—in part, perhaps, because it would hinder further pursuit of the bribery inquiries. But much more potenially damaging to them was that in ousting Trevor, angering Foley and Harley, and bringing on an early general election, they ended by setting up the new Speaker and his kinsman as rivals for the leadership of the Whigs in the Commons. Indeed, Foley—as Guy reported in June 1695—was 'positive that by a little pains' the Whigs in the lower House could be induced to 'totally leave Wharton and Montagu'.[93]

Well before the end of William's second parliament, Foley and Harley had demonstrated that they were capable of devising expedients to finance the war, such as Foley's 'million project' and his scheme to hypothecate a portion of the land tax. By mid-1695, then, they seem to have figured in Guy's view, and also in Sunderland's, as plausible alternatives to Wharton and Montagu if the Comptroller and the Chancellor of the Exchequer continued in their unruly ways. In turn, after the election results appeared to confirm Guy's forecast that Foley would probably be able to retain the Chair without the Court's backing, both Sunderland and Shrewsbury probably counselled William to enjoin Littleton to stay away. But despite Guy's extensive contacts with Foley and Harley during the summer and autumn of 1695, they were only willing to serve on their own terms, and the election of a substantial number of new Whig members strengthened their position in the opening months of the new parliament.[94] Certainly, the Whiggery professed by such inexperienced members as Lord Devonshire's two sons and Lords Ashley and Spencer was easily yoked both to old reform measures, chiefly the treason trials bill, and to the new projects that Harley and Foley sponsored during the first half of the 1695–96 session—the council of trade and a land bank. New members they might be, but otherwise they bore a distinct resemblance to those 'old parliament Whigs' to whom one of Locke's correspondents facetiously alluded in 1694 when she apologised for a lapse in her letters by remarking, 'it is as awkward a thing for an old maid to write a love letter as for an old parliament Whig to turn courtier'.[95]

No better illustration can be provided than Robert Molesworth, the author of the controversial *Account of Denmark*, published late in 1693 and noted by Sir Edward Harley as 'an extraordinary book' for its analysis of how that kingdom lost its liberties.[96] The former envoy to Denmark was recommended by Shrewsbury, Somers, and Trenchard for an Excise Commissionership in June 1694, not long after he returned to England, and he also had Robert Harley's help when he searched unsuccessfully for a vacant seat in the Commons that autumn. Similarly, though Molesworth figures as a staunch Court supporter in the four extant parliamentary lists for 1696 and was one of the ministerialists' slate for Commissioners of Accounts that February, he himself saw no contradiction between votes in favour of the association and Fenwick's attainder and votes for the reform of treason trials and the tack of the electoral qualifications bill. Molesworth also managed to combine backing for the parliamentary council of trade with approval of Wharton's resolution to subject its members to an abjuration oath.[97] With support from such Whig members as well from the bulk of the Tories, Foley and Harley—at the head of 'the country party, as it is called'—laid down the terms on which they were prepared to serve the King, and a concerned Sunderland in early 1696 urged a reluctant William to accept them.[98]

In the event, William—after agreeing to the land bank scheme—never had to decide whether to yield to the pressure for a parliamentary council of trade, and during the 1696–97 session the Junto more than regained the ground they had earlier lost. By the spring of 1697, they seemed closer than ever before to success in their bid for dominance. William himself had been brought to lobby for the attainder of Sir John Fenwick in order to vindicate the reputation of the Junto's patron, Shrewsbury. In April 1697 the King was also ready to recommend personally the Exchequer bill subscription—a venture that, as Somers put it to Wharton, 'the nation depends on ... at least I am sure the Whigs depend upon it'.[99] Then, too, analysis of the four extant parliamentary lists from the first two sessions of William's third parliament has led some students of the reign to conclude that 'what happened in 1696' was 'the virtual completion of the process' begun in 1693 'in which Whig and Court on the one hand, and Tory and Country on the other' became 'synonymous terms'.[100] Thus, of the sixty-nine members who were blacklisted as supporters of the 'Sacheverell clause' in 1690 and who are recorded as voting in 1696 on the price of guineas and on the attainder, only fourteen divided against the ministry on one or both questions.[101] Again, of the fifty-five members who were blacklisted as supporters of regency in 1689 and who are recorded as voting on the price of guineas and the attainder, only eight (seven of them placemen) supported the ministry on one or both questions.[102]

However, as the case of the switching voters in the two unlisted divisions of 31 January 1696 on the council of trade resolutions indicates, the actual situation in William's third parliament was rather more fluid than the lists alone would suggest. Besides the presence of a sizeable number of Whigs on the backbenches whose votes were being competed for by Montagu and his associates and by Foley and Harley, there were still more than thirty placemen with Tory inclinations sitting in the Commons during the 1696–97 session. To be sure, some of these Tory placemen—mainly associates of the Duke of Leeds—were in danger of removal from their posts by April 1697. Yet, their offence in the King's eyes was not that they were Tories but rather that they had failed to support ministerial measures during the past session. In fact, William was unwilling to have only 'one kind of men' displaced, and so Leeds remained, as did Charles Bertie (Treasurer of the Ordnance) and Peregrine Bertie (Vice-Chamberlain).[103] Hence, while the Junto, utilising Whig strength in the Commons and extending their grip upon office, may be said to have achieved a 'qualified form of party government' by the end of the war, the qualifications deserve underlining.[104]

One major qualification was the Junto's weakness in the King's closet. William's 'inner council' for English affairs in the mid-1690s consisted of Sunderland, Shrewsbury, and Somers; of the three, Somers was the least in the King's confidence, while Sunderland still had the principal voice in the disposition of royal patronage. As Matthew Prior rather undiplomatically observed to his patron Montagu in May 1697 in the course of his pursuit of the secretaryship to the Irish lords justices: 'If this secretary [Prior's competitor], whoever he is, was recommended or is protected by my Lord Sunderland, there is no hope of our succeeding.'[105] In part, Sunderland remained so influential because the King had never lost his distaste for the parties' lust for control. Nor had the Junto given William much reason to change his attitude. It had been necessity, not desire, that had impelled the King to withdraw his favour from the Tory ministers in 1693 and 1694. And at least at the outset of his career as minister 'behind the curtain', Sunderland had spoken of setting the King's business 'right without doing anything . . . that interferes between Whigs and Tories or shall lessen the prerogative'.[106] This was to promise more on both scores than even that virtuoso was able to perform, especially after the loss of the Turkey convoy. Furthermore, by 1695 Wharton and Montagu were reportedly of the view that the Junto could do without Sunderland as their broker, though Shrewsbury and Somers were not so rash. Despite the Whig tidal wave provoked by the discovery of the assassination plot, Shrewsbury and Somers were glad of Sunderland's aid at the height of the liquidity crisis that summer, and the Duke's subsequent physical collapse made the Earl as indispensable as he had been in 1693. Nor did Shrewsbury's return to business in March 1697 greatly improve the Junto's position. The Duke and the Earl were now on more intimate terms than ever before, and one old Whitehall hand was convinced that 'the secret and weight of the administration is wholly in them two'.[107] Even worse, Shrewsbury's health remained precarious; his relapse of April 1697 was followed by another in early August, so that by September 1697 Vernon was busily scouting out another post for himself in the conviction that his master was going to give up the seals and retire.[108]

As the Junto's concern over Shrewsbury's health and his future intentions betrays their dependence upon him to counter Sunderland's counsel and the King's own inclinations, so the second major qualification to their apparent predominance by the end of the war relates to the character of the ministerialist majorities in parliament. In the Lords, as the divisions on the attainder of Sir John Fenwick attest, the Junto had to rely upon courtiers and bishops for numerical superiority, though the elevation of Somers and Russell to the peerage in April 1697 (fifteen months after Wharton had succeeded to his father's barony) did add substantially to their debating strength there. In the Commons, the Junto continued to draw some support for official measures from a diminishing band of Tory placemen, but it was the backbench Whigs who might hearken either to Montagu and Littleton or to Foley and Harley who remained the most critical element in William's third House of Commons. Since Mary's death, the rivalry between the Speaker and Harley on one side and the Junto on the other had intensified. And while the Speaker's and his kinsman's political credit had been lessened by the land bank's failure, it had not been destroyed.

Thus, it was by no means certain that the Junto could repeat their successes of 1696–97 in subsequent sessions. As Vernon observed to Shrewsbury late in September 1697, the coming of peace might well prompt a reordering of priorities both in St Stephen's Chapel and among the political nation generally. For this reason, Vernon wondered whether the King might not be wise to call an election immediately rather than to delay until 1698 when the triennial act would require a dissolution:[109]

The people are now in much better humour and relish the peace more than they will do a year hence when they shall find taxes in a good measure continued, troops lying heavier upon them as being in greater numbers dispersed about the country, and that there will not be so quick a consumption for their goods nor their corn and cattle bear so high a price as in time of war.

I should think this the likeliest time to get rid of most of the non-associators, and I suppose the boroughs and cities would take some care to send those who should not abridge the freedom of their choice and restrain it only to landed men. Besides, this parliament is almost jaded with giving and may think of recommending themselves to future elections by holding their hands.

Only time would tell whether Sunderland's unrestrained optimism about the political results of the peace or Vernon's more cautious weighing of the postwar possibilities was the more prescient.

Notes to Chapter IX

1 HMC Downshire, I, 381.

2 BL Add. MS. 42592, f. 40, also ff. 27–8, 35–8, 41–2, including annotated transcripts of the Prince's declarations; CSPD, 1694–1695, pp. 286–7, HMC Buccleuch, II, 113–14.

3 Letters of Humphrey Prideaux . . . to John Ellis 1674–1722, ed. E. Thompson (Camden Society, 2nd s. XV, 1875), p. 156.

4 Cf. Baxter, William III, p. 341 and n. 32.

5 CSPD, 1694–1695, pp. 363, 364. The original is in PRO, SP 8/15 No. 69, and the handwriting of this well-known unsigned paper (sometimes attributed to Godolphin) is Coningsby's.

6 BL Loan 29/141 (unfoliated), to R. Harley, 5 August 1692. See also The State of Parties, and of the Public (1692[–3]), reprinted in PH, v, xlv–vii.

7 CSPD, 1693, p. 408; KAO, Chevening MS. 78, R. Yard to A. Stanhope, 21 November 1693.

8 Northants RO, Buccleuch MSS., Vernon letters, I, 67, 11 February.

9 Somers's alarmist view is noted in a minute of Trumbull's headed 'Lord Keeper about Council of Trade' (30 December 1695) in Berkshire RO, Trumbull Add. MS. 116.

10 See R. Lees, 'Parliament and the Proposal for a Council of Trade, 1695–6', EHR LIV (1939), 60. However, Aaron Smith was divested of the Solicitorship to the Treasury, ostensibly at least for his repeated failure to submit his accounts to the Board: S. Baxter, The Development of the Treasury 1660–1702 (1957), pp. 246 and n. 3, 249.

11 Cf. CTB, Introduction to vols. XI–XVII, pp. clv–clxxii; D. Rubini, Court and Country 1688–1702 (1967), chapter 3, esp. p. 88. Shaw's characterisation of the Commission has often been criticised, but he was less prone than Rubini to make demonstrably mistaken assertions. And see J. A. Downie, 'The Commission of Public Accounts and the Formation of the Country Party', EHR LXXXXI (1976).

12 E.g. BL Harleian MSS. 1489, f. 54, and 1492, ff. 10, 14–16. See also BL Loan 29/45B, f. 75.

13 HMC Portland, VIII, passim.

14 CSPD, 1694–1695, p. 363.

15 Middlesex RO, Jersey MS. 510/62, 25 August/4 September 1696.

16 Luttrell, Parliamentary Diary, p. 250; CJ, X, 701, 707, 710. Cf. M. Thomson, 'Parliament and Foreign Policy, 1689–1714', William III and Louis XIV, ed. R. Hatton (Liverpool, 1968), pp. 130–1.

17 CJ, XI, 24, 309; KU, F. Bonnet, 19/29 April 1695; BL Add. MS. 17677PP, ff. 237–8, L'Hermitage, 19/29 April 1695. And see HMC Buccleuch, II, 78.

18 Vernon Corr., I, 110. And see Archives, III, i, 489; Klopp, Der Fall des Hauses Stuart, VII, 316.

19 Most of these men ended their lives in prison years after William's own death.

20 Macaulay, History, VI, 2689–90 (Salisbury was also in trouble with the Lords on another score at the same time).

21 The quotation is from A Letter to a Member of Parliament (1698), reprinted in PH, v, cl.

22 R. Walker, 'The Newspaper Press in the Reign of William III', HJ XVII (1974), 691–710; G. Gibbs, 'The Revolution in Foreign Policy', BAGR, pp. 73–5.

23 NU, Portland MSS. PwA 2706–7, ? to Earl of Athlone, 1 and 22 February 1695.

24 Kenyon, Sunderland, p. 262 note; Shrewsbury Corr., p. 19 and ff.

25 NU, Portland MS. PwA 1248, [Sunderland to Portland], 29 July 1695.

26 Shrewsbury Corr., p. 533.

27 This and the next paragraph, where not otherwise indicated, are based on Baxter, William III, pp. 326–7, 348–52.

28 Huygens, Journaal, II, 337, also 176, 467, 561; HMC Buccleuch, II, 401–2, 403; Vernon Corr., I, 70, 209.

29 Berkshire RO, Trumbull Add. MS. 116, cabinet minute, 10 November 1695.

30 Compare on the subject of William's alleged homosexuality, H. and B. Van der Zee, William and Mary (New York, 1973), pp. 421–4; John Miller, The Life and Times of William and Mary (1974), p. 181.

31 HMC Bath, III, 83. And see HMC Buccleuch, II, 388; NU, Portland MS. PwA 152, list of prospective brides for William drawn up by Blancard for Portland.

32 CSPD, 1691–1692, pp. 543–4 (misdated, original in PRO, SP 8/13 No. 7); Burnet, History, IV, 269–70. See also E. Turner, 'The Lords Justices of England', EHR XXIX (1914), 453–76.

33 J. Carter, 'The Revolution and the Constitution', BAGR, p. 51.

34 The following discussion draws on and amends J. Carter, 'Cabinet Records for the Reign of William III', EHR LXXVIII (1963), 95–114.

35 Thus, a meeting of 18 December 1695 at Whitehall which the King did not attend is none the less referred to by Trumbull in his minute as a 'cabinet'; Berkshire RO, Trumbull Add. MS. 116. See also HMC Buccleuch, II, 324.

36 It is worth noting that Trumbull's complaint during the summer of 1696 that since the King's departure he had been 'wholly excluded from coming to the D[uke] of Shrewsbury's office' suggests that such meetings continued to be held when the King went abroad; Berkshire RO, Trumbull Add. MS. 125.

37 Romney did attend on 22 April 1697, but then that day he had been named a Lord Justice.

38 Peter Lord King, The Life and Letters of John Locke (1884), pp. 245–6.

39 I. K. Steele, The Politics of Colonial Policy: The Board of Trade in Colonial

Administration 1696–1720 (Oxford, 1968), chapter 2. See also J. Ehrman, *The Navy in the War of William III 1689–1697* (Cambridge, 1953), pp. 571–2.

40 HMC *Portland*, III, 576, 577. Compare BL Add. MS. 9729, f. 142, R. Henley to W. Blathwayt, 9 June.

41 *CJ*, XI, 573; Bodl. Locke MS. C4, f. 180, S. Brownover to Locke, 26 November 1696.

42 For subsequent Commons' attitudes to the Board, see Steele, *Politics of Colonial Policy*, p. 59.

43 *Shrewsbury Corr.*, p. 351; NU, Portland MS. PwA 940, 13 August 1697.

44 J. Horsefield, *British Monetary Experiments 1650–1710* (1960), app. 2.

45 The seamen's bill was discussed at three meetings where the King was present and at four meetings he did not attend. Members of the Admiralty Board were summoned to two of the latter meetings. Berkshire RO, Trumbull Add. MS. 116; HMC *Buccleuch*, II, 274, 275, 290–1.

46 For the projectors, see C. Brooks, 'Taxation, Finance and Public Opinion, 1688–1714' (unpublished Ph.D. thesis, University of Cambridge, 1970), chapters 7–8.

47 BL Harleian MS. 1274, f. 10. And see Wing H1416–17 (misdated).

48 BL Add. MS. 5540, f. 81, T. Day to J. Cary *et al.*, 5 December 1695. See also the mocking 'poem of state' against Neale and Barbon (both near bankrupts) as projectors; *Poems on Affairs of State*, V, ed. W. J. Cameron (New Haven, 1971), 493–7.

49 Berkshire RO, Trumbull bound MS. 50, T. Bateman to Sir W. Trumbull, 10 May 1698. And see Browning, *Danby*, III, 179; CSPD, 1690–1691, p. 512.

50 NU, Portland MS. PwA 1238, [to Portland], 13 July 1694.

51 NU, Portland MSS. PwA 1212, [Sunderland to Portland], 3 May 1693, and PwA 506, [H. Guy to Portland], 5 July 1695; BL Loan 29/187, f. 284, [R. Harley] to his father, 28 August 1694; CSPD, 1696, p. 215.

52 CSPD, 1696, p. 395; CTB, XI, 58, 60.

53 CTB, XI, 65.

54 *Shrewsbury Corr.*, p. 156.

55 Dalrymple, *Memoirs*, II, app. iii, 240; Browning, *Danby*, II, 212.

56 Northants RO, Buccleuch MSS, Vernon letters, I, 12 and 24, 27 October 19 November 1696.

57 BL Loan 29/187, f. 28, [R. Harley] to his father, 9 February 1693; *Vernon Corr.*, I, 83.

58 *Vernon Corr.*, I, 26, 30, 33, 36, 37, 58–9.

59 Berkshire RO, Trumbull Add. MS. 125.

60 Berkshire RO, Trumbull MS. 'Sunderland' bound vol. (unfoliated), 'Saturday'.

61 Browning, *Danby*, III, 178. For the arrangements in the next reign, see H. Snyder, 'Godolphin and Harley: A Study of Their Partnership in Politics', *Huntington Library Quarterly*, XXX (1967), 248; G. Holmes, *British Politics in the Age of Anne* (1967), p. 365 and note.

62 CSPD, 1694–1695 p. 362.

63 Bodl. Rawlinson Letters 104, f. 104, ? to T. Hoskins, 9 May [1695].

64 Lamberty, *Mémoires*, II, 199.

65 *Poems on Affairs of State*, V, 430–8. The three were Lord Cutts, Henry Guy, and Vice-Chamberlain Peregrine Bertie junior.

66 A. B., *A Letter to Mr. Secretary Trenchard* (1694, Wing F752), p. 10.

67 Bodl. Carte MS. 103 f. 256, 18 February 1696. See also *Memoirs of Ailesbury*, pp. 436–7. For reference to the Whigs' frequenting of Richard's Coffee-house, see *Somers' Tracts*, X, 211; Wing B2083, C445.

68 *Vernon Corr.*, I, 34.

69 *Vernon Corr.*, I, 121. And see Klopp, *Der Fall des Hauses Stuart*, VII, 510–11.

70 BL Loan 29/138 (unfoliated), to R. Harley, 15 October 1690. Note, however, that Hampden was talking about votes on election petitions.

71 Excluded from the total of ninety-one are (1) M.P.s elected in 1690 but unseated on petition, and (2) M.P.s chosen in by-elections who themselves did not survive until the dissolution.

72 The partisan leanings of the new members have been deduced from the positions attributed to the fifty-nine of them who continued to sit in William's third parliament in I. Burton *et al.*, *Political Parties in the Reigns of William III and Anne: The Evidence of Division Lists* (BIHR, special supplement 7, 1968), app. A.

73 For this list, see Appendix C.

74 Reprinted in PH, v, ciii.

75 *Correspondentie*, I, ii, 38–9. Cf. Baxter, *William III*, p. 278.

76 CSPD, 1694–1695, p. 365.

77 See Appendix D.

78 SR, VI, 461 (my italics).

79 BL Add. MS. 46527, f. 22, J. Vernon to Lord Lexington, 13 November 1694. See also BL Loan 29/187, f. 278, Sir C. Musgrave to R. Harley, 20 August 1694.

80 A *Letter from the Grecian Coffee House* (1701, BL 515 L8 No. 15), p. 9.

81 Berkshire RO, Trumbull Add. MS. 117, 3 July 1696 (copy). Moore's brother does not seem to have been successful and Moore remained in opposition.

82 BL Loan 29/313, bundle 7, F. Gwyn to R. Harley, 11 August 1694; and 29/187, f. 278, Sir C. Musgrave to R. Harley, 20 August 1694.

83 NU, Portland MS. PwA 936, C. Montagu to [Portland], 11 June 1695. See also PRO, SP 8/13 No. 6, a list of offices held for life or during good behaviour, [1689].

84 NU, Portland MS. PwA 1240, [Sunderland to Portland], 5 August 1694.

85 Dorset RO, Trenchard MS. D60/x36, 2 December 1693 (draft).

86 For the aspersions, see HMC *Portland* III, 510. The pamphlet quoted is A *Dialogue betwixt Whig and Tory* (1693), reprinted in ST, II, 391.

87 *The State of Parties* in PH, v, xxxviii–xxxix.

88 BL Loan 29/142 (unfoliated), 16 January 1694.

89 *Shrewsbury Corr.*, p. 26; BL Loan 29/187, f. 284, [R. Harley] to his father, 28 August 1694.

90 See Appendix C.

91 Somers's inability to leash Montagu in the mid-1690s is attested to not only by Guy but also by Locke's college; Bodl. Locke MS. C8, f. 214, 10 March 1696.

92 HMC *Portland*, III, 556.

93 NU, Portland MS. PwA 503, [H. Guy to Portland], 14 June 1695.

94 Sixty or so new Whig M.P.s appear on the parliamentary lists drawn up in 1695–96.

95 Bodl. Locke MS. C15, f. 29, M. Lockhart, 12 January [1694].

96 BL Loan 29/187, f. 212, [to A. Harley], 19 December 1693. For Molesworth in general, see E. L. Ellis, 'The Whig Junto in Relation to the Development of Party Politics and Party Organisation from its Inception to 1714' (unpublished D.Phil. thesis, University of Oxford, 1961), app. C.

97 CSPD, 1694–1695, pp. 184–5; HMC *Portland*, VIII, 43; HMC *Kenyon*, p. 399.

98 Berkshire RO, Trumbull MS. 'Ellis' bound vol., J. Ellis to Trumbull, 4 February 1696. For other references at this time to a 'country party', see KAO, Chevening MS. 78, R. Yard to A. Stanhope, 11 February 1696; HMC *Kenyon*, I, 386–7; HMC *Hastings*, II, 255.

99 Bodl. Carte MS. 228, f. 126, [21] April 1697.

100 Burton, *Political Parties*, p. 33.

101 Burton and his co-authors wrongly identify Sir William Drake as a supporter of the 'Sacheverell clause' and fail to include Robert Harley as one.

102 The seven Tory placemen were Charles Bertie, Lord Cornbury, Charles Fox, Charles Godolphin, Edward Nicholas, Lord Ranelagh, and Francis Robartes.

103 MSP, II, 431.

104 E. Ellis, 'William III and the Politicians', BAGR, p. 131.

105 HMC *Bath*, III, 114 and ff.

106 NU, Portland MS. PwA 1212, to [Portland], 10 July 1693.

107 HMC *Roxburghe, etc.*, p. 132.

108 *Vernon Corr.*, I, 375–6.

109 Northants RO, Buccleuch MSS., Vernon letters, I, 146, 30 September 1697.

X

RETREAT IN VICTORY

1697–1698

For all the enthusiastic rejoicing that greeted William on his public entry to London on 16 November 1697, the Treaty of Ryswick was no guarantee of either peace abroad or tranquillity at home. The international prospects did not seem particularly auspicious in the autumn of 1697. The 'haughty demeanour' of France in the final stages of the peace negotiations left William 'with apprehensions for the future', especially since the demise of the ailing and childless Carlos II of Spain could hardly be staved off much longer. So the King was concerned to keep England in 'a condition to insure and preserve' the peace, not least by continuing in service a substantial proportion of the 87,000 troops on foot at the war's end.[1] Nor was the 'new world' that Sunderland had hailed in England upon the news of the peace easy to settle. The most immediate disruption that threatened stemmed from Shrewsbury's renewed efforts to unburden himself of the seals. Plagued by continuing ill health and dismayed by new accusations of infidelity levelled against him before the Lords Justices in August 1697 by self-confessed counterfeiters and other denizens of London's underworld, the Duke made known both to the King and to Somers and Orford on 6 September that he was determined to resign.[2]

The danger that 'ruin to the building' would follow the removal of this 'corner stone' prompted Somers and Orford to put forward Wharton as Shrewsbury's successor—a suggestion with which Sunderland seemed prepared to concur. But the Whig leaders soon realised it would not be easy to secure this appointment. For one thing, it appeared that Wharton was not keen to serve as Trumbull's junior. And for another, the Junto were suspicious of the Lord Chamberlain, for all his professions, and not without cause. Sunderland, who knew only too well William's antipathy to Wharton, had plans of his own and now he approached Vernon to revive an idea he had broached the previous winter. This was to make Vernon Secretary, and thereby to reduce both Secretaries to mere administrators—'little men', as Vernon put it, 'framed for a dependence on a premier minister'.[3] Yet Sunderland did not intend to set up Vernon in open opposition to Wharton; rather, the under-secretary was to be kept in reserve in case of an emergency. Thus, as Shrewsbury prepared in late October 1697 to journey to town in order to deliver up the seals to William on his return to England, Vernon warned the Duke he would be[4]

coming into a strange intricacy. My Lord Chamberlain in some companies declares for my Lord Wharton, and knows there is no such thing intended. My Lord Wharton shows a willingness to accept of it, and at the bottom has no mind to it, or, as your Grace foresees, will soon be weary of it. Your Grace will be vehemently pressed to stay in, and you resolve against it. One you know is secretly designed for Secretary, and he is utterly incapable of it.

The complexity over the Secretaryship was, in turn, shaped in no small part by the Junto's fears that 'no friend of theirs' was likely to be given the seals and that Shrewsbury's resignation would set in motion a general 'change of hands'.[5] As early as May 1696, Sunderland had observed that the Whigs were frightened that William would dispense with their services after a peace; in April 1697, it was being 'buzzed about' in Whig circles that Sunderland was 'bringing the Lords Rochester, Marlborough, and Godolphin into play'; in July, Sir Joseph Williamson was informed that Sunderland and Rochester 'have had one, or more meetings of late, which alarms some people very much'; and in October 1697, Orford himself remarked that 'endeavours are used to persuade the Whigs that if they are not willing to do the King's business . . . in the parliament, the Tories are resolved to bid for the King'.[6]

Undoubtedly, some Tories were hopeful that the coming of peace might free William from his dependence upon the Whigs. As Sir Robert Southwell observed to Robert Harley in late September 1697: 'Perhaps the government will take strength by using the abilities of some, who only for the notion or suspicion of being Tories were clamoured at.'[7] But Southwell was not really a party man, and other Tories seem to have been more intent upon attacking their rivals than in ingratiating themselves with the King. While Henry Guy, invoking Harley's help, sought to reforge old links with Churchmen such as Musgrave, and Viscount Weymouth was offering to assist in reconciling 'the two great northern men', Musgrave and Lonsdale, Sir Christopher's response to Guy's approaches was 'a very dry one'.[8] Moreover, in mid-November 1697, the staunch Whig Sir Francis Drake reported from the West Country that 'our high blades of the clergy are very wroth and uneasy, and will be sure to do all the mischief they can'.[9] Their cry, Drake reported, was 'the Church is in utmost danger', and this old refrain may well have been revived in reaction to the provocative and widely-publicised conduct of Sir Humphrey Edwin (Lord Mayor of London) in attending a Nonconformist assembly of worship in his official regalia earlier that month. Certainly, Edwin's indiscretion (though not without precedent) was used to focus public attention on occasional conformity—a practice indulged in by Dissenters in order to qualify for municipal posts not only in London and the larger provincial towns but also in certain smaller parliamentary boroughs in which the votes of a few members of the corporation might determine the choice of M.P.s.[10]

Clerical ire may also have been aroused by the reports circulating in the late summer and early autumn of 1697 that Archbishop Thomas Tenison and some of his episcopal brethren were reviving old projects of ecclesiastical accommodation at home to add further glory to the peace abroad. Comprehension, indeed, was as touchy a subject among many Anglican clergy as was occasional conformity among their lay sympathisers. As Burnet commented, there were 'two different parties among the clergy; one was firm and faithful to the present government' and 'wished for a favourable opportunity of making such alterations, in some few rites and ceremonies, as might bring into the Church those, who were not at too great a distance from it'. But 'this moderate party', though it included many of the bishops appointed by William and Mary (including Burnet himself), was a distinct minority within the establishment. Burnet believed that 'the bulk of the clergy', despite taking the oaths, were 'cold in serving' the government, 'were always blaming the administration', 'expressed a great esteem for Jacobites [i.e. the non-juring clerics], and in all elections, gave their votes to those who leaned that way', and 'showed great resentments against the Dissenters, and were enemies to the toleration, and seemed resolved never to consent to any alteration in their favour'.[11]

Comprehension had foundered in 1689 in convocation; since then, the King had not allowed that assembly to do business in spite of the many problems the clergy confronted in the wake of toleration. These problems, and particularly the dissemination of heterodox and anti-clerical writings after the lapse of the censorship, had been invoked by Francis Atterbury and his co-authors in A Letter to a Convocation Man which launched late in 1696 a campaign to secure an acting convocation.[12] Since 1695, writers such as Stephen Nye and John Toland (an Irish protégé of Lord Ashley) had been able to expound their views freely, and the bishops seemed unable to have their publications suppressed, thanks to the Whigs' distaste for bills to regulate printing and publication. So to the old 'enemy', the Dissenters, there had been added a new foe in the persons of the propagators of anti-Trinitarianism and anti-clericalism. Seemingly, Dissenters and the heterodox had little in common with one another; still, both benefited from the patronage of individual Whigs.[13] And though attempts in the mid-1690s to weaken the Whigs by reviving the cry of 'the Church in danger' had had little success, it was possible that now the war was finally ended the airing of these vexed questions in church–state relations would redound to the Tories' political advantage.

Despite the clamour over occasional conformity, comprehension, and the spread of heterodoxy, the principal public controversy in late 1697 was not the state of the Church but the question of a 'standing army'. Furthermore, this was an issue, by contrast to the ecclesiastical one, on which it was easy for Whig country gentlemen to join hands with the Tories in the Commons. Speculation about William's plans for the army had begun as soon as the peace was announced, and in early October Foley informed Harley that 'the scheme met with is £2,000,000 per annum to be settled, of which £800,000 for army, £600,000 for navy, and £600,000 for civil list'.[14] £800,000 would have sufficed for roughly 25,000 men. But even that number was far too many for the 'old Whig' co-authors (John Trenchard and Walter Moyle) of An Argument, Showing a Standing Army is Inconsistent with a Free Government—the single most damaging cannonade in the pamphlet bombardment on this subject that began in the weeks before parliament reassembled. Trenchard, a distant relative of the late Secretary of State and a man of considerable wealth, had been a firm supporter of the Revolution; both he and his young friend Moyle (M.P. for Saltash, and at one time on good terms with Charles Montagu) were fond admirers of republican Rome and members of a wider circle which embraced Robert Molesworth, John Toland, and Lord Ashley.[15]

Actually, as Harley discovered when he came up to town in late November, a 'scheme' for the 1697–98 session had yet to be agreed upon by the ministry.[16] William had been hoping to prevail for the maintenance of at least 30,000 men. But once he returned to England, he realised that the task of persuasion would be much more difficult than it had appeared from the other side of the Channel. As he gloomily informed Heinsius on 26 November: 'The members who have come from the provinces seem to be strongly prejudiced against this measure and infinite pains are taken to discredit it in the eyes of the public by speeches and by pamphlets.'[17]

While William still had to settle with his ministers just how many troops to request, he was intent on seeing that 'nothing is neglected to oppose' the clamour against a standing army.[18] Somers, for one, was busy preparing a reply to Trenchard and Moyle, and the Lord Chancellor was able to make a strong case that the danger to the peace of Europe more than balanced the risk to domestic liberty that might be posed by a body of troops maintained with *parliamentary* authorisation.[19] The King also sought to allay the agitation by intimating in late November that the Huguenot regiments he originally had planned to retain would be disbanded. At the same time, William and Sunderland also sought to ease Junto fears that a general 'change of hands' was in the offing. Montagu, as first Lord of the Treasury, was sworn a cabinet councillor, and preparations for the coming session were discussed among the King, the principal ministers, and the chief Whig managers in the Commons.[20]

Yet in spite of William's desire to retain the Junto's services, he was not prepared to make Wharton Secretary. And since Wharton himself was unwilling to solicit openly for the post, it was possible for his friends to join the King in pressing Shrewsbury to retain the seals some time longer. Hence, when the Duke left London for Gloucestershire the morning of 1 December, he carried the seals back with him upon the assurance that there was no expectation that he should actually attend the business of his post.[21] But in the meantime, Trumbull had renewed his importunities to be relieved of his position. Sunderland flatly refused to assist Sir William in securing the King's leave for him to retire; even so, Trumbull could not be dissuaded for he had found that the Earl's acceptance of the Lord Chamberlain's staff in April 1697 had not really eased his own isolation within the administration. Then, too, it must have been painful for Sir William to be reminded by the importunate John Dutton Colt (still soliciting for a place) that 'Lord Sunderland has never yet failed his promise, nor those who depended of him'.[22] The final straw was Trumbull's discovery on 30 November that the Windsor prebend he had been promised for his own brother Ralph was to go to one of Princess Anne's nominees instead. With Albemarle as his intermediary, he finally gained an interview with the King and delivered up his seals to him at Kensington early the following evening, 1 December.[23]

Thus, William was again confronted, only hours after Shrewsbury's departure, with the troublesome decision of choosing a new Secretary of State. However, the search for a successor was not a protracted one. Early on 2 December, the Lord Chamberlain informed Vernon that William would announce his appointment at that afternoon's meeting of the cabinet council, and all the under-secretary's protestations were brushed aside. Sunderland's apparent failure to consult the Junto before proceeding with Vernon's elevation at first provoked little direct response from them. Somers had been forewarned by Shrewsbury earlier in the autumn that Sunderland had Vernon in mind in the event of a vacancy, and in any case the under-secretary was likely to make a more amiable and reliable colleague than Trumbull. Somers's principal concern, then, was to reassure Wharton that neither he nor any of the other friends of the Comptroller had been party to this *fait accompli*.[24] Whether this would suffice to appease Wharton (already resentful of the frustration of his Irish pretensions) remained to be seen, but Somers was hopeful. No doubt the Lord Chancellor would have been rather more perturbed had he suspected William and Sunderland of offering the seals to Harley before entrusting them to Vernon.

Whether or not this was one of the two occasions during William's reign when Harley, according to his own and to his brother's memoirs, was offered the Secretaryship, we know he did have an interview at Kensington with the King the evening of 1 December. Harley, however, was unwilling to trust more to the post than to tell his father he had been with William and had responded to him 'what became an honest man with all decency'.[25] His reticence makes it impossible to be certain what subjects were discussed, but it is apparent that even had Harley been eager to do so he could not now offer William any great hope of securing parliamentary approval for a large peacetime force for he was well aware that 'the heat against an army rather increases than otherwise'.[26]

Once the session opened on 3 December 1697, the King's servants quickly discovered how difficult their lot would be. To be sure, William's speech—in which he reminded members of the large debts outstanding, urged the necessity for a 'land force' as well as a strong fleet, and expressed the hope that peace would give him the 'leisure' to reform any abuses in royal administration, to promote trade, and to discourage 'profaneness and immorality'—was promptly answered by a Commons' address promising their assistance and support.[27] But when the question was put on the second day of business, 7 December, whether to proceed first on the speech in general or on supply in particular, a sharp dispute flared up. Harley, seconded by Granville, Boyle, and Seymour, spoke for the former method; Coningsby, backed by Pelham, moved the latter, and his motion barely carried on a previous question by 156 to 153.[28] Then on the 8th, the Commons did approve a resolution of credit for £600,000, but a division over whether any of this loan could be used to pay the troops was averted only after Montagu suggested that the House vote that the money should be 'for the use of the fleet, and other exigencies, and necessary services'.[29]

Yet these were only preliminary skirmishes, and the ministerialists were girding their loins for the expected clash on the main issue on 10 December. Normally the Privy Council sat on Thursday evenings, but on the 9th the usual meeting was called off so that the managers could attend an assembly at the Rose; there it was 'resolved to bring it to this question: whether a land force be necessary to be kept up for the year '98'. This, so Vernon reported to Shrewsbury, 'they think can't be well withstood'. But Harley and his friends also arrived at St Stephen's Chapel on the 10th with 'a question ready prepared', and they succeeded in getting one of their number, John Conyers, into the chair of the committee of the whole. Harley was, then, the first to be recognised when the debate began, and he took the opportunity to move that all troops raised since 1680 should be disbanded.[30] This, in effect, would have allowed William to keep no more than 8,000 men in England, and then only by 'connivance' of parliament, but so general was the support for Harley's proposal that the ministerialists did not venture to divide the committee that day.[31] Instead, on the 11th—after various figures ranging from 10,000 to 16,000 were broached as substitutes for the somewhat uncertain 1680 total referred to in Harley's resolution (did that, for instance, include the troops then stationed at Tangier?)—a motion to recommit the whole resolution was put to a vote in the full House, only to be rejected 185 to 148.

Just what the division of 11 December signified was itself a subject of conflict-ing interpretation. Harley's friend and fellow countryman Robert Price claimed that had the question been put that day, as at one time seemed likely, for a specific figure of 12,000 men, the minority 'would not have had 100'. But Vernon believed that had William been willing to authorise his spokesmen to propose the total of 15,000 that the King had told some he would be content with, that number would have been carried on the 11th.[32] Probably Vernon was unduly optimistic, though there can be no doubt that the ministerialists' lack of instructions did not help. But amidst these differing assessments, what is un-mistakable is the Whig split over the army question. Among those who spoke in favour of Harley's motion on the 10th were such normally staunch ministerial supporters as William Norris, Sir William Strickland, Sir Herbert Croft, and Sir William St Quintin, and they were joined in the division on the 11th by the Duke of Devonshire's two sons, Sir Richard Onslow, and even Treasury Commis-sioner Pelham.[33]

After their triumph over the army, Harley and the Whig defectors did not seek to obstruct a generous settlement of the civil list for the King's life. At a Rose Club meeting on 18 December, the ministerialists and their backbench friends agreed to press for £600,000 to £700,000 yearly. And on the 20th, the higher figure was approved without a division after Montagu reminded members that in addition to the £600,000 resolved upon for the civil expenses of the crown by the Convention parliament, £50,000 was needed now for James II's queen (as part of the understanding reached between Portland and Boufflers for James's removal from St Germain) and at least £25,000 more was desired in order to set up a separate establishment for Anne's eight-year-old son William, the young Duke of Gloucester, who was second in the line of succession only to his mother.[34] Musgrave and Seymour did attempt to have this resolution recom-mitted on the 21st, as they warned of the danger of trusting any monarch with so much for life and suggested the difficulties in the way of finding that amount. But when the Commons divided, the Churchmen were isolated in opposition and overwhelmed 225 to 86.[35]

During the debates on the civil list of 20–21 December, the King's character and achievements inspired encomia and prompted the Commons to 'leap over' their usual procedure of careful scrutiny of the particulars before voting supply. Yet the occasion was also taken by several of the minority on the 21st—particu-larly John Granville and Sir Thomas Dyke—to declaim on the dangers of Wil-liam's seeming confidence in the infamous Sunderland.[36] Nor were these the first shafts launched in the Lord Chamberlain's direction after he had ventured out from 'behind the curtain'. Before the session, there had been talk of moving an impeachment against him; during the army debates, his service under another monarch who kept up a large standing force had been recalled by several M.P.s; and on 18 December, the bumptious lawyer James Sloane (Wharton's secretary as Chief Justice in Eyre) joined the chorus against Sunderland, provoking fellow members to 'ask one another whether my Lord Chamberlain and Lord Wharton were upon ill terms'.[37] And in the wake of the aspersions cast against Sunderland in the debate of the 21st, it was noised about that the Earl of Abingdon's heir, Lord Norris, would lead off a frontal assault upon the Lord Chamberlain on the 23rd, and that Norris was counting upon Whig as well as Tory support in the attempt.[38]

Although Sunderland found himself in late December threatened 'by some of both sides', his rapidly mounting anxiety can be traced at least as far back as the pre-sessional manoeuvres over the disposal of the seals. As early as 3 December, the Lord Chamberlain spoke to Harley of resigning, complaining that 'I have been used too much to courts, but I know not how to live in this'.[39] Nor were his laments simply formulae to secure Harley's assistance either in the ministry or in parliament. On the 5th, Sunderland tendered his white staff to the King, but William refused to accept it. The developments of the succeeding weeks only heightened the Lord Chamberlain's malaise. He did try to pacify Wharton by promising, when he met with the Junto on the 7th, that he would support the Comptroller's candidacy, should Shrewsbury take the occasion of his under-secretary's promotion to give up his Secretaryship. However, he was not put to the test on this occasion, since the Duke—when informed of Vernon's eleva-tion—agreed to retain the seals. Yet not even the King's offer to Shrewsbury of the new post of Governor to the Duke of Gloucester could tempt Shrewsbury back to town. So Sunderland was left without Shrewsbury's assistance at this critical juncture, and Wharton remained unappeased.[40]

In turn, Sunderland's efforts and those of his friends to protect him against the parliamentary assault they anticipated were of little avail. Certainly, Mon-mouth's readiness to stand forth as 'a champion' of the Lord Chamberlain was no help, while Sunderland's approaches to the Tories only added to the existing 'jealousies' among the Whig ministerialists by giving the appearance that he was attempting to negotiate a 'change of hands'. The result was that when the King himself spoke to the Comptroller, on the eve of the projected attack of the 23rd, to ask him 'to engage his friends to stand by' the Lord Chamberlain, Wharton's reply showed so 'great coldness' that William thought it best not to tell Sunder-land.[41]

For all the rumours, the Commons' sitting on 23 December turned out to be an anticlimax as members droned through a lengthy debate on the disposition of the hammered coin still in circulation without any sign of Lord Norris and his band. Even so, Sunderland did not breathe any easier as members dispersed for the Christmas recess. Instead, on the 26th, as three weeks before, he pressed William to release him from his post, and this time he was not prepared to accept a refusal. When Sunderland came out of the King's closet that day, he gave up his key of office to Vernon, and the new Secretary took it in the mistaken belief that William had yielded. The King was aghast upon learning of this subterfuge, and he dispatched Vernon with the key to Guy's house at Earl's Court where Sunderland had taken refuge. None the less, the Secretary could not induce Sunderland to take it back. As the Earl explained himself to Vernon: 'It was not on account of the parliament only that he came to this resolution, for he had otherwise led the life of a dog, having done all that was in his power for the service of a party whom he could never oblige to live easily with him or to treat him with common civility.'[42] In addition, Sunderland exclaimed to Vernon that 'there was no rock like to what he suffered', in this as in previous years, 'by being ground as he had between Lord Monmouth and Lord Wharton', while Somers was informed that the Earl laid 'the greatest measure of guilt' at 'Whar-ton's door'.[43]

The Lord Chancellor, in writing of Sunderland's resignation to Shrewsbury, was too discreet to provide his own version of events. All he would say was that 'several things concurred' in the Earl's departure, 'most of them unnecessarily brought about, by [Sunderland's] endeavouring to be oversure in being supported, in case any attempt should be against him'. Others, like Methuen, agreed that 'the heads' of the Tories had not been engaged in 'a formed design' against the Lord Chamberlain, while also citing the 'great distrust' the Junto had conceived of Sunderland 'upon his advances made to Lord Rochester and others'.[44]

But what chiefly disturbed Somers about the Lord Chamberlain's resignation was that, with both Shrewsbury and Sunderland out of business, William would be 'left extremely destitute' of ministers—that is, in Vernon's words, of those 'he may be free with'. Of the King's three confidential English advisers since 1694, the Lord Chancellor now remained as the King's 'only minister' and his burdensome duties in Chancery during the law terms prevented him 'attending as often as it would be necessary' to take on a greater share in the guidance of the administration.[45] The 'naked' state of the Junto was, indeed, all too visible to friends and foes alike.[46] Thus, as the old year drew to a close the Whig leaders fervently joined with William in pressing the Chamberlain's staff upon Shrewsbury. Moreover, Somers and Orford, along with some of their close friends in the Commons (particularly Edward Clarke and Sir Henry Hobart), even expressed their regret to Sunderland at his resignation and assured him 'they should not have been backward in their respects to him when it came to the trial'.[47] However, Shrewsbury was no more eager to contemplate a regular attendance at Kensington as Lord Chamberlain than he was to resume active service at Whitehall as Secretary, while any serious consideration of an accommodation with Sunderland was delayed by the course of the Commons' proceedings in early 1698.

The new year opened with the Junto's foes, emboldened by the Whigs' disarray over the army and by the recent events at Court, preparing to launch a series of attacks upon Montagu. On 4 January, an inquiry into fraudulent endorsements of Exchequer bills was initiated amid rumours that some Treasury lords were involved, and a week later the Chancellor of the Exchequer again figured as the chief target of an order that Lowndes should lay before the Commons a list of all royal grants passed in 1697.[48] But Montagu's enemies soon discovered they had chosen to fight on swampy terrain. Admittedly, the Whigs remained divided over the question of the army. And when the ministerialists at William's insistence made an attempt on 8 January to secure £500,000 for guards and garrisons (a sum sufficient for nearly 15,000 men), they were outvoted 188 to 164. There were a few converts, notably Henry Boyle, but Onslow and Pelham again spoke and voted with the majority along with Irish Lord Chancellor Methuen (who had warned William beforehand against the manoeuvre) and Molesworth (who explained that his mind was altered in the course of the eight hours of debate).[49] The King, in the end, had to settle for £350,000 for the army, which was reckoned to be enough to support 5,000 foot and 5,000 horse. The only consoling note was the Commons' decision to award half pay to the disbanded English officers; this, so the new Earl of Jersey (the former Lord Villiers) observed, was 'the best thing, or the only good one, since the voting of the revenue for life'.[50]

Montagu, however, fared better, as the Whigs began to feel themselves 'stronger and more united', both by Sunderland's departure and by the apparent resolution of the army issue.[51] The Chancellor of the Exchequer was able to demonstrate in convincing fashion that he had no part in the fraudulent endorsements of Exchequer bills perpetrated by John Knight and Bartholomew Burton; rather, he had taken the lead in tracking down the culprits as soon as evidence of the conspiracy had come to light in the autumn of 1697. By 18 January, then, those who had started the inquiry were reported to be now 'willing to let it fall'.[52] Two days later, the question of recent royal grants also seemed about to be put to sleep as the Whigs carried a vote 162 to 119 in favour of taking into consideration all grants passed since 1660. Seymour and Granville were only the most prominent members of the opposition whose families had benefited by large gifts from Charles II, and Methuen (who voted with the majority on this occasion) thought that this resolution 'will in probability put an end to the matter'.[53]

Yet Montagu was not content to stand on the defensive. On 18 January, he wrote to Shrewsbury of 'carrying the war into the enemy's country', and in succeeding days it became clear that he aimed principally at Charles Duncombe, Burton's predecessor as Cashier of the Excise and an old acquaintance of both Monmouth and Sunderland. Duncombe had long been a thorn in Montagu's side in the Exchequer and in the City; he was also, in Montagu's view, 'the Iago of the whole villainy' directed against him. Sunderland, too, was suspected of a hand in the attacks against the Chancellor of the Exchequer, though in mid-January the Earl made his first specific overtures to the Junto for a reconciliation.[54] But neither Shrewsbury's warning to Montagu not 'to alienate the King's mind' by 'doing anything to confirm the opinion some have laboured to give him that the Whigs have a natural sourness that makes them not to be lived with' nor Sunderland's offers of friendship could sway Montagu in his determination to deal with Duncombe. Although Sunderland promised in writing to 'labour like a horse' for the Whigs' nominee for Shrewsbury's Secretaryship, to abandon Duncombe (though he hoped Guy and Montagu could still come to terms), and 'never [to] look towards business but upon the invitation' of Shrewsbury and the Junto, Montagu proceeded with his counter-attack.[55] And thanks to Duncombe's 'own lavishness of tongue' when he was examined in the Commons on 25 January upon Montagu's charges that he had been party to the fraudulent endorsements, a motion to commit him to the Tower passed without a division, as his friends apparently felt that this course (as in Guy's case in 1695) was the lesser evil.[56] But even this did not satisfy the Chancellor of the Exchequer, and on 1 February the Commons voted without dividing to expel Duncombe from the House and to bring in a bill of pains and penalties against him.

Now that Duncombe seemed to be down, Montagu expressed himself ready for an arrangement with Sunderland. In his view, and in Orford's, any accommodation would have to include Shrewsbury's acceptance of the Chamberlainship and the bestowal of the seals on Wharton and the Lord Presidency on Tankerville. Vernon's first reaction on 5 February was that those conditions seemed 'reasonable', but not all were enamoured of them. Wharton, for one, did not want to hear of Sunderland's return on any terms; the Comptroller, with the assistance of a 'fair lady' (presumably Lady Orkney), was instead dabbling with a project to make Albemarle 'the minister'. Then, too, some of the Junto's associates were at best lukewarm, and Treasury Commissioner Smith declared that if Sunderland were allowed back he would himself 'have nothing to do with public business'.[57]

It is true that Somers, who favoured a *rapprochement* with Sunderland, believed Smith's mind might be altered. But soon Vernon began to express second thoughts about the King's likely reaction to Orford's and Montagu's terms; much as William wanted Sunderland back, Vernon suspected the King would dislike the projected arrangements 'as too like a design to engross him, which he will hardly give way to'. Above all, there remained the question of whether Shrewsbury, 'the corner stone' now as before, could be induced to discard his yearning 'to be once again my own master'.[58] Hence, when the Duke let it be known in mid-February 1698 that he intended to come up to town in early March, further negotiations were suspended until his arrival.

Meanwhile, the Commons' proceedings were distinguished chiefly by new partisan clashes and by disappointments and delays in the King's business. At the beginning of March, the Commons had still to complete their review of the estimates for 1698 and the debts outstanding from years past. Furthermore, only one major levy had been tentatively approved; this was a three-shilling tax on land that was proposed by Harley, Musgrave, 'and that party'. The same members were also behind the order of 7 February for the preparation of five separate bills for resuming all royal grants since 1660. With 'the current run[ning] so strong' against the grantees, especially William's Dutch servants, the ministerialists did not attempt to oppose resumption, at least at this stage.[59]

The King's 'chagrin' at the challenge to his grants could only have been reinforced by the Whigs' successes in the continuing confrontations between Montagu and his enemies. On 14 February, the bill against Duncombe was committed, after an attempt to adjourn lost 161 to 107; on the 16th, an unexpected revival of the attack upon Montagu for his recent grant was decisively defeated 209 to 97, even though more than twenty M.P.s took the floor to speak on the minority side; and on the 22nd, a move to condemn the Treasury Commission for its handling of Exchequer bill payments was rejected 170 to 88.[60] These votes, combined with the delays on supply, left William, as Shrewsbury had warned Montagu, 'weary and peevish', and by late February the King was complaining to Heinsius about 'private animosities and party quarrels'.[61] Then, too, the ministerialists' failure in late February and early March even to attempt to get an increase in the number of marines in the Navy, coupled with the loss of their move to procure the payment of a token portion of the arrears due former allies, did nothing to improve William's disposition.[62]

Even more disappointing was the outcome of the King's meeting with Shrewsbury at Windsor during the second week of March. At the outset, the Duke felt well enough to accompany William foxhunting, and he appeared 'resolved to return to business'. But a fit of spitting blood on the evening of the 11th incapacitated the Duke, and it made William and others who saw him in that condition for the first time conclude that 'his health will never permit him to follow the King'.[63] Even so, nothing was settled for another month, and while the Duke convalesced at one of Wharton's houses outside London, the Whigs at Westminster did little to untangle the log-jam on ways and means. Thus, when the King came to the Lords on 2 April, before setting out for Newmarket for the races and to see Shrewsbury, there was only one supply bill ready for his approval —the land tax. So there still remained over £4,600,000 to be found to pay the estimates for 1698 and to satisfy those debts and deficiencies which the Commons had resolved to make good in 1698.[64]

In the light of Shrewsbury's collapse at Windsor, William was not surprised when he met the Duke at Newmarket to find him bent upon retirement. Shrewsbury resolutely refused the Chamberlainship, despite assurances from the King and the Junto that a regular attendance at Court was not expected. All the Duke would consent to was to keep the seals until the end of the 1697–98 session. After months of delays, then, William was left without either Shrewsbury or Sunderland. Under these circumstances, he could hardly be persuaded to reconsider his veto of Wharton, though pressure upon him to 'gratify' the Comptroller somehow—if not with the seals, then with the Chamberlain's staff—mounted. Indeed, it was now intimated that 'my affairs will not be concluded to my satisfaction in parliament' unless something was done for Wharton.[65]

Certainly, things could not go on as they were. Methuen observed to Lord Galway on 19 April that 'the present managers' have 'a great distrust of the King and proceed in his business accordingly', while Somers subsequently recalled that William 'declined speaking of his business to any in his service all the winter, and that in such a manner as if he was not unwilling it should be known'.[66] However, upon his return from Newmarket, the King did what he could with the Junto to remove 'any suspicions as if he were altered towards them and for putting the public business into a quicker motion'. In separate talks with Somers on 24 April, Orford on the 26th, and Montagu on the 28th, William stated that his objections to Wharton were 'particular and personal', that 'he neither could or would' consider 'changing of hands', and that all he desired was 'some latitude for his choice' of a new Secretary, 'provided it was still among the party'.[67] Naturally, this could not altogether satisfy the three, since by now they were too far committed on Wharton's behalf to propose any alternative to him, but at least these conversations presaged some progress on ways and means in the Commons.

During April, a variety of projects had been mooted in the lower House, and by the end of the month two were well advanced: an additional duty on coal and a new quarterly poll. Together, it was estimated that they would bring in about £1,000,000. There was also the possibility of raising another £600,000 or so by a 25 per cent capital assessment on the value of all royal grants made since 1660. This levy had been proposed by the Speaker's son Thomas on 8 April as a substitute for the five resumption bills, and his suggestion was unanimously approved after Montagu spoke in its favour. Even so, the bill to implement this resolution was delayed by complications in drafting, and it had yet to be considered as May began. And by then, the Commons were on the verge of again taking up a more familiar scheme of raising a loan from the traders to the East Indies.[68]

In early March 1698, a proposal had been 'handed about' St Stephen's Chapel which indicated that the East India Company might advance £600,000 to the government in return for a parliamentary charter. At that time, Vernon expected this project to be promoted by 'the Speaker and his friends' as a means of providing the money for the civil list and so making their court at Kensington.[69] But Foley and Harley did not embrace the plan even when it was specifically proposed by a backbencher in committee of the whole on 12 April. For the moment, the project was left in abeyance, amid reports that members of the Company had not yet agreed among themselves on the terms they were prepared to offer. Subsequently, a general meeting of the Company did approve a specific proposal, and by late April Vernon noted that William was anxious to have 'a trial' of that offer in parliament.[70]

In the meantime, the interloping traders had agreed among themselves on a counter-offer, and this year they were able to secure the backing of Montagu and the other Whig Treasury lords. Hence, when Sir John Fleet, speaking for the Company, informed the Commons on 4 May that his associates were willing to lend £700,000 to the government in return for a thirty-one-year monopoly of the trade, Montagu responded that he had good reason to believe that were the interlopers allowed to engage freely in the trade £2,000,00 at 8 per cent could be raised. On the 5th, the Commons appointed a committee to receive both proposals, and Montagu went off with Smith to Kensington to explain the interlopers' scheme to William. The King was at first sceptical that so large a sum could be secured, but he and other doubters were considerably impressed by the rapid progress of a preliminary subscription organised by the new interloping leaders, Samuel Shepherd and Sir Henry Furness. Within a fortnight over £1, 200,000 had been pledged, and on 24–25 May resolutions to implement the scheme were approved in committee of the whole. When these resolutions were reported on the 26th, the Company 'mustered up all their force' in a thin House; but after an attempt to amend the first was lost 126 to 99, the rest passed unopposed.[71]

The success of the interlopers' proposals enabled Montagu to devise a 'handsome provision' for the civil list on 27 May. The present debt of nearly £600,000 on the excise segment of the ordinary revenue was to be cleared off, the doubled duties of tunnage and poundage would be paid to the King for life after the present grant expired at the end of 1699, and in the meantime William would be appropriated £400,000 from the projected East India loan. These proposals were unanimously approved, with the proviso that any surplus above £700,000 that the civil list revenues might yield in years to come would be subject to parliament's disposal. £700,000 was, to be sure, less than the £1,200,000 the Convention parliament had decided that the King needed for the government's ordinary expenditures. But under the new arrangements, the King would not be expected to maintain guards and garrisons or to pay for the 'ordinary' of the fleet; these parliament would provide for separately. Moreover, the £700,000 was to be given for life. William, so Vernon informed Shrewsbury, 'never appeared in better humour' than upon hearing of the terms Montagu had secured, and it was observed that the grant had been made 'in so particular and extraordinary manner that it may be said his Majesty has his revenue settled in the manner of a rent charge'.[72]

Nevertheless, not until 5 July was William able to put an end to the 1697–98 session, for the East India Company fought a furious last-ditch stand against the supersession of the charter of 1693. Even after the East India bill was at last engrossed by the Commons on 23 June by a vote of 120 to 80, Somers did not think it could 'be depended upon that it will pass' in the Lords.[73] Both 'art and power' had to be invoked to get it through the upper House. Price reported on 2 July that Lord President Leeds, 'who was against the bill and had four proxies', was 'sent for out of the House and so was the Earl of Burlington, who had three others', before the bill was finally committed 65 to 48 late that day.[74] As Montagu recounted the affair to Shrewsbury on 16 July, he acknowledged:[75]

I have been in such a storm of business as never blew out of any quarter before. I was not ignorant of what I undertook, nor insensible of the opposition I should meet with from such a set of men as the East India Company, but really the dispute was more obstinate than I did expect. I saw no other way but something of that kind to make any tolerable end of the session and fix the civil list, and therefore I thought it ought to be risked. But in the progress, the contest ran so high I repented heartily it was ever attempted. But notwithstanding all the opposition that the wit or malice of the party could give in the House, we kept our scheme entire. And though, since the act passed, there has been more industry used to run it down as a chimera and an idle notion, the subscriptions began on Thursday at one [the 14th] and were completed tonight at seven.

The subscription of the entire £2,000,000 in only three days was an impressive testimony to the City's restored financial confidence, and it came little more than two years after the failure of the land bank project. Yet it should not be overlooked that though the Commons settled the civil list, provided for the estimates for 1698, and paid off £1,600,000 in navy and army arrears, they did not make good their resolutions of 28 January 1698 to satisfy over £1,500,000 in deficiencies on the supply for 1697.[76] Overall, the lengthy session gave time to complete no fewer than 107 statutes, and in addition to settling the East India trade parliament also legislated for the African trade. This year, the Royal African Company secured the statutory charter it had sought on several earlier occasions during the 1690s on condition that it open up the slave trade to all comers.[77]

Apart from the financial and commercial measures of the 1697–98 session, perhaps the most interest was generated by acts against James II's adherents and against blasphemy and profaneness. The first reached the statute book early in 1698 without much difficulty; in turn, its requirement that all who had been in France during the war must obtain a royal licence if they wished to remain in or to enter England caused a noticeable Jacobite exodus from the realm. Among those forced into exile was the Earl of Ailesbury, despite his efforts at the war's end to make his peace at Court by asking to be permitted to kiss the King's hand.[78]

The effectiveness of the act against blasphemy and profaneness, which was chiefly aimed against those who questioned orthodox Trinitarian doctrine (and so was known as the 'anti-Socinian' bill), remained to be tested after it finally received the King's approval at the end of the session. The bill was a sequel to the Commons' address of 15 February 1698, which had been moved by Sir John Phillips at the urging of Edward Harley, Robert's younger brother. The lower House's debate on Phillips's motion to request William to put into execution existing laws against 'profaneness and immorality' and to give orders 'for the suppressing' of heterodox books, had been marked by criticism of the episcopate's 'remissness for suffering such blasphemers to go unpunished'.[79] In response, Archbishop Tenison introduced in the Lords a bill to impose curbs on the kind of heterodox works cited in the Commons' debate and also in A Letter to a Convocation Man. His bill against atheism and blasphemy was sent down to the Commons in early March, only to be laid aside for one of their own brought in by Phillips. Yet there were also many M.P.s, among them Treasury Commissioners Montagu and Smith, who were opposed to both Tenison's and Phillips's proposals 'as setting up inquisitions'. Even so, their delaying tactics in the lower House did not pose as serious a threat to Phillips's bill as did the Lords' attempt to amend it so as to bring Jews within its scope, but in the end the peers gave way.[80]

Meanwhile, other controversial bills had been derailed or sidetracked. The most prominent of these was the bill of pains and penalties against Duncombe, which the Commons had sent up to the Lords on 26 February by a vote of 138 to 103, despite the defections of Attorney-General Trevor and Treasury Commissioners Fox and Pelham.[81] There it ran into fierce opposition from a combination of Tories, headed by Leeds, Rochester, and Nottingham, and of disaffected Whigs, such as Bolton and Peterborough (the former Earl of Monmouth who had taken his new title on the death of his Catholic kinsman in the summer of 1697). Although the bill was backed by Normanby, Godolphin, and Marlborough, it was rejected 48 to 47 on 15 March when some courtiers, including Romney and Albemarle, left before the division, 'not thinking there was any danger of losing it', and others including Burlington and Dorset voted against it.[82]

While Duncombe survived singed but whole from Montagu's fire, a number of 'country' projects also went awry. One was Sir Edward Seymour's bill, first offered in 1696–97, to check the expanding Irish woollen textile industry, which was now perceived as a serious competitor by the West Country and other home producers. This year, Seymour's measure was passed by the Commons. But then Methuen, acting for the Irish administration, secured the assistance of Godolphin, Marlborough, and Rochester. With their help, he staved off passage in the Lords by engaging on his own and his Dublin colleagues' behalf to 'settle' the matter in Ireland, so as to avoid provoking a new dispute there over the rights of the Irish parliament vis-à-vis both the English parliament and the crown.[83]

Other much-vaunted opposition projects did not even get through the Commons. Difficulties in assessing the projected levy on all beneficial royal grants made since 1660, coupled with the success of Montagu's East India proposals, led to the demise of that measure.[84] A similar fate befell Sir Richard Onslow's bill for reforming the militia. Opponents of a standing army had stressed the desirability of relying instead upon an improved militia, but when it came to adopting Onslow's reform bill there was little enthusiasm. The measure was committed on 7 March, but Sir William Williams's objection that to create a permanent, trained reserve among the militia would in effect be to establish a standing local tax and a standing army seems to have reflected others' opinions as well. So, after several poorly-attended sittings on the bill in committee of the whole, it was dropped in late April, ostensibly because of 'difficulties' in 'framing' the proposed reforms.[85]

The demise of the militia bill was accompanied by a discernible alteration in the Commons' temper on the question of the size of the army. As reports, first heard in February 1698, of the declining health of Carlos II of Spain continued to come in, M.P.s' zeal for disbanding diminished. Although he knew that substantially more than 10,000 troops were still on foot in England, Harley told Montagu early in June 1698 that he would not offer any appropriation clause to the East India bill to go along with similar clauses he had inserted in the poll and coal measures. Instead, a clause drafted by Lowndes, which made no mention of further sums for disbanding, was adopted.[86] So William resolved to keep up 16,000 men in England and ordered the Treasury to provide £650,000 for the service of the army, and he also decided to send over to Ireland the five Huguenot regiments in English pay which had been left behind in the Low Countries the previous autumn.[87]

The King's concern was to maintain a credible bargaining position in his

on-going negotiations with Louis for the partition of the Spanish monarchy upon
Carlos II's death. Conversations on this subject had been initiated by the French
a few weeks after the Earl of Portland arrived in Paris late in January 1698 on a
special embassy to Louis XIV. These preliminary talks had been carried further
by Count Tallard after he came to London on a return embassy in March, and
in an audience with the King on 1 April Tallard spelled out the French proposals.
By this time, William had had a chance to sound out sentiment in England as to
what might be expected from parliament upon the death of the last Spanish
Habsburg king. The verdict had not been encouraging. Neither Shrewsbury nor
the others whom the King consulted thought that a land army comparable in
size to that of the last war would be supported.[88] William decided, then, it would
be prudent for him to try to avert a new conflict by concluding an agreement
with France, in conjunction with the Dutch Republic. Yet, he was fearful that
it would be very difficult to contrive a security to bind the French to whatever
terms were arranged—a point driven home by Louis's unwillingness to remove
James II from St Germain, much less from France, even though Portland thought
he had reached an understanding with Boufflers on this point during their talks
in the summer of 1697. Even so, the King proceeded with the negotiations, and
he did so without consulting either the Imperialists or any of his English
servants.[89]

Whether William would have been quite so secretive had Shrewsbury and
Sunderland still been active in his service is not clear, but he does not seem to
have discussed the negotiations with Sunderland when the Earl arrived in town
at the end of the 1697–98 session. In any case, Sunderland's trip was a failure.
For all his conciliatory words to the Junto, they wanted no part of him. And
thanks especially to the success of the East India project, the King showed no
disposition to press them on this score after he was bluntly told 'his service
would suffer ... much in it'. So Sunderland had little choice but to declare
'a joy, greater than it was possible for him to express' that William had been
pleased 'to suffer him to retire to Althorp and never to think of business'.[90]
This was only to put a good face on the Junto's success which appeared to
vindicate Vernon's judgement of January 1698 that 'those who are strongest in
the House of Commons, and in possession of the management, methinks should
not be in danger of being discarded for the sake of any one man'. Thus, Montagu
jubilantly announced to Shrewsbury that 'I think we are got clear of that fireship
for ever. If he annoys us now, it must be [by] hoisting the enemy's colours;
and, under that declaration, I do not fear him.'[91]

There were, then, only two changes in the commission of Lords Justices named
for the summer of 1698 as William hastened in mid-July, in spite of the murmur-
ings of some of his subjects, to make ready to go to the Continent. To replace
Sunderland and Shrewsbury, Montagu and Marlborough were appointed on
16 July, along with seven hold-overs from the summer of 1697. Marlborough's
selection had been preceded in mid-June by the long-anticipated announcement
of his appointment as Governor to the Duke of Gloucester, along with that of
Bishop Burnet as Preceptor. Lady Marlborough continued high in the Princess's
favour, and her husband was certainly Anne's choice for the Governorship when
William solicited her nomination in late December 1697.[92] But Marlborough's
relations with the King had also shown a great improvement over the past year
or so. Vernon had noticed after Sunderland's resignation that Marlborough was

frequently with William, and when the Earl was named as Gloucester's Governor he was also admitted to the cabinet council.[93]

Marlborough's renewed prominence contrasted with Wharton's continuing failure to secure a ministerial post. Since Shrewsbury agreed in June to retain the seals until William came back from the Continent, it was possible once more to put off the question of his successor. The King did offer Wharton, after Shrewsbury declined it, an embassy to Madrid. But despite the importance of that task in the current diplomatic situation, the Comptroller does not seem to have been tempted. Hence, the only other appointments decided upon before the King's departure were in the Excise.[94]

William had resolved on the eve of the 1697–98 session upon a purge of the Excise Commission because of the declining yield of the excises and the quarrels among the incumbent commissioners. Subsequently, he had decided to hold his hand until the end of the session.[95] As rumour had it that all the present commissioners save Clarke were to be removed, the aspirants were many. Then, too, Montagu was not above encouraging M.P.s' expectations in order to forward the King's business in the Commons. Thus, the close of the session brought together 'a large band of solicitors, who look', Vernon observed, 'as if they depended on promises that had been made them, when the parliament was sitting'.[96] To avoid being tormented by the disappointed, William delayed filling in and signing the warrant for reconstituting the commission until the eve of his voyage, and the names of the five new commissioners, along with the four incumbents, were announced only after he had sailed. The new commissioners included four M.P.s, among them Montagu's younger brother Christopher, and brought the number of M.P.s on that board to six of nine.[97] Then, later in the summer, another M.P., Sir William St Quintin, was added to the Customs Board as a supernumerary commissioner, reportedly for moving the motion of thanks to Montagu on 16 February 1698, and his appointment temporarily brought the total of M.P.s on that commission to five of eight.[98]

In the meantime, the election campaign was in full swing. William had sometimes felt during the winter of 1697–98 that the principal concern of M.P.s was to court popular favour for the new triennial rite, and as early as January Locke reported from Essex that there 'had been great feasting lately' near by in preparation for the coming elections.[99] Even so, William's decision to call new elections immediately after the end of the 1697–98 session, instead of waiting until his return from the Continent, seemed 'a great surprise to some gentlemen. And the more they dislike it', Vernon remarked, 'the Whigs are the better satisfied in it.'[100]

However, the prompt dissolution was just about the only feature of the ensuing campaign that the Junto found pleasing, for it quickly became apparent there was abroad 'a strange spirit of distinguishing between the Court and Country party [which] visibly discovers itself in several elections'.[101] The main complaints, as Somers recalled after the elections, were against taxes and placemen. The latter were the targets of a number of election pamphlets, particularly John Toland's *The Danger of Mercenary Parliaments* and the anonymous *A Letter to a Country Gentleman Setting forth the Cause of the Decay and Ruin of Trade: To Which is Annexed A List of the Names of some Gentlemen, who were Members of the Last Parliament and now are (or lately were) in Public Employments.*[102] Nor were such grievances expressed only in print. Wharton's candidates at the Buckinghamshire election were confronted with placards reading 'No Courtier, No Pensioner, No Judas'; Macclesfield's nominee at Lancaster, Roger Kirkby (Governor of Chester Castle), was denounced in doggerel both as a refugee from the bailiffs and as one who had voted for 'Taxes on living, dead, glass, windows, malt / On leather, parchment, paper, money, salt'; and in Worcestershire, Thomas Foley senior came in a distant third in the poll, in part because of resentment 'that he had taken up a great deal of money at small interest and put it into the [Ex]chequer and banks at great interest, which made him depend upon the Court'. Then, too, an echo of the standing army controversy was heard in the Cornish borough of Liskeard where the incumbent, William Brydges, was condemned for his vote against disbanding.[103]

Although 'people are so galled with taxes that they kick and wince at every one', the ministerialists were not without their defenders in the press.[104] One pamphleteer, after reminding readers of the assassination conspiracy of 1696 and the presence of as many as a hundred non-associators in the last House of Commons, neatly turned Toland's 'neo-Harringtonian' analysis against him by arguing that on the occasion of the plot and also at other times ''twas as fortunate for England that numbers had places and preferments, depending upon the pleasure of the government, as it had been that the Church lands were, upon the dissolution of the religious houses, ... distributed amongst the nobility and gentry'.[105] Again, in a broadside hastily run out to distinguish between the 'Courtiers so-called' and 'the New Country party so-called', the latter were stigmatised as adherents of 'the late King James' working for his restoration 'under pretence of easing the people of taxes'.[106] Moreover, such arguments were also employed at the constituency level. At Abingdon, the non-associator Simon Harcourt was denounced as 'disaffected' by his opponent Hucks, who stood with Wharton's backing. Hucks also bid for support by promising to ease the borough of military quartering and to use the Excise post he hoped to obtain 'to help the people of that town in their excise'. Similarly, at Exeter, the lawyer Sir Bartholomew Shower (standing as Sir Edward Seymour's partner) was traduced as a supporter of the repeal of the test in James II's day and as a 'counsel for traitors' since 1688.[107]

Shower was not one to suffer such aspersions in silence, even though they were true. His counter-attack included both an avowal of his loyalty to the Church (as befitted one of the reputed co-authors of A Letter to a Convocation Man) and a condemnation of occasional conformity—a familiar phenomenon in Exeter. Elsewhere, too, the effects of those divisions within the Church observed at this time by Burnet were apparent. The ministerialist supporter who wrote A Prospect taken of England, divided in the Election of the next Parliament grouped the 'moderate churchmen and the Dissenters' with the 'Courtiers so-called' and associated the 'high churchmen' and the 'non-jurors' with 'the New Country party so-called'.[108] In Berkshire and Oxfordshire, the cry of the 'Church in danger' was raised by some 'hot heads' who portrayed recent Nonconformist attempts to set up a nationwide 'correspondence' to pursue 'the reformation of manners' as a plot against the ecclesiastical establishment.[109] Alerts also went out from Cambridge University dons to anxious country parsons of 'the great industry the Genevites used to get men of their set into the House of Commons'.[110] Simultaneously, in Oxford Sir William Trumbull was laid by as a candidate for the University, thanks 'to the zealous applications' of 'one factious part of it'—the men of Christ Church (Atterbury's college) and their friends, who were said to be eager 'to show how far they can go in affronting the King and government'.[111]

Not only was the 1698 campaign marked by 'the most dangerous division of a Court and a Country party', with each having wings within the Church, but it also saw a return to the level of contests recorded in 1690.[112] Altogether, 106 constituencies are known to have been polled or controverted, and it was observed in Buckinghamshire that some candidates behaved as if the recent legislation against treating was 'only waste paper'.[113] Yet in spite of the rancorous electoral propaganda, the substantial number of contests, and the choice of 187 new members (134 without any prior experience), some thought the returns did not presage any drastic shift in the parliamentary outlook. On 1 August, Paul Foley stated that the change 'appears to be many in number but very little in my opinion as to the main influence of things'; on the 23rd, under-secretary Yard commented that 'in the general we are very well pleased at Court and expect to have a greater majority in this House of Commons than the last'; and early in September, Lord Digby concluded a careful comparison of the old and the new Commons with the judgement that the Churchmen 'have not much mended'.[114] Others, however, detected an anti-ministerial swing, despite the short interval between the end of the session and the elections.[115] Somers reckoned on 16 August that the new Commons 'will be somewhat difficult to be dealt with, though several of the leading men of the opposite party are left out', such as Francis Gwyn (later returned at a by-election) and William Bromley; similarly, Nottingham was of the opinion on the 27th that the new House 'is much better than the last', though he regretted the failure to stand again of some Churchmen, including Sir Thomas Dyke.[116] Still others, such as Vernon, were loath to make any predictions, save that 'it is certain the animosities they [the new Commons] have one against another will be strong'.[117]

More quantitative assessments, both by contemporaries and by ourselves, lend credence to facets of each of these sets of qualitative judgements. To begin with, they show that the large number of incumbent placemen did not fare quite as well as their counterparts in other general elections of the reign. This was indicated by a printed list of the results, put out in August, in which the compiler used 'a mark more than he tells what is signified by it—the star is for new members and a cross for those that have places (as is supposed), though he is mistaken in several of them'.[118] Our own computations indicate that of the 132 incumbent placemen, 93 (70 per cent) were re-elected. Among the 39 who were not, there were a few who chose not to run again, notably the ageing Sir Robert Howard and Sir Stephen Fox and the disgruntled Attorney-General Sir Thomas Trevor. But there were also younger ministerialists such as Sir Henry Hobart (killed in a post-election duel in Norfolk), Lord Winchester, and Harry Mordaunt who were defeated at the polls. Moreover, the 39 departing placemen were not fully replaced; only 32 of the new members already held office.[119] Yet, it is also evident that a relatively low proportion of non-associators were returned. Only 52 (55 per cent) of all the 94 non-associators still sitting at the dissolution were re-elected, as compared to 65 per cent of all other incumbents, and the publication prior to the campaign of several lists of their names may have had an adverse effect in some instances.[120] Finally, we may instance the results of a contemporary's detailed comparison of the old and the new Commons, perhaps in general terms of Court and Country or possibly with specific reference to support for or opposition to the maintenance of a peacetime army. The unknown analyst's tabulations, which take into account almost all members, may be summed up as follows:[121]

	Old Commons	Re-elected	New members	New Commons
Court or army	281	179 (64%)	62	241
Country or anti-army	210	132 (63%)	95	227

This computation survives in manuscript among Harley's papers, but it does not accord with his own judgement. While the anonymous compiler reckoned that the swing away from the Court would come mainly from the new M.P.s, Harley's opinion on the eve of the 1698–99 session was that 'if there be any alteration, it will not proceed from the new members but from the change of opinions in some of the old'.[122]

As his subjects were mulling over the election results, William was on the verge of concluding the negotiations with Louis, for the King was convinced that Carlos II could not outlive October. In mid-August, the King communicated the proposed terms to Secretary Vernon and Lord Chancellor Somers, leaving it to the latter's discretion 'to whom else you would think proper to impart them'. Hitherto, Somers had been told only that France was showing 'some inclination' to arrange a peaceful settlement of the Spanish succession; now, he and Vernon were informed that the conditions were 'pretty near this nature':[123]

that the Electoral Prince of Bavaria shall have the kingdoms of Spain, the Indies, the Low Countries and all that depends upon the Spanish dominions, except the kingdoms of Naples and of Sicily, Sardinia, the province of Guipuscoa on this side of the Pyrenees, Fontarabia and St Sebastian, Final and the places of Tuscany, of which Spain stands now possessed, in consideration of which France is absolutely to renounce the right it pretends to the succession of Spain. Milan is to be given to the Archduke, second son to the Emperor.

Somers, who was then convalescing at Tunbridge Wells, instructed Vernon to communicate the terms to Orford, Montagu, and Shrewsbury. Orford and Montagu were in town when the King's and Portland's letters were shown them, and they informed Shrewsbury when they met the Duke (by prior arrangement) a few days later at Wharton's seat at Winchendon. Hence, when the Chancellor replied to William on 28 August, he was speaking both for himself and for the others.[124]

The Whig ministers' response was cautious, and Somers's letter raised three specific points. First, he accepted the need for an agreement, seeing that in England 'there is a deadness and want of spirit in the nation universally, so as not at all to be disposed to the thought of entering into a new war and that they seem to be tired out with taxes to a degree, beyond what was discerned, till it appeared upon the occasion of the late elections'. Second, he voiced a fear of French insincerity and asked what security England would have that Louis would abide by whatever settlement was reached. Third, he indicated some reservations about the particular conditions. In his view, Final and Guipuscoa in French hands would become unwelcome 'bridles' upon the successors to Milan and Spain, and France's acquisition of Sicily would endanger England's Mediterranean trade. He also advised William that could England 'be some ways gainer by this transaction', perhaps by the Elector of Bavaria conceding to Englishmen trading privileges in Spanish America, 'or in any other manner, it would wonderfully endear your Majesty to your English subjects'.[125]

In the end, however, Somers and the others were not prepared to oppose the King's judgement, and they left it to him to 'conclude only upon that which is most safe and prudent'.[126] Moreover, even before Portland's letter of 26 August reached Vernon in London with the warning that these terms were unlikely to be bettered and might be withdrawn if not quickly accepted, a blank commission under the great seal which was needed to conclude the agreement was dispatched to William by express in secrecy. Acting under this commission, Portland and Sir Joseph Williamson signed the Partition Treaty for England in mid-September 1698, with the two final and secret articles being communicated only to Vernon and Somers through whose hands the treaty had to pass.[127]

Unhappily for William, the King of Spain's health proved less fragile than anticipated, and the seeming improvement in his condition during the autumn of 1698 posed new problems. For one thing, it was necessary to try to keep secret all the terms of the new treaty. And for a second, Carlos II's survival removed the principal justification in many Englishmen's eyes for William's maintenance of a good many more than the 10,000 troops for whom the Commons had authorised pay in January 1698. While the terms of the treaty were under consideration in August, Vernon had observed to Shrewsbury that 'the number of troops kept up' will 'be excused or aggravated according to what shall happen to the King of Spain'. Earlier, there had been a stir in London, shortly before the King's departure for the Continent in late July, that the five Huguenot regiments 'which have been kept, as it were, concealed in Flanders' were to be sent to Ireland, and Somers warned William then of the resentment such a step would engender. But William had been assured by Methuen that the parliament in Dublin could be induced to maintain those regiments, and he was prepared to gamble on the English reaction.[128]

The King's refusal to heed Somers's caution about the Huguenot regiments was just one instance of the influence that Methuen had obtained, at least in Irish matters, after Sunderland's departure. The Lord Chancellor of Ireland had been recommended for that post by Sunderland and Shrewsbury, while Somers studiously avoided backing him, and Methuen's assurances about the Huguenot regiments kept him in the King's good graces even though he had voted with the opposition over money for the army on 8 January 1698.[129] Methuen had also undertaken to settle the main issues in dispute between England and Ireland: the Westminster parliament's desire to limit the burgeoning woollens industry of Ireland, and the Dublin parliament's zeal to break the shackles upon its independence imposed by Poynings's law. In these matters, he prompted William, or so he bragged to Galway, 'to take resolutions in his closet and declare them in the cabinet council in such manner as to prevent contradiction'.[130] Throughout, Somers had been at odds with Methuen, at least partly because the Lord Chancellor's friends Yonge and Clarke were anxious to have effective restrictions imposed upon Ireland's woollen exports. Thus, there was a strong tinge of *Schadenfreude* in Somers's sour comments to Shrewsbury over the mounting controversies in the Irish parliamentary session that began in late September 1698.

However vexing Irish affairs were, by the autumn of 1698 Somers had more serious worries than whether he and his colleagues in London could bear 'the blame of spoiling the session in Ireland' as a result of the changes the English Privy Council made in the draft woollens and linen bills sent over from Dublin.[131] In the Lord Chancellor's view, the very existence of the Junto ministry was now in doubt. The dangers, as Somers expounded them to Shrewsbury in a long letter of late October, were threefold. First, there was the King's disenchantment with the Junto, especially now that Shrewsbury was gone and Sunderland was excluded. On this point, Somers instanced not only the King's coldness to the Whig ministers during much of the previous session but also that William 'would in no sort declare himself' before the general election, perhaps 'to see first which faction would have the majority in the new parliament'. Second, there was the 'ill foot' on which the elections had been fought, and Somers feared that 'the complaints of taxes and offices' would also 'mislead many well-intentioned gentlemen' in the coming session. Third, there was the lack of suffi-cient 'men of business' (as opposed to mere administrators) in office, and the prospects of recruiting such men, given William's 'prejudices to some' and 'fondness for others of a different party', appeared slim. Moreover, though Somers was now resigned to Shrewsbury's withdrawal, which was formalised a few weeks later by the Duke's resignation of the seals, the Lord Chancellor was upset by another precipitate move by Montagu. Montagu's unexpected decision to claim the Auditorship of the Receipt for his brother Christopher (presumably as a stand-in for himself) when Sir Robert Howard died early in September 1698 left Somers in 'great disquiet'. Montagu had acted without waiting for William's approval on the grounds that the post was not in the King's but in the Treasury Commission's gift, and he had also acted 'without the advice or knowledge of many of his best friends', including Somers. Thus, the Lord Chancellor lamented to Shrewsbury, it is hard to see how Montagu's move could 'turn out well for the public. If he quits the Treasury, somebody, wholly of another sort, will succeed. If he keeps both places, I fear it will be a new subject of envy.'[132]

In this fashion, Vernon's gloomiest anticipations were being realised within little more than a year after the signing of the peace. One by one, the links in that 'chain of ministry' which had been in 'the possession of the Whigs' at war's end seemed to be snapping. And now, so Somers gloomily concluded his rumina-tions to Shrewsbury in October 1698, only the 'almost impossibility' that Sunderland or anyone else could succeed in 'finding a set of Tories who will unite' seemed to stand between the Junto and a general 'change of hands'.[133]

Notes to Chapter X

1 *Archives*, III, i, 123.
2 *Shrewsbury Corr.*, pp. 174, 179.
3 *Vernon Corr.*, I, 359, 379–81, 386, 390–2, 399, 404–5. And see CSPD, 1697, pp. 400–1.
4 *Vernon Corr.*, I, 431.
5 *Shrewsbury Corr.*, p. 503; *Vernon Corr.*, I, 381.
6 NU, Portland MS. PwA 1251, [Sunderland to Portland], 23 May 1696; Bodl. Locke MS. C8, f. 227, J. Freke to Locke, 6 April 1697; PRO, SP 84/223, J. Ellis to Sir J. Williamson, 16 July 1697; *Shrewsbury Corr.*, p. 502. See also HMC *Portland*, III, 593; Longleat, Thynne MS. 24, f. 78; BL Loan 29/78 (unfoliated), [E. Harley] to his father, 23 November 1697; ST, II, 566.
7 BL Loan 29/156 (unfoliated), 27 September.

8 BL Loan 29/188, ff. 203, 205, H. Guy to R. Harley, 23, 25 September; Levens, Bagot MSS., Grahme correspondence, Viscount Weymouth to J. Grahme, 28 September.

9 HMC *Fitzherbert*, p. 46.

10 *CSPD*, 1697, p. 467; BL Add. MS. 30000A, ff. 371, 373, L. F. Bonnet, 9/19 and 13/23 November; Althorp, Savile MSS., box 10, Viscount Weymouth to Marquess of Halifax, 9 November; Wing B895, D834, D837. For a precedent, see BL Add. MS. 17677 OO, f. 382, L'Hermitage, 6/16 November 1694.

11 Burnet, *History*, IV, 392–3. And see H. Horwitz, 'Comprehension in the Later Seventeenth Century: A Postscript', *Church History* XXXIV (1965), 343–5.

12 Reprinted in *Somers' Tracts*, IX, 412–33. And see G. V. Bennett, *The Tory Crisis in Church and State 1688–1730* (Oxford, 1975), pp. 47–50.

13 J. Simms, 'John Toland (1670–1722), a Donegal heretic', *Irish Historical Studies* XVI (1968–9), 308–13; J. Toland, *The Life of John Milton* (1699, Wing T1776), pp. 77–9; BL Add. MS. 40773, f. 333, J. Vernon to Portland, 29 April 1699.

14 BL Loan 29/188, f. 212, 5 October.

15 L. Schwoerer, 'No Standing Armies!' (Baltimore, 1974), chapter 8, a useful summary of the pamphlet literature; C. Robbins, *The Eighteenth Century Commonwealthmen* (Cambridge, Mass., 1959), chapter 4. And see BL Egerton MS. 929, f. 9, W. Moyle to C. Montagu, 11 August [1696].

16 BL Loan 29/188, f. 245, [R. Harley] to his father, 23 November.

17 *Correspondentie*, I, i, 212.

18 *Correspondentie*, I, i, 212.

19 Somers's 'balancing letter' is reprinted in ST, II, 585–9.

20 HMC *Portland*, III, 593; Berkshire RO, Trumbull Add. MS. 125, diary entries for 21 and 28 November.

21 *Shrewsbury Corr.*, pp. 179, 507–8.

22 HMC *Downshire*, I, 768.

23 Berkshire RO, Trumbull Add. MS. 125, November entries.

24 *Shrewsbury Corr.*, pp. 504–6.

25 BL Loan 29/188, f. 250, 4 December (misattributed in HMC *Portland*, III, 594); BL Loan 29/165, misc. 97, p. 3; HMC *Portland*, IV, 451; BL Lansdowne MS. 885, ff. 15–16. Possibly, the offer made was of the reversion to Sir R. Howard's Auditorship, for Howard was thought, mistakenly, to be on the verge of death at the time: HMC *Portland*, III, 593; Luttrell, *Brief Relation*, IV, 313.

26 HMC *Portland*, III, 593.

27 CJ, XII, 1.

28 *CSPD*, 1697, p. 502. Among the minority on the 7th were Palmes and some of his Yorkshire associates, and at least one reason may have been Palmes's sense of grievance over his son's problems as Teller; Kenyon, *Sunderland*, p. 291 and note.

29 CJ, XII, 4. And see BL Add. MS. 17677RR, ff. 527–8, L'Hermitage, 10/20 December.

30 Northants RO, Buccleuch MSS., Vernon letters, I, 162–3, 9 and 11 December.

31 *CSPD*, 1697, pp. 506–8; BL Add. MS. 17677RR, f. 528.

32 Longleat, Thynne MS. 24, f. 356, R. Price to Viscount Weymouth, 11 December; Bodl. Carte MS. 130, f. 385, R. Price to [Duke of Beaufort], 11 December; Northants RO, Buccleuch MSS., Vernon letters, I, 163. See also *CSPD*, 1697, pp. 511–12; BL Add. MS. 30000A, f. 397, L. F. Bonnet, 14/24 December.

33 *CSPD*, 1697, pp. 511–12, 513.

34 Northants RO, Buccleuch MSS., Vernon letters, I, 167, 18 December. Cf. [N. Hooke], *An Account of the Conduct of the Dowager Duchess of Marlborough* (1742), p. 117.

35 *CSPD*, 1697, pp. 522–4; BL Add. MS. 30000A, ff. 409–10, L. F. Bonnet, 24 December/3 January.

36 BL Loan 29/188, f. 257, [R. Harley] to his father, 21 December; *Vernon Corr.*, I, 445.

37 Berkshire RO, Trumbull Add. MS. 125, 28 November; Longleat, Thynne MS. 24, f. 378; Northants RO, Buccleuch MSS., Vernon letters, I, 167.

38 *Vernon Corr.*, I, 446; Burnet, *History*, IV, 377.

39 *Vernon Corr.*, I, 446; HMC *Portland*, III, 594.

40 BL Loan 29/188, f. 259, [R. Harley] to his father, 28 December; *Shrewsbury Corr.*, p. 506; BL Add. MS. 40771, f. 135, J. Vernon to Shrewsbury, 17 December; *CSPD*, 1697, p. 520.

41 *Vernon Corr.*, I, 447, 446; *Shrewsbury Corr.*, p. 521; Northants RO, Buccleuch MSS.,

Vernon letters, I, 166, 17 December; Blenheim, Sunderland letterbook III, J. Methuen to [Lord Galway], 28 December.

42 *Shrewsbury Corr.*, p. 511, 510.

43 *Vernon Corr.*, I, 449; *Shrewsbury Corr.*, p. 521.

44 *Shrewsbury Corr.*, p. 521, also 523; Blenheim, Sunderland letterbook III, J. Methuen to [Lord Galway], 28 December. And see BL Loan 29/188, f. 259.

45 *Shrewsbury Corr.*, pp. 511, 521; Grimblot, *Letters*, I, 181.

46 HMC *Portland*, III, 594. And see Blenheim, Sunderland letterbook III, J. Methuen to [Lord Galway], 30 December.

47 *Vernon Corr.*, I, 455–6; NU, Portland MS. PwA 1395, [Shrewsbury to Portland], 30 December. E. S. de Beer speculates that the Whigs backed Locke as a 'compromise candidate' for the seals in early 1698, but I am doubtful: 'John Locke: the Appointment Offered to him in 1698', *BIHR* XL (1967), 213–19.

48 *CSPD*, 1698, p. 15; Bodl. Carte MS. 130, f. 387, R. Price to [Duke of Beaufort], 6 January; *Vernon Corr.*, I, 461, 465; BL Loan 29/189, f. 3, [E. Harley] to his father, 3 January.

49 House of Lords RO, Commons' Lib. MS. 12, ff. 104–5, notes of the debate. See also HMC *Portland* III, 595; Northants RO, Buccleuch MSS., Vernon letters, I, 177, 8 January; *CSPD*, 1698, p. 23; Blenheim, Sunderland letterbook III, J. Methuen to [Lord Galway], 8 January..

50 Middlesex RO, Jersey MS. 510/132, 18 January. And see *Vernon Corr.*, I, 460–1; *CSPD*, 1698, p. 29; BL Loan 29/189, f. 8, [R. Harley] to his father, 18 January; *Correspondentie*, I, i, 221.

51 *Vernon Corr.*, I, 473.

52 *CSPD*, 1698, p. 140. See also CTB, XIII, 35–6 and ff.

53 Blenheim, Sunderland letterbook III, J. Methuen to [Lord Galway], 20 January; *CSPD*, 1698, p. 38; PRO, PRO 30/15/4/682, xxxi, R. Yard to Earl of Manchester, 28 January. Cf. Kenyon, *Sunderland*, p. 303.

54 *Shrewsbury Corr.*, pp. 528–9, 532. See also *Vernon Corr.*, I, 469–70; *CSPD*, 1698, p. 38.

55 *Shrewsbury Corr.*, p. 530; *Vernon Corr.*, I, 469–70.

56 *Vernon Corr.*, I, 477–8; *CSPD*, 1698, pp. 43–4.

57 *Shrewsbury Corr.*, pp. 532–3; BL Add. MS. 15895, f. 20, Shrewsbury to C. Montagu, 4 February; *Vernon Corr.*, I, 483–4, 486–7 (1 February), and II, 2. For a projected match between Albemarle and Rochester's daughter, see Middlesex RO, Jersey MSS. 510/124, 132.

58 *Vernon Corr.*, II, 5, also 8, 10–11; BL Add. MS. 15895, f. 20.

59 *Vernon Corr.*, II, 3; *CSPD*, 1698, pp. 77–8; BL Add. MS. 30000B, ff. 34–5, L. F. Bonnet, 8/18 February. The Irish bill did reserve one-third to the King's disposal.

60 BL Add. MS. 30000B, ff. 34–5; *CSPD*, 1698, pp. 89, 96, 102; BL Loan 29/189, f. 24, [E. Harley] to his father, 19 February; *Vernon Corr.*, II, 15–16, 18–19.

61 BL Add. MS. 15895, f. 20; Grimblot, *Letters*, I, 197.

62 *Vernon Corr.*, I, 482, and II, 1–2, 20–1; Northants RO, Buccleuch MSS., Vernon letters, I, 75, 8 March; *CSPD*, 1698, pp. 113, 118, 128–9, 134–5.

63 *Correspondentie*, I, i, 265–6; Middlesex RO, Jersey MS. 510/136, Jersey to R. Hill, 29 March. See also BL Add. MS. 40771, f. 153, Shrewsbury to Vernon, 8 March; *Vernon Corr.*, II, 23, 24–5.

64 CJ, XII, 14, 17, 44, 58, 152. See also W. R. Ward, *The English Land Tax in the Eighteenth Century* (Oxford, 1953), pp. 3, 21–2.

65 *Correspondentie*, I, i, 297.

66 Blenheim, Sunderland letterbook III; *Shrewsbury Corr.*, p. 560. See also PRO, PRO 31/3/180, Tallard au Roi, 9/19 May.

67 Northants RO, Buccleuch MSS., Vernon letters, II, 21, 28 April; *Shrewsbury Corr.*, p. 536; *Vernon Corr.*, II, 69.

68 *CSPD*, 1698, pp. 184, 195, 225; BL Add. MS. 17677SS, ff. 219–20, L'Hermitage, 8/18 April.

69 Northants RO, Buccleuch MSS., Vernon letters, I, 72, 1 March [1698]; *Vernon Corr.*, II, 21. The old Company had been approached by 'persons of considerable rank in the government' to promote such a loan in December 1697; Wing C1082, p. 5; East India Office Lib., old Co. Court Book B/41, f. 234, also 270.

70 *CSPD*, 1698, p. 188; East India Office Lib., old Co. Court Book B/41, f. 272; *Vernon Corr.*, II, 68.

71 Vernon Corr., II, 88, also 73, 75–6. And see CSPD, 1698, pp. 226–7, 258–9.

72 Vernon Corr., II, 90; CSPD, 1698, p. 272.

73 Shrewsbury Corr., p. 540. And see Bodl. Add. MS. A191, f. 67, T. Tenison to G. Burnet, 17 June; Bodl. Carte MS. 233, f. 54, Somers to [Wharton], 25 June.

74 Bodl. Carte MS. 130, f. 391, to [Duke of Beaufort], 2 July. And see Grimblot, Letters, II, 61, 64; BL Add. MS. 30000B, f. 159, L. F. Bonnet, 5/15 July; Northants RO, Buccleuch MSS., Vernon letters, II, 52, 2 July; LJ, XVI, 316.

75 Shrewsbury Corr., pp. 543–4.

76 CTB, XIII, 100.

77 K. G. Davies, The Royal African Company (1957), pp. 126–33.

78 BL Add. MS. 41807, f. 1, J. Vernon's note, [December 1697].

79 BL Loan 29/189, f. 21, [E. Harley] to his father, 12 February; CJ, XII, 102–3. For Harley's earlier interest in such legislation, see BL Loan 29/186, f. 225.

80 HLM, 1697–1699, pp. 112–13; Bodl. Ballard MS. 38, f. 186, T. Rowney to A. Charlett, 5 March; CSPD, 1698, pp. 128, 154, 169–70, 257; Berkshire RO, Trumbull MS. 'Jenkins' bound vol., G. Dolben to Sir W. Trumbull, 31 March; CJ, XII, 280.

81 PRO, PRO 30/15/4/682, xliv, R. Yard to Earl of Manchester, 1 March; CSPD, 1698, p. 114; Vernon Corr., II, 19.

82 Bodl. Carte MS. 130, f. 392, 15 March, R. Price to [Duke of Beaufort]; CSPD, 1698, pp. 129, 139–40, 145; Vernon Corr., II, 23–4, 27. See also Macaulay, History, VI, 2761–8.

83 H. Kearney, 'The Political Background to English Mercantilism, 1695–1700', Economic History Review, 2nd s., XI (1957), 484–96.

84 BL Add. MS. 30000B, f. 115, L. F. Bonnet, 10/20 May; CSPD, 1698, p. 242; Althorp, Savile MSS., box 2, Nottingham to Marquess of Halifax, 21 May.

85 CSPD, 1698, p. 134; BL Add. MS. 17677SS, ff. 204–5, L'Hermitage, 25 March/4 April. Text and summary in BL Loan 29/278 (unfoliated); BL Add. MS. 42593, ff. 79–84. Cf. J. R. Western, The English Militia in the Eighteenth Century (1957), pp. 88–9.

86 Vernon Corr., II, 179–80 (20 August), and 85, 94, 98, 103; Correspondentie, I, i, 297; HMC Bath, II, 223; BL Add. MS. 17677SS f. 301, L'Hermitage, 24 June/4 July. For Tallard's suspicions, see Grimblot, Letters, II, 27.

87 Burnet, History, IV, 384; CTB, XIII, 103; Grimblot, Letters, II, 85–6.

88 Correspondentie, I, i, 275; Archives, III, ii, 113–14; Northants RO, Buccleuch MSS., Vernon letters, II, 3, 1 April.

89 Correspondentie, I, i, 278–9, 293.

90 Vernon Corr., II, 105 (12 July), 122–3; Shrewsbury Corr., p. 545. And see Archives, III, ii, 238; Kenyon, Sunderland, pp. 305–7.

91 Vernon Corr., I, 474, also 466–7; Shrewsbury Corr., p. 524.

92 William had first offered the Governorship to Shrewsbury: BL Add. MS. 30000A, f. 411, L. F. Bonnet, 24 December/3 January; Vernon Corr., I, 444. See also Burnet, History, IV, 385–6; Middlesex RO, Jersey MS. 510/138, Jersey to R. Hill, 31 May.

93 Vernon Corr., II, 12, 104, 106.

94 Vernon Corr., II, 127, 131–2; Shrewsbury Corr., pp. 553–4.

95 CTB, XIII, 29–31, 38–9, 41–2, 93–4; Calendar of Treasury Papers, 1697–1702, pp. 161–2; CSPD, 1697, p. 492; Northants RO, Buccleuch MSS., Vernon letters, II, 21, 28 April 1698.

96 Vernon Corr., II, 123. And see Luttrell, Brief Relation, IV, 315; PH, V, cxiii–iv; Hunt. Stowe MS. 26, James Brydges's diary, 11 February, 31 March, 29 June 1698.

97 HMC Le Fleming, p. 352; HMC Portland, III, 598. The other five M.P.s were the incumbents Clarke and Foot Onslow, and the new members William Fleming, William Carr, and Sir William Ashurst.

98 Bodl. MS. Eng. hist. b209, Sir Richard Cocks's diary, f. 83 v.

99 Correspondentie, I, i, 249, 255; The Correspondence of John Locke and Edward Clarke, ed. B. Rand (1927). p. 531.

100 Northants RO, Buccleuch MSS., Vernon letters, II, 53, 5 July.

101 Vernon Corr., II, 143, also 126.

102 Shrewsbury Corr., p. 560. Both tracts are reprinted in PH, V.

103 Verney Letters of the Eighteenth Century, ed. Margaret Lady Verney, I (1930), 156; Westmorland RO, Le Fleming MS. 5294; BL Add. MS. 29570, f. 44, Sir C. Lyttleton to Viscount Hatton, 13 August; Cornwall RO, BO 23/72.

104 CSPD, 1698, p. 377.

105 The True Englishman's Choice of Parliament Men (1698, Wing T2698), p. 3.

106 A Prospect taken of England, divided in the Election of the next Parliament (1698), reprinted in HMC Portland, VIII, 54.

107 CJ, XII, 543–6; NLW, Kemys Tynte unsorted correspondence, T. Lloyd to Sir C. Kemys, 3 March 1699; CSPD, 1698, pp. 377–8.

108 CSPD, 1698, pp. 377–8; HMC Portland, VIII, 54.

109 BL Loan 29/48, bundle 5, R. Stretton to Sir E. Harley. And see Vernon Corr., II, 128–129, 133–4, 156; Wing B22, S4583.

110 The Diary and Letter Book of the Rev. Thomas Brockbank, ed. R. Lomax (Chetham Society, n.s. LXXXIX, 1930), p. 138. And see Bodl. Rawlinson Letters 91, f. 449, ? to T. Turner, 9 August.

111 HMC Downshire, I, 781. And see Bodl. Tanner MS. 22, f. 16, A. Charlett to [T. Tanner], 4 August.

112 MSP, II, 435.

113 Verney MSS., reel 50, Sir R. Hill to J. Verney, 22 July. Cf. Cumberland RO, Lowther correspondence, Sir J. Lowther to Viscount Lonsdale, 26 and 28 July. And see Appendix A.

114 BL Loan 29/75 (unfoliated). P. Foley to Sir E. Harley; KAO, Chevening MS. 78, R. Yard to A. Stanhope; BL Egerton MS. 2540, f. 115, Lord Digby to E. Nicholas, 3 September.

115 Both Charlett and Harley thought the changes would have been greater had the elections been later: Bodl. Tanner MS. 22, f. 119, A. Charlett to T. Tanner, [August]; Chatsworth MSS., correspondence 102.O, R. Harley to H. Boyle, 16 November.

116 Shrewsbury Corr., p. 554, also 555; Althorp, Savile MSS., box 2, Nottingham to Marquess of Halifax, 27 August.

117 Correspondentie, I, ii, 100.

118 BL Add. MS 40772, f. 8, J. Vernon to the King, 20 August (compare Correspondentie, I, ii, 88, 90). Varying editions of A Compleat List of the Knights, Citizens, and Burgesses of the New Parliament are in BL 1850 c6 No. 16 and Hunt. 347521.

119 Appendix D. And see Northants RO, Buccleuch MSS., Vernon letters, II, 63, 30 July.

120 In addition to the list circulated in March 1696, see Advice to Freeholders ... With a List of Non-Associators ([?1698], Hunt. 314291).

121 BL Loan 29/35, bundle 12, printed in H. Horwitz, 'Parties, Connections, and Parliamentary Politics, 1689–1714: Review and Revision', Journal of British Studies VI (1966), 55–69. See also Appendix C.

122 Chatsworth MSS., correspondence 102.O. See also Correspondentie, I, ii, 100.

123 Grimblot, Letters, II, 121; Correspondentie, I, ii, 88.

124 Correspondentie, I, ii, 89–92; Vernon Corr., II, 154–5. Neither Wharton, Marlborough, nor Godolphin, though present at the Winchendon house party, seems to have been made party to the secret.

125 Grimblot, Letters, II, 143–5.

126 Correspondentie, I, ii, 96, 99–100.

127 Correspondentie, I, ii, 94–7, 101–3; BL Add. MS. 40772, f. 13, J. Vernon to Somers, 22 August. And see Grimblot, Letters, II, 149.

128 Vernon Corr., II, 179 (20 August), 181; Shrewsbury Corr., pp. 538, 544, 558. And see Grimblot, Letters, II, 81; Middlesex RO, Jersey MS. 510/138.

129 Shrewsbury Corr., pp. 451, 456; Vernon Corr., I, 146–7, 152, 160; Grimblot, Letters, II, 247–9 (27 January [1698]), 184–6.

130 Blenheim, Sunderland's letterbook III, 14 April 1698.

131 Shrewsbury Corr., pp. 557–8 (cf. MSP, II, 433–4). See also MSP, II, 432; HMC Buccleuch, II, 615–16.

132 Shrewsbury Corr., p. 560. See also HMC Rutland, II, 163; CTB, XIV, 108–9.

133 CSPD, 1695 and addenda, p. 45; MSP, II, 436.

XI

THE COURT AT BAY

1698-1700

The autumn of 1698 found the Junto uneasily anticipating storms to come in the new parliament, yet they were not of a mind to yield their place in the sun without a struggle. Admittedly, Shrewsbury's departure had been a serious blow to their position at Kensington and the divisions among the Whigs in the Commons had weakened their ascendency at Westminster. Moreover, the resentment of heavy taxes and the distrust of placemen that had been manifest in the provinces during the ensuing general election had been accompanied by the return of a good many untried members. Even so, the enactment of the new East India project and the concomitant settlement of the civil list before the dissolution had partially assuaged the King's dissatisfaction at the loss of both Shrewsbury and Sunderland. Then, too, the opposition to the army in St Stephen's Chapel had succeeded only because Whigs such as Strickland and Norris, Onslow and Croft had joined with Harley and the Churchmen, and defections on this issue did not mean that the Whig backbenchers were prepared to turn upon the Junto. Furthermore, despite the ties that Harley and Speaker Foley had formed since the early 1690s with leading Tory Commoners such as Musgrave, Gwyn, and Granville, they seemed to have only very loose links with the foremost Tory peers, especially Rochester, Leeds, and Nottingham. Thus, the Junto did not appear immediately threatened by any 'shadow cabinet' waiting in the wings to replace them.

The lack of unity among the Junto's foes was apparent in the manoeuvring over the choice of a Speaker in the new House of Commons during the autumn of 1698. Immediately after the general election, various names were mentioned —chiefly Paul Foley, Simon Harcourt, and the newcomer Sir Bartholomew Shower.[1] Yet, contrary to Vernon's expectation, there was little enthusiasm for the first; his relative evenhandedness in the Chair during the last parliament meant, as Harley found out when he came up to town late in the autumn, that 'our friend will not be borne, unless it be done at Kensington'. Rumours did circulate that Foley would be set up by the Court 'by way of compromise', and at the same time two main opposition candidates emerged.[2] First in the field early in October 1698 was John Granville. Sponsored by Rochester, and backed also by Leeds and Nottingham, he appeared a formidable opponent for the Junto's choice, Sir Thomas Littleton, not least because he, too, could lay claim to considerable experience as chairman in committees of the whole.[3] Second to announce his bid was Sir Edward Seymour, who, it was said, 'sets himself up'. Nor could Seymour be persuaded to withdraw, despite repeated attempts by various Tory notables.

Instead, he was seen 'buttling' with Montagu in town on 23 November, and the two old opponents also dined together on the 24th, prompting stories that Sir Edward intended to come in 'between Court and Country'. Seymour's conduct, arising perhaps from a desire 'not to be too much pressed about his accounts' as Treasurer to the Navy under Charles II (which still had to pass Exchequer audit and which the Treasury had recently 'called upon [him] to make an end of'), aroused the fury of Granville's friends.[4] And Anthony Hammond, in his *Considerations upon the Choice of a Speaker* (published on the eve of parliament's scheduled opening on 29 November), not only condemned Littleton as unfit for the Chair by reason of his post at the Treasury but also lashed out at Seymour as an 'old prostitute of the explod'd Pension'd Parliament' of Charles II's reign.[5]

With Granville and Seymour competing for votes, the chief fear of Littleton's backers was that the King—delayed in Holland by contrary winds—might yet be persuaded to sponsor Foley again. Even Secretary Vernon, whose promotion upon Sunderland's recommendation had not been forgotten, was exposed to Junto suspicions on this score. But Vernon did not believe William intended to 'put such a hardship' upon Littleton 'as to set him aside a second time'. He also was of the opinion that for the King to do so 'would have a very ill effect upon his business, since all that I think will carry it on are engaged for Sir Thomas'. So when William finally arrived at Kensington late on 4 December, Vernon broached Littleton's candidacy and was pleased to find his master 'very inclinable to him'.[6] On the 6th, then, Sir Thomas was nominated in the Commons by Lord Hartington, and there were supporting speeches from Lord Spencer, Treasury Commissioners Montagu, Smith, and Pelham, and Sir Richard Onslow. He was opposed by Sir John Bolles, Lord Norris, Hammond, and a few others, but since the Junto's foes had been unable to agree upon a candidate of their own, the question for Littleton was carried 242 to 135.[7]

Littleton's success was an encouraging beginning, yet the Junto knew full well that it did not mean 'everything that was aimed at [by William] might be effected'.[8] Above all, they were doubtful that more than 10,000 men could be kept up and uncertain whether a majority could be mustered even to retain in English pay the Dutch regiments, which, so many members had hoped, would by this time have been sent back to Holland.[9] After Carlos II's apparent resuscitation, the pamphlet campaign against a standing army had been revived by John Trenchard and his friends. Trenchard's *A Short History of Standing Armies in England*, written with information provided by Harley, appeared in late November 1698. It alleged that while Charles II in 1680 had a military establishment of only 6,950 men in England, 7,800 in Ireland, and approximately 3,000 in Tangiers, William now had on foot 24,741 in England, 24,891 in Ireland, 4,769 in Scotland, and 5,568 in Holland—a grand total of 59,969.[10] This was a grossly exaggerated account of the current strength of William's army, yet Somers thought it best to advise the King to deal with the new House of Commons by 'proceeding nicely and letting them conceive much was left to themselves'.[11]

William did accept the Chancellor's draft for his opening speech of 9 December; this was skilfully worded 'so as to satisfy' him and yet provide 'no handle for cavilling' by the administration's critics.[12] The King began by recommending consideration of 'what strength ought to be maintained at sea and what force kept up at land for this year', while reminding members 'that the flourishing of trade, the supporting of credit, and the quiet of people's minds at home will depend upon the opinion they have of their security'. Next, he urged 'the making some further progress' in satisfying the debts left from the war. And last, he mentioned the desirability of measures to relieve the poor effectually, to advance trade, and for 'further discouraging of vice and profaneness'.[13]

But as in the 1697–98 session, even Somers's pen could not ease men's anxieties on the subject of the army. When the nearly four hundred M.P.s in attendance on 14 December took William's speech under consideration, Lord Spencer's motion for a supply was laid aside. Instead, the Commons were urged to return to the prewar practice of deliberating first upon the state of the nation, especially 'since the army had not been so far disbanded as was agreeable to the sense and opinion of the last parliament, which was a cloud upon the minds of gentlemen that sat there'.[14] Since the 'managers' were unwilling 'to lose their credit' completely 'by a further opposition' on this point, the army's foes got their way.[15] 16 December was fixed for the further discussion of the King's speech, and Lord Ranelagh was ordered to lay before the House precise lists of the troops in England and Ireland.

The totals of the lists that Lord Ranelagh brought in on 16 December were well below those alleged by Trenchard: 14,834 men in England and 15,488 in Ireland. Still, they were too large for most members. Once the Commons went into committee of the whole that day, Harley immediately moved for a maximum of 7,000 men in England for 1699. 'Many speeches' in support of his motion followed, and among the points raised were the threat to liberty posed by a large standing army, the need to reduce the public debt, the security afforded by the fleet, and William's own promises in 1688 to send home his Dutch forces. Even so, Vernon believed that the Commons might have agreed to 10,000 men 'if any had authority to propose it' to them. But, he reported to Shrewsbury, 'it was now as the last year that his Majesty would not declare himself on that point, thinking less than the present number insufficient'.[16]

The result was that Harley's motion on 16 December was not contested either in committee or on the floor the following day when the full House, on Jack Howe's urging, also stipulated that the 7,000 consist solely of 'his Majesty's natural born subjects of England'. Granted, the Commons did then vote down a motion for 10,000 men in Ireland and instead approved a 12,000 man establishment for that kingdom. But while the Catholic danger in Ireland had to be taken into account, the troops there were to be limited to 'his Majesty's natural born subjects'.[17] This formula allowed Scots to serve but it would compel the disbanding of the Huguenot regiments which the Dublin parliament, despite strong opposition encouraged by the young Duke of Ormonde (Rochester's son-in-law), had two months earlier agreed to maintain.

Not surprisingly, these votes were a great disappointment to the King. What was unexpected was the sharpness of his reaction. On 20 December, William wrote Heinsius that 'I am so chagrined at what passes in the lower House with regard to the troops that I can hardly turn my mind to any other matters'.[18] Nor was he prepared to absolve the Junto of blame for these rebuffs, despite Somers's earlier warning that the Speakership and the army were quite separate questions. Thus, when Montagu and others 'in great places' voiced reservations about the disbanding bill upon its second reading on 23 December, one of their friends on the backbenches thought that they behaved 'as if they had been chid for their passiveness' and 'as if they now spoke rather to answer the King's expectation than with any hopes or design to hinder the commitment of the bill'.[19] Even so, the ministerial leaders did decide to try to rally their usual supporters for the committee stage, which was set for Wednesday, 4 January 1699—a day after the Commons were to be called over at the end of the Christmas recess. During the holidays, 'people's pulses' were taken to gauge support for an increase to 10,000 men and for including the Dutch guards in that number. Yet the success of such an attempt seemed dubious, especially, as Vernon commented, 'if the King shall not be pleased to approve' the effort 'so that country gentlemen may understand their departing from their former resolution will be well accepted of, though it may not fully answer what his Majesty expected'.[20]

This William was far from ready to do; instead, he was talking about leaving England, perhaps permanently. The first evidence the King was thinking in such drastic terms is his letter to Heinsius of 20 December in which he spoke of taking 'resolutions of extremity' and of seeing the Pensionary in Holland sooner than planned.[21] In succeeding days, he dropped similar hints in his own Court, though at first Somers and others did not regard them as 'in good earnest'. However, an interview with William on 29 December convinced the Chancellor that his master was not merely making an effort to get the Junto 'to exert ourselves'. What the King told him was that he intended

when the next Wednesday's [4 January] business was over to come to the parliament and tell them that he came over to rescue the nation from the ruin impending over them, in which he succeeded, and had brought them to the end of a dangerous war without any great misfortune; that now they had peace, and might provide for their own safety; that he saw they were entertaining distrust and jealousies of him, so as not to do what was necessary for themselves; that he was, therefore, determined to leave England, but before he went would consent to any law they would offer for appointing commissioners of both Houses to administer the government, and then they would not be jealous of themselves.

Somers, in an earlier conversation with William on the subject, had treated the idea of his leaving as 'the most extravagant and absurd that ever was entertained'. Now, seeing that the King was firmly resolved, all he could say was that he hoped William would accept the great seal back before he departed, since 'I had it from him when he was King and desired he would receive it from me while he was so'.[22]

The new year of 1699 began, then, on a very ominous note, and the proceedings on 4 January did nothing to improve the situation. Despite all misgivings, Secretary Vernon opened the debate by moving the Commons to give leave to the committee to alter the figure of 7,000 men in the disbanding bill, and he was supported by several other ministerialists. However, Smith was conspicuously silent, Pelham spoke out against any change (instancing Carlos II's improved health and the prospects of a peace between the Imperialists and the Turks), and Pelham was joined by such leading backbench Whigs as Onslow and Hartington.[23] Another Whig country gentleman who spoke in opposition to Vernon's motion was a new parliamentary diarist, Sir Richard Cocks (M.P. for Gloucestershire); this was his maiden speech and he carefully wrote out his text in extenso. The diminutive Cocks avowed that he was convinced 7,000 men were ample if a ruler had the affections of his subject; if he did not, as in James II's case, then a much larger force would not suffice.[24]

In the face of continuing Whig disunity over the army, Montagu again avoided calling a division 'lest the majority that may be for lessening the forces should stick together in all other points'.[25] Thus, the only change in the bill made in committee was to allow Scots and Irishmen among the 7,000. And as the Commons refused to hear either of more men or of foreigners, so the King seemed to persist in his own resolution. As he told Heinsius on 6 January, 'I shall soon see myself compelled to take a step that will amaze' parliament.[26]

But while Edward Harley jubilantly reported to his father on 10 January that the 'Court now own that they are not able to contest' the disbanding bill in the Commons, when that measure came up for final reading on the 18th, there was a division.[27] The proceedings that day were summarised by one Whig M.P. as follows:[28]

Upon the third reading of the bill for disbanding the army, a rider was prepared (so I was informed) to except the King's troop of Dutch guards, consisting of about 200 horse, which probably would have been complied withal by the House, but Lord Coningsby beginning to express himself against the bill itself, and being heard with more quiet and attention than had been usual for the House to give to such as before spoke against the provision of the bill, it encouraged him and others to debate at large against the bill itself.

In the debate, the King's servants were joined 'voluntarily and without any concert' by a number of Whig country gentlemen—Sir William Blackett, Sir John Mainwaring, Sir John Phillips, and Richard Norton—and also by 'some citizens and merchants'. At first, the bill's leading advocates did not deign to reply, but 'seeing themselves pelted from all corners of the House', Musgrave and then others at last spoke in defence. 'No new topics were used on either side', but Montagu did underline repeated Court warnings of a continuing Jacobite danger by informing the Commons that James II and his queen had refused to accept the £50,000 annual 'pension' (compensation for Mary of Modena's dowry) intended for them 'rather than remove further from England' than St Germain.[29]

For all this, when the question for the passage of the disbanding bill, as it stood, was put after nearly five hours' debate on 18 January 1699, the affirmative carried it 221 to 154. Moreover, the minority (alleged to include 120 placemen) was promptly blacklisted in letters sent down to the country, and this list, which was compiled by Robert Price and a few friends shortly after the House rose, was later published as well.[30] But despite the defeat, Vernon believed that the division would 'yet have some good effect'; in particular, the 3,000 marines presently on the navy establishment 'will at least be secured by it, which were threatened before, many of those who went out for the bill declaring they are willing to make this addition'. And assuming the marines to be out of danger, Vernon wrote to Shrewsbury on the 21st that 'if there could be found a way of superadding the Dutch regiment of foot guards, I am of opinion his Majesty would be well enough satisfied. I do not find but many are disposed to pay him this personal respect, but how practicable it is I am not able to judge.'[31]

In fact, the ministerialists' choice of tactics to provide for the King's guards was circumscribed narrowly by the terms of the disbanding bill. The bill imposed severe penalties on any foreign troops left in the realm after 26 March 1699 and it also contained a clause of credit for £800,000 to meet the costs of disbanding. That clause, proposed by Foley on 12 January and acquiesced in by the King's servants, had the effect of making this a money bill in the eyes of the Commons.[32]

Hence, to press for its amendment or rejection in the Lords or to veto it would be likely to disrupt completely the current session. James Johnston observed on 20 January that 'if it be rejected we shall have no troops at all, for we shall have no money', and Harley put it even more starkly on the 21st: 'There is no medium, I think, but disbanding the army or keeping it up, shutting up the Exchequer, governing by sword and edicts.'[33] Consequently, though the disbanding bill was severely criticised by many peers, and particularly by Somers and Tankerville, the upper House approved it on 30 January without a single alteration.[34]

In the meantime, the Chancellor had been closeted at length with William, and the results of their conferences were apparent when the King came to the Lords in his robes of state on 1 February 1699. William accepted the disbanding bill without any mention of leaving the realm. But he did declare that 'the only reason which has induced me to pass' it is 'my fixed opinion that nothing can be so fatal to us as that any distrust or jealousy should arise between me and my people'. 'The nation', he warned, 'is left too much exposed' by the bill, and it was 'incumbent' upon parliament to take whatever measures are 'necessary for the safety of the kingdom and the preservation of the peace'.[35]

At first, Vernon thought this forthright speech would have a good effect, and both Houses promptly voted addresses of thanks. Furthermore, when Howe moved on 3 February to add a clause to the Commons' address to ask the King 'to set marks of his indignation on such as should presume to possess him with opinions that this House could come any resolutions that are either unkind to your Majesty or unsafe to the kingdom', Boyle spoke against the proposed amendment and it was dropped.[36] Then the House went into committee to debate the number of men for the navy for 1699. Admiral Rooke and Treasury Commissioner Pelham spoke for 15,000, and there seemed little occasion for dispute until Shower inquired whether any of this number were to be marines. He was followed by Musgrave, who moved an addition to the proposed resolution that would have limited the 15,000 to seamen, but upon a division this restriction was rejected 130 to 124. To be sure, a further fight on the floor over the marines was anticipated, but in the meantime the Junto were attempting to restore Whig unity by 'setting up the Rose Club again', and a meeting was called for 4 February in preparation for the Commons' consideration of William's speech on the 6th.[37]

The difficulty, as Vernon explained it to Shrewsbury on 2 February, was that the opposition in the Commons had secured 'the lead' in the course of the struggle over disbanding, and they were not about to relinquish it now. This was evident in the handling of the inquiries into mismanagement and corruption at the Admiralty which Harley and Foley had set on foot before the Christmas recess. At first, the Secretary had thought that 'they will make little of it', but after the sitting of 28 January he had to change his tune.[38] The point at issue that day was the delay in sending Admiral Matthew Aylmer's squadron to the Straits during the summer of 1698. With some members of the Navy Board providing detailed information to the Admiralty's critics, with Sir Robert Rich ill and Admiral Rooke sitting silent, the other Admiralty Commissioners in the Commons had a hard time of it, despite their plea that the delay was occasioned by a shortage of ready cash to pay for provisions. After seven hours of debate, there was a trial of strength upon a motion for adjournment. This the ministerialists lost 175 to 141, and then Aylmer's late sailing was voted 'prejudicial to England and a great mismanagement'.[39]

In the wake of this vote, some of the Admiralty Commissioners began to talk of resigning, while their enemies started to scent blood. Edward Harley observed that 'this is the first successful attack' and that 'there are things of a much higher nature that can be charged'.[40] Similarly, when Walter Moyle (who had lost his seat in the general election) heard of the division of 28 January, he wrote from Cornwall to his friend Hammond:[41]

Your vote against the Admiralty ... will certainly be the forerunner of the downfall of the baffled party. Now you have made a breach upon the body, it will be easy to hunt them singly from the herd, and run them down as you please. Ministry hunting is a noble sport. ... It is wisely done of you to flesh your young members with an easy prey, and reserve the Lords of the Treasury for the last triumph of the sessions.

With the Commons in this 'temper' towards 'men in employments', the Whig backbenchers asked all placemen to stay away from the Rose Club meeting of 4 February. In the absence of Montagu and his colleagues, the Rose Club decided not to venture upon an effort to secure the Dutch guards for William and simply to put off the consideration of the royal speech once more. But such a vote was 'not in their power, for the other party would have it take its course'. Harley took the lead on 6 February and proposed that the Commons answer the King's expressions of concern for the kingdom's security by bringing in a new bill for reforming the militia. And his suggestion 'was readily closed with' by the Whig country gentlemen, 'as if it were a good deliverance from a debate that was perhaps apprehended on all sides'.[42] Only the Lords were prepared to respond more positively. On the 8th, they voted 54 to 38 that they were 'ready and willing to enter into any expedient', short of a prorogation, 'consisting with the forms of parliament', for providing for the retention of the Dutch guards.[43]

However, even the suggestion of interference by the Lords was enough to make the Commons see red, and the leaders of the Country opposition exploited such reactions skilfully. In a preconcerted move on 10 February, Edward Harley presented a petition against a defaulting tax receiver, Michael Wickes, who had secured a seat in the Commons for Malmesbury (against Wharton's candidate) and was now standing upon his privilege as an M.P. against his creditors, including the crown. The younger Harley used this petition as grounds to seek leave to bring in a bill against placemen, so as to avoid like cases in future. Next, Sir John Bolles drew attention to the presence in St Stephen's Chapel of other financial officials who, he alleged, were ineligible to serve under the terms of the long-neglected section of the lottery act of 1694 that barred holders of new financial offices from sitting in the Commons.[44]

The Commons responded to this new assault against the Court by naming Edward Harley, John Howe, and Sir Richard Onslow to bring in a bill to limit the number of officials who could sit in the House and then proceeded to expel several of those whom Bolles had instanced. The first to be ousted was James Isaacson (one of the Commissioners of Stamped Paper) after a motion to adjourn was lost on the 10th by 164 to 111. Isaacson was followed on 13 February by his colleague on that commision, Henry Cornish, and the next day two more placemen were expelled. These proceedings, in Vernon's words, had 'a great tendency to garble the House', and since it was said that as many as thirty more members might be removed, these endangered M.P.s were kept 'in awe'.[45]

It was under these conditions that both sides mustered all their available supporters for what was to prove the 'tuggingest' day of the 1698–99 session. At issue on 18 February was the report of the committee of the whole's resolution of 4 February for 15,000 men for the fleet, and on the first question the ministerialists carried that figure 189 to 184. But then an amendment to specify that all must be 'seamen' was moved and approved 187 to 178. This meant that the 3,000 marines would have to be removed from the establishment and that the King would be saddled with a fleet substantially larger than he had desired.[46]

Two days later on 20 February, still another placeman was expelled by a vote of 184 to 133, as the opposition returned to the attack. The offensive they mounted now was three-pronged. First, there was the place bill brought in by Onslow on the 20th. This differed from its predecessors of William's second parliament in being a selective measure. The Treasury Commissioners, the Secretaries of State, and certain other major civil officials and military officers (approximately forty altogether) would remain eligible to sit in the Commons, but all those not so specified would have been unconditionally barred.[47] Second, there was the continuing inquiry into naval maladministration, which was being directed now more and more against Orford personally.[48] And third, there was the old East India Company's attempt to regain some of the ground it had lost the previous year to its rivals. What the old Company requested in its petition to the Commons on 25 February was the enactment of a statute to secure the continuance of its right to trade as a separate entity until the end of the twenty-one-year term of the royal charter of 1693. Until Montagu had thrown the government's weight behind the interlopers in 1698, the struggle over the control of the East India trade had not divided the Commons along partisan lines. But now, the old Company's petition was supported, at least in Sir Richard Cocks's estimation, by 'those that were for distressing the government', and leave for such a bill was voted 175 to 148 on the 27th as Francis Gwyn joined Sir Thomas Cook in telling for the majority.[49]

Not all the opposition's projects proved successful. After the Commons passed the new place bill on 15 March, the Lords never proceeded beyond a first reading. Then, too, the Commons themselves voted down the old East India Company's bill by 149 to 139 when it was read a second time on 9 March. Furthermore, on the 15th the House also rejected 141 to 140 a motion to condemn Orford for peculation in provisioning the fleet when he had been in command in the Mediterranean. Admittedly, the outcomes of the divisions on 9 and 15 March were somewhat fortuitous. The backers of the East India bill claimed that the Court had procured its defeat by luring their younger colleagues to the Cockpit on the 9th to see the baiting of a tiger by a pack of mastiffs, so allowing 'the lion Montagu an opportunity to prey' in St Stephen's Chapel, though this story was denied by Cocks who noted 'there were as many of [one] side' absent 'as of the other side'.[50] Similarly, Orford's escape, despite Thomas Papillon's vigorous condemnation of his victualling accounts, was facilitated when it accidentally emerged during the debate on the 15th that the Admiral had sworn to the truth of his expenditures before he received payment for them. Then, too, it was reported that George Churchill, hitherto one of Orford's most severe critics, was persuaded by his brother Marlborough to absent himself that day, while the teller for the majority on the 16th reckoned he had gained two additional votes by an accidental 'overreach in the counting'.[51] At best, then, these votes were holding actions by the ministerialists, and so was the rejection 164 to 160 a few days later of a motion to address William to dismiss the present Admiralty Commissioners.[52]

Certainly, none of the Commons' divisions of early and mid-March provided any grounds for William's new attempt to secure an abridgement of the disbanding act. Those to whom he broached his move warned him against it. None the less, on 18 March William sent a handwritten message to the Commons by Lord Ranelagh to inform them that his Dutch guards were ready to embark and would leave 'immediately, unless, out of consideration to him, the House be disposed to find a way for continuing them longer in his service'.[53]

The King's initiative was coldly received. Some spoke of sending Ranelagh to the Tower, but the fact that the message was in William's own hand and the consideration 'that the King could do no wrong' persuaded the lower House to let that motion fall. Harley took the occasion to jibe at the ministers, observing ironically that they could not be presumed to have advised it, 'at least those of them that were members, for if they had desired the continuance of the Dutch here they could have proposed it when they had so many opportunities of doing it regularly, and with greater prospects of success, while the disbanding bill was depending in the House'.[54] Howe went further in asserting that even were it possible to repeal part of an act so recently passed, to give foreigners any preference over natives would be undesirable. In the end, a motion to appoint a day to consider the King's message was rejected without a division on the 18th, and then a select committee was named to draft a representation of the reasons why the Commons could not comply. The text that Lord Norris brought in two days later was in the King's and in others' opinion 'a very impertinent one'. Yet efforts to soften it were unavailing on the 20th. First, a motion to recommit was defeated 175 to 156, and then a motion to delete a reference to William's 1688 declarations was lost 163 to 157.[55]

Despite this new rebuff, William did not revive his idea of withdrawing from England, and the Dutch regiments sailed without him. But his obviously unwilling compliance was hardly designed to put the Commons in any good humour as they struggled to finish their work on supply, and there was a good deal of foot-dragging over making good deficiencies in the yield of previous parliamentary grants. When this problem was first debated in late February, Howe went so far as to say that 'this was a good parliament and that a good parliament was not obliged to maintain the credit of a bad one, such as the last'.[56] Even so, not all were as irresponsible as Howe, and eventually the Commons on 17 April agreed upon a miscellaneous collection of duties, chiefly on paper and parchment (to be given for five years), which would almost suffice to pay the interest charges on the loans that had been necessitated by these deficiencies.[57]

However, the clauses that the Commons added to the paper bill and to the three-shilling land tax (which was to cover the costs of disbanding and the estimates for 1699) were highly objectionable to the King. The amendment inserted in the land tax bill on 19 April was to establish a commission to take account of the forfeited estates in Ireland, as a preliminary to their disposal by parliament. A list of commissioners was also included in the bill. The Commons agreed that none of the seven commissioners was to be an M.P., but in the ballot two of the leading Irish opponents of the Huguenot regiments and the pamphleteer John Trenchard garnered the most votes.[58] The amendment inserted in the paper duty bill also concerned the Irish forfeitures; it imposed penalties on any who disobeyed the warrants issued by the parliamentary commissioners in the course of their inquiries.

These tacks to supply bills did not go down well with the peers. Although a motion to delete the additions to the land tax bill failed by half a dozen votes on 27 April, the tack to the paper bill was successfully excised. Yet, rather than accept the Lords' alteration of a supply measure, the Commons allowed the paper duty bill to die.[59]

All in all, when the King came to Westminster on 5 May 1699 to bring 'this miserable session' to an end, he was not in a mood to give thanks for anything, save for the members' departure.[60] Thus, he prorogued parliament saying:[61]

If any thing shall be found wanting for our safety, the support of the public credit ... and for discharge of the debts occasioned by the war, or towards the advancing of trade, the suppressing of vice, and the employing of the poor, which were all the things I proposed to your consideration when we met first, I cannot doubt but that effectual care will be taken of them next winter, and I wish no inconvenience may happen in the meantime.

Although parliament had failed to act on most of the King's recommendations, a rash of private bills had been passed; of the eighty-five acts approved, only twenty-six were public bills. One of the more notable of the public statutes was Seymour's Irish woollens bill, adopted after the Dublin parliament failed to impose sufficiently heavy export duties on Irish textiles to satisfy English producers. Also approved, after virtually 'every card in the lobbyist's deck' was played, was a measure to open up the Russia Company to the Baltic merchants and the tobacco contractors dealing with the Czar.[62] On the other side of the ledger, the unsuccessful bills included a new attempt to regulate the press. This was passed by the Lords in January 1699, with backing from the bishops including Burnet, but it was rejected by the Commons on 1 February.[63] Another 'reform' bill, Sir John Phillips's measure for suppressing vice and profaneness, also failed in the Commons as it was condemned by some as an 'inquisition' and disparaged by others who argued that 'those that would not take the old and new testament for a rule of life would never be reformed by an act of parliament'.[64]

As the 1698–99 session drew to a close, there was speculation that William would not meet again with his fourth parliament, and the sharpness of the King's parting words seemed to indicate he was resolved upon a dissolution. However, some of his servants, notably Somers and Vernon, feared that a new parliament 'would be worse' than the present one, and by-elections held during the recess tended to confirm their gloomy predictions.[65] Whether William was seriously considering a dissolution is not clear, but he showed no eagerness to make drastic changes in the ministry at the session's end. Even had he been able to find a Tory alternative to the Junto, it is not likely he would have embraced it. In late March 1699, Somers informed Shrewsbury that 'the behaviour of one party of men this session has convinced the King (as he says often and very plainly) that he himself is aimed at, and not ministers or party otherwise than in order to prejudice him'. As Burnet later recalled, 'many hard things' had been said during the session against William himself, and it was evident that one of the sorest points was his seeming preference for things Dutch—his guards, his courtiers, his estate at Loo.[66]

Yet, if William was not prepared to call a new parliament or to embrace the

Tories, he also showed no sign of reconsidering his views on Wharton after Shrewsbury finally returned the seals to him in December 1698. All that was left, then, in the spring of 1699 was a resort to that 'pieced business' which Somers had foreseen with dismay the previous autumn—that is, a reversion to the type of composite ministry, lacking both unity and direction, that had characterised the early years of the reign.[67] Thus, the Earl of Jersey (the former Lord Villiers), who had served faithfully in the peace negotiations and was now on close terms with Albemarle, was (as had been expected for months) named to succeed Shrewsbury as principal Secretary; Leeds was finally dismissed, after he refused to resign, and the Earl of Pembroke, who had served inconspicuously and unobjectionably as Lord Privy Seal since 1692, was elevated to the Lord Presidency; and Viscount Lonsdale (the former Sir John Lowther of Lowther) reluctantly came out of retirement to serve as Lord Privy Seal.[68]

These three peers were nominally Tories, yet each was primarily a loyal servant of the King. Hence, when there had been talk during the middle of the 1697–98 session of the appointments of Lonsdale and Jersey, Secretary Vernon had expressed a concern that 'we be not picking out moderate men so long till the warm, sprightly men on both sides grow discontented'. But by the spring of 1699, Vernon himself was urging Shrewsbury to do his utmost for 'moderation' when the Duke met the King, first at Newmarket and later at Windsor.[69]

The main difficulty Vernon anticipated at the end of the 1698–99 session was keeping the Junto in temper. It was not only that the leading Whig ministers had no desire for and little confidence in a 'pieced business'; in addition, Montagu, Orford, and some of their associates seemed to prefer being 'easy' in lucrative, lesser places to soldiering on in responsible posts in the face of parliamentary attacks. Montagu was looking forward to taking up the Auditorship in the Exchequer that his brother was keeping warm for him, Smith had high hopes of gaining a tellership that had recently been vacated by death, and Orford—whose joint tenure of the Navy Treasurership and an Admiralty Commissionership had been condemned by the Commons during the last session—seemed inclined to resign the latter or, perhaps, to retire altogether.[70] The King, then, went out of his way, with aid from Somers and Shrewsbury, to keep these men in their present places. Montagu was given permission to hold the Auditor's place in conjunction with his seat on the Treasury Board, Smith was induced to remain on that Board by being made Chancellor of the Exchequer in succession to Montagu, and Orford was persuaded to stay on as head of the Admiralty and to give up the Treasurership on the understanding that he would have the principal voice in selecting both his new colleagues on a reconstituted Admiralty Commission and his successor as Treasurer.[71] At the same time, the vacant Teller's place was given to Godolphin's son, who had recently been wed to one of Marlborough's daughters.

The arrangements that the King had agreed to in order to keep the Junto in place were jeopardised in mid-May by Orford's sudden change of mind. Apparently his choler was aroused by two developments. One was an imbroglio over the choice of his successor as Treasurer of the Navy. Sir Thomas Littleton was soliciting for the position (which his father once held), but Orford wanted it for Lord Hartington. The second was William's reluctance to drop Admiral Rooke from the Admiralty Commission, though Orford felt that Rooke had not come to his defence during the previous session and would not accept Rooke's justification for his conduct. Even so, Orford never gave the King the chance to decide which, if he must choose, of the two Admirals he preferred to retain in his service. Instead, Orford abruptly resigned from the Admiralty on 15 May and then complained bitterly to any who would listen that all his requests to William had been refused and that Sunderland still 'governed everything'. His resignation was followed by those of all his remaining colleagues at the Admiralty except Rooke and Rich. At the same time, Littleton was about to resign from the Treasury Board to take up the Treasurership of the Navy, while Pelham—more and more at odds with his three Junto colleagues—was to be ousted.[72]

The upshot, then, was a considerable reshuffle of places, in which the Earl of Tankerville, head of the Board of Trade since its inception in 1696 and a leading Whig spokesman in the Lords, was the key figure. In March 1699, Vernon was informed that Orford, presuming there was no chance for Wharton, would have preferred Tankerville to Jersey for the seals. Had the Junto united behind Tankerville in 1698, probably the King would have acquiesced, but by early 1699 he had settled upon Jersey. So Tankerville was now offered the chance to succeed Orford as first Commissioner of the Admiralty. Rather than take up so exposed a post, the Earl reportedly declared that 'he would be drawn through a horse pond'.[73] In turn, the headship of the Admiralty was offered to another Commissioner of Trade, the Earl of Bridgwater (Lord Winchester's brother-in-law), and he in his dutiful, plodding way accepted. Then, the Board over which Bridgwater was to preside was reduced in size from seven to five members, and the two incumbents Rooke and Rich were joined by Lord Haversham and Admiral David Mitchell in a commission of 'his Majesty's own framing'.[74]

However, William had to restrain his personal preferences in reconstituting the Treasury Board so as to keep Montagu and Smith from resigning. This consideration ruled out the selection of Richard Hill, a protégé of Lords Rochester and Ranelagh, who had forsaken a clerical career to serve very capably as deputy Paymaster in Flanders during the war. Instead, Tankerville was chosen along with Henry Boyle, who had supported ministerial measures consistently since his grandfather Lord Burlington died early in 1698, to fill the vacancies left by Littleton's and Pelham's departures. In addition, Montagu was authorised to offer Fox's seat at that Board to Sir William Blackett, one of the Whig country gentlemen who had spoken against disbanding on 18 January 1699, but Sir William declined and so Sir Stephen remained, at least for the moment.[75] At the same time, the vacant seats at the Board of Trade were bestowed upon the Whig Earl of Stamford (who had refused a similar offer three years before) and upon the courtier Lord Lexington (who had recently returned from his embassy to Vienna).

Thus, the new appointees in the spring of 1699 included a motley array of Whigs and courtiers, while of the Junto Somers remained as Lord Chancellor, Montagu as first lord of the Treasury, and Wharton as Comptroller of the Household. And it was a measure of the disfavour into which Leeds and all his clan had fallen that the King displaced the Duke himself and ousted Charles Bertie from the Treasurership of the Ordnance in order to satisfy the pretensions of Harry Mordaunt, whose candidacy was backed strongly by Shrewsbury and Wharton.[76] So when William sailed for Holland on 2 June 1699, he left behind a commission of Lords Justices that included three new faces—Lonsdale, Jersey, and Bridgwater in place of Orford, Dorset, and Romney.

Romney was omitted from the commission of Lords Justices so that he might

accompany William across the Channel to act as first Gentleman of the Bedchamber now that Portland had again withdrawn from Court. Portland's first
retirement from William's service in early 1697 had ended when he accepted the
embassy to Paris in January 1698, but he had never come to terms with Albemarle
and now he could not be dissuaded from withdrawing for good. The King was
greatly distressed personally at Portland's decision which also came at a delicate
time in the renewed negotiations with Louis over the disposition of Carlos II's
domains. The first Partition Treaty had been nullified by the sudden death of the
young Electoral Prince of Bavaria in January 1699, and Portland had been kept
busy during the spring of 1699 in discussions with Tallard in London over some
alternative arrangement.[77] But despite William's unhappiness at Portland's
departure, he was not prepared to give up Albemarle in order to keep his old
friend. Nor was the King willing to forgo his trip to Loo 'to breathe a little', and
so he ignored Sunderland's unsolicited warning of April 1699 that his departure
would confirm the prevailing opinion 'he can not bear the being in England when
it is possible for him to help it'.[78]

The setbacks of the 1698–99 session and the King's dismay at Portland's
retirement were partly balanced by two other developments. One was the tentative agreement that William reached on the eve of his trip to the Continent with
Louis on a new division of the Spanish monarchy; the other was the prospect of
Shrewsbury's return to office. Precisely when and under what circumstances the
Duke 'promised' to take the Chamberlain's staff is not known, but in May 1699
Shrewsbury was already arranging to visit Sunderland at Althorp.[79] Marlborough
did warn the Duke in early June from London that 'so much jealousy reigns' here
that there is 'little encouragement' to 'meddle with anything', but when Shrewsbury and Sunderland met later that month they were 'very well satisfied with
one another'.[80] Apparently, Sunderland took this opportunity to renew his
offers to labour on the Junto's behalf in conjunction with Shrewsbury, though
the Earl was fearful that Orford especially would be implacable. Sunderland put
it this way to the Duke in early August:[81]

I believe nothing is more certain than that the moderation you mention and intend is the
only means to do good, provided the true measures are carried on steadily, which is not
practicable, unless there is first established a confidence between the King and those he
chiefly employs, that no jealousies may be of either side.

But Sunderland's was not an easy prescription to fill, especially as Shrewsbury's
activities were arousing the suspicions of the Junto, who were as yet uncertain
about the Duke's intentions. Shrewsbury had arranged to meet the Junto in mid-
August at Boughton (the Earl of Montagu's Northamptonshire mansion), but
only Charles Montagu of the four eventually appeared. Moreover, when the
Duke arrived in town on the 23rd, he found that the Chancellor had left only
six hours earlier to take the waters at Tunbridge Wells. So Vernon, after talking
to both Shrewsbury and Montagu, had to report to William on the 25th that
'these meetings that were thought to be big with intrigue have produced nothing'.
'Nothing has been communicated to the Duke of what they [the Junto] proposed
to themselves, so he likewise left it in doubts what he will do in the winter.'[82] The
King was greatly concerned to learn of the 'cold reception' Shrewsbury had
encountered, but his fears were eased by Vernon's account of the meeting between the Duke and the Lord Chancellor at Tunbridge Wells in early September.

The two spoke cordially and frankly, and Somers expressed 'a real satisfaction in the thoughts he had of seeing [Shrewsbury] in business' once more.[83]

With the stage set for Shrewsbury's re-entry, it only remained for William's return to England in late October to end the Duke's retirement. Despite the usual political speculation, the announcement of his appointment came as a surprise to many. Harley, for one, did not know what to make of it, and from Herefordshire he wrote inquiringly to his 'oracle' Trumbull: 'Is he a volunteer or pressed into the service? Is he to scaffold up the old building or be a master workman in erecting new?' In strikingly similar tones, Moyle in Cornwall asked of Hammond: 'Is he once more to be placed at the head of a sinking party, or is he to be put again between the two horns of the monarch's dilemma, the seals or the Tower?'[84] Nor was the political scene much clarified by two other pre-sessional appointments. One was the selection of George Churchill to succeed the deceased Sir Robert Rich at the Admiralty; Vernon believed this to be a sensible choice, but it put Orford 'out of humour' once more.[85] The second was necessitated by Montagu's resignation from the Treasury Commission and his installation as Auditor of the Receipt. Somers did 'not wholly approve' Montagu's decision, but he could not dissuade him, and on the evening of 15 November (with parliament scheduled to reassemble the next day) William accepted Montagu's resignation.[86] Tankerville succeeded as first lord of the Treasury, and Richard Hill, at the recommendation of his 'constant patrons' Rochester and Ranelagh, was named as the fifth commissioner.[87]

Rochester's part in Hill's appointment was only one sign of his renewed favour. The King dined with him on 3 November, and a long conference between the two at Kensington a few days later revived talk of that Earl's return to the King's service. Meanwhile, Harley had arrived in town, and on the 11th Vernon called at his lodgings to arrange a meeting between him and Shrewsbury. No account of the Duke's talk with Harley survives, but any tentative understanding that they might have reached was hindered by the frailties of nature. On 13 November, the ailing Paul Foley died at his seat in Herefordshire, and Harley hastily left town. At the same time, Shrewsbury's 'indisposition' flared up again. Even before he saw Harley, a new bout of haemorrhaging had led the Duke to talk of going abroad for the winter. He did remain in town for the opening of the 1699–1700 session, but on 21 November he retreated once more to the country.[88]

Shrewsbury's departure left William in difficulties. The alterations he had made at the end of the 1698–99 session, even supplemented by those announced on the eve of the current one, did not provide the necessary manpower to implement effectively any specific 'scheme'. The appointments of Jersey and Lonsdale, and also of Hill and Churchill, when taken in conjunction with the resignations of Orford and Montagu, certainly diluted the Whig element in the ministry. At the same time, Shrewsbury's withdrawal, coupled with the failure by William to designate any new 'minister' such as Rochester or any new 'manager' of the Commons such as Harley, left the composite administration without clear-cut leadership in the cabinet or in the Commons. Nor were such difficulties likely to be overcome by the King's innovation of a 'drawing room' at Kensington, with the Princess presiding as hostess, every Monday evening during the 1699–1700 session, even though this new departure had the merits of giving Anne at least a ceremonial role and of making William a little more accessible to members of parliament.[89]

It would appear, then, that William intended no more this session than to stand—as Somers had advised in September—'on the defensive'.[90] Montagu stayed on in the cabinet despite his departure from the Treasury, and he was joined there by the newcomers Tankerville, Bridgwater, Jersey, and Lonsdale. Then, too, the speech the King delivered to parliament on 16 November was much more cordial in tone than his parting words of 4 May. He began by excusing his summons of the members out of their 'countries' with a reference to the need to provide 'for the safety of the kingdom by sea and land' for the coming year 'before we are at the end of what was granted for that purpose the past session'. He spoke next of the advisability of taking care of the government's debts and deficiencies, and he instanced a sum owing to Prince George of Denmark arising out of arrangements made in conjunction with the Treaty of Altena of 1689. The specific mention of this debt can be read as another sign of William's desire to improve relations with the Princess, while to make his financial requests go down the smoother he stressed he sought nothing 'for any personal use of mine'. In addition, he spoke of smuggling, 'the increase of the poor', and 'the depravation of manners' as problems deserving legislative attention. Such a discourse, the King observed to the Pensionary, might be expected to have a good effect elsewhere, but 'people here have such a strange temper that I dare not form any expectation'.[91]

William's caution was borne out in the months that followed. When the Commons took up his opening speech, Seymour, Howe, and Musgrave quickly fastened upon the contrast between his words now and those of May 1699. They complained both that the ministers had given distorted accounts to the King of the Commons' proceedings during the 1698–99 session and that the Junto's followers in the county commissions misrepresented the majority's resolutions to the country.[92] The lower House responded to these charges by agreeing without a division on 28 November to address William against such misinterpretations. Moreover, committees were named to examine all new borough charters granted during the reign and all changes made in the county commissions since Somers had been entrusted with the great seal.[93]

The Lord Chancellor soon found himself the target of another set of complaints. These arose out of the commission issued under the great seal in early 1697 to Captain William Kidd, whose subsequent piracies had already given rise during the 1698–99 session to fears of an attack upon the ministers.[94] Kidd's venture, which had been initiated as a result of requests from the old East India Company for protection of its vessels against freebooters in the Indian Ocean, was sponsored by Orford, Shrewsbury, and Somers, and they were to receive the lion's share of any pirate booty that the Captain seized. But the project had gone awry when Kidd took to piracy himself, and the subscribers and their agent Lord Bellomont (now Governor of New York and New England) had had to exert themselves to have the Captain captured.

Kidd's affair was raised in the Commons on 2 December by Arthur Moore, a prominent figure in the old Company, and Howe and Musgrave promptly seconded Moore's demand for an inquiry. Their strategy was first to get the venture condemned and then to turn upon Kidd's sponsors, who had had the grant of the pirates' booty passed under the names of some of their personal servants. But after the Commons adjourned on 2 December, Orford, Montagu, Smith, and Boyle met at the Lord Chancellor's, and they decided to 'own' who the sponsors were, to defend the legality of the grant, and to excuse the scheme as a well-intentioned mistake that had been partially retrieved by Governor Bellomont's capture of Kidd in July 1699. As part of their defence, additional papers detailing Kidd's seizure were readied for submission to the Commons, and on the 4th the lower House accepted these materials as laid before them by Secretary Vernon. Thus, the stage was set for a full-scale debate on the affair.[95]

The royal grant to Kidd's sponsors was debated for over nine hours on 6 December in terms of a prepared question brought in by Sir Bartholomew Shower which condemned grants of pirates' goods as 'dishonourable to the King, against the law of nations, contrary to the laws and statutes of the realm, invasive of property, and destructive of trade and commerce'.[96] After Vernon recounted the history of the venture and identified the subscribers, the principal point argued by the forty or so M.P.s who spoke was the legality of the grant, and only Shower, Harcourt, and Edward Harley among the many lawyers in the House were willing to maintain the charge. Finally at 9 p.m. the question was put and defeated 189 to 133—a sizeable majority, so Vernon judged, 'as this House is constituted'.[97] Certainly, the opposition leaders were disappointed. There were complaints that nearly sixty of their friends had either 'sneaked' out before the division or 'had no patience and so went out', and Howe denounced the deserters as 'a crew of rogues'.[98]

Even 'more remarkable', in Vernon's view, was the defeat on 13 December of a motion for the removal of Burnet from his Preceptorship to the Duke of Gloucester. The Bishop, who had been chosen despite Anne's dislike of him, had always had many detractors. So when Sir John Bolles and Sir John Packington set upon him on the occasion of a debate upon Prince George's debt on the 12th, their reflections put the Commons in a jocular mood. But when those two Churchmen, with Seymour's backing, sought to press their assault the next day, the motion against Burnet was rejected 173 to 133, in spite of his Scots birth, his alleged advocacy of 'conquest' justifications of the Revolution, and his supposed Socinian leanings.[99]

These and lesser checks to Junto foes, among them the division on 18 December on Foot Onslow's election for Guildford that was carried in his favour 185 to 109, 'though all the grandees of the other side divided against him', gave Vernon additional grounds for optimism. As he wrote to Shrewsbury after that division, 'one may observe what a strength there is like to be in the Whig party, if they do not moulder again by being put upon unpopular things'.[100] To avoid new causes of odium in the Commons, the ministerialists seemed determined to keep on the defensive, even when their opponents sought to provoke them. They left it to others to take the lead upon supply. Furthermore, after the report of the commissioners on the Irish forfeitures was presented on 15 December, Montagu and Coningsby spoke 'very frankly' for a motion to bring in a bill to resume the King's grants, and the former declared his own grant would not influence him.[101] In this way, they hoped to defuse a potentially explosive issue which had been rendered even more volatile now that it was clear how large the grants were that William had made to Portland and Albemarle. The ministerialists also seemed to be intent on steering clear of a discussion of the charges levelled against the report by a minority of three commissioners. Though the three sent letters to the Speakers of both Houses in which they made various accusations against their four colleagues, among them that they had maliciously included in the report an account of the King's grant to Lady Orkney despite the fact that the lands she had been given were not forfeitures but the Duke of York's Irish estates, no attempt was made at first in either the Commons or the Lords to take up these criticisms.[102]

'The heat of the session seem[ed] much abated', then, when the Commons adjourned for Christmas on 22 December 1699, and attention shifted from parliament to the Court where both Sunderland and Shrewsbury were expected. Sunderland's trip had been planned for some time. After a year of negotiations, a marriage between his heir Lord Spencer and Marlborough's daughter Anne had been agreed upon in September 1699, and the ceremony had been scheduled to be held in town in early January 1700. Shrewsbury's journey, however, seems to have been taken on impulse, and, after meeting William at Hampton Court in late December, the Duke did not stay for William's return there in early January. Pleading a relapse, Shrewsbury withdrew to the country again, and the meeting with the Duke that Sunderland had hoped for had to be postponed indefinitely. Yet Sunderland stayed on in town, probably because William asked him to carry on the efforts to reach an understanding with Harley that Shrewsbury had made before the beginning of the session.[103]

Harley's pre-eminence in the Commons this year was more marked than ever before. As James Lowther (Lonsdale's nephew, M.P. for Carlisle, and an official in the Ordnance) remarked in January 1700: 'Mr Harley now manages the whole business of supply, and the House hath hitherto entirely approved of his scheme.'[104] Harley's 'scheme', so far as supply was concerned, was clear enough. First, the estimates were to be reduced, and so he took the lead in proposing only 7,000 men for the fleet on 20 December. Then on 12 January, Harley 'maintained almost himself' a long debate over the size of the 'ordinary' of the Navy, and in the end a sharp cutback was made in official requests.[105] Yet, though it had been generally expected before the session began that the large proportion of cavalry William had kept up among the 7,000 troops of 1699 would provoke complaints, when the army estimates were discussed on 20 January Harley showed himself averse to 'disputes about the horse or foot' and proposed simply that £300,000 should again be voted for guards and garrisons.[106] Second, he was intent upon reducing current taxation below the 1699 level. His view was that a two-shilling levy on land, when supplemented by the otherwise unappropriated customs duties, the surplus of the civil list revenues, and an improved yield from the excise, would suffice to raise the £1,300,000 in estimates for 1700 that had been approved by late January.[107] Third, Harley was determined that the Irish forfeitures, which the commissioners calculated to be worth about £1,600,000 at thirteen years' purchase, should be applied to the payment of the debts and deficiencies. Thus, when Vernon and his colleagues, under pressure from William to secure an amendment to the Irish forfeitures bill to reserve one-third of the estates to his own disposal, proposed such a clause on 18 January, Harley delivered the 'best' speech of the day against it. Harley, so Sir Richard Cocks noted, 'wondered anybody had confidence to demand only a part [for the King] for we intended to give him all', and he argued that it was for William's 'honour to have the public obligations made good' and contended the Commons 'ought to be just before we were bountiful'.[108] As Vernon had anticipated, Harley was expressing the sentiments of a sizeable majority, and the ministerialists did not even venture a division.

In any case, the ministerialists had been dispirited anew by the Commons' proceedings during the week before the debate on the forfeitures. Their deliberate attempt to involve the lower House in the new controversy over the Scottish East India Company's settlement at Darien had been successfully challenged by Harley, who believed that the Commons 'should not declare themselves one way or another, so as they may reserve themselves to be arbiters' between William and his northern subjects. The Scots in 1699 were nearly up in arms over the measures the King had taken in pursuance of English parliamentary resolutions of 1695–1696 and more recent Spanish diplomatic protests to discourage that Company's colony at Darien. Yet Harley criticised as needlessly provocative Sir Rowland Gwynne's motion of 15 January to have the Commons' earlier address against the Scottish company read. The highly-charged debate that day concluded with the rejection of Gwynne's motion 191 to 190, and all that was done was to order a recent pamphlet defending the Darien venture to be burnt by the common hangman.[109]

The ministerialists also suffered another setback on 15 January. Two days earlier, they had reacted to a motion by Sir John Leveson-Gower to have the Irish commissioners' report printed by openly criticising its biases. Gower's motion was dropped, but Montagu went too far in asserting that the majority on the commission had been instructed by some English M.P.s to include Lady Orkney's grant on the grounds that 'the report would signify nothing without it and that [it] would reflect on the King more than any other grant'.[110] As he made this charge, the Chancellor of the Exchequer appeared to be looking right at Harcourt. In turn, after Harcourt and the other concerned M.P.s had time over the weekend to check their correspondence to be sure that they had not in fact been so indiscreet, they responded on 15 January with angry demands upon Montagu for proof of his accusation. Under pressure to name his sources, Montagu finally pointed to Methuen, only to have the Irish Lord Chancellor claim Montagu had misunderstood what he had told him. The upshot was that Montagu's allegation was condemned as 'false and scandalous', the minority commissioners were discredited for originating the story Methuen had retailed to Montagu, and Montagu and Methuen remained at odds with one another for the rest of the session.[111]

It was these discouragements, coupled with the general support for a complete resumption of the Irish grants, that led the ministerialists to avoid dividing for the King's third on 18 January. Nor did they contest Howe's two resolutions, offered in response to the motion for the King's third, that (1) the grants had increased the nation's debts and (2) those who had either advised them or been instrumental in passing them had acted in derogation of the King and contrary to their official trust and duty. Montagu and Smith simply retorted that other members of parliament, referring particularly to Godolphin and Seymour during their service at the Treasury, had been party to the passing of the Irish grants. And so, as Vernon lamented to Shrewsbury in late January, 'these late proceedings give the other party a great triumph and the Whigs are miserably run down'.[112]

With 'some men ... humbled who were insolent and others ... ready to take both their places and behaviour', the only good point Sunderland could discern in late January 1700 was that it seemed, now that a two-shilling land tax bill had been ordered, the session would soon be over.[113] However, before it finally came to an end nearly three months later, the ministerialists had to endure many more defeats. One galling setback came on 9 February over the bill to incorporate the old East India Company for the remainder of the twenty-one-year term of its 1693 charter. This year, by contrast to the last, the ministerialists did not even attempt to oppose the measure and they simply sought to add to it a clause to safeguard the new Company's privileges. Yet this amendment was rejected by the Commons 165 to 140. A second rebuff was the Commons' approval of an addition to the combined bill for resumption of the Irish grants and imposition of the two-shilling land tax. This amendment, moved by Edward Harley, was to bar all Excise officers from sitting in the Commons, and it was accepted 158 to 98 on 18 March. Also included in the land tax measure was another clause, moved by Robert Harley, which was to empower the government to farm the collection of the excise. The chief reason offered for this proposal was the inefficiency of direct collection, but Vernon suspected the real concern was to get rid of the many sub-ordinate excisemen, since it was thought 'elections are more influenced by those officers than any others'.[114] A third victory for the opposition came on 26 March when the Commons, who had by then dropped their earlier bill to establish £200 in landed income as a qualification for service as a Justice of the Peace, agreed to address the King against the many changes in the commissions of the peace made since Somers had taken the great seal. By a vote of 119 to 113, it was agreed to request William to restore to the bench 'gentlemen of quality and good estates'. Moreover, when the ministerialists moved an amendment to limit the restoration to men 'well affected' to the King and his government, it was rejected 120 to 112.[115]

For all their many victories in divisions against the Court and its Whig servants, the 'other gentlemen', as Vernon referred to them, did not even now 'appear so united as to make a fixed party'.[116] Matthew Prior had remarked a year earlier to Portland that 'those who have obstructed the King's business' and 'compose that which they call the country party' included many who 'are and have been always Whigs'. Furthermore, the shrewder among these Whig country gentlemen regarded their present Tory allies, in Walter Moyle's words, as fit to be 'our protectors in the House of Commons' but to be avoided as 'our governors in the ministry'.[117] This wariness of the Tory leaders, combined with respect for the target, made many backbench Whigs reluctant to support the renewed assault upon Lord Chancellor Somers that was initiated by James Brydges on 13 February 1700.

Brydges, an unsuccessful suitor for a place on the Excise Board in 1698, was the son of the Jacobite Lord Chandos of Herefordshire.[118] Montagu at that time had encouraged him to oppose Paul Foley's candidacy for re-election for the city of Hereford, but after being disappointed in his designs in London Brydges had been returned with Foley. His first act as a member of the 1698–1700 parliament had been to vote against Littleton as Speaker; since then, he had been active as a member of the opposition. And now Brydges, invoking the Commons' resolutions of 18 January against the passing of the Irish grants, proposed an additional resolution that 'the procuring or obtaining of grants of estates, belonging to the crown, by any public minister, concerned in the directing or passing such grants, to or for their own use or benefit, whilst the nation lay under the heavy taxes of the late war, was highly injurious to his Majesty, prejudicial to the state, and a violation of the trust reposed in them'.[119]

Although Brydges, and others who backed his convoluted resolution, denied it was aimed at the English fee farms Somers had accepted in 1697 to sustain the dignity of his new peerage, these disclaimers were swept aside by Sir Richard Cocks and other Whig country gentlemen. We will, Cocks avowed, 'do as much for the public and go as far as any', but we will not support 'anything that has any private look or end in it'. With the Whigs again rallying to the Lord Chancellor's defence, as they had in Kidd's affair, Brydges's motion was rejected in the largest division of the session by 232 to 182. And Harley, in deference to such sentiments, averred in a renewed debate over royal grants on 15 February that 'he was not for removing the ministry but for laying down such rules that might prevent these evils for the future', so provoking Thomas Coke (a staunch Derbyshire Churchman newly returned in 1698) to stalk out angrily from St Stephen's Chapel 'cursing all house meeting dogs, meaning Robert Harley'.[120]

Just what Harley himself was aiming at is not easy to discern. He was in touch with Sunderland again, and rumours went the rounds that he might be named Secretary in place of Jersey, who was already weary of the burdens of his new post. Vernon professed his own willingness to lay down if that would facilitate a composition with Harley, and he reported in late February that Montagu 'has talked of late as if he wished' Harley 'were in employment'. However, Sunderland found Harley still 'averse to the meddling with any employment', and Vernon reckoned that even were Harley interested, 'he would not put himself under my Lord Chancellor or Mr Montagu, who are still called the ministers, though there are none that I see who take upon them any management'.[121] In all probability, Harley's chief concern at this juncture was to complete the destruction of the Junto's hold upon the royal administration while maintaining the precarious unity of the motley band of Churchmen and Whigs who accepted him as their 'general'.[122] Hence, as Vernon was speculating about Harley's intentions, Harley himself was writing to his father in early March to explain he could not yet leave London since 'the critical time of the session is now [and] all their arts are using towards ruining all [that] hath been done, by divisions, lies, and other usual methods'.[123]

In fact, the climax of the 1699–1700 session did not arrive until early April. Nor was it the Whig ministers who provoked the great crisis between the two Houses over the Irish forfeitures bill. Their fault, rather, was that they seemed to William to eschew any 'management', and his resentment of the Commons' majority and discontent with the Junto left him prey in the spring of 1700 to courtiers who were prepared to encourage the feelings he had long harboured against his fourth House of Commons. Certainly, it was generally assumed that Albemarle, Portland, and Lady Orkney were principally responsible for William's attempt to prevent the passage of the combined bill to resume the Irish forfeitures and to impose a two-shilling land tax.[124]

By the time the Commons finally sent the resumption bill up to the Lords on 2 April, it was loaded down with a host of amendments. Most were clauses to exempt particular grantees and purchasers of granted estates; these had been passed by the Commons despite their earlier resolution not to admit any individual petitions against the revocation. In addition, there were the Harleys' amendments to bar Excise officials from the Commons and to permit the farming of the excises. Hence, it was not difficult to rouse the peers against the bill. Some were personally affected by the intended resumption, others regarded the bill as an encroachment upon the King's prerogative, and most were already very sensitive on the subject of 'tacks' to money bills.

Although there was ample fuel among the peers to feed the flames, Sunderland had warned William that to encourage the Lords to reject or to obstruct the bill would be foolhardy. When the King ignored this advice, Somers and Marlborough sought to dissociate themselves from the attempt by absenting themselves from the Court and from the upper House. It was, then, Lonsdale and Wharton who were most active in 'stirring up' the peers to amend the bill, and while the former acted out of loyalty to his master's instructions, the latter was simply bent on making trouble. In turn, the Lord Privy Seal and the Comptroller were followed by several other cabinet councillors, particularly Archbishop Tenison and the Earl of Pembroke who 'came blindly into it, as supposing the King had some scheme in reserve for carrying on the public business' in case the measure was lost in a dispute between the two Houses.[125] And when the peers, with 'the court lords' in the van, voted 56 to 33 on 6 April to delete the clause excluding Excise officials from the Commons, the stage was set for what one observer described as the gravest confrontation between the Lords and the Commons since the Revolution.[126]

The Commons' response on 8 April was unequivocal. The peers' alterations were rejected *nemine contradicente*, the Irish commission's report was ordered to be printed, and a resolution was passed against any Privy Councillor who had secured 'exorbitant grants' for himself. There were also loud denunciations of the King's foreign servants and of the ministers, as well as talk of impeachments should the Lords persist. Yet on the 9th the upper House adhered to its amendment, though this vote was carried only by 47 to 34. Moreover, when Albemarle arrived a few minutes after that division, he explained that he had come to vote for dropping the amendment.[127]

Albemarle's change of mind seemed to indicate that William had taken alarm and was about to retreat. But having encouraged the peers to defend their privileges against the Commons, it was not so easy to get them to recede. Even after a free conference between the two Houses was held the afternoon of the 10th, the Lords seemed prepared to 'adhere' once more, and the Commons were informed they had done so by a vote of 40 to 37. At this report, Harley rose to declare[128]

that it was time to think of England and that since that was the last time probably they were to sit there, to show that they were not quite insensible. Then the word 'foreigners' in cabinets and councils wrought all up into high wrath, as locking of doors, and yet Harry B[oyle], attending to the duty incumbent, got out, frighted the principal Secretary out of his wits, Lord Jer[sey], that all the Dutch would be banished ...

Upon receipt of this news, Jersey sent off a message to William, who was waiting at the Cockpit with the robes of state so that he might be able to come quickly to Westminster Palace. William responded by giving Jersey permission to solicit the Archbishop and others to give up the contest. Meanwhile, the Lords had been occupied in examining the proxies on the previous division, and it appeared that there were six valid proxies for the negative and only three for the affirmative, so making the result of the division to 'adhere' a tie at 43 to 43. The Lords' usual rule of procedure was that in case of a tie, the question was to be treated as having been defeated, but now the peers began to quarrel about whether the question had been to desist from their amendment or to reject the entire bill. As the upper House tried to unravel this tangle, Jersey and Romney were busy urging members to change sides and agree to the Commons' bill without any changes. Nobody but the two courtiers themselves was prepared to do so, yet their switch and the deliberate departure of several of the bishops was sufficient. When the next division was finally called, there were 39 for agreeing with the Commons and only 34 against. Then the Lords promptly adjourned without waiting for William to come to them in order to pass the bill and so to put an immediate end to the session.[129]

In the meantime, there had been speeches in the Commons against Albemarle and Portland, but the opposition leaders did not 'prosecute them to a question, their business being, as they openly declared, to break the ministry'.[130] And once the news of the Lords' retreat reached St Stephen's Chapel, the principal fire was directed against Somers. Harcourt and Sir John Leveson-Gower were for impeaching the Lord Chancellor, but after Musgrave pointed out there would not be time this session to prosecute an impeachment, an address for his removal was proposed. Once again, however, Somers was defended both by his friends in office and by backbenchers such as Sir William Blackett, Richard Norton, and Lord Hartington, so the proposed address was rejected 167 to 106. Yet many of those who rallied to Somers were not prepared to speak or vote for William's foreign servants, and the result was that a ministerialist motion to adjourn was voted down 154 to 143. Thus, the long sitting of 10 April concluded with the uncontested passage of a resolution, proposed by Hartington, which called for the removal of all foreigners save Prince George from the King's 'councils' in England and Ireland.[131]

Had Jersey persuaded the Lords to await the King's arrival on 10 April, the 1699–1700 session could have been ended without this last affront to William. As it was, when the King came to Westminster the next morning, he made no parting speech, since he could not bring himself to express any thanks for the Irish bill. However, he did pass it, along with the bill to incorporate the old East India Company which he had postponed approving for nearly six weeks. This delay had not had the intended effect of promoting a compromise between the rival companies, but it did mean that of the sixty-two acts that reached the statute book this session sixty were passed on the 11th.

Among the new statutes were at least three others besides the Irish and East India measures which were unwelcome to the King. The act to prohibit the wearing of Indian textiles in England after September 1702 would satisfy vocal segments of the domestic industry, especially in East Anglia and London, who had been pressing for some such measure since the mid-1690s, but when the prohibition came into force it would reduce the yield of an important element of the customs. Furthermore the act to restrain 'the growth of popery', a product of an agitation led by Howe whose principal concern, so Vernon thought, was exposing the government's lenience towards its Catholic subjects, was likely to produce difficulties with foreign allies if it were rigorously enforced.[132]

Apart from the Irish bill, probably the most galling enactment to William of the 1699–1700 session was the statute to establish a commission of five to 'examine and determine' the debts of the army, the navy, and the transport service. Allegations that millions of pounds voted for the war had been embezzled or mis-spent had been made both in the Commons and in print, particularly by Charles Davenant who was now the opposition's chief author. Meanwhile, out of doors the disbanded troops were clamouring for their arrears, and on 27 February

1700 a group of them staged a near riot in the parliamentary precincts. Their target seems to have been Harley, who had been named (with Harcourt) a fortnight before to bring in a bill of accounts but had yet to do so. Whether it was true, as some claimed, that this year, as the last, the opposition did not really want to pursue accusations they knew they could not prove, on 29 February Harley laid the draft bill before the Commons.[183] Subsequently, the selection of commissioners divided the opposition leaders; Howe wanted M.P.s to be eligible and hinted at his own readiness to serve, even without pay, but Harley and Musgrave carried the day against him.[184] Harley was not anxious to revive the type of accounts commission on which he had long served himself, but he did not object to the addition of a rider to the bill on 6 April which instructed the new commissioners to state the accounts of the Prize Office. This amendment, adopted in the midst of the dispute between the two Houses over the Irish bill, was another bid to discomfit the Court, for it appears to have been deliberately aimed at bringing to light William's grant of prizes to the 'great favourite', Albemarle.[185]

While William had to stomach these measures and their reflections on his conduct, bills he had recommended failed to secure parliamentary approval. Despite his repeated exhortations, little was done to improve the system of poor relief. A bill was brought in by Sir Rowland Gwynne to require every town to establish workhouses, but when the Commons heard that the City of Bristol had spent over £5,000 on its own workhouse which employed only a relatively small number of the poor, thoughts of 'any general scheme' were laid aside.[186] Again, though the Lords did pass a bill for negotiating a union between England and Scotland at the King's urging, the Commons threw this measure out by an overwhelming voice vote on 5 March. Instead, the project of an Anglo-Scottish union was made one more occasion for reflections upon William. Shower told the Commons that as the Scots objected to being ruled *in absentia*, so might the English, who were treated in the same fashion for half the year while the King was at Loo spending the civil list revenue drawn from their taxes.[137]

In such an atmosphere, it is no wonder that William complained to Heinsius in April 1700 that 'it has in truth been the most dismal session I have ever had'.[138] But the King can hardly escape all responsibility for its unfortunate conclusion, and his sense of resentment carried him a step further after the prorogation. Although Somers was accused by his enemies in the Commons of advising the Lords' resistance to the Irish bill, William had been angered by the Chancellor's refusal to involve himself in the attempt to block the resumption of the grants. As before in the 1698–1700 parliament, the King either would not or could not understand how the Junto leaders could find majorities to forestall their own condemnation and not be able to muster the necessary votes to sustain his measures. So vexed was William on this score that it is possible, as rumour had it, that he even considered yielding Somers up to his enemies in the Commons if that would bring some concessions over the revocation.[139]

In any event, when the Lord Chancellor came to Hampton Court on 25 April to attend a Privy Council meeting and saw the King for the first time in nearly a month, he was met with a request that he resign. On what advice, if any, William was acting cannot be determined; both Shrewsbury and Sunderland were then at Hampton Court, and as usual the latter received credit for a decision of which he may have disapproved.[140] But the King had made his mind up, and when

Somers, who had offered to resign early in the session, now declined to go voluntarily, he was dismissed on 27 April.[141]

Somers's removal, less than a fortnight after Sir Edward Seymour had unexpectedly appeared at Kensington to congratulate William upon his 'deliverance' from the storm over the Irish bill, seemed to many to be the prelude to a complete ministerial reconstruction.[142] But while the town gossiped, the King could find no one to accept the great seal. This failure to have a successor in the wings is strong evidence that the Lord Chancellor's dismissal was not arranged by Sunderland as the first step in an elaborate plan. Both Chief Justice Holt and Attorney-General Trevor could not be persuaded to accept, despite all the arguments employed by Sunderland and Trumbull with the former, and by Harley and Rochester with the latter.[143] More than a fortnight passed without a successor being found, and in mid-May Robert Molesworth observed that 'you never knew such confusion in affairs'.[144]

As the search for a replacement for Somers continued, Shrewsbury was pondering a new royal offer to serve both as Groom of the Stole (in succession to Portland) and as Lord Lieutenant of Ireland. The King's newest attempt to gratify the Duke can be taken as another indication that William, though momentarily gripped by passion over the question of the Irish forfeitures (as he had been over disbanding earlier), had not abandoned his preference for men of 'moderation' and his antipathy to even the appearance that his favour was being engrossed by a single party. His fear of domination by a party had after all been a precipitating and persistent element in the progressive disintegration of the seemingly invincible Junto ministry after the Treaty of Ryswick, just as his pressure upon the Whig managers to espouse unpopular royal policies in the Commons had contributed to Harley's and his allies' seizure of the lead in St Stephen's Chapel. Three increasingly chaotic parliamentary sessions had followed the peace, and now the principal political question before the King and the kingdom was whether William, whose own health was of growing concern to his physicians and servants, could find a way to re-establish a ministry which would provide for co-operation between the crown and the Commons.

Notes to Chapter XI

1 Bodl. Ballard MS. 5, f. 131, E. Gibson to A. Charlett; *Vernon Corr.*, II, 148, 159.

2 BL Loan 29/189, f. 43, to his father, 3 December; Northants RO, Buccleuch MSS., Vernon letters, II, 104, 27 October. See also D. Rubini, *Court and Country 1688–1702* (1967), pp. 191–4.

3 NLW, Chirk Castle MS. F6458, Sir J. Leveson Gower to E. Kynaston, 11 October; Althorp, Savile MSS., box 4, J. Granville to Marquess of Halifax, 15 October, and box 2, Nottingham to same, 19 November; BL Egerton MS. 2540, f. 132, Lord D[igby] to E. Nicholas, 5 December.

4 Bodl. Carte MS. 130, f. 394, R. Price to [Duke of Beaufort], 26 November; BL Add. MS. 40773, f. 5, J. Vernon to the King, 2 December; CTB, XIII, 107–8, and XIV, 21, 23, 69.

5. Reprinted in ST, II, 651–3. Hammond was a non-associator; for his authorship, see Bodl. Rawlinson MS. A245, f. 64.

6 NRO, Buccleuch MSS., Vernon letters, II, 104, 27 October; *Vernon Corr.*, II, 223–4, and 217–22.

7 *Vernon Corr.*, II, 226–7; CSPD, 1698, p. 424. And see (? William Cowper's) account in Hertfordshire RO, Panshanger MS. D/EP/77, pp. 1–2.

8 *Shrewsbury Corr.*, p. 569.

9 *Vernon Corr.*, II, 230; Grimblot, *Letters*, II, 81.

10 Reprinted in *ST*, II, 671–3. And see BL Loan 29/282 (unfoliated), two letters of Trenchard to Harley, undated.

11 *Shrewsbury Corr.*, p. 569.

12 *Vernon Corr.*, II, 230.

13 *LJ*, XVI, 352.

14 Hertfordshire RO, Panshanger MS. D/EP/77, pp. 4–5. See also BL Add. MS. 40773, f. 36, J. Vernon to Earl of Jersey, 15 December; BL Add. MS. 33512, f. 155, J. Thurbarne to Sandwich corporation, 14 December.

15 *Vernon Corr.*, II, 235.

16 Northants RO, Buccleuch MSS., Vernon letters, II, 121, 17 December (cf. *Vernon Corr.*, II, 236). And see Hertfordshire RO, Panshanger MS. D/EP/77, pp. 6–7.

17 *CJ*, XII, 359, 360. And see *CSPD*, 1698, p. 428; Hertfordshire RO, Panshanger MS. D/EP/77, pp. 9–13. Ormonde, though a general and a Gentleman of the Bedchamber, aspired to play his grandfather's role in Dublin.

18 *Archives*, III, ii, 258–9.

19 Hertfordshire RO, Panshanger MS. D/EP/77, p. 17. And see *Vernon Corr.*, II, 237, 239, 240; House of Lords RO, Commons' Lib. MS. 12, ff. 108–9; Northants RO, Buccleuch MSS., Vernon letters, II, 123, 22 December.

20 *Vernon Corr.*, II, 240–3. And see *Shrewsbury Corr.*, p. 573.

21 *Archives*, III, ii, 258–9.

22 *Shrewsbury Corr.*, pp. 572–3. For the text of the speech William had drafted to deliver to parliament, see the facsimile in Macaulay, *History*, VI, 2867–9.

23 Hertfordshire RO, Panshanger MS. D/EP/77, pp. 19–21; House of Lords RO, Commons' Lib. MS. 12, ff. 109, 100–1; BL Add. MS. 17677TT, f. 61, L'Hermitage, 6/16 January; *Vernon Corr.*, II, 246; BL Loan 29/189, f. 53, [R. Harley], to his father, 7 January.

24 Bodl. MS. Eng. hist. b209, f. 93 v.

25 *Vernon Corr.*, II, 245, and 244, 246.

26 *Archives*, III, ii, 275.

27 HMC *Portland*, III, 601.

28 Hertfordshire RO, Panshanger MS. D/EP/77, pp. 26–7. See also Grimblot, *Letters*, II, 244–5; BL Add. MS. 30000C, f. 16, L. F. Bonnet, 20/30 January.

29 *Vernon Corr.*, II, 253; Hertfordshire RO, Panshanger MS. D/EP/77, p. 27; House of Lords RO, Commons' Lib. MS. 12, ff. 131–2, 87; *Hatton Corr.*, II, 238.

30 Bodl. Carte MS. 130, f. 397, R. Price to [Duke of Beaufort], 19 January. And see Appendix C.

31 *CSPD*, 1699–1700, p. 27; *Vernon Corr.*, II, 255, also 253–4.

32 *Vernon Corr.*, II, 251; BL Add. MS. 17677TT, f. 67, L'Hermitage, 13/23 January.

33 HMC *Johnstone*, p. 107; HMC *Portland*, III, 601.

34 *Vernon Corr.*, II, 255, 257; BL Add. MS. 30000C, ff. 24–5, L. F. Bonnet, 31 January/10 February.

35 *CJ*, XII, 468. And see BL Add. MS. 30000C, f. 25.

36 Hertfordshire RO, Panshanger MS. D/EP/77, pp. 30–1; *CSPD*, 1699–1700, p. 40.

37 *Vernon Corr.*, II, 258. And see Northants RO, Buccleuch MSS., Vernon letters, II, 140, 4 February; *CSPD*, 1699–1700, p. 42.

38 *Vernon Corr.*, II, 259, 238–9, 248–50. Vernon subsequently referred to the opposition leaders (Musgrave, Seymour, and Howe) as 'the managers'; Northants RO, Buccleuch MSS., Vernon letters, II, 147, 21 February.

39 *CJ*, XII, 618; BL Loan 29/78 (unfoliated), [E. Harley] to his father, 28 January; *Vernon Corr.*, II, 257; *CSPD*, 1699–1700, p. 12; BL Add. MS. 17677TT, ff. 84–5, L'Hermitage, 31 January/10 February.

40 BL Loan 29/78 (unfoliated), [E. Harley] to his father, 28 January; *CSPD*, 1699–1700, p. 37.

41 *The Whole Works of Walter Moyle, esq.*, ed. A. Hammond (1727), pp. 14–15.

42 Northants RO, Buccleuch MSS., Vernon letters, II, 140, 4 February; *Vernon Corr.*, II, 262, 263. This year's bill got no further than its predecessor of 1697–98.

43 *LJ*, XVI, 377. And see *HLM*, 1697–1699, pp. 284–5; BL Add. MS. 40773, f. 161, J. Vernon to Earl of Jersey, 9 February; Grimblot, *Letters*, II, 272.

44 Grimblot, *Letters*, II, 277–8; HMC *Portland*, III, 602; BL Add. MS. 17677TT, ff. 97, 101, L'Hermitage, 14/24 and 17/27 February.

45 Northants RO, Buccleuch MSS., Vernon letters, II, 143, 11 February. See also BL Add.

MS. 17677TT, f. 99, L'Hermitage, 14/24 February; KAO, Chevening MS. 78, T. Hopkins to A. Stanhope, 21 February; Cumberland RO, Lowther letters, J. to Sir J. Lowther.

46 Northants RO, Buccleuch MSS., Vernon letters, II, 145, 16 February; Bodl. MS. Eng. hist. b209, f. 93; CSPD, 1699–1700, pp. 66–7; BL Add. MS. 17677TT, f. 105, L'Hermitage, 21 February/3 March; BL Add. MS. 30000C, f.; 53, L. F. Bonnet, 21 February/3 March.

47 BL Add. MS. 17677TT, ff. 118–19, L'Hermitage, 10/20 March; KAO, Chevening MS. 78, T. Hopkins to A. Stanhope, 21 February; HLM, 1697–1699, pp. 382–3.

48 Northants RO, Buccleuch MSS., Vernon letters, II, 145, 16 February.

49 Bodl. MS. Eng. hist. b209, f. 91. See also Northants RO, Buccleuch MSS., Vernon letters, II, 154, 9 March.

50 Bodl. Carte MS. 130, f. 401, R. Price to [Duke of Beaufort], 11 March; Bodl. MS. Eng. hist. b209, f. 91. And see Northants RO, Buccleuch MSS., Vernon letters, II, 154.

51 Northants RO, Buccleuch MSS., Vernon letters, II, 157, 16 March; BL Add. MS. 17677TT, f. 130, L'Hermitage, 24 March/3 April. Papillon's vehemence against Orford was ascribed by Cocks to his fear of attack; Bodl. MS. Eng. hist. b209, f. 93 v.

52 Vernon Corr., II, 270–1; HMC Portland, III, 603. And see Bodl. MS. Eng. hist. b209, f. 79, for an explanation of Thomas Foley senior and Salwey Winnington's defection on this vote.

53 CJ, XII, 602. And see Vernon Corr., II, 269.

54 Vernon Corr., II, 269. And see Hunt. Hastings MS. 7890, [N. Johnston] to Earl of Huntingdon, 21 March; BL Add. MS. 30000C, f. 71, L. F. Bonnet, 21/31 March; Bodl. Tanner MS. 22, f. 6.

55 Archives, III, ii, 374. See also Vernon Corr., II, 270; CJ, XII, 602.

56 Bodl. MS. Eng. hist. b209, f. 91. See also Northants RO, Buccleuch MSS., Vernon letters, II, 147, 21 February.

57 Northants RO, Buccleuch MSS., Vernon letters, II, 169, 13 April.

58 Vernon Corr., II, 275. And see BL Loan 29/207, f. 98.

59 HLM, 1697–1699, pp. 424–34; CSPD, 1699–1700, p. 150.

60 Archives, III, ii, 410.

61 LJ, XVI, 466.

62 J. Price, 'The Tobacco Adventure to Russia' (Transactions of the American Philosophical Society, n.s. LI, 1961, part i), esp. pp. 38–46. Previous bills had failed in 1696–97 and 1697–98.

63 HLM, 1697–1699, pp. 271–6; BL Add. MS. 30000C, f. 6, L. F. Bonnet, 6/16 January; Bodl. Carte MS. 228, f. 268, newsletter, 17 January.

64 Northants RO, Buccleuch MSS., Vernon letters, II, 133, 17 January. See also BL Loan 29/189, f. 67, E. Harley to his father, 11 February.

65 HMC Johnstone, p. 100; BL Add. MS. 40774, f. 155, J. Vernon to the King, 25 August. See also BL Loan 29/189, f. 143, [R. Harley] to his father, 2 December 1699.

66 Shrewsbury Corr., p. 582; Burnet, History, IV, 403–4. There was also a furore in April 1699 when Ormonde threatened to resign his regiment over a dispute with Albemarle.

67 MSP, II, 436; Shrewsbury Corr., p. 570.

68 Vernon Corr., I, 411–12; HMC Bath, III, 301, 304; BL Add. MS. 40773, f. 327, J. Vernon to M. Prior, 27 March 1699; Browning, Danby, I, 544–8; C. Firth, 'The Memoirs of the First Lord Lonsdale', EHR xxx (1915), 97.

69 Vernon Corr., I, 467, and II, 274, 279.

70 MSP, II, 436; Shrewsbury Corr., pp. 562, 584.

71 Shrewsbury Corr., pp. 571, 584; Northants RO, Buccleuch MSS., Vernon letters, II, 165 and 184, 4 April, 15 May; Vernon Corr., II, 272–3.

72 Northants RO, Buccleuch MSS., Vernon letters, II, 175 and 181, 22 April, 6 May; Vernon Corr., II, 272–3, 280–1, 289–90; HMC Buccleuch, II, 622–3; BL Add. MS. 40774, f. 25, J. Vernon to the King, 2 June; Cumberland RO, Lowther letters, J. to Sir J. Lowther, 10 June.

73 Northants RO, Buccleuch MSS., Vernon letters, II, 155, 11 March; Vernon Corr., II, 287, 291; BL Add. MS. 17677TT, f. 177, L'Hermitage, 23 May/2 June.

74 BL Add. MS. 40774, f. 206, J. Vernon to Earl of Jersey, 3 October.

75 Vernon Corr., II, 288, 294, 299; CSPD, 1669–1700, p. 217; Northumberland RO, Blackett MS. ZBL 194, C. Montagu to Sir W. Blackett, 11 and 27 May (copies). Fox had almost resigned the previous autumn over his son's displacement.

76 Northants RO, Buccleuch MSS., Vernon letters, II, 158–9, 18 and 21 March; Vernon

Corr., II, 283–4, 285; BL Add. MS. 29575, ff. 472 and 476, C. to Viscount Hatton, 25 and 30 May.

77 *Correspondentie*, I, i, 338. And see Burnet, *History*, IV, 412–13.

78 Grimblot, *Letters*, II, 334; *Correspondentie*, I, ii, 111. And see Klopp, *Der Fall des Hauses Stuart*, VIII, 352.

79 For Vernon's subsequent reference to these 'promises', see BL Add. MS. 40774, f. 171, to the King, 12 September. See also *Shrewsbury Corr.*, pp. 582, 584, 588.

80 HMC *Buccleuch*, II, 623; BL Add. MS. 40774, f. 82, J. Vernon to the King, 4 July.

81 *Shrewsbury Corr.*, p. 591, also 589–90.

82 BL Add. MS. 40774, f. 155. See also Kenyon, *Sunderland*, p. 312.

83 BL Add. MS. 40774, f. 177, the King to J. Vernon, 5/15 September, and f. 171, J. Vernon to the King, 12 September.

84 HMC *Downshire*, I, 794; *The Whole Works of Walter Moyle*, p. 19 (1 November). Moyle's allusion is to the story that the Duke was frightened back into office in 1694.

85 Northants RO, Buccleuch MSS., Vernon letters, II, 248, 28 October. And see BL Add. MS. 40774, ff. 54 and 200, J. Vernon to the King, 16 June, 3 October.

86 *Historical and Political Memoirs*, ed. C. Cole (1735), pp. 82, 81.

87 Bodl. Rawlinson MS. C936, f. 114, J. Ellis to G. Stepney, 14 November.

88 *Historical and Political Memoirs*, p. 76; BL Add. MS. 17677TT, f. 289, L'Hermitage, 10/20 November; *Vernon Corr.*, II, 364–5 (and see D. Somerville, 'The Dates in the Vernon Correspondence', *EHR*, XLVIII (1933), 628–9); *Shrewsbury Corr.*, p. 594–5; Luttrell, *Brief Relation*, IV, 585.

89 HMC *Cowper*, II, 394; Luttrell, *Brief Relation*, IV, 587.

90 *Vernon Corr.*, II, 359.

91 *CJ*, XIII, 2; *Archives*, III, ii, 527–8.

92 HMC *Johnstone*, p. 113; BL Add. MS. 30000C, ff. 247–8, L. F. Bonnet, 28 November/8 December; Bodl. MS. Eng. hist. b209, f. 85 v.; *Vernon Corr.*, II, 368–9, 370.

93 Burnet, *Supplement*, pp. 545–6 (Harley's memorandum); *Vernon Corr.*, II, 436.

94 Northants RO, Buccleuch MSS., Vernon letters, II, 113, 29 November 1698. And see *CJ*, XIII, 12–39.

95 *Vernon Corr.*, II, 371–3.

96 Bodl. Locke MS. C8, f. 230, J. Freke to Locke, 7 December. See also *Vernon Corr.*, II, 375–6, 378–81; Bodl. MS. Eng. hist. b209, f. 85.

97 *Vernon Corr.*, II, 381. See also Bodl. Locke MS. C8, f. 230; New York Public Lib., Hardwicke MS. 33, pp. 127–43, Sir J. Jekyll's speech in Somers's defence.

98 Bodl. Carte MS. 130, f. 406, R. Price to [Duke of Beaufort], 6 December; Duke of Manchester, *Court and Society from Elizabeth to Anne* (1864), II, 54.

99 *Vernon Corr.*, II, 386–9; Bodl. MS. Eng. hist. b209, f. 85; BL Add. MS. 17677TT, L'Hermitage, f. 321, 15/25 December.

100 *Vernon Corr.*, II, 393–4.

101 Manchester, *Court and Society*, II, 54; BL Add. MS. 30000C, f. 283, L. F. Bonnet, 19/29 December.

102 *Vernon Corr.*, II, 386. And see *HLM*, 1699–1700, pp. 14–54.

103 *Vernon Corr.*, II, 391, 399–403; Kenyon, *Sunderland*, pp. 308–9, 313–14.

104 Cumberland RO, Lowther letters, to Sir J. Lowther, 20 January. See also *Vernon Corr.*, II, 415.

105 BL Loan 29/189, f. 157, [E. Harley] to his father, 13 January; *Vernon Corr.*, II, 396–7, 405–6.

106 BL Add. MS. 30000C, f. 234, L. F. Bonnet, 14/24 November; *Vernon Corr.*, II, 415. See also Northants RO, Buccleuch MSS., Vernon letters, III, 49, 23 March.

107 *Vernon Corr.*, II, 422. And see *CJ*, XIII, 39, 90, 124–5, 136.

108 Bodl. MS. Eng. hist. b209, f. 84 v. See also *Vernon Corr.*, II, 406, 411–12.

109 *Vernon Corr.*, II, 406–8.

110 BL Add. MS. 29576, ff. 11–12, [C. to Viscount Hatton], 20 January. And see *Vernon Corr.*, II, 406.

111 *CJ*, XIII, 123–5. And see Northants RO, Buccleuch MSS., Vernon letters, III, 27, 1 February; *Vernon Corr.*, II, 429–30.

112 *Vernon Corr.*, II, 412–13.

113 *Shrewsbury Corr.*, p. 613.

114 *Vernon Corr.*, II, 439, also 451–2, 452–3.

115 CJ, XIII, 301. See also PRO, PRO 30/15/4/684, xxvii, R. Yard to Earl of Manchester, 28 March; Northants RO, Buccleuch MSS., Vernon letters, III, 50, 26 March.

116 Vernon Corr., II, 268 (5 March, [1700]).

117 HMC Bath, III, 324; The Whole Works of Walter Moyle, p. 19. See also Original Letters of John Locke, Alg. Sidney, and Lord Shaftesbury, ed. T. Forster (1847), p. 83.

118 For Brydges's version, Hunt. Stowe MS. 26, 11 February, 13 March, 29 June, 6 December, 1698; for Montagu's, Bodl. MS. Eng. hist. b209, f. 67.

119 CJ, XIII, 208.

120 Bodl. MS. Eng. hist. b209, ff. 84, 83 v. See also PRO, PRO 30/15/4/684, xii, R. Yard to Earl of Manchester, 15 February; BL Loan 29/78 (unfoliated), E. Harley to his father, 'Thursday, 11 o'clock' [15 February]; Vernon Corr., II, 430-1, 444.

121 Vernon Corr., II, 431, 444, also 267-8, 435. See also BL Loan 29/165, misc. 97, p. 6.

122 For Harley as 'general', BL Loan 29/136 (unfoliated) T. Foley to R. Harley, 10 April 1700, and 29/300, bundle 9, Sir H. Mackworth to R. Harley, 17 October 1701.

123 BL Loan 29/189, f. 167, 5 March (cf. HMC Portland, III, 616).

124 Vernon Corr., III, 8.

125 Correspondentie, I, i, 350, 351; Vernon Corr., III, 9-10, also 3, 16, 17. And see Northants RO, Buccleuch MSS., Vernon letters, III, 55, 6 April; HLM, 1699-1702, pp. 141-2.

126 Vernon Corr., III, 7; BL Add. MS. 30000D, ff. 127-8, L. F. Bonnet, 9/20 April. See also Northants RO, Buccleuch MSS., Vernon letters, III, 55.

127 Vernon Corr., III, 12-15, 17.

128 BL Add. MS. 28053, f. 402, ? to Earl of Torrington, 11 April. Cf. Dartmouth's note in Burnet, History, IV, 439.

129 BL Add. MS. 28053, f. 402; Vernon Corr., III, 19-21, 24.

130 Cumberland RO, Lowther letters, J. to Sir J. Lowther, 13 April.

131 Vernon Corr., III, 21-5; BL Add. MS. 28053, f. 402.

132 Vernon Corr., II, 428-9, 431, 453-4; BL Add. MS. 17677UU, f. 154, L'Hermitage, 13/23 February; Northants RO, Buccleuch MSS., Vernon letters, III, 44, 12 March.

133 BL Add. MS. 17677UU, ff. 162-3, L'Hermitage, 19/29 February; BL Add. MS. 30000D, ff. 118-19, L. F. Bonnet, 2/13 April; HMC Portland, III, 615; ST, III, 304-5.

134 Northants RO, Buccleuch MSS., Vernon letters, III, 52, 28 March; Vernon Corr., III, 2.

135 ST, III, 304-5. See also Vernon Corr., II, 85-7, 89.

136 Northants RO, Buccleuch MSS., Vernon letters, III, 29, 6 February.

137 PRO, PRO 30/15/4/684, xix, R. Yard to Earl of Manchester, 7 March; BL Add. MS. 30000D, f. 84, L. F. Bonnet, 9/19 March.

138 Archives, III, iii, 100.

139 Vernon Corr., III, 3-4; HMC Portland, V, 452.

140 Note Sunderland's note to Harley headed 'Thursday' [? 11 April 1700], BL Loan 29/158, bundle 2: it reads, 'Since your friends moved for an address, I am almost as well satisfied, as if it had been agreed to.'

141 Burnet, History, IV, 442-6; Ralph, History, II, 854-5; Luttrell, Brief Relation, IV, 638, 639; HMC Portland, III, 618; Vernon Corr., III, 35, 43-4.

142 Vernon Corr., III, 35-6; Bodl. Ballard MS. 10, f. 40, [T. Tanner] to A. Charlett, 30 April; BL Add. MS. 17677UU, f. 230, L'Hermitage, 7/18 May.

143 HMC Portland, III, 618, 619; HMC Downshire, I, 796; Leicestershire RO, Finch correspondence, bundle 22, E. Southwell to Nottingham, 11 May. For rumours that Methuen might be named, see BL Add. MS. 17677UU, f. 230; H. Fox Bourne, The Life of John Locke (New York, 1876), II, 400-3.

144 HMC Various, VIII, 221.

XII

THE RAGE OF PARTY

1700–1702

The turbulent end to the 1699–1700 parliamentary session, followed by Lord Chancellor Somers's dismissal in late April 1700, seemed to many to presage a reconstitution of the ministry and, probably, a new parliament as well. Yet, after William's encouragement of the Lords' challenge to the Commons over the Irish bill had backfired and in the face of the difficulties in finding someone to take the great seal, the King was afflicted with second thoughts about the wisdom of 'running from one extreme to another'.[1] In any case, he still hoped to persuade Shrewsbury to return to business, and the appointment of Serjeant Nathan Wright as Lord Keeper on 21 May was no more than a stopgap. Although Wright was no favourite of Somers, he had distinguished himself as counsel against Fenwick in 1696 and he was generally reputed a Whig.[2] Sunderland, then, told Vernon that the Serjeant had taken on his new responsibilities 'with a foresight that he should not hold them long'.[3]

Sunderland's characterisation of Wright's appointment reflected his own active promotion during May of a plan to 'piece up' the ministry again with the Whigs, and the Earl was even hopeful that Somers would be restored if the former Lord Chancellor desired it. Thus, Shrewsbury's aid was invoked to mediate between William and Somers, and Sunderland let it be known that the King was 'very desirous to retain the party, if they could be brought into any disposition to serve him, and he approved very well that no alterations should be made, that the same parliament should meet again, and none to be removed out of their employments'.[4] But this was merely to recapitulate under the most unfavourable circumstances the futile efforts of the past two years to shore up relations between William and the Junto, and none of those who figured in Sunderland's project showed any eagerness for or confidence in these new overtures. Furthermore, by late May Shrewsbury had made his mind up to lay aside all thoughts of accepting the King's latest offers and to resign the Chamberlain's staff as well.[5]

The Duke's decision convinced Sunderland of the impracticability of a Whig restoration. The Earl left for Althorp on 28 May; then, despite urgent royal summons, he refused to return to Court, saying he would only be blamed anew for advising measures he actually opposed. Vernon told Shrewsbury on 22 June:[6]

He keeps to his resolution of not stirring from Althorp and declares by the grace of God, he will meddle no more. He says the King has nothing to do but to refer everything to his council, and to act above board by the advice of those who are by their employments entitled to give it; and if he has those about him who are not fit for those trusts, it is his fault they are not better chosen.

With Shrewsbury and Sunderland unwilling to assist and with the Junto out of office and out of temper, William had no alternative but to look elsewhere. Before he left for Holland early in July 1700, he had frequent talks with Rochester and with Harley, though the results of these consultations were not immediately apparent. The commission of Lords Justices that the King left behind included only two new faces: Wright in place of Somers and Tankerville in place of Montagu. Nor did the other appointments announced at this juncture fulfil the expectations of a change of hands. Jersey and Romney simply acquired new dignities, the former as Chamberlain and the latter as Groom of the Stole. In turn, Romney's Bedchamber place was bestowed upon the Whiggish Earl of Carlisle after Lord Hartington declined it, while Jersey's Secretaryship was left vacant for the time being. Moreover, though a reshuffle was necessary at the Excise Office, since four of the seven M.P.s on that commission chose to resign rather than to forfeit their seats in the Commons under the terms of the place clause in the resumption act, the new commissioners designated in late June were not party men.[7]

Nevertheless, William does seem to have decided before he left London to make Rochester Lord Lieutenant of Ireland and to restore Godolphin to the Treasury. One reason for delaying these appointments until his return was Godolphin's reluctance to serve under Tankerville, who outranked him. But Londale's demise (after a lingering illness) a few days after William's departure promptly gave rise to thoughts of promoting Tankerville out of Godolphin's way.[8] Yet, even should Rochester and Godolphin return to office, it remained an open question whether to call new elections. Vernon's prediction in late May was that the King would eventually decide this 'according to the prospect of being assisted by one or the other party', and the Secretary observed to Shrewsbury that it 'looks to me as if there was to be an auction of offices next winter, that shall go to the fairest bidders'.[9]

The topic of a dissolution also figured largely in the ciphered correspondences conducted between Guy and Harley and between Harley and Musgrave during the King's absence.[10] Then, too, these letters make clear the vital role that Harley would play, whether in the old or in a new House of Commons. He was the pivot upon which all turned. Thus, Rochester, who hitherto had not been on familiar terms with Harley, worked to gain his confidence, and the Earl was warmly recommended to Harley as a man deserving of trust by their mutual friend Francis Gwyn.[11] Furthermore, to judge from Vernon's reports to Shrewsbury in June and early July, it was Harley's assurances of 'moderation', so long as the Junto did not take the offensive, that persuaded William it would be feasible to proceed with the ministerial reconstruction that had been anticipated ever since the signing of the Treaty of Ryswick.[12]

The eventual decision on a dissolution was greatly influenced by two un-expected events. The first was the death of Princess Anne's only surviving child, William Duke of Gloucester, early in the morning of 30 July 1700. When he celebrated his eleventh birthday the week before, the Duke seemed in good health, but a few days' illness left the realm without a recognised successor after the Princess. Immediately, talk of a second marriage for William revived, while the King himself met with his cousin, the Electress Sophia of Hanover, at Loo in September. Inclusion of the Hanoverians in the line of succession, given William's reluctance to remarry and his increasingly poor health, seemed a more likely solution, but the King feared there would be strong opposition to Sophia and her offspring. Some Scots were talking of refusing to accept any successor designated by an English parliament, unless they were accorded commercial concessions by England. And in England, though Vernon reported that those with whom Guy 'converses' were 'zealous for the King's marriage and for adding the House of Hanover to the settlement', the Secretary warned that some Whigs might 'go a little awkwardly into this business'.[13]

Certainly, the prospect of another foreign ruler roused little enthusiasm in England, and some suspected that the Whigs still cherished hopes of establishing a 'commonwealth'.[14] Then, too, Gloucester's death acted as a tonic to the Jacobites, and soon the Earl of Manchester (the English ambassador in Paris) was relaying to Vernon the news that one of the late Lord Preston's brothers had arrived at St Germain, supposedly 'sent over by Sir C[hristopher] M[usgrav]e and other parliament men, with proposals in order to get the succession settled upon the pretended Prince of Wales on certain conditions'. Manchester added that this emissary also brought assurances that his friends in England 'would propose to the House not to assist in the execution of the treaty'.[15]

This was the second Partition Treaty; its main points had been settled a year before, but ratification had then been held up for many months, chiefly because of opposition in the United Provinces. The terms of this agreement, by which the main portion of the Spanish monarchy was to go to the Imperial claimant while France was to receive Final, Guipuscoa, and the kingdoms of Naples and Sicily, were found objectionable not only in Amsterdam but also in London. William's English ministers had had no hand in the negotiations, and when the agreement was finally communicated to them in late February 1700, on the eve of the signing, they had criticised various of its provisions. Subsequently, the treaty was unofficially published in London just after William left for the Continent in July 1700, and this disclosure provoked many protests, especially from those who feared French encroachment upon England's Mediterranean commerce.[16] Nor were the principal beneficiaries of the treaty, the Imperialists, much more enthusiastic when they were officially informed of the terms, though their cautious reception also owed something to the profound disgust they anticipated among Spaniards at this renewed provision for the dismemberment of their once great monarchy. Only France, it appeared, was satisfied with the arrangements, so much so that Louis in the summer of 1700 professed a willingness to exchange Naples and Sicily for Savoy and Piedmont, partly to appease commercial interests in the Maritime Powers and partly to gratify the importunate Duke of Savoy, who was excited at the prospect of acquiring a royal estate. Yet, when Carlos II finally died on 21 October 1700, leaving a new will aimed at forestalling partition by bequeathing his realms to one of Louis's grandsons on condition they be accepted in toto (if not, they were to be offered on the same terms to one of the House of Austria), Louis decided to accept the will rather than to try to implement the treaty.

The news of Louis's choice reached William on 4 November 1700, only a fortnight after he had returned to England, and the King was astonished at 'this unheard of proceeding'. It was bad enough that the Maritime Powers had been made France's 'dupes'; even worse, too many in England seemed ready to agree that it would be best to have the French accept the will.[17] Those who drew this conclusion argued that the danger to England posed by the incorporation of

Naples and Sicily in the French monarchy was greater than any that might follow from the Duke of Anjou's succession to the entire Spanish monarchy, since once Louis's grandson went to Spain and was surrounded with Spanish councillors he would soon act as a Spaniard and not as a Frenchman. And this was the view that both Rochester and Godolphin put to William in separate audiences held on the heels of the express from Paris.[18]

Rochester's and Godolphin's preference for the will may have been the reason for a new delay in the ministerial alterations that, a few days earlier, had seemed virtually assured now that Shrewsbury was ready to set out for the Continent in search of better health. On 28 October when the Duke came to Hampton Court to take leave of the King, his old servant Vernon informed Manchester that William had told Tankerville of his own imminent promotion to the Privy Seal. And it was 'expected', Vernon added, that Godolphin would succeed Tankerville at the Treasury. Then, too, James Brydges noted in his diary on 31 October, after a visit to Marlborough's town house where he found his host in the company of Godolphin, Guy, and Coningsby, that Marlborough did not deny the reports that 'in probability' he would be named Jersey's successor as Secretary of State.[19]

But when William announced his new appointments in council on 5 November, there were several surprises. Although Tankerville received the Privy Seal, neither Godolphin nor Marlborough nor Rochester was named. Instead, Sir Charles Hedges, a judge of the Admiralty and esteemed a 'moderate' despite his employment as counsel to James II's ecclesiastical commission, was chosen to fill the vacant Secretaryship. Nor were anxious Tories such as Viscount Weymouth reassured by reports that Hedges's sponsor was Lord Chamberlain Jersey, who, it was said, 'grows very much a minister and is in a fair way of being very great'. Jersey, after all, seems to have been suspected by Guy and his correspondents as the one 'who obstructs all' at Court, and his influence with Albemarle was added cause for alarm.[20]

However, Whig rejoicing that William was drawing back from his advances to their adversaries proved premature.[21] Harley, who had hastened up to town as soon as he was notified of the King's return, joined with Godolphin and Rochester to counter any notions of halting with the changes announced on 5 November, and their success was soon apparent. On 1 December, Godolphin was sworn of the cabinet council and a few days later the King signed a warrant designating him first lord of the Treasury. Then, on the 12th Rochester's appointment as Lord Lieutenant of Ireland was announced, and it was also made known that he would not leave for Dublin until the coming parliamentary session was over. A week later, William proclaimed the dissolution of his fourth parliament, as he was now convinced, in Seymour's words, that 'partitions and successions are too great to be begun in the fag end of a parliament'. Furthermore, the King—in response to Rochester's insistent request—declared that when the new parliament met in February 1701, the Convocation of Canterbury would be allowed to act for the first time since 1689.[22]

The ministerial changes, the dissolution, and the promise of an acting convocation (four years after A Letter to a Convocation Man had been published) seemed in the words of the former Lord Ashley, who had recently succeeded as Earl of Shaftesbury, to be a sudden 'turn' by the Court to 'the now popular Tories, who by acting the part of patriots have got great repute' and now were being 'restored to what they naturally belong to, a high and absolute Court and

Church interest'.[23] Then, too, Harley's involvement in these courses, coupled with his 'several meetings with the clergy' and his 'two journeys' to Oxford University before the King's return, surprised those who knew his Dissenting origins and his 'ten years' opposition to the Court'.[24] To be sure, Harley refused a post in the new ministry, yet there is no doubt he had been instrumental in persuading William to take the plunge, not least by assuring the King that a new House of Commons could be relied upon to provide for the Hanoverian succession without imposing any new limitations on William's own powers.[25]

Even so, the King still did not see eye to eye with his new advisers on the Spanish succession. As he stated his position to a specially-summoned gathering on 26 December of the two Secretaries of State, Jersey, Godolphin, and Rochester, he believed that those who thought 'that Spain would have separate interests from France' would 'find themselves mistaken', at least 'for many years' to come. The recent orders sent from Madrid to the governors of the various Spanish territories 'to obey the King of France in whatever related to their affairs' were clear evidence of this. Most immediately threatened were the Dutch garrisons in the barrier fortresses of the Spanish Netherlands; in the face of this imminent danger to the Dutch, William could 'not see how we could think ourselves in any state of safety'. In his opinion, Anglo-Dutch security could only be preserved by the maintenance of the existing ties between the two states and by the negotiation of new alliances—above all, with the Emperor. Yet, as William explained, Vienna was not likely to make such alliances without promises of assistance in the pursuit of her pretensions upon the Spanish monarchy; indeed, his soundings suggested that the Imperialists aimed at 'no less than the whole succession of Spain'. This the King did not think 'practicable', and in any event there seemed little point in proceeding upon such alliances until 'he saw how they would be made good' by the new parliament.[26]

In reply, Rochester and Godolphin urged William to omit no measures to secure England's interests by peaceable means, and in particular they pressed him to recognise Anjou as King of Spain. They also warned that 'they did not think the parliament' would be 'brought into a war against Spain or if the dismembering any part of that monarchy were made the grounds of it'. All they would concede was 'that alliances will be very necessary and what the people would come into if they were made only with regard to common security'. They concluded, then, that if the King's fears were justified, the best strategy would be a 'temporising' one, for 'the more time should be gained the nation would be in a better posture to defend itself'.[27]

The debate over the Spanish succession was not confined to the King's councils; it was also taken up in the spate of pamphlets published as the election campaign got under way in late December 1700. The Dutch resident believed that foreign policy was actually the main electoral issue: 'No longer do they invoke the names of Whigs and Tories; rather, the distinction in some places is reported to be peace or war.'[28] In William's view, however, the division was still a partisan one. The Whigs supported a war if necessary while the Tories favoured a peace if at all possible, and he was heartened to find 'to my great surprise that they begin to talk here of the necessity of a war in a more decided manner than I could ever have imagined'.[29]

Although the future of England's Mediterranean trade was an important concern in the public controversy over foreign policy, the effects of the continuing struggle for control of the East Indian trade were, probably, more evident in many constituencies. Before the dissolution, William had sought to defuse this controversy by encouraging new talks between the rival companies, and his promotion in December 1700 of Montagu to the peerage as Baron Halifax was intended to further an accommodation by removing the new Company's principal advocate from the Commons. But the old Company was even less interested in a compromise than they had been the previous winter; they hoped that the change of hands at Whitehall would enable them to supersede their competitors and they planned to offer an alternative subscription of £2,000,000 at 5 per cent to the new parliament. The new Company's leadership reacted to this threat by trying to secure a sizeable representation in St Stephen's Chapel, and by early January 1701 it was reported that 'the old and new company is the great distinction' in elections 'in and about London'.[30] The struggle between the two corporations may also have contributed to the spread of grossly exaggerated accounts that there were three thousand candidates vying for seats in the new Commons.[31] Certainly, the East Indiamen attracted considerable attention, not least when they ventured out into venal provincial boroughs. On occasion, as at Malmesbury, the new Company men acted in conjunction with established electoral interests (Wharton's, in that instance), but often they lacked such allies. And their appearance not only aroused the resentment of local gentlemen but also occasioned late in January the publication of *The Freeholders' Plea Against Stock-Jobbing Elections*.[32]

It is also possible that the well-lined purses of the East Indiamen helped to reduce the total number of contests; only 86 are known, as compared to the 1698 total of 106. Certainly, the new Company men did quite well; 67 have been identified in the list of returns, including a core of 28 active supporters, as compared to 17 old Company sympathisers, six of them active supporters. These figures indicate a resounding new Company success, but it is not so easy to interpret the overall results. Altogether 361 (70 per cent) of the sitting members were returned, including 75 per cent of those who had been blacklisted as opponents of the disbanding bill of January 1699. Among the 152 new M.P.s, there were also some whose views were well known, including such returning Whig stalwarts as Harry Mordaunt and Sir William Strickland and such Country Whigs as Maurice Ashley (the Earl of Shaftesbury's brother) and Robert Monckton. But the inclinations of the 108 members who had never sat before were more difficult to forecast, though this group included the two great rivals of the early eighteenth century, Henry St John and Robert Walpole.[33]

Contemporary verdicts on the outcome of the election do not provide much help, save in their agreement that the Tories had failed to achieve the sweeping victory they had anticipated. Some Whigs were 'very sanguine that this will be a good parliament', and the Brandenburg resident was told that for every four Tories there were seven Whigs.[34] But against these assessments, there were reports of sizeable Tory gains in the West and in the North. Thus, while Guy bemoaned the initial returns, when the results were in Harley let it be known he 'approve[d] well enough of the elections, notwithstanding the indirect practices and the briberies'.[35]

Given the differences between William and his new ministers over foreign policy and the uncertain political balance in the Commons, the new parliament began and continued under the influence of a triangle of forces. First, there was the King himself, anxious to act positively against France yet realising that he could not proceed very far without parliamentary backing. Second, there were the new ministers, eager to consolidate their position in the King's councils but aware that many of their friends in the Commons were loath to contemplate the burdens of a new war. And third, there were the old ministers (now all in the Lords) and their associates in the lower House, inclined to a vigorous anti-French line but not prepared to acquiesce in their rivals' new-found favour.

The opening of the session was a fitting prologue. The late Speaker, Sir Thomas Littleton, formally offered his services to the King, only to be told by William in an interview on 3 February that he 'judged it more for his interest to have Mr Harley'. The King also asked Sir Thomas to stay away from St Stephen's Chapel when the Commons assembled to choose his successor. Littleton, who still held the post of Treasurer of the Navy, obeyed, but many of his Whig friends were not disposed to yield without a struggle. As one of them, Sir Richard Cocks, recorded in his diary; we 'met at the Rose in order to oppose Mr Harley, because we did not like the preceptor [Rochester] at all nor the pupil very well'.[36] The upshot was that after Seymour proposed Harley to the Commons on 10 February, Lord Hartington rose to nominate Sir Richard Onslow. However, the Clerk, Paul Jodrell, who was presiding until the Chair was filled, recognised Sir John Leveson-Gower instead, and he seconded Seymour. Only then was Hartington given the chance to speak, and, after reflecting upon Littleton's absence and Harley's backing by the Court, he named Onslow 'as a more indifferent' choice. Hartington was supported by Lord Spencer, Sir William Strickland, Sir John Mainwaring, and Cocks himself. But when the question was put for Harley, the placemen—who had sat silent during the debate—joined with the Tories to carry the division 249 to 125.[37]

It was Harley, then, who led the Commons up to the Lords on 11 February 1701 to hear the King's speech. William began by urging the 'early and effectual' consideration of a further settlement of the English succession 'in the Protestant line'. Next, he desired the members' 'mature' resolutions on the great 'alteration in the affairs abroad' since Carlos II's death. In addition, he recommended the maintenance of a strong fleet as well as provision for the unfunded debts and the deficiencies remaining from the last war. Finally, he exhorted the Lords and the Commons to proceed vigorously and unanimously, declaring that the appearance 'we are firmly united among ourselves' would greatly contribute 'to our safety at home' and 'to our being considerable abroad'.[38]

The responses to the King's speech betrayed substantial differences both within each House and between them. The peers were the first to act. When they deliberated on the speech on 12 February, Lords Peterborough and Haversham urged a strongly-worded answer in denunciation of recent French measures. Normanby, Nottingham, and Rochester spoke for a simple vote of thanks, but the next day the Lords adopted an address encouraging William to enter into alliances 'for the preservation of the balance of Europe'.[39] However, the address also included a request for the submission to parliament of all treaties made since Ryswick. Moreover, at the suggestion of the Tory peers, the Lords agreed to seek the Commons' concurrence in their resolutions.

As the Tories seem to have intended, the Commons rejected the idea of a joint address, thereby diminishing somewhat the force of the Lords' votes.[40] Yet the lower House itself divided over the wording of its address. At issue was whether to include an assurance of support for 'effectual measures' to maintain the 'peace of Europe'. This formulation was opposed as premature by Thomas Pelham and as liable 'insensibly' to 'engage us in a war' by Jack Howe, but Treasury Commissioners Boyle and Smith urged it strongly and it was carried 181 to 163. 'The friends of the old ministry and most of the courtiers' voted in the affirmative, while the minority included Howe, Seymour, Musgrave, Gwyn (newly appointed Rochester's secretary in Dublin), and Rochester's heir Lord Hyde.[41]

Although the Whigs gained the upper hand in the first division of the 1701 session in the Commons, it was doubtful whether their advantage would survive the inquiry already under way in St Stephen's Chapel into the new Company's electioneering activities. The corporation's proceedings were severely condemned by Seymour on 13 February, and it was agreed to undertake an investigation of the briberies alleged against Samuel Shepherd senior and his associates. On the 15th, the elections of two other prominent new Company men, Sir Gilbert Heathcote and Sir Henry Furness, were also challenged by the Tories. The charge against them was that under the terms of the lottery act of 1694 they were ineligible to serve because they were trustees for the circulation of Exchequer bills. On the 18th, the Commons voted 186 to 181 to expel Furness; on the 22nd, Heathcote followed by a vote of 176 to 165; and before the session was over, eight more new Company men, including Shepherd and his two sons, lost their seats for electoral misconduct.[42]

While the parties jockeyed for position in parliament, elsewhere those who favoured an Anglo-French confrontation also exerted themselves. Among the pro-war elements may be numbered the Melfort faction at James II's court. Their leader did his best to speed a clash by the provocative letter he deliberately allowed to fall into English hands, which William then communicated to the Commons on 17 February. The French quickly disowned Melfort's statement that Louis was considering sponsorship of a new Jacobite invasion plan, but the letter was an uncovenanted advantage to the advocates of a strong anti-French line. After the Melfort letter reached London, the King instructed the Dutch ambassador to present him with a memorial, purporting to come from the Estates General. This memorial rationalised the Republic's recent recognition of Anjou as Philip V of Spain as an attempt to gain the release of the Dutch garrisons in the Spanish Netherlands and it called upon England to ready the 10,000 men and twenty ships promised to the United Provinces in case of attack by the 1678 treaty between the Maritime Powers.[43]

On 18 February, Secretary Hedges presented the Dutch ambassador's memorial to the Commons, and they took it under consideration in committee on the 20th. The effect, so William informed Heinsius, was all he could have wished. The initial response of some leading Tories was that England should follow the Dutch in recognising Philip, and it was even insinuated that William favoured this course. But this notion was denounced by Robert Monckton, a firm supporter of disbandment in 1697–98, as but a preliminary to the recognition of the pretended Prince of Wales. Hartington and other Whigs chimed in on this note, and they seemed to have the support of a majority of those present. In the end, the Commons agreed on a resolution in which they pledged to make good the terms of the 1678 treaty, if the need arose, and requested the King 'to enter into such negotiations, in concert with the States General . . . and other potentates, as may most effectually conduce to the mutual safety of these kingdoms, and the States

General, and the preservation of the peace of Europe'.[44] No wonder that William, in an unusual burst of cordiality, fêted the several hundred members of the Commons—among them, Seymour, Musgrave, and Granville—who carried the ensuing address to Kensington on 21 February.[45]

Despite earlier fears of Jacobite and 'republican' opposition, unanimity was also the order of the day when the Commons turned to regulate the succession to the throne. After the vote of solidarity with the Dutch was approved by the lower House on 20 February, Harley had urged the members to go on to deal with the succession, and on the 26th Hartington moved to take up the question in committee the following Saturday, 1 March.[46] That day, two resolutions were considered in what one M.P. described as 'the fullest committee I ever saw', and with Harley in the lead the four hundred or so present passed both 'without any dispute'.[47] The first resolution called for the settlement of the crown on the next Protestant line after William, Anne, and the heirs of their bodies; the second urged the making of 'further provision' for the 'security of the rights and liberties of the people'.[48] However, when Lord Spencer then sought to name the Hanoverian line, the chairman Conyers ruled that his motion would not be in order until the full House passed on the initial resolutions. Two days later, a prolonged debate over the committee's report ended with a vote in favour of formulating the new safeguards before designating the successors.[49]

The task of devising additional securities for Englishmen's 'rights and liberties' was tackled in committee on 5, 10, and 11 March. With some dispute but no divisions, nine provisions were formulated. They combined hitherto unsuccessful Country proposals, largely justified by reference to the preliminary version of the Declaration of Rights, with restrictions upon foreigners that reflected the experiences of William's reign and the precedents provided by the marriage contract between Mary Tudor and Philip II of Spain.[50] The former included resolutions that all major affairs of state should be transacted in the Privy Council, with members signing their advices (one); royal pardons should not be pleadable to impeachments (six); all placemen and pensioners should be excluded from the Commons (eight); and judges' tenure should be during good behaviour with their salaries 'ascertained and established' (nine). The latter comprehended resolutions that barred foreigners from the royal service and from both Houses of parliament (two), as well as from receiving royal grants (three); stated that the kingdom should not be 'obliged' to go to war in defence of lands not attached to the English crown (four); stipulated that the successor must join in communion with the established Church (five); and prohbited the successor from leaving the British Isles without parliamentary consent (seven).[51]

These limitations on the monarch's prerogative and influence encountered relatively little resistance in committee. As Blathwayt observed gloomily to Stepney: 'the parties strive to outdo one another ... [in] weakening the crown'. 'There was too great a concurrence of all sorts', though 'some on both sides' did try to stem the torrent and reminded their colleagues that no parliament could tie the hands of its successors.[52] Moreover, when the committee took up the question of the successor on 11 March, the chief competition was over who would have the honour of actually nominating the Electress and her house. Spencer's renewed attempt early that day was again ruled out of order, and so it was Sir John Bolles who had the distinction of proposing the motion in a 'very handsome speech' several hours later. Sir John was seconded by Sir Rowland Gwynne and the designation of the Hanoverian line was carried 'without debate'.[53] Then on the 12th, the full House approved all these resolutions with only minor alterations and a bill was ordered to implement them.

Despite the appearance of consensus, there were still some who were doubtful of the fate of the succession bill. The King was reported to be displeased with some of the intended limitations as reflections upon his rule, and there was also concern lest the new constitutional provisions prove unacceptable to the Lords.[54] Then, too, the prominent role accorded Bolles in the Commons' proceedings, which included his service in the chair of the committee of the whole on the bill, raised questions about the sincerity of the measure's sponsors, since Sir John was already showing clear signs of the mental instability that later overcame him.[55] Subsequently, the Commons' delays during late March and April on the bill, coupled with the thin attendance when the measure was considered in committee, reinforced suspicions that many M.P.s did not take it seriously.[56]

However, the only open opposition to the succession bill came at the report stage in the Commons on 10 May when the Whig placemen moved in a half-empty House to have the section excluding office-holders thrown out. Littleton proposed this deletion and warned of the 'jealousies that this clause would perpetually make between the King and the people', and Boyle seconded him. Sir Godfrey Copley responded with a motion, seconded by Edward Harley, to send the Serjeant at Arms into Westminster Hall to summon members to attend. And while the Serjeant made his rounds, Cocks entertained those present with a speech in defence of the threatened provision. When the attackers found the House filling up, they retreated, and the bill was finally dispatched to the Lords on 14 May without amendment.[57]

The Lords also proceeded on the succession bill with a considerable degree of unanimity. There was some talk of additions, particularly an amendment to limit the monarch's power to create new peers. But this proposal received only a lukewarm reception, chiefly because it was anticipated the Commons would be hostile to any attempt to make the peerage a more exclusive body. Moreover, though many peers were said to disapprove of the restrictive clauses imposed by the Commons, they decided apparently it was the better part of prudence to secure the designation of a Protestant successor now and to worry later about revising the conditions to be put upon him. Thus, the Lords passed the bill on 22 May without amendment.[58]

Although the bill of succession was approved without a division in either House, the Commons and the Lords had in the meantime found ample material for controversy—both among themselves and with each other. Indeed, the day that the Commons approved the heads of the succession bill (12 March), the Lords began to open Pandora's box by taking up the various treaties the King had laid before them in answer to their vote of 13 February. Chief among them was the second Partition Treaty, for William had not seen fit to submit its predecessor, and on 14 March Normanby and Nottingham eloquently condemned both the terms of the treaty of 1700 and the King's failure to take proper advice before concluding it. Godolphin and Rochester voiced their objections in rather milder fashion, and they proposed that the Lords address the King to advise that in future he should act in consultation with the Privy Council and Parliament. This debate concluded with an order creating a committee, which was chaired by Nottingham, to formulate the terms of such an address.[59]

However, the heads reported by Nottingham on 15 March provoked sharp criticism from the Whigs, and several of the more tendentious were deleted. Furthermore, Portland, who had received the King's permission to offer specifics in response to the charge that William had acted without consultation, disclosed that the terms of the treaty had been considered at a gathering of leading royal servants that was held at his house shortly before the ratifications had been exchanged in late February 1700. Those present, Portland stated, were Pembroke, Lonsdale, Jersey, Marlborough, Somers, the new baron Halifax, and Secretary Vernon. His account was then confirmed and amplified by some of the others, and Marlborough summarised the objections Somers and he had expressed at that gathering to the terms of the agreement with Louis XIV.[60]

Portland's and Marlborough's testimony made it clear that William had not concluded the second Partition Treaty without soliciting the views of his English ministers, though he had not followed their advice. The critics of the treaty suffered a further setback on 18 March when Wharton proposed that the Lords add to their projected address a condemnation of Louis for violating the agreement and an advice that in future dealings with France the King should 'proceed with such caution as may carry along with it a real security'. The Comptroller's amendment was opposed by Normanby, Nottingham, Rochester, and Godolphin, but after a motion to adjourn failed 38 to 31, Wharton's addition was approved.[61] This and other amendments, as Vernon gleefully observed, 'much change the nature' of the intended address and they were carried 'by such as were no favourers' of it. Moreover, when the Tories on 20 March sought to have the revised text communicated to the Commons before presentation to the King, the majority—no doubt recalling the fate of their last attempt at a joint address— rejected the motion 45 to 27.[62]

Meanwhile, William was busy demonstrating his newfound commitment to acting in conjunction with parliament. The clerks in Hedges's office were kept hard at work translating and transcribing current diplomatic documents for parliamentary consumption. And on 18 March, Hedges presented the Commons with copies of papers relating to the negotiations currently being conducted with the French at The Hague in an attempt to secure the interests of the Maritime Powers by peaceful means.[63] But though the lower House readily agreed on the 21st to thank the King for this account, a Court attempt to include thanks for his care of 'the peace of Europe' was defeated 193 to 187, with Granville and Gwyn telling for the majority. Instead, it was resolved to represent the 'ill consequences' of the second Partition Treaty, and on the 24th Seymour reported a draft of the proposed address. This attributed the 'dangers which now threaten both this kingdom and the peace of Europe' to that agreement, and the Commons approved the text only a few hours before the Lords were due to present their own rather different address on the subject.[64]

On 24 March, the Commons also agreed to take up in committee of the whole on the 29th the Lords' findings on the making of the 1700 treaty, which Howe now likened to 'a combination of three robbers to rob the fourth'. He was called to order by Goodwin Wharton for these defamatory words, but the Speaker claimed he had not heard Howe say them. Unabashed, Howe went on to explain that 'kings can do no harm and that he reflected only upon the ministry' in office when the treaty had been made. Sir William Strickland's retort to this was equally blunt: 'If kings can do no wrong', he declared, 'then we have injuriously expelled King James; if his councillors are to blame, then we are more in fault for they [Rochester and Godolphin] are councillors still.'[65]

These partisan exchanges in the Commons on 24 March were only a prelude to the clashes of the 28th and 29th, and, as in the 1699–1700 session, Somers was the principal target of the new ministry's supporters. On the 28th, the Kidd grant was revived against the former Lord Chancellor, even though the Captain had not said anything incriminating concerning his sponsors during his previous examinations before both the Admiralty and the Commons. With the placemen dividing along party lines, a motion to condemn the grant as void and illegal lost by 198 to 185. Similarly, though the impeachment of Portland for his part in the making of the second Partition Treaty was carried without a division on the 29th, Somers escaped censure for sealing it. Despite Harley's warning that to exculpate Somers would be to lay an 'axe to the very roots of our constitution', the 'old ministry men' defeated the motion against him 189 to 182.[66]

For all the bitterness of these confrontations between the parties, by early April 1701 the French ambassador in London was convinced that a war was certain, though probably not this year. In Tallard's view, the principal point at issue between the parties was which one would hold office when the war did break out.[67] Tallard's feelings were only reinforced by the Commons' response to a new royal message received on 31 March. This gave an account of France's refusal to offer anything more than a renewal of the Treaty of Ryswick to the Maritime Powers' demand for 'security', and William also transmitted a second (and this time genuine) request from the States General for the readying of the English aid promised in the treaty of 1678. When the Commons discussed the message on 2 April, the first to speak was James Brydges. Although he had been one of the Junto's most vociferous foes, he now only 'lightly reflected' upon past miscarriages so as not to 'widen our breaches when we should unite'. Brydges did allude to the government's debts and to the realm's unpreparedness for war, but he 'concluded with the danger of leaving France in the possession of all Spain'. Seymour continued in much the same vein: he was 'for saving his stake in the hedge, and he and his all, upon occasion, should be offered to the public; he was not for declaring against war nor being too forward in it, but for supporting the Dutch according to the treaty—to be seconds, not principals'. Then Heneage Finch proposed that the Commons 'assure' the King they would 'effectually enable him to support' the 1678 treaty and also advise him to continue the negotiations with France 'in concert with the States General' and 'to take such measures therein as may most conduce to their security'.[68]

While the Tories offered cautious support for the Dutch, other members wished to go further. The intrepid Lord Cutts, one of William's generals, offered an addition to the projected address to state that the Commons did not regard the renewal of the Treaty of Ryswick by France as a 'sufficient' security, and he was seconded by Hartington. But their amendment was opposed by the supporters of the original motion who claimed that it was tantamount to a declaration of war. Even so, it was reported that Cutts's addition would have been carried by forty votes, had not Secretary Hedges, reminding the members of William's wish for unanimity, urged that it be dropped. Finally, Cutts himself acceded to Hedges's suggestion, and the lengthy debate concluded with the passage *nemine contradicente* of Finch's motion. Then the House immediately went into committee and approved a resolution to supply the 10,000 men and twenty ships which England was supposed to furnish the Dutch under the terms of the 1678 treaty. William, despite Hedges's intervention, would have preferred the inclusion of Cutts's amendment, yet at least he was now able to assure Heinsius, in firmer terms than ever before, that England would not abandon the United Provinces.[69]

However, the King had not anticipated the new storm over the Partition treaties that blew up during the next few days. Hitherto, parliamentary attention had been focused on the 1700 agreement. But the Commons' request to the Lords on 2 April for the materials that the peers had accumulated concerning Portland's part in that negotiation, and particularly the evidence of his transactions with Vernon, referred to in the Tory lords' protest of 20 March against the majority's refusal to transmit their address to the Commons, opened a new scene. The Commons were seeking elucidation of the account Portland had given in the Lords on 15 March as to how he had become involved in the making of the 1700 treaty. In his statement Portland had alluded to a correspondence with Vernon— a correspondence he mistakenly placed in the summer of 1699, but which actually dated from the previous summer. When the Lords delayed replying to the Commons' request, while they tried themselves to resolve the contradictions in Portland's account, the Commons pressed their own member Vernon to explain the matter. In rectifying the Earl's mistake, the Secretary said enough to provoke the lower House to ask William on 8 April for the submission to them of the first Partition Treaty and related documents. And once these papers were laid before them on the 11th, along with the report of a conference with the Lords held on the 9th, the Commons' next request was for copies of the letters between Vernon and Portland of 1698.[70]

The object of the Commons' investigation was not Portland, whose part in the making of the treaties was not in doubt, but Somers. To be sure, Brydges had spoken on 2 April of the need for national unity, but he and his friends had lost none of their fear of and zeal against the Junto. This was evident in their continuing efforts to use Kidd's case against the old ministers. On 31 March, Seymour informed the lower House that Kidd had written him to intimate he had revelations to make, but when the Captain was summoned later that day to the Bar he said nothing of substance. Again, on 10 April a story made the rounds in the Commons that Kidd, though he was supposed to be incarcerated in Newgate, had been seen at Lord Halifax's house with Somers, and the House went to the length of summoning the Keeper of Newgate to ascertain the truth of this unfounded report.[71]

These false starts, and also the defeats of 28–29 March, were all made good on 14 April, after the Vernon–Portland correspondence was read out to the Commons by their Clerk. Sir Bartholomew Shower, after denouncing the terms of the first Partition Treaty as worse than those of the second, moved that Somers be impeached for sealing the instrument of ratification in 1698 without a warrant, and he was seconded by Harcourt. Littleton and Hartington distinguished themselves on the other side, but it was Somers himself who led his own defence. When he was advised of the impending vote, he sought permission to address the Commons and his request was granted over the objections of his accusers. In a half-hour speech that evoked general admiration, the former Lord Chancellor laid bare his own part in the conclusion of the first Partition Treaty and submitted in his vindication a copy of the letter of 28 August 1698 he had written to the King. Had his friends called for a division immediately after he departed, many thought Somers would have escaped once more. But it was not until 11 p.m., when something of the favourable impression Somers had made had worn off, that the Commons divided, and the motion to impeach was carried 198 to 188. Then, without further debate, impeachments were also voted against Orford and Halifax by substantially larger margins.[72]

The passage of the vote of impeachment against Somers, after so many unsuccessful attempts, was variously explained. Some pointed to Harley's statement from the Chair of the question against Somers in a fashion that presupposed his guilt; others commented that the division came at a time when many of his lawyer friends in the Commons were absent on circuit, and it was also observed that the Whigs had been weakened by the many election cases decided against their friends, especially those linked with the new East India Company.[73] But in the main, the Whigs laid the blame upon the Court. Sir Richard Cocks, in denouncing the political cowardice of placemen such as Lord Cutts who absented themselves on 14 April, spoke of 'the courtiers' as men who 'prefer the rising sun before God, country, friend, and everything'. By his reckoning, only Charles Godfrey, Sir Walter Yonge, Sir William St Quintin, Thomas Stringer, 'and two or three more' of the many Whigs still in place stood by Somers.[74] In turn, the Commons' passage on 15 April by a vote of 162 to 107 of a motion to address William to remove Somers and the other three lords under impeachment 'from his council and presence for ever' led the Earl of Shaftesbury to exclaim that 'our friends are given up as a peace offering to the Tory party, who have promised all shall go smoothly and without opposition to the King on these terms of their disabling the late ministry from coming into places again'.[75] The Whigs' fears were then intensified by the unexpected news that reached London in early May by way of the *Paris Gazette* that William, though he had not announced it in England, had recognised the Duke of Anjou in mid-April.[76]

But while the Whigs lamented that 'the King had given up' both 'his friends' and 'his cause', the Tories were by no means confident of their position.[77] It is true that late April brought reports Nottingham would be named Lord Chancellor in place of Wright, Seymour would succeed the dying Tankerville as Lord Privy Seal, and Musgrave and Howe would be named Privy Councillors. However, the Tory Commoners in question thought these rumours had been spread by their enemies in order to discredit them with their own friends on the back benches.[78] Moreover, Nottingham's friend Weymouth was of the opinion at the beginning of May that 'matters are still under the old uncertainty' between 'what they call the old and the new ministry': 'the old is not out nor the new in'.[79]

There was some cause for Weymouth's pessimism. After all, William did not dismiss the four lords from the Privy Council, much less purge their many friends still in place, and his recognition of Philip did not signify any lessening of his desire for forceful action against France. Moreover, out of doors a clamour for more vigorous measures against Louis was mounting, just as the new ministers were finding it difficult to restrain some of their more unruly supporters in the lower House over ways and means. By the beginning of May, the Commons had approved the expenditure of roughly £2,400,000 for the fleet, guards and garrisons, and payment of interest on the outstanding debts and deficiencies. But towards that sum they had so far voted only a three-shilling land tax. £900,000 more still had to be found, plus whatever would be needed for the forces that were to be sent to the Netherlands.

When the Commons resumed consideration of ways and means on 2 May in committee, the proposal that attracted most attention was one offered by Howe for reducing the civil list from £700,000 to £600,000. Howe justified this cutback on the grounds that neither the £50,000 per annum intended for Mary of Modena nor the charges of the late Duke of Gloucester's establishment were now being paid. Harley, Seymour, Harcourt, and other adherents of the new ministry tried to block this proposal, and they instanced the King's debts of over £500,000. But Howe's suggestions appealed to many backbenchers, and the committee instructed its chairman to move the full House to adopt it.[80] Three days later, the Commons did so by a vote of 214 to 169 in what Cocks described as 'the oddest division that ever was'. As he explained, among the 'new ministry' men Sir Joseph Tredenham, Anthony Hammond, and Sir Thomas Powis, 'altered by gifts or hopes', spoke against the proposal. But Seymour now spoke for it, Harcourt and Granville divided for it, and Musgrave stayed away from the House. Among the 'old ministry' men, Sir Rowland Gwynne spoke against the plan and Boyle was one of the tellers for the minority. But many other Whigs, including Hartington and Cocks himself, voted with the majority, not least 'because they were dissatisfied with the King's giving up the Lord Somers'.[81] And the result of this combination against the Court was, as under-secretary Ellis observed, to 'put our ministry into very great disorder, as tending much to the diminution of their credit with the King, since they have so little authority with their party as not to be able to restrain them from passing unreasonable and extravagant things only to lessen the King'.[82]

As the new ministers consulted how to overturn this unwelcome resolution, they and their adherents also had to reckon with the rising popular fervour for war, as evidenced in the recent adoption by the grand juries of Kent, Warwickshire, and Cheshire of addresses urging prompt action by the Commons to make good their earlier votes of support for the Dutch.[83] On 8 May, the Kent address was presented to the lower House in the form of a petition by one of the knights of the shire, Thomas Meredith, but earlier that day his colleague Sir Thomas Hales had alerted Seymour so that the Tories were ready when five of the signers of the petition appeared at the Bar to 'own it'. Seymour and Harcourt joined in denouncing the petitioners as 'tools of the late ministry', but they were not intimidated and refused to admit that they might have been misled. So the Commons, who were both generally inclined against receiving instructions from out of doors and particularly alarmed at the prospect of additional addresses of this nature, voted the Kentish petition 'a scandalous, insolent, and seditious' paper, 'tending to destroy the constitution of parliaments', and placed the five petitioners under arrest.[84]

During the next fortnight, the new ministry also managed to make up some of the ground lost on other fronts, as even the most rabid of their friends in the Commons showed signs of realising the political pitfalls before them. The most positive gesture came from Howe on 9 May when the lower House took up the latest Dutch plea for aid, which was accompanied by a strong message from William. Howe began by declaring that 'the liberties of Europe were in danger from France' and went on to explain that 'now there was occasion we should show the world that we were misrepresented'; 'we would manage things so that we would not be principals and yet not neglect anything that was necessary for our safety'. Although some Whigs reproached Howe for this belated recognition of the gravity of the French threat, the House concluded by adopting with virtual unanimity a resolution promising to assist William 'to support his allies in maintaining the liberties of Europe'.[85] Furthermore, the Commons requested that the King submit to them an estimate of the charges of the 10,000 men to be sent to the Republic. William jubilantly communicated these votes to Heinsius, noting that the French would be taken aback, especially by the invocation of the 'liberties of Europe', and observing that he could proceed now to negotiate with the Imperialists. Moreover, when the Lords considered the Dutch request the next day, it was remarked that Normanby spoke in support of an even stronger address in which the peers explicitly recommended renewal of the Anglo–Imperial alliance.[86]

After the Tories signalled their willingness to support a more vigorous anti-French line, their leaders sought to retrieve the vote of 5 May for reducing the civil list. The first tack they tried was to substitute a plan to take £3,000 a week from the civil list receipts for a term of years and apply those funds to meet the charges of a substantial loan to be used to pay for the estimates already approved for 1701. Seymour offered this proposal in committee on 21 May, and he was joined by Harley, Musgrave, Harcourt, Brydges, and other members of what some called the 'new Court party'. But Howe stood out for his original scheme, along with Sir Godfrey Copley, and they were supported by many Whigs including Hartington and Onslow. This combination was able to carry an amendment to Seymour's motion which stipulated that in addition to the £3,000 per week the public should have whatever surplus remained of the civil list receipts above £600,000. This addition, in effect, was simply a recasting of the resolution of the 5th, and when the composite motion was reported to the full House on the 23rd, a final attempt to alter it was made. The compromise at last arrived at that day was slightly more favourable to the King, if only in principle. £3,700 per week was to be taken from the civil list revenues for five years, and it was calculated that on the basis of the receipts in 1700 William would be left with approximately £600,000 per annum. However, he would retain his title to the whole £700,000 for life. It was also reckoned that £3,700 per week would suffice to cover the charges of a loan of at least £820,000, and so only £300,000 more would be needed to pay both the estimates and the costs of assisting the Dutch.[87]

As the Tories showed themselves more courtly as May proceeded, so William made several significant moves in support of his new ministers. On 15 May, Whig attempts in the Lords to attack the advisers of the dissolution of December 1700 were defeated with the aid of Albemarle's, Jersey's, and Archbishop Tenison's votes. The same day, the London common council rejected by a single vote a petition in support of war with France, and their decision was attributed to the Court's influence. In turn, when the long-awaited bid by the old East India Company to take over the new Company's loan to the government was reported to the Commons on the 17th, the proposition was left to lie on the Table by common consent on the grounds that to proceed with it might endanger the public credit.[88]

However, the most striking instance of the interplay among the King, the parties, and opinion out of doors came early in June as the Commons advanced to the final stages of the three money bills: the land tax, the civil list loan scheme, and a bill continuing a variety of miscellaneous duties which was intended to raise the last £300,000 in supply. By this time, it was apparent that the agitation for war had not been stilled by either the committal of the Kentish petitioners.

the Commons' address of 14 May against endeavours 'to raise tumults and sedi-
tions' which was provoked by the delivery of the hectoring 'Legion' memorial
to Speaker Harley, or the defeat of the petitioning campaign in the City.[89]
Instead, it was reported that more than a hundred M.P.s had received letters from
their constituencies urging more forceful measures against France, and on 8 June
Godolphin worriedly acquainted Nottingham that he had been 'informed from
some members of the House of Commons, who came yesterday out of the country,
that the people are generally unsatisfied with the proceedings of the parliament'.
Godolphin's hope was that the Commons would act 'to support the interest and
credit of our friends, with respect to the people and the King'. Thus, he suggested
that William, when he came to Westminster in response to a recent reminder
about the many bills awaiting his assent, should take that opportunity to give
'rise' to 'some vote' by the Commons 'which may leave a good impression' at
the end of the session and discourage talk of a new parliament.[90]

Godolphin's plan was approved by a 'general meeting' of the Tory parliamentary leadership a few days later and implemented on 12 June.[91] William came
that day to the Lords, approved the bill of succession and various other measures,
and then went on to thank the two Houses for their 'repeated assurances' of
support for alliances to preserve the 'liberty of Europe' and their 'ready compliance' with his requests for aid to the Dutch. All he asked now was that they
quickly complete the public business still before them, since 'the posture of
affairs abroad does absolutely require my presence' there. In response to this cue
from the throne, Seymour and Shower promptly proposed, and the Commons
agreed, to thank William for his 'approbation' of their proceedings and to 'unanimously assure' him of their support for such alliances as he should conclude 'in
conjunction with the Emperor and the States-General, for the preservation of the
liberties of Europe, the prosperity and peace of England, and for reducing the
exorbitant power of France'.[92]

Although the Commons' resolution of 12 June was disparaged by the Whigs as
a 'sham', they had to admit that Godolphin's 'artifices' had the effect of 'blind-
[ing] the people'.[93] But on another front, the Whigs could claim to have out-
manoeuvred their adversaries. Since Somers and Orford were confident that the
articles of impeachment drawn up against them by the Commons would not
survive critical scrutiny, they repeatedly pressed the Lords during May to give
them speedy trials. But when the Lords attempted to get the Commons to move
ahead with the impeachment proceedings, the majority in the lower House
retorted by charging the peers with encroachment upon the Commons' privilege
of choosing the order in which the trials should be held and with arbitrary dictation in regulating the procedure for the trials. The increasingly sharp exchanges
between the two Houses over these issues in late May and early June led the
Lords to vote by a margin of ten to put off deliberations on the land tax bill after
it was sent up to them by the Commons on 10 June. Then, new fuel was added to
these flames on the 13th by Lord Haversham's reflections on the Commons'
conduct of the impeachments, which he made to the face of the Commons'
managers at a conference between the two Houses. Haversham accused the Commons of acting partially by impeaching only some of those who had been involved
in the negotiation of the two Partition treaties, and he suggested that their conduct was clear proof that they did not really take seriously their articles against
the three Junto lords and Portland.[94]

Haversham's particular target was Jersey. The Lord Chamberlain had been one of the signers of the second Partition Treaty, and the Commons' averseness to impeach him was generally reputed to be the result of his willingness to support the new ministers in the King's closet. Moreover, these suspicions had seemed to be confirmed in mid-May when Haversham's son, Maurice Thompson, was ruled out of order by Speaker Harley for moving Jersey's impeachment during a debate on the articles against Somers.[95] Now, the Commons used the Lords' refusal to censure Haversham as a justification for their own decision not to proceed with the trials of the four lords. But the majority in the upper House were not to be deterred, and they continued to hold up the passage of the supply bills until they had disposed of the impeachments.

The first of the four lords to be tried was Somers. The Commons ordered their members to stay away on the 17th, but many attended as spectators. As expected, Somers was acquitted 56 to 32, with the verdict being received with 'three great hussa's in the Court and in the Hall as were upon the acquittal of the bishops in King James his time'.[96] The Commons' retort on the 20th was a resolution that 'all the ill consequences which may, at this time, attend the delay of the supplies' should be 'imputed to those who, to procure an indemnity for their own enormous crimes, have used their utmost endeavours to make a breach between the two Houses'. Yet, before the Lords approved the three money bills on 24 June, they also acquitted Orford and resolved that 'whatsoever ill consequences may arise from the so long deferring the supplies for this year's service are to be attributed to the fatal counsel of putting off the meeting of a parliament so long, and to the unnecessary delays of the House of Commons'.[97]

When the King came to Westminster late on 24 June to close the session, the two Houses had been sitting for over four months, yet they had passed only forty-nine acts, and of this total just thirteen were public measures. Some of the more noteworthy bills of the 1701 session which failed to reach the statute book were casualties of the virtually continuous clashing between the two Houses. Besides rejecting the Commons' bill to fix minimum property qualifications for justices of the peace, the Lords also blocked passage of the lower House's bill of accounts. That measure had begun as a bill to continue the commission of 1700 to state the military departments' debts, but it was later enlarged to provide for the creation of a new parliamentary commission of accounts. This addition was the work of Hammond, Howe, Tredenham, and other Tory backbenchers, and seven of their number, headed by Sir Godfrey Copley, were chosen in the ballot of 16 June to serve on this commission. Its purpose was to make good repeated charges that millions of pounds granted for the last war remained to be accounted for, and for this reason Harley, Musgrave, Seymour, and Harcourt showed little zeal for the project lest it further weaken the new ministry's position with the King. Yet, when their friends insisted, the Speaker and those Tories of his mind could only stand by and allow the bill to be sent up to the Lords. Fortunately for them, the Lords' attempt to alter the composition of the new commission, along with other amendments they inserted, made the measure unacceptable to the Commons' majority. Hence, the bill of accounts' demise could subsequently be adduced as one more count in the indictments drawn up against the Lords' proceedings in the pamphlet warfare that broke out once the 1701 session was over.[98]

Other, potentially more drastic 'reform' bills failed to gain the approval of even the lower House. One was a proposal, sponsored by Seymour and prompted by the conduct of the new East India Company in the 1700–01 election, to open up the narrower borough constituencies that were as a group particularly susceptible to bribery by outsiders. According to Luttrell, the remedy Sir Edward offered was that 'in boroughs where there are not fifty electors', the freeholders of the surrounding hundred should 'join in choosing members'. But since more than forty boroughs would have been affected, Seymour's plan was 'like knocking at a wasp's nest' and it never was reported out of committee.[99]

Seymour's fellow Churchman, Sir John Packington, was the sponsor of another bill which might have had far-reaching effects. His bill 'for the preservation of the Protestant religion' sought to prohibit the translation of bishops from one diocese to another. Sir John was bent on limiting the Court's influence over the bishops' votes in the Lords by curbing the crown's power to move loyal prelates from poorer to richer sees, and it was reported that he had been roused to action by the prospect that Burnet, the target of his shafts in the last parliament, was about to be promoted from Salisbury to Winchester.[100] Packington's bill was also brought forward at a time when the lower house of convocation had initiated a quarrel with the bishops' house over the right of adjournment, and its aspersions on the past conduct of the episcopate did reflect Sir John's and his friends' sympathy with the 'high Church' majority headed by Atterbury in the lower house. In addition, the measure touched on another tender point—occasional conformity. Although he was not anxious to publicise his role in his home county of Gloucestershire where there were many Dissenting voters, the section of the bill that penalised occasional conformists was inserted at John Howe's suggestion.[101] But as with Seymour's bill to reform the choice of burgesses to the Commons, so Packington's bill to reform the translation of bishops was never reported out of committee.

Despite the many clashes of the 1701 session between the two Houses and despite the relatively scanty legislative harvest, when Speaker Harley presented the supply bills to William for his assent on 24 April he took pains in his speech to stress the Commons' accomplishments. More money had been voted than ever before in peacetime; in addition, two acts of permanent significance, which were initiated by the lower House, had been passed.[102] One was Sir John Leveson-Gower's bill to regulate members of parliament's privilege of freedom from arrest and so end a long-standing abuse.[103] The second was the bill of succession. Yet no sooner had the latter reached the statute book than it was noticed that the section barring placemen from the Commons (as well as that nullifying pardons to impeachments) lacked the qualifying phrase, attached to the rest of the restrictive clauses, that it should take effect only after the first Hanoverian came to the throne. This omission was probably an oversight. When James Lowther, himself a placeman, commented on this point in a letter of September 1701, he claimed it was not 'so designed', and his testimony is corroborated by the circumstance that the Commons had included in the land tax act of 1701 a clause which barred Customs officials henceforth from sitting in the lower House.[104] This provision, in a bill which was transmitted to the Lords after the upper House had already passed the bill of succession, would have been redundant had it been assumed that the general exclusion of placemen stipulated in the succession act was to come into force immediately. But whatever the intention, there was now a chance that there would be an attempt at the beginning of the next meeting of parliament to insist upon a literal construction of this section of the act of succession.[105]

However, the principal subject for speculation as the King made ready to leave for the Continent was the future of the new ministry and the present parliament. Nor did Sunderland's appearance at Court immediately after the prorogation clarify William's intentions.[106] Admittedly, the King had given no sign of being ready to satisfy Whig desires for a dissolution. Rather, when he was warned by Jersey on 24 June that the peers, having already condemned the Commons' conduct, were about to approve Bolton's motion for an address asking him to call new elections, William had 'almost forced his way' into the Lords to put an end to the 1701 session in a speech in which he referred to 'our meeting again in the winter'.[107] Yet the King also seemed reluctant to commit himself unreservedly to the new ministers, who were pressing him to make further changes in the ministry, to alter the episcopal commission of 1695 which was charged with making nominations to ecclesiastical vacancies in the crown's gift, and to revamp the commissions of the peace and the London lieutenancy.[108]

The only major new appointment William made in the summer of 1701 was his selection of Marlborough as general of the forces being sent to the United Provinces and as plenipotentiary for the forthcoming negotiations at The Hague; the Earl's military command, his first since 1692, was publicly announced before the two Houses divided over the impeachments. Yet Marlborough was no party man, and the King's choice represented a realistic appreciation of the utility of associating one so much in Princess Anne's confidence with the measures to be taken against France, especially as William's own physical condition remained a source of concern.[109] Similarly, Edward Northey, named Attorney-General after Sir Thomas Trevor was promoted to the bench, was a moderate; his appointment, which was recommended by Lord Chief Justice Holt, also put paid to the hopes of several Tory legal notables, Shower, Conyers, Harcourt, and Powis.[110] Furthermore, after Tankerville died on 24 June, William avoided choosing a successor by the expedient of creating a commission to hold the Privy Seal temporarily. Thus, the only unexpected face among the seven Lords Justices he named for the summer of 1701 was the Duke of Somerset; he was reckoned a supporter of the new ministry, but hitherto he had distinguished himself chiefly by his friendship to the Princess and the aristocratic haughtiness he had in common with his kinsman Sir Edward Seymour. The Duke was joined on the commission by Godolphin, and by all the surviving Lords Justices from the summer of 1700, save for Marlborough who was to accompany William.

Although the appointments of Marlborough, Northey, and Somerset were not the decisive alterations the Tories desired, they did represent a continuation of the course upon which the King had embarked in dissolving the 1698–1700 parliament. Furthermore, William did yield partially to his ministers' importunities for local changes. He left behind instructions for the enlargement of the London lieutenancy, and during the course of the summer a host of new commissions of the peace were issued by Lord Keeper Wright. In some jurisdictions, particularly Warwickshire, Hampshire, and Wiltshire, Wright not only added the names of eligible Tories but also omitted those of some Whigs.[111] The chief impetus for these changes, as was usual, came from the localities, but the recommendations of individual Tory M.P.s and peers were strongly backed up by Rochester when they were challenged. Thus, when the King, in response to the arguments of the Earl of Carlisle (who made a special trip to Loo to present his case), hesitated over the alterations that had been set in motion in Westmorland on Musgrave's recommendation, Rochester put off his trip to Ireland.[112] In late August, Carlisle was forced to concede defeat to Rochester, who in this instance was supported by Harley, and Normanby reported the outcome to Nottingham in an optimistic vein:[113]

The consequence is of some use, and (as the preachers have it) may be of application; for our friend's insisting brought it about again and will always do so as certainly as that of a House [the Commons] which shall be nameless; and then I appeal to your good judgement if we ought to blame any besides ourselves when any repulse of consequence is acquiesced in.

As the Tories strained to exploit their majority in the Commons, so the Whigs exerted themselves to secure a dissolution. The Whigs' strategy was to convince the King by new manifestations of popular zeal for the war and of opposition to the present House of Commons that it would be both advantageous and safe for him to venture upon fresh elections. Thus, while the pamphleteers on each side (among them, allegedly, both Harley and Somers) rushed into print to expose the vices or to expatiate on the virtues of the Commons' majority, the Whigs also launched a campaign to secure favourable addresses from the county grand juries again being assembled for the assizes.[114] Their first successes came in Buckinghamshire and Hampshire late in July, and similar addresses were approved in August in Nottinghamshire and Yorkshire. But none of these grand juries acted unanimously, and late in August Seymour was instrumental in persuading the Devonshire grand jury to approve an address commending the Commons' proceedings during the past session.[115]

Had the Whigs been forced to depend solely upon mobilising opinion out of doors, it is doubtful whether they could have persuaded the King to risk a dissolution. As William explained himself to Sunderland at the beginning of September, he was afraid that 'if he should quit those he now employs, and that the others should not be able to serve him, then he shall have no resource. This inclines him to try again what the present ministry and their party will do; with a resolution to change upon the first occasion they shall give.' Sunderland, who had apparently come to a firm but still secret understanding with Somers, answered the King's request for advice very bluntly. The Tories, in his opinion, were either Jacobites or were unmanageable by their supposed leaders, and he expressed astonishment that 'after a thirteen years' experience the King will not judge right of things he knows, but will be undone infallibly by believing himself more cunning than a whole party by whom he is beset, and who wheedles him every day; and of which, in his whole reign, he never yet could gain any one man'. The Earl's counsel, then, was that William should return to England as soon as possible, summon Somers ('the life, the soul, and the spirit of his party, and can answer for it'), and ask the former Lord Chancellor 'what he and his friends can do, and will do, and what they expect, and the methods they would propose'.[116]

Sunderland's advice was clear, but William had not always heeded it before. That he eventually did so in the autumn of 1701 may in large part be attributed to the course of developments abroad. Initially, Louis's acceptance of Carlos II's will had brought substantial advantages to France: the expulsion of the Dutch garrisons from the barrier fortresses in the Spanish Netherlands; the Dutch and, later, the English recognition of Philip; and the signing in June of a Franco-

Portuguese alliance. But then the tide began to ebb. The Imperialists' decision to take up arms in Italy was vigorously implemented by Prince Eugene, and his successes were followed by the conclusion at The Hague in late August of a renewed grand alliance. Marlborough bore the burden of the negotiations for England, and it was eventually agreed that the Maritime Powers and the House of Austria would unite in a bid (1) to reclaim a sizeable portion of Carlos II's European domains for a Habsburg claimant, (2) to assure the Dutch of their barrier against France, (3) to guarantee the English their Mediterranean trade, and (4) to allow England and the United Provinces to take what they could of the Spanish West Indies.

Despite the growing resistance to their pretensions, the French showed no signs during the summer of 1701 of easing the hard line they had adopted after the acceptance of the will. The formation in early July of a French-dominated company to exploit the Spanish American trade was promptly followed by the termination of the French envoy's stay at The Hague. D'Avaux's abrupt departure aroused fears that his master would immediately unleash his forces against the Republic. Louis did not go this far, but in early September an edict to bar most English goods from entering France was readied for his promulgation. Then James II died on 5 September and the French monarch, in a decision which few had expected, recognised the exiled English king's son as James III, rightful sovereign of the British kingdoms. Louis was warned by his ministers that he was taking a grave risk of provoking a final rupture with England by so clear a breach of the spirit (if not the letter) of the Treaty of Ryswick, yet even the French councillors were taken aback by the vehemence of the English reaction. William immediately gave orders for breaking off diplomatic relations with Louis, and in England the news of the proclamation of James III sparked a new and more powerful wave of addresses that was begun by the London common council's declaration of 26 September against the 'pretended Prince of Wales' and for war.[117]

Simultaneously, William decided—despite the screed against a dissolution penned for his eyes by Godolphin—to take the first step on the course Sunderland had mapped out for him. On 30 September, the King dispatched Lord Galway to England, ostensibly so that Galway might prepare himself for a mission to Venice but actually so that he could 'discourse fully and plainly' with Somers.[118] In his conversations with Galway, and then with William himself upon the King's return to England on 4 November, Somers made out a persuasive case for calling a new general election. Then, too, he was able to back up his arguments with the thirty or so addresses, most 'tending to dissolving the parliament', which were presented to William after he reached London.[119]

Somers built his case on three main contentions. First, Tory promises of support for the war and their assurances that the quarrels between the two Houses would not be revived were undependable. Neither 'their will nor their power' could be relied upon; some of their number were Jacobites, and the nominal leaders of the party either would not or could not control the rank and file. Second, the dangers of hesitation were great. If the King did not act, the Whigs would 'look upon themselves as utterly abandoned' and would think only 'of measures to procure safety' for themselves. Then, too, should renewed disputes break out between the two Houses in a second session of the present parliament, so compelling the King to order a dissolution then, there was a grave risk of 'ill elections'. Third, the hazards of an immediate dissolution were not too great. Since 'Court and Country' was 'not the present question', the Whigs could be expected to do well. And even should they somehow fail to secure a majority, widespread public support for war would ensure that the new House of Commons would do 'what the King will desire'.[120]

Sunderland's and Somers's arguments were probably decisive, though when Albemarle wrote to the Pensionary after William made up his mind the Earl laid the main stress on the King's fears that the Tories 'by principles and inclination' were likely to 'favour the pretended Prince of Wales'.[121] In any case, when William put the proposition of a dissolution before a cabinet council held at Hampton Court on 9 November, it came as a surprise to some of his servants. Actually, neither of the two leading ministers was present: Rochester was still in Ireland; Godolphin was at the Princess's court at Windsor, having been lulled into a false sense of security by the King's charge to him the day before to draft a speech for the opening of the next session. When Godolphin returned on the 10th, William informed him he had decided upon new elections, and the King accepted the resignation the first lord of the Treasury immediately tendered. Despite Godolphin's departure, when the proclamation for a dissolution was discussed at a meeting of the Privy Council on the 11th, Wright, Pembroke, Jersey, Hedges, and some others present argued against its issuance. Even after William made his own views clear, the Privy Council only approved the proclamation by a majority of three.[122]

Although William was determined to have a new parliament, he decided—despite Sunderland's advice to the contrary—to await the election results before proceeding any further with changes in the ministry. He delayed replacing Godolphin, he held off appointing new sheriffs, and he also seems to have tried to induce Harley to agree to stand with Court backing again for the Chair in the new House of Commons. Harley's response was to inform William's emissaries—among them the Duke of Somerset—that 'the hands' which the King 'had trusted himself into would not permit' him to accept such an offer. At the same time, Harley encouraged his own disheartened friends by telling them that the unexpected dissolution 'may be turned to our advantage'.[123]

For all Harley's defiant words, the Tories embarked on the 1701 campaign under some considerable disadvantages. Their opponents had been stirring up sentiment against them for the past six months, and the dissolution proclamation, with its favourable references to the recent addresses and its expression of the King's desire to have 'good Englishmen and Protestants' chosen, seemed to send the Tories into the election 'with libels affixed to our backs'.[124] Furthermore, the indiscretion of Charles Davenant, Anthony Hammond, and John Tredenham in being found with the French Secretary Poussin at the Blue Posts Tavern the evening that official notice to leave England was served on the Frenchman helped the Whigs to stigmatise their opponents as Francophiles and Jacobites. The incident, with suitable insinuations, was first publicised in a pamphlet which appeared in early October, after Vernon's under-secretary, Hopkins, in the company of Lord Halifax and several friends, had gathered supporting testimony from witnesses.[125] Then, when the election was called, the label of 'Poussineer' was attached to 164 other members of the old Commons in the widely-circulated *A List of One Unanimous Club of Members . . . that Met at the Vine Tavern in Long Acre.*[126] In reply, the Tories concentrated mainly on the misdeeds of the

Junto and their followers—the 'modern Whigs', as Davenant called them—and they were charged with subservience to the Court, perversion of their official powers when in office, and gross corruption.

Nor did the paper warfare cease once the elections were over. In a number of constituencies the selection of M.P.s was followed by the framing of 'instructions' to guide them. These instructions purported to come from the electors themselves and their recommendations were usually couched in partisan terms. Although each side's instructions tended to follow a more or less standard pattern, in Westminster, where all inhabitants could vote, thousands of hands were actually secured to the local version.[127] One of the first instructions to be drawn up and printed was directed to Harcourt, the successful Tory incumbent at Abingdon; he was urged to inquire into the advisers of the dissolution, to pursue the impeachments against the four lords, and to continue the investigation of the public accounts.[128] But the majority of the nearly twenty instructions were Whig productions which came from the three metropolitan constituencies, York, Bristol, several counties, and some smaller boroughs.[129] They urged (in the words of the Buckinghamshire version) the grant of 'the most effective and most equal supplies', the restoration of the public credit, support of the King's alliances against 'the exorbitant power of France', consideration of 'all ways for maintaining' the Protestant succession, the exposure of any 'among us' sympathetic 'to the new Pretender which the French would impose upon us', and the avoidance of 'disputes and animosities' between the two Houses.[130]

Despite the highly partisan and voluminous outpouring from the press, only ninety-one constituencies are known to have been contested—just five more than the figure recorded in the 1700–01 election.[131] But this time, the East Indiamen conducted themselves in a much more restrained fashion, partly perhaps because of the many disqualifications the new Company men had incurred in the last parliament but mainly because of the success of Godolphin and Halifax, assisted by Sir Basil Firebrace, in mediating an accommodation between the two Companies during the summer and autumn of 1701.[132] Another notable feature of the 1701 election was the high proportion of incumbents returned. Three-quarters of the sitting members were re-elected, and among the 126 new members forty-eight had sat before, including two distinguished figures who had last served in 1689, Isaac Newton and Sir Christopher Wren. However, the blacklisted 'Poussineers' did not fare quite so well as other incumbents; 29 per cent failed to be returned, as compared to only 22 per cent of all other incumbents, and among the losers were Howe, Hammond, and Davenant.

Contemporaries' assessments of the returns, as after the previous election, varied considerably. The Whig Lord Spencer carefully (if not completely precisely) computed his friends' gains and losses, and concluded that the Whigs had gained fifty-two seats formerly held by Tories and lost only twenty-three that they themselves had held. Others of Spencer's associates were even more sanguine, and the foreign envoys were given to understand that the Whigs had secured the advantage by thirty votes or more, without taking into account the twenty to thirty Tory placemen who might be expected to defer to the King's wishes.[133] But the Tories in town informed their friends in the country that 'the majority runs against' the Whigs and that there was a good chance to have 'our old friend Harley in the Chair' once more.[134] Thus, well before all the returns were in, Godolphin began urging Harley to come back quickly to town, since 'we have a very fair expectation of taking such a step in the very first day of the sessions as may be a sufficient indication of all that is like to follow'. Simultaneously, Bishop Trelawney of Exeter was being pressed to hasten up his unusually full 'squadron' of Tory M.P.s from Cornwall and Devon, and similar whips went out to other provinces.[135] Moreover, Harley's own calculations corresponded with those of his friends. A marked list of the new Commons, corrected in his own hand, lists 253 in column A (supporters), 229 in column B (opponents), and 14 in column C (uncertain).[136] As for the Court, the reckoning there, according to under-secretary Ellis, was that the elections 'seem pretty equal on both sides, so that to which of them the King inclines will be the predominant'.[137]

William now made his preference clear. On 17 December, a meeting attended by over 60 M.P.s was informed that the King favoured Littleton for the Chair; in the week following, the Whig Earl of Carlisle, who had taken an active part in the northern elections, was named to succeed Godolphin at the Treasury; and on the 29th, Secretary Hedges was dismissed after he persisted in refusing to promise his vote to Littleton.[138] Hedges's refusal is also a measure of the determination of Harley's supporters, and the pull of party loyalty on the Tory placemen was even more strikingly demonstrated when the Commons debated the choice of a Speaker on 30 December. Among those who spoke in Harley's behalf was Admiral Rooke, who had just succeeded as first lord of the Admiralty after Haversham's sudden resignation in mid-December; ironically, Rooke's principal argument against Littleton was that Sir Thomas's place as Treasurer of the Navy rendered him unfit for the Chair. Moreover, when the House divided on the question for Littleton, it was observed that at least fifteen placemen—among them, Marlborough's two brothers—voted in the negative.[139]

The defection of the Tory placemen was, however, only one of the factors invoked by James Lowther to explain why his (and others') confident predictions of a 'great majority' for Littleton were confounded in Sir Thomas's defeat 216 to 212 and in the ensuing election of Harley. Lowther also instanced the absence of many northern M.P.s (while others reported the Tories had 'not so much as one wanting either in Wales or Cornwall'), the temporary disadvantage of Littleton's friends by having as many as eleven of their number chosen for two constituencies, and the scruples of 'several' who were unwilling to vote for a placeman but 'are very hearty in other matters'.[140] And while Lowther sought to discount Harley's victory, William—in relaying the news to Heinsius—expressed the hope that public business would, none the less, 'go on well'.[141]

Lowther's expectations that the Whigs would be able to consolidate their position at Court and in the Commons seemed to be borne out, at least in part, during the first weeks of the new parliament. In two early skirmishes over election petitions on 5 January, the Whigs gained the upper hand by votes of 134 to 120 and 187 to 176.[142] Furthermore, the King followed up his appointment of Carlisle by naming Halifax's kinsman, Manchester (a committed Whig), to succeed Hedges and by designating the new convert Somerset as Lord President. To make room for the Duke, Pembroke was named Lord Admiral (the first of the reign); thus, the Admiralty Commission whose members had formed the core of the Harleyite defection over the Speaker's election was superseded. These changes were followed on 25 January by Rochester's dismissal from the Lord Lieutenancy of Ireland, and there was talk that Jersey, who had fallen out with Albemarle, and also Wright were in danger of losing their posts.[143]

While the Whigs appeared on the ascendant at Court, the King's business was favourably and speedily dealt with by the Commons. William's opening speech, drafted by Somers, was not only the longest but possibly the most eloquent of the reign. Despite the length of his speech, the King's appearance at Westminster did not seem to tire him, and it was remarked he looked better than he had for several years.[144] William began by recalling to his audience 'that just sense of the common danger of Europe and that resentment of the late proceedings of the French king' that had been expressed in the addresses presented to him before the dissolution. He then went on to indicate the steps that would be necessary to counter Louis. At home, there was a need for 'further effectual' measures for securing the Protestant succession; abroad, he had concluded several alliances and still others were being negotiated. These treaties he promised to lay before parliament, and he urged that no time be lost in enabling him to make good the commitments that had been made in response to the votes of the 1701 parliament. A strong fleet was necessary, and so was an army 'in proportion' to that of the allies. He also exhorted the Commons 'to take care of the public credit, which cannot be preserved but by keeping sacred that maxim—that they shall never be losers who trust to a parliamentary security'. In addition, he reminded the members that as he had approved various bills for the examination of the public accounts during the last war, so he would now give his assent to 'any further way of examination' that might be desired in order to discover whether there had been 'misapplications and mismanagements' and whether the existing debts 'really' had arisen out of deficiencies in the funds voted. Finally, he voiced the wish that the members would lay aside all differences and disputes so that he might stand as 'the common father of all my people' and so that the only 'distinction' among us in future would be 'of those who are for the Protestant religion and the present establishment and of those who mean a Popish prince and a French government'.[145]

In response, both Houses unanimously voted strong addresses of support, and the Commons hastened to make good their resolutions by approving without division both the troop quota that Marlborough had negotiated at The Hague and the detailed military estimates for the coming year. The supply agreed upon by early February amounted to nearly £3,600,000, and this figure did not include the charge of those outstanding unfunded debts that the Commons also voted to make good. Moreover, by the end of February, ways and means to raise the bulk of this sum had been settled. A four-shilling land tax bill was ordered on 12 February, and a malt tax was tentatively approved 208 to 114 on the 20th.[146]

This was rapid progress for the Commons, and it was made possible by the Tories' readiness to vie with the Whigs in demonstrating compliance with the King's requests. Actually, the Tories were often in the van. The addresses of thanks were proposed by Normanby and Nottingham in the Lords, by Hedges and Thomas Coke in the Commons. Similarly, it was Harley who took the lead in committee of the whole on 31 January in offering proposals for the payment of the outstanding debts by adding them to the 'general mortgage' Montagu had devised in 1697 and by extending those duties presently committed to pay off former deficiencies for several more years. These proposals, Cocks sourly remarked, were 'contradictory to' Harley's 'and his party's former disposition'; they were offered now, in his view, 'to ingratiate themselves with the people against the next dissolution, which they imagined might be shortly'.[147] Again, it was Seymour who moved an address on 12 January to ask William to include in his new treaties an article which would bind the allies not to make peace before England had received 'reparation' from France for Louis's recognition of James III. The King was only too happy to comply with this request, since it appeared to ensure that England would enter the war as a principal. To be sure, there were occasions when Seymour and other Tories appeared to be dragging their feet—for instance, when he and Finch tried to get the Commons to vote that the 7,000 men in garrison in England should be counted towards the kingdom's quota of 40,000. But in this attempt and others they found only a few ready to join them, with Harley particularly quick to dissociate himself.[148]

Nor was that 'emulation' of the parties that Ellis had hopefully anticipated before the 1701–02 session confined to questions of foreign policy and supply. When Wharton, Haversham, and Shaftesbury moved the Lords on 2 January for leave to bring in a bill for the abjuration of James III, Hedges followed suit in the Commons on the 9th. However, the apparent consensus on abjuration did not mask for long the real differences between the two parties on this score. What the Whig lords proposed was a voluntary oath; no penalty was to be imposed upon refusers, yet the abjuration was to be tendered to each member of both Houses and their responses were to be recorded. This was to be that 'right test' which Shaftesbury, at least, had had in mind even before James II's death to sift 'the tares' from 'our wheat', and so serve as a 'national index'.[149] To forestall this and to appease the scruples of those in their ranks who might submit to but would never volunteer for an abjuration, the Tories advocated a compulsory oath. This was the tack adopted by the Tory peers in their unsuccessful resistance to the Whig bill in the Lords. And when Hedges laid his measure before the Commons on 13 January, just before the peers' bill was transmitted to them, it specified a mandatory oath. The lower House considered both bills on the 17th and agreed without much ado to proceed on their own on the grounds that the Lords' measure imposed a pecuniary penalty on any member of parliament who took his seat before having the abjuration tendered to him. But on the 20th, the Whigs proposed an instruction to the committee of the whole charged with the lower House's bill to make the abjuration voluntary. A prolonged debate ensued, but in the end their motion was rejected 188 to 187.[150]

The Tories' success in retaining a compulsory abjuration went hand in hand with the initial results of the well-attended and often lengthy evening sessions of the Committee on Privileges and Elections which sometimes sat 'till 2 or 3 o'clock in the morning'.[151] The Whigs had been able to get that committee to proceed first upon several petitions against sitting Tory members, but when the cases were heard they found they could not unseat them. On 16 January, the Tory M.P. for Maldon was triumphant 201 to 173, and in succeeding days his colleagues for Hertford and Maidstone were victorious 188 to 142 and 153 to 76. In turn, the Maldon resolution was confirmed on report by the full House on the 27th by 226 to 208.[152]

However, these setbacks did not discourage the Whigs from challenging another section of Hedges's abjuration bill when it was considered in committee of the whole on 28 January. In question was the portion of the oath which bound those who took it to swear to 'support, maintain, and defend the government and constitution of this realm, in King, Lords, and Commons, and the Church of England, as it is by law established'.[153] The Whigs objected that the first part of this section was ambiguous and that the obligation to swear to support the Church of England would prevent most Dissenters from taking the abjuration. By way of compromise, one of the Foleys suggested that an obligation to maintain the toleration might be included as well. But that suggestion was little to the taste of many Tories, and when the amended clause was finally put to the question after six hours of wrangling it was rejected *in toto* 173 to 155.[154]

With first one party and then the other gaining the advantage in the virtually evenly-divided Commons, the next clash came on 7 February over the report of the Maidstone election. The Whig petitioner in this case was Thomas Colepepper, one of the five Kentish petitioners of May 1701, and his zeal had not been cooled by his confinement then. During the 1701 election he had denounced his opponent as a traitor and distributed 'many quires of reflecting papers'; more recently, he had written to the Speaker to condemn the proceedings of the last parliament. Not only, then, did the House censure Colepepper and order his arrest anew, but it also agreed, upon Heneage Finch's motion, to deliberate in committee of the whole on 17 February on 'the rights, liberties, and privileges of the House of Commons'.[155]

It was widely anticipated that the sitting of 17 February would be 'the greatest day' of the 1701–02 session, but the proceedings ended quite inconclusively. At first, there was little debate, as the Whigs refrained from challenging three Tory resolutions which (1) condemned the assertion that the House of Commons 'is not the only representative of the commons of England'; (2) denied the claim that 'the House of Commons have no power of commitment but of their own members'; and (3) denounced published attacks upon the House and upon particular M.P.s as a violation of the Commons' 'rights and privileges'.[156] After their adoption, the Whigs moved to adjourn the committee, but William Bromley of Warwickshire (now sitting for Oxford University) proposed a fourth resolution stating that to address for a dissolution was 'tending to sedition'. This the Whigs opposed 'with courage and heat', and they appeared to have the support of a number of weathercock backbenchers. Rather than venture upon a division on Bromley's suggested resolution, the Tories now called the question that the chairman Granville should leave the chair. Amid mounting disorder, aggravated by the collapse of Sir William Strickland (one of the leading Whig speakers of the day) with a stroke, Granville left the chair without even waiting to be instructed to report the first three resolutions. Then, despite Whig protests at Granville's irregular conduct, Harley hastily adjourned the Commons.[157]

Nevertheless, the lack of a decisive division on 17 February only acted as a spur to both sides. On the 19th, the Tories moved and the House ordered that there be another sitting in committee on the same subject on the 26th; on the 24th, Hartington countered for the Whigs by gaining the Commons' consent to a motion that the committee on the 26th should also consider 'the rights and liberties of all the commons of England'.[158] The proceedings on the 26th were opened by Henry St John, who was already gaining for himself a reputation as one of the Tories' most able speakers. The resolution he moved and Thomas Coke seconded stated that 'the House of Commons had not right done them in the matter of the impeachments in the last parliament'. After a debate lasting till almost 10 p.m., the motion was rejected, despite support from Harley, by 235 to 221 in the largest division of William's reign. Then Hartington, pressing home the Whigs' advantage, moved two resolutions. The first was to uphold the subject's right to address for 'the calling, sitting, and dissolving' of parliaments; the second was to sustain the subject's right to 'a speedy trial' of 'any accusation', including an impeachment, against him. These were adopted without a division. And before the sitting ended, Hartington's resolutions, along with those of the 17th, were reported to the full House which wearily approved all five without further debate.[159]

The Whig successes of 26 February, so many members believed, would result in 'a shorter session than we expected'.[160] Certainly, all that was needed to complete the business of supply was agreement on the means to raise the last £300,000 of the charge for 1702. Then, too, by late February the Commons' abjuration bill was almost ready for the royal assent. When Hedges's measure was reported from committee on 10 February, the full House confirmed the amendment voted on 28 January by 187 to 166. Then on the 19th, the Whigs, joined on this occasion by the Harleys and the Foleys, voted down Bolles's proposed rider against occasional conformity 203 to 139.[161] Similarly, a majority in the Lords repulsed all Tory attempts to sidetrack the abjuration bill there, but the peers did make two amendments to the Commons' measure. One extended the oath to 'all ecclesiastical persons'. The other, which was aimed at dispelling Tory tales that William and the Whigs were intent upon removing Anne from the line of succession to the throne, imposed penalties of high treason upon any who sought either the death or the exclusion of the Princess.[162] The allegations of a plot against Anne are hard to accept at face value, but they may represent a reaction to pre-sessional reports that the Whigs would seek to 'improve' the succession act of 1701 and that they would propose an invitation to the Electoral Prince of Hanover to take up residence in England as a further safeguard for the Protestant succession.[163]

Probably, it was only a coincidence that the Lords' amendment in Anne's favour was incorporated in the abjuration bill on 23 February, two days after William suffered a broken collarbone when his horse stumbled and fell in Richmond Park. The King's injury was regarded by his physicians as more of an inconvenience than a cause for serious concern, and he appeared in public again early in March.[164] Nevertheless, when an opportunity arose to press parliament to consider once more a project that William had long favoured—the achievement of an 'entire union' between England and Scotland—he did not wait until he could personally come to Westminster to recommend it from the throne. This opportunity was unintentionally provided by Nottingham on 24 February when that Earl, professing his zeal for the Protestant succession despite his recent denunciations of abjuration, reminded the Lords that the Scots had yet to settle their crown on the Hanoverians. So Nottingham suggested that the Lords address William to call new elections in his northern kingdom, since the Scottish parliament chosen in 1689 (and still in being) had no mandate to make a new settlement. His proposal found little favour with the peers, but it did prompt Somerset to say that he knew William intended to propose negotiations for a union to parliament. This the King did by message on 28 February, and it was reported that a majority of the peers and 'all the Whig party' in the Commons seemed prepared to respond favourably to the royal initiative.[165]

Although neither the amendment to the abjuration bill on 23 February in defence of Anne's rights nor the King's message of the 28th recommending union with Scotland was inspired by any sense of impending mortality, on

4 March William came down with a cold and a fever. Possibly the royal physicians' concern that William should exercise his legs while convalescing from his fall contributed to this, for after napping on a chair in the draughty gallery at Kensington where he had been walking the King awoke feeling ill. His condition quickly worsened, and on the evening of the 6th a specially-summoned cabinet council was told that the doctors now feared for his life. The King weakened still further that night, so much so that on Saturday, the 7th, the ministers decided it would be advisable to get his hand to a commission to give his assent *in absentia* to the abjuration and malt tax bills that were being rushed through their final stages in the Lords.[166]

Yet even in this moment of crisis, partisan advantage was not ignored by some. When the Lords, alerted to William's rapid decline, sent down to the Commons around midday on 7 March to ask them not to adjourn until further notice, Bolles was in the process of proposing that the lower House recess till Monday. Despite the Lords' request, Seymour and Bromley then spoke in favour of Bolles's motion; their argument was that 'when the King was so ill it was not fit for us to sit and that the acts passed by commission would not have that [? force] and virtue and might be questioned' if 'it should happen that the King's under-standing was lessened by the indisposition he laboured under'. However, many suspected that the chief object of Bolles's motion was 'to elude the abjuration', and so the Commons rejected it. Several hours later, the same members renewed the motion for adjournment. But the lower House, informed that Lord Keeper Wright was at Kensington waiting for the King to waken from a fevered sleep in order to secure his signature to the commission, decided to recess only until 6 p.m. At the appointed hour, the Commons were called up to the Lords to witness the royal commissioners pass the two public bills and one private measure. Then they returned to St Stephen's Chapel and adjourned until 9 a.m. the next day.[167]

In fact, the ministers had acted just in time. Early on Sunday morning, 8 March 1702, William received the sacrament, and at about 8 a.m. he breathed his last. However, his sixth parliament—unlike any previous parliament in similar circumstances—sat on, at least temporarily, by virtue of the 1696 statute for 'the continuing, meeting, and sitting of a parliament in case of the death' of the sovereign. For another two and a half months the Lords and the Commons continued to meet and to do business, so enabling the new Queen and her ministers to proceed without delay upon the measures for war that the late King had worked so hard to set in motion. At least in this respect, this posthumous session was an appropriate epilogue to William's reign and an apt testimony to the new prominence parliament had assumed during his thirteen years on the throne both in the governance of the realm and in the eyes of the political nation.

Notes to Chapter XII

1 *Vernon Corr.*, III, 79.

2 BL Add. MS. 17677UU, ff. 240–1, L'Hermitage, 21 May/1 June; BL Add. MS. 30000D, f. 179, L. F. Bonnet, 21 May/1 June, but cf. f. 216, 28 June/9 July. See also Bodl. Ballard MS. 11, f. 166, E. Warcupp to A. Charlett 25 February 1700[–1].

3 *Vernon Corr.*, III, 59. Cf. HMC *Downshire*, I, 797.

4 *Vernon Corr.*, III, 50. And see Kenyon, *Sunderland*, pp. 316–17.

5 Note his wavering letter to Coningsby of 13 May from Heythorp; BL Add. MS. 57861, f. 48.

6 *Vernon Corr.*, III, 91.

7 HMC *Portland*, III, 619–22; *Vernon Corr.*, III, 82, 94–5, 105. Bateman reported to Trumbull that Godolphin had declined an offer of Jersey's Secretaryship; Berkshire RO, Trumbull bound MS. 50, 28 June.

8 Grimblot, *Letters*, II, 429; HMC *Bath*, III, 417, 418; *Vernon Corr.*, III, 97–8, 113, 115–16.

9 *Vernon Corr.* III, 55, 56.

10 To read the Musgrave–Harley correspondence, it is only necessary to add 36 to each number used in the Guy–Harley cipher. Of these, the most important, in addition to those correctly identified by the editor, are: 65, Albemarle; 74, Weymouth; 77, Somers; 80, Seymour; 81, Montagu; 84, Marlborough; 87, Shrewsbury; 88, Sir T. Trevor; 95, ? Coningsby; 99, Musgrave; 105, Howe; 106, ? Jersey; 130, cabinet council; 136, Whigs; 137, Tories; 163, Methuen; 195, London; 196, Oxford.

11 HMC *Portland*, III, 619, 623.

12 *Vernon Corr.*, III, 88–91, 96, 104–5, 106–7, 110, 113–14; Northants RO, Buccleuch MSS., Vernon letters, III, 93, 13 July.

13 *Vernon Corr.*, III, 130, also 118–19. And see Ralph, *History*, II, 884–5; BL Add. MS. 30000D, f. 250, L. F. Bonnet, 6/17 August.

14 HMC *Portland*, IV, 3; *Vernon Corr.*, III, 129, 134; BL Add. MS. 30000D, ff. 273–4, L. F. Bonnet, 6/17 September; BL Loan 29/165, misc. 97 (R. Harley's memoirs), p. 8.

15 *Historical and Political Memoirs*, ed. C. Cole (1735), pp. 234–5.

16 BL Add. MS. 30000D, f. 230. L. F. Bonnet, 16/27 July; HMC *Cowper*, II, 400–1; CSPD, 1700–1702, p. 90.

17 *Archives*, III, iii, 235.

18 Baxter, *William III*, p. 379. For Harley's similar response, HMC *Portland*, III, 634.

19 *Historical and Political Memoirs*, p. 239; Hunt. Stowe MS. 26, II, 31 October.

20 *Historical and Political Memoirs*, p. 269; HMC *Portland*, III, 630–1. And see BL Add. MS. 28052, f. 100, C. Trelawney to S. Godolphin, 7 November; Duke of Manchester, *Court and Society from Elizabeth to Anne* (1864), II, 82; BL Loan 29/189, f. 275, Weymouth to R. Harley, 15 November; BL Add. MS. 17677UU, f. 346, L'Hermitage, 15/26 November; Berkshire RO, Trumbull bound MS. 50, T. Bateman to Sir W. Trumbull, 1 and 8 November; Cumberland RO, Lowther letters, J. to Sir J. Lowther, 14 November.

21 *Original Letters of Locke, Alg. Sidney, and Lord Shaftesbury*, ed. T. Forster (1847), pp. 75–7; Longleat, Thynne MS. 25, f. 70, R Price to Weymouth, 9 November.

22 HMC *Portland*, IV, 8. And see *The Epistolary Correspondence of Francis Atterbury*, ed. J. Nichols (1799), III, 8–9, 28; Burnet, *History*, IV, 519; G. V. Bennett, *The Tory Crisis in Church and State 1688–1730* (Oxford, 1975), pp. 55–6.

23 *Original Letters of Locke*, p. 76.

24 BL Loan 29/165, misc. 97, p. 7; Bodl. Ballard MS. 6, f. 41, T. Tanner to A. Charlett, 12 February 1701.

25 BL Loan 29/165, misc. 97, pp. 8–9. And see *Vernon Corr.*, III, 85.

26 Vernon's account in BL Add. MS. 40781, 190–1. Compare Tindal, *The Continuation*, XV, 168–70.

27 BL Add. MS. 40781, f. 191.

28 BL Add. MS. 17677WW, f. 115, L'Hermitage, 31 December/11 January.

29 *Archives*, III, iii, 405, 415.

30 Bodl. Ballard MS. 6, f. 35, E. Gibson to A. Charlett, 9 January. See also Longleat, Thynne MS. 25, f. 34, Sir H. Gough to Weymouth, 30 November; PRO, CO 77/16 (unfoliated), Vernon's memorandum, 4 December; R. Walcott, 'The East India Interest and the General Election of 1700–1701', EHR LXXI (1956), 223–39.

31 BL Add. MS. 17677WW, f. 9, Geldermalsen, 7/18 January; BL Add. MS. 30000E, f. 3, L. F. Bonnet, 7/18 January, Cf. HMC *Portland*, IV, 10.

32 BL 8248 bb 26 No. 8. And see A. Browne, 'Lord Halifax and the Malmesbury Election, 1701', *Wiltshire Archaeological and Natural History Magazine* XLVII (1935–6), 500–503.

33 See Appendices A and D, and Walcott, 'The East India Interest', p. 237.

34 Bodl. Locke MS. C12, f. 122, J. Freke to J. Locke, 28 January; BL Add. MS. 30000E, f. 27, L. F. Bonnet, 4/15 February.

35 HMC *Portland*, IV, 12, 13, 14. And see Devon RO, Exeter diocesan letters, Bishop

Trelawney to Dean Cook, 18 January; D. Rubini, *Court and Country 1688–1702* (1967), p. 206.

36 Bodl. MS. Eng. hist. b209, f. 79 v. See also *Historical and Political Memoirs*, p. 303.

37 Besides Cocks's account, see Hunt, 236002 (MS. account in a volume of the *Votes*); Cumberland RO, Lowther letters, J. to Sir J. Lowther, 11 February; BL Add. MS. 30000E, f. 34, L. F. Bonnet, 11/22 February. Cf. CJ, XIII, 325.

38 LJ, XVI, 594.

39 LJ, XVI, 597, 596; HLM, 1699–1702, p. 144; BL Add. MS. 17677WW, f. 157, L'Hermitage, 14/25 February.

40 BL Add. MS. 29568, f. 6, J. Verney to Viscount Hatton, 13 February.

41 CJ, XIII, 332–3; Bodl. MS. Eng. hist. b209, f. 78; House of Lords RO, Commons' Lib. MS. 12, f. 63. See also PRO, PRO 31/3/187, Tallard to Torcy, 15/26 February; Klopp, *Der Fall des Hauses Stuart*, IX, 158; ARA Heinsius MS. 733, L'Hermitage, 18 February/1 March.

42 Walcott, 'The East India Interest', pp. 238–9; Bodl. MS. Eng. hist. b209, f. 77; Bodl. Ballard MS. 11, f. 166, E. Warcupp to A. Charlett, 25 February.

43 G. H. Jones, *The Main Stream of Jacobitism* (Cambridge, Mass., 1954), pp. 59–60; Baxter, *William III*, p. 383.

44 CJ, XIII, 349. And see *Archives*, III, iii, 441; Burnet, *History*, IV, 474–5; ARA Heinsius MS. 733, L'Hermitage, 21 February/4 March, 25 February/8 March; *Original Letters of Locke*, pp. 123–4 (misplaced); BL Add. MS. 30000E, f. 48, L. F. Bonnet, 21 February/4 March.

45 ARA Heinsius MS. 733, 25 February/8 March supplement.

46 BL Add. MS. 17677WW, ff. 169, 177, L'Hermitage, 21 February/4 March, 28 February/11 March; Klopp, *Der Fall des Hauses Stuart*, IX, 165.

47 BL Add. MS. 29568, f. 9, J. Verney to Viscount Hatton, 1 March; BL Add. MS. 30000E, f. 68, L. F. Bonnet 7/8 March.

48 CJ, XIII, 375–6. And see Burnet, *History*, IV, 498.

49 BL Add. MS. 17677WW, f. 180, L'Hermitage, 4/15 March; CJ, XIII, 375–6; BL Add. MS. 29568, f. 9.

50 BL Add. MS. 30000E, ff. 69–70, 73, L. F. Bonnet, 7/18 and 11/12 March; Burnet, *History*, IV, 498; Bodl. MS. Eng. hist. b209, f. 78.

51 CJ, XIII, 400–1.

52 Yale Univ. Lib., Osborn Collection, Phillipps MS. 7462, pp. 197–8, 11 March. And see BL Add. MS. 17677WW, ff. 183–4, 189, L'Hermitage, 7/18 and 11/22 March.

53 BL Add. MS. 29568, f. 11, J. Verney to Viscount Hatton, 11 March; Liverpool RO, Norris letters 2/182, W. Clayton to Mayor of Liverpool, 11 March.

54 ARA Heinsius MS. 733, L'Hermitage, 14/25 March supplement; BL Loan 29/165, misc. 97, p. 15.

55 For Bolles's mental health, *Vernon Corr.*, II, 337–8; CSPD, 1700–1702, p. 505; HLM, 1708–1710, p. 273.

56 Burnet, *History*, IV, 498–500. Compare Earl Cowper, 'An Impartial History of Parties', reprinted in W. Dunham *et al.*, *Complaint and Reform in England 1436–1714* (1938), pp. 916–17. And see Bodl. MS. Eng. hist. b209, ff. 78, 73 v.; PRO, PRO 31/3/188, Poussin to Torcy, 8/19 May; BL Add. MS, 30000E, f. 183, L. F. Bonnet, 13/24 May.

57 Bodl. MS. Eng. hist. b209, f. 73.

58 BL Add. MS. 30000E, f. 211, L. F. Bonnet, 23 May/3 June; Burnet, *History*, V, 501. And see ST, III, 192–3.

59 BL Add. MS. 7076, f. 100, J. Tucker to G. Stepney, 14 March; BL Add. MS. 30000E, ff. 91–2, L. F. Bonnet, 17/28 March. And see HLM, 1699–1702, pp. 220–4.

60 BL Add. MS. 7076, f. 102, J. Tucker to G. Stepney, 17 March; BL Add. MS. 30000E, ff. 92–3, L. F. Bonnet, 17/28 March; Klopp, *Der Fall des Hauses Stuart*, IX, 194. Cf. Burnet, *History*, IV, 481–2; Tindal, *The Continuation*, XV, 167–9.

61 LJ, XVI, 626; Burnet, *History*, IV, 482–3.

62 *Historical and Political Memoirs*, p. 348. See also *Original Letters of Locke*, p. 129; BL Add. MS. 17677WW, f. 196, L'Hermitage, 21 March/1 April; Leicestershire RO, Finch correspondence, bundle 22, Duke of Leeds to [Lady Leominster], 18 March; HLM, 1699–1702, p. 222; LJ, XVI, 629; BL Add. MS. 30000E, f. 96, L. F. Bonnet, 21 March/1 April.

63 BL Add. MS. 7076, ff. 102–3.

64 CJ, XIII, 419, 424–5. William thought both addresses 'very impertinent'; *Archives*, III, iii, 486.

65 Bodl. MS. Eng. hist. b209, f. 78. See also Devon RO, Seymour MS. M/L18:01/1, Sir T. Aleyn to 'Sister' Bonnell, 29 March.

66 Bodl. MS. Eng. hist. b209, ff. 78, 77 v. See also PRO, PRO 31/3/188, Tallard *au roi*, 29 March/9 April; BL Add. MS 30000E, f. 121, L. F. Bonnet, 1/12 April; Klopp, *Der Fall des Hauses Stuart*, IX, 208–9.

67 PRO, PRO 31/3/188, Tallard *au roi*, 3/14 April.

68 Bodl. MS. Eng. hist. b209, f. 77; CJ, XIII, 466.

69 Bodl. MS. Eng. hist. b209, f. 77; PRO, PRO 31/3/188, Tallard *au roi*, 3/14 April; ARA Heinsius MS. 733, L'Hermitage, 4/15 April; *Archives*, III, iii, 492, 504.

70 ARA Heinsius MS. 733, L'Hermitage, 4/15 April; BL Add. MS. 30000E, f. 141, L. F. Bonnet, 15/26 April; HLM, 1699–1702, pp. 223–4; Burnet, *History*, IV, 485–7, and Hardwicke's note. For later claims that the Prize Office inquiry had been exploited to put pressure on Vernon (once a Commissioner of Prizes), see ST, III, 308; cf. *Vernon Corr.*, III, 144–5, 148.

71 A *Full Account of the Proceedings in Relation to Capt. Kidd* (1701), reprinted in ST, III, 254–5; Luttrell, *Brief Relation*, V, 37; BL Add. MS. 17677WW, f. 225, L'Hermitage, 11/22 April.

72 Bodl. MS. Eng. hist. b209 f. 76 and v.; BL Add. MS. 29568, f. 13, J. Verney to Viscount Hatton, 15 April. Cf. Dartmouth's note in Burnet, *History*, IV, 491.

73 BL Add. MS. 30000E, f. 144, L. F. Bonnet, 15/26 April; Bodl. Ballard MS. 6, f. 57, E. Gibson to A. Charlett, 17 April; Cumberland RO, Lowther letters, J. to Sir J. Lowther, 19 April. While Harley may not have wished to have the impeachments moved, there can be no doubt he supported them vigorously when they were initiated: cf. HMC *Portland*, V, 646; BL Loan 29/165, misc. 97, p. 13.

74 Bodl. MS. Eng. hist. b209, f. 76. Earlier, Smith had resigned from the Treasury, and the vacant seat was given to Thomas Pelham.

75 CJ, XIII, 492; *Original Letters of Locke*, p. 93. And see Dartmouth's note in Burnet, *History*, IV, 488; HMC *Portland*, V, 646; BL Add. MS. 29568, f. 13; PRO, PRO 31/3/188, Poussin to Torcy, 17/28 April.

76 Burnet, *History*, IV, 494; *Archives*, III, iii, 519.

77 *Original Letters of Locke*, p. 96. See also BL Add. MS. 17677WW, f. 244, L'Hermitage, 2/13 May.

78 PRO, PRO 31/3/188, Poussin to Torcy, 5/16 May; BL Add. MS. 17677WW, ff. 239–240, L'Hermitage, 25 April/6 May; BL Add. MS. 7074, ff. 13–14, J. Ellis to G. Stepney, 2 May.

79 Levens, Bagot correspondence, to J. Grahme, 2 May.

80 Bodl. MS. Eng. hist. b209, f. 74 and v.; BL Add. MS. 30000E, f. 171, L. F. Bonnet, 6/17 May.

81 Bodl. MS. Eng. hist. b209, f. 74. See also BL Add. MS. 17677WW, f. 246, L'Hermitage, 6/17 May; BL Add. MS. 30000E, ff. 171–3.

82 BL Add. MS. 7074, f. 15, to G. Stepney, 6 May. And see BL Loan 29/165, misc. 97, pp. 13–14.

83 BL Add. MS. 30000E, ff. 173–4, L. F. Bonnet, 6/17 May. See also Surrey RO, Somers MS. O/1/9, Sir J. Jekyll to Somers, Chester, 30 April.

84 Bodl. MS. Eng. hist. b209, f. 73 v.; CJ, XIII, 518. And see *The History of the Kentish Petition* (1701), reprinted in *Somers' Tracts*, XI, 242–7; BL Add. MS. 17677WW, f. 250, L'Hermitage, 9/20 May.

85 Bodl. MS. Eng. hist. b209, f. 73 v.; CJ, XIII, 523. And see BL Add. MS. 7076, ff. 110–11, J. Tucker to G. Stepney, 9 May; *Original Letters of Locke*, pp. 98–9; PRO, PRO 31/3/188, Poussin to Torcy, 12/23 May; BL Add. MS. 30000E, ff. 185–6, L. F. Bonnet, 13/24 May.

86 *Archives*, III, iii, 525; BL Add. MS. 17677WW, f. 256, L'Hermitage, 13/24 May. Rochester, reportedly, left the chamber rather than vote on the address; BL Add. MS. 30000E, f. 189, L. F. Bonnet, 13/24 May.

87 Bodl. MS. Eng. hist. b209, ff. 70, 69 v. See also PRO, PRO 31/3/188, Poussin to Torcy, 22 May/2 June. Other calculations suggested the King might net somewhat more.

88 Bodl. MS. Eng. hist. b209, ff. 72 v., 71, 70; Bodl. Ballard MS. 36, f. 6, G. Harbin to A. Charlett, 17 May; Luttrell, *Brief Relation*, V, 44, 46, 50; BL Add MS. 30000E, f. 199, L. F. Bonnet, 20/31 May; Burnet, *History*, IV, 510–11.

89 For the 'Memorial', see CJ, XIII, 549; Bodl. MS. Eng. hist. b209, ff. 72 v.–71; *Somers' Tracts*, XI, 255–9, also 264–75.

90 Northants RO, Finch–Hatton MS. 4053, [8 June]. See also BL Add. MS. 30000E, f. 235, L. F. Bonnet, 3/14 June.

91 BL Add. MS. 30000E, ff. 283–4, L. F. Bonnet, 20 June/1 July; ARA Heinsius MS. 733, L'Hermitage, 20 June/1 July. See also Bodl. MS. Eng. hist. b209, f. 66 v.

92 LJ, XVI, 739; CJ, XIII, 626. And see BL Add. M. 30000E, ff. 260–2, 283–4, L. F. Bonnet, 13/24 June, 20 June/1 July; BL Add. MS. 17677WW, f. 292, L'Hermitage, 13/24 June.

93 Original Letters of Locke, p. 103.

94 HLM, 1699–1702, pp. 295–300, also 388–9; BL Add. MS. 7074, f. 29, J. Ellis to G. Stepney, 10 June; CJ, XIII, 629. Cf. C. Kirby, 'The Four Lords and the Partition Treaty', American Historical Review LII (1946–7), 477–90.

95 Bodl. MS. Eng. hist. b209, f. 71. And see BL Add. MS. 30000E, f. 130, L. F. Bonnet, 4/15 April; PRO, PRO 31/3/188, Poussin to Torcy, 17/28 April.

96 Cumberland RO, Lowther letters, J. to Sir J. Lowther, 21 June. And see Appendix B.

97 CJ, XIII, 639; LJ, XVI, 766. And see HMC Downshire, I, 803–4.

98 PRO, PRO 31/3/188, Poussin to Torcy, 9/20 June; Vernon Corr., III, 149–50; HLM, 1699–1702, pp. 393–4; HMC Cowper, II, 428, 432–3. For tracts pro and con, see ST, III, 302–312; Bodl. Pamphlet 238 No. 16.

99 Luttrell, Brief Relation, v, 45; Bodl. MS. Eng. hist. b209, f. 74. For a possible draft, see BL Loan 29/35, bundle 32. See also [J. Humfrey], Letters to Parliament-Men (1701, Hunt. 55552, with a MS. letter from Humfrey to R. Harley), pp. 7–9; The Representative of London and Westminster in Parliament (1702), reprinted in Somers' Tracts, XII, 401–2.

100 Text in A Letter from a Clergyman in the Country to a Dignified Clergyman in London, Vindicating the Bill (1701, Bodl. Gough Pamphlet 2961 No. 4). And see Bodl. MS. Eng. hist. b209, f. 77; BL Add. MS. 30000E, f. 75, L. F. Bonnet, 11/22 March; Original Letters of Locke, p. 90; An Answer to a Letter from a Clergyman in the Country to a Dignified Clergyman in London (1701[–2], Bodl. Pamphlet 238 No. 12).

101 Bodl. MS. Eng. hist. b209, f. 77. And see Rev. D. Williams's protest against the clause to Harley in BL Loan 29/190, f. 56, 26 March.

102 PH, V, 1322.

103 BL Add. MS. 30000E, f. 219, L. F. Bonnet, 27 May/7 June. See also Bodl. MS. Eng. hist. b209, f. 67 v.; Dartmouth's note in Burnet, History, IV, 492.

104 Luttrell, Brief Relation, v, 67; Cumberland RO, Lowther letters, to Sir J. Lowther, 23 September; SR, VII, 711. Cf. Rubini, Court and Country, pp. 176–7 and app. C.

105 As late as February 1702, Lowther was still fearful such an attempt might be made; Cumberland RO, Lowther letters, to Sir J. Lowther, 3 February. And see KU, L. F. Bonnet, 23 December/3 January 1701/2; A Full and True Relation of a horrid and detestable Conspiracy (1701, Guildhall 2111).

106 Vernon Corr., III, 150, 151–2, HMC Downshire, I, 803–4; BL Add. MS. 57861, f. 69, J. Vernon to Lord Coningsby, 3 July; PRO, PRO 31/3/189, Poussin to Torcy, 7/18 July; The Marlborough–Godolphin Correspondence, ed. H. L. Snyder (Oxford, 1975), 1, 7, 10, 12.

107 HMC Cowper, II, 430; LJ, XVI, 770. And see ARA Heinsius MS. 733, L'Hermitage, 24 June/5 July and supplement.

108 MSP, II, 444; BL Add. MS. 7074, f. 36, J. Ellis to G. Stepney, 27 June; HMC Cowper, II, 434; Burnet, History, IV, 527; BL Add. MS. 57861, f. 69. Yonge and St Quintin resigned their seats at the Customs Board in conformity with the new place clause, so that commission had to be reconstituted; Marlborough–Godolphin Correspondence, I, 29 and n. 4.

109 BL Add. MS. 30000E, f. 235, L. F. Bonnet, 3/14 June; HMC Cowper II, 432; BL Add. MS. 7076, f. 120, J. Tucker to G. Stepney, 1 July.

110 Cumberland RO, Lowther letters, J. to Sir J. Lowther, 1 July. For allegations that William had also consented to Haversham's removal from the Admiralty, but that Vernon stalled his ouster in the King's absence: HMC Cowper, II, 437, 439; cf. Burnet, History, IV, 527.

111 L. Glassey, 'The Commission of the Peace, 1675–1720' (unpublished D.Phil. thesis, University of Oxford, 1972), pp. 218–20; BL Add. MS. 40775, f. 16, J. Vernon to the King, 17 July, and f. 35, same to Marlborough, 25 July; Luttrell, Brief Relation, v, 73. Cf. BL Loan 29/29, bundle 11, T. Edwards's petition, printed in G. Holmes and W. Speck, The Divided Society: Party Conflict in England 1694–1716 (1967), p. 47.

112 Cumberland RO, Lowther letters, J. to Sir J. Lowther, 19 and 21 August, 4 September; BL Loan 29/186, f. 81, Sir C. Musgrave to R. Harley, 11 August; Vernon Corr., III, 155; BL Add. MS. 40775, ff. 47, 57, J. Vernon to the King, 1 and 5 August.

113 Leicestershire RO, Finch correspondence, bundle 22, 16 September.

114 *Vernon Corr.*, III, 155–6. See Harley's holograph draft for *A Letter from the Grecian Coffee House* (1701, BL 515 L8 No. 15) and his letter to Davenant of 6 October, both in BL Loan 29/7, bundle 1.

115 BL Add. MS. 40775, ff. 61, 67, 102, J. Vernon to the King, 8, 12, and 29 August, and f. 72, same to J. Methuen, 14 August. And see Luttrell, *Brief Relation*, V, 79, 88; *Original Letters of Locke*, p. 110.

116 *MSP*, II, 443, 446. And see *Marlborough–Godolphin Correspondence*, I, 12, 18; Kenyon, *Sunderland*, pp. 321–2.

117 Luttrell, *Brief Relation*, V, 94.

118 *Marlborough–Godolphin Correspondence*, I, 31–3; *MSP*, II, 452–3. And see BL Add. MS. 30000E, f. 383, L. F. Bonnet, 31 October/11 November.

119 Luttrell, *Brief Relation*, V, 107; BL Loan 29/165, misc. 97, p. 16. Most of these addresses were printed in the *London Gazette*, No. 3751–62.

120 *MSP*, II, 453–6.

121 Compare Baxter, *William III*, p. 393, quoting Albemarle's letter of 11/22 November; Klopp, *Der Fall des Hauses Stuart*, IX, 422–5, 498.

122 BL Loan 29/165, misc. 97, pp. 16–17; BL Add. MS. 17677WW, f. 372, de Saumiere, 18/29 November; BL Add. MS. 30000E, f. 395, L. F. Bonnet, 14/25 November, printed in Holmes, *The Divided Society*, p. 170.

123 BL Loan 29/165, misc. 97, p. 17; HMC *Downshire*, I, 811. And see *MSP*, II, 457–61; Luttrell, *Brief Relation*, V, 110; BL Add. MS, 30000E, f. 406, L. F. Bonnet, 25 November/6 December.

124 *CJ*. XIII, 644; HMC *Downshire*, I, 810–11. See also BL Add. MS. 30000E, f. 397, L. F. Bonnet, 14/25 November.

125 BL Add. MS. 40775, f. 109, J. Vernon's notes of 23 September, and f. 198, J. Vernon to the King, 26 September; BL Egerton MS. 920, f. 21, J. Vernon to W. Blathwayt, 23 September; HMC *Portland*, IV, 24.

126 Reprinted in *Somers' Tracts*, XII, 212–15. And see *An Answer to an Infamous Libel Entituled A List* (1701, Hunt. 57049), esp. p. 6.

127 ARA Heinsius MS. 730, J. Robethon to A. Heinsius, 2/13 December.

128 *A Letter from Abingdon, to a Friend in London* (1701, Hunt. 329567); also, *The Statesmen of Abingdon* (1702, BL T1990 No. 6).

129 Most were printed, along with the few Tory ones, in *The Electors' Right Asserted* (Hunt. 247062); this appeared a few days before parliament opened.

130 *The Electors' Right Asserted*, p. 14, reprinted in Holmes, *The Divided Society*, pp. 125–6.

131 See Appendix A.

132 PRO, C110/28, J. Dolben to T. Pitt, 19 July 1701; BL Add. MS. 40775, f. 95, J. Vernon to the King, 15 August 1701; HMC *Portland*, IV, 22 ff.

133 H. Snyder, 'Party Configurations in the Early Eighteenth-Century House of Commons', *BIHR* XLV (1972), 54–8. And see BL Add. MS. 30000E, f. 420, L. F. Bonnet, 16/27 December, printed in Holmes, *The Divided Society*, p. 19; BL Add. MS. 17677WW, f. 395, L'Hermitage, 16/27 December; ARA Heinsius MS. 730, J. Robethon to Heinsius, 16/27 December.

134 West Sussex RO, Winterton letters 850, R. Goulston to Sir E. Turnour, 16 December.

135 HMC *Portland*, IV, 29; HMC *Cowper*, II, 443. It was reported that despite the efforts of Lord Radnor (recently reappointed Lord Warden of the Stannaries), thirty-seven or thirty-eight of the forty-four Cornish M.P.s were Tories: Warwickshire RO, Mordaunt MSS. CR1368, vol. iii, No. 66, T. Morice to Sir J. Mordaunt, 9 December.

136 BL Harleian MS. 7556, ff. 96–100 (the remainder of the 513 returns are accounted for by sixteen double elections and by Shower's death); compare W. A. Speck, *Tory and Whig: The Struggle in the Constituencies 1701–1715* (1970), p. 112. And see Appendix C.

137 BL Add. MS. 7074, f. 72, to G. Stepney, 16 December.

138 Cumberland RO, Lowther letters, J. to Sir J. Lowther, 18 December; KU, F. L. Bonnet, 23 December/3 January; BL Add. MS. 7074, f. 77, J. Ellis to G. Stepney, 30 December.

139 Scottish RO, Leven & Melville MSS. GD 26, section 13, No. 120, anon. letter from London, 2 January. See also *Original Letters of Locke*, pp. 120–1; ARA Heinsius MS. 733, L'Hermitage, 30 December/10 January. All those placemen known to have defected were, in fact, listed by Harley among his expected supporters.

140 Cumberland RO, Lowther letters, to Sir J. Lowther, 18 and 30 December, and 1 January; Scottish RO, GD 26, section 13, No. 120.

141 *Archives*, III, iii, 621.

142 *Original Letters of Locke*, p. 122; ARA Heinsius MS. 790, J. Robethon to Heinsius, 13/24 January.

143 ARA Heinsius MS. 792, L'Hermitage, 26 December/6 January, 27 January/7 February; BL Add. MS. 30000E, ff. 411–12, L. F. Bonnet, 2/13 December; Yale Univ. Lib., Osborn Collection, Phillipps MS. 7462, p. 93, W. Blathwayt to G. Stepney, 19 December.

144 Hardwicke's note in Burnet, *History*, IV, 546; Baxter, *William III*, p. 396.

145 CJ, XIII, 646–7. Compare Lord Shaftesbury's *Paradoxes of State* (1702), reprinted in ST, III, 373–81; and see *Original Letters of Locke*, p. 122.

146 Luttrell, *Brief Relation*, V, 144.

147 Bodl. MS. Eng. hist. b210, f. 2. And see KU, L. F. Bonnet, 2/13 and 6/17 January.

148 HMC *Roxburghe, etc.*, p. 153; BL Add. MS. 17677XX, f. 169, L'Hermitage, 13/24 January; KU, L. F. Bonnet, 16/27 January; Cumberland RO, Lowther letters, J. to Sir J. Lowther, 3 February. And see *Minutes Taken from the Speech of Sir E. S. upon his Election* (1701, Bodl. 1419 e3378 No. 5).

149 *Original Letters of Locke*, pp. 111, 122, And see LJ, XVII, 9; BL Add. MS. 17677XX, f. 165, L'Hermitage, 9/20 January; HLM, 1699–1702, pp. 413–16.

150 Burnet, *History*, IV, 550–1; BL Add. MS. 40803, f. 10, newsletter to H. Greg, 20 January; KAO, Chevening MS. 81, R. Yard to A. Stanhope, 20 January.

151 William Salt Lib., Bagot MS. 141/6/5/60, W. Bagot to his wife, 29 January.

152 Cumberland RO, Lowther letters, J. to Sir J. Lowther, 8 January; KU, L. F. Bonnet, 9/20 January; Luttrell, *Brief Relation*, V, 131, 132; ARA Heinsius MS. 790, J. Robethon to Heinsius, 27 January/7 February; BL Add. MS. 40803, f. 11, newsletter to H. Greg, 23 January.

153 BL Add. MS. 40803, ff. 14–15, newsletter to H. Greg, 30 January. See also BL Add. MS. 17677XX, f. 193, L'Hermitage, 30 January/10 February; CJ, XIII, 739.

154 Bodl. MS. Eng. hist. b210, f. 1, KU, L. F. Bonnet, 30 January/10 February; ARA Heinsius MS. 790, J. Robethon to A. Heinsius, 3/14 February.

155 Bodl. MS. Eng. hist. b210, f. 2 v.; CJ, XIII, 735.

156 Bodl. Locke MS. C12, f. 170, P. King to J. Locke, [17 February]; CJ, XIII, 767. Cf. Luttrell, *Brief Relation*, V, 143.

157 Bodl. Locke MS. C12, f. 170. And see Bodl. MS. Eng. hist. b210, f. 4; KU, L. F. Bonnet, 20 February/3 March; HMC *Various*, VIII, 85; *Original Letters of Locke*, p. 126; BL Add. MS. 17677XX, ff. 224–7, 20 February/3 March.

158 CJ, XIII, 759. And see ARA Heinsius MS. 792, L'Hermitage, 20 February/3 March; Bodl. MS. Eng. hist. b210, f. 5.

159 CJ, XIII, 767. And see Bodl. MS. Eng. hist. b210, f. 5 and v.; *Original Letters of Locke*, pp. 126–8; Bodl. Ballard MS. 36, ff. 32–3, W. P[ercival] to A. Charlett, 27 February.

160 Liverpool RO, Norris letters 2/242, T. Johnson to R. Norris, 28 February. See also Cumberland RO, Lowther letters, J. to Sir J. Lowther, 28 February.

161 Bodl. MS. Eng. hist. b210, ff. 3, 4 v.; *An Account of some Late Designs to Create a Misunderstanding Betwixt the King and his People* (1702, BL 8133 c58 No. 3), p. 23.

162 HLM, 1699–1702, pp. 478–80; ARA Heinsius MS. 790, J. Robethon to Heinsius, 26 January/7 February; Burnet, *History*, IV, 522–4, and Dartmouth's note.

163 Yale Univ. Lib., Osborn Collection, Phillipps MS. 7462, p. 87, W. Blathwayt to G. Stepney, [torn] November 1701; BL Add. MS. 17677XX, f. 164, L'Hermitage, 26 December/6 January. During the winter Toland published a tract advocating an invitation, which provoked at least one reply: Bodl. Gough Pamphlet 1124 No. 13; BL T1625 No. 2.

164 Baxter, *William III*, pp. 396–7 (but the 21st was a Saturday).

165 HMC *Roxburghe, etc.*, pp. 154, 155; Burnet, *History*, IV, 558.

166 Baxter, *William III*, p. 397.

167 Bodl. MS. Eng. hist. b210, f. 6 v. And see HMC *Rutland*, II, 169; Burnet, *History*, IV, 559.

XIII

CONCLUSION

It is now a commonplace in the historiography of the Glorious Revolution to emphasise the inconclusiveness of the immediate settlement in 1689; there is less agreement, however, among historians in assessing the wide-ranging changes that occurred, often in an *ad hoc* fashion, in the constitutional framework, the political order, and the organisation of the government during William's reign. None the less, there can be little doubt that the alterations in relations between the crown and the houses of parliament between 1689 and 1702 were of profound importance.

To begin with, annual parliamentary sessions gradually became accepted as normal practice in the years after the Revolution. Yearly meetings of the two Houses were not required by the Declaration of Rights, the settlement of the ordinary revenue in 1690, or the triennial act. Rather, they were necessitated at first by the war with France. After the war's end, William had little alternative but to continue them. Although he did secure a permanent settlement of the 'civil list' in 1697–98, so long as he wished to retain any kind of army within England he needed parliamentary funding. And since the Commons were only prepared to vote suplies for the army and the fleet on a year-by-year basis, annual sessions continued to be held in peacetime, even though no mutiny act was passed between 1697 and 1702.[1]

While financial needs dictated yearly parliamentary meetings throughout the reign and the triennial act required new elections at least once every three years during the second half of the reign, William did retain the capacity to influence the composition of both the Lords and the Commons. The prerogative of creating new temporal peers and promoting present ones to higher rank was never questioned, save by a few peers during the Lords' debates in 1701 over the act of succession.[2] Altogether, William created twenty-seven temporal peers (including six sons called to the Lords in their fathers' baronies) and raised sixteen others to higher rank.[3] Many of these honours were distributed in two sizeable groups: the first in the spring of 1689, the second in the spring of 1694 at the end of the first parliamentary session conducted under Sunderland's auspices. Most so honoured on these and other occasions were men who had substantial claims on the royal favour; among them were five of the King's foreign servants, along with a number of prominent Revolution activists and many of those commoners who served in major ministerial posts.[4] By the end of the reign, then, thirty-six of the 162 lay peers owed their present titles to William.

The King's power to name new bishops also survived intact. An attempt was made in the Commons in 1701 to restrict his right to translate prelates to more desirable sees, but it failed. William had the opportunity to name twenty-one clerics to the episcopal bench in the course of his reign, and, thanks to a series of deaths among incumbents and to the deprivation of the non-juring bishops, fourteen of these appointments were made between 1689 and 1691. In addition, he transferred five of his own appointees and two pre-Revolution bishops to richer dioceses. The new bishops and their translated colleagues were singled out less for Court or political service than for their personal ability and their commitment to the Revolution settlement in church and state; the overall result by March 1702 was that eighteen of the twenty-six incumbents were William's nominees.[5]

The cumulative effects of the King's creations, promotions, and episcopal appointments, coupled with the withdrawal of a few non-juring temporal peers, was to enhance greatly the Court's voting strength in the Lords—the House in which resistance to the grant of the crown had centred. For instance, among the majority of sixty-eight who voted in favour of the third reading of the bill to attaint Sir John Fenwick in December 1696 were nineteen lay peers who owed their present titles to William and twelve bishops appointed by him; among the minority of sixty-one were seven lay lords who had been honoured by William and only three of his episcopal appointees. Again, among the fifty-six peers who opposed Lord Somers's impeachment in June 1701 were eleven lay lords who owed their present titles to William and eleven bishops he had appointed; among the minority of thirty-one were only three lay lords who had been honoured by him while the three bishops who voted for the impeachment had been chosen by his predecessors.[6]

Although William made considerable use of his powers of ennoblement and episcopal appointment, he was more restrained in the deployment of the crown's electoral resources. The crown, as an important employer and landlord, possessed a strong potential interest over at least one seat in perhaps as many as twenty boroughs.[7] In addition, the King might indirectly influence the outcome in many other constituencies by signalling the type of candidate he wished to have returned either in the proclamation of dissolution or through alterations in the commissions of the peace and of the lieutenancy. Indeed, Morrice observed in late 1690 that 'if there should be a new parliament, the choice will be much according to his Majesty's pleasure, if he thinks fit to exert his interest to the utmost, for the Lords of the Admiralty, the Commissioners of the Navy, the Victualling Office, the Excise Office, the Commissioners of the Custom House, the sheriffs, etc. do influence so many corporations they would turn the balance'.[8] But Morrice was writing at a time when it appeared that the parties' electoral appeal was roughly equal and at a moment when the King's victory at the Boyne had enhanced his personal prestige. Similar circumstances did not prevail during all five of the general elections of the reign, and in any case William never attempted to exploit the crown's interest in a systematic way. The King was also wary of making major ministerial alterations or extensive changes in the local commissions before elections.[9] In 1690 and in 1701, he held his hand on new ministerial appointments until the returns were in, though in 1700 the reconstitution of the ministry preceded the dissolution. Again, the most sweeping purge of the county commissions during the reign came in the year after the assassination plot of 1696, and by the time the next election was held in mid-1698 the Junto suspected that the King had sought to avoid committing himself to them. Still, William often did provide some indication of his desires in a general way. In 1690, he informally recommended the choice of moderate Churchmen; in 1695, he went on a progress through the Midlands at election time; and in November 1701 the Tories interpreted his dissolution proclamation as a slur upon the late Commons' majority.

The King's reluctance to make particular recommendations to individual constituencies or to exert the full weight of royal prestige at election times left elections 'free', as the Declaration of Rights had urged, from royal interference for the most part. But William and his advisers did seek to dispose of both the old and the many new posts in the administration in a manner calculated to advance the King's business in the Commons. And despite the exclusion of certain categories of officials from the Commons that were enacted between 1694 and 1701, the number of placemen (including holders of military commissions) sitting in the lower House rose from a total of 101 in January 1690 to 132 in March 1702. Moreover, on some occasions, the placemen provided a substantial proportion of the votes for Court measures; probably the most striking instance was the division of 18 January 1699 on the disbanding bill when ninety-five of the minority of 156 were placemen.[10]

Yet as the disbanding division also attests, the significance of the increasing number of placemen in the Commons can easily be exaggerated. Virtually every House of Commons during the reigns of William's Stuart predecessors included a substantial official contingent, ranging in size (depending on the criteria of classification) from one-fifth to nearly one-third of the total membership.[11] As in earlier decades, too, the bulk of these official members in the 1690s were returned to the Commons on their own or on private patrons' electoral interests. During William's reign, country gentlemen did complain of the intrusion of career military men in the House, but in social terms the more threatening, though transitory, challenge to gentry predominance was posed by the widespread corruption practised by the new East India Company and its backers in the first 1701 election. Then, too, the official element in the Lords, even without including the members of the episcopate in the reckoning, was much larger proportionately than it was in the Commons. The lay peerage supplied the majority of cabinet councillors and members of the Lords also predominated on the crown's pension list. In the light of the number of peers, lay and spiritual, who owed their seats in the Lords to William or derived a significant share of their income from the crown, it is hardly surprising that the King and his ministers could under most circumstances expect fewer difficulties in managing the Lords than the Commons. It was, after all, the upper House which blocked the place bills of 1692–93 and 1698–99 and which attempted to forestall disbandment and the resumption of the Irish forfeitures.

However, neither the Court's strength in the Lords nor the presence of a sizeable group of placemen in the Commons saved William from having to yield a good deal of ground to parliament, and especially to the Commons, during his years on the throne. In the first place, the lower House assumed a considerable measure of control over the employment of the vast supplies it voted. During the 1690s, the submission of detailed estimates and the formulation of precise appropriation clauses became a matter of course. It is true that the expedient, first utilised in November 1693, of authorising loans to the government on the strength of taxes to be approved later in the session was adopted in 1696–97 and in each of the postwar meetings, despite the care the Commons had taken in 1693 to enter a note in their *Journal* that this decision was not to constitute a precedent.[12] But such resolutions of credit were only a minor, though very helpful, short cut. Furthermore, the Commons' own procedures were often supplemented by the work of their Commissioners of Accounts. Between 1691 and 1697, the King's officials had to live with the prying and poking of successive commissions. Then, with war imminent in January 1702, William offered to approve the creation of a new Commission of Accounts, though he died before the measure was ready for his signature. And in the interim the Commons had created in 1700 a commission to examine the army, navy, and transport debts, though M.P.s were not eligible to serve on that body.[13] Moreover, throughout the reign the Commons were successful in preventing the Lords from choosing any members of these Commissions of Accounts and in forestalling virtually every attempt the peers made to amend money bills or to alter monetary provisions (very broadly construed) in other measures.

In the second place, the Commons gradually assumed a greater role in the formulation of policy, even in the sphere of foreign affairs that was supposedly reserved to the crown. After William sought the 'advice' of parliament in November 1692, he found it politic to comply with the Commons' request for copies of the treaties of the Grand Alliance.[14] The King did manage without real difficulty to retain a free hand in negotiating peace with France in 1696–97, but thereafter he increasingly felt constrained to act in the light of parliamentary opinion. Thus, he embarked on the negotiation of a partition treaty in 1698 because he believed he would not be able to induce his subjects to join as a 'principal' any new coalition against France. In turn, when Louis's acceptance of Carlos II's will abrogated the second Partition Treaty, William recognised the necessity of securing parliamentary backing for the alliances he wished to make, and in 1701 he deliberately sought enabling addresses from the Commons for each major step in The Hague negotiations. At the same time he informed Heinsius that it would not be possible to include any secret articles in the proposed treaty with the Emperor 'since I must communicate it to parliament'.[15] And even after William decided upon a dissolution in November 1701, he accepted Marlborough's insistent counsel that the troop quotas for the new alliance be submitted to the next parliament.[16]

In the third place, the Commons exploited their financial leverage to secure the passage of a series of bills for limiting the royal prerogative and expanding subjects' liberties. The most notable were the triennial act of 1694 and the act to reform trials for treason of 1696. Admittedly, the former reached the statute book only after clauses requiring annual sessions and general elections at regular three-year intervals were omitted; similarly, the latter was finally enacted only when the Commons accepted the Lords' perennial amendment to enlarge the composition of the Lord Steward's court. But by resorting to tacks to money bills, the Commons secured the exclusion from St Stephen's Chapel first of holders of new revenue posts (1694), next of excise officials (1700), and finally of customs officials as well (1701). These measures, coupled with the reform provisions of the act of succession, meant that by 1702 most of the major constitutional proposals in the preliminary version of the Declaration of Rights had either been embodied in statute or accepted in practice.

In the fourth place, the annual and prolonged parliamentary sessions of the reign resulted in an increasing amount of legislation. 809 bills were enacted between 1689 and 1702; by comparison, only 533 reached the statute book between 1660 and 1684.[17] In part, the increase was simply a function of parliament's greater availability: during William's reign, parliaments sat for approximately fifty-three and a half months—over a full year more than the total duration of Charles II's parliaments. As the Brandenburg resident remarked late in the reign: 'One can infer that it is the frequent parliaments which England has enjoyed during this reign that has given rise to an infinity of acts made for the public good.'[18] The longer duration of parliamentary sessions after 1689 may also have affected the improving 'success ratio' of bills introduced. During the first half of William's reign, the ratio of bills introduced in either House to enactments was one to two; by Anne's reign that ratio had risen to approximately two to three.[19] To some extent, the greater recourse to parliamentary legislation after the Revolution reflected the enhanced authority of statute. This is most apparent in the case of commercial companies which had previously operated under royal charters. Thus, once the old East India Company was alerted in early 1689 by the Commons' censure of its proceedings at St Helena that most M.P.s thought that martial law commissions and other quasi-sovereign powers 'ought not to be granted by the crown or otherwise than by act of parliament', the corporation repeatedly presented petitions to the lower House requesting the grant of a parliamentary charter.[20] The Company did accept a new royal charter in 1693, yet it continued to seek a statutory establishment in order to secure its position both at home and abroad. Other trading companies followed suit, and some were more successful than the old East India Company. One of them was the Hudson's Bay Company; and once its directors secured a parliamentary charter by private act in May 1690, they promptly wrote to their agents in the Bay in triumphant tones that 'whatever was eluded as prerogative before' by interlopers 'is now the law of our land and as such to be enforced'.[21]

In all these respects, then, William III—though not the earliest English ruler to reign by virtue of a 'parliamentary title'—stands out as the first of England's parliamentary monarchs.[22] His dependence upon parliament also made him more vulnerable than any of his predecessors to partisan pressure in the choice of his servants. Admittedly, William never ceased to struggle against the parties' efforts to gain dominance within his ministries and to convert his patronage to their own uses. The King's reluctance to exert to the full the crown's potential electoral interest and influence stemmed, in large part, from his unwillingness to put these resources at the disposal of the men of party. Yet time and again, parliamentary considerations were uppermost in his mind when he chose his ministers, and between 1694 and 1698 the Whigs came close to achieving a form of 'party government'. Indeed, the bolder among them even believed they could dispense with the services of the Earl of Sunderland as intermediary between them and the King. And perhaps they might have been able to do without him had they remained 'strongest in the House of Commons and in possession of the management' there.[23]

But this was easier said than done, even by the Junto. As James Morgan remarked on the occasion of the ministerial changes in late 1700: 'Contending factions and interests of parties does always keep up a civil war at Court, and set up and pull down everything by turn as they are strongest and most prevailing. They do it by turns, and there is no certainty but vicissitude to themselves and their creatures which wax and wane with them.'[24] Furthermore, the King had to contend not only with the parties' strivings for predominance within his government but also with the parties' fluctuating strengths within the Commons.

The instability of English politics between 1660 and 1688 is amply evidenced by Clarendon's fall, the Exclusion crisis, and the Glorious Revolution. Then, too, though the Revolution 'preserved' parliament and the Declaration of Rights was intended to prevent for the future the ills of Stuart rule, there remained the possibility of a Jacobite restoration. During the early years of William's reign, it seemed that James, taking advantage of the 'looseness' of the new government, might regain his throne with the aid of the French and the assistance of disaffected Englishmen. It is true that none of the prominent figures who was suspected, usually with reason, of making his peace at St Germain—Shrewsbury, Halifax, Monmouth, Russell, Godolphin, and Marlborough—ever really exerted himself in the old King's cause. Even so, fears of crypto-Jacobitism, especially within Tory ranks, were revived towards the end of the reign, and the alarm was not only sounded publicly by the Whigs but it was also voiced privately by some around William.

Nevertheless, it was the conflict over issues and the competition for places among those loyal to William that principally shaped domestic politics between 1689 and 1702. Pre-Revolution issues were not all resolved in 1689, the Revolution itself was a subject of controversy, and the King's policies engendered new disputes. And despite the enlargement of the government apparatus during the war, there was never a shortage of suitors for offices of profit in the crown's gift. Indeed, William is said to have exclaimed on occasion 'that he wished every man, that was in any office, immortal', so that he would not be badgered about the disposition of their posts.[25] The competition for place was affected, in turn, by the enhanced importance of parliament. Seats in the Commons were more and more stepping-stones to office, so that Harley's prediction before the general election of 1695 that the new triennial legislation would help to 'render gentlemen less willing to spend money to come into the House' proved to be mistaken.[26] As Lord Cheyne observed five years later to Sir John Verney (an often disappointed candidate in Buckinghamshire): 'In truth, a seat in parliament is not worth the pains we undergo to attain, but a place at Court with a seat there is most people's aim.'[27] Simultaneously, frequent elections accentuated the difficulties of electoral patrons and ministerial managers alike. 'These frequent parliaments', James Lowther predicted in January 1702, 'will make it impracticable for any one set of men to hold the ministry long.'[28]

The political parties had to live with other handicaps as well. To begin with, party still suffered from the taint of self-interested 'faction'; in theory, at least, parties had no legitimate role in the political process.[29] The parties had also to contend with the King's resistance to their pretensions, while the party leaders lacked the means to organise systematically and discipline firmly their putative followings. In practice, they operated in hand-to-mouth fashion—employing appeals to principle to rally the faithful, utilising the attractions of office to tempt the ambitious, and relying upon ties of friendship, kinship, and dependence to reinforce these bonds. To complicate matters, both Whigs and Tories had a dual and sometimes conflicting inheritance from the past: the partisan alignments formed during the Exclusion crisis overlaid, without wholly superseding, the opposition between Court and Country that was first articulated under the early Stuarts.

The complexity and the fluidity of partisan groupings during William's reign are apparent in contemporary terminology. Few observers of the political scene could escape employing the party labels. Under-secretary Yard, for instance, apologised to his correspondent Stanhope for his frequent references to 'the Whigs', 'the Tories', and 'the Court party'. But while he confessed these were 'very improper expressions' of the 'vulgar style', he continued to invoke them for 'distinctions' sake'.[30] Yet, such 'distinctions' themselves needed further explanation. In 1689, the old Nonconformist Morrice used the labels 'the Whigs', the 'English interest', and the 'Country party' almost interchangeably. But in 1695–1696 when under-secretary Ellis referred to 'the country party, as it is called', he meant the opposition to the then predominantly Junto ministry.[31] And this association between 'the country' and the rivals of the Junto was made much more explicit in the latter years of the reign when men spoke of the 'Church (or Country) party', the 'Country or Church party', and of those who went 'under the honourable appellation of Patriots and Churchmen'.[32]

Contemporary usage was a reasonably accurate reflection of how the play of national questions aligned men in parliament and also shaped sentiment out of doors. Over the course of the reign, controversy revolved around four broad issues: (1) the relations between church and state; (2) the legitimacy of the Revolution; (3) the limitation of royal prerogative and influence; and (4) the conduct and financing of foreign affairs. The first two were sources of division from the outset, and whenever they were raised men tended to align along a Whig–Tory axis. The second two were not as controversial initially, but as they came increasingly to the fore in the early and mid-1690s men tended to align along a Court–Country axis. To add to the confusion, during William's second, third, and fourth parliaments, and sometimes on other occasions too, the two sets of issues and the resultant alignments overlapped. The juxtaposition in close proximity of Whig–Tory and Court–Country divisions was especially frequent in the third and fourth sessions of the 1690–95 parliament, in the first and third sessions of the 1695–98 parliament, and in both sessions of the 1698–1700 parliament. Often, the paucity of the extant evidence obscures our view of how members voted, but sometimes, most notably in the case of the two divisions on the council of trade resolutions of 30 January 1696, the same individuals can be identified as dividing in rapid succession along Court–Country and Whig–Tory lines.

However, the situation in the early 1690s and again late in the decade also involved the rivalry for place and power; men, as well as measures, were in question. Between 1691 and 1694 it was the Tory ministers who were under fire; between 1698 and 1700 it was the Whig ministers who were under attack. And just as in the first instance Clarges, Musgrave, and other Churchmen on the backbenches rallied to defend Nottingham and his admirals, so in the second Lord Hartington, Cocks, and other backbench Whigs helped to beat off the assaults on Montagu, Orford, and Somers. Political groupings were further complicated by the appearance in the 1690s of a 'flying squadron' led by Paul Foley and Robert Harley. At the beginning of the reign, the Foleys and Harleys can be identified as Whigs; in the early and mid-1690s, Paul Foley and Robert Harley increasingly dissociated themselves from the emerging Junto (and some of their own kinsmen) by stressing measures, not men; in the late 1690s, especially after Foley's death, Harley came to the fore in the attack upon both Junto measures and ministers; and in William's last year Harley was denounced even by country Whigs such as Sir Richard Cocks and the Earl of Shaftesbury as 'a pupil' of Rochester and a man 'desperately engaged in party'.[33]

In part, it was Harley's leadership of the campaign to 'blast' the Junto that provoked such bitter condemnation from men who earlier had joined him in pressing for a parliamentary council of trade and for disbandment of the army. Yet at the same time, the increasingly close association between Harley and the Tories was reflected in the positions the combined forces of 'Patriots and Churchmen' adopted on national issues in the postwar years. In particular, the earlier gulf between them over Whig–Tory questions was narrowed considerably. Robert Harley and his younger brother Edward, though never completely disavowing their Dissenting associations, took a significant part in the revival of agitation about the state of the Church. Edward Harley was in the van of the Commons' campaign in the 1697–98 and 1698–99 sessions to stamp out blasphemy and profaneness, and Robert was at great pains 'to appear a Churchman'.[34] Meanwhile, the Tories sought to counter allegations of Jacobitism by backing the Hanoverian succession and by sponsoring a compulsory abjuration. It is true that old prejudices were not wholly overcome. Some Tories resisted the new abjuration in 1702, and it was observed that the Harleys and their kinsmen voted against Bolles's attempt to attach a clause against occasional conformity to the abjuration bill.

'Patriots' and 'Churchmen' found it easier to unite on what had been primarily Court–Country questions during the war. The two elements acted in concert during William's fourth parliament in support of place bills and in opposition to the Irish grantees and the new East India Company. Again, in 1701 they joined in pushing the reform provisions in the act of succession. As some Whigs ironically observed at that time: "tis a little strange that the old arbitrary and high prerogative men should be the persons who are for destroying the prerogative' and that those 'who are pleased to call themselves the Church party' should include 'the greatest part of the Dissenters, viz. the Harleys, Foleys, Winningtons, Joliffes, etc.'[35] But the result was that by the last year of the reign, as in 1689, the major issues of the day divided men along Whig–Tory lines. Moreover, the conflict within the Church between the 'high' and the 'moderate' clergy, which was exacerbated by the disputes between the two Houses of the Convocation of Canterbury in 1701, was driving the Williamite bishops into 'an uneasy dependence' on the Whigs.[36] And just as the general election of early 1690 was fought out, at least in national terms, between the two parties, so was the general election of late 1701.

What remains to be considered in analysing the shifting party groupings of William's reign is the extent to which individual M.P.s changed their allegiance from Whig to Tory and vice versa. The surviving evidence precludes any unqualified answer and sets definite limits to the inquiry. An initial limit derives from the very considerable turnover among the members who sat in William's six Houses of Commons. Overall, 863 (64 per cent) of the 1,354 M.P.s elected between January 1689 and March 1702 served in two or more parliaments during the reign.[37] Yet, of the members chosen in the general election of late 1701, only 125 had sat in the Convention parliament.[38] A further limit is set by the small number of extant 'division' lists. Even if we treat the list of members refusing the voluntary association in 1696 as a division list, the total for the reign is a mere eight, and of these only two give both sides of the 'division'. Still another limit to this inquiry arises from our procedure of treating each of the votes in question as a partisan one; in fact, the list of M.P.s who opposed disbanding on 18 January 1699 derives from a primarily Court–Country division.

Within these limits, comparison and analysis of the 'division' lists does yield some suggestive results. In the first place, the names of 421 (49 per cent) of the 863 M.P.s who sat in two or more of William's Houses of Commons appear on at least two of the lists.[39] Of these 421, 361 (86 per cent) can be said to have voted consistently—that is, only on the 'Whig' or only on the 'Tory' side. In the second place, the largest single element among the sixty who voted inconsistently is composed of twenty Tory officials and military men whose deviations from partisan orthodoxy were usually a result of their places and commissions. Only eleven of the sixty can be identified as shifting from a Whig to a Tory allegiance during the reign and just five (four of them placemen) moved in the opposite direction.[40]

It would be foolhardy to place too much weight on this quantitative analysis given its limited scope and arbitrary assumptions.[41] Yet the relatively small number of incumbents who appear to have changed their party alliances, coupled with the substantial turnover of members, does point to the significance of the untried M.P.s in each new parliament. Vernon, speculating on the wisdom of a dissolution in the summer of 1700, put it this way: 'an old one [Commons] having formed themselves into parties whereas a number of new men break the designs of party men'.[42] Even so, new members did not arrive at Westminster devoid of principles, prejudices, and prior commitments.[43] In many cases, electoral patrons took into account the political views of candidates seeking their support. To cite only one instance, when Sir Michael Biddulph approached Lord Stanhope for his backing at Lichfield in early 1701 he pledged to 'always vote' as his prospective partner Richard Dyott did.[44] Similarly, there were at least some candidates who stood, as William Lowther did at Pontefract in late 1701, in order to prevent the choice of a man of contrary 'principle'.[45]

In general, it is apparent from the barrage of political propaganda published before and during the elections of the reign that national issues were being put before the electorate—an electorate still growing in number.[46] But the effects that the press and the pulpit had upon the election results are not easy to gauge. Certainly, the incidence of contests was relatively high by comparison to the rest of the seventeenth century: the total ranged from a low of 60 in 1689 to highs of 106 in 1690 and 1698, and the average of *known* contests for the six general elections held between 1689 and 1702 was 88. Still, contests remained the exception, and only 87 of the 269 English and Welsh constituencies were polled in three or more of these campaigns.[47] Then, too, neither the published propaganda nor the references to national questions and party loyalties made by individual candidates or their backers can by themselves explain the behaviour of the electors even in frequently contested constituencies. Such explanations must await the results of the continuing research concentrating on individual constituencies and drawing upon the pollbook evidence surviving for a scattering of contests from the early 1690s onwards, but the first tentative findings of these inquiries do stress the importance of a 'floating vote' that was responding to 'the ebb and flow of political issues'.[48]

Where pollbooks are lacking, other approaches may offer at least pointers.

And a survey of the distribution of contested seats during the six general elections between 1689 and 1702 does suggest that the relatively high incidence of contests reflected not only the struggle for dominance among local 'interests' but also the play of 'public opinion' on national questions. For one thing, the seats most likely to be contested were in the larger constituencies—those presumably less susceptible to manipulation by aspiring or established electoral patrons. English counties and boroughs with 500 or more voters were contested on average 2·4 times in these six elections; those with 100 to 499 voters, 2·0 times; those with less than 100, 1·9 times. For a second, constituencies in the south-eastern third of England (the region in which the London press might be expected to exert the greatest influence) were contested more often than those elsewhere. There were proportionally more seats in the North with 500 or more voters than in any other region, yet the south-eastern constituencies were contested on average 2·5 times, the northern ones 2·0 times, the south-western ones 1·9 times and the Welsh ones only 0·6 times.[49]

While electors would appear, then, to have been responding to some (incalculable) degree to national issues that were defined in parliament and debated in the press, the impact of these questions seems to have differed from region to region. And these differences may also be reflected in the divergent recruitment patterns of the party men in the Commons. Among the 361 partisans identified on the basis of the division lists there were 201 Tories and 160 Whigs. Of the former, nearly half (94) were returned from the over-represented south-western third of England, with another dozen being returned for Wales. Of the latter, fewer than one-third (51) sat for south-western seats and only two for Welsh ones. No wonder that Whigs such as the Earl of Shaftesbury exclaimed against the 'over proportion' of members returned from the 'western corner' (especially Wales and Cornwall)![50]

The distribution of contested seats and the recruitment of party men reveal a complex interplay between local and national, provincial and metropolitan sentiments and circumstances. Similar interactions can be discerned in the Commons' responses to the changes William's reign brought in the central government's activities.[51] For if one of the principal results of the Revolution was to assure the continued control by local notables of most aspects of day-to-day administration, the demands of the King's foreign policy threatened to upset the balance between the capital and the provinces. During the 1690s, the number of central government agents at work over the kingdom was growing, particularly the rapidly-multiplying and widely-disliked breed of excisemen.[52] Furthermore, the high taxes and the large loans raised to finance the war produced a redistribution of coin and capital. A sizeable proportion of the government's receipts was, no doubt, expended outside London by way of payments for the quartering of troops and for the purchase of war supplies. Yet the net effect, accentuated after the Irish theatre of the war was closed down, was to drain wealth from the North and the West to the benefit of the South-east.[53]

Had it not been for the Commons, the ramifications of wartime finance and administration might well have been even more far-reaching. The Commons, after all, were dominated numerically by provincial country gentlemen. Moreover, a few of their number—most notably Foley and Harley—were capable of formulating constructive alternatives to ministerial proposals. To be sure, the

1694 plan to hypothecate the land tax was not adopted and the land bank project of 1696 was a casualty of the credit squeeze. Nor were Foley and Harley able to prevent the proliferation of specific excises. Yet they did succeed in warding off a general excise, and the land tax, administered by local notables in commission, remained the staple tax in the parliamentary repertoire. Furthermore, by legislating against the intervention of excisemen in elections, by reviving the Commons' power (conceded to the crown in 1696–97) to nominate commissioners for the land tax, and by excluding Excise and Customs officials from sitting in the Commons, Foley, Harley, and the country gentlemen did limit considerably the administrative and political effects of war finance and revenue collection.[54]

In turn, the Commons' own decisions on these and related questions were also shaped by regional and sectional differences. One obvious example is provided by the recurring clashes over the proportioning of the land tax. The revised pound rate levy approved in 1692–93, which was then made permanent after the war, represented a victory for the under-assessed North and West over the East and South-east.[55] Another source of repeated sectional conflict was the determination of the particular commodities to be subjected to excises and customs duties. Foley and Harley not only opposed a general excise; they also led a stubborn, though eventually losing struggle against excises on leather and leather goods—an effort prompted in no small part by the importance of tanning and of leatherworking to both the graziers and artisans of Herefordshire and the Marches.[56] Similarly, when Edward Clarke and Sir Walter Yonge deserted the ministry in 1697 to lead the successful resistance to the proposed additional wine duties, they did so out of concern for the expanding traffic in textiles between the South-west and Portugal.[57] A third focal point of sectional conflict was provided by the bills to regulate the status of the overseas trading companies. In part, the contests provoked by the efforts of the old, royally-chartered companies to secure parliamentary establishments were fought out between rival 'gangs' of London traders.[58] But the conflict over the East India trade also pitted provincial against metropolitan merchants and importers of foreign textiles against domestic producers.

The increased resort to statute during William's reign, coupled with the conflicts of interest many of these bills provoked, contributed to making lobbying of members both more intense and more sophisticated. During the 1690s, the London printers began to do a substantial trade in 'Cases', 'Reasons', and similar pieces offering arguments for or against individual measures; produced in runs of several hundreds, they were then distributed gratis to M.P.s.[59] In addition, members' support was often solicited in the Commons' lobby, on occasion by regularly-rotating delegations of Quakers or East India traders.[60] Some interest groups also took care to ensure that friendly and able members were present in order to chair committees dealing with measures of concern to them.[61] Nor was it only the new East India Company which thought it worth while to get directors and supporters returned to the Commons; the directors of the Lead Mine Adventurers helped to find a seat for Sir Humphrey Mackworth in the parliament of 1701 in the belief he would be 'useful to our company'.[62] And if nothing else worked, bribery might be attempted.[63]

While the corruption of individual M.P.s and ministers by interests seeking favourable treatment gave rise to the spectacular East India Company scandal of 1695, in general the Commons displayed far more concern over the threat to 'free' elections and 'impartial' deliberations posed by the growth of government patronage. Some attention was also paid, though only spasmodically, to the problem of officials enriching themselves out of parliamentary supplies. Even so, accusations that individual officials had diverted public money to their own use (e.g. the cases of Lord Falkland in 1693–94 and of Charles Whitaker, the Admiralty Solicitor, in 1701) or had claimed unreasonable fees or perquisites (e.g. the case of Henry Priestman, Commissioner of the Admiralty, in 1699) were often politically inspired.[64] So too was the inquiry into Exchequer bill frauds in 1698, which was aimed at Charles Montagu.[65]

Yet there can be no doubt that many sections of the royal administration did afford rich opportunities for fraud and peculation: navy victualling, the clothing of the army, land tax remittances, and the 'course' of the lower Exchequer, to mention only the more prominent examples.[66] Despite this, parliament preferred individual inquiries to effective remedial action. The Commission of Accounts, it is true, did devote much time to scrutinising official expenditures, and members of the commission also took the lead in devising new provisions against false musters. But even statutes had to be enforced, and in practice Army Paymaster Ranelagh, pleading royal instructions, issued moneys without regard to the muster roll figures. Similarly, the clause in the mutiny act of 1694–95 intended to end the sale of army commissions proved a dead letter.[67] Moreover, Ranelagh was prepared in 1697 to divert to private uses the prize money (some £20,000, he estimated) accruing upon winning malt lottery tickets assigned to his and other government offices. To be sure, the Commissioners of the Treasury were of opinion this would violate a parliamentary clause of appropriation, but Ranelagh —invoking Albemarle's favour—suggested that 'the King's pleasure, ought, and will, be too hard for opposition' on any score from the Treasury.[68] In the meantime, the legislation repeatedly proposed to bar the sale of civil offices never reached the statute book; rather, it was William's own 'rule' against granting either offices for life or reversions that was the chief barrier to alienation of offices in the crown's gift.[69]

By and large, it was left up to the King himself to regulate other facets of the executive as well. Moreover, after the end of the war the size of the governmental establishment was reduced, especially on the military side.[70] This reduction might have been carried a good deal further had Harley's proposal in 1700 to return to farming the excise proved financially attractive, but when the offers of the prospective farmers did not come up to expectations direct collection was retained.[71] Harley is also known to have been hostile to the commitment that the Commons did make in January 1698 to put disbanded native army officers on half pay.[72] Nor did he display any great zeal, at least before January 1702, in making adequate provision for the government's large unfunded debts even though they had resulted mainly from the deficiencies of parliamentary levies. In fact, until January 1702 Harley's chief contribution was to push through the resumption of the Irish forfeitures, but they were not enough even to satisfy the army's arrears.[73]

Although the King and his ministers had to struggle between 1699 and 1701 to maintain the government's credit in the face of inadequate parliamentary provision for past deficiencies and also of the old East India Company's attempts to overturn its rival, there was no longer any need to innovate. The Board of Trade was kept on foot, the Treasury and the Admiralty remained in commission, and the routine of cabinet meetings was maintained as a means of administrative co-ordination.[74] Moreover, since many excises, customs duties, and other levies had already been committed by statute for years, sometimes even decades, in advance, the operation of the revenue agencies was only marginally affected by the return to peacetime conditions. The long-term obligation of these revenues did pose some difficulties when the Commons were confronted during the last two parliaments of the reign with the need to finance rearmament. Yet until William's death, ways and means were devised without recourse to any strikingly new expedients. And simultaneously, the administrative tasks of mobilisation were dealt with by a generally experienced body of officials able to draw upon 'the lessons' of the previous war.[75]

What was true for the King's administration also largely held for the Commons. The only innovation in the House's financial procedures in the postwar years was its regular recourse to resolutions of credit. The Commons did revert to prewar practice in the 1698–99 session by taking up 'the state of the nation' before supply, but members showed no inclination to halt the House's increased use of committees of the whole for the transaction of the principal public business.[76] In the meantime, with Treasury Secretary Lowndes (first returned in 1695) assuming a prominent role in the preparation of financial bills, standards of parliamentary draftsmanship appear to have improved.[77] At the least, there seem to have been no more slips of the sort that made the paper and parchment tax of 1693–94 almost unworkable.[78] Then, too, the regularisation of proceedings may have been facilitated by the adoption at the beginning of the 1699–1700 session of a group of eight 'usual orders' of procedure. Yet these 'usual orders' mostly related to private business and they also varied somewhat from session to session well into Anne's reign.[79]

In any case, neither the alterations in the Commons' procedures over the course of the reign nor the House's enhanced stature after the Revolution much affected some features of life in St Stephen's Chapel. It was customary, apparently, for new Speakers to urge members to behave themselves decorously and to conform to the customary rules in debate, but these injunctions seem to have been honoured mainly in the breach.[80] Sir Richard Cocks, for example, complained that 'there is such a noise one can scarce hear or mind what is said', and Sir Anthony Keck reportedly characterised the Commons as a 'bear garden'.[81] Another perennial problem was absenteeism. In the proposals for reform he drafted in preparation for the meeting of the Convention in January 1689, Thomas Erle (already an experienced member) included an item 'that care be taken that those that are chosen to be parliament men daily attend' the House and that a penalty be imposed on those absent 'without just cause'.[82] But nothing was done, and the average attendance at divisions in the House during the reign was 238—less than half the total membership and approximately the same proportion that attended in the 1670s.[83]

Detailed analysis of the surviving records of the 1691–92 and 1692–93 sessions indicates that the bulk of the Commons' business was transacted by a minority of 'working' members, consisting of about one-quarter of the total membership.[84] By comparison to their colleagues (both the occasionally active and the wholly inactive), this group contained a higher proportion of placemen and lawyers.[85] But it also included many who had neither official connections with the government nor legal practices to serve. Some were country gentlemen such as William Brockman, a zealous member ready to castigate the less diligent.[86] Others were substantial townsmen, returned for such boroughs as Bristol, Hull, Liverpool, Great Yarmouth, and Sandwich. These were towns which still expected from their M.P.s both regular accounts of the Commons' proceedings and a solicitous attendance upon constituency interests not only in St Stephen's Chapel but also at Whitehall.[87]

Debates in both the full House and committees of the whole were dominated by an even smaller subgroup among the active M.P.s, which consisted of fifty to sixty members. This nucleus of frequent speakers can be distinguished both from the rest of the working members and from all their other colleagues by the high proportion of placemen it included and also by the debaters' much longer average term of service in the Commons. During the 1691–92 and 1692–93 sessions, a handful of hostile politicians, comprising approximately 15 per cent of the group of frequent speakers, bore the burden of opposition, while nearly 60 per cent of the most vocal M.P.s held offices of profit, though not all these placemen were supporting the ministry then in office. These placemen, and their counterparts in other sessions, were mainly politicians rather than career officials, and one of their qualifications for office was their ability and readiness to speak in the House. At the same time, their dual service provided a critical link between the King's administration and the Commons.

In the absence of comparative research, it is impossible to be sure that the patterns of participation in debate and in the other work of the Commons during William's reign differed substantially from those that prevailed in Charles II's. Probably they did not. Yet in many other respects the two reigns were separated by a wide gulf. In part, this separation was a result of the Revolution. But it was also, and even more, the product of William's war, of his consequent dependence upon parliament and the concomitant expansion of the executive, and of the responses to these changes in parliament and among the political nation. William's leading political aides—Carmarthen, Sunderland, and the tentative combination of Rochester and Godolphin—had all learned the parliamentary 'art' in the Cavalier parliament, but they had to practise it in conjunction with new House of Commons men and under altered circumstances. Carmarthen was only partially successful in making the transition, hampered as he was by the King's limited confidence and by his feuds with the leaders of the West country Church-men—Sir Edward Seymour and the Granvilles. Sunderland, relying upon the developing Whig Junto, was much more successful, at least for a time. But it was Rochester and Godolphin who eventually secured the assistance of the most able and skilful of the House of Commons men who came of age during the 1690s, Robert Harley.

Whether Harley, working in conjunction with Godolphin and Marlborough, the principal figures in the ministry that Anne chose at her accession, would be able to retain his lead in the Commons remained to be determined. But the Queen and the 'duumvirs' made it clear at the outset of the new reign that they were ready to mobilise the kingdom's resources 'to reduce the exorbitant power of France'.[88] And in choosing to commit England to renewed war as a principal, despite objections from some of the new Tory ministers, it was apparent that Anne and her chief advisers would not only be dependent upon the administrative apparatus and financial methods elaborated in the previous reign but that they would also have to cope with many of the political problems that had perplexed and bedevilled William III.

Notes to Chapter XIII

1 There was also no mutiny act in force during 1692.

2 BL Add. MS. 30000E, f. 211, L. F. Bonnet, 23 May/3 June 1701.

3 The figures in A. S. Turberville, *The House of Lords in the Reign of William III* (Oxford, 1913), pp. 7–11, are not reliable.

4 On occasion, however, the royal prerogative was employed as a substitute for a cash or land grant; Surrey RO, Somers MSS., copy of the Queen's warrant, 12 March 1691, giving the Earl of Bath, as part of the marriage portion of Lady Isabella Ouwerkerk, a patent for making an English baron or, in default thereof, £10,000. See also HMC *Frankland–Russell–Astley*, pp. 92–3; NU, Portland MS. PwA 1254, [Sunderland to Portland], 20 June [1696]; Bodl. Carte MS. 231, f. 38.

5 G. Bennett, 'King William III and the Episcopate', in *Essays in Modern English Church History*, ed. G. V. Bennett (1966), esp. pp. 118–22, 127–9.

6 See Appendix B. See also F. James, 'The Bishops in Politics, 1688–1714', in *Conflicts in Stuart England*, ed. W. A. Aiken (1960), pp. 232–3, 250.

7 Compare R. Walcott, *English Politics in the Early Eighteenth Century* (Oxford, 1956), pp. 36–9 and app. II; W. A. Speck, *Tory & Whig: The Struggle in the Constituencies 1701–1715* (1970), pp. 72–3.

8 DWL Morrice MS. R, p. 221, also 201.

9 The result, on occasion, was that individual placemen competed with one another for seats in constituencies where the government had some influence; J. H. Plumb, *The Growth of Political Stability in England 1675–1725* (1967), pp. 75–82. Walcott asserts that nineteen placemen were returned on the government's interest in the election of late 1701, but few in fact were official nominees; *English Politics*, pp. 38–9.

10 See Appendix D. Note, too, that the January 1690 figure is abnormally low because virtually no Irish appointments had as yet been made.

11 For instance, 133 of the 507 members of the Commons in 1664 were royal servants, office-holders, or recipients of favours or bounty; J. Jones, 'Court Dependents in 1664', *BIHR* XXXIV (1961), 81–91.

12 *CJ*, XI, 7, 580, and XII, 39, 401, and XIII, 344, 656.

13 Before his death William did, however, approve the bill to renew the 1700 commission to examine the army, navy, and transport debts.

14 Luttrell, *Parliamentary Diary*, p. 250; *CJ*, X, 701, 707, 710. Note also that those who in 1699 opposed paying the debt to Prince George which had been incurred in connection with the Treaty of Altena argued that since that agreement was not 'amongst the several treaties which were laid before the House' parliament had no obligation to do so; Bodl. Carte MS. 130, f. 406, R. Price to [Duke of Beaufort], 11 December 1699.

15 *Archives*, III, iii, 519. See also BL Add. MS. 7074, f. 7, J. Ellis to G. Stepney, 28 March 1701. In fact, the secret article in the 1689 treaty with the Imperialists which pledged Anglo-Dutch support for the Austrian claim to the Spanish succession was invoked by those who attacked Somers's sealing of the first Partition Treaty; BL Add. MS. 17677WW, f. 223, L'Hermitage, 11/22 April 1701.

16 *The Marlborough–Godolphin Correspondence*, ed. H. L. Snyder (Oxford, 1975), I, 13–14, 20, 38, 40.

17 D. Hinton, 'The Decline of Parliamentary Government under Elizabeth I and the Early Stuarts', *Cambridge Historical Journal* XIII (1957), 116; P. D. G. Thomas, *The House of Commons in the Eighteenth Century* (Oxford, 1971), p. 61.

18 BL Add. MS. 30000D, f. 110, 26 March/6 April 1700. See also *The Diary of John Evelyn*, ed. E. S. de Beer (Oxford, 1955), V, 209, and n. 6.

19 I am indebted to Sheila Lambert for the information for Anne's reign. See also her *Bills and Acts* (Cambridge, 1971), especially chapters 5 and 9, for the artificiality of the contemporary distinction between 'private' and 'public' legislation.

20 East India Office Lib., E/3/92, old Co. dispatch book, p. 59, to St Helena, 15 June 1689; *CJ*, X, 168.

21 *Hudson's Bay Copy Booke of Letters Commissions Instructions Outward 1688–1696*, ed. E. E. Rich (Hudson's Bay Record Society, vol. XX, 1957), p. 100.

22 M. Levine, 'A Parliamentary Title to the Crown in Tudor England', *Huntington Library Quarterly* XXV (1962), 121–7.

23 *Vernon Corr.*, I, 474.

24 Hunt. Stowe MS. 58, vol. 1, ff. 16–17, to James Brydges, 25 November 1700. I am obliged to Professor Clayton Roberts for bringing this letter to my attention.

25 Blenheim MS. C1–23, Godolphin to Sunderland, 8 August 1709, quoted in H. Snyder, 'Godolphin and Harley: A Study of their Partnership in Politics', *Huntington Library Quarterly* XXX (1967), 245 n. 2.

26 BL Loan 29/154 (unfoliated), to R. Probert (copy), 24 September 1695.

27 Verney MSS., reel 51, 21 December 1700. And see HMC *Ancaster*, pp. 249–50.

28 Cumberland RO, Lowther letters, to Sir J. Lowther, 22 January 1702.

29 J. A. W. Gunn, *Factions No More* (1971), esp. the editorial introduction.

30 KAO, Chevening MS. 78, 13 September 1692, 13 February 1694, 27 January 1696.

31 DWL Morrice MSS. Q, 624, 644, 654, and R, 84, 91; Berkshire RO, Trumbull MS. 'Ellis' bound vol., to Sir W. Trumbull, 4 February 1696.

32 BL Add. MS. 22851, f. 121, J. Craggs to T. Pitt, 25 February 1702; Bodl. Ballard MS. 11, f. 166, E. Warcupp to A. Charlett, 25 February 1700[–1]; Bodl. Ballard MS. 23, f. 108, [Mr Lloyd] to A. Charlett, 14 June 1701. See also the discussions of changing party labels in two tracts of 1701–02: *Harleian Miscellany* (1808–11), VIII, 186; ST, III, 351.

33 Bodl. MS. Eng. hist. b209, f. 79 v., February 1701; *Original Letters of John Locke, Alg. Sidney, and Lord Shaftesbury*, ed. T. Forster (1847), p. 128, February 1702.

34 A. Trevor, *The Life and Times of William the Third* (1835), II, 478–9, Hooper's memoirs, 1701. See also BL Loan 29/165, misc. 97, p. 7; G. Holmes, *British Politics in the Age of Anne* (1967), p. 260, quoting Harley's draft letter to Archbishop Tenison.

35 Trinity College MSS., King correspondence 780, 787, [E.] Burridge to Archbishop King, 1 and 17 April 1701. These observations are reiterated, in very similar terms, by the author (allegedly Lord Somers) of *Jura Populi Anglicani* (1701), reprinted in ST, III, 260–1.

36 Bennett, 'King William III and the Episcopate', p. 130.

37 The distribution is: 491 M.P.s served in one parliament during the reign, 329 in two, 210 in three, 154 in four, 93 in five, and 77 in six.

38 Thus, of the twenty-member 'Harley–Foley connection' constructed by Walcott for the 1701–02 parliament, only four had sat in the Convention parliament. Two of these, Harley himself and Sir Michael Warton, had been blacklisted as supporters of the 'Sacheverell clause', and another, the elder Thomas Mansell, had been blacklisted as a supporter of regency: *English Politics*, pp. 214–15. Walcott does not include in the 'connection' the only two other 'Sacheverellites' sitting in 1701–02 who were to be blacklisted (Henry Lee and John Lewknor), along with Harley and Warton, as supporting the attempt to revive the impeachments against the four lords. In addition to these four, forty-three other 'Sacheverellites' were elected to William's last parliament.

39 Appendix C includes a list of all 421 M.P.s, as well as a description of all the division lists. Limiting the analysis to M.P.s who sat for two or more parliaments excludes only thirty-two M.P.s with at least two recorded votes; twenty-six of these voted consistently, six did not.

40 The eleven Whigs include, beside the four listed in note 38, Sir R. Cotton of Cheshire, W. Duncombe, Philip Foley, Sir E. Harley, J. Howe, T. Pitt, and Sir W. Williams (the Exclusionist Speaker). The five Tories are Sir R. Cotton of Cambridgeshire, Lord Cornbury, Lord Ranelagh, F. Robartes, and Sir J. Turner (the only backbencher).

41 For an analysis of the Lords' division lists, see Appendix B.

42 *Vernon Corr.*, III, 114. And see the suggestive comments in *The Parliamentary Lists of the Early Eighteenth Century*, ed. A. Newman (Leicester, 1973), pp. 74–5, 84.

43 For lists compiled soon after the general elections of 1695, 1698, and late 1701 which attempt to classify the political leanings of both old and new M.P.s, see Appendix C.

44 HMC *Cowper*, II, 419. Stanhope later complained Biddulph had broken his pledge, p. 451.

45 Leeds Reference Lib., Temple Newsam MS. C9/150, to Lord Irwin, 17 November 1701.

46 J. Plumb, 'The Growth of the Electorate in England from 1600 to 1715', *Past & Present*, No. 45 (November 1969), esp. 110–16. And see Bodl. MS. Eng. hist. b209, f. 84, the Commons' vote on the Orford case in February 1700.

47 See Appendix A. Compare M. Hirst, *The Representative of the People?* (Cambridge, 1975), app. iv.

48 W. Speck *et al.*, 'Computer Analysis of Poll Books: A Further Report', *BIHR* XLVIII (1975), 65 and ff. See also R. Hopkinson, 'Elections in Cumberland and Westmorland 1695–1723' (unpublished Ph.D. thesis, University of Newcastle, 1973).

49 Constituency sizes and the regional classification have been derived from Speck, *Tory & Whig*, app. E and p. 67.

50 *Original Letters of Locke*, p. 128. Cf. Speck, *Tory & Whig*, pp. 66–7.

51 See also A. Everitt, *Change in the Provinces: The Seventeenth Century* (Occasional Papers, 2nd s. No. 1, Department of English Local History, Leicester University, 1969).

52 For a contemporary's conservative estimate of the number of new excisemen taken on between 1689 and 1699, see Wing R947, pp. 41–3.

53 D. W. Jones, 'London Overseas-Merchant Groups at the End of the Seventeenth Century and the Moves against the East India Company' (unpublished D.Phil. thesis, University of Oxford, 1970), p. 89 and *passim*.

54 C. Brooks, 'Public Finance and Political Stability: The Administration of the Land Tax, 1688–1720', *HJ* XVII (1974), 281–300.

55 For disputes over this issue early in the reign, see Lamberty, *Mémoires*, II, 167, 662–3; Luttrell, *Parliamentary Diary*, pp. 61–2, 311–13.

56 *HMC Portland*, III, 550, 562.

57 For the struggles over the salt taxes, see E. Hughes, *Studies in Administration and Finance 1558–1825* (Manchester, 1934), pp. 225–37.

58 J. Price, 'The Tobacco Adventure to Russia' (*Transactions of the American Philosophical Society*, n.s. No. 51, part i, 1961), pp. 31–2. See also M. Kammen, *Empire and Interest* (Philadelphia, 1970), chapters 2–3.

59 L. W. Hanson, *Contemporary Printed Sources for British and Irish Economic History 1701–1750* (Cambridge, 1963), p. xvii.

60 E. Kirby, 'The Quakers' Efforts to Secure Civil and Religious Liberty 1660–1696', *JMH* VII (1935), 413; BL Add. MS. 17677PP, ff. 463–4, L'Hermitage, 13/23 December 1695. See also N. Hunt, *Two Early Political Associations* (Oxford, 1961), pp. 18–48.

61 *HMC Downshire*, I, 775; Bodl. Rawlinson MS. C449, f. 6.

62 NLW, Nanteos letters, Duke of Leeds to W. Powell, 15 October 1700, and Sir H. Mackworth to same, 27 October 1700. And see Newcastle Univ., Misc. MS. 85 (Montagu Papers), C. Montagu to G. Baker, 21 December 1697 (I owe this reference to Dr Joyce Ellis).

63 Not all the money collected for purposes of bribery went to corrupt the purported targets. In 1699, a Commons' inquiry into an alleged case of bribery related to the distillers' bill revealed that Dalby Thomas had raised money from the distillers on 'a pretence of obstructing' the measure, but had actually 'intended to put the money into [his] own pockets'. Cumberland RO, Lowther letters, J. to Sir J. Lowther, 25 February 1698[–9].

64 Both Whitaker and Priestman were Orford's 'creatures'.

65 For attempts in the 1701 and 1701–02 parliaments to restrict Montagu's fees as Auditor of the Exchequer: Bodl. MSS. Eng. hist. b209, f. 69, and b210, f. 5 v.; *CJ*, XIII, 578, 841, 850; *SR*, VIII 37–8.

66 Plumb, *Growth of Political Stability*, pp. 117, 121; S. Baxter, *The Development of the Treasury 1660–1702* (1957), p. 166. The 1696–97 act regulating Exchequer procedure was officially sponsored and was drafted by Lowndes; H. Roseveare, *The Treasury* (1969), p. 75.

67 R. E. Scouller, *The Armies of Queen Anne* (Oxford, 1966), pp. 30–2, 70; *SR*, VI, 587–8.

68 Baker Library (Harvard University), Ranelagh–Blathwayt letters, Nos. 17 and 20, [1697] and 27 August 1697.

69 For William's 'rule' and its operation, see *CTB*, XIII, 105, 106, and XIV, 125; *CSPD*, 1699–1700, p. 227; *Correspondentie*, I, ii, 117–18. See also *CTB*, XIII, 58, 234; BL Add. MS. 33084, ff. 162–4; J. Sainty, 'A Reform in the Tenures of Offices during the Reign of Charles II', *BIHR* XLI (1968), esp. 162–4.

70 For the fleet's demobilisation, see J. Ehrman, *The Navy in the War of William III 1689–1697* (Cambridge 1953), pp. 612–19.

71 Hughes, *Studies in Administration and Finance*, pp. 190–7.

72 BL Loan 29/189, f. 8, [R. Harley] to his father, 18 January 1698.

73 W. Shaw, *CTB*, Introduction to vols. XI–XVII, pp. ccvii–ccxx.

74 While many cabinet minutes for the postwar years survive among Vernon's papers, those attending are rarely listed: for the exceptions see BL Add. MS. 40781, ff. 1, 141; *Vernon Corr.*, II, 39; *CTB*, XV, 90, 91; BL Add. MS. 40775, f. 367. Vernon noted that in succeeding Trumbull as Secretary, he was sworn 'Clerk' of the cabinet; *Vernon Corr.*, I, 434.

75 Ehrman, *The Navy*, p. 622.

76 Even so, many non-financial 'public' bills continued to be entrusted to select committees, sometimes with a stipulation that all who attended could vote. Cf. Thomas, *House of Commons in the Eighteenth Century*, p. 51.

77 For samples of Lowndes's work, see PRO, T48/4. See also BL Add. MS. 36914, f. 1, printed in Hughes, *Studies in Administration and Finance*, p. 228.

78 BL Egerton MS. 920, f. 112, J. Vernon to W. Blathwayt, 1 June 1694.

79 B. Kemp, *Votes and Standing Orders of the House of Commons: The Beginning* (House of Commons Library, Document No. 8, 1971), pp. 9, 42.

80 See BL Loan 29/161, misc. 17, Harley's notes for his acceptance speeches to the Commons in February and December 1701 and October 1702.

81 Bodl. MS. Eng. hist. b209, f. 91 v. See also CSPD, 1698, p. 34 ('reflections were grown so common of late'); BL Add. MS. 42592, f. 174, W. Brockman's notes ('great affairs of the nation are made personal').

82 Churchill College, Erle MS., 4/4.

83 For sessional averages, see *English Historical Documents 1660–1714*, ed. A. Browning (1966), pp. 956–7.

84 This and the paragraph following are a partial summary of T. Moore and H. Horwitz, 'Who Runs the House?', *JMH* XLIII (1971), 205–27.

85 For the diverse reactions of two placemen to their double burden at Whitehall and, Westminster, see HMC *Le Fleming*, p. 345; Cumberland RO, Lowther letters, J. to Sir J. Lowther, 29 April 1699.

86 BL Add. MS. 42592, f. 174.

87 For the correspondence of M.P.s for these boroughs with their 'masters', see BL Add. MS. 5540, f. 79 and ff.; Hull RO, letters 1117 and ff.; Liverpool RO, Norris letters; Great Yarmouth RO, 36/15/1–56; BL Add. MS. 33512, f. 118 and ff. For correspondences of country gentlemen with their boroughs, see *Letter-books of John Hervey, first Earl of Bristol*, [ed. S. H. A. Hervey] (Wells, 1894), I, 73–4, and ff.; HMC *Eighth Report*, pp. 392–3. See also R. Latham, 'The Payment of Parliamentary Wages—the Last Phase', *EHR* LXVI (1951), 31; *Merchants and Merchandise in Seventeenth Century Bristol*, ed. P. McGrath (Bristol Record Society, vol. XIX, 1955), esp. p. 163 n. 1. Compare Hirst, *The Representative of the People?*, pp. 164, 179.

88 Anne's first speech to parliament; PH, VI, 5.

CONTESTED ELECTIONS

1689-1702

The following table lists all known contests (marked by an 'x'). Where pollbooks or lists of voters are extant, the entry appears in italics ('*x*'). Those cases in which there is evidence of a canvass, but not of a contest, are also noted ('c'). In seven instances, W. A. Speck in *Tory & Whig: The Struggle in the Constituencies 1701–1715* (1970), app. E, lists contests for the 1701 election for which I can only find evidence of canvasses; these seven cases are marked '?'.

The majority of contested elections were controverted, but the ratio of contested to controverted elections varied significantly from one general election to the next: 1689, thirty-two controverted elections of sixty contested; 1690, seventy-six of 106; 1695, fifty-six of seventy-eight; 1698, forty-five of 106; 1700–01, forty-seven of eighty-six; 1701, forty-six of ninety-one.

Constituency	1689	1690	1695	1698	1700–01	1701	By-elections
Bedfordshire			x	x			
Bedford		x					
Berkshire		x	c				
Abingdon	x			x		x	1689
Reading	x	*x*	x	x	x	c	
Wallingford	x					x	
Windsor	x	x		c			1689
Buckinghamshire			c	x	*x*	x	1696; 1696
Agmondesham			x	x	x	x	
Aylesbury			x	x		x	1691; 1699
Buckingham	x	x	x		c		
Great Marlow		x					
Wendover	c						
Wycombe				x			
Cambridgeshire	c		c	x			1694; 1697
Cambridge University	*x*	x	*x*	x		x	*1692*
Cambridge			c	x		x	
Cheshire		x	c			x	
Chester	c	x	x	x	x	x	
Cornwall		c	c				
Bodmin							
Bossiney					x		
Callington							
Camelford		c	c				
Fowey				x	*x*	x	
Grampound							
Helston		x					
Launceston		x			c		1692
Liskeard				x			
East Looe							
West Looe							
Lostwithiel				x	x	x	1701

Constituency	1689	1690	1695	1698	1700–01	1701	By-elections
Michael	x	x	x	x	x	x	1689; 1697
Newport					x		1690; 1699
Penryn							1699
St Germans							
St Ives		x		x	x	x	
St Mawes			x	x	x	x	1696
Saltash				c			
Tregoney		x	x			x	
Truro	x	x					
Cumberland					c	x	
Carlisle		x	x	c	x	x	
Cockermouth		x	x	x	x	x	
Derbyshire	x	x			x	x	
Derby			x	x	x	x	
Devonshire							
Ashburton							
Barnstaple			c				
Beer Alston							
Dartmouth		x		x	x		1689; 1700
Exeter			x	x		x	1689
Honiton					x		
Okehampton			c	x	c		
Plymouth				x			1689
Plympton	x	x			x		1690
Tavistock		x	x	c	x	x	1696
Tiverton			c		c		
Totnes			x		x		
Dorset							
Bridport		x	x				1697
Corfe Castle		c		x		x	1699
Dorchester		x	c		x		1689
Lyme Regis	x		c			x	
Poole	x		c	x	c		
Shaftesbury			x		x		
Wareham		x	c				
Weymouth and Melcombe Regis				x	c		1702
Durham County			c	x		x	
Durham	x		c	x	x	c	
Essex	x	x	x	x	x	x	1693; 1694
Colchester	x	x	x				
Harwich	x	x		x	x		
Malden	x		x	x		x	1693
Gloucestershire	c	x	c	x	x	x	1696
Bristol	x	x	x	x		x	
Cirencester	x	x	x	c	x	x	
Gloucester		x	c			?	
Tewkesbury	x		x				
Herefordshire		c		c	c		1690
Hereford		c	c	c	x	x	1689
Leominster		x	c	c	x	x	
Weobley	x		c	x	x	x	1691
Hertfordshire		x	x	x			1697
Hertford	x	x		x	x	x	1701
St Albans		x			x	x	1701
Huntingdonshire			x				
Huntingdon			c		x		

Constituency	1689	1690	1695	1698	1700–01	1701	By-elections
Kent	x	c	c			x	1691
Canterbury			x				
Maidstone		x		x		x	
Queenborough		x	c				
Rochester		x				x	
Lancashire	c				x	c	
Clitheroe	c		x	x			1693; 1694
Lancaster	x			x			
Liverpool		c	x		x	x	1694
Newton		x					
Preston	x	x	x	x	x	x	1690
Wigan		c	x	x	x	x	1693
Leicestershire		x	x	c	x	c	
Leicester		x		c			
Lincolnshire			x				
Boston					c		
Grantham		x				x	1697
Great Grimsby		x			x	x	1699
Lincoln			x	x		?	
Stamford	x		x				
Middlesex	x	x	x		x	x	1695
London	c	x	x	x	x	x	1693; 1701
Westminster	x	x	x	x	x	x	1691
Monmouthshire			c				
Monmouth				c			
Norfolk	x	x		x	x	x	
Castle Rising							
King's Lynn							
Norwich				x		x	
Thetford	x	x		x	x	c	1699; 1700
Yarmouth						x	
Northamptonshire		c	x	x	c	x	
Brackley				x		x	
Higham Ferrers		c			x		
Northampton		c	c	c			1701
Peterborough				c	x	?	
Northumberland				x	c	x	
Berwick			x	x			
Morpeth			x				
Newcastle upon Tyne					c	c	
Nottinghamshire				x		x	
Newark				x	x	x	1693
Nottingham			x		x	?	1699
Retford					x	x	
Oxfordshire	x	x		x	c		1699
Banbury		x			x		1700
Oxford University			c	x	x		1701
Oxford		x	x	x		x	
Woodstock			c		c		
Rutland			x				
Shropshire		c	x			x	
Bishop's Castle			c	x	x	x	1695
Bridgnorth				x		x	
Ludlow		x	x	x		x	
Shrewsbury		x					
Wenlock	x	x					

Constituency	1689	1690	1695	1698	1700–01	1701	By-elections
Somerset		x	c	x			
Bath	x	x	x	x			1690
Bridgwater				x			1692
Ilchester	x		c	x	x		
Milborne Port			c	c		x	1702
Minehead				x			
Taunton	x		x	x			1701
Wells		x	x				
Hampshire				x			
Andover	x		c			x	
Christchurch		x	x				
Lymington	x	x	x		x		
Newport			c		x		1699
Newtown			x				
Petersfield	x		c				
Portsmouth		x	x				1696; 1696
Southampton		x	x		c		1689; 1699
Stockbridge		x	x				1689; 1689; 1691; 1693
Whitchurch			x				
Winchester		x			x		
Yarmouth			x				
Staffordshire				x			
Lichfield		x	c	x	x		
Newcastle under Lyme				c			1699
Stafford		x	c		c	c	
Tamworth	x	x		x	x		
Suffolk	x	x		x	x		
Aldeburgh		x					
Bury St Edmunds		x	x			x	
Dunwich	x		x	x			1701
Eye							
Ipswich	x	x	x	x	x	x	
Orford			c	x	x	x	
Sudbury	x				x		1699
Surrey			x	x		x	
Bletchingly		x	x		x		
Gatton				c			
Guildford	x			x			
Haslemere				x			
Reigate	x	x	x	x		x	
Southwark	x	x	x	x	x	x	
Sussex			x		c	x	
Arundel		x	c		x		1694
Bramber		x	c	x	x	x	
Chichester		x	x	x			
Grinstead	x		x				
Horsham			c			x	
Lewes							
Midhurst			c	x			
Shoreham			c	x	x	x	
Steyning					c		1701; 1701
Warwickshire		x	x		c		
Coventry		x		x	c	x	
Warwick		x	c	x		x	
Westmoreland	c	c	c		x	x	
Appleby					x	x	

Constituency	1689	1690	1695	1698	1700–01	1701	By-elections
Wiltshire		x				x	
Bedwin				x		x	
Calne					x	x	1691
Chippenham					x		1690; 1691; 1694
Cricklade	x	x	x	x			
Devizes	x	x	x				
Downton			c		x		
Heytesbury							
Hindon				x		x	1698
Ludgershall		x		x			1695
Malmesbury		x		x	x	x	
Marlborough	x	x	x	x	x		
Old Sarum	x						1689
Salisbury	x	x	c		x		
Westbury							
Wilton		x		c	x	c	
Wootton Bassett		x	c				
Worcestershire		x		x	x	x	
Bewdley					x		
Droitwich		x		x	x		1701
Evesham		c	x	x	c	c	1698
Worcester				x		?	1693
Yorkshire	c			x			
Aldborough		x		x	c	c	1696
Beverley			c			x	
Boroughbridge		x	c	x			
Hedon							
Kingston upon Hull		c	x		x	?	
Knaresborough	x	x					
Malton							
Northallerton			c		c		
Pontefract		x	x	x	x	c	1700
Richmond			c			c	
Ripon	x		c			x	
Scarborough			c			x	1693
Thirsk			x				
York		x	c	x		x	
Dover		x		x	c	?	1697
Hastings		x		x		x	
Hythe		x		c			
New Romney	x	x	x			x	1696
Rye	x	x		x			
Sandwich	x	x	x	x	x	x	1698; 1701
Seaford							
Winchelsea					x	x	
Anglesey							
Beaumaris	x			c			
Breconshire			x				1697
Brecon	x	x		x			
Cardiganshire	x	x					
Cardigan						x	
Carmarthenshire						x	1701
Carmarthen							
Caernarvonshire							
Caernarvon							
Denbighshire							
Denbigh		x		x	x		

Constituency	1689	1690	1695	1698	1700–01	1701	By-elections
Flintshire							
Flint							1697
Glamorganshire							
Cardiff							
Merioneth							
Montgomeryshire							
Montgomery							
Pembrokeshire					x		
Haverfordwest							
Pembroke							
Radnorshire			c	c	c		1692
New Radnor	x	x					

Appendix B

HOUSE OF LORDS VOTES
1689-1702

In some respects, the Lords *Journal* and the surviving House of Lords manuscripts are much fuller than the surviving House of Commons materials. The Lords *Journal* lists peers in attendance for each sitting and the Lords manuscripts include records of proxies for the first, second, and third of William's six parliaments. Moreover, numerous signed protests are printed in the Lords *Journal*, and on twenty-four occasions during William's reign twenty or more peers subscribed individually to such protests.

None the less, extant Lords division lists for the period 1689-1702 are few and far between. Only four are known to survive, but each of these does relate to a major and controversial question—the regency proposal of January 1689, the attainder of Sir John Fenwick in December 1696, and the impeachment of the Junto lords in June 1701. The first is a list of the forty-eight peers (and one teller) who supported the regency motion; moreover, from other contemporary evidence (principally, the list of those in attendance on 29 January) it is possible to identify all those who opposed the regency proposal that day. The second is a list of the sixty-eight peers for and the sixty-one against the third reading of the attainder bill on 23 December 1696. And the third and fourth are lists of those who voted for and against acquitting Lord Somers and the Earl of Orford, fifty-six to thirty-two on 17 June 1701 and forty-three to nil on 23 June, respectively.

From these lists, we have drawn up the following table, listing the votes of all the peers who voted in two or more of the divisions involved. The table is arranged as follows.

Column one: party designation. Those voting only on the 'Whig' side (against regency, for attainder, against conviction) are indicated by the mark 'W'; those voting only on the 'Tory' side (for regency, against attainder, for conviction) are indicated by the mark 'T'; those voting on both sides are indicated by the mark 'M' (mixed). These total, respectively, forty-four 'W's, twenty-eight 'T's, and twenty-three 'M's—that is, 76 per cent of those voting twice or more voted consistently and 24 per cent did not.

Column two: names of peers. The peers are grouped by rank (dukes, earls, etc.) and within each rank they are arranged alphabetically according to the title (or diocese) they held at William's death. Earlier titles or dioceses held during William's reign are indicated in parentheses.

Column three: Vote on the regency proposal, pro or con. (The list of supporters of regency is printed in *Clar. Corr.*, II, 256 note.)

Column four: Vote on the Fenwick attainder, pro or con. (Slightly varying lists for this division may be found in *PH*, v, 1154-5; BL Add. MS. 47608, part v; and Northants RO, Buccleuch MSS., Vernon letters, I, 41, 23 December 1696.) In addition, a single asterisk is used to designate those peers who were part of a Court-Whig network of proxy-givers and proxy-holders during the 1695-98 parliament; a dagger for those who were part of a Tory network during this parliament. (For a discussion of these proxy groupings, see H. Horwitz, 'The Structure of Parliamentary Politics', in *BAGR*, p. 104.)

Column five: Vote on the impeachment of Lord Somers, pro conviction or con. (Since those voting on Orford's impeachment took, respectively, the same positions as they had done on Somers's, this vote is not indicated separately. The source, in both cases, is *HLM*, 1699-1702, p. 300.)

Column six: 'C' (with a date following) indicates that the individual peer was created a peer, called to the Lords in his father's barony, or appointed a bishop by William. 'P' (with a date following) indicates that the individual was promoted in the peerage or translated to a more attractive diocese by William.

Party	Name	Regency	Fenwick	Impeach	Create/Promote
	Dukes				
W	Bolton (Winchester)	con	pro*		P 1689
M	Devonshire (Devonshire)	con	con*	con	P 1694
W	Newcastle (Clare)	con	pro*	con	P 1694
W	Norfolk	con	pro*		
T	Northumberland	pro	con	pro	
T	Ormonde	pro	con		
W	St Albans		pro*	con	
W	Schomberg		pro*	con	Father C 1689
T	Somerset	pro	con*	pro	
M	Southampton	pro	pro		
	Earls				
T	Abingdon	pro	con†		
M	Bath		con	con	
T	Berkeley, first Earl	pro	con†		
W	Berkeley, second Earl (Berkeley)		pro†	con	C 1689
W	Bolingbroke	con	pro		
W	Bradford (Newport)	con	pro		P 1694
W	Bridgwater	con	pro*		
M	Bristol	con	con		
T	Burlington, first Earl	pro	con†		
M	Burlington, second Earl (Clifford)		con†	con	C 1694
M	Carlisle		con	con	
M	Caernarvon		con†	con	
T	Craven	pro	con*		
M	Derby	con	pro	pro	
M	Dorset	con	con	con	
W	Essex		pro	con	
T	Feversham	pro	con	pro	
M	Huntingdon	con	con†		
T	Kent	pro	con†		
W	Macclesfield		pro*	con	
W	Manchester	con	pro		
W	Montagu (Montagu)	con	pro	con	P 1689
T	Nottingham	pro	con†	pro	
M	Oxford	con	pro*	pro	
M	Peterborough (Mordaunt, Monmouth)	con	pro	pro	P 1689
W	Portland		pro*	con	C 1689
W	Radnor	con	pro*	con	
W	Rivers		pro	con	
T	Rochester	pro	con†	pro	
W	Rochford		pro*	con	C 1695
W	Romney (Sidney)		pro	con	C 1689; P 1694
W	Scarborough (Lumley)	con	pro*	con	P 1689, 1690
T	Scarsdale	pro	con†	pro	
W	Stamford	con	pro	con	
W	Suffolk		pro*	con	
M	Sussex	con	con*		
W	Tankerville (Grey of Warke)	con	pro		P 1695
T	Thanet	pro	con†	pro	
M	Warrington		pro	pro	Father P 1689

Party	Name	Regency	Fenwick	Impeach	Create/Promote
	Viscounts				
M	Longueville (Grey of Ruthin)	con	con		P 1690
	Weymouth	pro	con†	pro	
	Barons				
W	Abergavenny		pro	con	
T	Arundel of Terrice	pro	con		
W	Berkeley of Stratton	con	pro		
T	Brooke	pro	con		
M	Byron	con	con†		
T	Chandos	pro	con		
W	Cornwallis	con	pro		
M	De la War	pro	pro†	pro	
W	Eure	con	pro†	con	
T	Ferrers	pro	con		
M	Fitzwalter		con	con	
T	Godolphin	pro	con*	pro	
M	Granville		con	con	C 1689
T	Guildford		con†	pro	
W	Haversham		pro	con	C 1695
W	Herbert of Cherbury		pro	con	C 1694
M	Howard of Esrick		pro	pro	
T	Hunsdon		con	pro	
T	Jeffries		con†	pro	
T	Jermyn	pro	con	pro	
M	Kingston		con†	con	
T	Leigh	pro	con*		
W	Lovelace		pro	con	
W	Lucas	con	pro*	con	
W	Osborne		pro†	con	C 1690
W	Ossulston		pro	con	
W	Rockingham		pro*	con	
W	Vaughan	con	pro		
W	Ward	con	pro		
W	Wharton		pro	con	
	Bishops				
W	Burnet of Salisbury		pro	con	C 1689
M	Compton of London	con	con	pro	
W	Cumberland of Peterborough		pro	con	C 1691
M	Fowler of Gloucester		con	con	C 1691
W	Gardiner of Lincoln		pro	con	C 1695
W	Hall of Bristol		pro	con	C 1691
W	Hough of Lichfield (Oxford)		pro	con	C 1690; P 1699
T	Mews of Winchester	pro	con		
W	Patrick of Ely (Chichester)		pro	con	C 1689; P 1691
T	Sprat of Rochester	pro	con	pro	
W	Tenison of Canterbury (Lincoln)		pro	con	C 1691; P 1694
T	Trelawney of Bristol (Exeter)		con	pro	P 1689
W	Williams of Chichester		pro	con	C 1696
T	Watson of St David's	pro	con		

Appendix C

HOUSE OF COMMONS VOTES

1689-1702

The extant House of Commons lists for William III's reign may be divided for our purposes into three categories (see also I. Burton and P. Riley, 'Division Lists of the Reigns of William III and Anne: What are They? How were they Compiled?', in *The Parliamentary Lists of the early Eighteenth Century: Their Compilation and Use*, ed. A. N. Newman (Leicester, 1973), pp. 17–29).

'Division' lists

1. Those opposed to making the Prince and Princess of Orange king and queen, 5 February 1689. 150 names.
    a. Original in *A Letter to a Friend, upon the Dissolving of the Late Parliament* (1690, Wing L 1657); a manuscript list had, apparently, been circulated during the Convention parliament.
    b. Reprinted, with annotations, in Browning, *Danby*, III, 164–72. And see H. Horwitz, 'The General Election of 1690', *Journal of British Studies* XI (November 1971), 82–3, 87 and n. 3.

2. Those in favour of the disabling clauses to the corporation bill, January 1690. 146 names.
    a. Original in *Some Queries Concerning the Election of Members for the Ensuing Parliament* (1690, Wing H 833).
    b. Reprinted, with annotations, in Browning, *Danby*, III, 164–72. And see H. Horwitz, 'The General Election of 1690', pp. 82–3, 87 and n. 3.

3. Those for and against fixing the price of guineas at 22 shillings, February–March 1696. 205 for and 175 against.
    a. Original in [S. Grascome], *An Account of the Proceedings in the House of Commons, in Relation to the Recoining of the Clipp'd Money, and Falling the Price of Guineas* (1696, Wing W 201).
    b. Reprinted in I. Burton *et al.*, *Political Parties in the Reigns of William III and Anne: The Evidence of Division Lists* (Bulletin of the Institute of Historical Research, special supplement 7, 1968). (This printing contains one error; William Try is not listed at all in the original.)

4. Those who refused the voluntary association, February–March 1696. 103 names.
    a. Original in various forms, many indicated in the annotations to the printed list in Browning, *Danby*, III, 187–213. Browning was unable to find any information about the attitude of three members—William Cary, Sir Thomas Estcourt, and John Speccot—but they are listed as refusing the association in a manuscript list in the House of Lords RO, House of Commons' *Votes*, IV.

5. Those for and against the third reading of the bill of attainder against Sir John Fenwick, 25 November 1696. 187 for and 161 against.
    a. Original in BL Add. MS. 47608 (unfoliated).
    b. Printed in I. Burton, *Political Parties*.

6. Those against the third reading of the disbanding bill, 18 January 1699. At least three separate versions of this list survive.
    a. BL Add. MS. 28091, f. 167, printed in Browning, *Danby*, III, 213–17. 154 names.
    b. *A List of the Members of the last House of Commons, Convened first to Sit on the 27th of September 1698 who Voted for a Standing Army* ([1701], Newberry Lib., Case 6a 160 No. 70). 159 names. The additions are Sir Edward Ayscough, Charles Dymocke, Edward Hyde (Viscount Cornbury), James Montagu, Sir Isaac Rebow, and Sir William St Quintin. Henry Trelawney is omitted.

c. NLW Carreg–Lwyd MSS. II, 74. 137 names. This omits all names on the list reprinted by Browning between Richard Hoar and Charles Mason (20); in addition, it omits Sir George Burrard, Sir Francis Drake, William Greenfield, Henry Henley, Sir Francis Molyneux, Thomas Molyneux, and Sir John Williams. It adds William Campion, Robert Crawford, Sir Thomas Felton, Sir Henry Goodricke, Charles Godolphin, Edward Hyde (Viscount Cornbury), Sir Henry Pickering, Henry Pelham, Christopher Stockdale, and John Tregagle.

7. Those opposed to making preparations for war in the 1701 parliament. 167 names.
a. Original in [T. Savage], *A List of One Unanimous Club of Members of the Late Parliament dissolved Nov. 11 1701, that met at the Vine Tavern in Long Acre* (1701; BL 8133 aa12).
b. Reprinted in [J. Drake], *Some Necessary Considerations relating to all future Elections of Members to serve in Parliament* (1702) which is reprinted in *Somers' Tracts*, XII, 212–15.
c. For further discussion, see R. Walcott, 'Division Lists of the House of Commons, 1688–1715', *BIHR*, XIV (1936–7), 26–7.

8. Those in favour of the impeachment of the four lords, 26 February 1702. 223 names.
a. Original in [J. Drake], *Some Necessary Considerations.*
b. Reprinted in *Somers' Tracts*, XII, 215–18.
c. See Walcott, 'Division Lists', p. 27.

II   *Forecasts of votes and characterisations of the general orientation of M.P.s.*

1. Samuel Grascome's list (spring 1693); Bodl. Rawlinson MS. D846, f. 5. This lists 230 members, in constituency order; however, no members from any constituency after Thirsk, Yorkshire, are listed (i.e. all Cinque Ports and Welsh members unlisted). Of the 230, 201 are listed with a 'C' (117 'C', forty-three 'CO', twenty-one 'CP', twenty 'COP'), twenty-five are listed without a 'C' (sixteen 'O', six 'P', three 'OP'), and four as 'Quere'. Our interpretation is that those listed with a 'C' were, in the compiler's view, supporters of the Court and that those listed without a 'C' were office-holders or pensioners who were in opposition to the Court.

2. Forecast for a division on the proposed council of trade (January 1696). 240 pro, 236 con, and twenty-eight doubtful.
a. Original in BL Loan 29/35, bundle 1.
b. Printed in I. Burton, *Political Parties.*

3. Forecast of opinion in the new parliament as compared to the last parliament (? August 1698), perhaps with reference to disbandment. 1695–98 parliament: 210 pro, 281 con, seven doubtful or unmarked. 1698–1700 parliament: 227 pro, 241 con, six doubtful or unmarked.
a. Original in BL Loan 29/35, bundle 12.
b. Printed in H. Horwitz, 'Parties, Connections and Parliamentary Politics, 1689–1714: Review and Revision', *Journal of British Studies* VI (November 1966), 62–9. And see I. Burton, *Political Parties*, p. 33 n. 2.

4. Party gains and losses in the 1701 election; marked list of the new 1701–02 parliament by the third Earl of Sunderland. Fifty-two Whig gains; twenty-three Whig losses.
a. Original in Blenheim MS. B1-1.
b. Printed in H. Snyder, 'Party Configurations in the Early Eighteenth-Century House of Commons', *BIHR* XLV (1972), 54–8.

5. Forecast of opinion in the new parliament of 1701–02, perhaps with reference to the Speakership, corrected in R. Harley's hand. The original is in BL Harleian MS. 7556, ff. 96–100. Compiled on the eve of the opening of the parliament, it lists all members returned in the election (including sixteen returned for two constituencies) and it omits only Sir Bartholomew Shower who died shortly after being returned for Exeter. 253 members are listed as 'A' (probable supporters of Harley's candidacy), 229 are listed as 'B' (probable opponents) and fourteen as 'C' (uncertain).

III   *Other lists*

1. BL Egerton MS. 3345, bundle 1. Four marked lists of the 1690–5 parliament and two of the 1698–1700 parliament. The markings are not explained, are not consistent with one another, and it has not been possible to formulate even tentative interpretations of their significance.

2. Berkshire RO, Trumbull Add. MS. 13, No. 68, printed (with some errors) in D. Rubini, *Court and Country 1688–1702* (1967), app. A. 171 names (winter 1694–5). This list cuts across both Court–Country and Whig–Tory lines. Its purpose has not been determined.

3. BL Loan 29/35, bundle 12. This appears to be a list of 'interests', drawn up late in the 1698–1700 parliament (January 1700 or later). Among the categories are 'Lord Som[ers] etc.', 'O[ld] E[ast India] C[ompany]', 'Places', 'Q'.

4. BL Add. MS. 28091, ff. 179–80, printed (with some errors) in Rubini, *Court and Country*, app. A. 228 names (late February–early March 1701). This is primarily a list of Tories, along with some Whig placemen—i.e. the combination that put Harley in the Chair on 10 February by a vote of 249 to 125. But given its probable date of compilation and its total of 228, it is difficult to associate this list with that division or any other division in this parliament.

From the lists in Section I above, we have identified 453 'party' men, listed in alphabetical order below. The criterion for inclusion was listing on two or more of the eight lists of Section I. 453 M.P.s fit this criterion, and of these all but thirty-two sat in at least two of the parliaments of the reign. The 453, in turn, were divided into three groups: Tories, those appearing only on 'Tory' lists; Whigs, those appearing only on 'Whig' lists; and Mixed, those appearing on both 'Tory' and 'Whig' lists. The 'Tory' lists are numbers 1, 3 (against), 4, 5 (against), 7, and 8. The 'Whig' lists are numbers 2, 3 (for), 5 (for), and 6. By this procedure, the 453 'partisans' were categorised as follows: 216 Tories fifteen sitting in only one parliament), 171 Whigs (eleven in only one parliament), and sixty-six Mixed (six in only one parliament).

In the table below, the following information about these 453 members is given in abbreviated fashion.

Column one: party designation, with asterisk to indicate those sitting in only one parliament.

Column two: name and years served in the Commons during William's reign. Those who also sat before 1689 are marked 'b', those after 1702, 'a'. In cases of members who served for only a portion of a parliament, months of entry or departure are given in those instances where it may be relevant to help to explain their omission from the forecast lists. Those with italicised names also appear as placemen in Appendix D.

Column three—first line: lists from Section I on which the individual M.P.s' names appear. The following abbreviations are used:

1689 a1—against making William and Mary king and queen
1690 a2—for the disabling clauses to the corporation bill
1696 b1—against lowering the price of guineas
1696 b2—for lowering the price of guineas
1696 c1—refusing the voluntary association
1696 d1—against attainting Sir John Fenwick
1696 d2—for attainting Sir John Fenwick
1699 a2—against disbanding
1701 a1—against making preparations for war
1702 a1—for the impeachment against the four lords

Column three—second line: lists from Section II on which the individual M.P.s' names appear. The following abbreviations are used:

1693 a1—those listed as 'O, P, OP' by Grascome
1693 a2—those listed with a 'C' by Grascome
1693 a3—those listed as 'Quere' by Grascome
1696 a1—pro council of trade
1696 a2—con council of trade
1696 a3—doubtful council of trade
1698 a1—pro ? disbanding
1698 a2—con ? disbanding
1698 a3—doubtful ? disbanding
1701 b1—losses, Sunderland election list of 1701
1701 b2—gains, Sunderland election list of 1701
1701 c1—pro ? Harley's candidacy in December 1701
1701 c2—con ? Harley's candidacy in December 1701
1701 c3—doubtful ? Harley's candidacy in December 1701

Party	Name/tenure	Votes/forecasts
W	Sir Edward Abney 1690–98	1696 b2; 1696 d2 1693 a2; 1696 a2; 1698 a2
T	Sir Edward Acton 1689–1702 a	1689 a1; 1696 b1; 1696 d1; 1701 a1; 1702 a1 1696 a1; 1698 a1; 1701 c1
T	*James Anderton* 1701–02 a	1701 a1; 1702 a1 1701 c1
W	Thomas Andrew 1689–98, 2/1701–02	1696 b2; 1696 d2 1693 a2; 1696 a2; 1698 a2; 1701 b2; 1701 c2
W	*Sir Matthew Andrews* 1689–98 b	1690 a2; 1696 b2; 1696 d2 1696 a3; 1698 a2
T	Andrew Archer 1690–98 a	1696 b1; 1696 c1; 1696 d1 1696 a1; 1698 a1
*W	George Ashby 1695–98 a	1696 b2; 1696 d2 1696 a2; 1698 a2
W	*Sir William Ashurst* 1689, 1695–1702 a	1690 a2; 1696 d2; 1699 a2 1696 a2; 1698 a2; 1701 c2
T	Sir Jacob Astley 1690–1701 ab	1696 b1; 1696 d1; 1701 a1 1696 a1; 1698 a1; 1701 b1
W	*Sir John Austen* 1689–99 b	1696 b2; 1696 d2 1696 a2; 1698 a2
W	*Robert Austen junior* 1695–98, 1702	1696 b2; 1696 d2 1696 a2; 1698 a2; 1701 c2
W	*Sir Edward Ayscoghe* 1689–99 b	1696 b2; 1696 d2; 1699 a2 1693 a2; 1696 a2; 1698 a2
*M	Thomas Babington 1689 b	1689 a1; 1690 a2
T	*John Backwell* 1690–1701 b	1696 b1; 1696 d1; 1701 a1 1696 a1; 1698 a1
T	Sir Edward Bacon 1700–1702 a	1701 a1; 1702 a1 1701 c1
*T	John Bagnold 1695–5/98	1696 b1; 1696 d1 1696 a1
M	(Sir) James Bankes 1698–1702 a	1699 a2; 1702 a1 1698 a2; 1701 c1
T	Caleb Banks 1689, 1691–96 b	1689 a1; 1696 b1; 1696 c1 1696 a1
T	Sir John Banks 1689–98 b	1689 a1; 1696 b1; 1696 c1; 1696 d1 1696 a1; 1698 a1
*T	Legh Banks 1695–98	1696 b1; 1696 c1; 1696 d1 1696 a1; 1698 a1
T	Sir John Barker 1689–11/96 b	1689 a1; 1696 b1; 1696 c1 1696 a1
T	Sir Samuel Barnardiston 1690–1702 b	1696 b1; 1696 d1; 1701 a1; 1702 a1 1693 a3; 1696 a1; 1698 a1; 1701 c1
W	Sir Thomas Barnardiston 1689, 10/1690–10/1698 b	1696 b2; 1696 d2 1693 a2; 1696 a1; 1698 a1
T	Sir Charles Barrington 1694–1702 a	1696 d1; 1701 a1; 1702 a1 1696 a1; 1698 a1; 1701 c1
W	*Richard Beke* 1689–1700 b	1696 d2; 1699 a2 1693 a2; 1696 a2; 1698 a2
M	*Sir Henry Bellasyse* 1695–1702 a	1696 b2; 1696 d2; 1699 a2; 1702 a1 1696 a1; 1698 a2; 1701 b1; 1701 c1
T	Thomas Bennett 1/1695–98 b	1696 b1; 1696 c1; 1696 d1 1696 a3; 1698 a1
T	Edward Berkeley 1689–1700 b	1689 a1; 1696 b1; 1696 c1 1696 a1; 1698 a1

Party	Name/tenure	Votes/forecasts
W	*John Berkeley, Viscount Fitzharding*	1696 b2; 1699 a2
	1691–1702 a	1693 a2; 1696 a2; 1698 a2; 1701 c2
M	*Charles Bertie*	1689 a1; 1696 b2; 1696 d2; 1701 a1; 1702 a1
	1689–1702 ab	1693 a2; 1696 a1; 1698 a2; 1701 c1
T	Henry Bertie	1689 a1; 1702 a1
	1689–95, 1702 ab	1701 c1
T	James Bertie	1696 b1; 1696 c1; 1696 d1
	1695–1702 a	1696 a1; 1698 a1; 1701 c1
M	*Peregrine Bertie junior*	1696 b2; 1696 d1
	5/1690–98, 1702 a	1693 a2; 1696 a1; 1698 a2; 1701 b2; 1701 c2
M	*Philip Bertie*	1696 b2; 1696 d1
	1694–98	1696 a1; 1698 a2
T	Robert Bertie	1696 b1; 1696 c1; 1696 d1
	1695–1702 a	1696 a1; 1698 a1; 1701 c1
T	*Philip Bickerstaffe*	1689 a1; 1696 d1
	1689–98 b	1693 a2; 1696 a1; 1698 a2
W	Sir Michael Biddulph	1690 a2; 1696 b2; 1696 d2
	1689, 1695–1700, 1702 ab	1696 a2; 1698 a2; 1701 c2
M	Sir William Blackett	1696 b1; 1699 a2
	1689–1700 ab	1696 a1; 1698 a2
W	(Sir) Francis Blake	1690 a2; 1699 a2
	1689–95, 1698–1700, 1702 a	1693 a2; 1696 a2; 1698 a2; 1701 c2
W	Henry Blake	1696 b2; 1696 d2; 1699 a2
	1695–1700, 1702	1696 a2; 1698 a2; 1701 c2
T	Sir John Bland	1701 a1; 1702 a1
	1690–95, 1698–1702 ab	1698 a1; 1701 c1
W	*William Blathwayt*	1696 b2; 1696 d2; 1699 a2
	11/1693–1702 a	1696 a2; 1698 a2; 1701 c2
T	Thomas Bliss	1701 a1; 1702 a1
	1698–1702 a	1698 a1; 1701 c1
T	*Thomas Blofield*	1696 b1; 1696 d1; 1701 a1
	1689–1701 a	1696 a1; 1698 a1; 1701 c1
T	Sir Charles Blois	1701 a1; 1702 a1
	1689–95, 1/1700–1702 a	1701 c1
W	Sir Thomas Pope Blount	1690 a2; 1696 b2; 1696 d2
	1689–97 b	1693 a2; 1696 a2
*T	George Bohun	1696 b1; 1696 c1; 1696 d1
	1695–98	1696 a3; 1698 a1
T	Richard Bold	1701 a1; 1702 a1
	1701–02 a	1701 c1
T	Sir John Bolles	1696 b1; 1696 c1; 1696 d1; 1701 a1; 1702 a1
	1690–1702	1696 a1; 1698 a1; 1701 c1
W	*George Booth*	1696 b2; 1696 d2; 1699 a2
	1689, 1692–1700, 4/1701–02	1693 a2; 1696 a2; 1698 a2; 1701 b2; 1701 c2
W	*Hugh Boscawen*	1690 a2; 1696 b2; 1696 d2; 1699 a2
	1689–6/1701 b	1693 a1; 1696 a2; 1698 a2; 1701 b2
*M	Sir William Bowes	1696 b1; 1696 d2
	1695–98 a	1696 a3; 1698 a1
W	Anthony Bowyer	1696 b2; 1696 d2
	1690–98 b	1693 a2; 1696 a2; 1698 a2
M	*Henry Boyle*	1690 a2; 1696 b1; 1696 d1; 1699 a2
	1689, 1692–1702 a	1696 a1; 1698 a2; 1701 c2
T	Sir Roger Bradshaigh	1696 b1; 1696 c1; 1696 d1
	1695–1702 a	1696 a1; 1698 a1; 1701 c3
W	Edward Brent	1696 b2; 1696 d2
	1690–4/98	1696 a2

Party	Name/tenure	Votes/forecasts
T	Edward Brereton	1689 a1; 1696 b1; 1696 c1; 1696 d1; 1702 a1
	1689–1702 a	1696 a1; 1698 a1; 1701 c1
M	*John Brewer*	1696 b2; 1702 a1
	1689–1702 a	1696 a1; 1698 a2; 1701 c3
T	William Bromley (Warwick)	1696 b1; 1696 c1; 1696 d1; 1701 a1; 1702 a1
	1690–98, 3/1701–02 a	1696 a1; 1698 a1; 1701 b1; 1701 c1
W	William Bromley (Worcester)	1690 a2; 1696 b2; 1696 d2
	1689–1700, 1702 ab	1693 a2; 1696 a2; 1698 a2; 1701 c2
T	William Brotherton	1696 b1; 1696 c1; 1696 d1; 1701 a1
	1694, 1695–1701	1696 a1; 1698 a1
M	Sir John Brownlow	1689 a1; 1690 a2
	1689–97	1696 a1
W	William Brownlow	1696 b2; 1696 d2; 1699 a2
	1689–1700	1693 a2; 1696 a2; 1698 a2
W	*George Rodney Brydges*	1696 b2; 1696 d2
	1690–98, 1701–02 a	1693 a2; 1696 a2; 1698 a2; 1701 c2
T	James Brydges	1701 a1; 1702 a1
	1698–1702 a	1698 a2; 1701 c1
T	Richard Viscount Bulkeley	1696 c1; 1702 a1
	1690–1702 a	1696 a1; 1698 a1; 1701 c1
*T	Francis Buller	1696 b1; 1696 c1; 1696 d1
	1695–3/98	1696 a1
T	Robert Burdet	1689 a1; 1696 b1; 1696 c1; 1696 d1
	1689–98 b	1696 a1; 1698 a1
M	*John Burrington*	1696 b1; 1696 d2
	1694–98	1696 a1; 1698 a2
T	Robert Byerley	1689 a1; 1696 b1; 1696 c1; 1702 a1
	1689, 1695–1702 a	1696 a1; 1698 a1; 1701 c1
T	Charles Caesar	1701 a1; 1702 a1
	1701–02 a	1701 c1
W	*William Campion*	1696 b2; 1696 d2; 1699 a2
	1689–98, 12/1698–1700, 1702	1696 a2; 1698 a2; 1701 c2
M	*William Carr*	1696 b1; 1699 a2
	1690–1702 a	1693 a2; 1696 a2; 1698 a2; 1701 c2
T	Sir Charles Carteret	1696 b1; 1696 c1; 1696 d1
	1690–1700	1696 a1; 1698 a1
T	Thomas Cartwright	1696 b1; 1696 c1; 1702 a1
	1695–98, 1702 a	1696 a2; 1698 a1; 1701 b1; 1701 c1
T	William Cary	1689 a1; 1696 c1; 1696 d1; 1702 a1
	1689–1702 ab	1696 a1; 1698 a1; 1701 c1
T	Henry Lord Cavendish	1696 b1; 1696 d1
	1695–1700	1696 a2; 1698 a1
T	John Cecil (Lord Burleigh)	1696 c1; 1696 d1
	1695–1700	1696 a1; 1698 a1
W	*James Chadwick*	1690 a2; 1696 b2; 1696 d2
	1689–97	1696 a2
M	Arthur Champneys	1696 b2; 1702 a1
	1690–1702 a	1693 a2; 1696 a2; 1698 a1; 1701 c1
W	*James Chase*	1696 b2; 1696 d2; 1699 a2
	1690–1702 a	1693 a1; 1696 a2; 1698 a2; 1701 c2
M	John Chetwynd	1689 a1; 1699 a2
	1689–95, 1698–99, 1701	1698 a2; 1701 b1
T	Charles Cheyne, Viscount Newhaven	1696 c1; 1696 d1
	1690–98 b	1696 a1
T	*William Cheyne, Viscount Newhaven*	1689 a1; 1696 d1; 1701 a1; 1702 a1
	1689–95, 2/1696–1702 ab	1693 a2; 1698 a1; 1701 b1; 1701 c1

Party	Name/tenure	Votes/forecasts
T	Sir Francis Child	1701 a1; 1702 a1
	1698–1702 a	1698 a2; 1701 c1
T	*Charles Churchill*	1701 a1; 1702 a1
	1701–02 a	1701 c1
T	*George Churchill*	1696 b1; 1702 a1
	1689–1702 ab	1693 a1; 1696 a1; 1698 a2; 1701 c1
W	*Edward Clarke*	1696 b2; 1696 d2; 1699 a2
	1690–1702 a	1693 a2; 1696 a2; 1698 a2; 1701 c2
T	Sir Gilbert Clarke	1696 b1; 1696 c1; 1696 d1
	1689–98 b	1696 a1; 1698 a1
W	*Sir Robert Clayton*	1690 a2; 1696 b2
	1689–1702 a	1693 a2; 1696 a2; 1698 a1; 1701 c2
T	William Clayton	1701 a1; 1702 a1
	1698–1702 a	1698 a2; 1701 c1
W	*Charles Cocks*	1696 b2; 1696 d2
	1694–1702 a	1696 a2; 1698 a2; 1701 c2
W	Sir Henry Dutton Colt	1696 b2; 1696 d2
	1695–98, 1702 a	1696 a2; 1698 a2; 1701 b2; 1701 c2
W	*John Dutton Colt*	1690 a2; 1696 b2; 1696 d2
	1689–98, 1701 b	1693 a2; 1696a2; 1701 b2
W	*Thomas (Lord) Coningsby*	1696 b2; 1696 d2; 1699 a2
	1689–1702 ab	1696 a2; 1698 a2; 1701 c3
T	Sir John Conway	1696 b1; 1696 c1; 1702 a1
	1695–1701, 2/1702 a	1696 a1; 1698 a1
T	*John Conyers*	1696 b1; 1696 d1; 1701 a1; 1702 a1
	1695–1702 a	1696 a1; 1698 a1; 1701 c1
T	Sir Thomas Cook	1701 a1; 1702 a1
	1694–95, 1698–1702 a	1698 a1; 1701 c1
T	Sir Godfrey Copley	1696 d1; 1701 a1; 1702 a1
	1695–1702 a	1696 a1; 1698 a1; 1701 c1
T	Sir John Cordell	1689 a1; 1701 a1
	1689, 1701 b	1701 b1
M	Henry Cornwall	1689 a1; 1699 a2
	1689–95, 1698–1701 ab	1698 a1
T	Sir William Coryton	1696 b1; 1696 c1; 1696 d1
	1689, 1695–1701 ab	1696 a1; 1698 a1
M	*Sir Robert Cotton* (Cambs.)	1689 a1; 1696 b2; 1696 d2; 1699 a2
	1689–1700, 2/1702 b	1693 a1; 1696 a2; 1698 a2
M	*Sir Robert Cotton* Bart.	1690 a2; 1696 b1; 1696 d1
	1689–1702 b	1696 a1; 1698 a1; 1701 c2
T	Thomas Coulson	1701 a1; 1702 a1
	1692–95, 1698–1702 a	1698 a1; 1701 c1
T	Francis Courtenay	1696 b1; 1696 c1
	1689–99	1696 a1; 1698 a1
T	William Courtenay (of Powdersham)	1701 a1; 1702 a1
	1701–02 a	1701 c1
T	William Coward	1696 b1; 1696 d1; 1702 a1
	1695–1702 ab	1696 a1; 1698 a1; 1701 c1
W	Sir William Cowper	1690 a2; 1696 b2; 1696 d2
	1689–1700 b	1693 a1; 1696 a2; 1698 a2
W	*William Cowper*	1696 b2; 1696 d2
	1695–1700, 3/1701–02 a	1696 a2; 1698 a2; 1701 c2
M	Charles Coxe (Southwark)	1696 b1; 1696 d2; 1699 a2
	1695–1702 a	1696 a1; 1698 a2; 1701 c2
T	Charles Coxe (Cirencester)	1701 a1; 1702 a1
	1698–1702 a	1698 a1; 1701 c1

Party	Name/tenure	Votes/forecasts
W	Sir Herbert Croft 1690–98 b	1696 b2; 1696 d2 1693 a2; 1696 a2; 1698 a2
W	*Courtenay Croker* 1695–1702	1696 b2; 1696 d2 1696 a2; 1698 a2; 1701 c2
W	*John Lord Cutts* 12/1693–1702 a	1696 b2; 1696 d2; 1699 a2 1696 a2; 1698 a2; 1701 c2
*T	William Daniel 1695–5/98	1696 b1; 1696 c1; 1696 d1 1696 a1
T	Sir Robert Dashwood 1689–98, 1699–1700	1696 c1; 1696 d1 1696 a1; 1698 a1
T	Sir Thomas Davall 1695–1702 a	1696 b1; 1701 a1; 1702 a1 1696 a1; 1698 a1; 1701 c1
T	Sir Robert Davers 1689–1701 a	1689 a1; 1696 b1; 1696 d1; 1701 a1 1696 a1; 1698 a1; 1701 b1
T	Robert Davey 1698–1702 a	1701 a1; 1702 a1 1698 a1; 1701 c1
W	Sir Thomas Day 1695–1700	1696 b2; 1696 d2 1696 a2; 1698 a2
T	Alexander Denton 1690–12/98	1696 b1; 1696 c1; 1696 d1 1696 a1; 1698 a1
T	William Lord Digby 1689–98	1689 a1; 1696 b1; 1696 c1; 1696 d1 1696 a1; 1698 a1
W	*Sir Basil Dixwell* 1689, 1695–1700	1696 b2; 1696 d2; 1699 a2 1696 a2; 1698 a2
T	*Gilbert Dolben* 1689–98, 1701–02 ab	1689 a1; 1696 b1; 1696 c1; 1696 d1; 1701 a1; 1702 a1 1693 a2; 1696 a1; 1698 a1; 1701 c1
T	*Thomas Done* 1689–98 b	1689 a1; 1696 b1; 1696 c1; 1696 d1 1696 a1; 1698 a1
W	*Thomas Dore* 1690–1702 a	1696 b2; 1696 d2; 1699 a2 1693 a2; 1696 a2; 1698 a2; 1701 c2
W	Richard Dowdeswell 1689–1702 a	1690 a2; 1696 b2; 1696 d2 1693 a2; 1696 a2; 1698 a2; 1701 c2
W	Sir Francis Drake 1689–95, 11/1696–1700 b	1690 a2; 1699 a2 1693 a2; 1698 a2
*T	Montagu Drake 1695–6/98	1696 b1; 1696 c1; 1696 d1 1696 a1
T	Sir William Drake Bart. 1690–1702 a	1696 b1; 1702 a1 1696 a1; 1698 a1; 1701 c1
W	Richard Duke 1695–1701 b	1696 d2; 1699 a2 1696 a2; 1698 a2; 1701 b2
W	*Edmund Dummer* 1695–98, 1701 a	1696 b2; 1696 d2 1696 a2; 1698 a2
T	*Anthony Duncombe* 1698–1702 a	1701 a1; 1702 a1 1698 a2; 1701 c1
M	*William Duncombe* 1689, 1695–98 b	1690 a2; 1696 b1 1696 a1; 1698 a1
W	Sir Ralph Dutton 1689–98 b	1690 a2; 1696 b2; 1696 d2 1693 a2; 1696 a2; 1698 a2
T	Sir Thomas Dyke 1689–98 b	1696 b1; 1696 c1; 1696 d1 1696 a1; 1698 a1
M	Charles Dymocke 1698–1702 a	1699 a2; 1702 a1 1698 a2; 1701 c1
W	Charles Egerton 1695–1702 a	1696 b2; 1696 d2; 1699 a2 1696 a2; 1698 a2; 1701 c2
T	Thomas Ekins 1698–1702	1701 a1; 1702 a1 1698 a1; 1701 c1

Party	Name/tenure	Votes/forecasts
T	Daniel Elliot	1696 b1; 1696 c1; 1696 d1
	1689–1700, 4/1701 b	1696 a1; 1698 a1
M	Sir William Ellis	1690 a2; 1696 b1; 1696 d2
	1689–1702 ab	1696 a1; 1698 a3; 1701 c1
T	William Elson	1696 b1; 1696 d1; 1701 a1; 1702 a1
	1695–98, 1701–02 a	1696 a1; 1698 a1; 1701 c1
W	(Sir) John Elwill	1690 a2; 1696 b2; 1696 d2
	1689, 1695–98 b	1696 a2; 1698 a2
M	George England	1690 a2; 1696 b1; 1696 d2
	1689–1701 b	1693 a2; 1696 a1; 1698 a1
W	*Thomas Erle*	1696 b2; 1696 d2; 1699 a2
	1689–1702 ab	1693 a2; 1696 a1; 1698 a2; 1701 c2
T	Sir Edward Ernle	1696 b1; 1696 d1
	1695–1700, 5/1701–02 a	1696 a1; 1698 a2; 1701 c2
T	Sir James Etheredge	1696 b1; 1696 c1; 1696 d1; 1701 a1; 1702 a1
	1695–1702 a	1696 a1; 1698 a1; 1701 c1
T	*William Ettrick*	1689 a1; 1696 b1; 1696 d1; 1701 a1; 1702 a1
	1689–1702 ab	1696 a1; 1698 a2; 1701 c1
W	(Sir) Stephen Evance	1696 b2; 1696 d2
	1690–98	1693 a2; 1696 a2; 1698 a2
W	Sir John Fagg	1690 a2; 1696 d2; 1699 a2
	1689–1/1701 b	1696 a2; 1698 a1
W	*Sir Henry Fane*	1690 a2; 1696 b2
	1690–98	1693 a2; 1696 a2; 1698 a2
M	*William Farrer*	1696 b1; 1696 d2
	1695–98, 1702 a	1696 a3; 1698 a2; 1701 b2; 1701 c2
W	(Sir) Thomas Felton	1696 b2; 1699 a2
	1690–2/1700, 1702 a	1693 a2; 1696 a2; 1698 a2; 1701 b2; 1701 c2
T	Heneage Finch	1696 b1; 1696 c1; 1696 d1; 1701 a1; 1702 a1
	1689–98, 1701–02 ab	1696 a1; 1698 a1; 1701 c1
T	William Fitch	1701 a1; 1702 a1
	1701–02 a	1701 c1
T	Sir John Fleet	1696 b1; 1701 a1
	3/1693–1700, 3/1701 a	1696 a3; 1698 a1
T	Henry Flemming	1696 b1; 1696 c1; 1696 d1; 1702 a1
	1689, 1695–98, 1/1700–02 a	1696 a1; 1698 a1; 1701 c1
W	Sir George Fletcher	1696 b2; 1696 d2; 1699 a2
	1689–1700 b	1696 a2; 1698 a2
M	*George Fletcher*	1699 a2; 1701 a1
	1698–1702 a	1698 a2; 1701 b2; 1701 c2
M	Philip Foley	1690 a2; 1696 b1; 1696 d1; 1701 a1
	1689–1700, 2/1701 b	1696 a1; 1698 a1
W	Thomas Foley senior	1690 a2; 1696 d2
	1690–98, 1/1699–2/1701 b	1696 a1; 1698 a2
T	Thomas Foley	1696 b1; 1696 d1; 1701 a1; 1702 a1
	1691–1702 a	1696 a1; 1698 a1; 1701 c1
T	Thomas Foley junior	1696 b1; 1696 d1; 1701 a1; 1702 a1
	1694–1702 a	1696 a1; 1698 a1; 1701 c1
W	(Sir) William Forrester	1696 b2; 1696 d2; 1699 a2
	1689–1702 ab	1693 a2; 1696 a2; 1698 a2; 1701 c2
T	Sir Humphrey Forster	1696 b1; 1696 d1
	1690–1701 b	1696 a1; 1698 a1
T	William Forster	1689 a1; 1696 b1; 1696 c1; 1696 d1
	1689–1700	1693 a2; 1696 a1; 1698 a1
W	Hugh Fortescue	1690 a2; 1696 b2; 1696 d2; 1699 a2
	1689–1702 a	1693 a2; 1696 a2; 1698 a2; 1701 c2

Party	Name/tenure	Votes/forecasts
T	Richard Fownes 1689–98, 4/1699–1702 ab	1689 a1; 1696 b1; 1696 c1; 1696 d1; 1701 a1 1696 a1; 1698 a1; 1701 c1
M	*Charles Fox* 1689–1700, 7/1701–02 ab	1689 a1; 1696 b2; 1696 d1; 1699 a2; 1702 a1 1693 a2; 1696 a1; 1698 a3; 1701 c1
W	*(Sir) Thomas Frankland* 1689–95, 12/1695–1702 ab	1696 b2; 1696 d2; 1699 a2 1693 a2; 1696 a2; 1698 a2; 1701 c2
T	Ralph Freeman junior 1697–1702 a	1701 a1; 1702 a1 1698 a1; 1701 c1
T	Thomas Freke (Dorset) 1689–1701 b	1696 b1; 1696 c1; 1696 d1; 1701 a1 1696 a1; 1698 a1; 1701 b1
W	Thomas Freke 1689, 1691–1700 ab	1690 a2; 1696 b2 1693 a2; 1696 a2; 1698 a2
T	Thomas Frewen 1689, 1694–98 b	1696 b1; 1696 d1 1696 a1; 1698 a1
M	Samuel Fuller 1689–98, 1701	1696 b1; 1696 d2 1693 a2; 1696 a1; 1698 a1; 1701 b2
T	John Gape 3/1701–02 a	1701 a1; 1702 a1 1701 b1; 1701 c1
T	Sir Charles Gerrard 1689–98 b	1689 a1; 1696 b1 1696 a1; 1698 a1
W	Fitton Gerrard 1689, 1694–95, 1697–1700	1690 a2; 1699 a2 1698 a2
*T	Thomas Gery 1695–98 a	1696 b1; 1696 d1 1696 a1; 1698 a1
W	*Charles Godfrey* 1689, 1691–1702 a	1690 a2; 1696 b2; 1696 d2; 1699 a2 1693 a2; 1696 a2; 1698 a2; 1701 c2
M	*Charles Godolphin* 1689–1701 b	1689 a1; 1696 b2; 1699 a2; 1701 a1 1693 a2; 1696 a2; 1698 a2
T	*Francis Godolphin* 1695–98, 1701–02 a	1696 d1; 1701 a1; 1702 a1 1696 a3; 1698 a2; 1701 c1
W	*Sir Henry Goodricke* 1689–1702 ab	1696 b2; 1699 a2 1693 a1; 1696 a2; 1698 a2; 1701 c2
T	Sir Henry Gough 1689–98, 3/1699–1701 ab	1689 a1; 1696 b1; 1696 c1; 1696 d1; 1701 a1 1696 a1; 1698 a1; 1701 b1
T	Richard Goulston 2/1701–02 a	1701 a1; 1702 a1 1701 c1
T	Henry Grahme 1701–02 a	1701 a1; 1702 a1 1701 c1
	Bernard Granville 1689–98 b	1696 b1; 1696 c1; 1696 d1 1693 a1; 1696 a1; 1698 a2
W	*Sir Bevil Granville* 1690–1700 b	1696 b2; 1699 a2 1693 a1; 1696 a1; 1698 a2
T	*John Granville* 1689–1702 ab	1696 b1; 1696 c1; 1696 d1; 1701 a1; 1702 a1 1693 a3; 1696 a1; 1698 a1; 1701 b1; 1701 c1
T	Francis Greville 1695–98, 1701–02 a	1696 b1; 1696 c1; 1696 d1; 1701 a1; 1702 a1 1696 a1; 1698 a1; 1701 c1
T	John Grey 1689–98 b	1689 a1; 1696 b1; 1696 c1; 1696 d1 1696 a1; 1698 a1
W	*Ralph Grey* 1695–98, 1701 b	1696 b2; 1696 d2 1696 a2; 1698 a2
T	Sir Thomas Grosvenor 1690–1700 b	1696 b1; 1696 c1; 1696 d1 1696 a1; 1698 a1
W	Thomas Guy 1695–1702 a	1696 b2; 1696 d2; 1699 a2 1696 a2; 1698 a2; 1701 c2
T	*Francis Gwyn* 1689–98, 1/1699–1702 ab	1689 a1; 1696 b1; 1696 c1; 1696 d1; 1701 a1; 1702 a1 1693 a1; 1696 a1; 1698 a1; 1701 b1; 1701 c1

Party	Name/tenure	Votes/forecasts
W	*Sir Rowland Gwynne*	1690 a2; 1696 b2; 1696 d2; 1699 a2
	1689–1702 b	1698 a2; 1701 c2
T	Sir Christopher Hales	1701 a1; 1702 a1
	1698–1701, 2/1702 a	1698 a1; 1701 c1
T	Richard Halford	1701 a1; 1702 a1
	1698–1702 a	1698 a1; 1701 c1
T	Thomas Halsey	1696 b1; 1696 d1; 1701 a1; 1702 a1
	1695–1702 ab	1696 a1; 1698 a1; 1701 c1
T	Anthony Hammond	1696 b1; 1696 c1; 1696 d1; 1701 a1
	1695–1701 a	1696 a1; 1698 a1; 1701 b1
T	Simon Harcourt	1696 b1; 1696 c1; 1696 d1; 1701 a1; 1702 a1
	1690–1702 a	1696 a1; 1698 a1; 1701 c1
M	Sir Edward Harley	1690 a2; 1696 d1
	1689, 1/1693–98 b	1696 a1; 1698 a1
T	Edward Harley	1696 d1; 1701 a1; 1702 a1
	1698–1700, 4/1701–02 a	1696 a2; 1698 a1; 1701 b1; 1701 c1
M	Robert Harley	1690 a2; 1696 b1; 1696 d1; 1701 a1; 1702 a1
	1689, 11/1690–1702 a	1696 a1; 1698 a1; 1701 c1
T	Thomas Harley	1701 a1; 1702 a1
	1698–1702 a	1698 a1; 1701 c1
T	Sir Eliab Harvey	1696 b1; 1696 c1; 1696 d1
	1693–99 b	1696 a1; 1698 a1
T	Michael Harvey	1696 b1; 1696 d1; 1701 a1
	1689–1701 b	1696 a3; 1698 a1; 1701 b1
T	William Harvey	1696 b1; 1696 c1
	1689–1702 a	1696 a1; 1698 a1; 1701 c1
W	*(Sir) John Hawles*	1690 a2; 1696 b2; 1696 d2; 1699 a2
	1689, 1695–1700, 3/1701–02 a	1696 a2; 1698 a2; 1701 c3
W	Nicholas Hedger	1696 b2; 1696 d2
	1690–98	1696 a3; 1698 a2
M	*Sir Charles Hedges*	1699 a2; 1702 a1
	1698–2/1700, 1701–02 a	1698 a2; 1701 c1
W	Henry Henley	1696 b2; 1696 d2; 1699 a2
	1695–1700 a	1696 a2; 1698 a2
W	*Robert Henley*	1696 d2; 1699 a2
	1695–1701	1696 a2; 1698 a2
M	*James Herbert*	1696 b2; 1701 a1; 1702 a1
	1689, 1695–1702 ab	1696 a1; 1698 a1; 1701 c1
T	Fredrick Herne	1701 a1; 1702 a1
	1698–1702 a	1698 a1; 1701 c1
T	Nathaniel Herne	1701 a1; 1702 a1
	1700–02 a	1701 c1
W	John Hervey	1696 b2; 1696 d2; 1699 a2
	1694–1702 a	1696 a2; 1701 c2
W	*Henry Heveningham*	1696 b2; 1699 a2
	1695–1700 b	1696 a2; 1698 a2
T	Robert Heysham	1701 a1; 1702 a1
	1698–1702 a	1698 a3; 1701 c1
W	Roger Hoar	1696 b2; 1696 d2; 1699 a2
	1695–99	1696 a2; 1698 a2
W	*Sir Henry Hobart*	1690 a2; 1696 b2; 1696 d2
	1689, 1694–98 b	1696 a2; 1698 a2
T	John Hoblyn	1696 b1; 1696 d1; 1701 a1; 1702 a1
	1695–1702 a	1696 a1; 1698 a1; 1701 c1
W	Thomas Hoby	1696 b2; 1696 d2
	1689–98 b	1693 a2; 1696 a2; 1698 a2

Party	Name/tenure	Votes/forecasts
T	*Henry Holmes* 4/1695–1702 a	1696 b1; 1696 c1; 1696 d1 1696 a2; 1698 a1; 1701 c1
W	*Sir William Honeywood* 1689–98 b	1690 a2; 1696 d2 1693 a2; 1696 a2; 1698 a2
T	Nicholas Hooper 1695–1702 a	1696 b1; 1696 d1; 1701 a1; 1702 a1 1696 a1; 1698 a1; 1701 c1
W	Sir Charles Hotham 4/1695–1702 a	1696 b2; 1696 d2 1696 a2; 1698 a2; 1701 c2
W	*Sir Robert Howard* 1689–98 b	1690 a2; 1696 b2 1693 a2; 1696 a2; 1698 a2
W	*Thomas Howard* 1689–4/1701 b	1690 a2; 1696 b2; 1699 a2 1693 a2; 1696 a2; 1698 a2; 1701 b2
M	William Howard 1695–1701	1696 b2; 1696 d1 1696 a2; 1698 a2
M	Sir James Howe 1698–1701 a	1699 a2; 1701 a1 1698 a1
M	*John Howe* 1689, 11/1690–1701 a	1690 a2; 1696 b1; 1696 c1; 1696 d1; 1701 a1 1696 a1; 1698 a1; 1701 b1
T	Richard Howe 1690–98, 1701 ab	1696 b1; 1696 c1; 1696 d1 1696 a1; 1698 a1; 1701 b1
W	*Sir Scrope Howe* 1689–98 ab	1690 a2; 1696 b2; 1696 d2 1693 a2; 1696 a2; 1698 a2
T	Sir George Hungerford 1695–1701 b	1696 d1; 1701 a1 1696 a2; 1698 a1; 1701 b1
T	John Hunt 1689–1701, 2/1702 ab	1689 a1; 1696 b1; 1696 d1; 1702 a1 1696 a1; 1698 a1
M	*Edward Hyde (Viscount Cornbury)* 1689–1701 b	1689 a1; 1696 b2; 1696 d2; 1699 a2 1693 a2; 1696 a2; 1698 a2; 1701 b2
T	Henry Lord Hyde 1692–1702 a	1696 b1; 1696 c1; 1696 d1; 1701 a1; 1702 a1 1696 a1; 1698 a1; 1701 c1
T	Robert Hyde 1689–98 ab	1689 a1; 1696 b1 1696 a1; 1698 a1
T	Sir Justinian Isham 1689, 1694–1702 ab	1689 a1; 1701 a1; 1702 a1 1696 a1; 1698 a1; 1701 c1
T	(Sir) Geoffrey Jeffreys 1690–98, 1701–02 a	1696 b1; 1696 c1; 1696 d1; 1701 a1; 1702 a1 1696 a1; 1698 a1; 1701 c1
T	John Jeffreys 11/1692–98, 1701–02	1696 b1; 1696 d1; 1701 a1; 1702 a1 1696 a1; 1698 a1; 1701 c1
W	*Jonathan Jennings* 1691–1701	1696 b2; 1696 d2; 1699 a2 1693 a2; 1696 a1; 1698 a2
T	Sir Robert Jenkinson 1689–1702 a	1689 a1; 1696 b1; 1696 c1; 1696 d1; 1701 a1; 1702 a1 1696 a1; 1698 a1; 1701 c1
T	William Jennens 1689–98, 1701–02 a	1696 b1; 1696 c1; 1701 a1; 1702 a1 1696 a1; 1698 a1; 1701 c1
T	Sir Henry Johnson 1689–1702 a	1689 a1; 1696 b1; 1701 a1; 1702 a1 1696 a1; 1698 a1; 1701 c1
T	William Johnson 1689–1702 a	1689 a1; 1696 b1; 1696 d1; 1702 a1 1696 a1; 1698 a1; 1701 c1
T	Edward Jones 1689, 1695–97 b	1689 a1; 1696 b1; 1696 c1; 1696 d1 1696 a1
M	*Richard Jones, Earl of Ranelagh* 1689–1702 ab	1689 a1; 1696 b2; 1699 a2 1693 a2; 1696 a2; 1698 a2; 1701 b2; 1701 c2
W	*James Kendall* 1689, 1695–1702 a	1696 b2; 1696 d2; 1699 a2 1696 a1; 1698 a2; 1701 c2
M	*Thomas King* 10/1696–1702 a	1696 d2; 1699 a2; 1702 a1 1698 a2; 1701 c2

Party	Name/tenure	Votes/forecasts
W	*Roger Kirkby*	1696 b2; 1696 d2; 1699 a2
	1689–1702 b	1693 a2; 1696 a2; 1698 a2; 1701 c2
*W	*John Knight*	1696 b2; 1696 d2
	1695–3/98	1696 a2
T	Edward Kynaston	1689 a1; 1696 b1; 1696 c1; 1696 d1
	1689–99 b	1696 a1; 1698 a1
T	John Kynaston	1696 b1; 1696 c1; 1696 d1
	1689–1702 a	1696 a1; 1698 a1; 1701 c1
T	Warwick Lake	1701 a1; 1702 a1
	1698–1702 a	1698 a1; 1701 c1
T	William Lambton	1689 a1; 1696 b1; 1696 d1; 1701 a1; 1702 a1
	1689–98, 1701–02 ab	1696 a1; 1698 a1; 1701 c1
W	John Lawton	1696 b2; 1696 d2
	1690–98 a	1696 a2; 1698 a2
M	Henry Lee	1690 a2; 1701 a1; 1702 a1
	1689–95, 1697–1702 ab	1698 a1; 1701 c1
W	(Sir) Thomas Lee	1696 b2; 1696 d2; 1699 a2
	1689–2/99, 1701–02	1693 a2; 1696 a2; 1698 a2; 1701 c2
T	Thomas Legh (of Ridge)	1701 a1; 1702 a1
	1698–1702 a	1698 a1; 1701 c1
T	Sir John Leveson-Gower	1696 b1; 1696 c1; 1696 d1; 1701 a1; 1702 a1
	1692–1702 ab	1696 a1; 1698 a1; 1701 c1
T	Richard Lewis	1689 a1; 1696 b1; 1696 c1
	1689–1701 b	1696 a1; 1698 a3
M	John Lewknor	1690 a2; 1696 b1; 1696 c1; 1702 a1
	1689–1702 ab	1696 a2; 1698 a1; 1701 c1
W	*Sir Thomas Littleton*	1690 a2; 1696 b2; 1696 d2
	1689–1702 a	1693 a2; 1696 a2; 1698 a2; 1701 c2
W	*William Lowndes*	1696 b2; 1699 a2
	1695–1702 a	1696 a2; 1698 a2; 1701 c3
W	*James Lowther*	1696 b2; 1699 a2
	1694–1702 a	1696 a2; 1698 a2; 1701 c2
W	*Sir John Lowther* (Whitehaven)	1690 a2; 1696 d2
	1689–1700 b	1693 a2; 1696 a2; 1698 a2
*W	Sir William Lowther	1696 b2; 1696 d2
	1695–98	1696 a2; 1698 a2
M	*Alexander Luttrell*	1699 a2; 1702 a1
	10/1690–1702 a	1693 a1; 1696 a1; 1698 a2; 1701 c1
W	(Sir) Henry Lyddell	1696 b2; 1696 d2
	1689, 1695–98, 1701–02 a	1696 a3; 1698 a2; 1701 c2
W	John Machell	1696 b2; 1696 d2; 1699 a2
	1689–1700 b	1693 a2; 1696 a2; 1698 a2
T	Sir Thomas Mackworth	1701 a1; 1702 a1
	1694–95, 1701–02 a	1701 c1
W	(Sir) John Mainwaring	1690 a2; 1696 b2; 1696 d2; 1699 a2
	1689–1702	1693 a2; 1696 a2; 1698 a2
T	John Manley	1696 b1; 1696 c1; 1696 d1; 1702 a1
	1695–98, 1702 a	1696 a1; 1698 a1; 1701 c1
T	Thomas Mansell (Margam)	1689 a1; 1696 b1; 1696 c1; 1696 d1; 1702 a1
	1689–98, 1699–1702 a	1696 a1; 1698 a1; 1701 c1
W	Sir Francis Masham	1696 b2; 1696 d2
	1690–98, 1701–02 a	1693 a2; 1696 a2; 1698 a2; 1701 c2
W	*Charles Mason*	1696 b2; 1696 d2; 1699 a2
	1695–5/1701, 1702 a	1696 a2; 1698 a2; 1701 c2
*M	Thomas Master	1689 a1; 1690 a2
	1689 b	

Party	Name/tenure	Votes/forecasts
W	Jasper Maudit 1694–98	1696 b2; 1696 d2 1696 a2; 1698 a2
T	Sir Richard Middleton 1689–1702 ab	1689 a1; 1696 b1; 1696 d1; 1702 a1 1696 a1; 1698 a1; 1701 c1
W	Sir Thomas Middleton 1689–98, 1699–1700 b	1690 a2; 1696 b2; 1696 d2 1693 a2; 1696 a2; 1698 a2
T	John Miller 1698–1702 a	1701 a1; 1702 a1 1698 a2; 1701 b1; 1701 c1
*W	*Robert Molesworth* 1695–98 a	1696 b2; 1696 d2 1696 a2; 1698 a2
W	Sir Francis Molyneux 1693–1/1700, 1702 a	1696 b2; 1696 d2; 1699 a2 1693 a2; 1696 a2; 1701 b2; 1701 c2
W	*Thomas Molyneux* 1695–1700, 1702	1696 b2; 1696 d2; 1699 a2 1696 a2; 1698 a2; 1701 c2
W	*Sir Thomas Mompesson* 1689–98, 1701 b	1690 a2; 1696 b2; 1696 d2 1693 a2; 1696 a2; 1698 a2
M	Robert Monckton 1695–98, 1701–02 a	1696 b2; 1696 d1 1696 a2; 1698 a1; 1701 c2
*M	William Monson 1695–98 a	1696 b2; 1696 d1 1696 a2; 1698 a2
W	*Charles Montagu* 1689–1700	1696 b2; 1696 d2; 1699 a2 1693 a2; 1696 a2; 1698 a2
W	*Christopher Montagu* 1695–1702 b	1696 d2; 1699 a2 1696 a2; 1698 a2; 1701 c2
*W	Heneage Montagu 1695–6/98	1696 b2; 1696 d2 1696 a2
W	Irby Montagu 1695–1701	1696 b2; 1696 d2; 1699 a2 1696 a2; 1698 a2; 1701 b2
W	James Montagu 1695–98, 12/1698–1700 a	1696 b2; 1696 d2; 1699 a2 1696 a2
T	Sir John Mordaunt 1698–1702 a	1701 a1; 1702 a1 1698 a1; 1701 c1
W	*Anthony Morgan* 1695–1702 a	1696 b2; 1696 d2; 1699 a2 1696 a2; 1698 a2; 1701 c2
*M	Francis Morley 1689	1689 a1; 1690 a2
T	Sir William Morley 1689–1700 b	1689 a1; 1696 b1; 1696 c1 1696 a2; 1698 a1
T	John Mountsteven 1695–1701 a	1696 c1; 1696 d1; 1701 a1 1696 a1; 1698 a1; 1701 b1
*W	Walter Moyle 1695–98	1696 b2; 1696 d2 1696 a2; 1698 a1
T	Sir Christopher Musgrave 1689–1702 ab	1689 a1; 1696 b1; 1696 c1; 1696 d1; 1701 a1; 1702 a1 1696 a1; 1698 a1; 1701 b1; 1701 c1
T	Nathaniel Napier 1695–1702 a	1701 a1; 1702 a1 1696 a1; 1698 a1; 1701 c1
W	*Thomas Neale* 12/1689–99 b	1696 b2; 1696 d2; 1699 a2 1693 a2; 1696 a2; 1698 a2
W	Richard Nevil 1695–1702 a	1696 b2; 1696 d2; 1699 a2 1696 a2; 1698 a2; 1701 c2
M	Sir Benjamin Newland 1689–12/99 b	1689 a1; 1696 b1; 1699 a2 1696 a1; 1698 a1
T	Andrew Newport 1689–98 b	1689 a1; 1696 b1; 1696 c1; 1696 d1 1696 a1; 1698 a1
M	*Edward Nicholas* 1689–1702 a	1689 a1; 1696 b2; 1699 a2; 1701 a1; 1702 a1 1693 a2; 1696 a1; 1698 a2; 1701 c1

Party	Name/tenure	Votes/forecasts
T	Sir Edward Norreys 1689–1702 ab	1696 b1; 1696 c1; 1696 d1; 1701 a1; 1702 a1 1696 a3; 1698 a1; 1701 c1
T	Francis Norreys 1701–02 a	1701 a1; 1702 a1 1701 c1
W	(Sir) William Norris 1695–1701	1696 b2; 1696 d2 1696 a2; 1698 a2
T	Charles North 1701–02 a	1701 a1; 1702 a1 1701 c1
T	Thomas Northmore 1695–1702 a	1701 a1; 1702 a1 1696 a1; 1698 a1; 1701 c1
W	Richard Norton 1/1693–1700 a	1696 d2; 1699 a2 1693 a2; 1696 a2; 1698 a2
W	Samuel Ogle 1690–1702 a	1696 b2; 1696 d2; 1699 a2 1693 a2; 1696 a2; 1698 a2; 1701 c2
W	Denzil Onslow 1689–1702 ab	1690 a2; 1696 b2; 1696 d2 1696 a2; 1698 a2; 1701 c2
W	Foot Onslow 1689–1700	1690 a2; 1696 b2; 1696 d2 1693 a2; 1696a2; 1698 a2
M	Sir Richard Onslow 1689–1702 ab	1690 a2; 1696 b2; 1696 d1 1693 a2; 1696 a2; 1698 a3; 1701 c2
W	Charles Osborne 1690–1700 b	1696 b2; 1699 a2 1693 a2; 1696 a1; 1698 a2
*W	George Oxenden 1695–98	1696 b2; 1696 d2 1696 a1; 1698 a2
T	Sir John Packington 1690–95, 1698–1702 a	1701 a1; 1702 a1 1698 a1; 1701 c1
T	Henry Paget 1690–98; 1701–02	1696 b1; 1696 d1 1696 a1; 1698 a1; 1701 c1
*W	Archdale Palmer 1695–98	1696 b2; 1696 d2 1696 a2; 1698 a2
T	Nathaniel Palmer 1689–98, 5/1699–1700, 1702 ab	1689 a1; 1696 b1; 1702 a1 1696 a1; 1698 a1; 1701 c1
W	William Palmes 1689–1702 ab	1690 a2; 1696 b2; 1696 d2; 1699 a2 1693 a2; 1696 a2; 1698 a2; 1701 c2
W	Thomas Papillon 1689–1700	1690 a2; 1696 b2; 1696 d2 1696 a2; 1698 a2
T	(Sir) Henry Parker 1689, 1695–1700 ab	1689 a1; 1696 b1; 1696 c1; 1696 d1 1696 a1; 1698 a1
T	Sir John Parsons 1689–98, 1701–02 ab	1696 b1; 1696 d1; 1701 a1 1696 a1; 1698 a2; 1701 c1
T	John Parsons 1690–98	1696 b1; 1696 c1 1696 a1; 1698 a1
M	Edward Pauncefort 1698–1702 a	1699 a2; 1702 a1 1698 a2; 1701 c1
*T	Robert Payne 1695–98	1696 b1; 1696 c1 1696 a2; 1698 a2
W	Henry Pelham 1690–1700, 1702	1696 b2; 1696 d2; 1699 a2 1696 a2; 1698 a2; 1701 b2; 1701 c2
W	Sir John Pelham 1689–98 a	1690 a2; 1696 d2 1693 a2; 1696 a2; 1698 a2
M	Thomas Pelham 1689–1702 ab	1696 b2; 1696 d1 1693 a2; 1696 a2; 1698 a2; 1701 c2
T	Alexander Pendarves 1689–98, 1/1699–1702 a	1689 a1; 1696 b1; 1701 a1; 1702 a1 1696 a1; 1701 c1
T	John Pery 1690–1700 a	1696 b1; 1696 d1 1696 a1; 1698 a1

Party	Name/tenure	Votes/forecasts
M	(Sir) John Phillips	1696 d1; 1699 a2
	1695–1702 a	1696 a1; 1698 a1; 1701 c2
T	Henry Pinnell	1696 b1; 1696 c1; 1696 d1; 1701 a1
	1695–1701 a	1696 a1; 1698 a1
M	Thomas Pitt	1690 a2; 1696 d1
	1689–98 a	1693 a2; 1698 a1
T	(Sir) John Pole	1689 a1; 1702 a1
	1689, 1698–1700, 1702 ab	1698 a1; 1701 c1
M	Alexander Popham	1696 b2; 1696 d2; 1702 a1
	1690–1702 a	1693 a1; 1696 a2; 1698 a2; 1701 c2
W	*Charles Powlett (Marquess of Winchester)*	1690 a2; 1696 b2
	1689–98	1693 a2; 1696 a2; 1698 a2
W	*William Lord Powlett*	1690 a2; 1696 b2; 1696 d2; 1699 a2
	1689–1702 a	1693 a2; 1696 a2; 1698 a2; 1701 c2
T	Sir Thomas Powis	1701 a1; 1702 a1
	1701–02 a	1701 c1
T	James Praed	1689 a1; 1702 a1
	1689–1702 ab	1696 a1; 1698 a1; 1701 c1
T	Robert Price	1696 b1; 1696 c1; 1696 d1; 1702 a1
	1690–1700, 1702 b	1696 a1; 1698 a1; 1701 c1
M	Jonathan Prideaux	1689 a1; 1690 a2; 1701 a1
	1689, 10/1690–95, 1701	
*W	*Henry Priestman*	1696 b2; 1696 d2
	1695–98	1696 a2; 1698 a2
W	Sir Roger Puleston	1696 b2; 1696 d2
	1689–97	1696 a1
W	*John Pulteney*	1696 b2; 1696 d2; 1699 a2
	1695–1702 a	1696 a2; 1698 a2; 1701 c2
W	*Sir Charles Raleigh*	1690 a2; 1696 b2; 1696 d2
	1689–4/98 b	1693 a2; 1696 a2
T	Morgan Randyll	1696 d1; 1702 a1
	1690–1702 ab	1696 a1; 1698 a1; 1701 c1
W	(Sir) Isaac Rebow	1690 a2; 1696 b2; 1696 d2; 1699 a2
	1689, 11/1692–1702 a	1693 a2; 1696 a2; 1698 a2; 1701 c2
T	Thomas Renda	1701 a1; 1702 a1
	1701–02 a	1701 c1
W	*Sir Robert Rich*	1690 a2; 1696 b2; 1696 d2; 1699 a2
	1689–99	1693 a2; 1696 a2; 1698 a2
W	Sir William Rich	1690 a2; 1696 b2; 1696 d2; 1699 a2
	1689–1700 a	1693 a2; 1696 a2; 1698 a2
M	*Francis Robartes*	1689 a1; 1696 b2
	1689–1702 ab	1693 a1; 1696 a1; 1698 a2; 1701 b2; 1701 c1
W	Russell Robartes	1696 b2; 1696 d2
	11/1693–1702 a	1696 a2; 1698 a2; 1701 c2
W	Sir Thomas Roberts	1696 b2; 1696 d2
	1691–98 a	1693 a2; 1696 a2; 1698 a2
T	Samuel Rolle	1696 b1; 1701 a1
	1689–1702 ab	1696 a1; 1698 a1; 1701 c1
T	Thomas Rowney	1696 b1; 1696 c1; 1696 d1; 1701 a1; 1702 a1
	1695–1702 a	1696 a1; 1698 a1; 1701 c1
W	Sir Rice Rudd	1696 d2; 1699 a2
	1689–1701 b	1696 a1; 1698 a2
W	Sir James Rushout	1690 a2; 1696 b2; 1696 d2
	1689–3/98 b	1696 a2
W	*Edward Russell (Admiral)*	1690 a2; 1696 b2; 1696 d2
	1689–97	1693 a2; 1696 a2

Party	Name/tenure	Votes/forecasts
W	*Edward Lord Russell*	1690 a2; 1696 b2; 1696 d2; 1699 a2
	1689–1702 ab	1693 a2; 1696 a2; 1698 a2; 1701 c2
W	James Lord Russell	1690 a2; 1696 b2; 1696 d2
	1689–1701 ab	1693 a2; 1696 a2; 1698 a2
W	*Robert Lord Russell*	1690 a2; 1696 b2; 1696 d2; 1699 a2
	1689–1702 ab	1693 a2; 1696 a2; 1698 a2; 1701 c2
W	Thomas Ryder	1696 b2; 1696 d2
	1690–95, 2/1696–98	1693 a2; 1698 a2
T	Robert Sacheverell	1701 a1; 1702 a1
	10/1699–6/1701, 1702 a	1701 b1; 1701 c1
T	Henry St John	1701 a1; 1702 a1
	1701–02 a	1701 c1
W	*Sir William St Quintin*	1696 b2; 1696 d2; 1699 a2
	1695–1702 a	1696 a2; 1698 a2; 1701 c2
T	John Sandford	1689 a1; 1696 b1; 1696 c1; 1696 d1
	1689, 9/1690–98 b	1696 a1; 1698 a1
W	Sir Richard Sandford	1696 b2; 1696 d2
	1695–1700, 5/1701–02 a	1696 a2; 1698 a2; 1701 b2; 1702 c2
*T	*Edwin Sandys*	1696 b1; 1696 d1
	1695–98	1696 a1; 1698 a1
T	*George Saunderson, Viscount Castleton*	1696 b1; 1696 c1; 1696 d1
	1689–98 b	1696 a1; 1698 a1
W	*George Sayer*	1696 b2; 1699 a2
	1695–1702 a	1696 a2; 1698 a2; 1701 c2
W	Sir William Scawen	1696 b2; 1696 d2; 1699 a2
	11/1693–1702 a	1696 a2; 1698 a2; 1701 c2
T	Francis Scobell	1701 a1; 1702 a1
	1690–95, 1/1699–1702 a	1701 c1
T	*Sir Edward Seymour*	1689 a1; 1696 b1; 1696 c1; 1696 d1; 1701 a1; 1702 a1
	1689–1702 ab	1693 a3; 1696 a1; 1698 a1; 1701 c1
T	*(Sir) Henry Seymour*	1701 a1; 1702 a1
	1/1699–1702 a	1701 c1
T	Henry Seymour (Portman)	1689 a1; 1701 a1; 1702 a1
	1689–95, 11/1696–1702 ab	1698 a1; 1701 c1
M	*William Seymour*	1699 a2; 1701 a1; 1702 a1
	1698–1702 a	1698 a2; 1701 c1
*W	(Sir) Edward Seyward	1696 b2; 1696 d2
	1695–98	1696 a2; 1698 a2
T	Peter Shakerley	1696 b1; 1696 c1; 1696 d1; 1701 a1; 1702 a1
	1690–1702 a	1696 a1; 1698 a1; 1701 c1
W	Bennett Sherrard	1696 b2; 1696 d2
	1689–98	1693 a2; 1696 a2; 1698 a2
W	Richard Slater	1696 b2; 1696 d2; 1699 a2
	1690–11/99 b	1693 a1; 1696 a2; 1698 a2
W	*James Sloane*	1696 b2; 1696 d2; 1699 a2
	1/1696–1700	1696 a1; 1698 a2
*T	Sir John Smith	1696 b1; 1696 c1; 1696 d1
	1695–98 b	1696 a1; 1698 a1
W	*John Smith*	1696 b2; 1696 d2; 1699 a2
	1689, 1691–1702 ab	1693 a2; 1696 a2; 1698 a2; 1701 c2
T	John Speccot	1689 a1; 1696 b1; 1696 c1
	1689–1701 b	1696 a1; 1698 a1; 1701 b1
W	John Speke	1696 b2; 1696 d2
	1690–98 b	1693 a2; 1696 a2; 1698 a2
W	Charles Lord Spencer	1696 d2; 1699 a2
	1695–1702 a	1696 a2; 1698 a2; 1701 c2

Party	Name/tenure	Votes/forecasts
W	*James Stanley*	1696 b2; 1696 d2; 1699 a2
	1689–1702 ab	1693 a2; 1696 a2; 1698 a2; 1701 c2
*M	Thomas Stephens	1696 b1; 1696 d2
	12/1695–98	1696 a3; 1698 a2
W	Christopher Stockdale	1696 b2; 1696 d2; 1699 a2
	4/1693–1702 a	1696 a2; 1698 a2; 1701 c2
T	Thomas Strangways	1689 a1; 1696 b1; 1696 c1; 1696 d1; 1701 a1; 1702 a1
	1689–1702 ab	1696 a1; 1698 a1; 1701 c1
W	Sir William Strickland	1690 a2; 1696 b2; 1696 d2
	1689–98, 1701–02 a	1693 a2; 1696 a2; 1698 a2; 1701 c2
*T	William Stringer	1696 b1; 1696 c1; 1696 d1
	1695–98	1696 a1; 1698 a1
T	Anthony Sturt	1696 b1; 1701 a1
	1695–1701 a	1696 a1; 1698 a1
T	Samuel Swift	1696 b1; 1696 c1; 1696 d1; 1701 a1; 1702 a1
	12/1693–2/94, 1695–1702 a	1696 a1; 1698 a1; 1701 c1
*W	Philip Sydney	1696 b2; 1696 d2
	1695–98	1696 a2; 1698 a2
T	*Sir Richard Temple*	1696 b1; 1696 d1
	1689–97 b	1693 a1; 1696 a1
W	*Maurice Thompson*	1696 b2; 1699 a2
	1695–1702 a	1696 a2; 1698 a2; 1701 c2
W	Sir John Thompson	1690 a2; 1696 b2
	1689–4/96 b	1696 a2
W	John Thornagh	1696 b2; 1696 d2; 1699 a2
	1689–1702 a	1693 a2; 1696 a2; 1698 a2; 1701 c2
T	Henry Thynne	1701 a1; 1702 a1
	1701–02 a	1701 b1; 1701 c1
T	Fredrick Tilney	1696 b1; 1702 a1
	1690–1700, 1702 a	1693 a2; 1696 a1; 1698 a1; 1701 c1
W	(Sir) *Thomas Tipping*	1690 a2; 1696 b2; 1699 a2
	1689, 1695–1700 b	1696 a2; 1698 a2
T	Sir Lionel Tollemache, Earl of Dysart	1701 a1; 1702 a1
	1698–1702 ab	1698 a1; 1701 c1
W	*Samuel Travers*	1696 b2; 1696 d2; 1699 a2
	1690–1700 a	1693 a2; 1696 a2; 1698 a2
W	*Sir Thomas Trawell*	1696 b2; 1696 d2; 1699 a2
	1690–1702 a	1693 a2; 1696 a2; 1698 a2; 1701 c2
T	John Tredenham	1696 b1; 1696 c1; 1701 a1; 1702 a1
	1690–1702 a	1696 a1; 1698 a1; 1701 c1
T	*Sir Joseph Tredenham*	1689 a1; 1701 a1; 1702 a1
	1689–95, 1698–1702 ab	1693 a1; 1698 a1; 1701 c1
*T	*Seymour Tredenham*	1696 b1; 1696 c1
	1695–11/96	1696 a1
M	*John Tregagle*	1699 a2; 1701 a1
	1697–1701	1698 a2
M	*Charles Trelawney*	1696 b1; 1699 a2; 1701 a1; 1702 a1
	1689–1702 ab	1696 a1; 1698 a2; 1701 c1
M	*Henry Trelawney*	1696 b2; 1699 a2; 1701 a1
	1689–2/1702 b	1693 a2; 1696 a1; 1698 a2; 1701 c1
W	Thomas Trenchard	1690 a2; 1696 b2
	1689, 12/1690–1702	1693 a2; 1696 a3; 1698 a2; 1701 b2; 1701 c2
T	Sir John Trevillian	1696 b1; 1696 c1; 1696 d1
	1695–98, 1701 a	1696 a1; 1698 a1; 1701 c1
T	William Try	1696 c1; 1696 d1
	1690–98 a	1696 a1; 1698 a1

Party	Name/tenure	Votes/forecasts
M	Sir John Turner	1689 a1; 1696 b2; 1696 d2; 1699 a2
	1689–1702 b	1696 a3; 1698 a2; 1701 c2
T	Sir Edward Turnour	1701 a1; 1702 a1
	1701–02 a	1701 c1
*T	Sir William Twisden	1696 b1; 1696 c1; 1696 d1
	1695–12/97 b	1696 a1
T	Edward Vaughan	1696 b1; 1696 d1; 1702 a1
	1689–1702 ab	1696 a1; 1698 a1; 1701 c1
T	Richard Vaughan (of Corte Derllis)	1696 b1; 1696 d1
	1689–1702 ab	1696 a1; 1698 a1; 1701 c2
T	Montagu Venables-Bertie, Lord	1689 a1; 1696 b1; 1696 c1; 1696 d1
	Norris: 1689–11/99	1696 a1; 1698 a1
T	John Verney	1696 d1; 1701 a1
	1695–1701 ab	1696 a1; 1698 a1; 1701 b1
W	*James Vernon*	1696 b2; 1696 d2; 1699 a2
	1695–1702 ab	1696 a2; 1698 a2; 1701 c2
T	Sir Richard Vivian	1701 a1; 1702 a1
	3/1701–02 a	1701 c1
T	Edmund Waller	1696 b1; 1696 d1
	1689–98	1696 a1; 1698 a1
W	Robert Walpole	1696 b2; 1696 d2
	1689–1700	1696 a2; 1698 a2
T	Sir Francis Warr	1689 a1; 1701 a1; 1702 a1
	1689–95, 11/1699–1700, 3/1701–02 ab	1701 c1
M	Sir Michael Warton	1690 a2; 1696 b1; 1696 d1; 1702 a1
	1689–1702 ab	1696 a1; 1698 a3; 1701 c1
*T	Isaac Watlington	1696 b1; 1696 d1
	1695–98	1696 a1; 1698 a1
M	George Weld	1689 a1; 1696 b1; 1696 c1; 1696 d1; 1699 a2
	1689–1701 b	1693 a1; 1696 a1; 1698 a1
T	Sir Michael Wentworth	1696 b1; 1696 c1
	1689, 5/1690–1/97 b	1696 a1
T	*John Weston*	1689 a1; 1701 a1
	1689, 1698–1702	1698 a1; 1701 c1
W	*Goodwin Wharton*	1696 b2; 1696 d2; 1699 a2
	12/1689–1702 ab	1693 a2; 1696 a2; 1698 a2; 1701 c2
W	*Thomas Wharton*	1690 a2; 1696 b2
	1689–2/96 b	1693 a2; 1696 a2
W	*Charles Whitaker*	1696 b2; 1696 d2
	1695–98, 1702 a	1696 a2; 1698 a2; 1701 b2; 1701 c2
W	John White	1696 b2; 1696 d2
	5/1689, 10/1691–98 b	1693 a2; 1696 a2; 1698 a2
T	Sir William Whitmore	1696 b1; 1696 d1
	1689–3/99 b	1696 a1; 1698 a1
M	Sir William Williams	1690 a2; 1696 b1; 1696 c1; 1696 d1
	1689, 1695–98 b	1696 a1; 1698 a1
W	*Sir Joseph Williamson*	1696 b2; 1696 d2
	1690–1701 b	1696 a1; 1698 a2; 1701 b2
T	Sir Francis Winnington	1696 b1; 1696 d1
	1692–98 b	1696 a1; 1698 a1
T	Salwey Winnington	1696 d1; 1701 a1; 1702 a1
	1694–1702 a	1696 a1; 1698 a1; 1701 c1
T	Sir John Wodehouse	1696 b1; 1696 c1; 1696 d1
	1695–98, 1702 a	1696 a1; 1698 a1; 1701 c1
T	(Sir) *William Wogan*	1689 a1; 1696 d1
	1689–1700 b	1696 a1; 1698 a1

Party	Name/tenure	Votes/forecasts
T	George Woodroofe	1696 b1; 1696 d1
	1695–98, 1701–02 a	1696 a1; 1698 a1; 1701 c1
M	Sir Francis Wyndham	1696 b1; 1696 d1; 1699 a2
	1695–1700, 1702 a	1696 a1; 1698 a2; 1701 b2; 1701 c2
*T	Sir Marmaduke Wyville	1696 c1; 1696 d1
	1695–98	1696 a3; 1698 a1
W	*Sir Walter Yonge*	1690 a2; 1696 b2; 1696 d2; 1699 a2
	1689–1702 ab	1693 a2; 1696 a2; 1698 a2; 1701 c2
W	Sir William Yorke	1690 a2; 1696 b2
	1689–98, 1701–02 b	1693 a2; 1696 a2; 1698 a1; 1701 c2

Appendix D

PLACEMEN IN THE HOUSE OF COMMONS
1689–1702

It is not easy to determine with great precision just how many members at any given point in time held places of profit under the crown. The following list has been compiled from two main types of sources: contemporary listings of all office-holders and contemporary listings of M.P.s with places. Of the former, the most important are the various editions of Edward Chamberlayne, *Angliae Notitia: Or the Present State of England* (16th edition of part i, 1687; 13th edition of part ii, 1687; 17th edition of part i, 1692; 17th edition of part ii, 1691; 18th edition; 1694, 19th edition, 1700; 20th edition, 1702; and 21st edition, 1704) and Guy Miege, *The New State of England* (1st edition, 1691; and succeeding editions of 1693, 1694, 1699, 1701, and 1703). In addition, *A New List of the Offices and Officers of England* (1697, Wing N654), *An Account of the Principal Officers, Civil and Military* (1697, Institute of Historical Research Library), and *A List of the Principal Officers, Civil and Military* (1702, Middlesex RO, Acc. 249/165) have been utilised.

The following contemporary listings of M.P.s with places have been employed as well:

1. PRO, SP 8/14, reprinted in Browning, *Danby*, III, 184–7. 102 names (after 1691–92 session). A slightly earlier version of this list, omitting only Peregrine Bertie junior, George Booth, Sir Stephen Fox, Sir John Guise, Lord William Powlett, and John Tredenham is in Nottingham Univ., Portland MS. PwA 2392.
2. BL Loan 29/206, ff. 170–1. Ninety-six names (after 1692–93 session), plus one name added later.
3. Bodl. Rawlinson MS. D846, ff. 1–3 (compiled by S. Grascome). 128 names (after 1692–93 session), plus nine added later.
4. BL Harleian MS. 6846, ff. 268–71. Eighty-five names (during 1693–94 session).
5. *A Letter to A Country Gentlemen: Setting Forth the Cause of the Decay and Ruin of Trade* (1698), reprinted in *The Harleian Miscellany* (1808–11) x, 367–71. Ninety-five names.
6. *A Compleat List of the Knights, Citizens and Burgesses of the New Parliament* (1698, BL 1850 c6 no. 16; an earlier version in Hunt. 347521). 110 names.
7. BL Loan 29/35, bundle 12 (see App. C, section II, no. 3); those marked with a dash. 124 names of members of the 1698–1700 parliament and thirty-two incumbents of the 1695–98 parliament who failed of re-election.

Besides these contemporary sources, I have also drawn upon the biographical notes compiled by Professor R. Walcott and by the 1660–1689 section of the History of Parliament Trust. All students of the political history of the later seventeenth and early eighteenth centuries owe much to the labours and the courtesy of Professor Walcott and the staff of the History of Parliament Trust.

Despite the efforts both of contemporaries and of twentieth-century scholars, the list of placemen I have compiled must be regarded as at best a tentative one. Not only may I have overlooked a few individuals but also it has been difficult to pin down in the cases of many known office-holders the exact dates of their tenures. The listing also is susceptible to criticism and correction on other scores—particularly my rough categorisation of the types of offices that individuals held and my identification of those holding places either for life or 'during good behaviour'. It should be added that no attempt has been made to include in this list M.P.s for whom close kinsmen were holding offices either in trust or as endowments (e.g. Guy Palmes's Exchequer tellership, which was bestowed upon him in recognition of his father William's parliamentary service). The list also excludes placemen in the Convention parliament who either did not survive or who lost their places before the dissolution of that parliament.

With these *caveats* in mind, the material in the list below may be summed up in this fashion:
placemen sitting at the dissolution of the 1689–90 parliament: 101
    incumbent placemen who failed to be re-elected as placemen in 1690: 11
placemen returned in the 1690 election: 90 incumbents and 29 new placemen: 119
placemen sitting in January 1693: 131
placemen sitting at the dissolution of the 1690–95 parliament: 120
    incumbent placemen who failed to be re-elected as placemen in 1695: 29
placemen returned in the 1695 election: 91 incumbents and 40 new placemen: 131
placemen sitting at the dissolution of the 1695–98 parliament: 132
    incumbent placemen who failed to be re-elected as placemen in 1698: 39
placemen returned in the 1698 election: 93 incumbents and 32 new placemen: 125
placemen sitting at the dissolution of the 1698–1700 parliament: 127
    incumbent placemen who failed to be re-elected as placemen in 1700–01: 32
placemen returned in the 1700–01 election: 95 incumbents and 25 new placemen: 120
placemen sitting at the dissolution of the 1700–01 parliament: 124
    incumbent placemen who failed to be re-elected as placemen in 1701: 20
placemen returned in the 1701 election: 104 incumbents and 26 new placemen: 130
placemen sitting at William's death: 132

The list below is arranged as follows:
    Column one: name, with asterisk indicating that the M.P. is also listed in App. C.
    Column two: years of service in the Commons during William's reign.
    Column three: years in office during William's reign.
    Column four: type of office; asterisk indicates that it was held either for life or during 'good behaviour'. The categories or types of offices employed are:
Army—armed forces (including garrison positions)
Central—central administration in London unless in one of categories below
Court—Court and Household positions
Legal 1—legal posts in the King's gift
Legal 2—King's Counsel and King's Serjeants
Legal 3—other legal posts
Overseas—Irish, colonial and diplomatic appointments
Pension—Pensions and grants
Revenue—posts in the provinces under the revenue services or in the royal land administration

Name	Service in the Commons	Tenure in office	Type
William Adderley	1690–93	?–death	Legal 3
*James Anderton	1701–02	1689–1702	Legal 2
*Sir Matthew Andrews	1689–98	1689–1702	Court
Matthew Appleyard	1689–95	1689–death	Revenue
Sir Henry Ashurst	1689–95, 1698–1700 1702	1689–91	Central
Henry Ashurst	1698–1702	1694–1702	Legal 2 and Central
*Sir William Ashurst	1689, 1695–1702	7/1698–1700	Central
Sir Richard Atkyns	1695–96	?1689–death	Army
Samuel Atkinson	1698–99	1689–1702	Central
*Sir John Austen	1689–99	1697–death	Central
Robert Austen	1689–96	1691–death	Central
*Robert Austen junior	1695–98, 1702	?1691–1702	Army
Matthew Aylmer	1697–1702	1689–1702	Army
		1697–1702	Central
*Sir Edward Ayscoghe	1689–99	1689–death	Central
*John Backwell	1690–1701	1689–death*	Revenue
Christopher Bale	1689–95	?1691–?94	Revenue
John Beaumont	1689–95	1689–95	Army
*Richard Beke	1689–1700	1689–1702	Central
*Sir Henry Bellasyse	1695–1702	?1689–1702	Army

Name	Service in the Commons	Tenure in office	Type
*John Bennett	1691–95	1689–1702	Legal 3 and Revenue
James Berkeley (Viscount Dursley)	1702	?1689–1702	Army
*John Berkeley, Viscount Fitzharding	1691–1702	1689–1702 / 1694–1702	Army / Central
*Charles Bertie	1689–1702	1689–99	Central
Peregrine Bertie senior	1689–95	1689–93	Revenue
*Peregrine Bertie junior	5/1690–98, 1702	1690–1702	Court
*Philip Bertie	1694–98	?1690–?1702	Revenue
Robert Bertie (Lord Willoughby)	1689–5/90	1689–97	Central
*Philip Bickerstaffe	1689–98	1689–1702*	Court
John Birch	1689–91	1689–death*	Central
John Birch	1701–02	1695–1702	Legal 2
*(Sir) Francis Blake	1689–95, 1698–1700 1702	1689–1702*	Legal 3
*William Blathwayt	11/1693–1702	1689–1702	Central
*Thomas Blofield	1689–1701	?1691–?96	Revenue
William Bokenham	1702	?1689–1702	Army
Nathaniel Bond	1695–98	?1689–1702	Legal 2
*George Booth	9–11/1689, 1692–1700, 4/1701–02	1689–94 / ?1694–1702	Central / Pension
*Hugh Boscawen	1689–6/1701	1689–death / 1696–death	Central / Revenue
John Boteler	1701–02	?–1702	Army
*Henry Boyle	1689, 1692–1702	1699–1702	Central
*John Brewer	1689–1702	1689–91	Central
*George Rodney Brydges	1690–98, 1701–02	?1701–02	Pension
William Brydges	1695–1702	1694–1702	Central
Jeremiah Bubb	1689–4/92	1689–death	Army and Central
John Burrard	1689–5/98	1689–death	Revenue
*John Burrington	1694–98	4/1695–1702	Central
James Butler	1690–95	?1689–?94	Army
*William Campion	1689–98, 12/1698–1700, 1702	?1689–?97	Revenue
Sir Henry Capel	1689–3/1692	1689–death	Central and Overseas
Adam Cardonnell	1702	?1689–1702	Central
Thomas Carew	3/1701–02	?1689–1702	Army
*William Carr	1690–1702	7/1698–1700	Central
Lawrence Carter	1698–1702	?1697–1702	Legal 2
Anthony Cary, Viscount Falkland	1689–94	1691–94	Central
William Cavendish (Marquess of Hartington)	1695–1701, 2/1702	1702	Court
*James Chadwick	1689–97	1694–death	Central
*James Chase	1690–1702	1689–1702	Court
*William Cheyne, Viscount Newhaven	1689–95, 2/1696–1702	2/1690–91	Central
Sir John Chicheley	1689–91	1689–6/90	Central
Henry Chivers	1689–95, 1697–1700, 3/1702	1689–?91	Army
George Cholmondeley	1690–95	1689–1702	Army and Court
*Charles Churchill	1701–02	1689–1702	Army
*George Churchill	1689–1702	1689–93 / 10/1700–02	Army / Central
*Edward Clarke	1690–1702	1694–1700	Central

Name	Service in the Commons	Tenure in office	Type
*Sir Robert Clayton	1689–1702	1689–97	Central
*Charles Cocks	2/1694–1702	1699–1702*	Legal 3
*John Dutton Colt	1689–98, 1–4/1701	1689–1700	Revenue
*Thomas (Lord) Coningsby	1689–1702	1689–1702	Central and Overseas
*John Conyers	1695–1702	?1693–1702	Legal 2
Richard Coote, Earl of Bellomont	1689–95	1689–93 1695–death	Court Overseas
Henry Cornish	1698–2/99	1692–1702	Central
*Sir Robert Cotton (Cambs.)	1689–1700, 2/1702	1691–1702	Central
*Sir Robert Cotton Bart.	1689–1702	1689–1702	Revenue
*William Cowper	1695–1700, 3/1701–02	1689–1702	Legal 2
Robert Crawford	1689–1702	1689–1702	Army
Richard Crawley	1702	?–1702	Legal 3
*Courtenay Croker	1695–1702	?1700–02	Revenue
Mitford Crowe	1701–02	?1699–1702	Overseas
William Culliford	1690–99	8/1690–93 1696–1702	Overseas Central
*John Lord Cutts	12/1693–1702	1689–1702	Army
Sir Samuel Dashwood	1690–95	1689–98	Central
Sir John Delaval	1702	?–1702	Army
*Sir Basil Dixwell	1689, 1695–1700	1691–1702	Central
Thomas Dodson	1702	?–1702	Army
*Gilbert Dolben	1689–98, 1701–02	1701–02	Overseas–Legal
*Thomas Done	1689–98	1689–1702*	Central
*Thomas Dore	1690–1702	1689–1702	Army
Robert Dormer	3/1699–1700, 1702	?–1702	Legal 3
John Drake	1/1699–1700, 2/1701–02	?1697–1702*	Legal 3
Joseph Dudley	8/1701–02	?1689–1702	Army
*Edmund Dummer	1695–98, 1701	?1690–99	Army
*Anthony Duncombe	1698–1702	1689–?1702 ?1695–1702	Army Central
(Sir) Charles Duncombe	1690–2/98, 1701	1689–97	Central
*William Duncombe	1689, 1695–98	1689–95 1695–97	Overseas Central
Sir Gervase Elwes	1690–98, 2/1700–02	1689–1702*	Revenue and Legal 3
*(Sir) John Elwill	1689, 1695–98	?1690–?97	Revenue
*Thomas Erle	1689–1702	1689–1702	Army
*William Ettrick	1689–1702	1689–1702	Revenue
*Sir Stephen Evance	1690–98	1689–1702	Court and Central
Thomas Lord Fairfax	1689–1702	1689–1702	Army
*Sir Henry Fane	1689–98	?1691–?92	Pension
*William Farrer	1695–98, 1702	1699–1702	Legal 2
*(Sir) Thomas Felton	1690–2/1700, 1702	1689–1702	Court
Edward Finch	1690–95	1689–6/92	Central
William Fleming	1696–1700	7/1698–1702	Central
*George Fletcher	1698–1702	?1692–1702	Army
*(Sir) William Forrester	1689–1702	1689–1702	Court
*Charles Fox	1689–1700, 7/1701–02	5/1690–7/98	Overseas
Sir Stephen Fox	1691–98, 2/1699–1702	1689–1702	Court and Central
'(Sir) Thomas Frankland	1689–95, 12/1695–1702	1689–1702	Central
Francis Gardiner	1695–98	?–?	Revenue
John Gauntlet	1695–1702	1689–1702	Central
Orlando Gee	1690–95	1689–1702*	Legal 3
John Gibson	1696–98, 2/1702	1689–1702	Army

Name	Service in the Commons	Tenure in office	Type
*Charles Godfrey	1689, 1691–1702	1689–93	Army
		1693–1702	Court and Pension
*Charles Godolphin	1689–1701	1689–1702	Revenue
		1691–1702	Central
*Francis Godolphin	1695–98, 1701–02	1699–1702*	Central
Sidney Godolphin	1690–95, 1698–1702	1689–1702	Army
*Sir Henry Goodricke	1689–1702	1689–1702	Central
*Sir Bevil Granville	1690–1700	1689–1702	Army
*John Granville	1689–1702	1689–12/90	Army
Henry Greenhill	1/1699–1700, 3/1701	?1694–1702	Central
Algernon Greville	1699–1700, 1702	?1697–1702	Army
*Ralph Grey	1695–98, 1701	1692–1702	Central
Sir John Guise	1689–11/1695	1–9/89	Army
		?9/1690–death	Pension
Henry Guy	1689–95	3/1690–4/95	Central
*Francis Gwyn	1689–98, 1/1699–1702	1689–1702*	Legal 3
		12/1700–1/02	Overseas
*Sir Rowland Gwynne	1689–1702	1689–4/92	Court
Richard Hampden	1689–95	1689–94	Central
William Harbord	1689–7/92	1689–death	Central and Irish
*(Sir) John Hawles	1689, 1695–1700, 3/1701–02	8/1695–1702	Legal 1
*Sir Charles Hedges	1698–2/1700, 1701–02	1689–1702	Legal 3
		11/1700–12/01	Central
Anthony Henley	1698–1700, 2/1702	1702	Pension
Sir Robert Henley	1691–11/92	1689–death*	Legal 3
*Robert Henley	1695–1701	?1689–1702	Central
Charles Herbert	1689–91	1689–death	Army and Revenue
Henry Herbert	1689–94	?1693–1702	Pension
*James Herbert	1689, 1695–1702	?1693–1702	Central
*Henry Heveningham	1695–1700	?1689–1702	Court
*Sir Henry Hobart	1689, 1694–98	1689–?91	Court
		1697–98	Central
*Henry Holmes	4/1695–1702	1689–96	Army
Sir Robert Holmes	1689–11/92	1689–death	Army
*Sir William Honeywood	1689–98	1689–1702	Central
Thomas Hopkins	1701	?1697–1702	Central
Thomas Hopson	1698–1702	?1689–1702	Army
Henry Howard (Lord Walden)	1694, 1695–98	1697–1702*	Central
Philip Howard	1689, 1701–02	1689–1702	Army and Pension
*Sir Robert Howard	1689–98	1689–death	Central
*Thomas Howard	1689–4/1701	1689–death*	Central
Emanuel Howe	1702	?1689–1702	Army and Court
*John Howe	1689, 11/1690–1701	1689–3/92	Court
*Sir Scrope Howe	1689–98	1689–1702	Court and Central
John Hungerford	1692–3/95	1689–1702*	Legal 3
Sir George Hutchins	1690–95	6/1690–3/93	Legal 1
John Hutton	1702	?–1702	Court
*Edward Hyde (Viscount Cornbury)	1689–1701	1689–1702	Army and Overseas
Henry Ireton	1698–1700	1689–1702	Army and Court
James Isaacson	1698–2/99	1694–2/99, 1700–02	Central
(Sir) Joseph Jekyll	1697–1702	1697–1702	Legal 1
Sir Edward Jennings	1690–91	1690–death	Central
Sir Jonathan Jennings	1689–95	1689–?97	Central

Name	Service in the Commons	Tenure in office	Type
*Jonathan Jennings	1691–1701	1691–1702	Central
William Jephson	1689–91	1689–death	Central
*Richard Jones, Earl of Ranelagh	1689–1702	1689–1702	Central
*James Kendall	1689, 1695–1702	1690–94, 1696–1699, 4/1701–02	Overseas and Central
Richard Kent	1690	1689–death	Central
Roger Kenyon	1690–95	1689–death*	Legal 3
*Thomas King	1696–1702	1689–1702	Army
*Roger Kirkby	1689–1702	1689–1702	Army and Central
Piercy Kirk	1689	1689–death	Army
Sir John Knatchbull	1689–95	2/1690–3/92	Central
*John Knight	1695–3/98	1689–97	Central
Thomas Lascelles	1689–97	?1693–death	Central
Sir Thomas Lee	1689–91	1689–death	Central
Richard Leveson	1692–95	1689–1702	Army
Richard Levinge	1690–95	?8/1690–94	Overseas–Legal
*Sir Thomas Littleton	1689–1702	1689–1702	Central
Francis Lloyd	1691–95	1689–1702	Legal 1
*William Lowndes	1695–1702	1689–1702	Central
*James Lowther	1694–1702	1696–1702	Central
Sir John Lowther of Lowther	1689–96	1689–94, 1700–01	Court and Central
*Sir John Lowther of White-haven	1689–1700	1689–96	Central
Henry Lumley	1701	1689–1702	Army
*Alexander Luttrell	10/1690–1702	1689–1702	Army
Francis Luttrell	1689–10/90	1689–death	Army
Dennis Lyddell	1701–02	?1689–1702	Central
Sir Robert Marsham	1698–1702	?1689–1702*	Legal 3
*Charles Mason	1695–5/1701, 1702	1689–? 1697–4/1701	Army Central
Sir Algernon May	1689	1689	Central
Baptist May	5/1690–95	1689–death*	Legal 3 and Revenue
Sir John Maynard	1689–10/90	1689–6/90	Legal 1
Simon Mayne	1691–95	1689–1702	Central
Philip Meadows	1698–1700	7/1698–1702	Central and Court
John Methuen	12/1690–1700, 1702	1689–1702* 1691–1702	Legal 3 Overseas–Legal
*Robert Molesworth	1695–98	1689–92, 1697–1702	Overseas
*Thomas Molyneux	1695–1700, 1702	1697–4/1701	Central
*Sir Thomas Mompesson	1689–98, 1701	1697–99	Central
Charles Montagu (Durham)	1695–1702	?1693–1702	Revenue
*Charles Montagu	1689–1700	1689–1702	Central
*Christopher Montagu	1695–1702	1694–?1700	Central
Harry Mordaunt	1692–98, 1701–02	1689–1702	Army, Court and Central
John Lord Mordaunt	1701–02	?1694–1702	Army
*Anthony Morgan	1695–1702	1689–1702	Army
Sir John Morgan	1689–1/93	1689–death	Army
George Morley	5/1701–02	1689–1702*	Legal 3
Sir John Morton	1689–95	1689–death	Court
John Mounsher	1702	?–1702	Central
Christopher Musgrave	1690–95	1689–1702	Central
Sir Robert Napier	1689–10/90, 1698–1700	?1693–?98	Court
Thomas Neale	1689–99	1689–death	Court and Central

Name	Service in the Commons	Tenure in office	Type
Thomas Newport	1695–98, 3/1699–2/1701	1699–1702	Central
Isaac Newton	1689, 1702	1696–1702	Central
*Edward Nicholas	1689–1702	?1689–1702	Central and Court
George Nicholas	1692–98	1689–1702*	Central
*(Sir) William Norris	1695–1701	10/1698–death	Overseas
*Charles North	1701–02	?–1702	Army
*Thomas Northmore	1695–1702	?–1702*	Legal 3
*Samuel Ogle	1690–1702	?1699–1702	Overseas
*Foot Onslow	1689–1700	1694–1702	Central
*Sir Richard Onslow	1689–1702	5/1690–2/93	Central
*Charles Osborne	1690–1700	7/1690–?99	Revenue
Thomas Owen	1701–02	?–1702*	Legal 3
*George Oxenden	1695–98	1689–1702	Legal 3
*Thomas Papillon	1689–1700	1689–99	Central
John Parkhurst	1689–95, 1698–1701	1689–1702	Central
Charles Lord Paston	1699–1700	?1694–1702	Army
*Edward Pauncefort	1698–1702	?1689–1702	Central and Court
*Henry Pelham	1690–1700, 1702	1697–1702	Central
*Thomas Pelham	1689–1702	1689–92, 1697–1699, 4/1701–02	Central
Alexander Pitfield	1698–1702	?–1702*	Legal
John Pollexfen	1689, 4/1690–95	1690–1702	Court and Central
Roger Pope	1699–1702	1689–1702	Army
Sir Charles Porter	1690–95	1689–95	Central and Overseas–Legal
John Povey	1697–1700	1689–1702	Central
Henry Powle	1689–11/90	1689–death	Legal 1
*Charles Powlett (Marquess of Winchester)	1689–98	1689–1702	Court and Overseas
*William Lord Powlett	1689–1702	8/1690–1702	Pension
*Robert Price	1690–1700, 1702	?12/1700–02	Legal 1
*Henry Priestman	1695–98	1690–99	Central
Mathew Prior	1701	1697–1702	Overseas and Central
*John Pulteney	1695–1702	1690–1702	Overseas and Central
Sir William Pulteney	1689–91	2/1690–death	Central
Richard Pye	1698–1700	?1689–1702	Revenue
Carew Raleigh	1698–1702	?1696–1702	Army
*Sir Charles Raleigh	1689–4/98	1689–death	Court and Revenue
Sir Richard Reynell	1690–95	8/1690–95	Overseas–Legal
*Sir Robert Rich	1689–99	1691–death	Central
*Francis Robartes	1689–1702	1692–1702	Overseas
Sir George Rooke	1698–1702	1689–1702	Army and Central
Anthony Rowe	1689, 3–10/1690, 11–12/1693, 2–3/1701	1689–1702	Court
*Edward Russell (Admiral)	1689–97	1689–99	Army and Central
*Edward Lord Russell	1689–1702	4/1693–1702	Court
*Robert Lord Russell	1689–1702	1689–1702	Central
Thomas Sackville	1689–93	4/1690–death	Court
George St Loe	1702	?1689–94 1697–1702	Central
*Sir William St Quintin	1695–1702	7/1698–1701	Central
*Edwin Sandys	1695–98	1689–?1702	Army
*George Saunderson, Viscount Castleton	1689–98	1689–94	Army
James Saunderson	1698–1700, 1702	?1692–1702	Central

Name	Service in the Commons	Tenure in office	Type
Nicholas Saunderson	1689–92	?1689–death	Central
Richard Savage (Viscount Colchester)	1689–94	?1698–1702	Army
*George Sayer	1695–1702	?1689–1702	Court
William Selwyn	1698–1701	1689–1702	Army
Charles Sergison	1698–1702	?1689–1702	Central
*Sir Edward Seymour	1689–1702	1692–94	Central
›Sir Henry Seymour	1699–1702	1689–1702*	Central
*William Seymour	1698–1702	1689–1702	Army
Sir Cloudesly Shovell	1695–1701	1689–1702	Army and Central
John Shrimpton	1702	1689–1702	Army
*James Sloane	1696–1700	1697–1702	Revenue
John Smith (Beaufort Buildings)	1698–1700	7/1698–1702	Central
*John Smith (Tidsworth)	1689, 1691–1702	1694–3/1701	Central
Simon Smith	1/1693–95	1689–95	Court
(Sir) John Somers	1689–93	1689–1700	Legal 1
William Spencer	3/1698–1702	?1689–1702	Court
Richard Staines	1689–98	1697–1702	Central
*James Stanley	1689–1702	1689–1702	Army and Court
James Stanhope	3/1702	?1692–1702	Army and Overseas
Sir William Stephens	1689–95	1689–?95	Army
Thomas Stringer	1698–1702	?1689–1702	Army and Legal 3
Christopher Tancred	1689–98	1689–1701	Court
John Taylor	1695–98, 1701	?1689–1702	Central
William Tempest	1690–95	1691–death*	Legal 3
*Sir Richard Temple	1689–97	1689–94	Central
Sir Richard Temple	1697–1702	?1689–1702	Army
*Maurice Thompson	1695–1702	?–1702	Army
William Thursby	1698–2/1701	1689–?1702	Legal 3
(Sir) Joseph Tiley	1695–98	?1697–1702	Legal 3
*(Sir) Thomas Tipping	1689, 1695–1700	1689–91	Army
Thomas Tollemache	1689, 1691–94	1689–death	Army
*Samuel Travers	1690–1700	4/1693–1702	Central
*Sir Thomas Trawell	1690–1702	?1694–1702	Army
Sir George Treby	1689, 5/1690–5/92	1689–1702	Legal 1
*Sir Joseph Tredenham	1689–95, 1698–1702	1689–96	Revenue
*Seymour Tredenham	1695–96	1692–death	Court and Revenue
*John Tregagle	1697–1701	1689–1702*	Revenue
*Charles Trelawney	1689–1702	1689–1702	Army
*Henry Trelawney	1689–2/1702	1689–1/92 1694–death	Army
(Sir) John Tremaine	1690–94	1689–death	Legal 2
(Sir) John Trenchard	1689–4/95	1689–death	Legal 1 and Central
Sir John Trevor	1689–3/95	?1689–11/92 11/1692–1702*	Legal 1
(Sir) Thomas Trevor	1692–98, 2–6/1701	1690–1702	Legal 1
Sir William Trumbull	1695–98	1689–1702* 1694–97	Central
Lionel Vane	1698–1702	?1697–1702*	Legal 3
*James Vernon	1695–1702	1689–1702	Central
Henry Vincent	1689–1702	1699–1702	Central
Walter Vincent	1689–11/92	?1689–death	Army
Thomas Vivian	1695–1700	1691–1702	Central
Robert Waller	1690–95	1689–?99	Revenue
William Walmesley	1701	1698–1702	Legal 3

Name	Service in the Commons	Tenure in office	Type
John Webb	1/1695–98, 1/1699–1702	1689–1702	Army
*John Weston	1689, 1698–1702	?1699–1702	Revenue and Court
*Goodwin Wharton	1689–1702	1689–1702	Army and Central
*Thomas Wharton	1689–2/96	1689–1702	Court
Thomas Wheate	1690–95	?1689–1702	Court
*Charles Whitaker	1695–98, 1702	1689–1702	Legal 3
Roger Whitley	1689, 1695–97	1689–death	Court
Thomas Whitley	1690–95	1689–death	Legal 3
Sir William Whitlock	1689–95	1689–96	Legal 2
John Wildman	1689	1689–91	Central
John Wildman junior	1689–95	1689–91	Central
*Sir Joseph Williamson	1690–1701	1689–death* 1697–99	Central
*(Sir) William Wogan	1689–1700	1689–1701	Legal 1
Richard Woolaston	3/1698–2/99, 3/1699–1702	?–1699	Central
Sir Christopher Wren	1–5/1689, 1702	1689–1702	Central
Sir Bourchier Wrey	1689–96	?1691–?92	Pension
Robert Yard	1702	1694–1702	Central
*Sir Walter Yonge	1689–1702	1694–1701	Central

Appendix E

THE TWENTY-EIGHT HEADS
of 2 February 1689 (*CJ*, XI7)

1. The pretended power of dispensing or suspending of laws, or the execution of laws, by regal prerogative, without consent of parliament, is illegal.
2. The commission for erecting the late Court of Commissioners for Ecclesiastical Causes, and all other commissions and courts of like nature, are illegal and pernicious.
3. Levying of money for or to the use of the Crown, by pretence of prerogative, without grant of parliament, for longer time, or in other manner, than the same shall be so granted, is illegal.
4. It is the right of the subjects to petition the King. And all commitments and prosecutions for such petitioning, are illegal.
5. The acts concerning the militia are grievous to the subject.
6. The raising or keeping a standing army within this kingdom in time of peace, unless it be with the consent of parliament, is against law.
7. It is necessary for the public safety, that the subjects, which are Protestants, should provide and keep arms for their common defence: and that the arms which have been seized, and taken from them, be restored.
8. The right and freedom of electing members of the House of Commons; and the rights and privileges of parliament, and members of parliament, as well in the intervals of parliament, as during their sitting; to be preserved.
9. That parliaments ought to sit frequently, and that their frequent sitting be secured.
10. No interrupting of any session of parliament, till the affairs, that are necessary to be dispatched at that time, are determined.
11. That the too long continuance of the same parliament be prevented.
12. No pardon to be pleadable to an impeachment in parliament.
13. Cities, universities, and towns corporate, and boroughs, and plantations, to be secured against *Quo Warrantos*, and surrenders, and mandates; and restored to their ancient rights.
14. None of the royal family to marry a papist.
15. Every king and queen of this realm, at the time of their entering into the exercise of their regal authority, to take an oath for maintaining the Protestant religion, and the laws and liberties of this nation; and that the coronation oath be reviewed.
16. Effectual provision to be made for the liberty of Protestants in the exercise of their religion, and for uniting all Protestants in the matter of public worship, as far as may be.
17. Constructions upon the statutes of treason, and trials, and proceedings, and writs of error, in cases of treason, to be regulated.
18. Judges commissions to be made *Quamdiu se bene gesserint*; and their salaries to be ascertained and established, to be paid out of the public revenue only; and not to be removed, nor suspended, from the execution of their office, but by due course of law.
19. The requiring excessive bail of persons committed in criminal cases, and imposing excessive fines, and illegal punishments, to be prevented.
20. Abuses in the appointing of sheriffs, and in the execution of their office, to be reformed.
21. Jurors to be duly impannelled and returned, and corrupt and false verdicts prevented.
22. Informations in the Court of King's Bench to be taken away.
23. The Chancery, and other courts of justice, and the fees of offices, to be regulated.
24. That the buying and selling of offices, may be effectually provided against.

25. That upon return of *Habeas Corpus*'s, and *Mandamus*'s, the subject may have liberty to traverse such returns.
26. That all grants of fines and forfeitures are illegal and void; and that all such persons as procure them, be liable to punishment.
27. That the abuses and oppressions in levying and collecting the hearth-money, be effectually redressed.
28. That the abuses and oppressions in levying and collecting the excise, be effectually redressed.

INDEX

M.P.s: *see* Parliament (M.P.s)
Macclesfield, Charles Gerard, first earl of: 117, 128
Macclesfield, Charles Gerard, styled Viscount Brandon, second earl of: 70, 117, 128, 132, 238
Mackworth, Sir Humphrey: 321
Madrid: 237, 279
Maidstone: 301, 302
Mails, tampering with: 51, 66
Mainwaring, Sir John: 251, 281
Maldon: 301
Malmesbury: 280
Malt, lottery tickets on: 322, *and see* Excises
'Management', 'Managers': *see* Parliament (Management)
Manchester: 136
Manchester, Charles Montagu, fourth earl of: 62, 97, 277, 278, 299
Manchester, Anne Yelverton, dowager countess of: 148
Manners, reformation of: 226, 238, 249, 256, 261; bill for suppressing vice and profaneness (1698–99), 256; *and see* Heterodoxy
Mansell, Thomas: 326
Marines: 231, 251, 252, 254, *and see* Army
Maritime Powers: 277, 282, 285, 286, 296, 325, *and see* Dutch
Marlborough, John, baron Churchill, first earl of: 5, 20, 28, 59, 60, 62, 66, 67, 76, 90, 93, 96, 103, 105, 110, 118, 125, 126, 128, 144, 153, 154, 171, 183, 184, 186, 223, 235, 236, 237, 246, 254, 259, 267, 278, 285, 294, 296, 299, 300, 305, 314, 316, 324
Marlborough, Sarah Jennings, countess of: 5, 40, 76, 236
Martial Law, commissions of: 58, *and see* Mutiny Acts
Mary I, Queen: 283
Mary II, Princess of Orange and Queen: 2, 4, 8, 10, 11, 12, 14, 17, 18, 28, 33, 34, 40, 46, 54, 55, 58, 59, 60, 61, 67, 68, 76, 77, 80, 84, 87, 88, 89, 92, 95, 96, 99, 100, 104, 108, 115, 116, 119, 123, 132, 143–4, 169, 171, 175, 203, 204, 211, 215, 216; act to make Mary regent (1690), 58, 60
Mary of Modena, Queen: 4, 71, 227, 251, 289
Maryites: 10, 12
Mastiffs: 254
May, Baptist: 96
Maynard, Sir John: 31, 59, 210
Mediterranean: squadron in, 135, 182; trade, 240, 277, 279, 296
Melfort, John Drummond, earl [Scottish] of: 282
Meredith, Thomas: 289
Methuen, John: 193, 205–6, 229, 230, 232, 235, 241, 264, 274, 305
'Middle Party': 35, 61, 95, *and see* Political Divisions, 'Trimmers'
Middlesex: 51
Middleton, Charles, earl [Scottish] of: 115, 199
Midlands, royal progress through: 157, 313

Milan: 240
'Million Project': *see* Annuities
Militia: 14, 86; bills to reform (1689, 1689–1690, 1690, 1691–92, 1697–98, 1698–99), 34, 35, 86, 100, 235, 253, 271; *and see* Army, County Commissions, King's Prerogative
Mines, royal, act and bill: *see* Sir Carbery Price
'The Minister', 'The Ministers': 229, 230, 260, 266, *and see* 'Premier Minister'
Ministerialists: *see* Placemen, Whigs
Ministers, Ministry: appointments and dismissals of (actual and rumoured), 40–41, 50, 52, 53, 57, 59, 66, 67, 76, 77, 84, 114–16, 117–19, 127–8, 166, 191–2, 193, 222–3, 225, 228, 229, 230–1, 232, 236–7, 242, 256–7, 260, 275–6, 278, 288, 294, 297, 299; attacks upon, 31, 32, 34, 40, 42, 56, 57, 65, 70, 71, 105, 136, 145, 147, 152, 252, 253, 254, 255, 261–2, 264, 266, 267, 268, 272, and impeachments of the four lords, 286, 287–8, 291–2, 294, 298, 302, 307, 326; divisions among: 14, 41, 57, 69, 71, 77–8, 115, 119, 217–18, 257, 260, *and see* Political Divisions; 'new' and 'old' ministry, 281, 282, 286, 288, 289; responsibility to parliament, 34, 38, 97, 107, 255, 283, 285–6; spokesmen in parliament, 53, 54, 97, 123, 136, 227, *and see* Parliament (Management); *and see* Cabinet Council, Council of Nine, King's Administration, Lords Justices, Privy Council
Mint, the: 179, 180, 188, *and see* Coinage
Mitchell, David, Admiral: 258
Molesworth, Robert: 134, 140, 165, 189, 216, 224, 229, 270
'Mob', the: 13
Mompesson, Sir Thomas: 54
Monasteries, dissolution: 238
Monckton, Robert: 280, 282
Monmouth, James Scott, duke of: 4, 114, 135
Monmouth, earl of: *see* third Earl of Peterborough
Mons: 68
Montagu, Ralph, baron and first earl of: 2, 6, 19, 20, 105, 118, 259
Montagu, Charles, *see* Baron Halifax
Montagu, Christopher: 237, 242, 257
Montagus, family of: 158
Moore, Arthur: 212, 221, 261
Moore, John: 68
Mordaunt, Viscount: *see* third Earl of Peterborough
Mordaunt, Harry: 106, 132, 138, 239, 258, 280
Morgan, James: 315
Morrice, Reverend Roger: 7, 9, 12, 13, 15, 24, 29, 44, 49, 53, 56, 65, 80, 81, 95, 312, 317
Moyle, Walter: 224, 225, 253, 260, 265, 277
Mulgrave, Earl of: *see* Marquess of Normanby
Muscovy, Czar of (Peter the Great): 256
Musgrave, Sir Christopher: 12, 22, 28, 29,